THE
ABC-CLIO
COMPANION TO

Women
in the
Workplace

Norman Rockwell's "Rosie the Riviter"

THE
ABC-CLIO
COMPANION TO

Women in the Workplace

Dorothy Schneider
and
Carl J. Schneider

ABC-CLIO

Copyright © 1993 by ABC-CLIO, Inc.

Library of Congress Cataloging-in-Publication Data

Schneider, Dorothy.
    The ABC-CLIO companion to women in the workplace/Dorothy Schneider and Carl J. Schneider.
      p. cm. — (ABC-CLIO companions to key issues in American history and life)
    Includes bibliographical references and index.
    1. Women—Employment—United States—History—Dictionaries.
I. Schneider, Carl J. II. Title. III. Series.
    HD6095.S34   1993   331.4'0973—dc20   93-23533

ISBN 0-87436-694-1

99 98 97 96 95 94   10 9 8 7 6 5 4 3 2

ABC-CLIO, Inc.
130 Cremona Drive, P.O. Box 1911
Santa Barbara, California 93116-1911

ABC-CLIO Companions to Key Issues in American History and Life

The ABC-CLIO Companion to the American Labor Movement
Paul F. Taylor

The ABC-CLIO Companion to the Civil Rights Movement
Mark Grossman

The ABC-CLIO Companion to Women in the Workplace
Dorothy Schneider and Carl J. Schneider

Forthcoming

The ABC-CLIO Companion to the American Peace Movement
Christine Anne Lunardini

The ABC-CLIO Companion to the Environmental Movement
Mark Grossman

The ABC-CLIO Companion to Women's Progress in America
Elizabeth Frost-Knappman

Contents

Preface, ix

Introduction, xi

Women in the Workplace, 1

Chronology, 307

Bibliography, 323

Illustration Credits, 357

Index, 359

Preface

All books on this subject necessarily rest on a false premise: that women's paid work and the work they contribute without pay to the welfare of their families and their communities are divisible. In fact, women weave a seamless web. On their daily agenda, most of them have to combine the needs of job and family—they tuck ideas and services for both into the folds of their schedules. Younger employed women drive their children to dancing lessons and Little League; older employed women shop for groceries for their parents and arrange for Meals on Wheels.

We lack the recklessness, the time, and the resources to take on working women's multiple lives and responsibilities. So we have confined this book to women's paid work—not even half, we figure, of the contribution women actually make to society.

Sometimes we have had to omit entries simply because we could uncover no reliable information on the subject. For information on Cuban-American women in the workplace, for instance, after bibliographic research had disclosed no sources adequate for our purposes, we called the National Association of Cuban-American Women, who referred us to the National Council of La Raza, who referred us to the National Association of Cuban-American Women. We also tried in vain the Cuban American Committee Research and Education Fund.

We have, of course, omitted many more distinguished American women in gainful employment than we have included. Since women's historical positions as outsiders have occasioned so many "firsts," we could not even begin to list all those who broke barriers. But generally we have selected either women who pioneered in their occupations or who secured significant improvements for other women in the workplace.

The ABC-CLIO Companions series is designed to provide the nonspecialist with concise, encyclopedic guides to key movements, major issues, and revolutions in American history. The encyclopedia entries are arranged in alphabetical order. Cross-references connect related terms and entries. A chronology of key events provides a handy overview, and a bibliography is provided to facilitate further research.

We owe gratitude for much of the information in this book and for much of our own education about women in the workplace to many who have generously helped us in their own areas of expertise: Catherine Blinder of Connecticut's Permanent Commission on the Status of Women; Linda Freeman of the National Association of State Universities and Land Grant Colleges; Elizabeth Norris of the

Young Women's Christian Association; Helen Wildermuth of the Connecticut Valley Real Estate Company; Rebecca McGreevy of Estée Lauder; Anne Penniman, Mary Attridge, Beverly Page, and Barbara Smith of the Essex, Connecticut, Library; Larry and Thetis Reeves of *Guest Guide* in Hartford, Connecticut; Christine Bobbish of the Connecticut Historical Society; Leslie Nolan of the Museum of the City of New York; Marie Wilson and Theresa Stanton of the Ms. Foundation for Women; Marie-Hélène Gold and Jane Knowles of the Schlesinger Library on the History of Women in America; freelance writers Paula Feder and Eleanor Stoddard; Joan Schneider of Edwards Brothers; Maggie Bierwirth of the staff of Congressman Sam Gejdenson; Gail Buckner and Linda Cherry of the International Association of Women Police; Chris Martin of the American Dental Association; Martha Weise Peredo of the National Council of La Raza; Jan Ballard of the American Animal Hospital Association; Carl Wise of the American Veterinary Medicine Association; and the anonymous but helpful and delightful representative of the Guerrilla Girls with whom we spoke. We thank Amy Catala, our editor, and Sallie Greenwood, illustrations editor for ABC-CLIO. Our agent, Elizabeth Knappman, has helped us particularly by her own interest in and knowledge of women's history.

Introduction

Women have multiple workplaces. They work long hours in the home. They volunteer in their communities. And they earn their livings in offices, in schools, in hospitals, in factories, on farms, in laboratories, and in hundreds of other settings.

This book focuses on that paid work, but the history of women's paid employment cannot be understood without an awareness of the responsibilities most women carry in their homes and those that many assume in their communities.

Certainly men also work in their homes and in their communities. Women, however, still bear most of the burden of child care, of cooking, of housework, and, increasingly, of elder care. Overwhelmingly, Americans still assume that women bear the primary responsibility for the care of house and family, and women still contribute many more hours of volunteer work than men.

This triple work load seriously affects women's view of and performance in their paid work. For many it limits the hours they can work for pay. It compels others to drop out of the work force, at least temporarily. It arouses guilt as women try to avoid shortchanging their employers, their families, or their communities. It stresses women and it fatigues them. The landmark *Women's Voices* poll, conducted in 1992 by the Ms. Foundation for Women, found a high level of concern among women about combining work and family. "There's just not enough hours in your day," said one participant. "You wish there were more, and you wish you could be there for more members of your family when they need you."

American society does little to ease and much to aggravate these difficulties. The United States notoriously lags behind other industrialized nations in providing child care and family leave. Only in 1993 has federal law required employers to offer *unpaid* family leave. In many ways the country still conducts its business in flagrant disregard of actualities, as if women worked only for pin money and as if married women and mothers did not work for pay.

COLONIAL DAYS: AN ECONOMY BASED ON HOUSEHOLD PRODUCTION

In the earliest days of colonial America, local governments and trading companies tried to attract white women to the New World. For a while Pennsylvania, Maryland, and Massachusetts offered land to unmarried women. A few British women were banished to the colonies in servitude to the Crown. Many more European women indentured themselves to get to North America, promising to work four to seven years in exchange for transportation. Although the first black women also came as indentured servants, most African women were kidnapped and sold into slavery here. These slave women experienced in the worst possible form the problem that still afflicts women as they try to do their paid work and care for their families. Forced to work for their slavemasters during the day, they had to cook, clean, wash, sew, and weave for their families at night.

In the seventeenth and eighteenth centuries, most American women, like most American men, worked at home, usually in a small town or rural setting. All members of the family contributed to the family support, laboring in the fields or in the house, in large part producing what they consumed. In this preindustrial society, writes Mimi Abramovitz, "Men farmed and fished while women manufactured a variety of goods for both use and trade."[1] But women and men interacted. Husbands might help with spinning, and wives usually knew how to operate their husbands' businesses, which under the common law they could inherit.

These heirs were fortunate. Other women were less so—single women without fathers or brothers, propertyless widows, deserted wives, and women with husbands who could not or would not work. Local communities struggled with the problem of their support. For those whom the authorities regarded as deserving, they provided funds and goods, or paid for their board, or searched for means by which such women could support themselves and their families.

Others, the "undeserving," might be institutionalized and set to forced labor. Some towns auctioned off the services of "undeserving" women to the lowest bidder—that is, to whomever would promise to support them for the least money, wringing labor from them. When they could, towns forcibly expelled the "undeserving," or palmed them off on another settlement, sometimes after whipping them. Salem, Massachusetts, for example, sent Margaret Page to jail "as a lazy, idle loitering person."[2] The Providence, Rhode Island, town fathers shipped off to Boston one Mrs. Hayman, whose husband had gone to sea six months earlier leaving her pregnant and homeless.

These ways of treating poor women were predicated on the belief that women ought to live in patriarchal families. The more closely a poor woman conformed to this ideal, the more probable it was that the authorities would regard her as deserving, that is, *involuntarily* lacking a male breadwinner. Women who failed to achieve this desideratum ought to support themselves. But how? Women found work in spinning, weaving, sewing, domestic service, and agriculture. Midwives not only assisted in births but also peddled herbs and nursed the sick. Women entrepreneurs operated small shops (typically dry-goods stores), taverns, boarding houses, and schools. Women published newspapers; eleven, including Elizabeth Timothy (d. 1757) of the *South Carolina Gazette* and Cornelia Smith Bradford (d. 1755) of Philadelphia's *American Weekly Mercury*, supported themselves as printers before the Revolutionary War. As troubles with England escalated in the late eighteenth century, demand for American-made goods increased, and women who made cloth, clothing, hats, and food products enjoyed expanded markets.

Some people went so far as to argue that women *should* enter the workplace, since their labor was needed and idleness was sinful. Yet throughout the eighteenth century, even as more women worked for pay, they faced increasing criticism and the ideal of the lady of leisure won more support. This ideal, obviously attainable only by upper-class and upper–middle-class women who lived in settled parts of the country, nonetheless encouraged condescending attitudes toward those who had to earn their own livings and support their families.

THE POST–REVOLUTIONARY WAR PERIOD: MOVING TOWARD INDUSTRIALIZATION

In the period after the Revolutionary War the United States was taking the first tentative steps toward industrialization, and "manufactory" owners were beginning to look for workers. Neatly enough, the same process that created that search also rendered some women "surplus." In particular, the transfer of textile manufacture out of the home reduced the need for women's household labor. Farmers began to need the labor of their daughters less and cash more.

Society, at once needing women's paid labor and clinging to the ideal of the traditional patriarchal family, sent women a mixed message: they ought to work, *but* they should center their lives on home and family. Accordingly, most women preferred to earn money, or to assist their male kin to earn money, at home. Many women accepted piecework at home on an "outwork" basis; for example, male shoemakers counted on their wives' labor to construct the uppers.

Some women, though, particularly young women in New England, began leaving their homes to work. Indeed, by 1820 women worked in at least 75 different manufacturing occupations.[3] But society's mixed message in effect instructed them not to commit fully to their paid work; and their employers argued that since these women employees would otherwise be idle, their work was insignificant and deserved only low pay. These attitudes added up to bad news for women. They contributed to a still-unresolved debate over the worth of women's work and the proper focus of women's energies.

The textile mills employed women by the hundreds. Women ran small businesses, even if only as street vendors. In addition, here and there women began to agitate for education that would enable them to enter one of the professions—most commonly teaching.

This impulse toward paid employment was a response both to economic necessity and to questioning about women's roles and women's rights. Before 1840, Elizabeth Cady (1815–1902), who had refused to promise to obey when she married Henry Stanton, had already talked with Lucretia Mott about convoking a women's rights convention. During the years when she was bearing her seven children, Stanton was agitating for a married woman's right to own property. Interests of wage-earning women and women's rights advocates interlocked. Married working women were beginning to think about owning their own labor and controlling their own earnings.

As the numbers of women leaving their homes during their working hours reached a significant mass and as women's rights advocates spoke out, other voices countered, insisting that society needed women's labor in the home, and only there, and that women, by natural moral superiority and divinely commanded self-sacrifice, are uniquely qualified to tend and train children. Eliza Farnham (1815–1864) based such an argument on her belief that women had been created for a higher sphere than men: men should support women so that, as mothers and homemakers, they could elevate the race. Women belong at home and not in gainful employment. (Farnham herself, in a pattern familiar among the more vocal female advocates of women's confinement to the home, divorced her first husband and earned money as a prison matron, a teacher of the blind, a lecturer, matron in an insane asylum, and an author.) From arguments like these evolved the nineteenth-century idea of separate spheres—the private sphere for women and the public sphere for men—and the ideal of "True Womanhood," saintly and nurturing.

Economic factors reinforced the ideals of the patriarchal family and True Womanhood. By the end of the depression years of the 1830s, employers depended less on women's labor. As cities grew and transportation improved, they could centralize jobs, so piecework done at home and the compensation for it dwindled. Factory wages were also declining. From the mid–1840s on, immigration increased, swelling the labor force. Correspondingly, society was discarding its expectations that women should contribute to the economy of the household. On the contrary, many argued that employers *ought not* pay women a living wage but instead keep them dependent on their husbands so as to keep those men sober and industrious—an idea that still echoed in the mind of Henry Ford in the early twentieth century. This dangerous argument, pressed to its logical end, transformed the exploitation of women workers into a boon for society.

The shift in attitudes changed women's expectations and the ways they thought about their own roles and duties. For centuries everyone had taken it as a natural part of the pattern of life that women and men alike should work and produce and that they should jointly feed, clothe, and house their families. With production moving into the factories, the need for women's labor inside the home had dropped significantly, yet society was urging families to keep women there. Well-off women stopped working for pay before or after marriage, and other women tended toward a pattern of quitting paid employment when they married—if their families could afford it. Men's lives changed too, as they alone shouldered the burden of family support and as their earning a "family wage" became a status symbol. The nineteenth century, theoretically so golden an era for family values, put multiple stresses and strains on family life.

These same factors lowered respect for and devalued women's paid work. It took an extraordinary woman to see her job as anything but a necessary evil that demeaned her in the eyes of the world. For conventional people, a married woman's work symbolized her husband's failure. The new attitudes also divided woman from woman, working woman from lady of leisure, and servant from mistress. In many households, the servant no longer worked alongside the housewife and no longer participated in family activities.

In 1840 only about 10 percent of all women took jobs outside their homes, and by 1860 at most 15 percent of all women were in the labor force.[4] These women were overwhelmingly young, single, and/or poor: widows, free blacks, migrants to the growing cities, and emigrants from foreign countries. Nonetheless, women still constituted about half of the workers in manufacturing.[5] In the countryside women still sold surplus products and did piecework at home.

THE CIVIL WAR AND ITS AFTERMATH

The Civil War changed the realities without much altering of the myths of True Womanhood and separate spheres for women and men. Not for the last time, the United States suddenly discovered that it needed women's paid work. The government opened clerical jobs to women. Schools hired so many women teachers that the profession began to feminize. The dreadful illnesses and wounds inflicted by the war created a need for the professionalization of nursing.

Thousands of women, north and south, whose male kinfolk had been slaughtered or disabled somehow had to make their own way in the postwar era. The editor of the Boston *Daily Evening Voice* advocated that such women be forced to move to the West, which needed teachers and domestics. Some of these women petitioned their state legislature to lease them land and furnish them with rations, tools, seeds, and instructions, so that they could raise their own food.[6] Impoverished southern farmers could no longer afford to support their daughters. Most of the black women newly freed from slavery and newly arrived immigrant women were desperately needed to contribute to the family economy.

Yet women continued to earn far less pay than men for the same jobs. Like men, they suffered under harsh working conditions. The post–Civil War period saw their protest and militancy, as women tried to protect themselves, organizing in trade unions and production cooperatives.

By 1870 a quarter of the wage earners in nonagricultural occupations were female. Seventy percent of these women were domestic servants. The other 30 percent were mostly industrial workers, over four-fifths of them employed in making clothes, and the other fifth a miscellany of teachers, store clerks, paper box makers, cigar makers, and printers.[7]

The conflict between the actuality of working women and the myth of True Womanhood roused concern—particularly in an economy oversupplied with labor, a lot of it unskilled or minimally skilled. Half persuaded by the myth they had helped to create, government, employers, and men's trade unions tried to get women out of the workplace and into marriage. They blamed women for men's low wages on the grounds that many women who "didn't need to work" were taking the jobs men deserved and settling for lower wages than men earned. Besides, they fretted, working for pay would make women unable to create harmonious families. Women's charitable organizations, buying this bill of goods, responded by providing boarding houses, clubs, discussion groups, and reading material for working women to keep them fit to bear and raise children.

Yet it was difficult to confine even the most quiescent middle- and upper-class True Women quietly to their homes. With their husbands away at work all day, women associated with other women in clubs, at church, or in the community—clubs dedicated to missionary ideals of doing good or to self-cultivation, clubs that would soon lead them out of the private sphere and into the public.

Meanwhile, women educators were giving the idea of True Womanhood and the domestic cult a new twist. If women were to stay in the home, then they ought to be competent to run it. Catharine Beecher advocated training in the domestic arts. Others pushed further: women as the shapers of young lives, women as keepers of morality, women as the supreme powers in the private sphere needed the best

possible education, fully equal to that of men. They set out to offer it at the Seven Sisters and other women's colleges. Beginning in the 1830s a few private men's colleges admitted women, often on the theory that they would improve the moral atmosphere for the male students. And some state land grant institutions, particularly in the Midwest and West, admitted women from their earliest days. By 1870 women constituted a fifth of all college students, and by 1880 almost a third.

Real education always causes trouble by questioning the status quo, and women's education was no exception. Particularly at women's colleges, faculty imbued women students with the idea that in return for their educations they had a duty to society, a lesson often internalized as a duty to change society. Many women alumnae—alarmingly many, in the minds of the authorities—chose not to marry, or if they did marry, to bear fewer or no children. Instead they worked for pay, as volunteers, or both. They were beginning to enter the professions—not just teaching and nursing, but medicine, the ministry, and the law.

THE PROGRESSIVE ERA

Among these college-educated women and their cohorts, the ideal of the "New Woman" began to replace that of the True Woman. The New Woman strode onto the scene about 1890. She was American, determined, competent, and independent. She was, wrote Dorothea Dix in 1915, a "husky young woman who can play golf all day and dance all night, and drive a motor car, and give first aid to the injured. . . ."[8] She perceived herself as a partner to men, with whom she associated freely, nevertheless a "nice girl." No homebody, she worked and played in the public sphere. The New Woman was of course as much a myth as the True Woman. But myths shape thought and behavior.

In fact, despite the horrified protests that greeted her, the myth of the New Woman fitted the work ethic and the

American temperament much more comfortably than that of the True Woman. The New Woman's independence, self-reliance, and willingness to work as a partner better suited a society in which the ruts left by covered wagons still cross-hatched the Great Plains and where the original white settlers still survived in the Midwest and the Southwest.

All over the country during the Progressive Era women were not only entering the public sphere but also creating an extensive, dense, interlocking network through which to change it. Technological advances were beginning to ease the burden of housework. Now, through their volunteer work, their clubs, and their settlement houses, women were joining together to reform society. Among them, even without the vote, they exercised remarkable influence by persuading, arguing, lobbying, raising money, and contributing countless hours of volunteer work.

The spirit of the time encouraged small individual efforts at solving local problems, which then trickled and flowed into more ambitious attacks on state and national problems. Volunteer women identified and tackled all sorts of problems—from sanitation to women's suffrage, from school reform to prohibition. They mounted major efforts to change conditions for women in the workplace, by personal influence, by protective legislation, and by supporting unions and strikes.

If education and changing ideas were altering the work force, so were economic factors. Among the large, poor working-class population, few men could command a wage sufficient for all the family needs, even though family size was shrinking. Unregulated working conditions caused high rates of disease and crippling among male industrial workers, whose families their wives or widows then had to support. Many men could find only seasonal work. Technological advances were displacing others. By 1890 sheer necessity was pushing married women into the workplace.

By 1900 a fifth of the female labor force was married.[9] More than 20 percent of women over ten years old worked for pay.[10] Almost 12 percent of all working women headed families, and 16.4 percent were the sole providers for their families.

The turn of the century found working women diversified both demographically and in the work they performed. Although most were young—some in that day of few child labor laws pathetically young—a third were over 35, at a time when a woman's life expectancy was about 48 years. They differed in marital status, motherhood, class, religion, and race. Native-born white women were entering the labor force in unprecedented numbers.

The range and variety of their work as described in the 1900 census astounds those who think of all women a century ago as homebodies. Many have heard of the professional women: the 1,010 lawyers counted in the 1900 census, the 2,193 journalists, the 3,405 clergy, the 787 dentists, and the 7,399 physicians and surgeons. And anyone can explain away as mavericks the 18 longshoremen, the 84 engineers and surveyors, the 95 theatrical managers, the 100 architects, the 409 electricians, even the 1,365 miners and quarriers. But who were those 8,246 women whom the census designated as "hunters, trappers, guides and scouts"?

The numbers of working women in unexpected occupations surprised even their feminist contemporaries. Nearly 3,000 women, wrote labor organizer Agnes Nestor, worked in the Chicago stockyards "... in the canneries, in the chipped beef rooms, in the packing rooms, packing, weighing, and painting cans, and sewing the bags for the hams."[11] And, Lydia Commander bragged in 1907, "There are 946 commercial travelers, 261 wholesale merchants, 1,271 officials of banks, 100 lumbermen, 113 woodchoppers, 84 civil engineers and surveyors, 1,932 stock raisers, 143 marble cutters,

595 butchers. There are even 10 wheel-wrights, 8 steam boilermakers, 2 roofers and slaters, 1 well-borer, and a licensed pilot on the Mississippi."[12] By 1907 women held nearly a quarter of the highly-skilled jobs of coremaking in Pittsburgh foundries.[13] In short, by 1900 women labored in 295 of the 303 occupations listed in the census.

Even more significant, women's working for pay was becoming commonplace, and women's attitudes about paid work were changing. Popular writers like Edna Ferber were setting before their readers the joys and benefits of earning one's own living. Ferber's skirt saleswoman Edna McChesney thanked fortune "that I wasn't cursed with a life of ease. These massage-at-ten-fitting-at-eleven-bridge-at-one women always look such hags at thirty-five."[14]

New Women turned away from the prospect of twiddling their thumbs at home as good daughters until they moved to other homes as good wives. "All the girls in my town expected to earn their own living," wrote a midwesterner. "Most of us went to work as soon as we were graduated from college or high school, or from the condensed form of instruction known as the business college ... no girl dreamed of remaining at home as a burden to the family to support.... When we met a new girl, we did not ask, 'Who is she?' We inquired, 'What does she do?'"[15]

Urbanization and technological advances were beginning to cut the farm population, but the 1900 census counted almost half a million women employed as agricultural laborers. More than half of them were apparently field hands and vegetable and fruit pickers, toiling all too often with their young children under miserable, hopeless conditions. Of these, almost three-fourths were black. In 1900 over half of all black Cotton Belt households hired out at least one daughter 16 or younger as a field laborer.[16] German-American, Swedish-American, Mexican-American, and Japanese-Amer-

ican women also tilled the fields across the United States.

Another 300,000 women, mostly white, were farmers, planters, and overseers—apparently women of property or at least of considerable responsibility and authority. Some inherited a family farm. Others bought land for themselves. Among those "farmers, planters, and overseers" were also the women who homesteaded their own land.

Thousands more women uncounted by the census—farm wives—contributed endless and often lifelong labor to the farm economy without pay and often without establishing by their labor any property rights in the farm.

By 1900 domestic servants were hard to find in many areas of the country. In the 1900 population of about 75,000,000, "only" about 1,000,000 women were in domestic service as maids, laundresses, cooks, companions, waitresses, and nurses.[17] About one household in ten had live-in servants, and seven out of ten housewives did their own work.[18] Middle-class housewives were more apt to employ part-time rather than full-time help. In 1900 only 26 percent of women in domestic service were native-born whites; 28 percent were foreign-born; another 19 percent were the daughters of immigrants; and 27 percent were black.[19] Southern housewives still relied on black women; southwestern householders turned to Mexican Americans; westerners sometimes employed Asian Americans; and rural midwesterners could still sometimes find native-born white "hired girls" to help them. For many married women, some form of domestic service was the only option. It was what they knew how to do. In 1910 married women constituted 55 percent of the janitors, 51 percent of the laundresses, and 39 percent of the servants.[20]

But to the puzzlement of employers, most working women regarded domestic service as a last resort. Even though it frequently paid more than factory work or work in a department store, its low status, its long hours, its lack of personal freedom, its often poor living conditions, and the unreasonable demands of some female employers, not to mention the sexual demands of the female employers' sons and husbands, made many women scorn it. Those forced into domestic work it tried to avoid living in, often setting themselves up as quasi-entrepreneurs hiring themselves out by the day.

Factory work was just one step up from domestic work. In 1900 factories employed about a quarter of women workers—almost 1,250,000.[21] Most of them were young, single immigrants. Seventy-five percent of them were foreign-born or the daughters of foreign-born parents. Much of their work was seasonal. They knew no security: according to a survey by the Women's Trade Union League, most of them held two to five different positions in the course of a year.[22]

They worked in many industries. They stripped tobacco and rolled and packed cigars. They assembled paper boxes. They dipped candies. They made artificial flowers and feathers. They processed food. Almost 40 percent of them labored in the needle trades, some in an "inside shop" that did cutting and sewing, some in a "contracting shop" that hired workers to finish garments, and some in their tenement dwellings as home workers. No one knew how many women toiled at home in such jobs, with or without the help of their families, right down to their two-year-old babies. They were paid on a piecework basis. In 1901 the New York State Department of Labor put the number of home workers within that state at 30,000, mostly Italian women.[23]

Most factories confined their women workers in hellish settings—dangerous, filthy, littered—for inordinately long hours and pitiably small wages. Bookbinders sometimes worked 24½ hours at a stretch. Women employees had to fight off the sexual advances of their bosses and endure suggestive comments. Employers, uncontrolled by minimum wage laws, paid women only what they had to, usually a quarter to two-thirds of what men earned.[24] Worse still, they eroded even the pittances they paid by such mean devices as setting the clocks back to prolong working hours or requiring women in the needle trades to furnish thread and findings and glovemakers to buy their own machines, paying as much as $65 for a machine that cost the employer $35. Fringe benefits, of course, did not exist, nor did sick days. Sometimes women even gave birth on the mill floor between the looms.[25]

All too few women in industry earned enough to live on. Most survived by residing with their families, turning over all their earnings, receiving car fare and lunch money back. "Women adrift" huddled together in overcrowded rooms, or tried to rent beds in charitable institutions for ten cents a night. Some of them eked out their wages by prostitution.

"The mill-girl is happy, isn't she?" everyone asked Marie Van Vorst after this middle-class woman disguised herself in cheap clothes and sought jobs in factories up and down the East Coast. "I thank Heaven that I can say truthfully," wrote Van Vorst, "that of all who came under my observation, not one who was of age to reflect was happy ... the most sane and hopeful indication for the future of the factory girl and the mill-hand is that she rebels, dreams of something better, and will in the fullness of time stretch toward it."[26]

She did indeed rebel, in many a strike—notably the Uprising of the 20,000 of 1909. From 1895 to 1905, women conducted 83 strikes completely on their own.[27] In 1900 San Francisco laundry workers rebelled against a system that forced them to stand for as long as 17 hours a day at mangles, just above the washroom with hot steam pouring up through the floor, "breathing air laden with particles of soda, ammonia, and other chemicals." They had to live in dormitories with four beds to a room, and to do without food after six P.M., though they often worked until midnight, for a wage of $8.10 a month plus room and board. Secretly unionizing, they won elimination of the boarding house system, shorter hours, higher pay, holidays, overtime, and a regular lunch hour. Their union thrived for years.[28] Women bookbinders, mostly native-born, comparatively well-educated whites, managed to unionize a quarter of their 14,000 work force.

Many of these labor actions found strong support among women's volunteer organizations, particularly the Women's Trade Union League. In a parallel effort to improve conditions for women in the workplace, these volunteer organizations dedicated ever more time and effort to passing protective legislation.

In 1900 almost 216,000 women worked in stores at tedious and low-paying jobs that they nevertheless rated as a notch or two above factory work.[29] The stores happily hired women, especially neatly dressed and well-spoken women, but only, of course, for the lower ranks. Store rules did not allow them to sit down or lean on their counters, required them to work impossibly long hours, particularly during the holiday seasons, and confined them to perhaps 20 minutes, perhaps less, to eat lunch. If they failed to clothe themselves with sufficient elegance, the male floorwalkers who supervised them might suggest that they make friends among the male customers.

In a brilliant stroke, some of these oppressed women turned to their middle- and upper-class women customers for help. The Consumers' League that resulted learned to exercise its members' persuasive and economic powers efficiently, improving working conditions not only in department stores but also in factories, and, not incidentally, promoting higher standards of product sanitation.

The dream of working-class girls and the haven of middle-class women entering the work force during the Progressive Era was the relatively new (to women) field of clerical work. Industry was ex-

panding, introducing machines, and applying the principles of "scientific management" to get the work done faster, more easily, and more cheaply. Demand for clerical workers soared. Young, single, white, native-born women, most often the daughters of native-born parents, flocked to meet it. The work was clean and respectable, suitable for "ladies." The number of women clerical workers grew from 7,000 in 1880 to 187,000 in 1900 to 1,421,000 in 1920.[30]

They could master the necessary skills relatively quickly and inexpensively. Young Women's Christian Associations taught typing and other clerical skills, and high schools eventually followed suit. Even if women learned their office skills in the more prestigious private business schools, they paid tuition as low as $10 a month, perhaps for as long as nine months, after which they could expect to start with wages of $10 a week.

The jobs they got were mostly new, differing from the clerical jobs of the nineteenth century, which often provided men with an apprenticeship in the business world and offered many of them almost unlimited upward mobility. The new jobs created by the rapid expansion of industry and the application of the principles of scientific management held out no such prospect. They were broken down into their component parts, deskilled, affording the employee little insight into or overview of the business, and almost no control over her own work. Employers wanted these jobs filled by women—workers to whom they could pay low wages, who would presumably leave the workplace to marry after a few years, whom they could train rapidly and interchange one for another with a minimum of disturbance. By preference employers hired young, attractive women to adorn the office, unmarried women with no prattle about the need for more wages to support families.

At the top of their ranks stood the private secretary. She had status. She expected file clerks and typists to call her

"Miss." She exercised far more control over her work than they. To some extent she could decide for herself when to do what. But her boss expected from her in the office some, if not all, of the personal services he expected from his wife at home. Often her pay did not adequately recompense her for the responsibilities she bore, and she usually could not aspire to a higher job.

Like private secretaries, office workers in small businesses performed more diverse tasks and exercised more control over their own work, especially in one-woman offices, than in large corporations. Indeed, then as now, they often knew more about the business than the men to whom they reported, but only rarely could they overcome the gender prejudice that denied them commensurate wages and promotion.

Still, in the Progressive Era, women were better off in clerical work than in most of the other jobs available to them. Both in status and in money, women office workers fared better than women in factories, stores, and domestic service. In the late nineteenth century, some women office workers even outearned teachers. The gap between office workers and other women narrowed as more women entered the lowest ranks of clerical work, as legislation and unionization improved the lot of factory women and store workers, and as teachers' pay rose with their standards of education.

Clerical workers could do little to protect themselves, for most of them were not the kind to think of unionizing. For years they clung to the status of "ladies," at the sacrifice of their own interests, identifying with their bosses rather than with other workers. Clerical work became a female ghetto and a refuge. As management deskilled the work available in the typing pools and file rooms, it sentenced women to "no-exit" jobs. At the same time, office work provided a kind of insurance for women who dropped in and out of the work force or needed to move from one city to another as familial demands changed.

Professional women differed from working-class women in all sorts of ways. Though they clustered in large cities, they were geographically mobile. Politically aware, they were strikingly active in reform work, and, of course, they had more money than working-class women. They faced staggering difficulties, but they found or created opportunities.

In the professions that they entered in increasing numbers, they had to battle the usual societal disapproval, sexual harassment, inequitable status and pay, and gender discrimination. Almost as often as not, professional women had to deny themselves marriage if they wanted a career. Only about a quarter of them dared to indulge themselves in what so many men have long taken for granted—the combination of satisfying professional work and a family.[31]

But these courageous and fortunate women enjoyed the advantage, unusual among women workers, of exercising considerable control over their own work. Better still, as women's presence and influence increased, they began to create their own conditions (as Henrietta Rodman fought for teachers' rights), even their own professions (pioneering like Elsie deWolfe in interior decorating and Alice Hamilton in industrial medicine), and their own professional associations in medicine, law, journalism, science, business, the arts, and education. Sometimes they worked their way into paid positions in club work and reform activity. The new professions of social work, home economics, public health nursing, and occupational and physical therapy not only absorbed the energies of thousands of women workers but also alleviated the suffering of a rapidly industrializing society.

All sorts of women undertook entrepreneurial ventures. Wives supplemented the family income by selling milk and eggs or taking in boarders or doing piecework. Domestics and private-duty nurses hired themselves out by the day. Women operated dressmaking and hat-making businesses from their homes or in small shops. They peddled goods on pushcarts. They ran two-thirds of the employment offices in big cities. They contracted to feed men at shearing and lumber camps; they raised animals for menageries; they grew violets. Now and then one of them flourished into big business, like African American Mme. C. J. Walker of hair-product fame.

World War I and its aftermath, however, made clear the dominant attitudes of American culture toward women's work. The country called on women for extensive volunteer work and demanded their services in the workplace for the duration of the war. Women took over jobs traditionally performed by men, including those from which they had long been barred because of alleged incapacities: lack of strength, lack of intelligence, lack of commitment, or lack of managerial ability. Black women, though even in wartime not enjoying the opportunities open to European Americans, suddenly were in demand in factories and offices that never had allowed them within their precincts.

When the war ended, the employers dismissed most of the women. The war had clearly demonstrated that the United States, however urgent its demands on women in emergencies, considered them a secondary labor force, available as needed, easily dispensed with when not. With all the pioneering activity, with all the labor reforms, with all the expansion of opportunities for women throughout the Progressive Era, suffragist Dr. Anna Howard Shaw still found it necessary to insist: "The time has come when we women have a right to ask that we shall be free to labor where our labor is needed, that we shall be free to serve in the capacity for which we are fitted."

BOOM AND BUST:
THE 1920S AND 1930S

After World War I, a new Victorianism assumed that women functioned best as wives and mothers and that they ought not work for money but instead devote themselves to good causes. On the other hand, the shorter hours and improved working conditions that resulted from the labor reforms of the Progressive Era combined with the easing of the burden of housework through technological advances to enable more women to work for pay—not sheerly out of grim necessity, but to raise the family's standard of living. Whereas in 1920 about a quarter of wage-earning women were married (and a quarter to a third of these did "homework"), by 1930 that proportion had moved up to almost a third.[32] At the same time, prosperity was changing the composition of the female labor force in other ways. Even as more women exercised a free choice to move into the labor market, others, whose husbands were earning more, chose to leave the labor force. Nevertheless, as late as 1930, immigrants and blacks constituted 57 percent of all employed women.[33] Women were also making important long-term commitments to professional work. For instance, during the 1920s women earned 12 of every 100 science and engineering doctorates, a higher proportion than they reached again until 1975.[34]

The prosperous growing economy needed women workers. They found jobs, not only in clerical work but also in advertising, sales, marketing, publishing, accounting, credit, and life insurance. They began to dominate the human services fields.

But unions kept on resisting women's "invasion" of the workplace, and employers continued to shunt most women into dead-end jobs and to deny them wages sufficient for economic independence. Between 1910 and 1940, 86–90 percent of all employed women worked in only ten different occupations.[35] Women workers suffered also in the 1920s for lack of the support that women's organizations had afforded them during the Progressive Era, as the club women who had united around the central women's issue of suffrage dispersed after the passage of the Nineteenth Amendment. The mood of the country had shifted from reforming to binging on the much touted "peace and prosperity." Many of the women moving into the labor force were suspicious of unions and susceptible to the paternalism of employers who offered them restrooms, suggestion boxes, and counselors, but not a living wage.

The Great Depression (1929–1939), with its suffering for families all over the nation, caused some odd quirks in hiring patterns. As men lost their jobs at catastrophic rates, some employers sought out women employees because their labor cost less. As a result, although women also were fired or laid off, women moved from 24.3 percent of all workers in 1930 to 25.1 percent in 1940.[36] Unions had perforce to recruit women members, increasing their numbers from 250,000 in 1929 to 800,000 in 1939.[37] Yet at the same time 2–4 million would-be women workers were unemployed; about a tenth of them headed households, and a fifth to a half of them had responsibilities for dependents.[38] Public sentiment and government propaganda criticized married women who worked on the grounds that they had no right to "take a job away from a man." Many institutions adopted a policy of refusing to hire married women. Despite these sanctions, married women continued to increase their representation in the labor force. In 1930, 11.7 percent of married women worked, and in 1940, 15.2.[39]

In 1930 almost 11 million women worked for pay; in 1940, about 13 million. Throughout the decade, more women worked at domestic service than in any other field, though the proportions dropped. By 1940, of every ten women workers, three were in clerical or sales work, two were factory operatives, two were in domestic service, one was a professional—most often a teacher or a nurse—and one was a service worker. They worked long hours—more than half of them more than 50 hours a week—and earned little. In 1937 they averaged $525 annually, against men's $1,027.[40]

The pathos of these figures is exceeded by the misery of the estimated 2,000,000 unemployed women. The Young Women's Christian Association reckoned that in 1933, 145,000 of them were homeless and footloose, most of them under the age of 18. Yet in a sense women workers were protected during the Great Depression by the lower wages customary for them and by men's not applying for "women's work." Traditionally-female areas such as clerical work and service occupations contracted less than those such as manufacturing, in which men were concentrated.

WORLD WAR II AND THE START OF THE COLD WAR (1939–1963)

The outbreak of war in Europe in 1939 ended the Great Depression and increased employment opportunities—at first mainly for men, but soon the United States again, as in earlier boom times and previous wars, felt the need for its secondary labor force and set out accordingly to alter ideals about femininity. By mid-1942 the government was already campaigning to lure women into the workplace, pressuring women's magazines to print stories and articles praising wage-earning women who "backed up the men at the front." The minimum age for employed women was lowered from 18 to 16. Popular songs, newsreels, movies, and newspapers all told women of their duty to go out to work. Relatively higher wages for women, particularly in "men's jobs," proved at least as persuasive. With all these lures, government and employers recruited perhaps 3.5 million more women than would have gone to work otherwise—about a quarter more than would have normally been expected.[41]

At war's end the same propaganda machine reversed its engines to push women out of shipyards and airplane factories and into their kitchens and nurseries. Despite all the pressure, despite the closing of many plants, despite massive firings and layoffs, many women chose not to leave the workplace. In a repeat of the postwar pattern of World War I, they moved instead into lower-paid work.

Five years after the end of the war, women's participation rate in the work force had doubled from the 16 percent of 1940 to 32 percent in 1950.[42] Many of the new employees were white middle-class married women with children. Typically they stayed at home with their young children, but took a job when the youngest child went to school—a pattern that eroded only in the late 1960s.

During the 1950s women's participation rate in the labor force crept up more. The cult of consumerism urged women to stay at home and consume. But this creed also whispered another message: earn money to consume more. In the immediate postwar years, savings from wartime earnings paid for many of the goods purchased under the force of the pent-up demand of wartime, when good citizens were supposed to "use it up; wear it out; make it do." Thereafter, many women clearly discerned that to consume more they needed more money, and they went out to earn it. Women constituted 29 percent of the work force in 1950, 35 percent by 1965.[43]

Despite the promotion of the Dick-and-Jane fantasy family during the 1950s, the authorities could not quite make up their minds about whether or not women ought to work. The Cold War made them nervous. Suppose it should heat up. Suppose the country suddenly needed its women in the workplace again. These fears enabled the Women's Bureau of the Department of Labor (founded in World War I at the behest of Progressive Era women) to open training programs for women in industry and to call for such needed supports for women workers as equal Social Security benefits, paid maternity leaves, and day care. In 1956 the AFL-CIO, concerned that falling rates for women workers (as compared to wartime wages and men's wages) might drag down pay scales generally, endorsed the ideal of equal pay for equal work.

On the other hand, pop psychologists were quick to accuse the wage-earning woman of destroying family life, creating neuroses in her children, neglecting her husband, and rejecting her own femininity.

THE NEW AGE OF WOMEN'S
LIBERATION (1963–1980)

The women seeping into the labor force in the 1950s, it turned out, had other ideas besides economic survival or raising their families' standard of living. Betty Friedan gave them voice in 1963 when she published *The Feminine Mystique*, which raised to the level of consciousness a lot of the concerns that working women had been mulling over, such as the relegation of so many women to the secondary labor force, the inequality of women's pay, and the injustice of not recognizing or rewarding so much of the work that women contribute to society, including housework. Why, women asked themselves and each other, must they put up with sexual harassment in the workplace? Why must they listen to the argument on the one hand that women are paid less because they need less and on the other hand that women are paid less because they are less skilled, particularly in those frequent instances when both statements are false? Why are men entitled to the comforts and pleasures of a family, but career women are expected to choose between work and marriage?

Although at first the women who whispered or shouted these questions were mostly middle-class, soon poor women, encouraged and trained by President Johnson's war on poverty, also began to break into higher-paying "men's jobs."

During the 1960s and 1970s, this kind of thinking resulted in action, both individual and organizational. A new women's movement attracted the support of millions of women and changed the lives of millions more.

Working women widened their support systems through networking. Women's organizations multiplied, both those general in interest and those specific to an occupation. With the country in a prosperous era and a prevailing mood of reform, they successfully lobbied for critical legislation to give women a fairer share and a fairer shake, from the Equal Pay Act of 1963 and the Civil Rights Act of 1964 to the Pregnancy Discrimination Act of 1978. Often at great financial and emotional expense, individual women bravely went to court to sue for fair treatment or a chance at a nontraditional job, or pushed the Equal Employment Opportunity Commission to help them. Women students flocked to law schools and used their newly acquired legal expertise to fight for women's rights. Through these combined efforts, affirmative action programs, executive orders, and judicial decisions redefined women's rights and opportunities in the workplace. They also accelerated the pace of women's entry into the work force. In the 1960s and the 1970s, the women's work force doubled from 22 million to 44 million. [44]

Married women continued to move in increasing numbers into the work force. By 1976, 62 percent of the female labor force were married; whereas in 1900, 62 percent had been single. The link between poverty and a wife's presence in the workplace had broken. The number of female-headed households had sharply increased. By 1978, with a rising divorce rate and more out-of-wedlock babies, the proportion of single-parent families, mostly headed by women, reached 18.9 percent of all families, more than double the proportion of 1950. From about 1970 on, mothers of young children flocked into the workplace, soon constituting its fastest-growing element. By 1978, 30 percent of mothers with children under a year old worked for pay, and 41 percent of mothers with children under two.[45]

The 1970s saw some movement by women into traditionally male-intensive jobs, especially by black women, who gained shares in both manufacturing and such male-dominated areas as communications, transportation, and government.[46] The ranks of women professionals began to swell, particularly in medicine and the law, and women competed to enter M.B.A. programs with their eyes on high-paid jobs in business.

Forces other than the women's movement also enlarged the women's work force. The expansion of a service economy that began in the early 1970s created many new jobs, especially low-skilled, entry-level positions in clerical work, retail sales, personal services, and human services—jobs with little prospect of upward mobility, the sorts of jobs traditionally held by women.[47] Employers hired more part-time and temporary workers. They further deskilled jobs, compartmentalizing and routinizing them. They shifted tasks downward to lower-status, lower-paid staff. Paralegals and a whole hierarchy of paramedics, mostly female, took over large portions of the work previously performed by highly trained lawyers and doctors, still mostly male.[48]

The activities of the women's movement in the 1960s and the 1970s are still bearing fruit—some of it bitter. Reactions and backlashes are inevitable, but most women in the early 1990s believe that the women's movement has improved their lives.[49]

THE 1980S AND 1990S AND BEYOND

The closer the view of events, the more distorted and the more difficult to balance and evaluate. During the 1980s and early 1990s, as in the 1920s, Americans turned away from trying to achieve a great society and turned to indulging in shopping until they dropped or went bankrupt.

Attempts to achieve equity for women nonetheless persisted, particularly in the private sector, even though the reluctance of the federal government to enforce existing legislation hampered them. Women's organizations lobbied for new legislation, such as the Women's Business Ownership Act passed in 1988 (but discontinued in 1992) and the Displaced Homemakers Self-Sufficiency Assistance Act. Organizations and individuals resorted to the courts to protect or procure their rights. Women won their first significant victory in equal pay for comparable work in the 1982 case of *AFSCME v. Washington*. In 1986 in *Meritor Savings Bank v. Vinson*, they fought successfully to broaden the definition of sexual discrimination to include sexual harassment. The outcome of all this activity remains to be evaluated by more distant and more objective eyes.

The 1980s and 1990s have aggravated the problems of child care and the difficulties of combining family and work responsibilities. Since 1980, women, often from economic necessity and the falling real income of their families, have continued to move into the workplace—especially mothers of young children. In the early 1990s, these new workers are still controversial, and cultural attitudes toward them are still ambivalent. Society generally still dictates that middle- and upper-class women should bear the primary burden of child care and punishes them if they delegate this to someone else, no matter how responsible. About poor women society is even more ambivalent, at once wanting them to raise their children responsibly and to earn a living for themselves and their children: "The exception to the rule that mothers not work outside the home has historically been the poor, unmarried, or widowed mother, whose employment has for the most part been seen as a preferable alternative to her economic dependency on the state."[50]

In the 1970s and 1980s, while highly educated, mostly white women penetrated traditionally male professions in significant numbers, blue-collar women fared less well. Deregulation and capital flight overseas contributed to the loss of manufacturing jobs. Employers saved money by hiring women rather than men, but they also hired part-timers and temporary workers rather than regular full-time workers, home workers (pieceworkers) rather than factory workers, underground off-the-books sweatshop workers rather than legal workers. Opportunities in the labor market expanded at an even lower rate for women of color than for white women.

But several facts proclaim themselves. Hundreds, indeed thousands, of organizations dedicated to promoting the welfare of women in the workplace are functioning. Attitudes toward women in the workplace have shifted significantly, with millions of men concerned, either out of personal interest in the earnings of their wives, or out of a sense of justice, or both. Women and men alike generally accept the idea that women are more likely than not to occupy the workplace—as 57 percent of all American women now do. Although sexism has not yet become as unacceptable as overt racism, sophisticated males deplore both equally. If there is anything to trickledown theories, their attitudes may ultimately triumph.

Some futurists predict hope and help for women in the changing demography of the United States, which indicates that in the twenty-first century the work force will consist of smaller proportions of white males and larger proportions of women and minorities. Some gurus at the Harvard Business School in the early 1990s are warning corporations that they will not be able to compete in the global economy unless they make better use of their women employees, i.e., give them a chance to exercise fully their talents and skills and some support in fulfilling their family responsibilities.

Women, however, know all too well that they have a long way to go. The comparable worth (pay equity) battle has hardly started. Only with great effort and sacrifice can managerial women in most companies crack the glass ceiling that allows them to see the top ranks of executives but not join them. Only with great effort and a degree of luck can many women climb above the sticky floor that keeps them glued to low-paid jobs. Women in executive suites, in classrooms, in offices, in the trades, in trucks, in police stations and firehouses, on fishing boats, and in mines encounter difficulty in dealing with male co-workers worried about their own jobs or masculinity and willing to indulge in the grossest sexual harassment to drive women out. Seventy-seven percent of all women are still in the 20 occupations that are 80 percent female.[51]

Besides these obvious problems, all workers, regardless of gender, are caught in a shift that may affect them as radically as the Industrial Revolution affected the lives of nineteenth-century workers. Global economic forces are changing the very shape of American business and industry. The economy is showing a tendency to divide the work force into two widely separated segments: one highly skilled, always learning—shifting and retraining several times in a work life—, creative, maintaining high personal satisfaction, high control over one's own work, and high pay; the other closely supervised and condemned to boringly repetitive and routine work. Women are overrepresented in the second segment. Job security and job benefits are decreasing, with only a small fraction of the work force protected by union contracts, and employers perforce turning more and more to consultative services, contract workers, part-time workers, temporary workers, and above all, off-shore workers.

Although after all these years American women in the workplace still carry their triple load of work, family, and community; although women workers, particularly the mothers of small children and the daughters responsible for elder care, are exhausted by their unending workdays, the *Women's Voices* poll shows them generally optimistic and hopeful. Indeed, on the whole, women are more likely to be satisfied with their work than men—44 percent of the women versus 38 percent of the men say they are very satisfied. Women's attitudes should reassure those establishment patriarchs who worry about family values, for women workers value families. They are tired and stressed, but they don't want to go back. "This is what I wanted to do." "I wanted to have it all, and I got it all. I wanted a husband, the kids and a career. And I love it."

But they have an agenda. As Radcliffe President Linda S. Wilson told a Congressional subcommittee in 1992, "The U.S. is the only industrialized nation in which basic workplace policies assume that women are not in the workplace."[52] It is this underlying assumption that women need changed.

Women need and want equal pay for equal work. "If I'm as qualified as you are, I certainly want the amount of money and the recognition. I think we're entitled to that as women." In the early 1990s, average earnings for women with a college degree were $26,000 per year, versus men's $39,000—a difference over a 40-year work life of $420,000.[53]

Women want healthcare benefits. "I'm afraid to get sick. I'm afraid to go to the doctor if I am sick because the insurance policies change every year as far as what they're going to cover and how much they're going to pay and what it's going to cost us." "There are so many kids who don't get glasses because the parents don't have any insurance. Or kids with hearing problems or kids who walk into school with ringworm and mom can't take them anywhere because they don't have the money."[54]

Women want flextime. Fifty-eight percent of all women and 67 percent of women who currently work full-time would prefer a job with flexible hours.[55]

On 13 December 1992, *The New York Times* reported a women's economic policy developed by women leaders for submission to President-Elect Clinton. It included such provisions as expanding the definition of "infrastructure" to include housing, child care, health, and recreation; increasing the minimum wage to a level that would support a family of three; signing legislation requiring larger companies to allow workers to take unpaid leave for personal or family medical emergencies; in federal employment awarding equal pay for work of equal value, and developing policies to allow employees to balance work and family responsibilities; and providing incentives to urban enterprise zone investors to focus on the employment needs of low-income women. These are the sorts of changes women need to meet their obligations.

The question looms whether, in a highly competitive global market, Americans can continue a system that disadvantages and underuses women. In our heterogeneous society, demographers tell us, several factors indicate a coming dearth of white males in the workplace: the level or declining participation of white men, the continuing rise in the percentage of working women, immigration patterns, and variations in birth rates among different ethnic groups. Between 1990 and 2000, about two-thirds of new work force entrants will be women, with women of color making up the greatest share. Black women will increase their employment by a third, and Latinas by a huge 85 percent.[56] In 1991, 45 percent of the work force was female; that percentage is expected to rise to 47 percent by the year 2000. In 1991, 57.4 percent of all women worked; government experts anticipate a rise to 62.6 percent by 2000.[57]

More women are preparing themselves for the world of work. In the 1980s the number of men receiving B.A. degrees declined from 473,611 to 438,097, while the number of women recipients climbed from 455,806 to 534,570; similar patterns held for M.A.s. From 1980 to 1986 the number of men earning M.B.A.s increased by 8.3 percent, the number of women by 69.7 percent.[58] Encouraging as these figures are for women fortunate enough to get to college, it's chilling to hear the estimate that in the year 2000 only 14 percent of jobs will be open to workers with less than a high school education, while in 1992 most women workers—58 percent—have a high school diploma or less.[59]

In increasing numbers women are starting their own businesses. The Foundation for Women Business Owners predicted 1992 as the year that more Americans would be working for women-owned businesses than for Fortune 500 companies.

Some forward-thinking companies are beginning to plan for the better utilization of working women. Societal attitudes toward women in the workplace have changed radically, particularly among young Americans. Women want to work, as the *Women's Voices* poll has amply demonstrated. Women need to work, many of them as the sole support of their families. Can the country finally stop relegating women to a secondary work force, pay them on their merit rather than on their gender, and give them the support systems they need to fulfill the obligations they fully recognize to their families, their employers, and their communities?

Another question remains. If and when women acquire more power, if and when they move in significant numbers into the trades and other nontraditional occupations, if and when more women become managers, will they change the nature of the workplace? Some theorists believe that they will make it safer, healthier, more cooperative and less authoritarian, more flexible, and more respectful of individual differences. Women will, in this theory, no longer work simply under "men's rules," but transfer to the workplace the standards and qualities with which they work in the home, humanizing employment, rendering it less stressful, and increasing its satisfaction. It is impossible to evaluate this bright prediction, but it is worth noting that many of the reforms that have improved the conditions under which most Americans labor were enacted first for women workers, and were initiated, fought for, and lobbied through by women.

Notes

1. Mimi Abramovitz, *Regulating the Lives of Women: Social Welfare Policy from Colonial Times to the Present* (Boston: South End Press, 1988), 51.

2. Ibid., 86.

3. Lynn Y. Weiner, *From Working Girl to Working Mother: The Female Labor Force in the United States, 1820–1980* (Chapel Hill: University of North Carolina Press, 1985), 31.

4. Alice Kessler-Harris, *Out to Work: A History of Wage-Earning Women in the United States* (Oxford: Oxford University Press, 1982), 46, 48.

5. Ibid., 48.

6. Alice Kessler-Harris, "Independence and Virtue in the Lives of Wage-Earning Women," in Judith Friedlander, Blanche Wiesen Cook, Alice Kessler-Harris, and Caroll Smith-Rosenberg, eds., *Women in Culture and Politics: A Century of Change* (Bloomington: Indiana University Press, 1986), 6–7.

7. Carole Turbin, "And We Nothing but Women: Irish Working Women in Troy," in Carol Ruth Berkin and Mary Beth Norton, *Women of America: A History* (Boston: Houghton Mifflin, 1979).

8. James R. McGovern, "The American Woman's Pre–World War I Freedom in Manners and Morals," *Journal of American History* LV (September 1968): 323.

9. Cindy Sondik Aron, introduction to Dorothy Richardson's *The Long Day: The Story of a New York Working Girl* (Charlottesville: University Press of Virginia, [1905], 1990), xviii.

10. Abramovitz, 221.

11. Agnes Nestor, *Woman's Labor Leader: The Autobiography of Agnes Nestor* (Rockford, IL: Bellevue Books, 1954), 63.

12. Lydia Kingsmill Commander, *The American Idea* (New York: Arno Press, [1907], 1972), 132.

13. Barbara Meyer Wertheimer, *We Were There: The Story of Working Women in America* (New York: Pantheon Books, 1977), 210.

14. Edna Ferber, *Personality Plus: Some Experiences of Emma McChesney and Her Son Jock* (New York: Frederick A. Stokes, 1914), 61.

15. Elizabeth Sears, "Business Women and Women in Business," *Harper's Monthly* 134 (January 1917): 274.

16. Carl N. Degler, *At Odds: Women and the Family in America from the Revolution to the Present* (New York: Oxford University Press, 1980), 409; and Jacqueline Jones, *Labor of Love, Labor of Sorrow: Black Women, Work, and the Family from Slavery to the Present* (New York: Basic Books, 1985), 91.

17. Degler, 309.

18. Nestor, 63.

19. Ruth Schwartz Cowan, *More Work for Mother: The Ironies of Household Technology from the Open Hearth to the Microwave* (New York: Basic Books, 1983), 170.

20. Sara M. Evans, *Born for Liberty* (New York: Free Press, 1989), 156–157.

21. Nancy Woloch, *Women and the American Experience* (New York: Alfred Knopf, 1984), 235.

22. Nancy Schrom Dye, *As Equals and As Sisters: Feminism, The Labor Movement, and the Women's Trade Union League of New York* (Columbia: University of Missouri Press, 1980), 73, 212.

23. Ibid., 18, 19.

24. Wertheimer, 214; and Andrew Sinclair, *The Emancipation of American Women* (New York: Harper and Row, 1965), 306. "Economist John Commons estimated that only 25 percent of all female wage earners made a living wage in 1914—a figure placed at $8. a week." Alice Kessler-Harris, *Women Have Always Worked: A Historical Overview* (New York: Feminist Press, 1981), 63.

25. Nestor, 158; Rheta Childe Dorr, *A Woman of Fifty* (New York: Arno Press, [1924], 1980), 123; and Wertheimer, 358.

26. Mrs. John Van Vorst and Marie

Van Vorst, *The Woman Who Toils, Being the Experiences of Two Gentlewomen as Factory Girls* (New York: Doubleday, Page, 1903), 267, 269.

27. Wertheimer, 204.

28. Ibid., 214 ff., passim.

29. David M. Katzman, *Seven Days a Week: Women and Domestic Service in Industrializing America* (New York: Oxford University Press, 1978), Table A-3.

30. Margery W. Davies, *Woman's Place Is at the Typewriter: Office Work and Office Workers, 1870–1930* (Philadelphia: Temple University Press, 1982), Table 4.

31. Degler, 385.

32. Weiner, 87; and Kessler-Harris, *Out to Work*, 229.

33. Barbara J. Harris, *Beyond Her Sphere: Women and the Professions in American History* (Westport, CT: Greenwood Press, 1978), 104.

34. Violet B. Haas and Carolyn C. Perrucci, eds., *Women in Scientific and Engineering Professions* (Ann Arbor: University of Michigan Press, 1984), 59.

35. Kessler-Harris, *Out to Work*, 249.

36. Ibid., 258.

37. Susan Ware, *Holding Their Own: American Women in the 1930s* (Boston: Twayne, 1982), 42.

38. Ibid., 32.

39. Ibid., 29.

40. Ibid., 21–28, passim.

41. Kessler-Harris, *Out to Work*, 276–277.

42. Ibid., 278.

43. Ibid., 301.

44. Susan Householder Van Horn, *Women, Work, and Fertility, 1900–1986* (New York: New York University Press, 1988), 135.

45. Weiner, 96–97.

46. Bette Woody, *Black Women in the Workplace: Impacts of Structural Change in the Economy* (Westport, CT: Greenwood Press, 1992), 69.

47. Ibid., 9–10.

48. Now some of the tasks of social workers with graduate degrees are being assumed by paraprofessionals called "welfare assistants." Ibid., 36.

49. See the report for *Women's Voices*, a 1992 poll sponsored by the Ms. Foundation for Women and the Center for Policy Alternatives. This poll, which oversampled poor women, Latina women, and African-American women, shows that 69 percent of women believe that the women's movement has improved women's lives, and 77 percent of them believe that women's lives have improved in the last 25 years.

50. Weiner, 119.

51. *Women's Voices: A Polling Report* (New York: Ms. Foundation for Women and Center for Policy Alternatives, 1992), 15.

52. *Radcliffe News* (Boston: Winter, 1993).

53. *Women's Voices: A Policy Guide* (New York: Ms. Foundation for Women and Center for Policy Alternatives, 1992), 5.

54. *Women's Voices: A Polling Report*, 15, 18.

55. Ibid., 13.

56. *Women's Voices: A Policy Guide*, 15.

57. U.S. Bureau of the Census, *Statistical Abstract of the United States: 1991* (111th ed., Washington, DC, 1991), Table 632.

58. Felice N. Schwartz, with Jean Zimmerman, *Breaking with Tradition: Women and Work, the New Facts of Life* (New York: Warner Books, 1992), 137–138. Schwartz capably advances and develops the argument for the necessity of better utilizing women workers.

59. *Women's Voices: A Policy Guide*, 15.

Abbott, Edith (1876–1957)

Like her sister Grace Abbott, Nebraska-born Edith Abbott interested herself in progressive ideas, social reform, pacifism, and equal rights for women. After earning a Ph.D. in economics from the University of Chicago, she went to work for the Women's Trade Union League and the Carnegie Institution. In a subsequent stay at Hull House she partnered her sister in working for a ten-hour law for working women, the unionization of women workers, and child labor legislation. Edith Abbott bore the responsibility for research. In her career she produced more than a hundred books and articles, directed toward the resolution of problems. She published her landmark study, *Women in Industry*, in 1910. She also helped to shift education for social work into the university. From 1924–1942 she served as dean of the School of Social Service Administration of the University of Chicago. With Sophonisba Breckinridge she founded the professional journal *Social Service Review* in 1927 and the University of Chicago Social Service Series.

See also Abbott, Grace; Breckinridge, Sophonisba Preston; Hull House; Social Workers; Unions; Women's Trade Union League.

Reference Barbara Sicherman et al., eds., *Notable American Women: The Modern Period* (1980).

Abbott, Grace (1878–1939)

This sister of Edith Abbott, social worker, director of the Children's Bureau, a native Nebraskan, earned a master's degree in political science from the University of Chicago in 1909. A resident of Hull House, she headed the Immigrants' Protective League, founded among other purposes to combat white slavery. In 1917, at the insistence of Julia Lathrop, Grace Abbott joined the Children's Bureau to supervise child labor law administration. When in 1918 the U.S. Supreme Court declared the child labor law unconstitutional, she championed a constitutional amendment abolishing child labor. In 1921 she became head of the Children's Bureau, where for several years she devoted herself to administering the Sheppard-Towner Act, which established child health and prenatal care centers. In the New Deal she helped to draft the Social Security Act. She finished her career as professor of public welfare at the University of Chicago.

See also Abbott, Edith; Hull House; New Deal; Sheppard-Towner Act; Social Security Act; White Slavery.

Reference Edward T. James et al., eds., *Notable American Women I* (1971).

Academic Women

In the nineteenth century, from the 1830s on, determined and energetic women like Mary Lyon labored to turn their vision of higher education for women into a reality by establishing institutions dedicated to that purpose. These institutions were sustained by women faculty of high quality and purpose, independent in thought and active in improving conditions for women as well as inspiring and training their students. Also in the 1830s, a few private men's colleges, notably Oberlin, allowed women students within their precincts on a separate and unequal basis, though they usually received women faculty only gradually, later, and reluctantly. Some land-grant institutions enabled by the Morrill Act of 1862—particularly state-supported institutions in the West—admitted citizens of their states without respect to gender, and in time women found a place on

1

their faculties. All in all, in 1879–1880 women constituted 36.6 percent of academic personnel.

Despite an explosive growth in higher education, the twentieth century saw a decline in the ratios of women faculty, down to 20 percent in 1910 and at only 22 percent in 1962. The climb upward from that nadir has been muddy and rutted. Women adminstrators were even fewer and farther between: for years, in most coeducational institutions including land-grant colleges and state universities, they were limited to deans of women and deans of home economics. Furthermore, in the twentieth century up until the 1970s, even women's colleges chose men as their presidents.

In the 1970s the legal requirements of nondiscrimination on the basis of sex and race were extended to college and university faculty and administrators by statute and executive order. Title IX of the Education Amendments Act (1972) applied the nondiscrimination provisions of Title VII of the Civil Rights Act of 1964 to educational institutions. Colleges and universities were required to set up affirmative action programs to employ more women and offer them a fair chance at promotion and tenure. Despite some remaining uncertainties (e.g., the battle over "goals" versus "quotas"), educational institutions at the end of the twentieth century must take positive steps to overcome the effects of past forms of exclusion, an exclusion that is demonstrated when there are fewer women in a particular position and rank than could reasonably be expected by the availability of qualified candidates. Degrees of compliance vary from campus to campus, as does the level of resentment on the part of some male faculty and administrators to a policy that to them equates special treatment with unfair advantage.

These legal changes have enabled academic women to instigate lawsuits to seek equitable treatment and restitution of lost benefits; though many among

them with viable complaints may have been discouraged by the fact that in the 60 sex discrimination cases in academia brought from 1972 to 1983 under the Equal Pay Act or Title VII of the Civil Rights Act, only six plaintiffs prevailed. Litigation initiated by academic women has turned primarily on issues of tenure and promotion. On these issues plaintiffs encounter difficulties, because courts have been reluctant to intervene in academic decisions where evaluations of scholarly research and teaching ability are subjective and confidential. Recent decisions, however, indicate the courts' greater willingness to hold colleges and universities accountable for discrimination. In *Kunda v. Muhlenberg College* (1980), for example, the Third Circuit Court held that the college had discriminated against Connie Rae Kunda in denying her tenure and promotion to assistant professor on the grounds that she lacked the master's degree, since three male members of her department had been promoted without the degree. The court found the college in violation of Title VII and awarded Kunda promotion and tenure.

The number of women in academe is growing in both the professoriate and administration, even in disciplines traditionally considered male reserves. Nevertheless, in 1987 with women students outnumbering men, women constituted only 27.3 percent of full-time college professors (*Chronicle of Higher Education Almanac*, 26 August 1992)—only eight percentage points more than in 1910, and nine percentage points *fewer* than in 1880. Opportunities for academic positions for women, especially at the full-professor level and in graduate departments, have not kept pace with the increased production of women with doctorates. Most faculty women are concentrated in the lower ranks and the lower-paid disciplines.

Carolyn Heilbrun, a distinguished scholar and former president of the Modern Languages Association, publicized the handicaps of academic women in 1992 when she resigned from Columbia University in protest against the way her department treated women, particularly those engaged in women's studies. Similarly Dr. Frances Conley, a neurosurgeon, called national attention to the plight of academic women when she resigned from Stanford University in 1991 because of her disgust at the sexual harassment inflicted by male colleagues. In effect, these scholars blew the whistle on their employers.

During the late 1980s the number of academic women heading institutions of higher learning rose, reaching 348 in 1992—about one in ten of the chief executive officers. (American Council of Education figures, quoted in *Women's Research Network News*, Winter 1993) Since 1975 these figures have more than doubled, with more women overseeing large institutions. Similarly the number of women presidents who are members of minority groups has risen from 22 in 1983 to 50 in 1992. Women are also moving into the higher ranks in fund-raising and development. But most academic women administrators cluster at the lower levels of management.

See also Abbott, Edith; Abbott, Grace; Affirmative Action; *Board of Trustees of Keene State College v. Sweeney;* Breckinridge, Sophonisba; Civil Rights Act of 1964; Clarke, Edith; Dykes, Eva B.; Education Amendments Act; Equal Pay Act; Gilson, Mary Barnett; Hamilton, Alice; Hamilton, Gordon; Home Economists; Hyde, Ida Henrietta; Kingsbury, Susan Myra; Kreps, Juanita Morris; Lyon, Mary; McClintock, Barbara; Magill, Helen; Mansfield, Arabella; Mayer, Maria Gertrude Goeppert; Mead, Margaret; Mitchell, Lucy Sprague; Mitchell, Maria; Mossell, Sadie Tanner; Nepotism; Nutting, Mary Adelaide; Packard, Sophia B.; Palmer, Alice Elvira Freeman; Part-Time Workers; Professional Women; Regan, Agnes Gertrude; Richards, Ellen Henrietta Swallow; Sabin, Florence Rena; Sex Discrimination; Sexual Harassment; Simpson, Georgiana; Smith, Sophia; Thomas, Martha Carey; Wheelock, Lucy; Willard, Emma Hart; Willard, Frances Elizabeth Caroline; Wolfson, Theresa; Woodbury, Helen Laura Sumner; Woolman, Mary Raphael Schenck; Yalow, Rosalyn S.; Young, Ella Flagg.

References Nadya Aisenberg and Mona Harrington, *Women of Academe: Outsiders in the Sacred Grove* (1988); Jessie Bernard, *Academic Women* (1964, 1974); Mariam K. Chamberlain, *Women in Academe: Progress and Prospects* (1991); Billie Wright Dzieck and Linda Weiner, *The Lecherous Professor: Sexual Harassment on Campus* (1990); Penina Migdal Glazer and Miriam Slater, *Unequal Colleagues* (1987); Elaine Kendall, *Peculiar Institutions: An Informal History of the Seven Sister Colleges* (1975–1976); Susan Gluck Mezey, *In Pursuit of Equality: Women, Public Policy and the Federal Courts* (1992); Michele Paludi and Richard B. Barickman, *Academic and Workplace Sexual Harassment: A Resource Manual* (1991); Paula Ries and Anne J. Stone, eds., *The American Woman, 1992–93: A Status Report* (1992); A. Simeone, *Academic Women: Working towards Equality* (1987); Barbara Miller Solomon, *In the Company of Educated Women* (1985); Stephanie L. Witt, *The Pursuit of Race and Gender Equity in American Academe* (1990).

Accountants and Bookkeepers

Accounting expanded as a profession after 1900 as businesses enlarged and recognized the need for more accurate statistics to control costs and identify markets. Although here as elsewhere discrimination hampered women, these fields were not as gender-segregated as business in general. Women found ample opportunities as lower-paid bookkeepers, few as higher-status accountants. In 1900, 31 percent of bookkeepers/cashiers and 6 percent of accountants/auditors were women; by 1940 the ranks of women bookkeepers/cashiers had swelled to 65 percent, but women accountants/auditors had grown only to 8 percent. Government and the insurance industry provided women with interesting jobs as statisticians and actuarial workers, but limited their pay and their upward mobility.

Although the number of women certified public accountants has been increasing year by year, the larger accounting firms have been reluctant to promote them to partner or principal. Women have countered through the courts. In the case of *Price Waterhouse v. Hopkins*, for example, the court, finding that the accounting firm had relied on stereotypical perceptions in judging Ann Hopkins' qualifications for promotion, awarded her a partnership as a remedy for this discrimination.

See also Business and Industry; Clerical Workers; Glass Ceiling; *Price Waterhouse v. Hopkins*; Professional Women; Sex Discrimination.

Reference Susan Gluck Mezey, *In Pursuit of Equality: Women, Public Policy and the Federal Courts* (1992).

Actresses
See Cinema; Comediennes; Theater.

Adams, Annette A. (1877–1956)
This California educator and attorney was the first American woman district attorney. She later became the presiding judge of California's Third District Court of Appeals.

See also Attorneys.

Reference Joan McCullough, *First of All* (1980).

ADC
See Aid to Families with Dependent Children.

Adkins v. Children's Hospital (1923)
In this case the United States Supreme Court ruled a District of Columbia minimum wage law for women unconstitutional, declaring that such protective legislation deprived women of their liberty of contract. This decision contradicted *Muller v. Oregon* and *Radice v. New York* and dealt a major blow to the segment of the women's movement that believed working women needed special protection and should be treated differently from male workers. The National Woman's Party, on the other hand, urged complete equality of the sexes and so sided with the court in this instance.

See also Minimum Wage; *Muller v. Oregon*; Protective Legislation; *Radice v. New York*; *West Coast Hotel Co. v. Parrish*.

Reference Judith Baer, *Women in American Law* (1991).

AFDC
See Aid to Families with Dependent Children.

Affirmative Action
This policy rests on Title VII of the Civil Rights Act of 1964 and subsequent statutes and executive orders designed to protect minority group members and women against discrimination in the workplace. What it means in practice has been controversial and its enforcement a source of conflict.

In the 1960s and 1970s, affirmative action evolved to require covered employers, who employ about a third of the labor force, to recruit actively minorities and women, to award them their fair proportion of places and promotions, and to rectify pay inequities. Individual employers had to set numerical goals and draw up a timetable for compliance to remedy "patterns and practices" of past discrimination and to avoid new instances of discrimination. Some employers had to make special efforts to recruit women into nontraditional occupations, usually with a timetable and goals. This interpretation of affirmative action presupposes that discrimination against women and minorities has been a systemic problem, not limited to individual cases.

The Reagan and Bush administrations, on the other hand, took the position that government should provide relief only to individuals victimized by overt discrimination. They argued against "goals," defining them as "quotas" that employers must fill regardless of qualifications. Imposing such goals, they said, causes "reverse discrimination" against workers not in the protected groups—notably white males—and thus violates Title VII.

In the Reagan/Bush interpretation, affirmative action may require an employer only to revise procedures for recruiting, hiring, promoting, and training employees in order to equalize opportunities for underrepresented groups. In its earlier, stronger, and more substantive form, affirmative action may require preferential treatment for underrepresented groups if their members have the necessary qualifications. This interpretation has aroused controversy, particularly in its application to women, who, it is argued, have not been subject to the same deprivations as racial minorities.

The future of affirmative action remains in doubt, partly because of the changes in the Supreme Court and partly because of society's unease with some of its ramifications. Its effectiveness may be disputed, but even with a hit-and-miss enforcement women have won at least partial victories in a variety of discrimination cases, and under it their rights and opportunities have expanded.

See also Civil Rights Act of 1964; Equal Employment Opportunity Commission; *Johnson v. Transportation Agency of Santa Clara*; Nontraditional Occupations; Office of Federal Contract Compliance Programs; Uniform Guidelines on Employee Selection Procedures.

References Susan D. Clayton and Faye J. Crosby, *Justice, Gender, and Affirmative Action* (1992); Richard A. Epstein, *Forbidden Grounds: The Case against Employment Discrimination Laws* (1992); Kathanne W. Greene, *Affirmative Action and Principles of Justice* (1989); Hudson Institute, *Opportunity 2000: Creative Affirmative Action Strategies for a Changing Workforce* (1988); Karen J. Maschke, *Litigation, Courts, and Women Workers* (1989); Susan Gluck Mezey, *In Pursuit of Equality: Women, Public Policy and the Federal Courts* (1992); Deborah L. Rhode, *Justice and Gender: Sex Discrimination and the Law* (1989).

AFL-CIO
See American Federation of Labor.

AFL-CIO Standing Committee on Salaried and Professional Women
This committee within the AFL-CIO encourages union organizing, conducts workshops and conferences on women's workplace issues, and publishes statistics on white-collar women.

See also American Federation of Labor.

Reference NWO: *A Directory of National Women's Organizations* (1992).

African Americans
See Black Americans.

AFSCME v. State of Washington (1982)
In this comparable worth case, the American Federation of State, County, and Municipal Employees (AFSCME) and other plaintiffs sued the State of Washington, some of its officials, and all state agencies, boards, and institutions of higher education on behalf of everyone who worked for the state in a position that had at least 70 percent female incumbents. They alleged that the state had discriminated against them by paying them less because they were in "women's jobs." The judge, basing his decision on Title VII of the Civil Rights Act of 1964, ruled for the plaintiffs, and awarded back pay and future raises. In 1985 the Washington legislature, which had already passed a bill in 1983 requiring annual increases in salaries of state employees to achieve equity based on comparable worth, authorized an appropriation to settle all claims in the case, with a deadline for acceptance. At this juncture the Ninth Circuit Court reversed the lower court's decision, but the state of Washington nonetheless settled with the plaintiffs in 1986 at an estimated cost of $482 million.

See also Civil Rights Act of 1964; Comparable Worth; Government Workers.

References Susan Gluck Mezey, *In Pursuit of Equality: Women, Public Policy, and the Federal Courts* (1992); Steven L. Willborn, *A Secretary and a Cook: Challenging Women's Wages in the Courts of the United States and Great Britain* (1989).

Agassiz, Elizabeth Cabot Cary (1822–1907)
Agassiz, the first president of Radcliffe College, grew up in comfortable circumstances in Boston. Educated at home, after a few years of social life she married the Swiss naturalist Louis Agassiz in 1850 and devoted herself to him and the children of his first marriage. Her notes on his lectures became the basis of some of his publications; with the skills and knowledge so acquired she herself wrote introductory guides to marine biology.

From 1854–1863, partly to supplement the family income, she ran a school for girls on the third floor of their house, in which her husband taught, while she acted as counselor to the girls and school administrator. She continued to assist her husband, accompanying him on lectures and expeditions. In 1867 the two coauthored *A Journey in Brazil*. She served as his scribe and sometimes wrote the only account of his discoveries. In 1873 she helped him plan and administer a coeducational school of natural history at Buzzard's Bay.

Louis Agassiz died in 1873, and a daughter-in-law a few days later, leaving Elizabeth Agassiz to bring up three foster-grandchildren and to write a biography of her husband. In her widowhood she also promoted the foundation of Radcliffe, which opened in 1879 as the Harvard Annex, incorporating in 1882 with Agassiz as president. Although Harvard professors taught all its classes, the Harvard Corporation delayed until 1893 before establishing a formal link between the institutions. Agassiz remained president of what had now become Radcliffe College, but in 1899 she insisted on assuming the title of "honorary president," gradually turning over control to Agnes Irwin. In 1903 Agassiz resigned, but a Harvard professor, not Irwin, succeeded her.

Throughout her presidency Agassiz insisted on equal standards with those of Harvard. She believed in educating women both for education's sake and to train women as teachers.

See also Academic Women.

References Edward T. James et al., eds., *Notable American Women I* (1971); Lucy A. Paton, *Elizabeth Cary Agassiz: A Biography* (1974).

Age Discrimination Acts

The Age Discrimination in Employment Act of 1967 (ADEA) prohibits employers of more than 20 persons from discriminating on the basis of age in hiring, firing, compensation, and other terms and conditions of employment, in referrals for employment, and in membership in a labor union. It covers workers 40–70 years old in most private industries and in state and local governments, and from 40 onward in the federal government. It forbids firing older workers in favor of younger workers, refusing to count experience as a substitute for educational qualifications, and forcing older workers to accept reduced wages in lieu of being fired in favor of younger workers.

Exceptions to ADEA may be allowed where age can be established as a bona fide occupational qualification (BFOQ), reasonably imposed by the requirements of a particular job or business. It exempts apprenticeship programs, and the courts have allowed exceptions for jobs in which a certain age is a BFOQ. ADEA permits special benefits for older workers and reduced benefits for them where the cost of providing benefits is greater than for younger workers and might discourage hiring older workers. The Equal Employment Opportunity Commission is the enforcing agency.

ADEA protects workers 40 and over from a "hostile work environment." But it does not provide damages for emotional suffering created by such an environment. In other words, a plaintiff who won a suit alleging that she had suffered repeated derogatory references to her age might get a court order to halt the behavior, but she could not collect damages because of it. But if she could prove that the behavior had contributed to a failure to promote her or include her in valuable training she might qualify for monetary damages.

Although ADEA applies to both men and women, it has particular significance for women because they frequently enter the labor market later in life than men, have fewer years of gainful employment left to them, and receive smaller pensions (if any) upon retirement. The apprenticeship exclusion works against women: an apprenticeship is frequently a prerequisite for entry into jobs from which women have traditionally been excluded (higher-skilled crafts and construction), and an age requirement (typically 25) for entry bars many women who often seek to enter an apprenticeship program later than men.

The Age Discrimination Act of 1975 (ADA) prohibits "unreasonable discrimination on the basis of age in programs or activities receiving Federal financial assistance." Since it does not define age, it applies at all ages. Federal departments or agencies that extend financial assistance are responsible for enforcement; if voluntary compliance fails, they may terminate assistance. The 1975 act is more limited than the 1967 act in that it affects only people in programs or activities that get money from the federal government. But the 1975 act is broader than the 1967 act in that it includes people in such programs and activities outside the 40–70 age bracket.

See also Bona Fide Occupational Qualification; Employment Retirement Income Security Act; Equal Employment Opportunity Commission; National Center for Women and Retirement Research; Older Women.

References Barbara A. Burnett, ed., *Every Woman's Legal Guide* (1983); Wayne N. Outten with Noah A. Kinigstein, *The Rights of Employees* (1983); *Working Woman* editors with Gay Bryant, *The Working Woman Report* (1984).

Agricultural Workers

Like domestic service, agricultural work has been a means by which successively arrived ethnic groups in North America have become wage earners. The male European immigrants who came before the late 19th century could usually claim or buy land, but blacks and more recent arrivals more often have worked for wages or as tenant farmers or sharecroppers.

Women's participation in agricultural work has varied according to their racial-ethnic group. Generally, women of color have worked in the fields more than European Americans—though among Puerto Ricans, for example, women have not traditionally farmed.

In the twentieth century, mechanization has dramatically reduced the absolute numbers of agricultural workers and their proportions in the work force, from more than 10 million in 1900 to fewer than three million in 1980; or from one worker in three to one in 30. Though in 1900, 44.2 percent of black women workers, 47.2 percent of Native American women workers, and 58.1 percent of Japanese-American women workers labored in agriculture, by 1980 only Chicanos had as many as 2.9 percent of their women workers in this occupation. Yet of the relatively few farm workers in 1990, women constituted 21 percent.

By homesteading, purchase, or inheritance, many American women have owned and operated their own farms. The 1900 census reported 307,788 mostly white women farmers, planters, and overseers. Like other farmers and ranchers, their representation has decreased with twentieth-century mechanization and the development of agribusiness.

See also Cannery and Agricultural Workers Industrial Union; Farm Wives; Farmers; Homesteaders; Migrant Laborers; Tenant Farmers; United Farm Workers.

References Teresa Amott and Julie Matthaei, *Race, Gender, and Work: A Multicultural Economic History of Women in the United States* (1991); Joan M. Jensen, *With These Hands: Women Working on the Land* (1981).

Aid for Dependent Children

See Aid to Families with Dependent Children.

Aid to Families with Dependent Children (AFDC)

This program, which originated in the Social Security Act of 1935, assists families headed by single mothers or mothers whose husbands have deserted. (Fathers, grandparents, siblings, uncles, aunts, stepfathers, stepmothers, stepbrothers, and stepsisters may also be caretakers in AFDC families.) When government thus substituted itself for the absent male breadwinner, it also assumed his traditional authority, issuing strict regulations, disobedience to which may debar the family from further help.

An agricultural worker harvests bell peppers in Collier County, Florida.

Although the Social Security Act set no "fit parent" provisos, some of the individual states through which the program is administered originally evaluated applicants' moral character and "employability." This separation of the sheep from the goats became more difficult with the rapid expansion of the program occasioned by population growth, changing family structures, labor market dislocations, and changes in the community ethic. And in 1968 a Supreme Court ruling forbade states to deny aid on the ground of "unsuitability" unless the child(ren) was/were removed from the home and provided with adequate care. The Kennedy and Johnson administrations introduced new efforts to rehabilitate family life.

This program regularly comes under attack by critics who insist that government should limit the reproductive choices of mothers receiving such assistance, or force them to work outside the home, or both. They also urge that the government force absent fathers to contribute to the support of their children—an attractive idea, but one hard to consider optimistically in the face of the defections in child support payments of fathers of all classes and economic levels.

Criticism of this sort has contributed to the establishment of such changes in AFDC as the Work Incentive Program (WIN), which requires welfare mothers deemed "inappropriate" to register for work, accept referrals for training, and accept bona fide work offers. In 1988 Congress passed the Family Support Act (FSA), designed to move people off AFDC through education, training, and employment.

AFDC, however meager (in no state above the national poverty level), increases poor women's choices, enabling them to strike, to refuse flagrantly exploitative jobs, and to leave battering husbands.

See also Child Care; Colonial America; Family Support Act of 1988; Great Depression; Job Training Partnership Act; Mothers' Pensions; Old Age Insurance Program; Social Security Act of 1935; Unemployment Insurance Program; Workfare.

References Mimi Abramovitz, *Regulating the Lives of Women: Social Welfare Policy from Colonial Times to the Present* (1988); Julia Teresa Quiroz and Regina Tosca, *For My Children: Mexican American Women, Work, and Welfare* (1992); Women's Enterprises of Boston, *Earning a Breadwinner's Wage: Nontraditional Jobs for Women on AFDC* (1978).

Airline Stewardesses
See Flight Attendants.

Aitken, Jane (1764–1832)
Forced by her father's death to assume responsibility for his debts and the care of her two younger sisters, Jane Aitken became a printer, bookbinder, and bookseller in her own right. Taking over her father's business, she won for herself a reputation for work of high quality and taste—head and shoulders above that of any other woman bookbinder at that time.

See also Bookbinders; Printers.

Reference Edward T. James et al., eds., *Notable American Women I* (1971).

Alliance of Minority Women for Business and Political Development
Founded in 1982, this 650-member organization of black women entrepreneurs supports their business efforts.

See also American Association of Black Women Entrepreneurs; Entrepreneurs.

American Association of Black Women Entrepreneurs
This organization was founded in 1983 as the Association of African-American Business Owners to increase the number of successful black women entrepreneurs by means of personal development programs, business training programs, networking, and legislative action. It enrolls 1,500 members and publishes the *Black Business Women's News*.

See also Alliance of Minority Women for Business and Political Development; Entrepreneurs.

American Association of Colored Teachers (AACT)

Shut out by many state affiliates of the National Education Association (NEA), many black teachers joined AACT. This group, later known as the American Teachers' Association, conceptualized teaching as a high-status position and ideologically stood closer to the NEA than to the American Federation of Teachers. Organized by educators from Hampton Institute and Tuskegee, AACT approached NEA in 1926 for affiliation but was repeatedly rejected, although the two organizations operated in a loosely coordinated fashion thereafter. In 1966 they finally merged, with the agreement that NEA would integrate its state associations within a year, with blacks in leadership positions.

See also American Federation of Teachers; National Education Association.

Reference Marjorie Murphy, *Blackboard Unions: The AFT and the NEA, 1900–1980* (1990).

American Association of University Women (AAUW)

Founded in 1891, this organization of 140,000 college and university graduates works for the advancement of women. Its study-action program includes projects on women's work and women's worth.

See also Palmer, Alice Elvira Freeman.

American Civil Liberties Union (ACLU)

The ACLU operates its Women's Rights Project to educate the public about women's rights, and uses the equal protection clause of the Constitution to fortify those rights. Founded in 1972, this project combats sex discrimination through class-action litigation, emphasizing nontraditional blue-collar employment, the rights of fertile women in the workplace, and equal pay for work of comparable worth.

The ACLU's National Task Force on Civil Liberties in the Workplace found that workers' civil rights are inadequately protected. It recommended the elimination of the doctrine of at-will employment and the enactment of legislation to safeguard against unjust discharge and to protect employees' privacy rights.

See also At-Will Employment; Blue-Collar Workers; Civil Rights; Comparable Worth; Sex Discrimination.

References Joyce Gelb and Marian Lief Palley, *Women and Public Policies* (1982); Wayne N. Outten with Noah A. Kinigstein, *The Rights of Employees* (1983); Susan Deller Ross and Ann Barcher, *The Rights of Women* (1984).

American Federation of Labor (AFL)

Founded in 1886 by craftsmen disaffected with the Knights of Labor, the AFL has traditionally tended to concentrate on the work force elite, its skilled workers and craftspeople. For fear that low pay for women would debase all wages, the new organization advocated equal pay and invited women to join its affiliates. Nonetheless, for many years its support of women workers was ambivalent and half-hearted. It appointed women organizers only intermittently: the first, in 1891, was Mary E. Kenney O'Sullivan. Its affiliates frequently excluded women from membership or negotiated lower pay scales for them. Its famed president, Samuel Gompers, believed that women should not work except in cases of economic necessity. The federation opposed protective legislation for women as a dangerous precedent.

In the early twentieth century, despite the encouragement and loyalty of the Women's Trade Union League (WTUL), the AFL still hemmed and hawed about organizing women or fighting for their rights. Its high fees and dues often excluded low-paid women workers. In the 1920s the AFL refused either to charter locals or women excluded from membershipby affiliates or to take action against those affiliates.

During the Great Depression the AFL wanted to increase male employment by closing jobs to women, particularly married women. Although it praised the Women's Bureau, it opposed legislative means of obtaining equal pay and continued to refuse help to WTUL organizers.

After 1938, when the AFL expelled the group that became the Congress of Industrial Unions (CIO), competition from this more liberal group somewhat changed AFL attitudes towards women. The International Ladies' Garment Workers' Union, which at first sided with the CIO, returned to the AFL fold in 1940. In 1955 the two groups merged into the AFL-CIO.

In the latter part of the twentieth century, as union membership and power have waned and the demographics of the workplace have changed drastically, the AFL-CIO has more ardently recruited women members, who now constitute the fastest-growing segment of its membership.

See also Coalition of Labor Union Women; Congress of Industrial Organizations; Great Depression; International Ladies' Garment Workers' Union; Jarrell, Helen Ira; Knights of Labor; Married Women's Employment; O'Sullivan, Mary Kenney; Parker, Julia Sarsfield O'Connor; Protective Legislation; Stevens, Alzina Parsons; Thorne, Florence Calvert; Unions; Valesh, Eva MacDonald; Women's Bureau; Women's Trade Union League.

References Philip S. Foner, *Women and the American Labor Movement* (1979); Carol Hymowitz and Michaele Weissman, *A History of Women in America* (1980); James J. Kenneally, "Women in the United States and Trade Unionism," in Norbert C. Soldon, ed., *The World of Women's Trade Unionism* (1985); Susan Ware, *Holding Their Own: American Women in the 1930s* (1982).

American Federation of Teachers (AFT)

This organization, formed in 1916, was organized on the basis of local unions, attaining national strength only in the 1950s. Its membership of rank-and-file teachers opposed the administrative hierarchy and close supervision.

In 1902 Chicago had seen the first school strike in the country, with students, teachers, and community ranged on one side and the school administration on the other. The same era had seen the growth of local teachers' unions, woman-led and feminist, like the powerful Chicago Teachers' Federation organized in 1897 and led by Margaret Haley and Catharine Goggin. Between 1902 and 1910, 11 of these local unions joined the American Federation of Labor (AFL). Some school boards responded with yellow-dog contracts.

In 1916 the new AFT, the first national teachers' union in the country, represented teacher unionism in opposition to the professionalism advocated by the National Education Association (NEA). Almost immediately the nature of the teacher unionist movement was altered, partly by the election of a man as AFT's first president—a move that not only softpedaled the feminist element but also exacerbated the differences between the elementary school teachers, almost all women, and the higher-paid high school teachers, about equally divided between women and men.

The AFT defended the academic freedom of teachers accused of lack of patriotism in the hysteria of World War I and in the communist scares that followed. Partly in consequence, in the interwar period the AFT lost members and divided male conservatives from male and female progressives. Tensions also arose between middle-class women teachers and male proletarian leaders. But the Great Depression brought a rapid growth in membership, particularly from Work Projects Administration teachers, and revitalized the union. It also brought ideological warfare between younger, more radical teachers (some of them communists) and older union members, a controversy ultimately won by the conservatives, who then resolved to oust all communists and fascists. Meanwhile women teachers were losing ground in the leadership.

After World War II both the NEA and the AFT confronted crises, not only because of rapid population growth and a shortage of teachers, coupled with a series of teachers' strikes from 1945–1948, but also because of Senator Joseph McCarthy's exploitation of the communist scare, particularly difficult for the AFT because of its "radical" past.

From its earliest days the AFT, in contrast to the NEA, had established a *relatively* good record in integrating its membership racially, incorporating black leadership, and demonstrating concern for the education of black children. By 1952 it had adopted a fairly extensive civil rights program on which it stood, despite the heavy difficulties encountered by local unions in segregationist states and significant membership losses. But with the conflicts in the late 1960s between the supporters of community control of the school and teachers' unions and the resulting confrontations between "black power" leaders and white union leaders, AFT's national reputation for supporting civil rights plummeted.

The national acceptance of unionization after World War II was reflected in a growing number of teacher strikes, though in 1952 the AFT affirmed its no-strike policy. But throughout the 1950s the organization edged closer to sanctioning unlimited collective bargaining. In 1962 new strike activity began, often with AFT involvement. Although these new strikes were repeatedly attributed to the increase in the number of young male teachers in high schools, teacher resentment against the centralized bureaucracies that ran the schools had grown more militant among both genders.

Intense competition between the AFT and the NEA to represent teachers in collective bargaining drained both organizations, causing the AFT in 1968 to propose merger. Negotiations dragged on for several years, but ultimately the NEA refused. At the same time AFT was beseiged internally by feminist demands for more power and for more organizational support for women's rights, helped on by Title IX of the Education Amendments Act of 1972 forbidding discrimination against women in education programs. In the 1970s and 1980s women and minorities gained new power in the AFT.

In the early 1990s AFT supported the concept of teacher accountability. Politically, however, it had also adopted a more conservative stance than NEA on social issues.

See also American Association of Colored Teachers; American Federation of Labor; Barker, Mary Cornelia; Education Amendments Act; Great Depression; National Education Association; Strikes; Teachers; Unions; World War I; World War II; Yellow-Dog Contract.

Reference Marjorie Murphy, *Blackboard Unions: The AFT and the NEA, 1900–1980* (1990).

American Missionary Association (AMA)

During the post–Civil War period, the American Missionary Association, founded in 1846 within the Congregational Church, sent Northern teachers, 90 percent of them white women, to educate former slaves. These teachers established schools and churches for the blacks, sharing with their students the abusive language heaped upon them by their local white communities. Gradually women's roles in the field lessened as in the 1870s the AMA shifted its attention to black colleges.

See also Jeanes Teachers.

References Lura Beam, *He Called Them by the Lightning: A Teacher's Odyssey in the Negro South, 1908–1919* (1967); Angela Howard Zophy and Frances M. Kavenik, eds., *Handbook of American Women's History* (1990).

American Society of Professional and Executive Women

Founded in 1979, this 25,200-member organization seeks to serve the interests of career women in all sectors of the economy through seminars, an information and library service, and executive recruitment. It publishes a quarterly, *Successful Women in Business*.

American Teachers' Association

See American Association of Colored Teachers.

American Woman's Educational Association (AWEA) (1852–1862)

AWEA, founded by Catharine Beecher, proposed to help women get educated and find jobs as nurturers. It contributed money to chosen women's colleges but failed in its goal of establishing departments of domestic economy.

See also Beecher, Catharine Esther.

Reference Angela Howard Zophy and Frances M. Kavenik, eds., *Handbook of American Women's History* (1990).

American Women's Economic Development Corporation (AWED)

Founded in 1977, this national nonprofit corporation, which trains and counsels women entrepreneurs, is partially underwritten by federal, state, and city agencies and by private companies and foundations. It offers in-house and telephone counseling sessions. Its hotline service provides quick answers to single questions in calls lasting up to 15 minutes. It trains women in many facets of running their businesses, including writing business plans. It sponsors roundtables, conferences, and seminars. More than 400 experienced business people volunteer their time as speakers, counselors, and instructors. AWED boasts a high success rate, with only half of one percent of the women it has trained and counseled having had to file for bankruptcy. Membership in AWED reduces fees for its services.

See also Catalyst; Entrepreneurs; Small Business Administration.

American Women's Hospital Service (AWHS)

The American Medical Women's Association founded AWHS in 1917 to enable women physicians to participate in World War I. The armed forces refused their services, except as contract physicians work-ing without rank or military benefits and at low pay. AWHS organized and paid for medical units completely staffed by women, which operated in France, sometimes in cooperation with the French army. After the armistice AWHS engaged in reconstruction efforts, which were gradually transmuted into service in many countries, including the United States, under the aegis of Dr. Esther Pohl Lovejoy. Although the military admitted women doctors into service in 1943 for the duration of World War II, only in the 1950s did they win permanent rank.

See also Military Women; Physicians; World War I; World War II.

References Esther Pohl Lovejoy, *Certain Samaritans* (1933); Dorothy Schneider and Carl J. Schneider, *Into the Breach: American Women Overseas in World War I* (1991).

Americans with Disabilities Act of 1990 (ADA)

This act extends to the 43,000,000 Americans with disabilities many protections of the Civil Rights Act of 1964. It forbids employers of more than 25 employees (15 employees after 26 July 1994) to discriminate on the basis of disability, provided the individual can do the job with or without reasonable accommodation. Accommodation may include the employer's making facilities accessible, restructuring jobs, acquiring or modifying equipment, or providing readers and interpreters. ADA, however, exempts employers from making accommodations that impose "undue hardship" on the operation of the business. Employers may not ask applicants about the existence, nature, or severity of disabilities but may inquire about their ability to perform specific job functions. The act also prohibits limiting, segregating, or classifying individuals on the basis of their disabilities. The Equal Employment Opportunity Commission is the enforcing agency.

See also Civil Rights Act of 1964; Equal Employment Opportunity Commission; Networking Project for Disabled Women and Girls; Rehabilitation Act of 1973.

Reference Connecticut Permanent Commission on the Status of Women, *Non Traditional Jobs for Women: A Resource Guide* (1991).

Anarchism

This philosophy rejects all forms of institutionalized authority (e.g., government, church, family), as necessarily exploitative, oppressive, and violent. It celebrates personal freedom and the inherent goodness of the individual freed from the shackles of authority. Although anarchism has played only a minor role in the American labor movement, it contributed idealism and ideological fervor through such leaders as Rose Pesotta and Emma Goldman.

See also Goldman, Emma; Pesotta, Rose.

Anderson, Marian (1902–1993)

Her local church paid for the musical training of this black contralto, who broke the racial barrier at the Metropolitan Opera. Born in Philadelphia, Anderson began singing for the Union Baptist Church when she was six, using the

Marian Anderson

money she earned for singing lessons. In 1939, despite the international reputation she had already established, the Daughters of the American Revolution barred her concert from their hall. Anna Eleanor Roosevelt led a protest that enabled Anderson to sing instead at the Lincoln Memorial. Anderson also worked for the civil rights movement and in 1958 served as a delegate to the United Nations.

See also Musicians; Roosevelt, Anna Eleanor.

Reference Jennifer S. Uglow, comp. and ed., *International Dictionary of Women's Biography* (1985).

Anderson, Mary (1872–1964)

This labor leader, who emigrated from Sweden at 16, headed the federal Women's Bureau of the Department of Labor from 1920 to 1944. As a worker in the shoe industry, she joined the Chicago Federation of Labor and the Chicago branch of the Women's Trade Union League (WTUL). After the Hart, Schaffner & Marx strike of 1910–1911, Margaret Dreier Robins put Anderson in charge of that company's new grievance procedure, as an employee of the WTUL.

During World War I Anderson was appointed to a committee on women in industry, through which she met Mary van Kleeck. Van Kleeck soon hired her to work in a women's branch of the Army's Ordnance Department and later in the Women in Industry Service (WIS) that preceded the Women's Bureau.

In 1919 Robins sent Anderson and Rose Schneiderman to represent women workers at the Paris Peace Conference. After van Kleeck's resignation Anderson directed WIS and then the Women's Bureau, where she served until 1944. During World War II she assisted women's access to jobs and training and upheld high working standards.

See also Robins, Margaret Dreier; Schneiderman, Rose; van Kleeck, Mary; Women's Bureau; Women's Trade Union League; World War I; World War II.

References Mary Anderson, *Woman at Work* (1951); Barbara Sicherman et al., eds., *Notable American Women: The Modern Period* (1980).

Apprentices

In colonial America young people learned their trades by apprenticeships. Parents might apprentice children as young as seven, the girls to learn domestic service, spinning, sewing, and weaving; the boys to learn cobbling, silversmithing, or cabinetmaking. Townships might similarly apprentice indigent children, orphans, or children whom they removed from "unsuitable" homes.

In hundreds of trades the apprenticeship system still survives. It offers the apprentice an opportunity to earn while learning. The modern apprentice not only spends several hours a week in a classroom but also works under the supervision of a skilled worker, a journeyperson. The beginning apprentice usually earns about half a journeyperson's wage, with raises every six months. In two to four years the apprentice receives a certificate as journeyperson.

Apprenticeship programs may be sponsored by unions or by employers. They *may* require a high school diploma or graduate equivalent diploma (GED), a driver's license, access to transportation, and good physical condition. State labor departments can furnish information about their availability. State apprenticeship laws and regulations vary around the country.

Women frequently experience difficulty in being accepted into apprenticeships and are consequently barred from work that would pay them more than they can earn in occupationally segregated "women's work." The maximum age limit for acceptance into many apprenticeships, often set at 25, operates against women, who, because of childbearing and family responsibilities, may enter the workplace later than men. The U.S. Department of Labor now requires affirmative action goals and timetables for women and minorities in apprenticeships. And women apprentices must receive equal treatment on the job.

See also Affirmative Action; Colonial America; *Occupational Outlook Handbook*; Taylor, Lucy Beaman Hobbs; Trades.

References Mimi Abramovitz, *Regulating the Lives of Women: Social Welfare Policy from Colonial Times to the Present* (1988); Teresa Amott and Julie Matthaei, *Race, Gender, and Work* (1991); Connecticut Permanent Commission on the Status of Women, *Non Traditional Jobs for Women* (1991); Connecticut Permanent Commission on the Status of Women, *Women in Apprenticeships: Steps to Building a Career* (1989).

Architects

Long before Columbus, Native American women often took the responsibility for building their dwellings, especially in the tribes of the Southwest and the Great Plains. There they selected the poles, butchered the buffalo for skins for the covering, and erected the tipi, learning their skills from their foremothers.

In the European-American community of the nineteenth century, women wrote some of the books that dealt with the design of the home. For instance Catharine Beecher's and Harriet Beecher Stowe's *Treatise: American Woman's Home* (1869) detailed plans for making houses more functional, more comfortable, better ventilated, and easier to clean. Some women designed their own homes and supervised their construction. Designer Harriet Morrison Irwin (1828–1897), who liked octagonal houses, patented a plan for a hexagonal house. In 1848 Louisa C. Tuthill published the first history of architecture in the United States.

But in the nineteenth century few women practiced architecture. Even late in the century getting trained presented difficulties for women, despite the emergence of architectural schools at land-grant universities that were open to women. Louise Blanchard Bethune, the first professional American woman architect, served an apprenticeship. Minerva Parker Nichols (1861–1949) learned catch-as-catch-can, partly in the Philadelphia Normal Art School, partly by drafting in an architect's office, and partly through a course in architectural drawing at the Franklin Institute. Sophia G. Hayden (c. 1868–1953) graduated from the regular architectural course at the Massachusetts Institute of Technology, its first alumna.

In 1916 the Cambridge School of Architecture and Landscape Architecture, the first architectural school for women in the United States, evolved out of the lessons that six young women persuaded an instructor at the Harvard School of Architecture to give them. Most of its students had already graduated from college. It provided unique encouragement to its women to practice their profession after graduation, meeting a problem that has haunted women graduate architects throughout the twentieth century. The school provided excellent training, insisting that students take a summer term after their first year, affording them guided study tours in Europe, and requiring an apprenticeship. In 1938 Smith College took over the school and in 1942 closed it, ostensibly for the duration of World War II, just as Harvard's Graduate School of Design serendipitously welcomed women students to fill the gaps left by men gone to war. The Cambridge School never reopened.

In the early 1990s women are ill-represented in the profession. According to the American Institute of Architects, their total female membership was 3,051 in 1992, or 7.5 percent of the total membership. Despite the outstanding successes achieved by Julia Morgan and other women architects, women in general have experienced difficulties in getting commissions from corporations and organizations. Many of them have resisted specialization, a trend in major firms. Most often women have been confined to domestic architecture. But Maya Ying Lin, now a New York–based architect, designed Washington's Vietnam Wall at 21 when she was a student at Yale, and went on to design the black granite Civil Rights Memorial in Montgomery, Alabama.

See also Barney, Nora Stanton Blatch; Beecher, Catharine Esther; Bethune, Louise Blanchard; Morgan, Julia; Professional Women; World War II.

References Dorothy May Anderson, *Women, Design and the Cambridge School* (1980); Doris Cole, *From Tipi to Skyscraper: A History of Women in Architecture* (1978); Lamia Doumato, *Architecture and Women* (1988).

Arizona Mine Strike of 1983

Women copper miners and women related to male miners were so prominent in this year-and-a-half strike that a police officer remarked, "If we could just get rid of these broads, we'd have it made." They struck in the tradition of their forerunners, women hired as miners during World War II, who pulled off a wildcat strike for better working conditions, and at the end of the war fought to hold on to their jobs. In the early 1970s a union-backed equal employment opportunity lawsuit had forced the hiring of more women.

A consortium of 20 miners' unions had negotiated for a new contract with all the major copper-producing companies. When the employer, Phelps Dodge, refused the contract, miners at four different sites walked out. Undaunted by arrests, handcuffs, chains, shackles, a flood, evictions, and injunctions, women walked the picket lines (one, composed entirely of women, was a mile long), endured the sexual harassment and the brandished guns of the scabs, raised money for food, established a day-care center for picketers' children, bartered for each other's skills and services, wrote letters that evoked sympathy and support from all over the country and from abroad, and organized speaking tours. They transformed themselves.

The strike ended inconclusively with the unions decertified, and the company deep in economic trouble. Despite the many arrests, no one went to prison. Strikers won suits against or settled for damages from the county and the sheriff for violation of their civil rights.

See also Injunctions; Scab; Sexual Harassment; Strikes; Trades; World War II.

References Barbara Kingsolver, *Holding the Line: Women in the Great Arizona Mine Strike of 1983* (1989).

Army Nurse Corps

After the catch-as-catch-can nursing experiences of all American wars up until the twentieth century, the military finally created the Army Nurse Corps in 1901 and the Navy Nurse Corps in 1908. Both were tiny, with the expectation that the American Red Cross would maintain a reserve pool of nurses who would either join the military corps in wartime or work alongside corps nurses. All through World War I military nurses worked under the handicap of no rank. In 1920 they received the ersatz "relative rank," and only in World War II actual rank. The military now attracts nurses, even in times of civilian shortages, because it offers them so much responsibility and authority.

See also McGee, Anita Newcomb; Nurses; World War I; World War II.

References Jeanne Holm, *Women in the Military: An Unfinished Revolution* (1982); Dorothy Schneider and Carl J. Schneider, *Into the Breach: American Women Overseas in World War I* (1991).

Artists

Women have experienced the same discrimination in the arts as in other occupations. Often their work has been relegated to the wrong side of the wavering division between arts and crafts. Recently enthusiasm for quilts and theorem paintings and the pottery of Native American women like Maria Montoya Martinez has blurred the distinction. But Judy Chicago still has trouble exhibiting her creations.

In more traditional art fields, Henrietta Deering Johnston (1670–1728/9) pioneered in pastel portraiture, and several eighteenth-century women painted miniatures. But women were not regularly enrolled in American art schools until the mid-nineteenth century, and, perforce, concentrated on still life and portraits. The last half of the nineteenth century saw an explosion of women artists. The Art Students League, founded in 1875, accepted women students and placed women on its governing board. The National Association of Women Painters and Sculptors spawned its own academy, sponsored exhibits, and funded scholarships. Women showed their work at the Philadelphia Centennial Exposition and the Chicago World's Columbian Exposition. Women helped to create the first major school of American neoclassical sculpture. Mary Cassatt and other American women explored the French Impressionist movement. In 1895 Cecilia Beaux became the first woman professor of art, with an appointment at the Pennsylvania Academy of the Fine Arts.

Women artists gained in prestige and numbers in the twentieth century. The first new movement, the Ash Can School, included the sculptor Mary Abastenia St. Leger Eberle (1878–1942), the painter Theresa Bernstein Meyerowitz, and several other women painters and illustrators. The landmark Armory Show of 1913 hung the works of more than 40 women. Marguerite Thompson Zorach (1887–1968) helped introduce fauvism and cubism to the United States between 1910 and 1920, and in 1925 founded the avant-garde New York Society of Women Artists. New galleries like Alfred Stieglitz's "291" offered fresh opportunities. The sculptor and art patron Gertrude Whitney (1875–1942) and Juliana Force, Whitney's agent and the director of the Whitney Museum, provided women and men artists alike with invaluable aid: models, studio space, display space, and purchases. In 1940 the comic strip "Brenda Starr" first appeared; it was drawn by the first syndicated woman cartoonist, Dale Messick. Georgia O'Keeffe (1887–1986) aroused the admiration of critics and the general public alike with her paintings of the American Southwest. In mid-century Helen Frankenthaler began color-field or stain painting. Kay Sage and Dorothea Tanning practiced surrealism, and Lee Krasner and Joni Mitchell abstract expressionism. The sculptor Louise Nevelson created her own unique art in wood.

Though women artists still disagree about its usefulness, the National Museum of Women in the Arts, founded in

1987 in Washington, D.C., has insistently called attention to the achievements of women in art. In New York City in the 1980s and 1990s the underground Guerrilla Girls, who style themselves the "conscience of the art world," have wittily protested the neglect of women by the art establishment.

See also Chicago, Judy; Force, Juliana Rieser; Hosmer, Harriet Goodhue; Lewis, Edmonia; Martinez, Maria Montoya; Peale, Anna Claypoole, Margaretta Angelica, and Sarah Miriam; Wheeler, Candace Thurber.

References *Anthology of Contemporary African-American Women Artists* (1992); Avis Berman, *Rebels on Eighth Street: Juliana Force and the Whitney Museum of American Art* (1990); Paula Chiarmonte, *Women Artists in the United States: Guide on the Fine and Decorative Arts, 1750–1986* (1990); Penny Dunford, *A Biographical Dictionary of Women Artists in Europe and America since 1850* (1990); William H. Gerdts, *Women Artists of America, 1707–1964* (1965); Ann S. Harris, *Women Artists, Fifteen Fifty to Nineteen Fifty* (1977); Nancy G. Heller, *Women Artists: An Illustrated History* (1987); Theresa Bernstein Meyerowitz, *William Bernstein Meyerowitz* (1986); Charlotte S. Rubinstein, *American Women Artists: From Early Indian Times to the Present* (1982); Charlotte Streifer Rubenstein, *American Women Sculptors* (1990); Eleanor Tufts, *American Women Artists, 1830–1930* (1987); Susan Waller, *Women Artists in the Modern Era: A Documentary History* (1991).

Asian Americans
See Chinese Americans, Filipina Americans, Japanese Americans, Korean Americans.

Assertiveness
Psychologists like Carol Gilligan believe that because of their upbringing many women lack the self-confidence and assertiveness necessary to succeed in the workplace, particularly as managers and in nontraditional occupations. They may try to conciliate when they should compete. Some women take training to increase their assertiveness.

See also Managers; Nontraditional Occupations.

Reference *Working Woman* editors with Gay Bryant, *The Working Woman Report: Succeeding in Business in the 80s* (1984).

Association of Executive and Professional Women
This umbrella organization supports executive and professional women and their networks in all segments of society.

Attorneys
Because it was possible to prepare for the law by reading or by studying under the guidance of a lawyer, women managed to enter the profession in small numbers early on. The first woman admitted to the bar in the United States was Arabella Mansfield, who in 1869 was permitted to take the Iowa bar examination despite a statute that limited membership to white males. Three years later Charlotte E. Ray, a graduate of Howard University School of Law, became the first black woman admitted to the bar (in Washington, D.C.).

As their numbers increased, women lawyers played important parts in social reform, particularly during the Progressive Era, and again during the women's movement of the 1960s and 1970s. In 1981 Sandra Day O'Connor became the first woman on the U.S. Supreme Court. By 1989 women were earning 40 percent of all law degrees awarded.

A critical point in a lawyer's career is the partnership decision, which, like tenure decisions in universities, is collegial, judgmental, and subject to the vagaries of the old boys' network. Since 1984 women's road to partnership has been eased by the Supreme Court decision in the case of *Hishon v. King & Spalding* that made partnership selection subject to the requirements of Title VII of the Civil Rights Act of 1964. A 1990 study in the *National Law Journal* (12 February 1990) showed a consistent increase in the number of women associates and partners in law firms.

See also Adams, Annette A.; Borchardt, Selma Munter; Bradwell, Myra Colby; Breckinridge, Sophonisba Preston; Brent, Margaret; Civil Rights Act of 1964; Equity Club; Harris, Patricia

Roberts; Hills, Carla Anderson; Hobby, Oveta Culp; Jordan, Barbara; Kelley, Florence; Kellor, Frances; King, Florence; Lockwood, Belva Ann Bennett McNall; Lytle, Lutie; Mansfield, Arabella; O'Connor, Sandra Day; *Price Waterhouse v. Hopkins;* Professional Women; Progressive Era; Shadd, Mary Ann; Ward, Hortense Sparks Malsch.

References Joan McCullough, *First of All* (1980); Susan Gluck Mezey, *In Pursuit of Equality: Women, Public Policy, and the Federal Courts* (1992); Paula Ries and Anne J. Stone, eds., *The American Woman, 1992–93: A Status Report* (1992); Sarah Ragle Weddington, *A Question of Choice* (1992).

At-Will Employment

Employment "at will" is a common law concept that permits an employer to fire workers with no reason except his determination of what is in his own interests. In the past under this doctrine employees were helpless against arbitrary discharge or discipline, unless they could find protection in union contracts, which typically required management to have "just cause" for discharging or firing any worker. Since the passage of the Civil Rights Act of 1964, the at-will employment doctrine has been weakened by law and by court decisions. Discrimination or harassment on the basis of sex, race, age, or union activity is now illegal. It is not always clear, however, to what extent workers are protected against firing or discipline on the basis of sexual preference, whistle-blowing, refusing to disobey a law when ordered to do so, marital status, arrest record, demeanor, or appearance. Court challenges to the at-will doctrine do not always succeed, and the law is complicated because so much of it lies within the jurisdiction of states, which differ in their exceptions to the at-will rule.

See also Civil Rights; Civil Rights Act of 1964; Just Cause; Sexual Preference; Unions; Whistle-Blowing.

References Wayne N. Outten with Noah A. Kinigstein, *The Rights of Employees* (1983); Michael Yates, *Labor Law Handbook* (1987).

Authors

See Writers and Publishers.

AWED Corporation

See American Women's Economic Development Corporation.

Ayer, Harriet Hubbard (1849–1903)

This entrepreneur and journalist grew up in comfort and privilege, graduating from a private school at age 15. The next year she married Herbert Copeland Ayer and between 1867 and 1877 bore three daughters while living the life of a wealthy society matron, traveling widely, and educating herself culturally. The couple separated in 1882 and divorced in 1886.

When her husband failed in business in 1883, Ayer undertook to support herself and her two surviving daughters, working as a decorator and furniture saleswoman. In 1886 she set up in business for herself as Recamier Preparations, manufacturing and marketing face cream and proving herself an advertising genius. Scandal erupted in 1889, with suit and countersuit between Ayer and one of her stockholders, whom she accused of illegally holding a block of her stock and trying to deprive her of her reason, alienate her children, and poison her. In 1893 her former husband and one of her daughters committed her to a private insane asylum and deprived her of control of her investments. Fourteen months later her lawyers succeeded in releasing her. She then took to the lecture platform, describing her incarceration and calling public attention to the plight of the insane and the allegedly insane.

In 1896 she began to write beauty advice for the New York *World.* In 1899 she published her columns in *Harriet Hubbard Ayer's Book: A Complete and Authentic Treatise on the Laws of Health and Beauty,* where she incorporated commonsense hints on the importance of bathing, sleep, fresh air, exercise, and good nutrition.

See also Entrepreneurs; Journalists.

References Margaret Hubbard Ayer and Isabella Taves, *The Three Lives of Harriet Hubbard Ayer* (1957); Edward T. James et al., eds., *Notable American Women I* (1971).

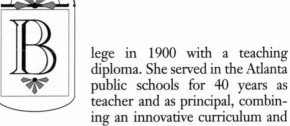

Bagley, Sarah G.
(active 1835–1847)

Out of her experiences as a worker in one of the cotton mills in Lowell, Massachusetts, Bagley became a labor activist and reformer, agitating for the ten-hour workday, higher wages, and better working conditions, and exhorting workers to organize and protest. Her commitment to the cause of working women led her in 1844 to organize the Lowell Female Labor Reform Association, branches of which soon appeared in other mill towns of New Hampshire and Massachusetts. She encouraged and supported the embryonic labor movement in New England as a publicist, organizer, and speaker. After 1847, when the presidency of the association passed to another mill worker, no further record of her life exists. The last record of her employment was with the newly opened telegraph office in Lowell—possibly as the first female telegraph operator.

See also Lowell Girls; Unions.

References Edward T. James et al., eds., *Notable American Women I* (1971); Madeleine B. Stern, *We the Women* (1962).

Bambace, Angela (1898–1975)

This union organizer, born in Brazil, immigrated to the United States at the age of six. Beginning work in the garment trade at 17, she immediately joined the International Ladies' Garment Workers' Union (ILGWU). She participated in many strikes and in 1936 began organizing. In 1956 she was elected vice president of ILGWU. She retired in 1973.

See also International Ladies' Garment Workers' Union; Strikes; Union Organizers.

References Judith O'Sullivan and Rosemary Gallick, *Workers and Allies* (n.d.); Barbara Sicherman et al., eds., *Notable American Women: The Modern Period* (1980).

Barker, Mary Cornelia (1879–1963)

This educator and labor leader, a native of Georgia, graduated from Agnes Scott College in 1900 with a teaching diploma. She served in the Atlanta public schools for 40 years as teacher and as principal, combining an innovative curriculum and teaching methods with firm discipline.

Throughout her career, even as an administrator, she battled for teachers' rights. She helped to found a teachers' association in Atlanta, served on its board and as its president, and worked to affiliate it with the American Federation of Teachers (AFT). In 1925 she was elected president of the national AFT, a position in which she increased the membership by 50 percent and led the organization to adopt a legislative program. She also encouraged black teachers to organize and negotiate.

Barker pushed her interest in labor organizing beyond the realm of teaching, showing special concern for the welfare of southern women factory workers. She helped organize the Southern Summer School for Women Workers in Industry, chairing its central committee from 1927–1944.

See also American Federation of Teachers; Southern Summer School for Women Workers in Industry.

Reference Barbara Sicherman et al., eds., *Notable American Women: The Modern Period* (1980).

Barnard, Kate (1875–1930)

Barnard, Commissioner of Charities and Corrections in Oklahoma 1907–1914, was the first woman elected to a major state office in the United States. A welfare leader and political reformer, she successfully lobbied for prison reform, labor laws, and compulsory education.

See also Government Workers.

Reference Edward T. James et al., *Notable American Women I* (1971).

Barney, Nora Stanton Blatch
(1883–1971)

This civil engineer, architect, and developer also worked as a political activist for women's suffrage and peace—not surprisingly, since she was the daughter of suffragist Harriot Stanton Blatch and the granddaughter of suffragist Elizabeth Cady Stanton. She had one daughter with her first husband, Lee de Forest, and another daughter and a son with her second husband, Morgan Barney. She was the first woman member of the American Society of Civil Engineers. As an architect she prided herself on her control over the plans for the houses she built and on her crew of skilled workmen.

See also Architects; Engineers.

Reference Barbara Sicherman et al., eds., *Notable American Women: The Modern Period* (1980).

Barnum, Gertrude (1866–1948)

A native of Illinois, this social worker and labor organizer was born into a conventional upper-middle-class family. In the late 1890s Barnum developed a social conscience, spent some years in Chicago settlement houses, and soon after the turn of the century began an involvement with the trade union movement and the cause of women in the workplace that continued until her retirement in 1919.

In 1905, as a national organizer for the Women's Trade Union League, she generated public sympathy for women striking for better working conditions in textile mills (Fall River, Massachusetts), laundries (Troy, New York), and corset factories (Aurora, Illinois). In 1911 the International Ladies' Garment Workers' Union took her on as a special agent, in which capacity she successfully solicited support for striking garment workers. Her union activities attracted national attention. In 1914 she served as President Wilson's special agent to the United States Commission on Industrial Relations, and in 1918–1919 as assistant director of the investigation service of the U.S. Department of Labor. She was also active in the women's suffrage movement.

See also International Ladies' Garment Workers' Union; Settlement Houses; Unions; Women's Trade Union League.

Reference Edward T. James et al., eds., *Notable American Women I* (1971).

Barry, Leonora Marie Kearney (1849–1930)

This union organizer, a native of Ireland, immigrated to the United States in 1852 and was educated in upper New York State, earning a teacher's certificate at 16. In 1871, after teaching for several years, she married painter and musician William E. Barry and subsequently bore three children; in 1881 both her husband and one daughter died. Left with two children to support, Barry started work as an unskilled hand in a mill, earning 65 cents in her first week.

That meager wage and the oppressive conditions of work drove her to join the Knights of Labor, where she soon rose to positions of leadership. As head of the national organization's Department of Women's Work she traveled extensively, troubleshooting and reporting on the wide-scale use of child labor and the deplorable conditions she found in the country's sweatshops. She also organized short-lived cooperative factories and a women's benefit fund. Possibly her most important legacy was the passage of the first factory inspection act in Pennsylvania (1889), for which she worked industriously, but for which she did not lobby on the grounds that it would not be ladylike. When she married for a second time (1890) she gave up her union activities, believing that women should not work outside the home unless compelled by economic necessity.

See also Knights of Labor; Union Organizers.

Reference Edward T. James et al., eds., *Notable American Women I* (1971).

Barton, Clara (1821–1912)

This founder and longtime president of the American Red Cross and pioneer in nursing grew up in Massachusetts. At 18 she began to teach, and in 1852 she founded one of New Jersey's first public schools; when it succeeded the town placed a man in charge. She resigned and secured a clerkship in the Patent Office in Washington, D.C.—perhaps the first regularly appointed woman civil servant.

When the Civil War began, Barton advertised for relief supplies, which she stored in her own rooms; with the help of friends she distributed them by mule team in the camps and on the battlefields of Virginia and Maryland. Her lifelong talent for friendship with men, her efficiency and resourcefulness, and her willingness to serve in any way necessary gained her the cooperation of the military and the title of the "Angel of the Battlefield."

With the development of the Sanitary Commission and other agencies, Barton's work diminished. But in the spring of 1864 she became head nurse under General Benjamin Butler, serving at several corps hospitals in Virginia. In early 1865 she set up an office at Annapolis to gather and collate information on missing men, which she distributed to northern newspapers. In 1866 Congress appropriated $15,000 to reimburse her for the expenses of this work, which she continued until 1868, at the same time lecturing on her war experiences.

During a stay in Switzerland necessitated by a physical breakdown, she learned of the International Committee of the Red Cross, formed in 1863 and ratified by the Geneva Treaty of 1864. She worked for that organization during the Franco-Prussian War. In 1877 she began an arduous campaign to organize an American Red Cross and persuade the American government to ratify the Geneva Treaty.

She reached the first goal in 1881, though not until 1900 did Congress issue a federal charter to the Red Cross. But from 1881 on Barton devoted herself as a volunteer to the presidency of the Red Cross, supervising relief in 21 disasters. In the Spanish-American War, at the age of 77, she again rode mule wagons to distribute tons of provisions, cooked soup for soldiers, and set up orphan asylums for Cuban children.

Like many another before and since, she clung to her position long after it demanded new methods that she could not

Clara Barton

supply. Only the federal government's withdrawal of patronage from the Red Cross forced her resignation in 1903. A lifelong feminist, she always supported equal pay for equal work.

See also Nurses.

References Edward T. James et al., eds., *Notable American Women I* (1971); Elizabeth B. Pryor, *Clara Barton, Professional Angel* (1987); Ishbel Ross, *Angel of the Battlefield* (1958).

Beals, Jessie Tarbox (1870–1942)

Beals, the first woman news photographer, was born in Canada, the daughter of American parents. She studied at the Collegiate Institute of Ontario and prepared to teach. At 17 she took a job in northwest Massachusetts. She acquired a camera by selling a subscription to the *Youth's Companion*—and found a career.

Soon in the interstices of teaching she was reading about and experimenting

Photographer Jessie Tarbox Beals at work

with photography, traveling the countryside looking for subjects, stationing herself to take commercial pictures of birds, and doing a land-office business in portraits at Chatauqua. After she married machinist Alfred T. Beals in 1897, she taught him photography and the two went on the road, taking whatever pictures they might sell. In their partnership Alfred Beals always had a secondary position. Although the marriage survived Jessie's bearing a daughter by another man in 1910, Jessie walked out of it in 1917.

Despite some hard times, Beals's career prospered. From 1900 until her death she sold her pictures to newspapers and major magazines; in 1903 the *Buffalo Inquirer and Courier* hired her as the world's first woman staff photographer. In 1904 she became the first woman credentialed to take pictures at the St. Louis World's Fair. In 1905 she opened a portrait studio in New York City. Her work spanned a wide spectrum of her craft: portraiture, news photography, social commentary, fashion, photojournalism, and pictorial photography.

See also Photographers.

Reference Alexander Alland, Sr., *Jessie Tarbox Beals, First Woman News Photographer* (1978).

Beecher, Catharine Esther (1800–1878)

All her life this educator and writer cherished her noted minister father, her family, and her home training in the household arts and morality. They shaped her educational theories. She believed that women should exert themselves only within the domestic sphere. There, she argued, they should assert authority to make responsible decisions. For this role they needed education.

After her fiancé died at sea in 1822, her father decided that she was called to a vocation beyond that of most women. To that end she and her sister Mary in 1823 opened a girls' school in Hartford, Connecticut, later known as the Hartford Female Seminary.

There, in accordance with her theories, girls practiced gymnastics and were trained in teaching and domestic science. In 1831 she opened another school, the Western Female Institute in Ohio, which six years later collapsed for want of money.

But her "western" experience had convinced Beecher of the necessity to found normal schools to train teachers for the West. Her book on the subject, *The Duty of American Women to Their Country* (1845), resulted in the creation of the Board of National Popular Education, with Beecher supervising teacher selection, training, and placement. Increasingly her interests turned to founding endowed nondenominational women's colleges in the West—for the purpose, needless to say, of training women as teachers and housewives. Accordingly she founded the American Woman's Educational Association, which established three schools, one of which survived.

To support herself, Beecher wrote books, including the influential *A Treatise on Domestic Economy for the Use of Young Ladies at Home and School* (1841), and *Treatise: American Woman's Home* (1869), coauthored with her sister Harriet Beecher Stowe. These books of household hints enjoyed great popularity. Above all she advocated systematization in the home; where it was employed, she believed, it would expand autonomous female responsibility. This sort of thinking reflected and contributed to the popular nineteenth-century theories of women's moral superiority, their duty to sacrifice themselves to their families, and their exercise of ultimate power in shaping the minds of children—rocking the cradle and ruling the world.

See also American Woman's Educational Association; Architects; Home Economists; Teachers.

References Mae E. Harveson, *Catharine Esther Beecher, Pioneer Educator* (1932, 1969); Edward T. James et al., eds., *Notable American Women I* (1971); Kathryn Kish Sklar, *Catharine Beecher: A Study in American Domesticity* (1973).

Bellanca, Dorothy Jacobs
(1894–1946)

This outstanding trade union organizer, a native Latvian who emigrated to the United States at six, went to work at 13 as a buttonhole-sewer in a man's overcoat factory in Baltimore. Soon after the turn of the century she began her lifelong career in the union movement; by 1914 she headed Local 170 of the United Garment Workers of America and by 1916 was serving on their executive board. Her activities thereafter won her national recognition as an organizer and negotiator. During the 1920s and 1930s she focused on organizing for the Amalgamated Clothing Workers of America, while she also worked for the Congress of Industrial Organizations' Textile Workers Organizing Committee. During the Great Depression and World War II she worked with various federal and state agencies concerned with problems of unemployment, maternity and child welfare, standards for the employment of women in defense industries, and discrimination in employment. Ever the activist, she entered New York state and city politics, helping to found the American Labor party in 1936, and unsuccessfully running for Congress from Brooklyn in 1938. Few other immigrant women achieved such prominence in the American labor movement.

See also Congress of Industrial Organizations; Great Depression; Mason, Lucy Randolph; Union Organizers; World War II.

References Edward T. James et al., eds., *Notable American Women I* (1971); Susan Ware, *Holding Their Own: American Women in the 1930s* (1982).

Benefits

Benefits, or fringe benefits, are forms of compensation in addition to wages. Most women in the workplace suffer the disadvantage not only of the gender gap in wages but also of the lack of adequate benefits. This lack originates in three areas: occupational segregation, which confines so many women to low-paid and low-benefit women's work; the engage-ment of so many women in part-time and temporary work, which usually offers few or no benefits; and the failure of society to require most employers to provide benefits critically important to women, like child care, paid maternity leave, and family leave.

Moreover, the mounting costs of benefits have contributed to the proliferation of part-time, temporary, and consulting work and a cutback in full-time employment. It often proves cheaper for an employer to pay a full-time employee overtime than to hire another employee.

Benefits have become so important in the late twentieth century that a job seeker with options may be as much influenced in her choice by the benefits offered as by the pay. Among those provided, health insurance for the employee and her family probably ranks first in importance in the minds of most workers. Its costs have soared astronomically in the 1980s and 1990s, and government, business, and even health care providers now recognize an existing crisis.

Although younger employees often fail to recognize their importance, pensions constitute another substantial part of an employee's benefits package. In 1990 only 23 percent of all women, compared to 46 percent of men, received pension benefits at retirement. Women's average pension income was only 60 percent that of men, and Social Security payments received by retired women were only 76 percent of men's.

As part of their benefits package, companies may offer disability insurance in the form of short-term insurance, like maternity leave, or long-term, which for the severely disabled may last a lifetime. The Employee Assistance Programs set up in the 1940s, primarily to deal with alcoholic employees, have evolved into packages that may include dependent-care referrals; financial, legal, and tax advice; family/marital counseling; physical fitness programs; stress counseling; crisis intervention; supervisory training; elder care; and assistance with on-the-job performance problems. These programs can even help the employee find care for an elderly parent in a different part of the country. (*New York Times*, 6 September 1992)

As costs mount and sensitivity to the individual needs of employees increases, more companies are developing flexible benefits, a cafeteria-style plan that allows employees to choose their benefits from a list of options. Typically such a plan awards employees a given number of credits and assigns a certain number of credits to each benefit; employees may choose up to their maximum credits. Sometimes the plan allows the employee to purchase more credits for a fee.

Among them all, employee benefits typically comprise a staggering 25 to 60 percent of compensation costs, with the national average standing at 40 percent.

See also Child Care; Compensation; Consultants; Elder Care; Family Leave; Gender Gap; Health Insurance; Maternity Leave; Occupational Segregation; Older Women; Part-Time Workers; Pensions; Temporary Workers; Welfare Work.

References Susan Gluck Mezey, *In Pursuit of Equality: Women, Public Policy and the Federal Courts* (1992); Nine to Five, National Association of Working Women, "Profile of Working Women" (1990); Paula Ries and Anne J. Stone, eds., *The American Woman, 1992–1993: A Status Report* (1992).

Benefits Package
See Benefits.

Bernays, Doris Fleischman (1892–1980)
About 1920 Bernays, along with her husband Edward, established the principles, practices, and ethics of the new field of public relations.

See also Communications.

Reference Carolyn Garrett Cline et al., *The Velvet Ghetto* (1986).

Bethune, Louise Blanchard (1856–1913)
Bethune, a native of upstate New York, was the first professional American woman architect. After high school she planned to enter the new architecture school at Cornell but instead apprenticed with a Buffalo architect. In 1881 she married a colleague, Robert Armour Bethune, and the two set up a wide-ranging practice in Buffalo. They designed chapels, factories, veterinary stables, armories, residences—whatever commissions came their way. Insofar as she did specialize, it was in school buildings.

In 1888 the American Institute of Architects elected her its first woman member; the next year she became its first woman fellow. In those early days of the profession she advocated equal pay for women, tried to improve standards by urging the licensing of architects, and refused to bid competitively—even on the women's building at the 1891 World's Columbian Exposition in Chicago. (Sophia G. Hayden, graduate of the regular architectural course at the Massachusetts Institute of Technology, won that competition.) Bethune, who had borne one child in 1883, retired in 1891 to devote herself to genealogy.

See also Architects; Equal Pay Act of 1963.

Reference Edward T. James et al., eds., *Notable American Women I* (1971).

Bethune, Mary McLeod (1875–1955)
This influential black leader fought to educate black people, to organize them to exercise political power, and to focus the attention of the nation on their problems. A native of South Carolina, child of former slaves, she was educated at Scotia Seminary in North Carolina and the Moody Bible Institute in Chicago. When the Presbyterian Mission Board turned her down as a missionary to Africa because she was black, McLeod began teaching in the South. In 1898 she married businessman Albert McLeod Bethune; their only child was born in 1899. In that year the couple separated, and Bethune went to Florida to open a mission school.

Five years later in Daytona Beach, she opened the school for girls that would eventually unite with Cookman Institute

Mary McLeod Bethune pickets for civil rights.

to form Bethune-Cookman College, over which she presided until 1942. Bethune sought new ways through which she and the school could serve the black community: the development of a high school program, a voter registration drive in the face of Ku Klux Klan threats, and a hospital for blacks. Even with the support of the Methodist Episcopal Church, she had to devote immense energies to fundraising.

During that time, Bethune was gaining a national reputation through her service with the National Association of Colored Women; in her presidency the organization built its first national headquarters and hired its first executive secretary. In 1935 she united the major national black women's associations in the National Council of Negro Women.

She cultivated a friendship with Eleanor Roosevelt, whom she educated on the problems of black Americans. She used her various appointments in the New Deal's National Youth Administration to increase opportunities for young blacks and to alert the public and the government to black problems. To strengthen the black presence and black influence in government, she created the Federal Council on Negro Affairs, a "black cabinet" to President Roosevelt.

Bethune gradually resigned her official responsibilities in the early 1940s. But she continued to speak and to struggle for black equality.

See also New Deal; Roosevelt, Anna Eleanor; Teachers.

References Rackham Holt, *Mary McLeod Bethune* (1964); Catherine Owens Peare, *Mary McLeod Bethune* (1951); Barbara Sicherman et al. eds., *Notable American Women: The Modern Period* (1980); Emma Gelders Sterne, *Mary McLeod Bethune* (1957); Jenifer S. Uglow, comp. and ed., *International Dictionary of Women's Biography*, (1985).

Bickerdyke, Mary Ann Ball (1817–1901)

"Mother" Bickerdyke, a Civil War hospital worker, helped to establish the profession of nursing. After a peripatetic childhood, a scrappy education, a few years perhaps as a domestic worker, and residence on an uncle's farm, she married in 1847. Robert Bickerdyke, her husband, a sign and house painter, died 12 years later, leaving her with three children. She supported them by practicing "botanic" medicine.

In 1861, leaving her children to be cared for by neighbors, she volunteered to distribute a relief fund raised by her Galesburg, Illinois, church for wounded and ill soldiers in nearby Cairo. Setting herself to work to ameliorate the ghastly conditions she found among them, Bickerdyke became the matron of the general hospital there; but, persuaded that she was needed even more at the front, she moved with Grant's army, toiling in tent field hospitals in Tennessee and Mississippi, laundering, cooking, distributing supplies, nursing, and searching the battlefields for the wounded. In April 1862, the Northwestern Sanitary Commission in Chicago, impressed by her rising fame, appointed her their agent in the field.

This brusque, energetic woman arrogated authority to herself, building support among the northern generals, and attacking medical officers whom she considered inefficient. In 1863 she became matron of a military hospital in Memphis, Tennessee. Indignant over its insufficient diet for patients, she went out to solicit farmers for cows and chickens, successfully transporting them to Memphis. Soon she was off again to join Grant's army at Vicksburg and later to travel with Sherman's army to Chattanooga and then on his march to the sea. Late in 1864, after a couple of months of accompanying hospital trains north and a speaking tour for the Sanitary Commission, she set out with a load of supplies to rejoin Sherman, but disembarked at Wilmington, North Carolina, to help the emaciated men lately freed from the notorious Andersonville prison, and wound up in Beaufort, North Carolina, as the war ended.

No subsequent experience ever matched those glory years of the Civil War. For a while Bickerdyke served as assistant superintendent of a Chicago charity for poor women and children. Her effort at running a boarding house as part of a project to resettle unemployed veterans failed financially. In 1870 she began work as a missionary for the New York Board of City Missions. Four years later she helped relieve a population afflicted by a plague of locusts in Illinois.

She spent her last 11 years in San Francisco, earning her living as a clerk at the mint and volunteering for charitable organizations, now and then traveling to Washington to help veterans procure pensions, visiting Soldiers' Homes, and helping to organize a branch of the Woman's Relief Corps of the Grand Army of the Republic. In 1886 Congress awarded her a small pension.

See also Civil War; Nurses.
References Nina Brown Baker, *Cyclone in Calico* (1952); Edward T. James et al., eds., *Notable American Women I* (1971).

Biological Clock

The twenties and early thirties of a woman's life present the optimal physical opportunity for her to conceive and bear children. As she ages, her "biological clock" ticks away this opportunity, but unless and until more employers better accommodate women's family responsibilities, working women may have to choose between interrupting their careers, sometimes permanently, or postponing childbearing well into their thirties. At that age they face greater dangers, both for the fetus and for themselves.

See also Child Care; Maternity Leave; Mommy Track.

Blache, Alice Guy (1873–1968)

The French-born Blache, perhaps the first woman filmmaker, moved to the United States in 1910 after a 12-year career with Gaumont, for whom she invented cinematographic equipment, directed, and produced. She operated her own American firm, the Solax Company, until the early 1920s, enjoying great success, and wondering why more women didn't choose directing as a career. Blache, at home in all genres, made notable technical advances. She may have been the first person to do narrative on screen. She advocated natural acting. Sometimes she shot on location.

See also Cinema.
References Ally Acker, *Reel Women* (1991); Gwendolyn Foster-Dixon and Wheeler Dixon, "Women Who Made the Movies" (videotape, 1991).

Black Americans

The first African women to come to North America were indentured servants who eventually earned their freedom. But slaves were brought to Virginia as early as 1619. By the mid-seventeenth century, law had begun to codify slavery, often by specifying different treatment for blacks than for whites, such as taxing the field work of white women but not that of blacks, thereby sending black women out to the fields. Most women slaves worked in the fields besides keeping house, bearing children, and caring for them. Free black women could usually find work only at jobs that no one else wanted, in domestic service or as unskilled labor, though an elite found their way into nursing or storekeeping.

After the Civil War and the freeing of the slaves, job opportunities changed little. A frightened white labor force fought black workers' competition however they could. Most black women workers toiled in agriculture or as domestic servants, seamstresses, laundresses, or hairdressers. A fraction found employment in the mills, and a few others succeeded as entrepreneurs or farmers. By prodigies of effort, 160 black women had become doctors, seven had become dentists, and ten had become lawyers by the turn of the twentieth century. But at that time domestic service and agriculture absorbed the labors of 88 percent of black women.

The urgent demand for teachers for black schools provided most of the professional openings for black women—13,525 of them by 1900. In the late nineteenth century, almost literally making bricks without straw, teachers like Lucy C. Laney, Nannie Helen Burroughs, Charlotte Hawkins Brown, and Mary McLeod Bethune founded schools for black youngsters. There the training, based on the philosophy of Booker T. Washington, stressed vocational education. For girls this usually meant home-making, with a sprinkling of academic subjects and emphasis on morality and thrift.

Women spearheaded the northward movement of blacks in the Great Migration of 1910 to 1930. Although in the North, too, blacks were usually reduced to jobs that no one else wanted, they still earned significantly more than in the South. The labor shortage of World War I opened new opportunities to them, but in the years between the wars they found almost as many closed doors as ever. Competing white workers fought to keep them out of jobs in offices, sales, and manufacturing. But a few black entrepreneurs succeeded, and the black middle class swelled with the arrival of 130,000 immigrants from the British West Indies between 1900 and 1924.

The Great Depression afflicted black workers even more heavily than whites, as housewives made do without domestic servants and white workers competed for jobs formerly staffed by blacks. Many relief measures did not apply to domestic service and agriculture, where most black women still labored.

Again in World War II government and employers urged women into the workplace, but even then they discriminated against blacks. This time, with the support of unions and the National Council of Negro Women, some black women workers responded militantly, as in 1944 when they stormed a Ford plant to demand jobs. Despite postwar setbacks, they achieved permanent gains, opening up jobs in factories and offices—gains on which they expanded in the 1950s. Between 1930 and 1960 they doubled their share of manufacturing jobs and multiplied their share of clerical and sales jobs eight times.

The Civil Rights Movement of the 1960s, particularly with the enactment of the Civil Rights Act of 1964, exerted pressure for new jobs for blacks on government, employers, and unions, and enabled blacks to enter new fields of endeavor. This progress stalled in the mid–1970s, as employers in search of cheap labor, lower taxes, and less government regulation moved their factories out of the United States, and stores fled from the cities to the malls. In the 1980s unemployment among black men and black teenagers of both genders rose alarmingly. In 1988, more black women were in the labor force than black men.

Although black women have narrowed the wage gap between themselves and white women, now in the late twentieth century they still suffer higher unemployment rates, have more trouble in finding full-time work, and are more likely to work in low-paid, low-status jobs.

See also American Missionary Association; Bethune, Mary McLeod; Civil Rights Act of 1964; Civil War; Domestic Servants; Entrepreneurs; Farmers; Great Depression; Indentured Servants; Slavery; Teachers; Tenant Farmers; Unemployment; Unions; Vocational Education; World War I; World War II.

References Teresa L. Amott and Julie A. Matthaei, *Race, Gender, and Work: A Multicultural Economic History of Women in the United States* (1991); Paula Giddings, *When and Where I Enter: The Impact of Black Women on Race and Sex in America* (1984); Darlene Clark Hine, ed., *Black Women in America: An Historical Encyclopedia* (1993); Jacqueline Jones, *Labor of Love, Labor of Sorrow: Black Women, Work and the Family from Slavery to the Present* (1985); Dorothy C. Salem, ed., *African-American Women: A Biographical Dictionary* (1993); Jessie Carney Smith, ed., *Notable Black American Women* (1992); Dorothy Sterling, *We Are Your Sisters: Black Women in the Nineteenth Century* (1984); Bette Woody, *Black Women in the Workplace* (1992).

Blackwell, Antoinette Louisa Brown (1825–1921)

The first American ordained woman minister of a recognized denomination, Blackwell grew up in upstate New York. She studied literature and theology at Oberlin College, which refused her degrees and a license to preach because she was a woman. Despite the protests of the clergy, she was ordained minister of the First Congregational Church in Butler and Savannah, Wayne County, New York in 1853. But her growing interest in social issues led her to work in slums and prisons. After her marriage in 1856 to Samuel Blackwell, brother of Elizabeth Blackwell, she studied and wrote about evolution in the leisure permitted her by bearing and caring for seven children. In later life as preacher and lecturer she encouraged women's advancement and professional aspirations and worked for women's suffrage.

See also Blackwell, Elizabeth; Brown, Olympia; Religion.

References Elizabeth Cazden, *Antoinette Brown Blackwell* (1983); Edward T. James et al., eds., *Notable American Women I* (1971).

Blackwell, Elizabeth (1821–1910)

The first woman in modern times to earn a degree in medicine, Blackwell was born in England and privately educated, studying the same subjects as her brothers. When she was 11 her family immigrated to the United States, where they moved from New York City to Jersey City to Cincinnati. Blackwell taught for seven years. Turned down by one medical school after another, she was finally admitted to Geneva College in upper New York State, though the townspeople ostracized her and the college at first barred her from classroom demonstrations. Nevertheless she earned her medical degree in 1849 and thereafter studied abroad.

After a dismal struggle to get started in practice, she, her sister Dr. Emily Blackwell, and her protegée Dr. Marie E. Zakrzewska opened the New York Infirmary for Women and Children in 1857. In 1859, after a stint in England to improve opportunities for women in medicine, she became the first woman entered on the Medical Register of the United Kingdom. During the Civil War her activities contributed to the establishment of the United States Sanitary Commission and she and Emily helped to select and train nurses. To offer American women improved medical training, she founded the Women's Medical College of the New York Infirmary in 1868, got it functioning, and then turned it over to Emily. Notable for its high standards, it continued to operate until 1899, when Cornell University Medical School at last brought itself to admit women. After 1869 Blackwell carried on her work in England. Throughout her medical career she emphasized the importance of hygiene and sanitation and criticized the excessive use of surgery.

See also Civil War; Zakrzewska, Marie Elizabeth.

References Elizabeth Blackwell, *Pioneer Work in Opening the Medical Profession to Women* (1895, 1914); Edward T. James et al., eds., *Notable American Women I* (1971); Ishbel Ross, *Child of Destiny* (1944).

Bloor, Ella Reeve (1862–1951)

"Mother" Bloor, a socialist union organizer, focused her entire life on improving the status of women. She grew up on Staten Island and in New Jersey, educated partly in the public schools and partly by her mother. At 19 she married an aspiring lawyer, Dan Ware; they had six children, but he disliked her political activism and they divorced in 1896. A second marriage to socialist Louis Cohen resulted in the birth of two more children and another divorce.

Bloor's volunteer activities had already led to an interest in the labor movement: in the early 1890s she had organized streetcar workers in Philadelphia. In 1905 she became a state organizer for the Socialist Labor party in Connecticut. In 1906 she documented for a government commission the charges against the meat-packing industry made by Upton Sinclair. Then for more than a decade she organized for the Socialist party and for labor unions. Disillusioned by the hysteria of World War I, she devoted the rest of her life to the Communist party, while continuing to organize labor. She was arrested more than 30 times, up to the age of 72.

See also Communist Party; Socialist Party; Union Organizers; Unions; World War I.

References Ella R. Bloor, *We Are Many: An Autobiography* (1940); *Notable American Women: The Modern Period.*

Blue-Collar Workers

The term "blue-collar" in its strictest sense pertains to wage earners wearing rough work clothes, often in jobs requiring manual labor. Partly because many of these jobs are skilled crafts, partly because many of them have been represented by strong unions, and partly because they have traditionally been male-dominated, they are higher paid than such "women's work" as clerical jobs. In the latter half of the twentieth century more women have entered blue-collar occupations, like bartending, bus driving, and the construction trades. The increase of women's participation in the blue-collar labor force has been accelerated by the passage of laws against discrimination in employment and wages.

See also Civil Rights Act of 1964; Equal Pay Act of 1963; Nontraditional Occupations; Pink-Collar Workers; Sexual Harassment; Trades; White-Collar Workers.

References Deborah L. Rhode, *Justice and Gender: Sex Discrimination and the Law* (1989); Ellen J. Rosen, *Bitter Choices: Blue Collar Women in and out of Work* (1987); Carroll W. Wilkinson, *Women in Nontraditional Occupations: References and Resources* (1991).

Board of Directors of Rotary International v. Rotary Club of Duarte (1987)

This case tested whether Rotary International's rules excluding women from membership violated California's Unruh Act, which entitled all persons regardless of sex to membership in business establishments. The U.S. Supreme Court held that Rotary's exclusion of women was discriminatory and in violation of California law; it further ruled that Rotary International's assertion of First Amendment rights to private association was not adversely affected by the admission of women to membership. Their admission to Rotary and similar organizations affords businesswomen important access to networking.

See also Business and Industry; Men-Only Clubs; Networking; *Roberts v. United States Jaycees.*

Reference Susan Gluck Mezey, *In Pursuit of Equality: Women, Public Policy and the Federal Courts* (1992).

Board of Trustees of Keene State College v. Sweeney (1978)

In this job discrimination case the college failed to provide the court with a legitimate nondiscriminatory reason for denying promotion to women instructors. The complaint of the women was thus sustained.

See also Academic Women; Civil Rights Act of 1964; Education Amendments Act.

References Judith Freeman Clark, *Almanac of American Women in the 20th Century* (1987); Susan Gluck Mezey, *In Pursuit of Equality: Women, Public Policy and the Federal Courts* (1992).

Boarding

In the nineteenth and early twentieth centuries, many women supplemented the family income, or earned it all, by taking in boarders, whom they housed and fed. Immigrant women took in "greenhorns" (new immigrants) and men working to accumulate enough money to send for their families. Rural women boarded the teacher as their contribution to her pay. Newlyweds not yet ready to invest in a home boarded; so did widowers and their children; so did students and young professional women and men; and so did workers who slaved in southern cotton mills.

Boarding became a lifestyle for many, ranging from the miserable, in situations where the boarders took turns in the beds and the landlady counted every penny and watered the milk, to the abundant, where boarders enjoyed each other's company and the landlady prided herself on her pie.

The system declined gradually; by 1930 only about 11 percent of families took in boarders, and the numbers have since fallen.

References Angela Howard Zophy and Frances M. Kavenik, eds., *Handbook of American Women's History* (1990); Dorothy Schneider and Carl J. Schneider, *Women in the Progressive Era* (1993).

Bona Fide Occupational Qualification (BFOQ)

Under special circumstances the prohibition in Title VII of the Civil Rights Act of 1964 against classifying people on the basis of race, sex, religion, or national origin may be waived if such distinctions are necessarily linked to the normal operation of a particular enterprise, i.e., are a BFOQ. It is up to the Equal Employment Opportunity Commission or the courts to interpret what legitimately constitutes a BFOQ.

Employers might, for example, successfully defend excluding women from particular jobs if they could convince the courts that those jobs present health or safety problems unique to women. But in *UAW v. Johnson Controls* (1991), the U.S. Supreme Court found against the employer, who had required all female employees under 70 who wanted jobs with high lead exposure (which might damage a developing fetus) to produce medical proof of sterilization or infertility. And an Alabama law that set minimum height and weight standards for state corrections officers, alleging a BFOQ for the adequate performance of their jobs, was struck down by the Supreme Court in *Dothard v. Rawlinson* (1977); the court noted that these standards disqualified 40 percent of the state's women but only one percent of its men.

See also *Cheatwood v. South Central Bell Telephone Co.*; Civil Rights Act of 1964; Disparate Impact; *Dothard v. Rawlinson*; Equal Employment Opportunity Commission; Fetal Protection Policies; Protective Legislation; Tests; *UAW v. Johnson Controls*.

Reference Robert E. Doherty, *Industrial and Labor Relations Terms* (1989).

Bookbinders

In colonial America the binding of books was generally a function of the printer. Male printers frequently depended upon the women in their families to acquire skills in this craft. The first woman binder of record was Elizabeth Short, who in 1714 bound 2,000 copies of the *Saybrook Platform* printed by her husband Peter. In later more industrially developed times the printer usually turned the binding function over to an outside craftsperson.

See also Aitken, Jane; Colonial America; O'Sullivan, Mary Kenney; Printers.

Bookkeeping

See Accountants and Bookkeepers; Clerical Workers.

Borchardt, Selma Munter (1895–1968)

This educator, attorney, and labor leader, a native of Washington, D.C., earned undergraduate degrees at Syracuse University, a master's and extensive credits toward a doctorate in sociology from Catholic University, and a degree from the Washington College of Law. Nonetheless she always credited the labor movement with being her greatest teacher.

In her working life she managed to combine as many interests as she did in her education. She committed herself to a career in public education, even while building a good-sized legal practice. Simultaneously she fought for teacher control over education. Active in the Washington teacher's union, she held offices in the national American Federation of Teachers (AFT), lending her legal expertise both to the AFT and to the American Federation of Labor. For more than

30 years she represented the AFT in Washington as its lobbyist. She also accepted appointments to government commissions, where she advised Franklin D. Roosevelt's National Youth Administration and helped to draft the United Nations Educational, Scientific and Cultural Organization (UNESCO) charter.

See also American Federation of Labor; American Federation of Teachers; Attorneys; Teachers.

Reference Notable American Women: The Modern Period.

Boycotts

To boycott is to refuse to deal with. Unions sometimes ask the public to refuse to buy the products of those employers against whom the unions have grievances. For example, the International Ladies' Garment Workers' union has a long history of boycotting the sale of nonunion-made garments. A secondary boycott may be directed against other companies not directly involved in a labor dispute. Certain types of secondary boycotts are outlawed in the Taft-Hartley Act and the Landrum-Griffin Act.

See also Clayton Anti-Trust Act; International Ladies' Garment Workers' Union; Norris–La-Guardia Act; Taft-Hartley Act; Unions; United Farm Workers.

Bradwell, Myra Colby (1831–1894)

This attorney was born in Vermont and in her childhood moved successively to New York State, Illinois, and Wisconsin. She taught for several years before her 1852 marriage to the penniless budding lawyer James Bolesworth Bradwell. He continued to read law while they taught and opened their own private school. In 1855 he passed the Illinois bar and with his brother-in-law built up a sizable practice, while Myra Bradwell bore four children.

During the Civil War she worked with the Northwestern Sanitary Commission; after the war she continued her involvement with the Soldiers' Aid Society and a Soldiers' Home, as well as with other charities. But she was also reading law. In 1868 she began to publish a legal newspaper and with her husband set up the Chicago Legal News Company. Under her presidency both enterprises flourished. The *Chicago Legal News* achieved wide influence, for 25 years molding opinion in midwestern legal circles to encourage regulation of railroads and large corporations, zoning ordinances, improved legal standards, the formation of bar associations, the establishment of law schools, and the compulsory retirement of judges. Above all she advocated the removal of women's legal disabilities.

In 1869 Myra Bradwell passed the Illinois bar examination, but the state supreme court denied her admission, a decision upheld by the U.S. Supreme Court. But in 1890, the Illinois bar finally admitted her and in 1892 the federal Supreme Court followed suit. Upon her death, her state bar association said: "No more powerful and convincing argument in favor of the admission of women to a participation in the administration of government was ever made than can be found in her character, conduct, and achievements." Her daughter, Bessie Bradwell Helmer, carried on her work.

See also Attorneys; Civil War; Mansfield, Arabella.

Reference Edward T. James et al., eds., *Notable American Women I* (1971).

Brandeis Brief

See Muller v. Oregon.

Bread and Roses Strike (Lawrence, Massachusetts, Textile Strike, 1912)

This strike was notable for the brutality of the employers' response, the originality of the strikers' tactics, and the militancy of the women strikers. It began when the mill owners cut the wages of all workers to compensate for profits lost as the result of protective legislation forbidding women and children to work more than 54 hours a week. This loss of wages, on top of unspeakable working and living conditions, outraged the working community, which responded by striking. Outside help for the strikers came from the newly organized Industrial Workers of the World, which created a spirit of solidarity among the many ethnic groups and encouraged the participation of women.

One-half of the 23,000 mostly foreign-born striking workers were women and children, workers that the American Federation of Labor had considered "unorganizable." Supporting the strikers were wives, sisters, and mothers of employees. Women often walked the picket lines rather than the men, on the theory that the police would hesitate to assault women—a false assumption. When they marched, the women put the young girls in the middle of their ranks, both to protect them and to call attention to them. (Half of the children of Lawrence worked in the mills.) Women threw stones at scabs, hung photographs of them in the local grocery stores, and poured scalding water on them from upper windows. Women formed "endless human chains" by linking arms, then went weaving and hooting through the neighborhoods and business sections. They cut out the backs of the uniforms of the soldiers called in to keep order. They stripped men unsympathetic to the strike. When police arrested one woman, others crowded into the police van: "Take us all or take no one." Housewives helped the strikers by feeding them and taking care of their children.

Police arrested 130 women during the strike, charging almost 90 percent of them with intimidation or assault on an officer. A policeman shot and killed Annie Lo-Pizzo. When the strikers tried to send their starving children to out-of-town sympathizers, police beat mothers and children waiting for the trains. The harshness and cruelty of the employers and the police eventually roused public support all over the country for the strikers.

Assisted by the Industrial Workers of the World, reformers like "Big Bill"

Haywood, Mary Heaton Vorse, Mary Harris Jones, Elizabeth Gurley Flynn, and the nationwide attention the strike attracted, the strikers won a settlement. But ultimately they lost, as one by one the textile mills left the Northeast for the non-unionized South.

See also American Federation of Labor; Flynn, Elizabeth Gurley; Industrial Workers of the World; Jones, Mary Harris; Protective Legislation; Scab; Strikes; Unions; Vorse, Mary Heaton.

References Ruth Milkman, ed. *Women, Work and Protest: A Century of U.S. Women's Labor History* (1985); Dorothy Schneider and Carl J. Schneider, *Women in the Progressive Era* (1993).

Breckinridge, Sophonisba Preston (1866–1948)

This social worker was one of the Hull House circle of reformers. The daughter of a distinguished liberal Kentucky family, she studied law after her graduation from Wellesley in 1888, and she became the first woman to pass the Kentucky bar. When her career as a lawyer floundered, she moved to Chicago and in 1901 earned a Ph.D. in political science at the University of Chicago, then a J.D. in 1904. After this extensive education she taught courses on the economic and legal aspects of family life in the university's department of household administration. In 1907 she also began to teach at the Chicago School of Civics and Philanthropy, which trained social workers. There she soon became dean and head of research, with Edith Abbott as her assistant.

Breckinridge and Abbott published three books on delinquent children based on direct observation, describing the breakdown of the family under urban conditions, books that they conceptualized as materials for social workers. This kind of research involved Breckinridge with welfare administration and social reforms. She investigated tenements, campaigned for a national child labor law, served in the state Consumers' League, helped organize Chicago's Immigrant Protective League, and worked with the

National Association for the Advancement of Colored People. Insisting on the importance of economic equality for women, she supported women's unions and drafted bills regulating wages and hours of women's employment, lobbying for the support of such measures by the Progressive party.

Despite all this whirlwind of activity and her involvement in the American Association of University Women, the peace movement, and the women's suffrage movement, Breckinridge devoted herself primarily to developing the profession of social work. Through her efforts the University of Chicago took over the Chicago School of Civics and Philanthropy as its Graduate School of Social Service, Breckinridge herself teaching there and serving also as assistant dean of women. She insisted on rigorous standards and full professional training for social workers. In her own teaching, in several books, and in the *Social Science Review*, which she helped found (1927) and edited, she emphasized the importance of the state in any program of social welfare. She retired from the university in 1942 but continued her other labors almost up to her death.

See also Abbott, Edith; American Association of University Women; Consumers' League; Hull House; Social Workers; Unions.

Reference Notable American Women I.

Brent, Margaret (n.d.)

This first female lawyer in the American colonies, who arrived in Maryland in 1638, amassed a fortune by acquiring large tracts of land.

See also Attorneys.

Reference Alice Kessler-Harris, *Out To Work: A History of Wage-Earning Women in the United States* (1982).

Bridge Job

This work carries a member of the labor force from a career job into retirement. It may be part-time or temporary; it may carry less responsibility than the career job. Sometimes the worker turns to a completely new field.

See also Older Women; Part-Time Workers; Temporary Workers.

Brookwood Labor College (1921–1937)

Established in Katonah, New York, by Fannia Mary Cohn, this project of the International Ladies' Garment Workers' Union was the first residential college for workers. At this cooperative institution, the students and faculty joined in the manual labor necessary for maintenance. It attracted labor notables from many countries. The informal but intensive classes, particularly in the social sciences, helped students to understand the country's problems and inspired them to carry their new knowledge back to their fellow workers. In the late 1920s and early 1930s the college was torn apart between the conservatism of sponsoring American Federation of Labor officials, who denounced it as subversive, and the radicalism of its director. It closed in 1937.

See also American Federation of Labor; Cohn, Fannia Mary; International Ladies' Garment Workers' Union; Workers' Education.

References Joyce L. Kornbluh and Mary Frederickson, eds., *Sisterhood and Solidarity: Workers' Education for Women* (1984); Rose Pesotta, *Bread upon the Waters* (1987).

Brown, Olympia (1835–1926)

This Universalist minister, a native of Michigan, took her undergraduate degree at Antioch College. There she was inspired by the example and preaching of Antoinette Brown Blackwell. In 1861 she entered the theological seminary of St. Lawrence University, graduating and being ordained in 1863—the first American woman ordained by full denominational authority. Until 1876 she served churches in Weymouth, Massachusetts, and Bridgeport, Connecticut, also involving herself in the women's suffrage movement.

In 1873 she married John Henry Willis but retained her maiden name. She bore two children, a son in 1874 and a daughter in 1876. In 1878 she accepted a call to a church in Racine, Wisconsin; her husband accompanied her, shifting his business. Nine years later she resigned; though she continued to preach and to serve in ministerial posts she devoted more of her time to the cause of women's suffrage. Even in her eighties she picketed the White House and burned President Wilson's speeches.

See also Blackwell, Antoinette Louisa Brown; Religion.

References Charlotte Cote, *Olympia Brown: The Battle for Equality* (1989); *Notable American Women* I.

Bryn Mawr Summer School for Women Workers (1921–1938)

Proposed by Bryn Mawr's president Carey Thomas, this residential six- to eight-week program to train labor activists served an international constituency of blue-collar women, teaching them economics, politics, and union history. Bryn Mawr dean Hilda Worthington Smith directed it, and the Women's Trade Union League provided major support. The experience politicized both students and faculty, the graduates often moving into union leadership, and their teachers into public service in labor and economics.

See also Blue-Collar Workers; Henry, Alice; Kingsbury, Susan Myra; Thomas, Martha Carey; Unions; Women's Trade Union League; Workers' Education.

References Dorothy M. Brown, *Setting a Course: American Women in the 1920s* (1987); Rita Heiler's film *The Women of Summer: Bryn Mawr Summer School for Women Workers, 1921–1938* (1985); Joyce L. Kornbluh and Mary Frederickson, eds., *Sisterhood and Solidarity: Workers' Education for Women* (1984); Florence Hemley Schneider, *Patterns of Workers' Education: The Story of the Bryn Mawr Summer School* (1941); Hilda Worthington Smith, *Women Workers at the Bryn Mawr Summer School* (1929).

Bureau of Vocational Information (BVI) (1911–1926)

Founded in New York as the Intercollegiate Bureau of Occupations and directed by Emma Hirth, the BVI reorganized itself in 1919, relegating placement to the United States Employment Bureau and concentrating on studying women in various occupations and informing women about how to obtain job training. Along with groups like the Institute of Women's Professions and the Women's Educational and Industrial Union, the BVI compiled guides to women's occupations. In 1924 the BVI issued *Training for the Professions and the Allied Occupations*, listing hundreds of occupations, their educational requirements, sources of training for them, and the duties they imposed.

See also Employment Agencies; *Occupational Outlook Handbook*; Vocational Guidance; Women's Educational and Industrial Union.

Reference Sharon Hartman Strom, *Beyond the Typewriter: Gender, Class, and the Origins of Modern American Office Work, 1900–1930* (1992).

Business and Industry

Women in business long preceded women formally educated for business, thanks to grim necessity, women's entrepreneurial and organizational talents, and the desire of local authorities to reduce the numbers dependent on charity. Even in colonial America, some women sold what they raised or made.

Although business colleges have always enrolled women and some coeducational colleges and universities have offered them business training, many institutions have put women on a secretarial track and men on a managerial track. Prestigious graduate programs long barred women: the Wharton School admitted them only in 1938, and the Harvard Graduate School of Business Administration only in 1963. Yet elite women's colleges, with the important exception of Bryn Mawr, refused to develop business programs until the late 1930s. Nonetheless by 1928 women were receiving more than 17 percent of the degrees in business from four-year colleges and universities, though these included degrees in secretarial science. In 1988–1989, women earned 46.7 percent of the undergraduate degrees in business and management, up from 8.7 percent 20 years earlier, and a third of the M.B.A.s. (*New York Times*, 16 October 1992)

With or without degrees, during the late nineteenth and all through the twentieth century, women have been making their way in business in increasing numbers. African-American Maggie Lena Walker (1867–1934) was America's first woman banker. In 1919 Brenda Vineyard Runyon opened the country's first all-woman bank and operated it until 1926. Mary Gindhard Roebling, president of the Trenton Trust Company of New Jersey, became the first woman stock exchange director in 1958, and in 1967 Muriel F. Siebert the first woman to buy a seat on the exchange.

See also Board of Directors of Rotary International *v. Rotary Club of Duarte*; Business and Professional Women's Clubs, Inc. of the U.S.A.; Catalyst; Clerical Workers; Colonial America; Communications; Entrepreneurs; Glass Ceiling; Human Resources Managers; Kreps, Juanita Morris; Managers; Networking; *Roberts v. United States Jaycees*; Seymour, Mary Foot; Siebert, Muriel F.

References Catalyst, *Building an Effective Corporate Women's Group* (1988); Catalyst, *Women in Corporate Management* (1990); Carolyn Garrett Cline, et al., *The Velvet Ghetto: The Impact of the Increasing Percentage of Women in Public Relations and Business Communication* (1986); Elizabeth A. Dexter, *Career Women of America, 1776–1840* (1950); Elizabeth A. Dexter, *Colonial Women of Affairs: Women in Business and Professions in America before 1776* (1972); L. Dusky and B. Zeitz, *The Best Companies for Women* (1988); Rosabeth Moss Kanter, *Men and Women of the Corporation* (1977); Rosabeth Moss Kanter, *When Giants Learn To Dance: Mastering the Challenge of Strategy, Management and Careers in the 1990s* (1989); Felice N. Schwartz with Jean Zimmerman, *Breaking with Tradition: Women and Work, the New Facts of Life* (1992).

Business and Professional Women's Clubs, Inc. of the U.S.A. (BPW/USA)

Founded in 1919, the National Federation of Business and Professional Women's Clubs, Inc. of the U.S.A., with its 125,000 members in 300 occupations, aims to enhance the status of working women. It supports the Business and Professional Women's Foundation and organizes the National Council on the Future of Women in the Workplace, which concerns itself with problems like dependent care and sensitizing employers to the needs of working women.

Business Owners

See Entrepreneurs.

Caldwell, Sarah (b. 1928)

Born in Missouri and raised in Arkansas, Caldwell has broken new ground for women musicians in conducting. A child prodigy, she studied violin at the New England Conservatory before she decided to become a conductor. In the early 1940s she was appointed to the faculty of the Opera Workshop at Tanglewood, and in 1952 she joined Boston University's music department. In 1957 she founded, and for many years directed, the Opera Company of Boston, where she distinguished herself by her staging and sense of theater and her introduction of many "firsts," including the first American stage appearance of singer Joan Sutherland and first performances of several operas. From about 1975 invitations came to conduct symphony orchestras and operas internationally, and in 1976 she debuted as the first woman conductor at the Metropolitan Opera in New York, hailed for her musicianship.

See also Musicians.
Reference Robert McHenry, ed., *Liberty's Women* (1980).

California Federal Savings and Loan v. Guerra (1987)

This case tested whether a California law requiring employers to grant women disability leave for pregnancy and childbirth constituted preferential treatment in violation of Title VII of the Civil Rights Act of 1964 and the Pregnancy Discrimination Act of 1978. The U.S. Supreme Court upheld the California statute (and thus its preferential features), noting that it advances women's equality in the workplace and allows women as well as men to have families without losing their jobs.

See also Civil Rights Act of 1964; Family and Medical Leave Act; Family Leave; Maternity Leave; Pregnancy; Pregnancy Discrimination Act.

Reference Susan Gluck Mezey, *In Pursuit of Equality: Women, Public Policy, and the Federal Courts* (1992).

Cannery and Agricultural Workers Industrial Union

This interracial union led the Great Strikes of California in the 1930s, seeking wage increases, an eight-hour day, overtime, abolition of piecework and child labor, and equal pay for women. The workers won Pyrrhic victories in many of these strikes, for as farmers mechanized, the numbers of employees plummeted.

See also Agricultural Workers; Strikes; Unions.
Reference Teresa Amott and Julie Matthaei, *Race, Gender, and Work: A Multicultural Economic History of Women in the United States* (1991).

Cary, Mary Ann Shadd

See Shadd, Mary Ann.

Catalyst

Founded in 1962, this organization helps employers encourage the career development of women and maintains a Corporate Board Resource to find qualified women for corporate boards, a speakers' bureau, and an information center on women in business.

See also American Women's Economic Development Corporation; Business and Industry.

La Causa

See United Farm Workers.

Center for Women Policy Studies (CWPS)

This nonmembership independent policy research and advocacy organization, founded in 1972, provides technical expertise on women's issues. In 1991 it established a National Brain Trust on Economic Opportunity for Low Income Women, which concentrates on higher education as a route to economic independence. Its Work and Family Policy Program investigates how women of color define and experience work and family issues. Its scholarly works have documented various kinds of systematic discrimination against women.

See also Clearinghouse on Women's Issues; Committee on Women's Employment and Related Social Issues.

Reference Joyce Gelb and Marian Lief Palley, *Women and Public Policies* (1982).

CETA
See Job Training Partnership Act.

Cheatwood v. South Central Bell Telephone Co. (1969)

In this early interpretation of bona fide occupational qualification the U.S. Supreme Court rejected the telephone company's argument that its refusal to consider Claudine Cheatwood (or any other woman) for the post of commercial representative was based upon requirements of the job. The company argued that the job required lifting heavy objects (up to 90 pounds), coping with flat tires, and entering bars and poolrooms—tasks that only men could perform. Moreover, women might not be able to find suitable restrooms. A landmark decision, the Cheatwood case required the employer to consider an applicant's individual competency and not rely upon assumptions about the capabilities of her gender.

See also Bona Fide Occupational Qualification; *Dothard v. Rawlinson*; Restrooms.

Chicago, Judy (b. 1939)

Born Judy Cohen in Chicago, Illinois, this painter and sculptor has focused her talents on female imagery in art and issues of female consciousness. Many of her themes are drawn from women's history. An ardent feminist, she legally changed her name to Judy Chicago in 1970 to signify her break with a male-oriented society. She studied at the Art Institute of Chicago and UCLA (B.A. 1962, M.A. 1964) and has exhibited her work in New York, Chicago, and various museums in California. She helped establish a women's art program at Fresno State College.

Chicago is perhaps best known for the Conference for Women Artists at the California Institute of the Arts, which she organized in 1972; the "Woman's Building" in Los Angeles (1973); and her textile and ceramic piece "The Dinner Party" (1979), which interpreted the lives of 39 women from classical to modern times. Her work also includes several books, a documentary film, a tapestry series, and other pieces illuminating aspects of women's lives.

See also Artists.

Reference Judith Freeman Clark, *Almanac of American Women in the 20th Century* (1987).

Judy Chicago

Chicago Training School for Active Workers in the Labor Movement
See Training School for Women Organizers.

Chicanas
See Hispanic Americans.

Child Care
Care for her children constitutes one of the most serious problems of the working mother. The problem grows more acute with the increase in working mothers and in single-parent families. But the United States lags far behind other industrial nations in providing child care, for the most part leaving mothers to wrestle with the problem alone. In 1987 only a few more than a million firms in the private sector and 74,000 government organizations furnished some benefits to help employees with child care, even including the possibility of flextime or part-time work.

In the nineteenth and early twentieth centuries, many children of working mothers received little or no care in their mothers' absence, working mothers generally leaving children old enough to dress and feed themselves to cope on their own. Although the first American day nursery was established in 1828, records show only six existed by 1880. Thereafter growth spurted, to 500 by 1912, under the leadership of women like the philanthropist Josephine Jewell Dodge, who in 1898 formed the National Federation of Day Nurseries. Usually these were open only to the children of women who had to work. And, of course, far too few existed to meet the need. Caretaking neighbors helped to fill the gap, along with proprietary day nurseries, where abuses were common. Some mothers "put out" their children with relatives better able to care for them, or in desperation committed them to the almshouse—a practice that led in the late nineteenth century to the development of orphanages and foster homes.

As an alternative to day nurseries and boarding out, Progressive Era reformers proposed mothers' pensions to fund mothers to stay in their own homes. Missouri enacted such a law in 1911; by 1935 all but two states provided Aid for Dependent Children.

The increasing number of married women entering the labor force in the 1920s usually fended for themselves. Well-off women hired servants to care for their children in their own homes. Most women, however, could not afford this kind of private care, especially given the dwindling number of servants, and had to turn instead to relatives and neighbors, proprietary day care, and the growing number of nursery schools, which promised not merely custodial care but also education. Nursery schools multiplied from 16 in 1923 to 108 by 1928. The charitable day nurseries established earlier changed with their clientele: since the destitute women they had been built for now presumably received Mothers' Pensions and no longer needed them, these nurseries turned instead to the children of working married women. The social workers in these day nurseries, however, often treated these mothers who "chose to work" as victims of a social-psychological problem in need of the caseworkers' expert remedies—an attitude that led to the marginalization of day nurseries. They revived briefly during the New Deal, which federally funded them for a time.

During World War II the government again interested itself in day nurseries. In 1941 Congress passed the Lanham Act, to meet on a 50-50 basis social service needs of communities affected by the war. Some companies desperately in need of employees created their own facilities: the Kaiser Shipbuilding Company opened a model on-site facility, with provisions for care of sick children and parental visitation. The company also arranged a service whereby the mother could pick up a prepared meal after work to carry home. But even during the war most working mothers had to rely on private arrangements, especially as facilities rarely provided care for babies under 18 months, and centers open to older children met less than 10 percent of the need.

After the war most of the existing child care facilities closed: by 1946 only 1,504 centers for 40,000 children still operated. Only in 1960 did society again acknowledge day-care as a social concern. In 1970 the White House Conference on Children urged massive federal funding for day-care, and the Comprehensive Child Development Act of 1971 recommended that government provide day-care for all children; Richard Nixon vetoed it. Early education programs alleviated the problem only partially, even though by 1979 51 percent of all children aged three to five were reported to be in preschool. In 1973 day-care centers, both for-profit and nonprofit (run by churches, welfare organizations, educational institutions, and other community associations) provided only 700,000 slots for the 6,000,000 preschoolers whose mothers worked. The Tax Reform Act of 1976 and the Revenue Act of 1978 gave some tax relief for parents who paid for day-care. Some parents were able to arrange part-time work, split shifts, and staggered hours; others exchanged child care in babysitting cooperatives.

More recently some companies have been allowing flextime and/or telecommuting. An increasing but still relatively small number of companies furnish some sort of day-care for employees' children, arguing that providing this facility benefits the company by giving it its pick of employees, and employees who are not tense with worry over their children. For instance, an Illinois automotive parts maker that offers a subsidized on-site day-care center and a summer camp has a waiting list of 5,000 would-be employees. But companies like these are the exception. Although a Hewitt Associates study shows that 74 percent of large companies offer some type of child care assistance, most of it takes the form of maintaining a list of child care providers or offering dependent care spending accounts: tax-free accounts that permit employees to set aside up to $5,000 of their pretax salaries annually to pay for child care. (*U.S. News and World Report*, 22 February 1993)

Smaller companies face special difficulties in meeting this need of working parents. Despite the low pay of most child care workers, staffing costs are formidable in these labor-intensive facilities. Some companies have had good results by providing emergency child care to help parents when their regular arrangements break down. Others have agreed to pay for emergency at-home care for up to three consecutive days. In 1991 the Stride Rite Corporation, a pioneer in on-site child care, opened an intergenerational day-care center to accommodate 55 children and 24 older adults, in acknowledgment of the increasing problem for workers of elder care.

The United States military, particularly the Air Force, has compiled one of the best (though still far from perfect) records for day-care provision. The quality of child care the military offers, however, varies markedly from service to service and post to post and suffers almost everywhere from hours too short for the needs of servicewomen (and servicemen). Moreover, the military provides little or no help for military personnel assigned overseas.

Almost all child care givers face the problem of low wages, part-time work, and no benefits. A 1989 study of the Child Care Employee Project found that they were paid 27 percent less in 1989 than in 1977.

All in all, most working parents are thrown back on their own resources for child care—even though by 1980 only about a quarter of American families still featured a working father and a mother who stayed home. Some, though a decreasing number, turn to relatives or friends for help. A few work out cooperative arrangements. Here and there two-parent families can arrange for flextime or part-time work, so that one or the other parent can be home at any given time. But most working mothers pay more than they can afford for child care, and/or put up with inferior quality. In 1990 child care was the fourth largest budget item for most working families; poor families spent 23 percent of their income on it. Yet at least a third of school-age children came home to empty houses.

See also Aid to Families with Dependent Children; Benefits; Dall, Caroline Wells Healey; Elder Care; Flextime; Lanham Act; Mothers' Pensions; New Deal; Part-Time Workers; Progressive Era; Telecommuting; World War II.

References Catalyst, *Corporate Child Care Options* (1987); Child Care Action Campaign, *Not Too Small To Care* (1992); Sylvia A. Hewlett, *A Lesser Life: The Myth of Women's Liberation in America* (1989); Nine to Five, National Association of Working Women, "Profile of Working Women" (1990); Paula Ries and Anne J. Stone, eds., *The American Woman, 1992–93: A Status Report* (1992); Sara E. Rix, ed., *The American Woman: 1988–89: A Status Report* (1988); Lynn Y. Weiner, *From Working Girl to Working Mother: The Female Labor Force in the United States, 1820–1980* (1985).

Chinese Americans

Beginning in the 1840s, American employers imported Chinese men to build railroads, operate mines, and work as domestic servants. In time some Chinese set up small businesses, farmed, or ranched, a handful of them helped by their wives. But of the 8,848 Chinese women who immigrated between 1850 and 1882, 6,000 were imported as prostitutes. After 1882, when the United States outlawed Chinese immigration, many Chinese women here married and/or earned their livings in a variety of other ways. But most Chinese-American men were stranded in the United States with their wives and families in China.

From 1882 to World War II, Chinese women could enter the United States only as the wives of merchants, a situation that encouraged Chinese men to establish small businesses. These women immigrants and their children often worked frantically for the success of the family business, particularly during the desperate days of the Great Depression. Some moved on to other work, first in domestic service and manufacturing, then into the professions (particularly teaching) and sales. But even as late as 1941 employers freely announced: "We do not hire Chinese."

World War II, the common enemy of Japan, and labor shortages effected in 1943 the repeal of the Chinese Exclusion Act, followed by a series of laws that opened the doors to Chinese immigration. The War Brides Act, as amended in 1947, allowed Chinese servicemen to bring their wives and children to the United States. And in 1952 the McCarran-Walter Immigration and Nationality Act allowed 30,000 Chinese who opposed the 1949 socialist revolution to come to America. With the Immigration Act of 1965, Chinese immigration spurted, particularly because Chinese-American men could at last send for their families.

Not only did Chinese-American women move into clerical work during this period, but many of the new immigrants were highly intelligent and educated women with professional capabilities. On the other hand, the wives who entered under the Immigration Act of 1965 have more often worked as sewing machine operators or in other dead-end jobs in clerical, sales, or restaurant work.

As a community, Chinese Americans have invested heavily and profitably in upward mobility for their sons and daughters through education, particularly in accounting and business. In 1980 almost a third of employed Chinese-American women held a managerial, administrative, or professional position.

See also Clerical Workers; Domestic Servants; Great Depression; Prostitutes; Teachers; World War II.

References Teresa Amott and Julie Matthaei, *Race, Gender, and Work: A Multicultural Economic History of Women in the United States* (1991); Lucie Cheng and Edna Bonacich, eds., *Labor Immigration under Capitalism: Asian Workers in the United States before World War II* (1984); Lucie Cheng Hirats, "Chinese Immigrant Women in Nineteenth-Century California," in Carol Ruth Berkin and Mary Beth Norton, *Women of America: A History* (1979); Roger Daniels, *Asian America: Chinese and Japanese in the United States since 1950* (1988).

Chisholm, Shirley St. Hill (b. 1924)

Chisholm was the first black woman elected to the U.S. House of Representatives. At three she went to live with her grandmother in Barbados and returned to the United States eight years later to complete her education at a Brooklyn girls' high school, as a sociology major at Brooklyn College, and with a master's in elementary education. After experience in teaching elementary school children, day-care, and child welfare, she served in the New York state assembly from 1964–1966. For her Congressional campaign in 1968, running against civil rights leader James Farmer, she mobilized the support of other black women, proclaiming herself "Unbossed and Unbought," and drawing her strength more from the people than from the Democratic party bosses. She served in the House of Representatives from 1969–1983. In 1972 she announced her candidacy for the Democratic presidential nomination, with Cissy Farenthal of Texas as her running mate.

See also Government Workers; Teachers.
Reference Susan Duffy, comp., *Shirley Chisholm: A Bibliography* (1988).

Christman, Elisabeth (1881–1975)

This labor organizer, a native of Germany, emigrated to the United States as a small child. She left her Chicago German-Lutheran school when she was 13 to work in a glove factory. In 1902 she helped to lead a labor action and form a local union and later the International Glove Makers Union of America, in which she held offices.

Christman also worked through the Women's Trade Union League (WTUL), serving on its national board and helping to administer its Chicago Training School for Active Workers in the Labor Movement. In her multiple roles she supported strikes, distinguishing herself for her patience in negotiating. Eventually in 1921 she accepted a full-time job as secretary-treasurer of the WTUL. In the New Deal she served on various presidential committees, and in World War II she worked with the Women's Bureau for equal pay for women in war industries. She wound up her career as legislative representative for the Amalgamated Clothing Workers of America. Even in retirement and in the hospital, she advised women employees in their negotiations with the hospital.

See also Nestor, Agnes; New Deal; Strikes; Training School for Women Organizers; Union Organizers; Women's Bureau; Women's Trade Union League; World War II.
Reference Barbara Sicherman et al., eds., *Notable American Women: The Modern Period* (1980).

Cinema

Throughout the history of American cinema, women have had noteworthy careers, not only as female stars, featured players, and extras, but also as directors, producers, editors, studio owners, writ-

Shirley Chisholm

ers, technicians, and innovators. The full scope of their participation in the film industry is only recently being acknowledged by its historians. Women never dominated the film industry; those who succeeded did so because they were talented and possessed of a tremendous drive.

As actresses women have gained fame and fortune ever since movies were first cranked out, but thousands more have met defeat in this quest. In 1928 Janet Gaynor became the first recipient of the Academy Award for best actress, and in 1931 Hattie McDaniel became the first black actress to win an Academy Award.

In the early years of the industry, the 1910s and 1920s, American women helped to make the movies by directing as well as acting in them. Indeed, in that period more women worked as directors than at any subsequent time until the 1980s. At all times the most frequent route for women into directing and producing has been through acting. Kathlyn Williams first reigned as a queen of silent serials; Ida Lupino (b. 1918) starred in the 1940s and 1950s and sacrificed a successful directing career when her husband objected to having two directors in the family; and Penny Marshall won fame as a television actress before achieving directorial success in the 1980s. But now and then women screenwriters have moved on to directing, like Alice Blache.

Typically women directors and producers have made realistic movies and have chosen subjects and themes important to women. As early as 1913 Kate Corbally was incorporating actual suffrage demonstrations in her movie "Eighty Million Women Want," and in 1916 Cleo Madison (1883–1964) directed and starred in "Her Defiance," an early feminist tract.

But they have also ranged far afield. In 1917 Ruth Ann Baldwin was writing, editing, and directing westerns. Lois Weber (1882–1939), hailed in 1916 as the "greatest woman director," built her career by exploring controversial themes

Silent-screen star Mary Pickford

of morality, like child labor, abortion, racism, prostitution, and capital punishment. She won critical acclaim for her work in some 400 films as director, writer, star, or producer. In 1917 she established her own studio. About the same time, Dorothy Davenport Reid (1895–1977), who always emphasized the importance of naturalistic acting, started her own company. Dorothy Arzner (1900–1979), perhaps the most famous of them all, directed 17 feature films between 1927 and 1943, among them such popular pictures as "The Bride Wore Red," "Craig's Wife," and "Christopher Strong." She gave many female stars important career opportunities, among them Rosalind Russell, Katherine Hepburn, Ruth Chatterton, and Irene Dunne. The French-born Germaine Dulac (1882–1942), after years of experimental avant-garde films, in her later life ran the newsreel units of Pathé and Gaumont.

According to a survey conducted by the Directors Guild of America in 1980 only 14 of the 7,332 feature movies made in the preceding 30 years were directed by a woman; in 1986, however, 36 features were made with women directors. Among the new generation of women directors are Susan Seidelman, Donna Deitch, Amy Heckerling, and Martha Coolidge, who are establishing a body of work that may challenge male sensibilities.

Margaret Booth (b. 1898), proud of her ability to be "one of the boys," pioneered in film editing during the 1950s and 1960s. Frances Marion's (1887–1973) unprecedented 50-year career as a highly successful screenwriter included 136 produced screenplays and three Oscars. Prolific Anita Loos (1893–1981), filmwriter, author, and creator of the irresistible Loreli Lee, turned "title writing" into sophisticated wit.

In 1993 some women have advanced in the executive ranks of the entertainment industry, like Lucie Salhany, chair of Fox Broadcasting, and Sherry Lansing, chair of Paramount Motion Pictures, the first women to hold the top post at a television network or movie studio. But women still get few of the highest jobs and they are typically paid less than their male counterparts. A 1991 survey by Women in Film showed only three women, versus 45 men, who held the title of president at any operation of the 20 entertainment companies surveyed. (*New York Times*, 17 January 1993) No women have cracked the top tiers of the major talent agencies.

See also Blache, Alice Guy; Comediennes; Theater; Writers and Publishers.

References Ally Acker, *Reel Women: Pioneers of the Cinema, 1896 to the Present* (1991); Gwendolyn Foster-Dixon and Wheeler Dixon, "Women Who Made the Movies" (videotape, 1991); Louise Heck-Rabi, *Women Filmmakers* (1984); Joan McCullough, *First of All: Significant "Firsts" by American Women* (1980); Barbara X. Quart, *Women Directors* (1989); Janet Todd, *Women and Film* (1988).

Civil Rights

The issues raised in the debate over workers' civil rights divide into two broad categories: (a) the problem of unjust discharges and discipline where the employee is denied essential due process,

and (b) the right of workers to privacy at work and home.

Some defenders of the constitutional rights of Americans allege that many American workers of both genders, particularly in the private sector, sacrifice freedom of speech, the right to due process, and privacy rights when they report to work. In ten states employers may fire employees for refusing to lie about their bosses' illegal conduct. In 21 states employers may fire workers for political expression. Most companies practice at-will employment, which entitles them to dismiss employees with or without a reason.

Those who interpret the constitution differently respond that those citizens who choose to exercise their rights must accept the consequences; that employees may indeed speak freely in the workplace but must then risk retaliation; that the due process clause does not extend into private dealings.

Unions and other employee advocates negotiate to extend these rights into the workplace. In most colleges and universities, for example, the American Association of University Professors insists on the right of even untenured faculty to due process.

But under the at-will employment doctrine, most employees hold their jobs at the pleasure of their employer, generally subject only to: (a) state and federal laws that prohibit discrimination on the basis of sex, race, religion, national origin, age, and disability, and (b) the provisions of union contracts to define and protect workers' rights. The decline in union membership in the past several decades leaves most of the labor force without union protection. On the job, government employees enjoy the protection of civil service law and the due process of law clause of the 5th and 14th amendments—safeguards not extended to the private sector workplace.

The question of privacy rights is exacerbated when employers root around in employees' lockers and desks for drugs and in their private lives for information about their life-styles: smoking off the job, drug use, drinking patterns, sexual orientation, and medical history. Millions of workers are subject to personality tests, business-related telephone call monitoring, drug tests, and camera and computer surveillance. The AIDS epidemic has heightened the debate over privacy rights versus societal rights by raising the question of mandatory HIV testing. Labor advocates and organizations like the American Civil Liberties Union argue that these practices deprive workers of their civil rights.

See also American Civil Liberties Union; At-Will Employment; Civil Rights Act of 1964; Electronic Monitoring; Fair Labor Standards Act; Genetic Discrimination; Unions; Whistle-Blowing.

References Judith A. Baer, *Women in American Law: The Struggle toward Equality from the New Deal to the Present* (1991); Lewis L. Maltby, *A State of Emergency in the American Workplace* (1990).

Civil Rights Act of 1964, Title VII

This law, by inadvertence, luck, and pressure from a few Congresswomen and women lobbyists, includes a ban on sex discrimination. Title VII also created the Equal Employment Opportunity Commission (EEOC) as its enforcement agency. The original law has been amended by the Equal Employment Opportunity Act of 1972 and the Pregnancy Discrimination Act of 1978. Employers found to have violated Title VII may be required to implement an affirmative action plan to eliminate discriminatory practices.

Title VII as amended prohibits discrimination in employment on the basis of race, color, religion, national origin, or sex by employers engaged in interstate commerce with 15 or more employees, labor unions, apprenticeship training program sponsors, educational institutions, employment agencies, and all federal, state, or municipal governments in reference to their civilian employees. The terms and conditions of employment include hiring and firing, promotion, compensation, training, seniority, benefits, apprenticeships, referrals, job and facility assignments, and classified advertisements. Employment policies that apply to both men and women and thus appear gender neutral may also be illegal if they can be shown to have the effect of discriminating against women in practice and have no relevance to job performance, e.g., a height requirement that excludes more women than men. Title VII prohibits employers from discriminating against women on grounds of pregnancy, maternity, or because they may in time become pregnant. It also prohibits sexual harassment in the workplace.

Title VII has enabled thousands of women to win back pay and to rectify other inequities (e.g., lower pay for women employees performing the same job as male employees and ability tests that discriminate against females). Women workers have won court cases involving sexual harassment, state protective laws, pregnancy-related policies, and wage discrimination. Under this law the courts have redefined sex discrimination and sexual harassment. In *Meritor Savings Bank v. Vinson*, the Supreme Court ruled that a hostile work environment may constitute sexual harassment, but in such instances courts may accept evidence regarding women's personal attire, manner, and sexual activities. And judges have so far hesitated to eliminate all discriminatory employment practices in wage and pregnancy issues.

In the 1980s a minority group of critics have questioned the principles of the Civil Rights Act of 1964 and similar legislation, arguing that discrimination is a salutary practice, not an evil. On the grounds of freedom of association these critics argue for "voluntary discrimination" and against governmentally sanctioned coercion. Employers, they say, should be allowed to hire whomever they wish, just as workers should be free to make whatever contractual arrangements they wish, without the intervention of government. Otherwise, they say, employers are forced to hire less qualified workers, American industry loses efficiency, and the system encourages "protected" minority groups to look at themselves as victims.

See also Affirmative Action; *AFSCME v. State of Washington*; Apprentices; Benefits; Civil Rights Act of 1991; Comparable Worth; Disparate Impact; *Dothard v. Rawlinson*; Education Amendments Act; Employment Agencies; Equal Employment Opportunity Commission; Equal Pay Act; *Frontiero v. Richardson*; *Johnson v. Transportation Agency of Santa Clara*; *Meritor Savings Bank v. Vinson*; *Nashville Gas Co. v. Satty*; Pay Equity; *Phillips v. Martin Marietta Corporation*; Pregnancy; Pregnancy Discrimination Act of 1978; *Price Waterhouse v. Hopkins*; *Radice v. New York*; Sex Discrimination; Sexual Harassment; Tests; *UAW v. Johnson Controls*.

References Barbara B. Bergmann, *The Economic Emergence of Women* (1986); Barbara A. Burnett, ed., *Every Woman's Legal Guide: Protecting Your Rights at Home, in the Workplace, in the Marketplace* (1983); Connecticut Permanent Commission on the Status of Women, "Non Traditional Jobs for Women: A Resource Guide" (1991); Richard A. Epstein, *Forbidden Grounds: The Case against Employment Discrimination Laws* (1992); Karen J. Maschke, *Litigation, Courts, and Women Workers* (1989).

Civil Rights Act of 1991

This law, passed in the wake of the Clarence Thomas nomination hearings, permits an employee to sue for damages in a case of sexual harassment, but it imposes severe limits on monetary awards to women, the disabled, and members of certain religious groups that do not apply in cases of race and national origin discrimination. It empowers the Equal Employment Opportunity Commission (EEOC) and the Department of Justice to seek monetary damages on behalf of victims of intentional discrimination, but damages are limited to $50,000 for employers of 100 or fewer and $300,000 for employers of more than 500.

See also Civil Rights Act of 1964; Equal Employment Opportunity Commission; *Franklin v. Gwinett County School District*; Pregnancy Discrimination Act of 1978; Sexual Harassment.

Reference William Petrocelli and Barbara Kate Repa, *Sexual Harassment on the Job* (1992).

Civil Service
See Government Workers.

Civil War (1861–1865)

The exigencies of the Civil War meshed with an unacknowledged need for action among energetic, competent women, propelling them out of their homes and into the public sphere, either as volunteers or as paid laborers. The war occasioned a demand for workers that exceeded the supply of males. A hundred thousand new jobs for women were created in northern factories, arsenals, and sewing rooms. Women replaced men as salesclerks and began to feminize teaching. Clerical positions previously held by men opened up. The first "government girls" were appointed to positions in the Treasury Department (clerks, copyists, currency counters, and workers in the mint); other departments followed the Treasury's lead. Many of these "government girls" continued to hold their jobs after the war's end and became a permanent part of the Washington scene. The Confederate government also employed women in its offices, but its defeat, of course, terminated their jobs. In all cases the women's working experience was accompanied by male resistance and rumors and allegations of impropriety, questions about seriousness of purpose, and slurs of inefficiency.

At the same time that demand for their services was rising, the number of women looking for work surged. The war's terrible slaughter left many women without economic support from a male and forced to earn their own livings, both during and after the war. By 1870, 10 percent of all industrial workers were female, about 88,000 more than in 1860. The census reports show that between

1860 and 1870 the numbers of women wage earners increased by more than 60 percent; the figures for the war years are slightly higher.

During the Civil War, too, not only Dorothea Dix and Clara Barton but thousands of other women as well contributed both volunteer and paid work to relieve the sufferings of the sick and wounded soldiers left in a sorry state by their governments.

See also Barton, Clara; Bickerdyke, Mary Ann Ball; Blackwell, Elizabeth; Bradwell, Myra Colby; Clerical Workers; Dix, Dorothea Lynde; Military Women; Teachers.

References James J. Kenneally, "Women in the United States and Trade Unionism," in Norbert C. Soldon, ed., *The World of Women's Trade Unionism: Comparative Historical Essays* (1985); Mary E. Massey, *Bonnet Brigades* (1966).

Civil Works Administration (CWA)
See New Deal.

Clarke, Edith (1883–1959)
This electrical engineer, who grew up in Maryland, used her inheritance to earn a degree in mathematics and astronomy at Vassar. After a brief and unhappy bout with teaching, she took civil engineering courses at the University of Wisconsin in 1911–1912 and turned a summer job as a "computer" with the American Telephone and Telegraph Company into a six-year tenure. When the United States entered World War I, she enrolled at the Massachusetts Institute of Technology; in 1919 she received the first electrical engineering degree that institution had ever granted a woman.

Unable to find work commensurate with her training, she spent a year in Turkey teaching physics and then in 1922 went to General Electric as an engineer. Her work focused on large electrical systems constructed by interconnecting smaller systems, working out predictive calculative devices that she patented. Later she moved on to apparatus and system analysis, writing numerous articles

and a book that became a standard graduate text. She left in 1945 to retire to a farm, but in 1947 she reemerged to teach for nine years at the University of Texas. The first woman elected a fellow of the American Institute of Electrical Engineers, in 1948, Clarke also won the Society of Women Engineers' Achievement Award in 1954.

See also Academic Women; Engineers; World War I.

Reference Notable American Women: The Modern Period.

Class Action
A lawsuit alleging discrimination may be brought by one or more individuals as representatives of a class of employees who have experienced discrimination. A class action suit is thus designed to provide relief not only for a single employee but for all others who have suffered from the same discriminatory employment practices.

Reference Barbara A. Burnett, ed., *Every Woman's Legal Guide* (1983).

Clayton Anti-Trust Act
This 1914 law was an attempt by reformers to give unions legal protection by exempting them from the provisions of the Sherman Anti-Trust Act of 1890. The Sherman Act had outlawed "every . . . combination . . . or conspiracy in restraint of trade or commerce among the several states." Though originally intended to control business monopolies, it had been used also to control union organizing, as, for instance, by court rulings that the use of a boycott constituted restraint of trade.

The Clayton Act stated that labor organizations were not illegal conspiracies, that "the labor of a human being is not a commodity or article of commerce," and that "no . . . injunction shall be granted in any case between an employer and employees . . . growing out of a dispute concerning terms or conditions of employment." At first regarded as a victory for organized labor (the executive committee of the American Federation of Labor hailed it as "labor's Magna Carta"), the Clayton Act fell short of expectations when the courts ruled that Congress did not intend to permit boycotts in support of organizing campaigns.

See also American Federation of Labor; Boycotts; Criminal Conspiracy; Injunctions; Taft-Hartley Act; Unions; Wagner Act.

References Michael Evan Gold, *An Introduction to Labor Law* (1989); Arthur S. Link, *Wilson II: The New Freedom* (1956).

Clearinghouse on Women's Issues (CWI)

Founded in 1972, this 400-member organization disseminates information on women's rights of all kinds, particularly the economic status of women.

See also Center for Women Policy Studies; Committee on Women's Employment and Related Social Issues.

Clergy
See Religion.

Clerical Workers

Up until the 1860s men had performed almost all of the clerical work in offices. During the Civil War, facing the shortage of male workers, the Treasury Department hired female clerks, at significantly lower wages than it was paying men. About the same time women were setting up their own businesses as copyists and beginning to work as stenographers, bookkeepers, and accountants. With the spreading adoption of the typewriter in the 1880s, women's office employment climbed sharply, as they qualified for the new typist jobs, and as the supply of literate male labor failed to meet the demand. Training was relatively inexpensive, short-term, and easily available, whether in private business colleges like those of Katharine Gibbs and Mary Foot Seymour or later in the public schools. In 1917 the Smith-Hughes Act provided federal moneys with which high schools offered agricultural and industrial education for boys, while training girls in home economics and "business" (typing, stenography, and bookkeeping). In the late nineteenth and early twentieth centuries women took over most clerical work. In 1900, 320,000 women were so employed; in 1930, 2,000,000; and in 1980, 12,000,000.

But the ground shifted beneath their feet. When earlier on young men had dominated the occupation, clerical jobs had often led to upward mobility, acting as apprenticeships during which young men learned the business and trained for managerial roles. The feminization of offices coincided with deskilling, breaking down tasks to their fundamentals, so that any one worker could easily replace another. Confined to one job in one department, women workers could hardly develop an understanding of the business. Moreover, even when they worked alongside male colleagues and did the same work, women did not enjoy the same access to promotion.

Women, with their high digital facility, their reputation for patience in repetitive tasks, and their lower wages, filled the typing and stenographic pools and the ranks of file clerks. Partly because at the turn of the century many of them thought of their working lives as ending with marriage, but even more because they had little or no choice, they accepted the lack of upward mobility and allowed their nurturing capabilities to be suborned into roles as "office wives." After all, office jobs beat domestic service and factory work, maybe even teaching. Through 1930 the salaries of clerical workers equaled or exceeded those of teachers, and clerical workers faced fewer marriage bars and fewer behavioral constraints than teachers.

But the lack of upward mobility together with the lack of control over their own work also prompted clerical workers to leave the labor force when they could. Most women clerical workers could hope

Marcella Sievers at her desk at the Standard Lime and Stone Company, Fond du Lac, Wisconsin, about 1910

to rise no higher than the lowest levels of management or a private secretary's job. While the female private secretary traditionally has been expected to execute a variety of tasks, make decisions—sometimes major ones—and smooth and brighten the life of her boss, except when she worked for an unusually powerful and supportive person or in an industry (like publishing) where a quirk of development might offer her unusual opportunities, her chances for advancement have hardly existed.

As in so many other occupations, European-American women at first dominated in clerical jobs. Only the labor shortages of World War II broke down racial barriers against women of color, a change consolidated by the gender-discrimination laws and affirmative action programs of the 1960s and 1970s. But they still bunch in lower-skilled clerical jobs, while more European-American women work as secretaries. Similarly,

class, age, and marital status have segmented clerical workers.

Unionization among clerical workers has been impeded by the suspicions of industrial unions, who have often suspected office workers of spying for management, by the split among male and female office workers occasioned by the segregation of women into low-status and low-pay jobs, and by the tendency of some office workers to identify their own interests with those of their employers. From 1900 on clerical workers sporadically attempted to form unions, such as the Telephone Operators' Department of the International Brotherhood of Electrical Workers, which succeeded for a few years. In general these efforts worked better among government clerical workers than in the private sector. By the end of the 1920s, almost none of these unions remained. But interest revived with the hardships of the Great Depression and the split between the American Federation of Labor and the more liberal, woman-worker-friendly Congress of Industrial Organizations (CIO). In the late 1930s the CIO chartered three unions for office workers: the United Office and Professional Workers of America, the United Federal Workers, and the State, County and Municipal Workers of America. The three grew until 1950, when the CIO expelled them for refusing to banish Communist members. (These unadorned statements of fact mask costly, self-sacrificial efforts here and there by office workers to negotiate collectively and to strike: for instance, in October 1937, 85 employees of the Efficient Letter Company—some of them temporary workers for $6 a week for up to 18 years—struck and won; many others lost.) Only in the latter part of the twentieth century have many secretaries and clerks come to refuse to identify with their bosses, to understand their own separate interests, and to unionize—with particular efforts from Nine to Five, the National Association of Working Women.

In 1990, 80 percent of all clerical workers were female—18.4 million women, or more than one out of four women in the workplace. The numbers of typists and data entry keyers are declining, while those of computer equipment operators are rising. But it seems likely that with increasing automation and the movement of data-keying overseas the proportional and perhaps the actual number of clerical workers will decline. More often than not, the clerical workers so displaced either leave the work force or drop into lower-paid and sometimes part-time service sector jobs.

See also Affirmative Action; American Federation of Labor; Apprentices; Congress of Industrial Organizations; Domestic Servants; Electronic Monitoring; Factory Workers; Gibbs, Katharine; Girl Fridays; Great Depression; Nine to Five; Part-Time Workers; Pink-Collar Workers; Scientific Management; Seymour, Mary Foot; Teachers; Telephone Operators' Department of the International Brotherhood of Electrical Workers; Temporary Workers; Unions; United Office and Professional Workers of America; World War II.

References Margery W. Davies, *Woman's Place Is at the Typewriter: Office Work and Office Workers, 1870–1930* (1983); Ruth Milkman, ed., *Women, Work and Protest* (1985); Nine to Five, National Association of Working Women, "Profile of Working Women" (1990); Sharon Hartman Strom, *Beyond the Typewriter: Gender, Class, and the Origins of Modern American Office Work, 1900–1930* (1992).

Closed Shop

This term applies to a company that hires only union workers. By the 1970s some 20 states had enacted "right-to-work" laws forbidding closed shops.

See also Taft-Hartley Act; Unions.

Coalition of Labor Union Women (CLUW)

This nationwide group for union women, founded in 1974, tries to sensitize organized labor and the public to the needs of working women and their families. It has focused on gaining more power for women within the unions. It endeavors to organize the unorganized, promote affirmative action, stimulate political action and legislation on women's issues, and increase women's participation in their unions. It provides a referral service and support to speed up grievance procedures for union and other working women. It also maintains a Center for Education and Research. It supports the Equal Rights Amendment. In 1980 CLUW president Joyce Miller became the first woman member of the executive council of the AFL-CIO.

See also Affirmative Action; Equal Rights Amendment; Nine to Five; Unions.

References James J. Kenneally, "Women in the United States and Trade Unionism," in Norbert C. Soldon, ed., *The World of Women's Trade Unionism* (1985); Ruth Milkman, ed., *Women, Work and Protest: A Century of U.S. Women's Labor History* (1985).

COBRA

See Consolidated Omnibus Budget Reconciliation Act.

Cochran, Jacqueline (1907–1980)

Floridian Cochran, the first woman to fly faster than the speed of sound, founded the Women's Airforce Service Pilots during World War II. After the war she piloted military jets and helped to plan the space program. She broke the sound barrier in 1953 and in 1964 flew at double the speed of sound. Cochran also established herself as an entrepreneur with her own cosmetics business.

See also Entrepreneurs; Military Women; Ninety-Nines; Pilots; World War II.

References Jacqueline Cochran, *The Stars at Noon* (1954); Jacqueline Cochran and Maryann Bucknum Brinley, *Jackie Cochran: An Autobiography* (1987).

Cohn, Fannia Mary (1885?–1962)

This labor educator and leader, a native of Russia born of middle-class but radical parents, immigrated to New York City in 1901. In 1905 she abandoned her plans for pharmacy school in favor of a career in the union movement. She began by working as a sleevemaker; by 1909 she was engaged in work for the International Ladies' Garment Workers' Union (ILGWU). In 1914 she attended the Chicago Training School for Active Workers in the Labor Movement but soon quit because she didn't like the courses. In 1915 she led the first successful strike of Chicago's dress and white goods workers.

As executive secretary of the Education Department of ILGWU and as a vice-president of that organization, Cohn fought for more women as members and as officers. She advocated a liberal education for workers, both for their own personal development and for their contributions to unions and to society generally. She helped to establish Brookwood Labor College, the Manumit School for Workers' Children, a recreational program for working-class children, and a clearinghouse for workers' education programs. She served devotedly even after the union no longer supported educational

programs nor paid her a salary. But after 1935 union politics gradually deprived her of responsibilities, forcing her retirement in 1962.

See also Brookwood Labor College; International Ladies' Garment Workers' Union; Strikes; Training School for Women Organizers; Unions; Workers' Education.

References Ricki Carole Myers Cohen, "Fannia Cohn and the International Ladies' Garment Workers' Union" (1976); *Notable American Women: The Modern Period.*

Coleman, Bessie (1896–1926)

Coleman, a barnstormer, was the world's first licensed black pilot.

See also Pilots.

Reference Angela Howard Zophy and Frances M. Kavenik, eds., *Handbook of American Women's History* (1990).

Collar Laundry Union of Troy, New York (1864–1869)

This unusually successful example of women's labor activity was, in its day, perhaps the only bona fide women's union in the country. With a membership of some 400 it managed to improve wages and working conditions and accumulate sufficient funds to support workers on strike or faced with illness. In the 1860s it won an increase in wages for its members and contributed substantially to the strike funds of male unions. Toward the end of the decade, though, management broke it with a lockout.

See also El Paso Laundry Workers' Union Strike; Strikes; Unions; Washerwoman's Strike.

References James J. Kenneally, "Women in the United States and Trade Unionism," in Norbert C. Soldon, ed., *The World of Women's Trade Unionism* (1985); Carole Turbin, "And We Are Nothing but Women: Irish Working Women in Troy," in Carol Ruth Berkin and Mary Beth Norton, *Women of America: A History* (1979); Carole Turbin, *Working Women of Collar City: Gender, Class, and Community in Troy, 1864–86* (1992).

Collective Bargaining

This term applies to the procedure of determining terms and conditions of employment by negotiation between labor and management. The National Labor Relations Act of 1935 guarantees the right of workers to negotiate with their employers collectively, as a group (usually a union) instead of as individuals.

See also Unions; Wagner Act.

Reference Michael Evan Gold, *Introduction to Labor Law* (1989).

Collins, Jennie (1827–1887)

This self-educated labor reformer was raised by her grandmother, whose death left her to shift for herself at 14. She worked for a while in the cotton mills of Lawrence and Lowell, Massachusetts, then as a domestic, and later in a tailoring firm.

After the Civil War Collins involved herself in the labor movement, particularly in the Working Women's League of Boston, which she helped to found. She supported strikes and boycotts, winning some fame among women suffragists as a militant labor orator.

Soon, though, she turned to less controversial undertakings. She opened a social center for Boston working women, Boffin's Bower, supported by employers of women's labor and by funds that Collins herself raised, sometimes by writing or lecturing. This venture included not only a workshop, recreational facilities, and help for the needy (whom Collins sought out), but also an employment agency. After she died the Helping Hand Society ran Boffin's Bower for a time.

See also Boycotts; Civil War; Employment Agencies; Strikes; Working Women's League.

Reference Edward T. James et al., eds., *Notable American Women I* (1971).

Colonial America

Before the American Revolution an important minority of free white women worked outside the home as shopkeepers, artisans, and merchants in a wide range of occupations. including virtually every enterprise in which men were engaged. Nonetheless employment opportunities for women outside the home or the family farm were severely limited. The colonial white woman located in a settled area could open a shop (typically a dry goods store), practice midwifery, run a small school in her home, or sell skills associated with housewifery, e.g., becoming a domestic servant, working as a seamstress, or opening a boarding house. A woman who had worked with her husband in a trade such as printing or bookbinding might take over the business when her husband died. In most cases women employed as artisans or merchants had learned the requisite skills from their husbands. The greater number of women working for pay outside the home were occupied in some aspect of the clothing trade, as seamstresses, tailoresses, or laundresses. Free black women could find work only as laundresses, house servants, or cooks.

In all cases women worked from necessity, either to increase the family's productivity or as widows to support themselves and their children. Single women (spinsters) without other means of support were encouraged to work rather than become dependent on poor relief. The prevailing social code expected women to work outside the home *if*—but only if—*necessary*, rather than end up in debtor's prison or in the poor house.

Women's legal position was based upon English common law, which distinguished between the rights of an unmarried and a married woman. Before marriage a woman could own property, enter into contracts, and generally order her life as she saw fit and as her birth family would permit. Upon marriage, however, she surrendered these rights and indeed her personhood to her husband; she could not own property in her own name, enter into contracts, or retain whatever wages she might earn by working outside the home. Legally wife and husband became one person, and that person was the husband. The subservient position of women under common law was partially mitigated by arrangements outside the common law system, notably by trusts and prenuptial agreements by which women could own and control property independently of their husbands. With foresight and determination women of acumen and strength of character, such as Elizabeth Murray Inman, could protect themselves from financial hardship brought about by husbandly mismanagement or worse of their property. But such cases were rare; most married women labored under legal disabilities.

Although in so many ways the colonial economy relied on women's work, from the beginning American society considered women secondary to men and paid them less. During the eighteenth century, their economic status declined even further, as the ideal of the lady of leisure won adherents. Though more women worked after the American Revolution than before, they faced more disapproval.

Historians disagree about the existence of economic discrimination against women in the colonial period. The shortage of women created a necessity for a broader economic role than was later the case. The same consideration opened wider economic opportunities for women in frontier America.

See also Boarding; Bookbinders; Coverture; Domestic Servants; Inman, Elizabeth Murray; Printers.

References Carol Ruth Berkin, *Within the Conjurer's Circle: Women in Colonial America* (1974); Carol Ruth Berkin and Mary Beth Norton, *Women of America: A History* (1979); Julia Spruill Cherry, *Women's Life and Work in the Southern Colonies* (1972); Elizabeth A. Dexter, *Colonial Women of Affairs* (1972); Philip S. Foner, *Women and the American Labor Movement* (1979, 1982); Barbara J. Harris, *Beyond Her Sphere: Women and the Professions in American History* (1978); Marlene Stein Wortman, ed., *Women in American Law, From Colonial Times to the New Deal* (1985).

Comediennes

Like many other women in the entertainment industry, comediennes typically build their careers in several areas—not only in cinema and theater but also in cabarets and radio, television, and recording studios. Many of them develop their own material; some write for others, selling jokes to established comics; and a few direct and produce.

One of the earliest, Lotta Crabtree (1847–1924), began performing in saloons at age eight, traveling by horseback from one mining camp to another. Her looks, her combination of innocence and impudence, and her daring as a young woman in showing her legs on stage won her success, and by the time she was 23 she had her own theater company. Marie Dressler (1869–1934) moved from light opera and legitimate theatre through vaudeville to films, through which she clowned her way to stardom, successfully making the transition to talking pictures in 1927, turning homeliness into an asset. Ruth Draper (1884–1956) developed her own genre of humorous monologues and won international fame in her character sketches.

But in the nineteenth century, most comediennes started in vaudeville, where they might give as many as six shows a day, crisscrossing the country, sleeping and eating catch-as-catch-can. If they made it into big-time vaudeville, they enjoyed more money and better working conditions—but of the nearly 20,000 entertainers in vaudeville's heyday, fewer than a thousand made the big-time and only a handful of comediennes starred. Sophie Tucker (1884–1966) gave up big tips as a singing waitress for vaudeville and burlesque, where she delighted audiences with her bawdy songs and "40-horse-power voice." She built her most enduring reputation in cabarets as the "last of the red-hot mamas."

By the 1920s vaudeville was beginning to decline, but cinema and radio offered new venues for comediennes—though most often they had to be part of husband-and-wife teams and to portray themselves as dumb or ditzy—like Gracie Allen (1906–1964) and Jane Ace (1905–1974). A rare exception was Hattie McDaniel (1898–1952), a black vaudeville headliner and radio comedy star who became the first black woman to win an Academy Award. But she, of course, was limited and demeaned by racial stereotyping.

Women who wanted to do stand-up comedy faced the worst of odds until the late 1960s, enduring societal disapproval and audience heckling. British-born Beatrice Herford (1868–1952) was one of the first women to develop the monologue, appearing first in England in 1895 and later in the United States, offering personality portraits, gently caricatured. To the usual difficulties African American Jackie "Moms" Mabley (1897–1975) added racial prejudice, which despite her half-century in show business kept her from national fame until 1967. She went on to win a gold record as a recording artist, always in the character of a cantankerous old woman. Unlike Mabley, who used raunchy jokes and political and social commentary, many stand-up comediennes based their humor on self-deprecation.

After World War II television offered comediennes an enormous new audience. Imogene Coca (b. 1908), who came to TV via musical comedy, nightclubs, vaudeville revues, and stock companies, developed an enviable reputation for gentle satire.

Near the end of the twentieth century opportunities for comediennes have proliferated: more than a fourth of the rising young stand-up comics are women. Self-disparagement is no longer required. They can now afford to tackle all sorts of subjects and may choose to present themselves as ladylike or blatantly aggressive—though, of course, the latter choice will have its price. They can even poke fun at men.

Cerebral-palsied Geri Jewell (b. 1956) has gained a success in the field unparalleled by any other disabled person. Robin Tyler has dared to present herself with a butch stage persona. And African American Whoopi Goldberg (b. 1950) is running off the charts with her successes in films, her "Spook Show," and her work for children's education. They (and the public) owe a lot to Elaine May (b. 1932) and Lily Tomlin (b. 1937), who with their feminist outlook have pioneered new kinds of women's comedy.

See also Cinema; Theater; World War II.

References Ally Acker, *Reel Women* (1991); Linda Martin and Kerry Segrave, *Women in Comedy* (1986); Mary Unterbrink, *Funny Women: American Comediennes, 1860–1985* (1987).

Commission on the Status of Women

See President's Commission on the Status of Women.

Committee on Women's Employment and Related Social Issues (WERSI)

Founded in 1981, this committee of the National Research Council of the National Academy of Sciences analyzes research related to women's employment, identifies areas that need research, assesses the impact of federal policies and programs related to women's employment, and considers the wider social implications of women's participation in the work force.

See also Center for Women Policy Studies; Clearinghouse on Women's Issues.

Communications

Public relations and business communication are popular fields for women, to the point that some experts see them as becoming feminized. By 1986 the membership of the International Association for Business Communicators was already more than 60 percent female. Like the field of human resources management, though its top people are often high-salaried, public relations offers staff jobs, not line jobs, unless workers choose to go into agency work.

See also Bernays, Doris Fleischman; Business and Industry; Human Resources Managers; Line Jobs; Staff Jobs.

Reference Caroline Garrett Cline et al., *The Velvet Ghetto: The Impact of the Increasing Percentage of Women in Public Relations and Business Communication* (1986).

Communist Party of the United States of America (CPUSA)

Inspired by the successful Bolshevik Revolution of 1917, the American Communist party followed the Soviet model and directives for most of its existence. Its revolutionary criticisms of the capitalist state and its preoccupation with ideological and doctrinal purity isolated it from the mass of American workers. Nonetheless, through its activities in organizing workers, supporting strikes, and protesting social and economic injustices, CPUSA was a factor in the American labor movement, especially during the Great Depression.

In the 1930s a substantial proportion of CPUSA's membership was women. In 1933, 16 percent of the 20,000 members were women; at the end of the decade, 30–40 percent; and by 1943, 46 percent of the estimated 83,000 members. Black women always constituted a small minority of female membership. The party generally dismissed feminism as a bourgeois reform and expected married party members to subordinate family relationships to organizational demands. Although it paid attention to specific women's issues only intermittently in the 1930s, its Women's Commission (headed first by Anna Damon and then by Margaret Cowl) reached out to working women and sought to represent their interests. Though only an occasional woman, like Dorothy Healey, rose to a high position of leadership, a number of women organized for the party, among them Peggy Dennis, Ella Reeve ("Mother") Bloor, Charlene Mitchell, Anna Burlak, Grace Hutchins, and Elizabeth Gurley Flynn.

See also Bloor, Ella Reeve; Flynn, Elizabeth Gurley; Great Depression; Healey, Dorothy; Industrial Workers of the World; Socialist Party; Strikes.

References Peggy Dennis, *The Autobiography of an American Communist* (1977); Theodore Draper, *The Roots of American Communism* (1957); Dorothy Healey and Maurice Isserman, *Dorothy Healey Remembers* (1990); Robert Schaffer, "Women and the Communist Party USA, 1930–1940" (1974);

Susan Ware, *Holding Their Own: American Women in the 1930s* (1982).

Commuter Marriages

As more women enter the workplace, couples sometimes find themselves forced to live apart by the business or professional demands of their careers. Whether they commute regularly between each other's residences or whether they endure long separations, the situation inflicts strains on the marital relationship. But some couples find that the arrangement more sharply defines the line between work and leisure and enhances their pleasure in their limited time together.

See also Dual-Career Couples; Nepotism.

Comparable Worth

Advocates of equal pay for jobs of comparable worth usually seek to narrow the gender gap between men's and women's pay. Instead of the present system in which employers compensate "women's jobs" at a lower rate than those dominated by men, these reformers would institute a system to evaluate jobs on the bases of skill, effort, responsibility, and working conditions, and reward equally jobs that measure the same. They would undertake these evaluations employer-by-employer and compensate for differences by raising the compensation of the lower-wage job.

This principle of comparable worth has evoked discussion intermittently since World War II. Wage discrimination claims based on comparable worth have so far had little success at the federal level; its advocates, mostly women's organizations, therefore have turned to state and local governments, where some comparable worth legislation has been enacted. A few state and local governments have adopted the principle in setting pay scales for their own employees. Neither courts nor legislatures have gladly embraced it, and most private employers actively oppose it. Despite the self-evident democratic justice of the principle, its critics point to the danger that its application might lower men's wages rather than raise women's and to the difficulty of determining what constitutes comparable worth. Opponents also argue that the principle might cause labor conflict, hamstring American business in international competition, and damage the patriarchal family. Some feminists fear that it might result in more occupational segregation, inflation, and unemployment for women workers.

See also AFSCME v. State of Washington; County of Washington v. Gunther; Gender Gap; Occupational Segregation; Pay Equity; Sex Discrimination; World War II.

References Henry J. Aaron and Cameran M. Lougy, *The Comparable Worth Controversy* (1986); Barbara A. Burnett, ed., *Every Woman's Legal Guide* (1983); Paula England, *Comparable Worth: Theories and Evidence* (1992); M. Anne Hill and Mark R. Killingsworth, eds., *Comparable Worth: Analyses and Evidence* (1989); Alice Kessler-Harris, *A Woman's Wage: Historical Meanings and Social Consequences* (1990); Susan Gluck Mezey, *In Pursuit of Equality: Women, Public Policy and the Federal Courts* (1992); Steven L. Willborn, *A Comparable Worth Primer* (1986); Steven L. Willborn, *A Secretary and a Cook: Challenging Women's Wages in the Courts of the United States and Great Britain* (1989).

Compensation

The term "compensation" is sometimes used as distinct from "wages" in that it includes both wages and benefits.

The decline of leisure for the American worker, the stress she suffers, and the consistent rise of productivity prompt some economists and sociologists to propose that employers offer workers a choice between compensation in money and compensation in time. Possibly, they suggest, workers would be happier, healthier, and even more productive if they did not moonlight, work long hours of overtime without compensatory time off, take work home at night, and/or forgo vacations as long as those enjoyed by European workers. With the yearly income of Americans on a per-person basis standing at 65 times

the average income of half the world's population, with the average American owning and consuming more than twice as much in 1990 as in 1948, would she or he profit more from increased leisure than from increased funds with which to raise the standard of living still higher?

See also Benefits; Leisure; Moonlighting; Productivity.

Reference Juliet B. Schor, *The Overworked American: The Unexpected Decline of Leisure* (1992).

Comprehensive Employment and Training Act of 1974 (CETA)

See Job Training Partnership Act.

Computer Monitoring

See Electronic Monitoring.

Computer-Related Health Problems

See Health Hazards.

Congress of Industrial Organizations (CIO)

Among the founders of this organization, first formed in the early 1930s as a committee within the American Federation of Labor (AFL), were the International Ladies' Garment Workers' Union and other women's groups. In 1938 the AFL expelled the CIO, which wanted to organize workers by industry rather than by craft.

The CIO dedicated itself to organizing workers without regard to race, skill, or sex. More active in promoting women's interests than the AFL, the CIO immediately committed itself to equal pay for "substantially the same work." Soon after its founding, it conducted an organizing drive in the textile industry, about 39 percent female, with the notable assistance of Lucy Randolph Mason. The CIO also enjoyed success among black women tobacco strippers and Hispanic women pecan shellers, as well as among such unions with large numbers of women workers as the United Electrical and Radio Workers of America. During World War II it urged equal pay legislation and full postwar employment with federal child care provisions. These accomplishments for women helped to modify the AFL's attitudes toward women.

Although by contrast with the AFL the CIO appeared friendly to women workers, throughout the 1930s and 1940s CIO male unionists signed contracts exchanging gains for blue-collar members for agreements eliminating the bargaining rights of clerical workers, overwhelmingly women. Similarly unions of white-collar workers, like insurance agents, shut out secretaries, stenographers, and file clerks. CIO industrial unions for the most part ignored clerical workers; in 1941 the United Auto Workers finally tried to unionize them—but half-heartedly. The CIO had granted charters to the United Office and Professional Workers of America (UOPWA), the United Federal Workers, and the State, County and Municipal Workers of America, but had limited the potential of the UOPWA and in 1950 expelled all three for refusing to eliminate communist members. In 1955 the AFL and the CIO merged.

See also American Federation of Labor; Child Care; Comparable Worth; International Ladies' Garment Workers' Union; Mason, Lucy Randolph; Pay Equity; Unions; World War II.

References James J. Kenneally, "Women in the United States and Trade Unionism," in Norbert C. Soldon, ed., *The World of Women's Trade Unionism* (1985); Ruth Milkman, ed., *Women, Work and Protest* (1985); Susan Ware, *Holding Their Own: American Women in the 1930s* (1982).

Congressional Caucus for Women's Issues (CCWI)

Founded in 1977, this nonpartisan segment of the U.S. House of Representatives tries to improve the status of women, especially with regard to Social Security, federal and private pensions, health, insurance, and child support enforcement.

See also Pensions; Social Security Act.

Consolidated Omnibus Budget Reconciliation Act of 1986 (COBRA)

COBRA requires employers to continue to provide health benefits for a limited period to unemployed workers and full-time workers forced onto reduced work schedules.

See also Benefits.

Reference Nine to Five, National Association of Working Women, "Working at the Margins: Part-Time and Temporary Workers in the United States" (1986).

Conspiracy
See Criminal Conspiracy.

Construction Workers

The construction industry is notorious for its hostility to women looking for jobs. To open up opportunities for women in this sector, the federal government has set specific affirmative action goals for all contractors who have government construction contracts, requiring them to take positive steps to ensure that 6.9 percent of their work force is female. In addition, federal construction contractors are required to maintain a working environment that is free of sexual harassment, intimidation, and coercion, and to assign at least two women to each construction project if possible.

The wide range of construction jobs accounts for the largest group of skilled workers in the country and among the highest paid. Although a traditional male bastion, the construction trades are slowly attracting more women: for instance, 18,000 women were working as carpenters in 1990, compared to 16,000 in 1980.

See also Affirmative Action; Blue-Collar Workers; Nontraditional Occupations; Sexual Harassment; Trades.

Reference Connecticut Permanent Commission on the Status of Women, *Non Traditional Jobs for Women* (1991).

Consultants

As companies aim for efficiency and higher productivity, many have reduced the numbers of their full-time employees, turning instead to part-time workers and consultants. This trend has both helped and harmed women. On the upside, women offering consultant services can sometimes build businesses in which they charge high fees—if they can find a niche and learn to market their services. On the downside, women lose the security and benefits that they would enjoy as full-time employees.

See also Benefits; Entrepreneurs; Part-Time Workers.

Consumers' League (CL)

This organization of middle-class women, founded in 1891, rallied department-store customers to protect clerks. These underpaid and overworked women, subject to the sexual harassment of the male floorwalkers who supervised them and of male customers as well as the exploitation of their employers, were forbidden even to sit down during their long working hours. If they fainted, they were laid out on cement basement floors to recuperate and resume work.

The members of the Consumers' League, not much given to confrontation, worked imaginatively to alleviate these woes. They became ombudswomen for the clerks, investigating claims and imposing their customer clout on store-owners. They supported unionization and strikes. They not only helped to enact protective legislation but also individually monitored stores to ensure its enforcement. They avoided boycotts, but achieved similar results by encouraging their members and the general public to shop at stores on their White List that met their standards for fair treatment of employees. Eventually the CL seal of approval became so influential that it was sought by manufacturers claiming fair and sanitary working conditions.

With its successes CL expanded its interests to include decent working conditions in the manufacture of clothing and other products, eventually even to the production of food. CL's longtime executive secretary, Florence Kelley, effectively advocated protective legislation for women workers on a national scale.

CL's influence began to decline about 1915. As the reform movement slowed, the feminist movement split over the issue of protective legislation vs. the Equal Rights Amendment, and the U.S. Supreme Court struck down measures enacted during the Progressive Era.

In the 1930s, under the leadership of Lucy Randolph Mason, CL became an adjunct of the New Deal, which embodied many of its goals in legislative proposals.

See also Boycotts; Equal Rights Amendment; Goldmark, Josephine Clara; Herrick, Elinore Morehouse; Kelley, Florence; Lowell, Josephine Shaw; Mason, Lucy Randolph; Nathan, Maud; New Deal; O'Reilly, Leonora; Perkins, Frances; Progressive Era; Protective Legislation; Sexual Harassment; Strikes; Wolfson, Theresa.

References Maud Nathan, *The Story of an Epoch-Making Movement* (1926); John A. Salmond, *Miss Lucy of the CIO: The Life and Times of Lucy Randolph Mason, 1882–1959* (1988); Dorothy Schneider and Carl J. Schneider, *Women in the Progressive Era* (1993).

Contingent Work Force

Throughout much of American history industry has profited by the existence of "disposable" workers, to be called in when needed and sent home when not. In this group black people and other minorities, old people, and women have figured prominently. In both world wars, for example, government and industry instructed women in their patriotic duty to enter the work force, and in their womanly obligations to leave it as men returned from military service. By necessity members of the contingent work force often have to resort to part-time work and temporary work.

See also Part-Time Workers; Temporary Workers; World War I; World War II.

Reference Richard S. Belous, *The Contingent Economy: The Growth of the Contemporary, Part-Time and Subcontracted Workforce* (1989).

Contract Labor

This system involves a middleman who contracts with an employer to provide so many laborers at specified wages for a specified period. Heavily used by Chinese, Korean, Mexican, and Filipino laborers, it opens up broad opportunities for exploitation, especially when the laborers speak no English. The contractor may not only charge an employment fee or percentage of wages but also loan money at high interest for transportation costs and insist that laborers buy necessities from him.

See also Migrant Laborers.

Reference Tricia Knoll, *Becoming Americans: Asian Sojourners, Immigrants, and Refugees in the Western United States* (1982).

Cooper Union

This tuition-free undergraduate college was established in New York City in 1859 for "the advancement of science and art." It pioneered as an evening engineering and art school, teaching craft skills like telegraphy to women as well as men.

See also Wheeler, Candace Thurber.

Cooperative Housekeeping

In the late 1860s Melusina Fay Peirce developed the idea of cooperative housekeeping to try to shift household tasks out of the home, thus solving the servant problem and relieving middle-class matrons of the drudgery of domestic labor. Various plans evolved in the decades before 1900, all requiring some degree of centralizing housework (including food preparation, laundry, child care, and sewing) in a communal workplace, with the work being done on shares or by wage-earners hired by the cooperative. The idea, however, enjoyed its heyday in the Progressive Era, with community dining clubs, cooperative child-care facilities, and cooperative laundries.

Just why most of these experiments failed no one knows, though experts have variously blamed the desire of businesses to sell more appliances, the demands of husbands for individualized catering to their preferences, families' desire for privacy, and the common undervaluing of the worth of the time and energies of married women.

In the late twentieth century some of the needs once scheduled to be met by cooperative housekeeping are finding other responses. The fast-food industry flourishes. When they can afford it, more people eat in restaurants; when they can't, they turn to buying TV dinners or other prepared foods. Workers pick up sandwiches or salads at the nearest supermarket instead of carrying lunchboxes prepared by loving hands at home. Old people eat food provided by Meals on Wheels or by their local senior citizens' dining facilities or by the kitchens of their retirement villages.

For women in the workplace, the advantages of some sort of communal solution to the problem of housework are clear. Women wage-earners need every possible aid to alleviate the burden of the second shift.

See also Child Care; Gilman, Charlotte Anna Perkins Stetson; Housekeeping; Progressive Era; Second Shift.

References Ruth Schwartz Cowan, *More Work for Mother* (1983); Dolores Hayden, *The Grand Domestic Revolution: A History of Feminist Designs for American Homes, Neighborhoods, and Cities* (1981); Harvey A. Levenstein, *Revolution at the Table* (1988); Juliet B. Schor, *The Overworked American: The Unexpected Decline of Leisure* (1992).

Cooperative Industries

The movement toward ownership of industries by their workers has not attained notable success in the United States. Off and on groups have attempted to form such cooperatives. After the Civil War, sewing women made desperate by sub-subsistence wages established cooperative contracting firms to eliminate the middlemen who had cut their wages in half—with limited success. The Shirt Sewers' Cooperative Union was formed by middle-class women attempting to give New York sewing women better wages; it employed about 40 women, but lasted only a few years. Other trades-women, particularly in printing estab-lishments and laundries, set up their own cooperative businesses.

Another wave of cooperatives appeared in the 1960s and 1970s, particularly among adherents of the counterculture. And in the late–twentieth-century era as industries have closed their employees have sometimes attempted to buy and run them, with mixed success.

See also Consumers' League; International Ladies' Garment Workers' Union; Ladies Indus-try Association; Petition Campaigns; Printers; Triangle Shirtwaist Fire; Unions; United Tail-oresses Society of New York; Uprising of the 20,000; Women's Trade Union League.

References Thomas R. Brooks, *Toil and Trouble: A History of American Labor* (1971); Alice Kessler-Harris, *Out To Work: A History of Wage-Earning Women in the United States* (1982); Gerda Lerner, ed., *The Female Experience: An American Documen-tary* (1977).

Cori, Gerty (1896–1957)
The first American woman to receive a Nobel Prize for medicine and physiology (shared with her husband and an Argen-tine scientist), Gerty Cori held marginal research appointments for much of her professional career because universities and research institutes where her hus-band worked had rules against husband and wife collaborating or policies about nepotism. In 1947, the year she won the Nobel Prize, Cori was finally made pro-fessor of biochemistry at Washington University in St. Louis. Her research was widely recognized in the scientific com-munity, and President Harry Truman named her to the board of the National Science Foundation. Gerty Cori man-aged the responsibilities of marriage and motherhood (she had one son) without interrupting her scientific career.

See also Nepotism; Professional Women; Sci-ence, Mathematics, and Science-Based Profes-sions.

Reference Barbara Sicherman et al., eds., *No-table American Women: The Modern Period* (1980).

Corning Glass Works v. Brennan (1974)
This Equal Pay Act case tested whether male employees of the Corning Glass Works on the night shift could be paid more than the female employees who worked the day shift, the company argu-ing that the working conditions were not similar. The U.S. Supreme Court found that the working conditions at Corning were not differentiated by time of day and therefore the pay disparity violated the Equal Pay Act.

See also Equal Pay Act; *Schultz v. Wheaton Glass Company.*

Reference Susan Gluck Mezey, *In Pursuit of Equality: Women, Public Policy and the Federal Courts* (1992).

Cottage Industry.
See Home Workers.

County of Washington v. Gunther (1986)
The issue in this comparable worth case was whether women can sue their em-ployers for wage discrimination even though their jobs are not identical with those of male employees. The U.S. Supreme Court upheld the right of wo-men to sue over sex-based wage disparity without meeting an equal work standard.

See also Comparable Worth; Equal Pay Act.

Reference Susan Gluck Mezey, *In Pursuit of Equality: Women, Public Policy and the Federal Courts* (1992).

Coverture
This English common law concept, preva-lent in colonial America, held that mar-riage changed a woman from a *feme sol* with property rights to a *feme covert* whose inheritance *and wages* belonged to her hus-band. A *feme covert* could not sue nor could she contest her husband's custody of their children. During and after the American Revolution some married women success-fully petitioned their legislatures to act as *feme sol* traders in the absence of their husbands. In the mid-nineteenth century coverture was replaced by the Married Women's Property Acts.

See also Colonial America; Married Women's Property Acts.

References Marlene Stein Wortman, ed., *Wo-men in American Law* (1985); Angela Howard Zophy and Frances M. Kavenik, eds., *Handbook of American Women's History* (1990).

Cattle ranching skills practiced by women contributed to the development of Wild West shows and rodeos. These sisters team up for branding on their Colorado ranch in 1894.

Cowgirls

The Wild West shows in which women like Annie Oakley, May Lillie, and Lucille Mulhall won fame ended with World War I, and cowgirls and cowboys alike moved into rodeo. New women stars emerged: Vera McGinnis Farra, who in 1924 was the first woman to wear long pants in competition; Bonnie Grey, who moonlighted as a stuntwoman for Western movie actors; Tad Lucas, who invented the "hang down" off the back of her cantering horse. In competition women like these roped calves and steers, vied in relays and barrel races, rode bulls and bareback broncs, and did trick riding.

The 1940s saw prize money for women disappear and women were relegated to posing and pageantry. Late in the decade Nancy Binford, a rancher and horse breeder; Thena Mae Farr, producer of the first all-girl rodeo; and other women founded the Girls Rodeo Association, now the Women's Professional Rodeo Association. The 100 actively competing members of this group train from childhood for the six approved events: bull riding, bareback bronc riding, tie-down and break-away calf roping, team roping, and barrel racing. In the 1990s they win big money in state and national competitions: Charmayne James-Rodman earned her eighth world title by the age of 14, and by 1990, still in her 20s, she had made over $1 million. In Hereford, Texas, Margaret Formby has founded and now directs the National Cowgirl Hall of Fame and Western Heritage Center.

See also Oakley, Annie; Sports.
Reference Patricia Hilliard, "Hero Rides Discrimination Out on a Rail" (1992).

Criminal Conspiracy

This common law doctrine holds that certain acts legal when performed by an individual become illegal when performed by a group. In early–nineteenth-century America, courts applied this doctrine to labor unions, which were held to be conspiracies and therefore illegal. The courts ruled that workers who formed unions were "conspiring" to obtain better wages and working conditions by their collective actions in strikes and boycotts. But by the end of the century juries had become reluctant to convict unionized workers of criminal conspiracy, and in many jurisdictions the law changed so that strikes could no longer be considered criminal conspiracy.

See also Boycotts; Clayton Anti-Trust Act; Injunctions; Strikes; Unions.

Reference Michael Yates, *Labor Law Handbook* (1987).

Dall, Caroline Wells Healey (1822–1912)

This strong-minded author and reformer, a comfortably off native of Boston much influenced by Transcendentalism, dedicated herself early to good works. From 1837 to 1842 she ran a nursery school for working women's children. Suddenly confronted by the financial reverses of her father, she supported herself as a teacher in Washington, D.C., from 1842–1844, while she was struggling also to provide education for free blacks there. In 1844 she married Unitarian minister Charles Henry Appleton Dall. Ten years after their marriage he set off alone as a missionary to India, where he worked until his death, leaving his wife and their two children behind.

This experience apparently prompted Dall to devote her considerable energies to women's rights, a subject on which she wrote extensively. In 1867 she published *The College, the Market, and the Court: or Woman's Relation to Education, Labor, and Law.* The book, demanding an end to gender-based discrimination in education and law, attributed discontent among contemporary women to a lack of opportunity to work. In later life she wrote on a variety of other subjects.

See also Child Care.

Dancers

In most forms of dance, from tap to ballet, American women have been performers and teachers rather than innovators and choreographers. But early in the twentieth century three American women invented modern dance: Isadora Duncan (1878–1927), Ruth St. Denis (1877–1968), and Martha Graham (1894–1992). After careful research, African American Katharine Dunham brought African elements to American dance. Agnes DeMille (1905–1993) choreographed dances drawing on American tradition and changed the use of dance in Broadway musicals. In the 1960s women like Twyla Tharp, Meredith Monk, Yvonne Rainer, Lucinda Childs, and Trish Brown contemporized the dance, stripping it down to austerity and changing its traditional gender distinctions. Graham's and Tharp's use of ballet dancers like Rudolf Nureyev, Margot Fonteyn, and Mikhail Baryshnikov has encouraged an interchange among the dance forms and influenced ballet choreography.

See also Duncan, Isadora; Graham, Martha; St. Denis, Ruth; Tallchief, Maria.

Dancer Judith Jamison

References Christy Adair, *Women and Dance: Sylphs and Sirens* (1992); Agnes DeMille, *Dance to the Piper* (1952); Twyla Tharp, *Push Comes to Shove* (1992).

Daughters of St. Crispin (DOSC)

This first national union of working women, a sister organization of the Knights of St. Crispin, was founded in 1868. It operated largely through loosely connected local lodges. In the 1860s and 1870s it championed equal rights for working women and debated the significance of women's suffrage for female industrial workers.

See also Unions.

Reference Mary H. Blewett, *Men, Women, and Work: Class, Gender, and Protest in the New England Shoe Industry, 1780–1910* (1988).

Day Care

See Child Care.

De la Cruz, Jessie Lopez (b. 1919)

This California-born Chicana labor organizer and advocate of land ownership labored for years in the fields before she became an organizer for the United Farm Workers in 1967. "It was very hard," she said, "being a woman organizer. Many of our people my age and older were raised with the old customs in Mexico: where the husband rules, he is king of his house. . . . Men gave us the most trouble—neighbors there in Parlier! They were for the union, but they were not taking orders from women, they said." In 1974 de la Cruz helped found National Land for People.

See also Agricultural Workers; Union Organizers; Unions; United Farm Workers.

References Ellen Cantarow, *Moving the Mountain: Women Working for Social Change* (1980); Susan Ware, *Modern American Women: A Documentary History* (1989).

Defense Advisory Council on Women in the Services (DACOWITS)

See Military Women.

Dentists

See Health Professionals and Paraprofessionals; Taylor, Lucy Beaman Hobbs.

Depression

See Great Depression.

Dewson, Mary Williams (1874–1962)

As a student, this reformer and social worker was mentored by the distinguished professors who taught her at Wellesley, women who gave her insight into contemporary social and economic problems. As she began work for the Women's Educational and Industrial Union in 1897, she became the protegée of social reformer Elizabeth Glendower Evans, who interested Dewson in methods of professionalizing housework, both to provide better jobs as domestic servants for factory workers and to liberate housewives for careers.

In her next job as superintendent of parole for the Massachusetts State Industrial School for Girls, Dewson experimented with penal reform, examining the effects of extrainstitutional care, social and psychological study of individual offenders, and close supervision by social workers. In 1912 she moved on to become the executive secretary of a new Massachusetts minimum wage investigating commission. There she planned and executed a statistical study of women's and children's compensation on which the first American minimum wage act was based.

For many years Dewson intermittently held influential volunteer and paid positions, extending her sphere nationwide. She worked for women's suffrage; she served overseas with the Red Cross in World War I; she fought for minimum wage laws; in 1930 she lobbied for New York's law limiting women's working hours to 48 per week.

From 1928 until about 1941 she worked for social justice legislation more indirectly by strengthening the role of women within the Democratic party and finding government jobs for women party workers—among others, Frances Perkins. Her ardor gained her the nickname "More Women Dewson." In the same period she helped to pass a New York unemployment insurance act and minimum wage laws in Ohio and Illinois. She contributed to the Social Security Act of 1935 and served as a member of the Social Security Board. She assisted Perkins as official industrial consultant.

See also Compensation; Domestic Servants; Evans, Elizabeth Gardiner Glendower; Government Workers; Minimum Wage; Perkins, Frances; Social Security Act of 1935; Social Workers; Women's Educational and Industrial Union; World War I.

Reference Susan Ware, *Partner and I: Molly Dewson, Feminism, and New Deal Politics* (1987).

Dickason, Gladys Marie (1903–1971)

This labor economist and organizer, a native of Oklahoma, earned an undergraduate degree from the University of Oklahoma in 1922 and a master's in economics and political science from Columbia in 1924. For several years she studied and taught on the college level, but in 1933, in the depths of the Great Depression, she left the academy to take a job with the Amalgamated Clothing Workers of America (ACWA), of which she was named research director in 1935. She also organized cotton-garment workers and negotiated on their behalf.

Her work grew in importance during the war years, and she was elected a vice-president of ACWA in 1946. After World War II she participated in national negotiations and led efforts to raise the minimum wage. Increasingly she turned to organizing and to insisting on the necessity for working women to assert themselves against male union members.

See also Great Depression; Minimum Wage; Union Organizers; Unions; World War II.

Directors and Producers

See Cinema.

Disability Insurance

See Benefits.

Disabled Workers

See Americans with Disabilities Act of 1990; Networking Project for Disabled Women and Girls; Rehabilitation Act of 1973.

Discrimination

See Age Discrimination Acts; Americans with Disabilities Act; Civil Rights Act of 1964; Sex Discrimination.

Disparate Impact

An employment requirement that is not discriminatory on its face, that appears neutral and fair in form, may in fact be discriminatory if its application has a disproportionate (disparate) impact upon women and minorities and thus reduces their employment opportunities. Height and weight requirements, for example, have been particularly effective as a way to keep women out of traditionally male jobs in police and fire departments or correctional institutions. Such requirements have been held by the courts to violate Title VII of the Civil Rights Act of 1964.

See also Bona Fide Occupational Qualification; Civil Rights Act of 1964; *Dothard v. Rawlinson*; *Griggs v. Duke Power Company*; Law Enforcement; Tests.

References Susan Gluck Mezey, *In Pursuit of Equality: Women, Public Policy and the Federal Courts* (1992); Michael Yates, *Labor Law Handbook* (1987).

Displaced Homemakers

While American widows with little or no history of paid employment have always faced economic problems, in the latter half of the twentieth century displaced homemakers have proliferated, their numbers rising to more than 15.6 million in 1989. These women have lost their primary financial support through widowhood, divorce, separation, a husband's long-term unemployment, disability, or desertion, or the discontinuation of public assistance. Almost 60 percent are poor or near poor; almost 45 percent have not completed high school; 25 percent are women of color.

Many of these women lack both economic resources and a history of paid employment. The more fortunate of the divorcées among them receive rehabilitative alimony for a limited period, during which they are expected to get training for a job. Others have been helped by the Comprehensive Employment and Training Act. Women bereft of adequate financial support in their 50s or 60s face particular difficulties, since they often have been out of the workplace for a long time, their skills are rusty or nonexistent, and their job-hunting is often frustrated by age discrimination.

By 1989, 27 states had passed displaced homemaker legislation and displaced homemaker programs were available in every state. Also in that year, however, a third of the 15.6 million displaced homemakers lived in poverty.

See also Age Discrimination Acts; Comprehensive Employment and Training Act; Displaced Homemakers Self-Sufficiency Assistance Act of 1990; Health Insurance; Job Training Partnership Act.

References Paula Ries and Anne J. Stone, eds., *The American Woman, 1992–93: A Status Report* (1992); Laurie Shields, *Displaced Homemakers: Organizing for a New Life* (1981).

Displaced Homemakers Self-Sufficiency Assistance Act of 1990

This law established the first federal training program specifically designed to meet the needs of displaced homemakers. It is intended to help states provide greater opportunities for them by expanding and coordinating existing preemployment programs and support services. As of late fall 1992, this legislation had not been funded.

See also Displaced Homemakers.

Reference Ms. Foundation for Women and the Center for Policy Alternatives, *Women's Voices: A Policy Guide* (1992).

Displaced Workers

As in the last quarter of the twentieth century the United States shifts to a service economy, as automation increases in factories and offices, and as industries move offshore, millions of workers are displaced—a term that the Department of Labor applies to a worker with three years or more tenure whose job has been eliminated by plant closing or relocation, slack work, or the abolition of the worker's position or shift. Usually these workers either get additional training, accept lower wages, or leave the work force completely; in any case they usually endure a long period of unemployment. Many more women than men withdraw: between 1979 and 1984, 20 percent of displaced women aged 20-61 withdrew, against 5 percent of men. The older the woman, the less chance she has of finding another job. Even when displaced workers find new employment, they often suffer a wage drop: a 1984 study showed that displaced white-collar and service sector males experienced an average earnings loss of 8.7 percent, while females lost on average 16.2 percent.

See also Service Sector; Unemployment; White-Collar Workers.

References Nadya Aisenberg and Mona Harrington, *Women of Academe: Outsiders in the Sacred Grove* (1988); Nine to Five, National Association of Working Women, "Profile of Working Women" (1990); Nine to Five, National Association of Working Women, "Social Insecurity: The Economic Marginalization of Older Female Workers" (1987).

Divorce

See Displaced Homemakers.

Dix, Dorothea Lynde (1802–1887)

This advocate of the rights of the mentally ill and superintendent of army nurses during the Civil War was a native of Maine. From the age of 14 she taught in her own schools or elsewhere while continuing her own education, and at 22 she published a popular elementary science textbook. Ill health interrupted such activities and for several years inflicted idleness.

But in 1841 volunteer work brought her to a knowledge of the miserable plight

Dorothea Lynde Dix

of the insane and she joined in efforts to protect them, surveying their condition and lobbying to ameliorate it, extending her efforts throughout much of the eastern half of the United States and many parts of Europe.

Her successes in these undertakings brought her fame. When the Civil War began, she accepted an appointment as superintendent of army nurses, recruiting skilled, able, plain-looking older women. Her rigid standards, her insistence on looking into every corner of the medical establishment, and her passion for detail caused conflicts and undermined her authority, but she persisted until 1866. She continued her volunteer activities until 1881, when ill health forced her hospitalization.

See also Civil War; Nurses.

References Edward T. James et al., *Notable American Women I* (1971); Helen Marshall, *Dorothea Dix: Forgotten Samaritan* (1937).

Domestic Feminists

Nineteenth-century advocates of what modern historians call "domestic feminism" accepted patriarchy but widened "woman's sphere" and advocated women's venturing outside the home for approved purposes. Domestic feminists did not want the vote. On the grounds of women's moral superiority, they deplored the struggle for equality. But they justified paid industrial and clerical work as proper for "true women" and supported reforms in married women's property rights.

See also Clerical Workers; Separate Spheres; Social Feminists.

Reference Angela Howard Zophy and Frances M. Kavenik, eds., *Handbook of American Women's History* (1990).

Domestic Servants

In the United States domestic service has historically been a job of low prestige and last resort. Early on this work was done, for keep or for money, by indigent widows and single women, orphans, indentured servants, female apprentices, or black female slaves. After the Civil War, domestic service constituted the principal source of employment of free black women. With the successive waves of immigration of different ethnic groups, it became more and more the province of the most recently arrived women, particularly Irish, German, and Scandinavian women, Chicanas (women of Mexican ancestry), and Asians.

The status and relationship of the servant to her employer gradually declined. In colonial America she had worked alongside the housewife and often participated in family activities (a relationship vestigially preserved until the early twentieth century in the midwestern "hired girl"). But in the mid-nineteenth century, the gap between mistress and servant widened, as the domestic code prescribed that "ladies" did not work, and domestic servants more often belonged to different ethnic or cultural groups from their employers.

Throughout the nineteenth century, middle class whites in most regions of the United States could afford part-time or full-time servants, though, it's

Seven women pose with items signifying their duties within a household in Black River Falls, Wisconsin, in the 1890s.

important to remember, the middle class then was relatively small. Never in American history could as many as half our families afford full-time servants, and from the latter part of the nineteenth century on, the numbers of household workers dropped. The vigorous efforts of middle-class women individually and in groups to recruit more domestic workers failed. Even the lure of better pay than they could earn in industry did not make up to prospective workers for the long hours, little or no privacy, often improvised living quarters, low status, and the boss always looking over their shoulders.

As women found other opportunities, those left in domestic service gradually freed themselves from the conditions they most disliked, such as living in and wearing uniforms. Many of them became independent contractors, women conducting small service businesses, who hired out their own labor to different employers for different days of the week.

The availability of other jobs has, in the twentieth century, reduced the supply of cooks, maids, and cleaning ladies and raised their wages. Gradually, more and more domestic work has been transferred to companies that prepare food, give child care, and tend the sick outside the home, or to individuals or companies that provide services in the home. And women still perform most of the domestic work for these companies, as building cleaners, hotel maids, day-care-center workers, health aides, caterers, cooks and kitchen workers, and waitresses.

Because domestic service involves so many different employers, many of whom employ only one person, regulating it and protecting its workers have been difficult. Consequently many protective labor laws have exempted domestic workers. Despite their eventual inclusion in the social security program, many evade it, grudgingly making payments into it.

See also Apprentices; Civil War; Colonial America; Indentured Servants; National Committee on Household Employment; Part-Time Workers; Social Security Act of 1935; Washerwoman's Strike.

References Teresa Amott and Julie Matthaei, *Race, Gender, and Work* (1991); Faye E. Dudden,

Serving Women: Household Service in Nineteenth-Century America (1983); David Katzman, *Seven Days a Week: Women and Domestic Service in Industrializing America* (1978).

Dothard v. Rawlinson (1977)

This case tested the legality of Alabama's prison regulations excluding women from serving as guards in positions requiring close physical proximity to male inmates. The U.S. Supreme Court upheld Alabama's argument that gender was a bona fide occupational qualification because women are naturally vulnerable to sexual assault and their presence would jeopardize prison security. But the court also ruled that Alabama's height and weight requirements for these positions had a disparate impact on women and were not bona fide occupational qualifications.

See also Bona Fide Occupational Qualification; Civil Rights Act of 1964; Disparate Impact; Sex Discrimination.

References Susan Gluck Mezey, *In Pursuit of Equality: Women, Public Policy and the Federal Courts* (1992); Deborah L. Rhode, *Justice and Gender: Sex Discrimination and the Law* (1989).

Dress for Success

As women moved into management in the 1960s and 1970s, "experts" like John T. Molloy issued reams of advice on the ways they should dress to present themselves as competent executives in the corporate business image. (A Guerrilla Girl comments that this project might better be titled "Undress for success.")

See also Dress Requirements; Guerrilla Girls; Rhoads Dress.

Reference *Working Woman* editors with Gay Bryant, *The Working Woman Report* (1984).

Dress Requirements

Differences in dress on the job have long functioned as status symbols, from the fashion editor wearing a hat all day to the waitress in employer-prescribed uniform. White-collar workers have distinguished themselves from blue-collar by wearing street clothes at work.

In some instances, uniforms have indicated professional or occupational standards. Until the 1960s nurses cherished their caps as marks of their educational attainments and professionalism. Policewomen and military women still show their rank, their medals, and their authority on the uniforms they proudly wear.

Besides status, however, employees' dress may also reflect employers' requirements. Up until the late twentieth century employers emphasized neatness and modesty of dress among women employees as evidence of "ladylike" qualities, of being careful of details, of being serious of mind. Telephone operators, office workers, and salesgirls in department stores, for example, had to dress to the satisfaction of their employers, even on their way to work. Many housewives wanted their maids and chauffeurs to wear uniforms and caps. On the other hand, nightclubs and some restaurants forced waitresses and "hatcheck girls" into skimpy, sexy costumes.

During the 1960s employers and their women employees fought pitched battles over the women wearing pants at work. Since then dress at work has become less formal and more comfortable, emphasizing practicality and safety. Nevertheless, executive women still dress for success and many working women recognize the need to differentiate between working clothes and recreational clothes—if only to spare themselves the accusation of inviting sexual harassment by their attire.

See also Blue-Collar Workers; Dress for Success; Military Women; Sexual Harassment; White-Collar Workers.

Dual-Career Couples

The rising numbers of women in the work force mean that in the late twentieth century more and more couples are bringing home two paychecks—in 1989, more than 25 million. About 18 percent of women in such couples earn more than their husbands.

Wives and husbands who both work for pay, while enjoying a double income, confront many on-the-job problems, besides difficulties in juggling household tasks and parental and child care. If both work for the same employer, they face suspicion of favoritism and nepotism, especially if one reports to the other. If they work for different employers, they may encounter problems in being assigned to the same location, especially if one or both are in line for promotion. Couples in such situations also must make complex decisions about adjusting their benefits, within the limits allowed by their employers, particularly now that some employers are trying to shift the responsibility for health insurance to the employer of the other spouse. Ideally, though, dual-career couples can be a team working together toward mutual goals, understanding one another's problems and interests, and supporting each other.

See also Benefits; Commuter Marriages; Health Insurance; Nepotism.

References Alice Nakamura and Masso Nakamura, *Second Paycheck: An Analysis of the Employment and Earning of Wives Compared with Unmarried Women and Men* (1985); Susan McRae, *Cross-Class Families: A Study of Wives' Occupational Superiority* (1986); Felice N. Schwartz, *Breaking with Tradition: Women and Work, the New Facts of Life* (1992); Cynthia Taeuber, comp. and ed., *Statistical Handbook on Women in America* (1991); *Working Woman* editors with Gay Bryant, *The Working Woman Report* (1984).

Duncan, Isadora (1878–1927)

This forerunner of modern dance, a native of San Francisco, led a helter-skelter financial life, from her childhood on. Her parents divorced soon after her birth, and her mother scrabbled for a living, leaving her children pretty much on their own, but passing on to them her antireligious beliefs and her opposition to accumulating material goods. By the time she was six, Isadora Duncan was teaching dance to other children, and at ten she left school to do it full-time. At 12 she joined with her siblings in presenting dance concerts, preferring her own improvisations to the ballet she briefly studied. Soon she moved with her mother to Chicago and then to New York, where she first danced and acted with Augustin Daly's company and later gave solo performances in private homes.

On she went to Europe, where she fell deeply under the influence of Greek art and culture. Her movements emphasized the natural freedom of expression that she believed originated in the solar plexus, the seat of the soul. Her gifts as a publicist enhanced her career and her genuine talent, expressiveness, charisma, and originality. Her personal life made her even more spectacular, especially when in 1905 she had a child by the stage designer Gordon Craig and in 1910 another by the wealthy Paris Eugene Singer. In 1913 both children died tragically in an automobile accident; another son, sired by an Italian sculptor, died in infancy.

Nonetheless Duncan carried on her career, trying desperately in France, Germany, the United States, South America, and Russia to support a school of the dance for children. A marriage in 1922 to

Dancers inspired by Isadora Duncan

a young Russian poet lasted only briefly. She left an invaluable heritage to the modern dance.

See also Dancers.

References Mary Desti, *The Untold Story: The Life of Isadora Duncan, 1921–1927* (1989); Isadora Duncan, *My Life* (1972); Edward T. James et al., eds., *Notable American Women I* (1971); Allan Ross Macdougall, *Isadora: A Revolutionary in Art and Love* (1960); Ilya I. Schneider, *Isadora Duncan: The Russian Years* (1981); Frances Steegmuller, ed., *Your Isadora: The Love Story of Isadora Duncan and Gordon Craig* (1974).

Dykes, Eva B. (n.d.)

In 1921 Dykes earned her Ph.D. from Radcliffe, one of the first three black women to hold the doctorate.

See also Magill, Helen; Mossell, Sadie Tanner; Simpson, Georgiana.

Earhart, Amelia Mary (1897–1937)

This pioneer aviator, a native of Kansas, graduated from a Chicago high school in 1916. The aces of World War I captured her imagination. After a few years of false starts, she moved to Los Angeles, where she took flying lessons from pioneer woman pilot Neta Snook. Earhart first soloed in 1921. At 25, with money earned here and there and borrowed on her valuables, she bought her first plane in which she set a soon-broken woman's altitude record of 14,000 feet. For several years she barnstormed in air shows.

In 1928 she gained fame for a transAtlantic flight, on which she acted as log-keeper. She used her fame to open opportunities in flying for women, as in helping to found the Ninety-Nines. During the 1930s she set one record after another. In 1932 she became the first woman to fly the Atlantic alone and the first pilot to cross by air more than once. She disappeared over the Pacific on an around-the-world flight in 1937.

See also Ninety-Nines; Pilots.

References Amelia Earhart, *The Fun of It* (1932); Amelia Earhart, *Last Flight* (1937); Muriel Earhart Morrissey, *Courage Is the Price* (1963).

Pilot Amelia Earhart poses with Denver Post *publisher Frederick Bonfils in 1931.*

Eastman, Crystal (1881–1928)

This pacifist social investigator found a role model in her minister mother. After earning a bachelor's degree from Vassar College and a master's in sociology from Columbia, she undertook the study of law, with an eye to effecting social reform. During her lifetime she devoted her considerable talents to advancing the economic independence of women, labor reform, human rights, and peace.

After she passed the bar, she worked on the significant labor study the Pittsburgh Survey; her findings, published in *Work Accidents and the Law* (1910) promoted the enactment of workmen's compensation laws. Eastman also served from 1909–1911 on the New York State Employers' Liability Commission, helping to pass such a law in that state.

She devoted most of the rest of her life to the causes of women's rights (including women's suffrage) and peace. She also contributed to her brother Max's radical journals, the *Masses* and the *Liberator*, writing articles on labor problems and feminism.

See also Attorneys; Workmen's Compensation.

Reference Edward T. James et al., eds., *Notable American Women I* (1971).

Eddy, Mary Baker (1821–1910)

Baker, the daughter of a Congregational minister, founded the Church of Christ,

Mary Baker Eddy

Massachusetts, and published the first edition of *Science and Health*, which went through 382 editions in her lifetime. She also wrote extensively for a monthly and a weekly house organ and in 1908 founded the *Christian Science Monitor*. In 1881 she obtained a charter for the Massachusetts Metaphysical College, where she trained Christian Science practitioners, most of them women. The network they formed and her charismatic teaching drew disciples, who in 1886 joined together in the National Christian Scientist Association. Though she spent much of her time after 1887 in seclusion, she retained her authority as head of her Church of Christ, Scientist, despite scandal and dissension.

See also Religion.

References Adam H. Dickey, *Memoirs of Mary Baker Eddy* (1927); Edward T. James et al., eds., *Notable American Women I* (1971); Sibyl Wilbur, *The Life of Mary Baker Eddy* (c. 1907).

Scientist. As a girl she irregularly attended the schools of her New Hampshire town and was tutored at home. In 1843 she married building contractor George Washington Glover, but a year later he died and she bore his son. Illness forced her to turn over the child's upbringing to her sister. In 1853 she married Daniel Patterson, a dentist, an experience whose misery only worsened her health.

After spending most of her life as a partial or complete invalid, she was successfully treated in 1862 by Phineas Parkhurst Quimby, a healer who believed the cause and cure of disease to be mental. After Quimby's death Eddy herself turned to healing, teaching—and altering—his theories. The doctrines she developed for her church emphasized the health, personal peace, comfort, and worldly success with which they would reward their adherents. She gained theological equity for women through the concept of a "Father-Mother God."

In 1875 Eddy gathered followers in her "Christian Scientists' Home" in Lynn,

Edson, Katherine Philips
(1870–1933)

This social reformer and government official grew up in Ohio, where her father, a woman's rights advocate, saw to her getting an education in music. In 1890 she married the musician Charles Farwell Edson; financial necessity forced them to turn from music to ranching in California. In this marriage she bore three children. The Edsons were divorced in 1925.

In California she began to participate in reform movements, campaigning for women's suffrage and working on municipal problems, particularly public health. By 1912 her reform interests had involved her in politics; in that year the governor, for whom she had campaigned, appointed her a special agent of the state Bureau of Labor Statistics. She contributed most significantly to minimum wage legislation for women. For 18 years she served on an Industrial Welfare Commission empowered to set minimum wages, maximum hours, and working standards, becoming its executive commissioner in 1916 and chief of the state Division of Industrial Welfare in 1927. Other governmental agencies, both federal and state, engaged her services. Even after the U.S. Supreme Court ruled against a District of Columbia minimum wage for women in *Adkins v. Children's Hospital* (1923), Edson and the other California commissioners kept on administering the California law.

In 1931 the winds of politics blew Edson out of office, but she spent the rest of her life advising her successor.

See also Adkins v. Children's Hospital; Government Workers; Minimum Wage; Protective Legislation.

Reference Edward T. James et al., eds., *Notable American Women I* (1971).

Education
See Academic Women; Teachers; Workers' Education.

Education Amendments Act of 1972
Title IX of this act forbids discrimination against women in any education program or activity receiving federal funds, thus rectifying omissions in the coverage of the Equal Pay Act and Title VII of the 1964 Civil Rights Act. The U.S. Supreme Court narrowed the application of the Education Amendments Act in the *Grove City College v. Bell* case of 1984, but in 1988 Congress amended the Civil Rights Act of 1964 to override the implications of that case. The federal agency granting funds is the enforcement agency, usually the Department of Education.

Title IX regulations interpret the act to include discrimination against women in job-oriented education programs. Additionally, they extend the ban on discrimination to include employees of educational institutions (not just students), thus covering hiring and firing, pay, and provisions for pregnancy and maternity benefits.

See also Civil Rights Act of 1964; Equal Pay Act; Pregnancy.

References Barbara A. Burnett, ed., *Every Woman's Legal Guide* (1983); Susan Gluck Mezey, *In Pursuit of Equality: Women, Public Policy and the Federal Courts* (1992); Marjorie Murphy, *Black-*

board Unions: The AFT and the NEA, 1900–1980 (1990); *Working Woman* editors with Gay Bryant, *The Working Woman Report* (1984).

EEOC
See Equal Employment Opportunity Commission.

Eight-Hour Day
Although workers' pressure for shorter hours began no later than the 1780s, only after 1850 did the work week decline significantly. The eight-hour-day movement, which began after the Civil War, took half a century to reach its goal. Although men benefited more than women from union-negotiated limitations on hours, women benefited earlier than men from legislated limitations.

See also Muller v. Oregon; Protective Legislation.

Reference Juliet B. Schor, *The Overworked American: The Unexpected Decline of Leisure* (1992).

Elder Care
With the graying of the population and the soaring costs of custodial care for older people, more workers confront the problem of caring for their kith and kin. Many of these workers belong to the sandwich generation, with responsibilities to both children and parents. In 1990 more than 2.2 million family members supplied unpaid help to aging relatives. Women bore a disproportionate share of this responsibility: 75 percent of caregivers were women, many of whom also worked full-time for pay outside their homes.

In 1993 the passage of the Family and Medical Leave Act (FMLA) acknowledged the existence of the problem. But difficulties compound because many elderly people live at a distance from their children and may be too frail for day-care.

In 1991 the Stride Rite Corporation, a pioneer in on-site child care, opened an intergenerational day-care center to accommodate 55 children and 24 older adults, in acknowledgment of the increasing problem of elder care.

See also Benefits; Child Care; Family and Medical Leave Act; Family Leave; Sandwich Generation.

Reference Nine to Five, National Association of Working Women, "Profile of Working Women" (1990).

Electronic Monitoring

Electronic monitoring enables employers to assess employee performance both quantitatively and qualitatively, as computers count keystrokes and keyboard errors and special headsets allow supervisors to eavesdrop on operators and telemarketers talking to customers and to each other. Some software programs even flash subliminal messages on computer screens urging operators to work faster. As many as 26,000,000 workers may be electronically monitored.

Unless this evaluation technique is carefully and considerately used, it presents difficulties. It may cause both employer and employee to elevate quantitative performance while ignoring quality. Workers complain about invasion of privacy, stress, and fear. A 1990 University of Wisconsin study suggested that these workers suffer more job stress than others and report twice as many wrist pains.

Some unions now negotiate in an effort to end monitoring abuses, insisting on the worker's right to know when she is being monitored, trying to establish fair standards for the practice, and setting up grievance procedures to appeal unfairly or incorrectly collected data. The Electronic Communications Privacy Act of 1986 provides that an employer monitoring communication should not listen to employees' private conversations unrelated to company business. A proposed Privacy for Consumers and Workers Act would require monitoring equipment to emit a periodic beep.

See also Civil Rights; Clerical Workers; Health Hazards; Unions.

References Nine to Five, National Association of Working Women, "Profile of Working Women" (1990); Nine to Five, National Association of Working Women "Stories of Mistrust and Manipulation" (1990); Paula Ries and Anne J. Stone, eds., *The American Woman, 1992–93: A Status Report* (1992).

El Paso Laundry Workers' Union (AFL) Strike of 1919

These laundry women, mostly Chicanas, struck in defense of their right to organize and in protest over their low wages. El Paso's Central Labor Union and several Mexican social organizations supported the strike financially. The laundry union purchased a laundry and began to operate it under union conditions. Employers defeated the strike by hiring other Chicanas as scabs.

See also Collar Laundry Union of Troy, New York; Scab; Strikes; Unions.

Reference Mario T. Garcia, *Desert Immigrants: The Mexicans of El Paso, 1880–1920* (1981).

Elizabethton, Tennessee, Strike of 1929

Young women in a single factory began this great strike. The Women's Trade Union League then sent a representative to help organize a United Textile Workers local union. The strike spread throughout the county and touched off textile strikes throughout the South. Striking women workers literally wrapped themselves in American flags, defied an injunction against picketing, and provoked the guardsmen called out against them. Negotiator Anna Weinstock of the Labor Department won a rehiring agreement, which management subsequently broke.

See also Gastonia, North Carolina, Strike of 1929; General Textile Strike of 1934; Injunctions; Strikes; Unions; Women's Trade Union League.

References Dorothy M. Brown, *Setting a Course: American Women in the 1920s* (1987); Angela Howard Zophy and Frances M. Kavenik, eds., *Handbook of American Women's History* (1990).

Employee Assistance Program (EAP)
See Benefits.

Employment Agencies

During the Progressive Era (1890–1920), reformers' research revealed the corruption of many employment agencies. Anyone could set up an agency; many women operated agencies from their homes. Too many operators assumed no responsibility for the nature of the work into which they were recruiting women, and some were merely covers for white slavers. Immigrants and black women migrating northward, ignorant of their new environment, were particularly vulnerable to the machinations of disreputable agencies. Women's groups interested in working women's welfare and the prevention of prostitution successfully lobbied for laws regulating the agencies and often personally oversaw their administration.

From 1910 to 1923 college administrators and alumnae founded 15 employment bureaus for graduates. The creation of the United States Employment Agency during World War I resolved many problems of women seeking employment. But employers still may choose to list choice jobs with private agencies, whose fees are sometimes chargeable to the employer. Some agencies, known as "headhunters," specialize in executive searches.

See also Bureau of Vocational Information; Intercollegiate Bureau of Occupations; Kellor, Frances; Matthews, Victoria Earle; Progressive Era; Prostitutes; Seymour, Mary Foot; United States Employment Service; White Rose Mission; White Slavery; Women's Educational and Industrial Union; Woman's Municipal League; Young Women's Christian Association.

References Mary E. Dreier, *Margaret Dreier Robins* (1950); Dorothy Schneider and Carl J. Schneider, *Women in the Progressive Era* (1993).

Employment at Will

See At-Will Employment.

Employment Retirement Income Security Act (ERISA) (1974)

This act, designed to protect the pension rights of workers, among other provisions requires companies to manage pension funds prudently, not to deny workers eligibility because of age or length of service, and to vest (assign to the employee) pension rights for employees with five years of work credit. The act also limits loss of benefits for employees who for reasons beyond their control have a break in their service and allows workers to make pension benefits available to spouses or other survivors. Additionally, it requires companies with existing pension plans to extend that benefit to part-time employees who work more than 1,000 hours a year.

ERISA does not cover public employees, nor does it set minimum pension payments or compel pension plans to make cost-of-living adjustments. Unions cannot force employers to bargain for increased pension benefits for workers already retired. By making pension plans more expensive, it has caused some employers to eliminate pension plans.

See also Benefits; Older Workers; Part-Time Workers; Pensions; Unions.

Reference Michael Yates, *Labor Law Handbook* (1987).

Engineers

Engineering, which expanded as a profession between 1890 and 1900, has not traditionally attracted women and has presented formidable obstacles to them. During its early history many technical institutes denied women entrance, and the few women trained at coeducational colleges and universities endured active hostility from their fellow students and found few job openings.

About 1916 Nora Stanton Blatch (Barney) lost her case against the American Society of Civil Engineers for excluding women. Marie Luhring, however, was elected to the American Society of Automotive Engineers in 1920. Of the 130,000 engineers counted in the 1920 census, only 41 were women. This exclusion cost women dearly, for engineering often provides access to corporate employment and upward mobility.

Despite the efforts of engineering schools to enroll women since the 1970s, engineering is still the most male-dominated of all the professions. In 1990 women still represented only 15 percent of engineers entering the work force and only 8.7 percent of all civilian engineers. Women engineers in many companies are still segregated in the lower ranks, with less opportunity than men to move into management.

But projected shortages of engineers suggest that companies will have to draw on women and minorities to meet their needs. The profession has grown more attractive to women, since much of it now requires analytical skill, small-scale design, and computer work. The newer specialties within the field are less male-identified and presumably less hostile to women. With the growth of "para-engineering" occupations, the work done by engineers has become more abstract, more creative, and more administrative. It is one of the five best-paid occupations for women. In 1986 starting salaries offered to women in electrical engineering averaged 100.3 percent of those offered to men.

Studies by Judith McIlwee and J. Gregg Robinson suggest that in companies where engineers as a group are powerful, they tend to shut women out. In companies where engineers are less powerful, women engineers flourish. Women tend to advance less than men in high-tech firms and electrical engineering, as much as or more than men in aerospace and mechanical engineering.

See also Barney, Nora Stanton Blatch; Clarke, Edith; Gilbreth, Lillian Evelyn Moller; Jemison, Mae Carol; King, Florence; Morgan, Julia; Professional Women; Richards, Ellen Henrietta Swallow; Roebling, Emily; Science, Mathematics, and Science-Based Professions.

References Ruth Carter and Gill Kirkup, *Women in Engineering* (1990); Beatriz C. Clewell and Bernice Anderson, *Women of Color in Science, Mathematics, and Engineering* (1991); Violet B. Haas and Carolyn C. Perrucci, eds., *Women in Scientific and Engineering Professions* (1984); Joan McCullough, *First of All* (1980); Judith S. McIlwee and J. Gregg Robinson, *Women in Engineering: Gender, Power,* *and Workplace Culture* (1992); Sharon Hartman Strom, *Beyond the Typewriter: Gender, Class, and the Origins of Modern American Office Work, 1900–1930* (1992).

Entertainers
See Cinema; Comediennes; Dancers; Musicians; Theater.

Entrepreneurs
In colonial America the law allowed widows to carry on their former husbands' businesses, and some of them successfully managed stores, newspapers, printing establishments, farms, and plantations. Others set up their own enterprises: midwifery practices, schools, inns, and cooking and sewing businesses. Daughters too might assume such responsibilities in the family's fiscal emergencies. Women sold what they raised or made.

Nineteenth-century industrialization and the changes wrought by the Civil War, however, did not demonstrably expand women's opportunities for business ventures. Women entrepreneurs of the period like Lydia Pinkham and Hetty Green usually enjoyed strong family support and/or set up businesses that catered to women customers. Most capable women of the period focused their energies in the public sphere on welfare work.

Later in the century, with the successive waves of immigrants of different ethnic groups, women's enterprises multiplied. Women of all races set up their own companies. Katharine Gibbs and Mary Foot Seymour seized on the opportunities provided by the typewriter to equip women with office training and employment. African American Mme. C. J. Walker employed thousands of workers in the hair-care industry. By 1900 most women entrepreneurs were engaged in service and retail-related businesses that are traditionally female areas, such as travel agencies, real estate, and clothing design. However an increasing number were starting businesses in such nontraditional areas as mining and construction.

In the twentieth century even more women have started their own businesses. Alice Foote MacDougall, for instance, deserted by her husband and left with three children, went into the wholesale coffee business in 1907, opening a chain of coffeehouses and restaurants. Olive Ann Mellor Beech (b. 1903) founded the Beech Aircraft Corporation with her husband in 1932; after his death in 1950 she took full control, expanding sales to over $200 million in 1978. Elizabeth Arden (c. 1884–1966), Helena Rubinstein (1882–1965), and Estée Lauder all founded cosmetic empires.

As of 1990 women's enterprises constituted 28 percent of all business in the country. Women-owned companies had almost 11 million employees, and the number was growing, at a time when Fortune 500 companies employed 12.3 million, with their numbers declining. Women continue to open businesses at twice the rate of men. By the year 2000, the Small Business Administration estimates, nearly 40 percent of all United States businesses will be owned by women. Yet in 1992 only about 1 percent of government contracts was awarded to women-owned businesses.

While most of the legal difficulties confronting women in business (including starting their own) have been eliminated, women still may face gender discrimination from bankers in obtaining credit, from customers, from suppliers, and from trade organizations. Therefore it is important for women entrepreneurs to seek out special programs and associations that provide support, information, and advice. More than half the states run programs where women can find help in developing their businesses, and several private associations offer sophisticated assistance.

See also American Women's Economic Development Corporation; Business and Industry; Cochran, Jacqueline; Colonial America; Consultants; Equal Credit Opportunity Act; Gibbs, Katharine; Gleason, Kate; Green, Hetty Howland Robinson; Hawes, Elizabeth; Inman, Elizabeth Murray; Pinkham, Lydia Estes; Rodgers, Elizabeth Flynn; Self-Employment Learning Project; Seymour, Mary Foot; Small Business Administration; Turnbo-Malone, Annie Minerva; Walker, Sarah Breedlove; Wheeler, Candace Thurber; Women's World Banking.

References Teresa Amott and Julie Matthaei, *Race, Gender, and Work: A Multicultural Economic History of Women in the United States* (1991); Mary Kay Ash, *Mary Kay* (1987); Barbara A. Burnett, ed., *Every Woman's Legal Guide* (1983); Robert Coffee and Richard Scase, *Women in Charge: The Experiences of Female Entrepreneurs* (1985); Oliver Hagan, Carol Rivchun, and Donald Sexton, eds., *Women-Owned Businesses* (1989); Patricia A. Morrall, *The Directory of Women Entrepreneurs* (1990); *National Directory of Women-Owned Business Firms* (1990); Organization for Economic Cooperation and Development Staff, *Enterprising Women: Local Initiatives for Job Creation* (1991).

Equal Credit Opportunity Act (1974)

This federal law bans discrimination against applicants for credit on the basis of sex, marital status, race, color, religion, national origin, age, receipt of public assistance, or good-faith exercise of federal consumer-protection rights. It covers all aspects of a credit transaction and all types of credit. Enforcement agencies include banking agencies and the Federal Trade Commission.

See also Entrepreneurs.

Reference *Working Woman* editors with Gay Bryant, *The Working Woman Report* (1984).

Equal Employment Opportunity Act (1972)

See Civil Rights Act of 1964; Equal Employment Opportunity Commission.

Equal Employment Opportunity Commission (EEOC)

EEOC is responsible for the enforcement of legislation that prohibits employers from discriminating in their employment practices on the basis of race, color, religion, national origin, or sex. Established by Title VII of the Civil Rights Act of

1964, EEOC's enforcement powers were originally limited to investigating charges of discrimination and seeking conciliation; it has subsequently been given authority by the Equal Employment Opportunity Act of 1972 to take enforcement action directly through the federal courts. The commission also administers the Age Discrimination in Employment Act and the Equal Pay Act.

EEOC has issued guidelines for employers to protect themselves against charges of discrimination. It has attempted to harmonize state protective labor laws with the Civil Rights Act, even on occasion overturning state laws. In court cases it has concentrated on class action suits. Illustrative of its role in pursuing the ban on sex discrimination is its action against the American Telephone and Telegraph Company (1973), which resulted in an out-of-court award of over $38 million in back pay to women employees.

The enforcement record of EEOC remains controversial: many organizations and people concerned about sexual discrimination have criticized the agency for its narrow definition of discrimination and its limited litigation policies.

See also Age Discrimination Acts; Civil Rights Act of 1964; Class Action; Equal Pay Act; Sexual Harassment.

References Robert E. Doherty, *Industrial and Labor Relations Terms: A Glossary* (1989); Alice Kessler-Harris, *Out To Work: A History of Wage-Earning Women in the United States* (1982); Karen J. Maschke, *Litigation, Courts, and Women Workers* (1989).

Equal Pay Act of 1963 as Amended by the Education Amendments Act of 1972

Lawsuits alleging wage discrimination on the basis of sex have revolved around narrow distinctions and conflicting legal theories, and their issue is almost always in doubt.

Efforts to equalize pay for men and women performing substantially the same work go back at least to 1919 and legislation enacted in Michigan, Mon-

tana, and Texas. During the emergency of World War II employers were theoretically required to pay equal wages for comparable work. The postwar drive for equal pay, spearheaded by the director of the Women's Bureau, Esther Peterson, encountered rough going until 1963, when the Equal Pay Act was signed into law.

The act was a compromise in which the term "equal pay for equal work" was substituted for "equal pay for comparable work." This substitution was critical, for most women in the early 1990s still work in sex-segregated jobs, and the act does not apply to them, since it is impossible to argue that they perform work exactly similar to men's. Even when such women do work more complicated than that of male colleagues, requiring more training and better judgment, this act does not protect them.

This act provides only that employers must pay men and women equally when both perform jobs under the same working conditions and requiring equal skill, effort, and responsibility. It exempts employers with no employees engaged in interstate commerce. The law prohibits unions from trying to cause employers to violate it, and employers from lowering the wages of one gender to comply with it. But it allows employers to pay women and men different wages based on factors other than sex: seniority, merit, or production. It does not cover domestic and agricultural workers, and it does not require that employers give women equal access to jobs. The Equal Employment Opportunity Commission (EEOC), the enforcement agency, may seek relief for victims, including salary raises, back pay, and additional damages up to the amount of the back pay award.

Although women have benefited from the Equal Pay Act in increased wages, the act itself is limited in what it can accomplish because of the equal work requirement. The law has relieved some underpaid women workers, but the U.S. Department of Labor, charged with making routine checks for violations and investigating individual complaints, has not exercised this authority assiduously. The breadth of the exceptions the law allows has also led to inconsistent court interpretations. The act has succeeded best in protecting workers in blue-collar jobs where the requirements are more clearly defined and vary but little.

See also Blue-Collar Workers; Civil Rights Act of 1964; Comparable Worth; *Corning Glass Works v. Brennan; County of Washington v. Gunther;* Education Amendments Act; Equal Employment Opportunity Commission; Fair Labor Standards Act; Pay Equity; *Schultz v. Wheaton Glass Company;* Unions; Women's Bureau.

References Barbara A. Burnett, ed., *Every Woman's Legal Guide* (1983); Connecticut Permanent Commission on the Status of Women, *Non Traditional Jobs for Women* (1991); Alice Kessler-Harris, *Out To Work: A History of Wage-Earning Women in the United States* (1982); Susan Gluck Mezey, *In Pursuit of Equality: Women, Public Policy and the Federal Courts* (1992); D. J. Treiman and H. I. Hartmann, *Women, Work and Wages: Equal Pay for Jobs of Equal Value* (1981); *Working Woman* editors with Gay Bryant, *The Working Woman Report* (1984).

Equal Rights Amendment (ERA)

"Equal Rights under the law shall not be denied or abridged by the United States or by any state on account of sex." This proposed constitutional amendment has long divided proponents of women's rights. Susan B. Anthony initiated the move for it in 1876. In 1920 suffragist leader Alice Paul, immediately after the passage of the 19th Amendment giving women the vote, started a drive to pass the ERA. In 1923 it failed ratification by three states. It remained a live issue thereafter and by 1972 both houses of Congress had passed the ERA, but it failed to secure the necessary states' ratifications. Since then it has been regularly reintroduced into the Congress.

The amendment has foundered mainly on two objections. The first, the question of whether it would make women subject to military draft, has lost force because of various plans to draft medical women and the participation of servicewomen in the Grenada and Panama incursions and particularly in Desert Shield and Desert Storm during the Gulf War of 1991. But some feminists continue to fear that the passage of ERA would deprive working women of the benefits of special protective legislation, benefits hard-won in the early part of the twentieth century. Others answer that these protections ought to apply to male as well as female workers, that their specificity makes women less attractive employees, and that they reduce women to the status of children.

See also Protective Legislation.

Reference Jane Mansbridge, *Why We Lost the ERA* (1986).

Equity Club

Founded in 1886 for women students and alumnae of the University of Michigan Law School, this was the first organization in the United States to provide a network for women attorneys. The club requested its members to write an annual letter discussing the issues most troublesome to them; the publication of these letters helped women lawyers in their struggle against opposition and prejudice.

See also Attorneys.

Reference Virginia G. Drachman, *Women Lawyers and the Origins of Professional Community in America: The Letters of the Equity Club, 1886 to 1890* (1992).

Evans, Elizabeth Gardiner Glendower (1856–1937)

This social reformer was privately educated in Boston. In 1882 she married Glendower Evans; he died in 1886, and she never remarried.

From 1886 until 1914 she devoted herself to the Massachusetts reformatory system. But in 1911 at the behest of Florence Kelley she financed and worked in the Massachusetts campaign that culminated in the first American minimum wage act for women. Her friendship with Mary Kenney O'Sullivan had already led her to activity in the Women's Trade Union League and support for strikes.

Throughout her life her interests broadened. From 1913 to 1935 she contributed to progressive journals and supported them financially. She also interested herself in women's suffrage, peace, and the American Civil Liberties Union.

See also American Civil Liberties Union; Kelley, Florence; Minimum Wage; O'Sullivan, Mary Kenney; Strikes; Women's Trade Union League.

Reference Edward T. James et al., eds., *Notable American Women I* (1971).

Executive Order 11246 as Amended by Executive Order 11375 and Executive Order 12086

These orders forbid contractors holding federal contracts or subcontracts of federal contracts of over $10,000 to discriminate on the basis of sex, race, color, religion, or national origin in all aspects of employment. They also require covered contrac-tors to formulate an affirmative action plan. The Office of Federal Contract Compliance Programs (OFCCP) of the Department of Labor is primarily responsible for enforcement and handles both individual and class complaints. Complaints must be filed within 180 days of the occurrence. OFCCP may seek appropriate relief for victims, including back pay.

See also Affirmative Action; Executive Orders; Office of Federal Contract Compliance Programs.

References Barbara A. Burnett, ed., *Every Woman's Legal Guide* (1983).

Executive Orders

Orders issued by the President of the United States (or chief executive of a state or municipality) pursuant to a constitutional or legislative authorization have the force of law.

See also Executive Order 11246.

Factory Workers

In the eighteenth century textile production began to move slowly out of the home into centralized workplaces—often as a means for towns to deal with their indigents. Because women had traditionally made cloth, employers wanted to recruit them as laborers in these new textile "manufactories." But most women hesitated, because the colonial family ethic insisted that women belonged at home. A respectable wife, widow, or daughter might spin at home, take in boarders, or work in someone else's home as a domestic servant, but she usually didn't go outside the home to work. Accordingly, for cheap labor employers often turned to the workhouses, which housed unmarried women and other "undeserving" poor. Indeed the first attempt in the colonies to organize female labor under one roof, in 1750, sprang from Boston's desire to get widows off its relief rolls.

But eventually, in the early nineteenth century poverty, the manufacture of more products in factories, and the factories' corresponding need for more labor changed the ethos, making it respectable for women to labor productively outside their homes, even while the need for their reproductive labor and their maintenance of family still persisted at home. The unsatisfactory conditions and pay for "outwork" in shoe production, palm-leaf hatmaking, and garment making turned many women toward factory work. At first only young single women considered this work, many of them middle-class farmers' daughters. But as competition increased and conditions in the factories deteriorated, they were replaced by former farm laborers, free blacks, black slaves contracted out by their owners, and, beginning in the 1840s, Irish immigrants who, married or not, had no choice but to try to earn wages outside the home.

By 1900 more than a quarter of European-American, Native American, and Chinese-American women workers held manufacturing jobs, though factories still excluded most black women and women of other ethnic groups; when they did employ them, they gave them the least desirable jobs. But the traditionally masculine crafts, like carpentry, masonry, plumbing, blacksmithing, cabinet-making, and machine-making, barred almost all women. And all kinds of factories confined women to ill-paid jobs on the lower levels.

There they were exploited, cheated, and sexually harassed. The conditions under which they labored were both demeaning and dangerous, as tragically demonstrated by the Triangle Shirtwaist fire. The general assumption that women worked only for pin money defied the reality that many of them either contributed to the support of their birth families or supported families of their own. Their pathetically low pay forced many a factory woman to live with her birth family. The "women adrift" among them were hard-pressed to survive.

During the late nineteenth and early twentieth centuries many European-American women found their way into sales, clerical, professional, and managerial jobs, to be replaced in factories by newly arrived immigrants and women of color.

Throughout their history, from the days of the Lowell Girls onward, factory-employed women have struggled to organize, to form unions, and to negotiate through collective bargaining. Their task was complicated by the differing traditions of the successive immigrant groups, by women's passive acculturation, by the

87

lack of commitment among women to a lifetime career, and above all by the relegation of women workers to a contingent work force. In general, only late in the twentieth century, with the phenomenal growth of female employment, have most unions begun to commit wholeheartedly to the ideal of equal treatment for women workers, let alone to the desideratum expressed in comparable worth.

The late twentieth century has seen a replay of the situation in factory work during the late nineteenth and early twentieth centuries, as illegal operators have exploited the labor of immigrants either illegally living in the United States or ignorant of its laws and consequently unable to defend themselves. Factory owners willing to revive sweatshops and piecework at home have turned to this exploitable group of new arrivals. Moreover, the need to cut costs occasioned by foreign competition has caused manufacturers to move their operations offshore, reducing the available factory jobs in the United States.

See also Bagley, Sarah G.; Collective Bargaining; Colonial America; Comparable Worth; Contingent Work Force; Farley, Harriet; Lowell Girls; Lynn, Massachusetts, Shoe Strike of 1860; Pieceworkers; Pin Money; Strikes; Triangle Shirtwaist Fire; Unions; Women Adrift; Workhouses.

References Mimi Abramovitz, *Regulating the Lives of Women: Social Welfare Policy from Colonial Times to the Present* (1988); Teresa Amott and Julie Matthaei, *Race, Gender, and Work: A Multicultural Economic History of Women in the United States* (1991); Mary H. Blewett, *Men, Women, and Work* (1988); Alice Kessler-Harris, *Out To Work: A History of Wage-Earning Women in the United States* (1982).

Fair Employment Practices Commissions

These state agencies monitor the enforcement of state fair employment practices laws; they hear and investigate complaints of discrimination.

See also Fair Labor Standards Act.

Reference Michael Yates, *Labor Law Handbook* (1987).

Fair Labor Standards Act (1938)

This New Deal measure made permanent the wages and hours regulations begun in the National Industrial Recovery Act codes, guaranteeing a minimum wage and a maximum work week and restricting child labor. This federal statute met many of the goals long advocated by women's organizations. Amendments to the act have increased the minimum wage and added to the categories of workers covered. The inclusion of domestic service as a covered category in 1973 was particularly significant.

See also Domestic Servants; Minimum Wage; National Industrial Recovery Act; New Deal; Norton, Mary Teresa Hopkins.

References Robert E. Doherty, *Industrial and Labor Relations Terms* (1989); Michael Yates, *Labor Law Handbook* (1987).

Family and Medical Leave Act (FMLA)

This act, vetoed by George Bush, was enacted into law in February 1993, in the earliest days of the Clinton administration. It requires employers of more than 50 people to provide 12 weeks unpaid leave each year for the birth or adoption of a child, the serious illness of a family member (including a parent), or the serious illness of an employee. FMLA continues health benefits and guarantees the same or a comparable job upon return.

Some employers worry about the expenses imposed upon them by these requirements. However, the experience of companies with even more liberal leave policies than those mandated shows that many workers avoid taking long leaves because they cannot afford the loss of wages. And a 1992 study authorized by the Families and Work Institute suggests that offering this kind of family leave may actually save companies money. Based on the experience of a large high-tech company that offers a year of unpaid parental leave, the study found that leaves actually cost less than the alternative—hiring and training a new employee.

The researchers reported that leaves do indeed cause inconvenience and cost money and recommended that companies minimize these by careful planning. The cost of a leave supported by rerouting or reassigning work or letting it go averaged 32 percent of a worker's annual salary (39 percent for management, 28 percent for nonmanagement). Replacing workers, on the other hand, cost 150 percent of a manager's salary and 75 percent of a nonmanager's. (*New York Times*, 31 January 1993 and 7 February 1993; *U.S. News and World Report*, 17 February 1993)

See also Child Care; Elder Care; Family Leave; Maternity Leave; Pregnancy; Pregnancy Discrimination Act.

Family Leave

Family leave includes maternity and paternity leave, as well as time to care for ailing family members (including parents)—problems becoming more urgent with the increase in working women and the graying of the population. Until 1993 paternity leaves rarely were available: even among employers with more than 100 workers, in the early 1990s only 1 percent offered paid paternity leaves, and only 18 percent unpaid leaves; among smaller firms the rate was sharply less. In 1992 Florida's Dade County became the first local government to mandate family leave, the law applying to Dade County companies and municipalities with more than 50 employees. In 1993 the situation changed radically with the passage of the Family and Medical Leave Act, requiring employers of more than 50 people to offer unpaid leaves of 12 weeks for specified family crises.

See also California Federal Savings and Loan v. Guerra; Child Care; Elder Care; Family and Medical Leave Act; Maternity Leave; Pregnancy.

References Catalyst, "Report on a National Study of Parental Leaves" (1986); Lisa Semetilli-Dann et al., *Family and Medical Leave: Strategies for Success* (1992); Robert Stumberg, Janice Steinschneider, and George Elser, *State Legislative Sourcebook on Family and Medical Leave* (1990); Edward P. Zigler and Meryl Frank, eds., *The Parental Leave Crisis: Toward a National Policy* (1988).

Family Support Act of 1988

In 1988 Congress passed the Family Support Act (FSA), designed to move people off Aid to Families with Dependent Children (AFDC) through education, training, and employment. FSA's Job Opportunities and Basic Skills programs mandate each state to establish an employment and training program for people who receive AFDC and establish federal guidelines for these programs, requiring states to provide child care and transportation for women participants and child care and Medicaid for those leaving AFDC for employment. This "workfare" legislation linked public assistance and individual initiative, in many cases making assistance dependent on the recipient's willingness to work for wages. Under its provisions, many recipients of AFDC could maintain eligiblity only by participating in job training or in low-paid, low-skill employment. The program provides for preemployment and some job training services.

See also Aid to Families with Dependent Children; Workfare.

References Ms. Foundation for Women and the Center for Policy Alternatives, *Women's Voices: A Policy Guide* (1992); Julia Teresa Quiroz and Regina Tosca, *For My Children: Mexican American Women, Work, and Welfare* (1992); Beverly Stadum, *Poor Women and Their Families* (1992).

Family Wage

The theory that the male breadwinner in a household is entitled to a wage that will enable him to support his dependents (and keep his wife and daughters at home) was an integral part of the work culture of men and their unions well into the twentieth century. The industrial ethic of the time excluded women from the workplace and exalted their role as homemakers and mothers. Some women workers (particularly if they anticipated marriage in their future) supported the patriarchal family and their men's demands for a family wage, rather than aligning with their female co-workers in pressing for equal pay for equal work, better hours, and decent working conditions for women. So generally accepted was this philosophy that even the term "living wage," though variously defined, has usually been applied only to men.

In the late twentieth century, with more and more women working outside the home, the concept of family wage is being extended to include women, many of whom are self-supporting heads of families.

See also Lynn, Massachusetts, Shoe Strike of 1860; Unions; Women's Wages.

References Mimi Abramovitz, *Regulating the Lives of Women: Social Welfare Policy from Colonial Times to the Present* (1988); Ava Baron, ed., *Work Engendered* (1991); Alice Kessler-Harris, *A Woman's Wage* (1990).

Farley, Harriet (ca. 1813–1907)

From 1842–1845, this mill worker edited the *Lowell Offering*, a magazine written for and by the Lowell Girls. Farley, like a number of her contemporaries, left her rural New England home for work in textile-manufacturing towns like Lowell, finding the experience liberating. Unlike her fellow mill worker Sarah Bagley, Farley refused to challenge the mill owners over wages, hours, and poor working conditions, believing that "the employers know best" about such matters. Instead, she championed the mill girls' intelligence and respectability, devoting pages of the *Lowell Offering* to essays and stories of moral uplift and inspiration. Inevitably Farley lost the support of the increasingly militant mill girls, and the *Offering* ceased publication in 1850.

See also Bagley, Sarah G.; Factory Workers; Lowell Girls.

Reference Edward T. James et al., eds., *Notable American Women I* (1971).

Farm Wives

The labor contributed by farm wives has been and is essential to the existence of most family farms. Yet even in the late twentieth century in many states these arduous lifelong labors fail to establish any property rights in the farm.

Until the industrialization and urbanization of the twentieth century, farming employed most American workers. Farm wives both worked in the fields and did the washing, cleaning, nursing, and cooking necessary to support male farm workers. Many women supplemented the farm income by selling milk, butter, eggs, chickens, cheese, honey, spun yarn, woven cloth, and the garden produce they grew. Others took in "outwork." Some prospered, particularly during the heyday of the family farm, up until about 1930, when more sophisticated farm machinery and improved farming methods enabled the development of agribusinesses. Many more, however, toiled away their lives on subsistence or sub-subsistence farms.

In the twentieth century mechanization and the development of agribusinesses have threatened the livelihoods of farmers and farm wives. Many women, in a desperate effort to hold onto the family farm, have taken on second (or third) jobs in town. Farm wives, sometimes in association with women farmers, have formed organizations to promote agriculture and the family farm, like the 35,000-member American Agri-Women, founded in 1974; and Women Involved in Farm Economics, an association of 22 state and 140 local groups founded in 1976.

See also Agricultural Workers; Farmers; Homesteaders; Migrant Laborers; Tenant Farmers.

References Margaret Jarman Hagood, *Mothers of the South: Portraiture of the White Tenant Farm Woman* (1939); Joan M. Jensen, *Loosening the Bonds: Mid-Atlantic Farm Women, 1750–1850* (1986); Joan M. Jensen, *With These Hands: Women Working on the Land* (1981); Jacqueline Jones, *Labor of Love, Labor of Sorrow: Black Women, Work and the Family from Slavery to the Present* (1985).

Farmers

From colonial days, American women have operated their own farms or managed farms during the absence of their male owners. They have acquired farms by inheritance, by purchase, and by homesteading. The 1900 census reported 307,788 mostly white women farmers, planters, and overseers. As with other farmers and ranchers, their numbers have decreased with twentieth-century mechanization and the development of agribusinesses.

See also Agricultural Workers; Brent, Margaret; Farm Wives; Homesteaders; Migrant Laborers; Pinckney, Eliza Lucas; Tenant Farmers.

References Teresa Amott and Julie Matthaei, *Race, Gender, and Work: A Multicultural Economic History of Women in the United States* (1991); Alice Kessler-Harris, *Out To Work: A History of Wage-Earning Women in the United States* (1982).

Farming Out

In colonial America municipalities bore sole responsibility for the maintenance of the poor. To save money on their relief rolls, towns often farmed out (auctioned off) to the lowest bidder the services of the "undeserving" poor white woman in exchange for her support, for which the successful bidder then charged the town. (The community designated as "deserving" and, therefore eligible for aid, women who conformed to received standards of work and family, whom the community deemed economically helpless through no fault of their own, like widows or wives of disabled men.) As the eighteenth century progressed, farming out was used as a punishment that lowered pauper costs and supplied cheap labor. Larger towns then turned to "contracting out" groups of poor people, sending them to a private house and paying the manager for maintaining them; the manager then could use their labor.

See also Apprentices; Colonial America; Indentured Servants; Slavery; Workhouses.

Reference Mimi Abramovitz, *Regulating the Lives of Women: Social Welfare Policy from Colonial Times to the Present* (1988).

Federal Emergency Relief Administration (FERA)

See New Deal.

Federation of Organizations for Professional Women

Founded in 1972, this association affiliates organizations in the cause of equity for women and tries to improve their educational and employment status.

Female Ghettos

See Occupational Segregation; Velvet Ghettos.

Female Society of Lynn and Vicinity for the Protection and Promotion of Female Industry

More than 1,000 women outworkers at shoebinding formed this organization in 1833 to secure higher wages and pay equal to that of men, a demand supported by male artisans. The protest failed and the society disintegrated within a year.

See also Lynn, Massachusetts, Shoe Strike of 1860; Shoemakers; Society of Shoebinders; Unions.

Feminist Majority Foundation

This think tank develops strategies to empower women in many areas, including economic equity.

Feminization

Some occupations once dominated by men have gradually been taken over by women, or feminized, for example, elementary school teaching after the Civil War and clerical work in the early twentieth century. Often a contributing reason has been the lower pay assigned to women workers, and/or the lesser prospects of advancement. Understandably, men in occupations becoming feminized often worry that the entrance of numbers of women will decrease their prestige and profitability.

An ongoing case in point is that of veterinary medicine. Since 1976 the number of women veterinarians has increased dramatically—more so than in any other previously male-dominated profession. And from 1980 to 1988 starting salaries in real dollars adjusted for the cost of living declined by 10 percent. Other careers, such as engineering, that require less time and money to learn, offer greater financial rewards. Has the increasing feminization of the profession accounted for these (comparative) financial woes? Certainly not solely, for the problem of low pay for long hours has haunted the veterinary profession ever since it began. But young men are turning to careers that offer greater earning potential.

See also Clerical Workers; Health Professionals and Paraprofessionals; Teachers.

Reference Sue Drum and H. Ellen Whiteley, *Women in Veterinary Medicine* (1992).

Fern, Fannie (Sara Payson Willis Parton) (1811–1872)

Fern, one of the first American women newspaper columnists, whose father founded the *Youth's Companion*, was educated in her birthplace, Boston, and at Catharine Beecher's academy. In 1837 she married the well-off Charles H. Eldredge, who died in 1846, leaving her with two daughters (another having predeceased her father). Her marriage in 1849 to Samuel P. Farrington ended in divorce after three years.

Economic necessity, particularly in the interstices between marriages, forced her to try one after another of the few occupations open to middle- and upper-class women. Attempts at sewing and teaching produced so little money that she had to give up one daughter to the child's paternal grandparents. In desperation in 1851 she began to write witty pieces for local magazines under the pen name Fanny Fern. Two years later the publisher James C. Derby printed a collection of these as *Fern Leaves from Fanny's Port-Folio*—a best-seller that was followed in 1854 by another such collection and one for the juvenile market.

In 1855 she became a weekly contributor to the *New York Ledger* at the dazzling pay of $100 per column. In this occupa-

tion she remained for the rest of her life, intermittently publishing collections of her columns and writing two novels. Usually she wrote humorously and saucily of domestic problems, but she also espoused issues like intellectual equality of the sexes, a single standard of morality, women's suffrage, and limitation of family size.

In 1856 she married the biographer James Parton; after her death he married her daughter.

See also Beecher, Catharine Esther; Journalists.

Reference Joyce W. Warren, *Fanny Fern: An Independent Woman* (1992); Edward T. James et al., eds., *Notable American Women III* (1971).

Ferraro, Geraldine (b. 1935)

The first woman to run for vice-president as a candidate of a major political party, Attorney Ferraro brought to the 1984 race her experience as assistant district attorney for Queens County, New York, and her three terms in the House of Representatives. Though defeated in the 1984 campaign, Ferraro afterward resumed her political career. In 1992 she unsuccessfully sought nomination for the U.S. Senate in the Democratic primary.

See also Attorneys; Government Workers.

Fertility

Throughout American history birth rates have decreased, while the numbers of women employed in gainful work have increased. But a correlation between these two phenomena is not clear. The sharpest drop, from almost 280 live births per 1,000 women aged 15–44 in 1800, to 130 in 1900, occurred during a century when most women still did their work, paid or unpaid, within the home; and from 1940 to 1960 both fertility rates and work participation increased significantly. Clearly participation in the work force is at most only one of several factors affecting fertility. Furthermore, women's decisions to join the work force result from a complex of causes, many economic, and many beyond the control of individual women.

Reference Susan Householder Van Horn, *Women, Work, and Fertility, 1900–1986* (1988).

Fetal Protection Policies

The exclusion of women of child-bearing age from jobs that might jeopardize the health of a fetus or a woman's reproductive potential has until recently been a policy of major American companies affecting multitudes of women workers. Such exclusionary policies, however, were never applied to male employees working under identical hazardous conditions that could damage their reproductive systems. Such sex-specific protection policies have been illegal since 1991, when the U.S. Supreme Court in *UAW v. Johnson Controls* held that they discriminated against women. Women and men are now equally free to determine whether they will accept the health risk.

See also Health Hazards; Pregnancy; Protective Legislation; *UAW v. Johnson Controls*.

Reference National Organization for Women Legal Defense & Education Fund, "Fetal-Protection Policy Fact Sheet" (1992).

Filipina Americans

Most Filipinas immigrated to the United States in one of three waves. The few in the first wave, 1909–1934, seldom joined the paid labor force. The war brides who came after World War II, married to white or Filipino servicemen, could find work in agriculture, canneries, or family businesses, or as domestic servants. The 1965 Immigration Act, providing for immigration of skilled professional workers, has bifurcated Filipina immigrant workers into a large group of poor women usually restricted to low-paid, seasonal work, often as hotel maids or in manufacturing and food-processing jobs, with little upward mobility; and a much smaller group of well-trained scientific professionals, especially in medicine. In 1980 Filipinas enjoyed 68 percent participation in the labor force. The profes-

sionals among them largely account for their earning on average a higher *median* income than any other racial-ethnic group of American working women.

See also Professional Women.

Reference Teresa Amott and Julie Matthaei, *Race, Gender, and Work: A Multicultural Economic History of Women in the United States* (1991).

Film
See Cinema.

Flexible Benefits
See Benefits.

Flexplace
See Home Workers; Telecommuting.

Flextime

This arrangement allows workers to choose their own starting and quitting times within limits set by management. They may put in a full eight-hour day on a staggered schedule or complete a workweek in four long days rather than five eight-hour days. A maxiflex system permits them to vary their hours every day. In 1980, 12 percent of workers used flextime. Companies, in return for more complicated scheduling, higher utility costs, and overtime adjustments, benefit by increased worker responsibility and initiative and higher productivity. Workers gain freedom to schedule leisure and personal and family tasks, and communities profit by decreased pressure on transportation facilities. Necessary communication among workers can often be effected during "core hours," typically between ten and three, when all workers are at the workplace. Flextime for supervisors presents obvious problems; usually supervisors need to be on the job during the same hours as the people they supervise.

In 1989 full-time men workers were more likely than full-time women workers to have flexible work schedules, but whites of both genders were more likely to have options about these schedules than African Americans and Hispanics and managerial or professional employees than technical/sales/administrative support workers. An employee may hesitate to use flextime if her/his manager opposes it.

See also Job Sharing.

References Catalyst, *Flexible Work Arrangements: Establishing Options for Managers and Professionals* (1989); Paula Ries and Anne J. Stone, eds., *The American Woman, 1992–93: A Status Report* (1992); Lynn Y. Weiner, *From Working Girl to Working Mother: The Female Labor Force in the United States, 1820–1980* (1985); Working Woman editors with Gay Bryant, *The Working Woman Report* (1984).

Flight Attendants

In the early days of aviation all jobs were designated for men. Ellen Church, who apparently had hoped to fly as a pilot, became the first stewardess (called a "sky girl") in 1930 and helped create a new occupation for women. World War II significantly increased the numbers of female flight attendants (the change of occupational name from "stewardesses"). But the airlines did not hire a black flight attendant until 1957, when Ruth Carol Taylor joined Mohawk Airlines. In 1980 about 50,000 Americans worked in this occupation.

For many years the airlines, which had first insisted on graduate nurses (a requirement dropped for lack of nurses during World War II), would employ only pretty, young, slender, unmarried women who were not pregnant; approved applicants were subject to such requirements as wearing girdles, hats, gloves, and makeup. The airline industry has been particularly prone to gender-related problems because it has exploited women flight attendants as an advertising asset—hence the importance placed on looks, age, and measurements.

Title VII of the Civil Rights Act of 1964 and the Age Discrimination Acts provided a legal basis for women flight attendants to challenge airline regulations about age, appearance, marital status, and maternity. Flight attendants used both their unions and the courts effectively. Restrictive policies began to fall in 1971, when Pan American Airways' refusal to hire a man as flight attendant was ruled a violation of Title VII (*Diaz v. Pan American Airways*). By 1978 the situation had changed to the point that some airlines provided maternity leaves.

See also Age Discrimination Acts; Civil Rights Act of 1964; Maternity Leave; Pilots; Unions; World War II.

References Judith A. Baer, *Women in American Law: The Struggle toward Equality from the New Deal to the Present* (1991); Joan McCullough, *First of All* (1980); Georgia Panter Nielsen, *From Sky Girl to Flight Attendant: Women and the Making of a Union* (1982).

Flint Auto Workers' Strike (1937)

In this sit-down strike the United Auto Workers (UAW) angered some women workers by forbidding their participation inside the plant. But they joined male strikers' wives in the Women's Emergency Brigade in a protective picket line between strikers and police and helped to organize logistics and support. When police fired into the crowd in the January 21 Battle of Bulls Run, women fought back with stones, lumps of coal, and milk bottles. After 44 days General Motors settled with recognition of UAW and a raise.

See also Strikes.

References Ruth Milkman, ed., *Women, Work and Protest* (1985); Angela Howard Zophy and Frances M. Kavenik, eds., *Handbook of American Women's History* (1990).

Floating Population
See Women Adrift.

Flynn, Elizabeth Gurley (1890–1964)

This radical labor organizer never forgot the poverty she saw as a child in New England mill towns and in New York City. In 1906 she began her career as a labor agitator, dropping out of high school to start a national career. A charismatic speaker, she devoted herself to the Industrial Workers of the World for ten years, traveling here and there to support strikes and to organize labor, often being arrested and usually attracting publicity. She figured prominently in the Lawrence, Massachusetts, Textile Strike of 1912, and the Paterson, New Jersey, Silk Strike of 1913.

Although in 1926 doctors warned her that continuing her career would jeopardize her life, in 1936 she became an organizer for the communist party, resumed public speaking, and began to write a feminist column for the communist *Daily Worker*, advocating on the one hand equal opportunity and equal pay but on the other hand protective legislation for women. During World War II she publicized women's contributions to the war effort and argued for unionizing new women workers, providing day care, and drafting women for industry and military service.

In 1951 she was convicted of conspiring to teach and advocate the overthrow of the United States government by force and violence; she served almost two and a half years in a federal penitentiary. In 1961 she was selected as the first woman national chair of the Communist party in the United States. She died while visiting Moscow in 1964.

See also Communist Party; Industrial Workers of the World; Bread and Roses Strike; Protective Legislation; Strikes; World War II.

Elizabeth Gurley Flynn speaks at Haledon, New Jersey, during a silk workers strike in 1913.

References Rosalyn Baxandall, *Words on Fire: The Life and Writing of Elizabeth Gurley Flynn* (1987); Elizabeth Gurley Flynn, *I Speak My Own Piece: Autobiography of "the Rebel Girl"* (1955); Barbara Sicherman et al., eds., *Notable American Women: The Modern Period* (1980).

Follett, Mary Parker (1868–1933)

This writer and lecturer in industrial management was educated in Massachusetts and England, earning her undergraduate degree at Radcliffe. As a social worker she helped to set up vocational guidance for Boston schoolchildren and the Boston Placement Bureau. Later she worked with the Boston Department of Vocational Guidance, which absorbed the placement bureau in 1917. That work led her to an interest in industrial relations.

Believing that confrontation between labor and management would defeat social justice, she advocated "integration" rather than conflict. All her work emphasized the psychological bases of organized human activity; she saw vocational guidance and successful industrial relations as a means to help people learn how to work and play together harmoniously and effectively. Her broadly based philosophy continues to influence current administrative thought.

See also Managers; Social Workers; Vocational Guidance.

Reference Edward T. James et al., *Notable American Women I* (1971).

Food Services

Job segregation by sex in the food service industry has varied over time and place. Historically, males have dominated the industry, but during the course of the twentieth century the number of women increased until by 1970 over 90 percent of the work of waiting on tables had been feminized. Although the lines separating male and female are constantly being redrawn, male domination of particular jobs (e.g., cooks, maîtres d'hôtel, and bartenders) still survives in the early 1990s, especially in the more prestigious and expensive restaurants; and women waitresses must still contemplate the possibility of downward mobility as they age.

In the past women also faced barriers in the form of ordinances and rules barring them from serving liquor, working at night, and tending bar, all under the guise of protecting their respectability and safety. Some of these restrictions were promoted by male waiters and bartenders as a way of reducing competition; and some waitresses supported such protective legislation because of women's special needs. Disputes over these restrictions were often bitter and heated, but in the end the courts held them to be violations of Title VII of the Civil Rights Act of 1964.

See also Civil Rights Act of 1964; Harvey Girls; Protective Legislation; Women's Protective Union.

References Ava Baron, ed., *Work Engendered* (1991); *The Waitresses' Handbook: A Guide to the Legal Rights of Waitresses and Other Restaurant Workers* (1986).

Force, Juliana Rieser (1876–1948)

This first director of the Whitney Museum of American Art, a native of Pennsylvania, devoted her life to increasing audiences for artists. After three semesters at Northfield Seminary for Young Ladies in Massachusetts, she taught in a business school, tried to write, and eventually went to New York City to freelance as a stenographer. In this work she met the heiress and sculptor Gertrude Whitney, who subsequently hired her full-time.

Together, with extraordinary sensitivity to the needs of artists, they built and maintained the Whitney Studio Club, the Whitney Studio Galleries, and the Whitney Museum. Force made a reputation throughout the art world for her taste, the collections of folk art and modern art that she assembled, and above all for her understanding of and generosity to artists.

See also Artists.

Reference Avis Berman, *Rebels on Eighth Street: Juliana Force and the Whitney Museum of American Art* (1990).

Franklin v. Gwinett County School District

In 1992 the U.S. Supreme Court ruled that sexually harassed students are entitled to seek monetary damages from their institutions, without a cap on the amount of damages. The decision also applies to other forms of sex discrimination in education and covers employees as well.

See also Civil Rights Act of 1991; Sex Discrimination; Sexual Harassment.

References National Organization for Women Legal Defense & Education Fund, "Legal Program Case Docket" (1992).

Friedan, Betty (b. 1921)

In the 1963 *The Feminine Mystique*, this feminist trumpeted to the public the frustration of educated women confined to the role of homemakers. She went on to cofound the National Organization for Women (NOW), of which she was the first president. Friedan's solution for the frustrations of women confined by their roles as housewives/mothers/consumers was meaningful and paid work outside the home.

See also National Organization for Women.

Reference Joyce Gelb and Marian Lief Palley, *Women and Public Policies* (1982).

Fringe Benefits
See Benefits.

Frontiero v. Richardson (1973)

In this case Lt. Sharon A. Frontiero challenged the constitutionality of military regulations that denied the husbands of military women the benefits available to wives of servicemen. The U.S. Supreme Court held that the regulation violated Frontiero's constitutional right to equal protection of the law.

See also Military Women; Sex Discrimination.

Reference Susan Gluck Mezey, *In Pursuit of Equality: Women, Public Policy and the Federal Courts* (1992).

Gastonia, North Carolina, Strike of 1929

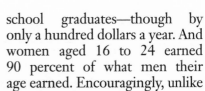

In this "City of Spindles," textile workers struck in April 1929; in response management evicted them from company-owned houses. In the tent city into which the homeless workers moved, violence erupted between police and workers, by then communist-supported, and deaths ensued on both sides. As in the Elizabethton, Tennessee, Strike of 1929, white women most actively waged this strike.

See also Communist Party; Elizabethton, Tennessee, Strike of 1929; General Textile Strike of 1934; Strikes.

Reference Dorothy M. Brown, *Setting a Course: American Women in the 1920s* (1987).

Gender Gap

Throughout the history of the United States a gender gap has yawned between men's pay and women's pay. The ratio of women's pay to men's pay increased from 1815 to the 1930s, most markedly with the Industrial Revolution in the early nineteenth century, and again with the surge of women into clerical work around the turn of the century. From the mid–1950s to the 1980s it stayed almost constant, hovering around 60 percent. Between 1981 and 1989, it rose from 59 percent to 68 percent. In the early 1990s women earn on average 72 cents for every dollar men earn.

Unfortunately the recent relative gain for women has resulted as much from the decline in men's earnings as from the rise in women's pay. On the other hand, the 1980s' gains occurred at the same time that more women were flooding into the work force. For the first time, the median earnings of women college graduates slightly exceeded those of male high school graduates—though by only a hundred dollars a year. And women aged 16 to 24 earned 90 percent of what men their age earned. Encouragingly, unlike their mothers, young women in the 1980s did not fall further behind their male peers as they aged. (*New York Times*, 8 October 1992) As legislation against sex discrimination has been enacted and as women have learned new skills, planned to remain in the labor force, and seen themselves as careerists, the gender gap has narrowed.

These gains were not obtained equally for all women. African-American women gained more than whites, earning about 28 percent more in 1989 than in 1969, though they still averaged only about 92 percent of white women's compensation. Between 1980 and 1987 women with work disabilities increased their average earnings by 8 percent, though they still earned only about 84 percent of the compensation of their counterparts without work disabilities. The gender gap widens with age, at least partly because so many older women workers are concentrated in traditionally low-paying, "women's occupations."

Between 1983 and 1991 several occupations narrowed the gender gap in their fields, so that women secretaries in 1993 earn 97 percent of the earnings of men secretaries (against 77 percent in 1983); women mechanics and repairers 104 percent; women police and firefighters 84 percent; women bank tellers 92 percent; women mathematicians and computer scientists 86 percent; and women public relations specialists 84 percent. On the other hand, between 1983 and 1991 women physicians slipped from 85 percent of men's earnings to a mere 54 percent, women lawyers from 89 percent to 75 percent, and women financial managers from

64 percent to 59 percent. (*Working Woman*, January 1993)

Differences between the genders in job experience, education, and length of tenure all helped to create the gender gap. Steven Willborn estimates that more than 25 percent of the gap derives from the longer hours that men work for pay: more hours each week, more weeks each year, more second jobs, more overtime. Some experts attribute another 40 percent of the wage gap to men's greater productivity. More arduous working conditions for men may account for another 5–10 percent. The Committee on Women's Employment of the National Academy of Sciences attributes 33–40 percent of the gap to occupational segregation of women into lower-paying jobs. Analysis of the causes of the gender gap is complicated by such factors as women's past patterns of work. For instance, the many older married women entering the labor force since 1940 with little or no experience and outmoded or no skills usually have perforce taken low-paying, dead-end jobs. Moreover, with their family responsibilities, women drop in and out of the work force more frequently than men.

But the National Longitudinal Study of the High School Class of 1972 by the U.S. Department of Education, which followed large numbers of women and men after their high school graduation, concluded that a serious gap still occurs when all these factors are eliminated. Although the women earned higher grades in high school and college, and although their total time on the job showed little difference from that of men, in 1985 the men were averaging $25,022 against the $18,970 of childless women and the $15,016 of women with children. Within the same occupation, men were paid more, though length of job experience or family responsibilities did not account for the gap.

So even allowing due weight to all the possible contributory factors, it's hard to discount the impact of an undervaluing of "women's work" in creating wage discrimination. The presence of large numbers of women in an occupation still signals low wages. In 1990, in jobs where women constituted 90 percent or more of the job force, average weekly pay was $285, but where women represented 10 percent or less, the pay averaged $460. Even within the same occupation, women earn less than men: in the sales occupations in 1990, for instance, women earned 57 percent of men's earnings, and among clerical workers, where women dominate, women earned only 75 percent of men's earnings. Similarly, male registered nurses in 1991 averaged $703 weekly, against $630 weekly for females.

Although in the decade from 1979–1989 the number of women working at or below minimum wage fell from 20 percent to less than 7 percent, almost twice as many women as men still earned minimum or less, and 18.5 percent of women in the service sector were still in that category.

To a limited extent individual women can alleviate their own situation *if* they can and will enter traditionally male fields. More education also will improve their earning power, though not as much as it improves that of men. Women who complete college earn more than double what female high school dropouts earn, though considerably less than college-educated men. Unemployment among women high school dropouts is about five times the level of college-educated women.

See also Comparable Worth; Married Women's Employment; Minimum Wage; National Committee on Pay Equity; Occupational Segregation; Part-Time Workers; Service Sector; Sex Discrimination; Temporary Workers; Wage Discrimination; Women's Wages.

References Claudia Goldin, *Understanding the Gender Gap: An Economic History of American Women* (1990); Ms. Foundation for Women and the Center for Policy Alternatives, *Women's Voices: A Policy Guide* (1992); Nine to Five, National Association of Working Women, "Profile of Working Women" (1990); Paula Ries and Anne J. Stone, eds., *The American Woman, 1992–93: A Status Report* (1992); Cynthia M. Taeuber, comp. and ed., *Statistical Handbook on Women in America* (1991); Steven L. Willborn, *A Secretary and a Cook:*

Challenging Women's Wages in the Courts of the United States and Great Britain (1989); Pamela Wilson, ed., Salaried and Professional Women: Relevant Statistics (1992).

Gender-Specific Occupations
See Occupational Segregation.

General Electric v. Gilbert
This 1976 U.S. Supreme Court decision ruled that denial of benefits for pregnancy-related disability and illness is not discrimination based on sex. The General Electric (GE) disability plan covered its employees for a wide variety of diseases and disabilities, but excluded disabilities arising from pregnancy and childbirth. In a 6–3 decision the court held that the GE plan did not constitute sex discrimination. The court announced that since pregnancy "is not a disease at all and is often a voluntarily undertaken desired condition" GE did not violate Title VII of the Civil Rights Act of 1964 when it excluded pregnancy from its disability plan.

Immediately after the decision, over 300 groups of women (primarily unions, but also including the National Organization for Women, the Women's Equity Action League, and the National Women's Political Caucus) lobbied Congress to place pregnancy on a par with other disabilities. Their activities resulted in the enactment of the Pregnancy Discrimination Act of 1978.

See also Civil Rights Act of 1964; Maternity Leave; National Organization for Women; Pregnancy; Pregnancy Discrimination Act; Sex Discrimination; Unions; Women's Equity Action League.

References Joyce Gelb and Marian Lief Palley, Women and Public Policies (1982); Susan Gluck Mezey, In Pursuit of Equality: Women, Public Policy and the Federal Courts (1992); Rita J. Simon and Gloria Danziger, Women's Movements in America (1991).

General Textile Strike of 1934
This strike occurred in the Piedmont, stretching from southern Virginia through the central Carolinas and into northern Georgia and Alabama, which at the time was the world's leading producer of yarn and cloth. The hopes raised in the workers by the National Industrial Recovery Act (NIRA) had been disappointed, as their complaints under its codes bore little result. When in May 1934 the Code Authority attacked overproduction with a 25-percent cut in machine hours, workers, already squeezed between short time and living costs, began a series of wildcat strikes, and in August the United Textile Workers (UTW) approved a walkout to begin September 1. By mid-September, 400,000 textile workers across the nation had struck—the largest single labor conflict in American history. Governors mobilized the National Guard, and the governor of Georgia declared martial law in the mill villages and put pickets into a detention camp.

Young women were vehemently conspicuous and audible on the picket lines. At some work sites well-organized strikers prevented anyone from entering the mills. At others employees still working and strikers battled one another with sticks and guns. Elsewhere National Guardsmen clubbed and bayoneted strikers. Deaths resulted. The strike ended on 22 September 1934, after President Franklin D. Roosevelt had personally intervened, promising the workers a federal investigation and asking employers to take strikers back. But the government set up no machinery to keep employers from firing unionists. The strike left the UTW in disarray, and the Supreme Court's 1935 declaration that NIRA was unconstitutional braked the federal program for economic recovery. In the aftermath of the strike employers ruthlessly attacked the union, blacklisted unionists, and evicted strikers from mill-owned houses. After this strike employers began to abandon the mill village system.

See also Elizabethton, Tennessee, Strike of 1929; Gastonia, North Carolina, Strike of 1929; National Industrial Recovery Act; Strikes.

Reference Jacquelyn Dowd Hall et al., Like a Family: The Making of a Southern Cotton Mill World (1987).

Genetic Discrimination

In the early 1990s workers and workers' rights advocates have begun to worry about the possibility of employers (and insurers) discriminating against potential employees on the basis of their genetic patterns. For instance, an employer might refuse to hire an applicant with a higher-than-average chance of developing a disease that would involve high costs for health care.

See also Civil Rights.

Gibbs, Katharine (1865–1934)

This entrepreneur founded the Katharine Gibbs Schools in Providence, Boston, and New York to prepare women for office work. Left a widow at 46 with two sons to support, she took courses at Simmons College, sold her jewelry to get capital, and devised a curriculum including business law and liberal arts as well as secretarial skills. She caught the wave of demand for secretaries in the Progressive Era, and her schools prospered.

See also Clerical Workers; Entrepreneurs; Progressive Era; Seymour, Mary Foot.

References Caroline Bird, *Enterprising Women* (1976); Charles Stephenson and Robert Asher, eds., *Life and Labor: Dimensions of American Working-Class History* (1986).

Gibson, Althea (b. 1927)

Gibson, the first black invited to play in the American Lawn Tennis Association championships, left school in her teens to work as a chicken cleaner. But other African Americans helped her through college, where she earned a degree in physical education. She won the Wimbledon and Forest Hills tournaments in 1957 and 1958 and the world professional tennis championship in 1960. In 1963 she joined the women's professional golf tour, and in 1975 became athletic commissioner of New Jersey.

See also Sports.

References Jennifer S. Uglow, comp and ed., *International Dictionary of Women's Biography* (1985); Angela Howard Zophy and Frances M. Kavenik, eds., *Handbook of American Women's History* (1990).

Gilbreth, Lillian Evelyn Moller (1878–1972)

This engineer, industrial psychologist, and efficiency expert took an undergraduate and a master's degree in literature. She interrupted her studies for a doctorate to marry contractor Frank Bunker Gilbreth in 1904. Besides bearing a dozen children in 17 years, Gilbreth published her *Psychology of Management* in 1914, earned a Ph.D. in psychology in 1915, and joined her husband in pioneer work in scientific management and motion study. The Gilbreths marketed to industry the technique of searching for the "one best way" to do a job fast, with minimal effort, and most comfortably for the worker. Between 1912 and 1920 they jointly wrote five books.

When her husband died in 1924 and companies canceled most of his contracts, Gilbreth supported her family by lecturing and offering management courses. She also began to apply the Gilbreth techniques to housekeeping, writing extensively on the subject. She strongly influenced the development of home management courses. She designed equipment and routines to enable handicapped persons to keep house. From 1935 to 1948 she served as professor of management at Purdue University and acted as consultant for careers for women. In 1931 she was the first recipient of the Gilbreth Medal of the Society of Industrial Engineers, and in 1966 she was awarded the Hoover Medal for distinguished public service by an engineer. She continued her work into her eighties.

See also Engineers; Home Economists; Housekeeping; Scientific Management.

References Frank Gilbreth, Jr., *Time Out for Happiness* (1970); Edna Yost, *Frank and Lillian Gilbreth: Partners for Life* (1949).

Gilder, Jeannette Leonard (1849–1916)

Gilder was the cofounder (1881) and, from 1901–1906, sole editor of the *Critic,*

Althea Gibson

an important magazine of literary criticism and review. Known primarily for her editorial skills, Gilder also worked as New York agent for a number of out-of-town authors and wrote pieces for the theater and various newspapers and magazines.

See also Journalists; Writers and Publishers.

Reference Edward T. James et al., eds., *Notable American Women II* (1971).

Gillespie, Mabel Edna (1877–1923)

This labor reformer, a native of Minnesota, studied at Radcliffe and then entered social settlement work. Throughout her life she involved herself with the problems and conditions of the working woman.

Her activities were legion. In 1904 she participated in an unsuccessful strike for the eight-hour day at Fall River, Massachusetts. She served as executive secretary of the Buffalo branch of the New York Consumers' League; as executive secretary of the Boston Women's Trade Union League (WTUL), on the executive board of the national WTUL, as a member of various state and local labor committees and agencies, as first president of the stenographers' union that she had organized, and as first woman member of the executive board of the Massachusetts State Federation of Labor. She successfully worked to affiliate the Boston WTUL with five established unions, thus gaining support from men's unions for efforts to organize women workers. After World War I she turned her attention to the education of women workers, serving on the administrative committee of the Bryn Mawr Summer School for Women Workers and helping to found the Boston Trade Union College (1919).

See also Bryn Mawr Summer School for Women Workers; Consumers' League; Strikes; Unions; Women's Trade Union League.

References Gladys Boone, *The Women's Trade Union Leagues in Great Britain and the U.S.* (1942); Edward T. James et al., eds., *Notable American Women II* (1971).

Gilman, Charlotte Anna Perkins Stetson (1860–1935)

An active and articulate feminist author and lecturer, Gilman focused on issues related to women's labor and social organization. A native of Connecticut and the daughter of a dysfunctional family, she grew up in poverty, her schooling limited. Still in her teens, she began to support herself as a commercial artist and art teacher. Her catastrophic first marriage, to artist Charles Stetson, brought on a nervous collapse, from which she apparently never completely recovered; after ten years they divorced in 1894, though she sent her daughter to live with Stetson and his new wife. Her second marriage, to attorney George Gilman in 1900, lasted until his death in 1934 but was childless. Unable to accept domestic responsibility, Gilman lectured and wrote articles and books. From 1909 to 1916 she edited and published the *Forerunner,* a monthly magazine that offered its readers literature, social commentary, and news—all on the position of women in society. Suffering from breast cancer, she committed suicide in 1935.

Gilman was arguably the leading intellectual of the woman's movement of her day. During the course of her career she worked with many of the country's leading women, including Jane Addams, who introduced her to Hull House and the settlement movement; Sarah Cooper,

Charlotte Perkins Gilman

with whom she helped plan the California Woman's Congresses of 1894 and 1895; and suffragist Carrie Chapman Catt. Throughout her career she stressed the virtues of female economic independence and the necessity of overcoming the limitations placed on women's activities and opportunities by the dominance of male values in American society. What she espoused, in fact, was a total reorganization of society in which women would assume their rightful place.

Her influential book, *Women and Economics* (1898), was published early in the Progressive Era, when women were moving out of the home into gainful employment or volunteer reform activities (and sometimes both). It dispassionately examined motherhood ("not as advantageous as believed"), stultifying domestic routines, and women's dependence upon men's approval for their support. To relieve mothers and housewives of domestic drudgery, she proposed replacing home child care with centralized nurseries staffed by trained personnel, providing day-care nurseries for working mothers, and organizing cooperative kitchens run by professional cooks trained in domestic science.

See also Cooperative Housekeeping; Hull House; Progressive Era.

References Charlotte Perkins Gilman, *The Living of Charlotte Perkins Gilman* (1935); Edward T. James et al., eds., *Notable American Women II* (1971).

Gilson, Mary Barnett (1877–?)

Gilson's investigation of saleswomen's jobs for the Boston Women's Educational and Industrial Union in 1910 led to work as a vocational counselor at the Boston Trade School for Girls. A conversion to the theories of scientific management rescued her from her disillusionment at finding that vocational guidance did not suffice to get women out of sweatshops. From 1913–1924 a job in Cleveland as welfare secretary (later service and employment manager) of Clothcraft Shops, where she was charged with systematizing employment and using welfare programs to improve the labor force, afforded her the opportunity to apply these theories.

She took over the responsibility of hiring from the foremen, trying to match the worker and the job and to promote from within, solely on the basis of merit and aptitude—methods she believed would help women workers by the creation of a non-gender-biased system. She was constrained, however, by union protocols and the tradition of higher wages for men. Inspired by the desire to help women gain equality in the workplace, Gilson tried to inculcate in them habits of industry and independence and to persuade them to delay marriage, which she believed decreased their efficiency. She and her work earned fame among personnel, office, and scientific managers generally.

The hard times after World War I, however, cut Gilson's programs; she left management, completed a Ph.D., studied unemployment, and in 1931 began to teach at the University of Chicago.

See also Academic Women; Human Resources Managers; Managers; Scientific Management; Unions; Vocational Guidance; Welfare Work; Women's Educational and Industrial Union.

Reference Sharon Hartman Strom, *Beyond the Typewriter: Gender, Class, and the Origins of Modern American Office Work, 1900–1930* (1992).

Girl Fridays

During the 1950s and the early 1960s, employers often advertised for "executive assistants" whom they termed "girl (or gal) Fridays," after Robinson Crusoe's helper. Ostensibly these jobs offered interesting work and upward mobility, but many women whom they attracted found themselves doing conventional secretarial work. When job ads were legally desegregated by the Civil Rights Act of 1964, employers revised their advertisements to "gal or guy Friday."

See also Civil Rights Act of 1964; Clerical Workers.

Given-Out Work

See Pieceworkers.

Glass Ceiling

This term describes the invisible barrier that keeps competent women from rising to the highest and most powerful jobs in their companies. Those who deny the existence of this barrier cite other reasons for the tiny number of women at the top, like women's family responsibilities and their unwillingness to put their jobs first. Studies like that of the Mobil Oil Corporation (1989) suggest, however, that these reasons are questionable: the study reports that although 27 percent of men refuse to relocate, only 19 percent of women refuse. A 1990 Wick and Co. study suggests that the prime reason that experienced professional and managerial women leave big corporations is that they perceive only limited opportunities to advance.

See also Sticky Floor.

References A. Morrison, R. White, and E. Van Velsor, *Breaking the Glass Ceiling* (1987); Paula Ries and Anne J. Stone, eds., *The American Woman, 1992–93: A Status Report* (1992).

Gleason, Kate (1865–1933)

This business promoter and community developer, though she studied intermittently over the years at what is now the Rochester Institute of Technology, owed the better part of her technical training to her father, who operated a small toolmaking shop in her childhood. From about 1888 she worked with him in marketing beveled gears. She worked primarily in sales, traveling in the United States and Europe.

In 1913 she left the family business to build her own career in banking and residential and industrial development, helping to launch several businesses and experimenting extensively with low-cost housing. In the late 1920s she drafted plans for poured-concrete suburban homes, a project that she was never able to finish. She left an estate of $1,400,000.

See also Entrepreneurs.

Reference Edward T. James et al., eds., *Notable American Women II* (1971).

Goesaert v. Cleary (1948)

In this case the U.S. Supreme Court upheld the constitutionality of a Michigan law under which women could not be licensed as bartenders unless they were related to male bar owners. The court accepted the state's contention that bartending presented dangers from which women could be protected only by a male relative. Interestingly, tavern waitresses were not considered to be in peril and were permitted to work without restriction.

Protective legislation of this kind that bars women from taking specific jobs has now been superseded by laws forbidding employers to discriminate on the basis of sex, beginning with the Civil Rights Act of 1964. But laws that bar women from jobs that might damage their reproductive systems or fetuses are still being tested.

See also Civil Rights Act of 1964; *Muller v. Oregon*; Protective Legislation; *Radice v. New York*; Separate Spheres; Sticky Floor; *UAW v. Johnson Controls*.

References Judith A. Baer, *Women in American Law* (1991); Susan Gluck Mezey, *In Pursuit of Equality: Women, Public Policy and the Federal Courts* (1992).

Goldman, Emma (1869–1940)

This anarchist lecturer earned her living through much of her life by manual labor and as a midwife. Born in Russia and educated mostly in Prussia, she went to work in 1881 in a glove factory but continued to read widely. In 1885 she immigrated to the United States. An unhappy marriage in 1887 to colleague factory worker Jacob Kersner ended in divorce but gave her American citizenship.

Moving to New York City in 1889, Goldman flung herself into the anarchist movement, advocating that the hungry steal and the oppressed attack the oppressors—even abetting such an attack. (In later years she backed away from the use of violence.) Always she bravely and passionately defended free speech. She

Emma Goldman

argued against marriage in favor of love freely given between mature men and women. She recommended birth control, openly though illicitly distributing birth control information. During World War I she spoke out against conscription. In short, she fought on every conceivable front for the total freedom of the individual from authority. Even while espousing such controversial ideas, she gained popularity as a lecturer.

Her speeches landed her in jail more than once. In 1908 the United States took away her citizenship and in 1919 deported her. She spent the rest of her life in Europe; in 1925 she married miner James Colton to acquire British citizenship.

See also Anarchism; Midwives.

References Richard Drinnon, *Rebel in Paradise: A Biography of Emma Goldman* (1961); Emma Goldman, *Living My Life* (1931); Edward T. James et al., eds., *Notable American Women II* (1971).

Goldmark, Josephine Clara (1877–1950)

This social researcher and publicist began her professional career in 1903 as publica-

tions secretary of the Consumers' League and chair of its committee for legal defense of labor laws. Her reputation rests on her meticulous studies of particular social and labor problems that provided data for legislative and court action. Her compilation of medical, economic, and social data relating to the effects of long working hours on women workers provided Louis D. Brandeis (her brother-in-law and future Supreme Court Justice) with the material for his successful defense before the U.S. Supreme Court of Oregon's legislation setting maximum working hours for women (*Muller v. Oregon*, 1908). Her career is marked by many such studies, in which she marshaled facts in support of efforts to protect workers' welfare. Thus her investigation of the Triangle Shirtwaist fire (1911) led to recommendations to protect the safety of factory workers. Her study (1923) of the nursing profession stressed the need for higher standards in nursing education and provided the factual basis for sweeping reforms.

See also Consumers' League; *Muller v. Oregon*; Nurses; Triangle Shirtwaist Fire.

Reference Edward T. James et al., eds., *Notable American Women II* (1971).

Government Workers

Federal, state, and local governments employ huge numbers of women. Beginning with the Civil War the federal government recruited them to replace men who had gone to war and to save money—a move imitated by state and municipal governments in the early twentieth century.

In 1870 the civil service opened some examinations to women, and by 1893 almost a third of employees in federal offices in Washington were women. Although white women gradually eroded civil-service discrimination, women were still barred from 64 percent of the exams for scientific and professional positions until after World War I: 87 percent of those for mechanical and manufacturing positions, and 15 percent of those for clerical positions. In 1919, the civil service opened all examinations to both women and men. The Classification Act of 1924 moved toward equal pay for equal work. But department heads still reserved the right to designate jobs for males or females. And the civil service discriminated against blacks until World War II.

In the 1990s civil-service examinations, fairly administered, control promotions, but access to the examinations may be difficult, particularly for women. Many of the jobs women hold offer little upward mobility. Veterans, 94 percent of whom are male, enjoy an advantage in competitive examinations. In 1990 women held only 31.3 percent of high-level state and local government jobs; African-American women held only 5.1 percent of top managerial positions.

As researcher Catherine White Berheide has pointed out, most women in state and local government worry more about the sticky floor, which keeps them from moving up from their low-wage, low-mobility jobs, than about the glass ceiling far above their heads. In 1990 in state and local governments women were concentrated in administrative support (clerical) jobs, where they constituted 87.4 percent of all workers, and among paraprofessionals (e.g., home health care aides and child support workers), where they made up 72.3 percent of the workers. Fifty-five percent of the approximately three million women in state and local government jobs work in the lowest-paying employment categories (under $20,000 a year, even after ten years of experience), versus 25 percent of men. Women of color are overrepresented here. Once a worker enters at these levels, she can advance only with the greatest difficulty. (*New York Times*, 11 November 1992)

Government employees outdo all other women in unionization by more than two to one. In 1985 unions and associations represented more than 40 percent of the 7.7 million women in the public sector.

With this critical mass unionized, public-sector women figure prominently in the struggle for better working conditions for women.

When toward the end of the nineteenth century women moved into the public arena, they began to hold local and state political appointments and elected offices. Jeannette Rankin was elected to the Congress in 1916, even before women's suffrage was federally enacted, and other women followed her after the ratification of the 19th amendment in 1920. Nellie Tayloe Ross succeeded her husband as governor of Wyoming in 1924, the first woman governor, and later served as the first woman director of the United States Mint. Patricia Roberts Harris was the first African-American woman ambassador, appointed to Luxembourg by Lyndon Johnson in 1965, and the first African-American woman in the president's cabinet, appointed secretary of housing and urban development by Jimmy Carter in 1977. When in 1972 African-American Congresswoman Shirley Chisholm declared herself a candidate for president of the United States, she prepared the way for Geraldine Ferraro's 1984 vice-presidential candidacy on the Democratic ticket. (The flamboyant Victoria Claflin Woodhull, who with her sister was one of the first American women to own a brokerage firm, had been nominated for the presidency in 1872 by the Radical Reformers party, which she had just founded. In 1884 and again in 1888 Belva Lockwood ran as the National Equal Rights party's candidate for president.) In 1974 Ella Grasso was elected governor of Connecticut, the first woman governor not preceded by her husband. Sandra Day O'Connor, appointed by Ronald Reagan in 1981, broke the barrier against women on the U.S. Supreme Court. In 1992 Texas had more than 100 women mayors. And in that year Tammy Baldwin became the first openly lesbian or gay candidate elected to the Wisconsin state legislature. (*National NOW Times*, January 1993)

The 1992 elections, 20 years after the outbreak of political activism of women in the 1970s, saw several of them prepared to run for high office. Four women won Senate seats, increasing women's representation there to six: Barbara Boxer and Diane Feinstein were elected the two senators from California. In the House of Representatives women raised their presence by almost 70 percent, from 28 to 47. Women also gained slightly in state legislatures, by about 2 percent. Seventy-one women now hold statewide elected offices at the executive level, a share of a little over 20 percent. (*New York Times*, 8 November 1992) Women, however, still constitute only 6 percent of the Senate, 10.8 percent of the House, and about 20 percent of the state legislatures. (*Chronicle of Higher Education*, 18 November 1992)

Minority women are gradually working their way into high governmental positions. In 1987 Wilma Mankiller became the first woman head of the Cherokee nation. In 1989 Ileana Ros-Lehtinen became the first Cuban American ever elected to Congress; Julia Chang Bloch became the first American ambassador of Asian descent; and Antonia Novello became the first woman and the first Hispanic American appointed Surgeon General. In 1991 Patricia F. Saiki took office as head of the Small Business Administration, the first Asian American in that position; Sharon Pratt Dixon was elected the first woman mayor of Washington, D.C.; and Unita Blackwell, mayor of a town of only 300 people, was the first woman to preside over the National Association of Black Mayors.

The movement of women into state and federal offices has been slow. In 1989, for instance, fewer women held appointed state cabinet posts than in 1988; however, the passions aroused by the women's issues of the 1990s, such as sexual harassment and the right of choice to birth control and abortion, may promote the election and appointment of more women at all levels. Besides the nonpartisan National Women's Political Caucus, each of the major parties in the 1990s has an organization to raise money for women candidates: the Republicans' WISH (Women in the Senate and House), and the Democrats' Emily's List (Early Money Is Like Yeast). As women move into elected offices, they gain power to appoint other women; for example, Governor Ann Richards appointed Lena Guerrero the first woman on the Texas Railroad Commission, which had long controlled the world price of oil. In 1990 the State Department signed a consent decree agreeing to recompense in some degree women denied appointments and honors because they were female.

See also Adams, Annette A.; Barnard, Kate; Barton, Clara; Bellanca, Dorothy Jacobs; Chisholm, Shirley St. Hill; Civil War; Dewson, Mary Williams; Edson, Katherine Philips; Ferraro, Geraldine; Glass Ceiling; Harris, Patricia Roberts; Hills, Carla Anderson; Hobby, Oveta Culp; Ickes, Anna Wilmarth Thompson; Jordan, Barbara; Kirkpatrick, Jeanne J.; Kreps, Juanita Morris; Law Enforcement; McCormick, Ruth Hanna; Martin, Anne Henrietta; Moskowitz, Belle Lindener Israels; Norton, Mary Teresa Hopkins; O'Connor, Sandra Day; O'Day, Caroline Love Goodwin; Perkins, Frances; Rankin, Jeannette Pickering; Ray, Dixy Lee; Roosevelt, Anna Eleanor; Sexual Harassment; Smith, Charlotte; Sticky Floor; Swartz, Maud O'Farrell; Valesh, Eva MacDonald; Veterans' Preference; Woodbury, Helen Laura Sumner; Woodward, Ellen Sullivan; World War I; World War II.

References James D. Barber and Barbara Kellerman, *Women Leaders in American Politics* (1986); Center for the American Woman and Politics Staff, comp., *Women in Public Office: A Biographical Directory and Statistical Analysis* (1978); Susan M. Hartmann, *From Margin to Mainstream: American Women and Politics since 1960* (1989); Frank P. Le-Veness and Jane P. Sweeney, eds., *Women Leaders in Contemporary U.S. Politics* (1987); Joan McCullough, *First of All* (1980); Celia Morris, *Storming the Status House: Running for Governor with Ann Richards and Dianne Feinstein* (1992); Carolyn Mulford, *Elizabeth Dole, Public Servant* (1992); Albert J. Nelson, *Emerging Influentials in State Legislatures: Women, Blacks, and Hispanics* (1991); Norma M. Riccucci, *Women, Minorities, and Unions in the Public Sector* (1990); Paula Ries and Anne J. Stone, eds., *The American Woman, 1992–93: A Status Report* (1992); Sharon Hartman Strom, *Beyond the Typewriter: Gender, Class, and the Origins of Modern American Office Work, 1900–1930* (1992); *Women in Congress, 1917–1990* (1991).

Graham, Martha (1894–1992)

This dancer and choreographer, who from 1926 until her death headed her own dance company, changed the course of modern dance. She developed a technique based on contraction and release of the torso and the dancer's relationship to the ground.

She attended the Cumnock School of Expression in California and joined the company of Denishawn, headed by Ruth St. Denis and Ted Shawn, with whom she debuted at 22. After appearing in the Greenwich Village Follies and teaching at the Eastman School of Dance in Rochester, New York, she gave her first concert in New York City. There she built her career, teaching privately and in the Neighborhood Playhouse and gradually putting together her own company. Although she gave up dancing in her 70s, she continued to choreograph and to teach throughout her long and productive life.

See also Dancers; St. Denis, Ruth.

Martha Graham with partner Bertram Ross in 1961

References Martha Graham, *Blood Memory* (1991); Jennifer S. Uglow, comp. and ed., *International Dictionary of Women's Biography* (1985).

Great Depression (1929–1939)

The stock market crash in the fall of 1929 initiated the longest and most severe depression in the history of the United States. By 1933 a quarter to a third of the labor force could not find work, the private agencies and municipalities on which Americans had always depended for relief and charity had long since run out of funds, and people literally fainted in the streets from hunger. Despite the vigorous economic experiments of Franklin D. Roosevelt's New Deal for almost a decade, the unemployment rate failed to drop below 20 percent until World War II demanded new production. The Great Depression's significance for women was ambiguous.

Ironically, during the Depression employers often chose women over men workers as cheap labor, while simultaneously society criticized women for taking jobs away from men. Propagandists concocted slogans like "Don't steal a job from a man." Twenty-six states prohibited employing married women. Serious writers like Norman Cousins proposed firing *all* women workers and replacing them with men, on the grounds that women shouldn't be working anyway. Public and private employers often refused to hire married women or fired them when they married. But light industry and service sectors of the economy that demanded women workers recovered faster than the heavy industries. Unions watching these trends grew more interested in organizing women.

But many of the New Deal efforts to relieve the unemployment and suffering of the Great Depression were directed solely toward men. As Meridel LeSueur noted in "Women on the Breadlines" (*New Masses*, January 1932), "It's one of the great mysteries of the city where women go when they are out of work and hungry. There are not many women in the bread line. There are no flop houses for women as there are for men, where a bed can be had for a quarter or less. You don't see women lying on the floor at the mission in the free flops. They obviously don't sleep in the jungle [camps created by homeless men] or under newspapers in the park. There is no law I suppose against their being in these places but the fact is they rarely are. Yet there must be as many women out of jobs in cities and suffering extreme poverty as there are men."

The National Industrial Recovery Act (NIRA) codes, despite their blatant sex discrimination in paying boys more than widows with dependent children for similar work, inadvertently raised women's wages faster than men's by significantly increasing minimum wages in industry—the lowest-paid sectors where so many women toiled. Similarly, NIRA administrators cut the normal work week of many unskilled women from 54 to 40 hours. By 1935, when NIRA was declared unconstitutional, women as well as men were protected by many industry-wide negotiated contracts.

In the long run the Great Depression and the New Deal solidified women's position in the marketplace, lowering the barriers between male and female jobs, and extending protective labor legislation from women only to men as well.

See also Minimum Wage; National Industrial Recovery Act; New Deal; Protective Labor Legislation; Sex Discrimination; Unions; White House Conference on the Emergency Needs of Women.

References Melvin Dubofsky and Stephen Burwood, eds., *Women and Minorities during the Great Depression: Selected Articles on Gender, Race, and Ethnicity* (1990); Alice Kessler-Harris, *Out To Work: A History of Wage-Earning Women in the United States* (1982); Louis Scharf, *To Work and To Wed: Female Employment and the Great Depression* (1980); Susan Ware, *Beyond Suffrage: Women in the New Deal* (1981); Susan Ware, *Holding Their Own: American Women in the 1930s* (1982); Susan Ware, *Modern American Women: A Documentary History* (1989).

Great Migration
See Black Americans.

Great Strikes of California
See Cannery and Agricultural Workers Industrial Union.

Greeley-Smith, Nixola (1880–1919)
This journalist worked briefly for the *St. Louis Post-Dispatch* but returned to New York City to work for the *Evening World* until her death. She was particularly successful in appealing to the woman reader; her forte was the personal interview. She was known at the time as one of journalism's most distinguished women.
See also Journalists.
Reference Ishbel Ross, *Ladies of the Press* (1974).

Green, Hetty Howland Robinson (1834–1916)
This "Witch of Wall Street," in her time "the richest woman in America," noted for her financial acumen and eccentricity, inherited a fortune accumulated in whaling and foreign trade and multiplied it, turning $10 million into $100 million. She grew up reading the financial pages to her grandfather and then her father. A hard-nosed woman brought up with the necessity of protecting her money, she married an older millionaire in 1867 and bore two children. After 1874 she devoted herself to her money, concentrating brilliantly on real estate. She was a shrewd woman without a sense of proportion.

When her husband went bankrupt in 1885, she refused to underwrite his debts, and a separation ensued. The miserly woman sought medical care for herself and her children at free clinics, wore rags, and lived in near-slums.
See also Entrepreneurs.
References Edward T. James et al., eds., *Notable American Women II* (1971); Boyden Sparkes and Samuel T. Moore, *Hetty Green: A Woman Who Loved Money* (1930); Jennifer S. Uglow, comp. and ed., *International Dictionary of Women's Biography* (1985).

Grievances

Enforcement of labor legislation (e.g. antidiscrimination and fair labor practices laws) depends largely upon individuals who believe they have a case and are willing to file a grievance with the appropriate agency or sue in the courts. Federal agencies like the Equal Employment Opportunity Commission may initiate cases if the agency heads (or the president who appointed them) are willing to be aggressive, which cannot always be counted on. Women employees who have cause to file a grievance face obstacles: the disapproval of employers and co-workers, unwelcome publicity, sacrifice of privacy, and hostile cross-examinations. Labor law is highly technical and subject to frequent change, and persons with a grievance are generally well-advised to seek legal counsel. Many employers provide in-house agencies to handle grievances, which employees should use in a good-will effort to find a remedy for the complaint. When these fail or in their absence, women have chalked up successes through the courts, by going public and influencing opinion, and by lobbying for legal protection.

See also Equal Employment Opportunity Commission.

References Judith A. Baer, *Women in American Law: The Struggle toward Equality from the New Deal to the Present* (1991); Wayne N. Outten with Noah A. Kinigstein, *The Rights of Employees* (1983); Michael Yates, *Labor Law Handbook* (1987).

Griggs v. Duke Power Company (1971)

The issue in this case was whether the Duke Power Company could require workers to pass professionally developed tests in lieu of a high school diploma to qualify for employment or to transfer to another department. The U.S. Supreme Court found that both the tests and the educational requirement were unrelated to work on the job and had a disparate impact on women and minorities. Thus the test and educational requirements, although appearing neutral, were in fact discriminatory.

In *Griggs* the plaintiffs were black employees of the power company, but the principle it enunciated set the stage for later cases where an ostensibly neutral requirement proved restrictive on women's employment opportunities.

See also Bona Fide Occupational Qualification; Disparate Impact; Tests.

Reference Susan Gluck Mezey, *In Pursuit of Equality: Women, Public Policy and the Federal Courts* (1992).

Guerrilla Girls

These witty and inventive New York women artists began operations in the 1980s to improve opportunities for women in art. They put before the public the facts about the lack of attention paid to women artists in shows, museum space, and reviews. They keep their identities secret: wearing gorilla costumes, they may overnight placard the city with posters lampooning the male art establishment. In 1993 they began to publish a journal.

See also Artists.

GUERRILLA GIRLS' POP QUIZ.

Q. If February is Black History Month and March is Women's History Month, what happens the rest of the year?

A. Discrimination.

GUERRILLA GIRLS CONSCIENCE OF THE ART WORLD

A poster designed by the Guerrilla Girls

Hackley, Emma Azalia Smith (1867–1922)

This black singer and choir director was born in Tennessee, grew up in Detroit, graduated from normal school, and then began to teach. In 1894 she married lawyer and editor Edwin Henry Hackley and moved to Denver, where she earned a bachelor's degree in music. For a few years she directed choirs and edited the women's section of her husband's newspaper, but in 1901 she left her husband and settled in Philadelphia.

Hackley carved a substantial career for herself as a singer, choral director, and music educator in Philadelphia, Chicago, and New York. She studied abroad and toured extensively in the United States. She also devoted her talents, influence, and energies to the advancement of black musicians, including Marian Anderson. She toured black organizations, schools, and musical associations, giving lectures and recitals. From 1912–1916 she tried to establish the Vocal Normal Institute in Chicago, only to be defeated by financial problems. She organized "Folk Song Festivals" in black churches and schools throughout the country.

See also Anderson, Marian; Musicians.

References Maude Cuney-Hare, *Negro Musicians and Their Music* (1936); M. Marguerite Davenport, *Azalia* (1947); Edward T. James et al., eds., *Notable American Women II* (1971).

Hale, Sarah Josepha Buell (1788–1879)

This magazine editor, a native of New Hampshire, was educated at home and at about age 18 opened her own school. In 1813 she married lawyer David Hale, but their happy marriage ended with his death in 1822. Left with five children to support, Hale opened a millinery shop and began to write. Her fiction and verse brought her an offer to edit a monthly woman's magazine that the Reverend John Lauris Blake proposed to establish.

Hale moved to Boston, where she edited the *Ladies' Magazine* (later the *American Ladies' Magazine*) for 13 years, filling it with articles on peace and "woman's sphere," and, unlike other editors, printing only original contributions. As editor of *Godey's Lady's Book* from 1837 to 1877 she combined business acumen with an unerring understanding of her readers' taste. Although highly traditional in her concept of woman's role in society (marriage and children represented woman's divinely appointed sphere), she did not entirely ignore some of the problems facing her sex as the country industrialized and urbanized and as more women entered the workplace. Moreover she consistently promoted education for women and believed that women, not men, should teach the young. She advocated exercise, proper diet, and sensible dress for women. By 1854 she was actually urging the necessity for all women to learn to support themselves. And she eventually backed the movement to win property rights for married women. In all cases though, she and *Godey's* preached caution rather than agitation for reforms.

See also Journalists.

References Isabelle Webb Entrikin, *Sarah Josepha Hale and "Godey's Lady's Book"* (1946); Ruth E. Finley, *The Lady of Godey's* (1931); Edward T. James et al., eds., *Notable American Women II* (1971).

Haley, Margaret Angela (1861–1939)

This teacher and union official, a native of Illinois, began her career at 15. By 1881 a teacher in Chicago, she soon joined the Chicago Teacher's Federation, in which for almost 40 years, from 1901 until her death, she was to serve as the full-time, salaried business agent. Under her leadership the federation became an effective political force, obtaining tenure for teachers, a pension system, and a voice through teachers' councils in determining school curriculum and discipline. She worked closely with the labor movement, was an organizer for the American Federation of Teachers, and in 1919 served on the executive committee of the newly formed Labor party along with Agnes Nestor. Throughout her career she fought for the welfare of teachers, a commitment that inevitably involved her in confrontations with Chicago's political machine. In 1850 Haley published *Woman's Record: or Sketches of All Distinguished Women, from 'the Beginning' till A.D. 1850.*

See also American Federation of Teachers; Nestor, Agnes; Teachers; Unions.

Reference Edward T. James et al., eds., *Notable American Women II* (1971).

Hamilton, Alice (1869–1970)

This physician pioneered industrial toxicology. A stimulating environment in her Indiana home endowed her with wit, moral earnestness, and high aspirations. Since she needed to support herself, she chose to study medicine at the University of Michigan and to intern at the Northwestern Hospital for Women and Children in Minneapolis and the New England Hospital for Women and Children, with postdoctoral studies at Michigan, in Germany, and at Johns Hopkins.

Accepting an appointment at Northwestern University's Women's Medical School, she moved into Hull House, where she lived and worked with Jane Addams, Julia Lathrop, and Florence Kelley. In 1902 she took a post as a bacteriologist at the Memorial Institute for Infectious Diseases, continuing her study and research.

After this long preparation she found her vocation in industrial diseases. In 1908 she began work on them for the state of Illinois, and in 1911 she became a special investigator for the federal government, concentrating first on the lead trades and later on rubber and munitions plants. Her brilliance and tact in working with employers changed their practices.

During World War I she focused on munitions industries. About 1920 she accepted a half-time position as assistant professor of industrial medicine at Harvard, its first woman professor. She continued to work also as consultant and advocate for industrial health reform, no longer needing to pioneer but now an established authority in the field she had created, and consequently forced to devote more of her time to administrative, political, and public relations functions. Her *Industrial Poisons in the United States* (1925), however, showed her still working on the cutting edge. After her forced retirement from Harvard in 1935, she became a consultant in the federal Division of Labor Standards.

From 1944–1949 she served as president of the Consumers' League, wrote her autobiography, and revised her 1934 textbook *Industrial Toxicology*. In her old age she had earned the right to say: "For me the satisfaction is that things are better now, and I had some part in it."

See also Consumers' League; Hull House; Kelley, Florence; Physicians; World War I.

References Alice Hamilton, *Exploring the Dangerous Trades* (1943); Barbara Sicherman, *Alice Hamilton: A Life in Letters* (1984); Barbara Sicherman et al., eds., *Notable American Women: The Modern Period* (1980).

Hamilton, Gordon (1892–1967)

This social work educator, a native of New Jersey, was educated at home and at Bryn Mawr. During World War I she worked for the Red Cross in Colorado and thereafter moved to New York, where she began her career in social work. She wielded her greatest influence during her 34 years on the faculty of the New York School of Social Work, where she mentored generations of social workers, and where she wrote her *Theory and Practice of Social Casework*. This important 1940 text focused on delivering concrete services; her 1951 revision added a concern for treating psychological problems.

See also Social Workers.

Reference Barbara Sicherman et al., eds., *Notable American Women: The Modern Period* (1980).

Harris, Patricia Roberts (1924–1985)

Attorney Patricia Harris was the first African-American woman ambassador, appointed to Luxembourg by Lyndon Johnson in 1965; and the first African-American woman in the president's cabinet, appointed Secretary of Housing and Urban Development by Jimmy Carter in 1977. In this cabinet post she initiated a drive to prevent discrimination against women seeking mortgage loans. In 1979 she became Secretary of Health, Education, and Welfare.

Educated at Howard University, the University of Chicago, American University, and George Washington University law school, she participated in the civil rights movement as a student. She worked for the Young Women's Christian Association from 1946 to 1949, and for the American Council on Human Rights from 1949 to 1953. After her marriage to William Harris in 1955 and a brief stint with the U.S. Department of Justice, she taught at Howard University law school; she retired from Howard to accept a partnership in a Washington law firm.

See also Attorneys; Government Workers; Young Women's Christian Association.

Reference Jennifer S. Uglow, comp and ed., *International Dictionary of Women's Biography* (1985).

Harvey Girls

These young women, mostly unmarried and always white, worked as waitresses in the chain of restaurants established by Fred Harvey along the Acheson, Topeka, and Santa Fe Railroad. From the 1880s until its decline after World War II, the Harvey system provided employment for tens of thousands of women. The company ensured their respectability at a time when waitressing was generally considered a socially inferior occupation, especially in the western regions served by the railroad, where public suspicion of waitresses was heightened by the high male-female ratio and the abundance of dance halls with their serving girls. In this set-

ting, the Harvey Girls set unusual standards of businesslike, professional service; their personal lives and conduct were regulated to eliminate public criticism of single girls working far from home and to calm the fears of the young women being hired (and their apprehensive parents). The girls were required to live in the clean, decent dormitories provided by their employer and were forbidden to wear makeup, chew gum, wear jewelry, or socialize with the male help. In return, they were treated well in terms of compensation and job security.

It was an exciting experience for the women, most of whom were recruited from eastern cities and communities. Many of them married railroad men, settled in the west, and became pillars of the community.

See also Lowell Girls; Mercer Girls; Waltham System.

Reference Lesley Poling-Kempes, *The Harvey Girls: Women Who Opened the West* (1989).

Hawes, Elizabeth (1903–1971)

This fashion designer, writer, and union organizer was a native of New Jersey. During her life she jumbled together her many interests.

In 1930 she embarked on a short-lived marriage to Ralph Jester, a sculptor; they were divorced in 1935. In 1937 she married film and theater director Joseph Losey and a year later bore a son; this marriage ended in 1944.

As a youngster of ten she began to make clothes and sell them; after she graduated from Vassar in 1925 with a degree in economics, she worked in Paris studying the fashion business and reporting on fashions. She opened her own business in the United States in 1928. In 1931 she became the first American designer to show a collection in Paris. As business flourished, she began a ready-to-wear line. A conviction that manufacturers changed fashions solely to increase sales disillusioned her, and she persuaded herself that the day of the ready-to-wear dress was ended. Accordingly she closed her business in 1940. The course of Hawes's thinking about fashion was reflected in her journalism for the *New Yorker* and *PM* and her books *Fashion Is Spinach* and *Why Is a Dress?*

From fashion Hawes moved on to war work at an aeronautical plant, where she supported union organizing efforts and wrote a book *Why Women Cry* based on her observations there. In 1944 she took a job with the United Auto Workers in Detroit, an experience that led to her book *Hurry Up Please It's Time*, urging working women to assert themselves.

In 1948 and 1952 Hawes made stabs at getting back into the fashion industry; they missed. But even in 1954 she was pleading with women in *It's Still Spinach* to be their own arbiters of fashion.

See also Entrepreneurs; Union Organizers.
Reference Barbara Sicherman et al., eds., *Notable American Women: The Modern Period* (1980).

Heads of Household

In 1990 women headed 11 million families, or 45 percent of black families, 23 percent of Latino families, and 13 percent of white families. Of all these women, 87 percent were in the work force. Their median annual income was $13,718, when the poverty level for a family of three was $10,060.

Reference Nine to Five, National Association of Working Women, "Profile of Working Women" (1990).

Healey, Dorothy (b. 1914)

Born in Colorado, Dorothy Healey joined the American Communist party in 1928 and became one of the few women to rise to a position of leadership, serving as leader of the Los Angeles district for over 20 years and as a member of the party's national committee. She was involved in the labor struggles of the migrant workers in California in the 1930s, a strike leader, and a political activist. Increasingly critical of the authoritarianism of the party and its subservience to the Soviet Union, she resigned in 1973.

See also Communist Party; Flynn, Elizabeth Gurley.
Reference Dorothy Healey and Maurice Isserman, *Dorothy Healey Remembers* (1990).

Health Hazards

Women in the workplace face both hazards specific to them, especially hazards to their reproductive health, and hazards common to both genders.

Bloodborne diseases threaten women particularly because so many of them are teachers and nurses, occupations with high exposure to body fluids, and because infections may cause severe consequences during pregnancy. These women run special risks of contracting other communicable diseases, such as measles and tuberculosis. But with women in so many diverse occupations employing new technology, more threats to their health have inevitably risen, from emanations from computer monitors and carpal tunnel syndrome for clerical workers to unexplored dangers presented by computer chips and toxic chemicals.

For instance, with millions of workers operating video display terminals, complaints of health problems have mounted. Workers report eye problems, stress, and pain and strain in back, neck, arms, and wrists. Some women computer operators have reported reproductive problems, for which no cause is known. Electronic monitoring may increase stress and fatigue. Good work-station design and illumination and frequent breaks may alleviate some of these difficulties. Engineers are now experimenting with redesigned keyboards, some of them vertical, some hollowed out, many widely separating the two hands.

Employers' justifiable fears about hiring women for jobs that may damage their reproductive systems or their fetuses clash with laws against sex discrimination. Court cases result, as in *UAW v. Johnson Controls*.

See also Clerical Workers; Electronic Monitoring; Fetal Protection Policies; Occupational Safety and Health Administration; Pregnancy; Pregnancy Discrimination Act of 1978; Sex Discrimination; *UAW v. Johnson Controls.*

References Wendy Chavkin, ed., *Double Exposure: Women's Health Hazards on the Job and at Home* (1984); Steve Fox, *Toxic Work: Women Workers at GTE Lenkurt* (1991); M. Frankenhauser et al., eds., *Women, Work, and Health* (1991); Regina H. Kenen, *Reproductive Hazards in the Workplace: Mending Jobs, Managing Pregnancies* (1992); Randy Rabinowitz, *Is Your Job Making You Sick?: A CLUW Handbook on Workplace Hazards* (n.d.).

Health Insurance

In the last quarter of the twentieth century, health insurance costs have been soaring. Government, business, and even health care providers now recognize a crisis. In response hard-pressed employers have created new forms of health insurance that seek to limit unnecessary use of doctors and hospitals, reduce coverage, shift the responsibility of the employee's spouse to the employee, or require employees to pick up part of the costs. (*New York Times,* 10 January 1993)

Consequently the proportion of workers holding health insurance through their jobs has been declining, and workers pay an increasingly high percentage of the cost. More men than women hold health insurance through their jobs, though this figure is skewed because working wives are often included on their husbands' policies. The decline in this benefit between 1980 and 1987 has been particularly notable among Hispanics, where it has fallen nearly 17 percentage points for men and nearly 7 for women. American reliance on private and employer-provided health insurance has left millions inadequately covered or completely uncovered.

The Consolidated Omnibus Budget Reconciliation Act of 1986 (COBRA) provides the possibility of continuing existing health insurance for unemployed workers and their families, for spouses and dependent children of retiring workers, and for displaced homemakers. Such persons may continue the same coverage at the group rate of the policies that formerly covered them, *provided* they pay the premiums.

The continuing escalation of health care costs, however, threatens the ability of ever more employers to provide health insurance. By the end of 1989, the average United States employer's medical benefit costs had increased to more than 13 percent of payroll, versus 5 percent of payroll in 1979.

See also Benefits; Consolidated Omnibus Budget Reconciliation Act; Displaced Homemakers.

References Susan Gluck Mezey, *In Pursuit of Equality: Women, Public Policy and the Federal Courts* (1992); Paula Ries and Anne J. Stone, eds., *The American Woman, 1992–93: A Status Report* (1992).

Health Professionals and Paraprofessionals

Women have always assumed much of the responsibility for the care of the sick and wounded. In the twentieth century they have diversified and professionalized the kinds of work they do in this area.

Some experts see the application of that principle of scientific management as a necessary element in the containment of health costs whereby work is performed at the least cost and at the lowest skill level practically possible. Some experts estimate that 75–80 percent of primary adult care and 90 percent of pediatric primary care could be safely entrusted to health professionals other than physicians. A whole hierarchy of people trained in medicine already exists. Except for physicians and physicians' assistants, most of them are women: nurse practitioners, midwives, nurse specialists, registered nurses, licensed practical nurses, paramedics, home health aides, psychiatric therapists, occupational therapists, physical therapists, speech therapists, medical social workers, medical records keepers, laboratory technicians, and others.

Although certainly in the minds of physicians these professions are hierarchically arranged, with physicians at the top of the pyramid, power struggles have inevitably arisen. The nurse or midwife or therapist or social worker or pharmacist often spends more time with the patient, knows the patient's circumstances better, and knows a great deal more than the physician about breast-feeding or speech problems or nutrition or the side-effects of combinations of drugs. In some cases these women offer a level of care and concern superior to that of physicians, partly because of their concentration in relatively few areas and partly because of their empathy for their women patients. For example, in 1986 the Congressional Office of Technology Assessment concluded that the quality of certified midwifery care was just as good as that provided by physicians and recommended the expansion of midwifery services. In December 1989, the *New England Journal of Medicine* reported that in birth centers, 73 percent of which were run by midwives, pregnancy outcomes were as good as those of hospitals and Caesarean-section rates much lower.

Dr. Susan Hayhurst was America's first woman pharmacist; she was already a physician when she earned her degree from the Philadelphia College of Pharmacy in 1883. In 1989 women constituted almost a third of all pharmacists, and in 1988 they earned almost 60 percent of the degrees awarded in the field. (*New York Times*, 18 October 1992)

America's first woman dentist was Dr. Emeline Roberts Jones, who in 1855 apprenticed to her dentist husband and later became his partner, continuing their practice after he died. Lucy Beaman Hobbs Taylor was the first woman to earn a dental degree. In 1989, although women constituted only 8.6 percent of dentists, they earned almost 25 percent of dentistry degrees awarded. According to the American Dental Association, the numbers of women in dental schools rose by 22.9 percent between 1983–1984 and 1992–1993, so that the later 1990s will see some increase over the 13,000 women dentists of 1993.

In 1903 Mignon Nicholson became the first woman veterinarian in the United States, graduating from McKillip College. In 1910 Elinor McGrath graduated from the Chicago Veterinary College and Florence Kimball from Cornell University. By 1936, 30 women had earned the degree of doctor of veterinary medicine. As late as 1963 the rosters showed only 277 women veterinarians. But about that time the profession recognized a growing need for veterinarians, and veterinary school enrollment surged—particularly the enrollment of women: from 1976–1986 total student enrollment increased by 2,648, and the number of female students by 3,397. More women are on the way: veterinary school enrollments in 1990–1991 showed about 60 percent women. More women than men go on to graduate work.

In the late twentieth century women have moved into the profession at a rate unprecedented not only for veterinarians but also for any such previously male-dominated profession. Of the 46,594 veterinarians in 1991, about 25 percent are women. Of veterinarians in private practice, in 1991 men averaged $57,502 and women $47,725; of those in public or corporate practice, men averaged $64,450 and women $43,962. Contributing factors to this disparity are the higher tendency of men than of women to own their own practices and the greater youth of women: since women entered the profession recently, they tend to be about ten years younger than men. Moreover, many women go into the relatively low-paid areas of small-animal practice and university teaching.

See also Midwives; Nurses; Physicians; Pinkham, Lydia Estes; Professional Women; Psychologists and Psychiatrists; Scientific Management; Slagle, Eleanor Clarke; Social Workers; Taylor, Lucy Beaman Hobbs.

References Jeanne Achterberg, *Woman as Healer* (1991); Rima D. Apple, ed., *Women, Health and Medicine in America* (1990); Center for Information Management, American Veterinary Medicine Association, "Economic Report on Veterinarians and Veterinary Medicine" (1993); Sue Drum and H. Ellen Whiteley, *Women in Veterinary Medicine*

(1992); Joan McCullough, *First of All* (1980); Paula Ries and Anne J. Stone, eds., *The American Woman, 1992–93: A Status Report* (1992).

Henrotin, Ellen Martin (1847–1922)

This club leader and labor reformer grew up and was educated in Connecticut and Europe. In 1868 she married Chicago financier Charles Henrotin; in this marriage she bore three sons. Activity in women's clubs led to an interest in social reform and women's issues. Her important contributions to the feminist emphasis of the 1893 Columbian Exposition led to her 1894 election as president of the General Federation of Women's Clubs, where she used her influence to win widespread support among women for improved labor conditions, among other reforms.

In her later years she interested herself particularly in women in industry, serving as president of the Women's Trade Union League from 1904–1907 and publicizing the horrifying conditions under which women and children then labored. She also concerned herself with the problems of prostitution and white slavery, advocating sex hygiene education in the schools.

See also Prostitutes; White Slavery; Women's Trade Union League.

Reference Edward T. James et al., eds., *Notable American Women II* (1971).

Henry, Alice (1857–1943)

Australian-born, Henry began her American career as a woman's union leader and labor journalist in 1906 when she became office secretary of the Chicago branch of the Women's Trade Union League (WTUL). She served the league in various ways: on a committee investigating conditions among women in the brewery industry, whose report did much to improve conditions and increase union membership; as author of a history of women and trade unionism; as field worker and union organizer; and as editor of the WTUL's magazine *Life and Labor* (1911–1915). Her concern for workers' education is represented in her service as director of the WTUL's training program of labor leaders in Chicago, and her work in planning and directing the Bryn Mawr Summer School for Women Workers in 1921.

See also Bryn Mawr Summer School for Women Workers; Union Organizers; Unions; Women's Trade Union League; Workers' Education.

References Jennifer S. Uglow, comp and ed., *International Dictionary of Women's Biography* (1985); Edward T. James et al., eds., *Notable American Women II* (1971).

Herrick, Elinore Morehouse (1895–1964)

This journalist and labor relations expert grew up in Massachusetts. She supported her undergraduate work at Barnard and journalism courses at Columbia by working as a cub reporter for the *New York World*. In 1916 she married Horace Terhune Herrick, a chemical engineer; in this marriage she bore two sons.

When her marriage dissolved about 1920, she had to work in factories to support her family. She moved up rapidly to the position of production manager, but there she hit a glass ceiling. In 1927 she managed to resume her college education at Antioch College, while she and her mother ran a boarding house and Herrick worked as administrative assistant to the college president and moonlighted by lecturing on problems in industry. She earned her A.B. in 1929.

From 1929–1933 Herrick served as executive secretary of the New York Consumers' League, preparing reports, drafting and lobbying for minimum wage and child labor legislation, and serving on state boards. She then moved on to regional work for the National Labor Relations Board of the New Deal, where her fair-mindedness won her respect from all sides. In 1942 Todd Shipyards Corporation appointed her its director of personnel and labor relations for its 150,000 employees. Foresightedly, she stressed the importance of retaining in the labor force after World War II women who wanted to work.

At war's end she went to the *New York Herald Tribune* as director of personnel and editorial writer, staying there until her retirement in 1955.

See also Boarding; Consumers' League; Glass Ceiling; Human Resources Managers; Journalists; Minimum Wage; New Deal; World War II.

Reference Barbara Sicherman et al., eds., *Notable American Women: The Modern Period* (1980).

Hills, Carla Anderson (b. 1934)

This attorney and politician, a Californian, was the first woman to serve as Secretary of Housing and Urban Development, appointed in 1975. She was educated at Stanford, Oxford, and the Yale University law school. In 1958 she married politician Roderick Hills; in that marriage she has borne four children. She worked as Assistant District Attorney in Los Angeles from 1958–1961 and then in private practice until 1974, when she accepted an appointment as Assistant Attorney General in the U.S. Justice Department. She has also served as a trade negotiator for the federal government.

See also Attorneys; Government Workers.

References Judith Freeman Clark, *Almanac of American Women in the 20th Century* (1987); Jennifer S. Uglow, comp. and ed., *International Dictionary of Women's Biography* (1985); Joan McCullough, *First of All* (1980).

Hispanic Americans

Because of immigration and their high fertility rates, Hispanics represent the fastest growing proportion of the United States population. Hispanic women rank below all other American women in educational attainment, labor-force participation, and median weekly earnings, clustering in low-skilled, low-paid jobs vulnerable to high rates of unemployment. As compared to other American women, Hispanic Americans are overrepresented in the service occupations and as dressmakers, assemblers, or machine operators. In the second quarter of 1987, they earned on average 87 percent as much as all United States women, 87 percent as much as Hispanic men, and 59 percent as much as white men.

In the workplace Hispanic women face the most severe difficulties because of their lack of education. In March 1987, Hispanic women had completed a median of 11.5 years of school, compared with 12.6 years for all American women. Only 7.5 percent of Hispanic women had graduated from college, compared with 16.5 percent of all American women. Among Hispanic women over 25, only half had graduated from high school, compared with three-fourths of all American women.

Obviously, poverty rates among Hispanic-American women run high. So, too, the percentage of families maintained by women: in 1987, 23.4 percent for all Hispanics, versus 16.2 percent for the United States population at large. Considerable disparities among Hispanic groups show up on this score: 19.2 percent of Mexican-American families are maintained by women, a staggering 43.3 percent of Puerto Rican families, 17.7 percent of Cuban families, and 25.5 percent of families from Central and South America.

The youthfulness of Hispanic-American women may significantly affect their future: their median age in 1987 was 25.8 years, compared to 32.9 years for all U.S. women. Younger Hispanics have begun to close the education gap and enter professional and managerial jobs.

MEXICAN AMERICANS

In 1845, Texas, formerly a part of Mexico, joined the United States. In 1848, the United States annexed Mexico's northern territories (now California, New Mexico, Utah, Nevada, Colorado, and Arizona); thereby, thousands of Spanish-speaking people and a quarter of a million Indians entered the population. The movement of Mexicans into the United States has continued, particularly because of the better wages and standard of living in the United States.

Mexican women and Chicanas, their descendants, have confronted barriers in the labor market, often being forced into jobs in agriculture, domestic service, and industry that other Americans disdain. In times of labor shortage, such as during the world wars, the United States has encouraged Mexican immigration, usually on a temporary basis, but otherwise it admits far fewer Mexicans than wish to immigrate, and in times of economic crisis like the Great Depression it has deported hundreds of thousands, including U.S. citizens. The illegal status of many immigrants from Mexico renders them particularly vulnerable to exploitation because of their fear of deportation; it also excludes them from Aid to Families with Dependent Children and the Social Security system.

Chicana workers still remain overconcentrated in low-paid, seasonal jobs and continue to suffer for lack of formal schooling, partly because of generations of child labor, particularly in agriculture, and partly because so many of them have belonged to families of migrant laborers.

PUERTO RICAN AMERICANS

From 1900, high unemployment in Puerto Rico encouraged emigration to the United States. During World War I, U.S. labor shortages and the granting of U.S. citizenship to Puerto Ricans in 1917 increased the pressure. Early on, most of the women immigrants stayed in their new American homes, perhaps taking in piecework, or caring for boarders or children. But some went into domestic service and some went outside their homes to manufacture garments and cigars.

The Great Depression sent about a fifth of immigrants back to Puerto Rico, in a forlorn hope for economic rescue, as the island became what John Gunther called "the poorhouse of the Caribbean." World War II again boomed emigration to the United States; by 1980, 40 percent of all Puerto Ricans were living in the United States, with their numbers still growing. But the women workers among them suffered rising unemployment during the postwar years, as the new clerical, service, and sales jobs they sought could not absorb all the displaced factory workers. Compared with the experiences of most other racial-ethnic groups, Puerto Rican women's participation in the United States labor force plummeted, though by 1980 it had risen again to 40 percent. In the early 1990s many still move back and forth between the United States and Puerto Rico in search of work, compounding their educational and linguistic difficulties.

See also Aid to Families with Dependent Children; Domestic Servants; Great Depression; Job Training Partnership Act; Migrant Laborers; La Mujer Obrera; Pieceworkers; Social Security Act of 1935; Unemployment; World War I; World War II.

References Edna Acosta-Belen, ed., *The Puerto Rican Woman* (1986); James Cockcroft, *Outlaws in the Promised Land: Mexican Immigrant Workers and America's Future* (1986); Teresa Amott and Julie Matthaei, *Race, Gender, and Work: A Multicultural Economic History of Women in the United States* (1991); Irene I . Blea, *La Chicana and the Interaction of Race, Class, and Gender* (1992); Marta Escutia and Margarita M. Prieto, *Hispanics in the Workforce, Part II: Hispanic Women* (1988).

Hobby, Oveta Culp (b. 1905)

This attorney and journalist, a native of Texas, was the first director of the Women's Army Auxiliary Corps and its successor, the Women's Army Corps, and the first Secretary of Health, Education, and Welfare, appointed by Dwight D. Eisenhower in 1952. She was the second woman (after Frances Perkins) to hold a cabinet post. Educated at the University of Texas law school, she served in Texas governmental positions for many years. In 1931 she married publisher and former governor William P. Hobby; in 1938 she became the executive vice-president and then the manager of his newspaper the *Houston Post*.

See also Attorneys; Government Workers; Journalists; Military Women; Perkins, Frances.

Reference Judith Freeman Clark, *Almanac of American Women in the 20th Century* (1987); Joan McCullough, *First of All* (1980).

Home Economists

The study of the family and domestic life dates back to Catharine Esther Beecher, influential in establishing courses in domestic science in the nineteenth century. In the early twentieth century leading women experts like Ellen Swallow Richards founded the American Home Economics Association (1909) and developed syllabi and courses for schools and women's clubs. Home economics became standard in high schools and colleges. In the 1920s Marion Talbot established a graduate program at the University of Chicago, and Martha Van Rensselaer led Cornell to preeminence in the field.

The teaching of home economics was encouraged by the Smith-Hughes Act and the Smith-Lever Act. The Smith-Hughes Act (1917), intended to advance vocational education, provided moneys with which high schools offered agricultural and industrial education for boys, while giving girls training in home economics and "business" (typing, stenography, and bookkeeping). Federal grants were to be matched by state or local funding. The act also established a Federal Board of Vocational Education. The Smith-Lever Act (1914) provided federal financing for home economics in land-grant colleges and universities.

The work of home economists affected women's home and work lives. The new home economics faculty and the teachers they trained established new standards of nutrition, efficiency, and cleanliness, which they carried into hundreds of thousands of homes through extension programs and club work. They raised the quality of life for many a family. They experimented with communal kitchens and with packaged meals that working women could carry home; with cooperative nurseries, communal laundries, and shopping groups. Sometimes, to be sure, they taught ahead of their knowledge, trying to substitute New England boiled dinners for the healthier diets of immigrants. Sometimes their passion for expertise and the "scientific approach" led them to advocate ludicrously rigid methods of child care. Sometimes they made housekeeping and family care seem so complicated as to call for trained scientists to perform them. All of these fed into the New Victorianism of the 1920s, which encouraged women to devote their energies to the home and made them responsible for the welfare and happiness of everyone in it.

But out of the home economists' work grew new occupations for women, not only in teaching but also in the corporate world, in hospitals, in hotels, and in the marketplace: in nutrition, hygiene, child care, extension work, and human relations.

See also Beecher, Catharine Esther; Child Care; Cooperative Housekeeping; Gilbreth, Lillian Evelyn Moller; Housekeeping; Richards, Ellen Henrietta Swallow; Vocational Education; Woolman, Mary Raphael Schenck.

References Joyce Antler, *The Educated Woman and Professionalization* (1987); Ruth Schwartz Cowan, *More Work for Mother: The Ironies of Household Technology from the Open Hearth to the Microwave* (1983); Martha F. Crow, *The American Country Girl* (1915, 1974); Elizabeth Ewen, *Immigrant Women in the Land of Dollars: Life and Culture on the Lower East Side, 1890–1925* (1985); Alice Kessler-Harris, *Out To Work* (1982); Harvey A. Levenstein, *Revolution at the Table: The Transformation of the American Diet* (1988); Angela Howard Zophy and Frances M. Kavenik, eds., *Handbook of Women's History* (1990).

Home Workers

Although historically this term has been applied most often to piecework done in the home, in the late twentieth century the availability of personal computers, modems, copiers, facsimile machines, and scanners has enabled many businesspeople to do some or all of their paid work at home, an arrangement sometimes referred to as flexplace or telecommuting. In 1992, 20,000,000 people in the United States were thus running a primary or secondary business, working at home a day or two each month, or catching up on business correspondence and planning at night or on weekends. Some were "corporate home workers" on the payroll of a company outside their home. (*New York Times*, 24 May 1992)

Critics see this trend as dangerous in its potential to take advantage of workers unprotected by unions and the possibility of unsafe working conditions. But reported increased productivity, the cut in commuting costs, and the greater freedom of the employee all argue for its growth.

Arguments over home work continue. The Deva catalog for spring 1993 reported a suit filed by the federal Department of Labor (DOL) against the company, which employs home sewers in rural Maryland. "This, despite [DOL's] having conducted in-depth interviews and time and motion studies at each stitcher's home. They had found conditions and pay to surpass all their standards. Amazingly, the DOL told us there would be no beef if we ceased making women's wear; men's and unisex wear were legal!" U.S. District Court Judge Herbert Murray refused to accept the government's argument that Deva was in violation of a law enacted in the 1940s to prevent sweat shops. Judge Murray found that Deva stitchers earn two to four times the prevailing minimum wage, and finding no violation whatever, the judge dismissed the case.

See also Entrepreneurs; Pieceworkers; Telecommuting; Unions.

References Catalyst, *Flexible Work Arrangements: Establishing Options for Managers and Professionals* (1989); *Working Woman* editors with Gay Bryant, *The Working Woman Report* (1984).

Homesteaders

American women first gained the right to homestead, that is, to claim federal land by right of residence and cultivation, by the Homesteading Act of 1862, providing that they were single and over 21, citizens or immigrants who had filed citizenship papers, or heads of household. The prospect of land ownership attracted many self-reliant women, so that about 12 percent of all claims were filed by women. Despite the enthusiasm of some of them, homesteading was trickier than advertised. Often homesteaders gained only land that no one else, not even the railroads, wanted, and many of them failed. Still, considering the alternatives open to women, homesteading provided a singularly attractive hope of land ownership to nineteenth-century American women.

References H. Elaine Lindgren, *Land in Her Own Name: Women as Homesteaders in North Dakota* (1991); Elinore Pruitt Stewart, *Letters of a Woman Homesteader* (1988).

Horney, Karen (1885–1952)

This German-born psychiatrist and pioneer in the psychology of women, educated in German universities and hospitals, married Oskar Horney in 1909; they separated in 1937. Even during their marriage, Horney turned over the care of their three daughters to governesses and concentrated on her work. Her own depression and fatigue aroused her interest in psychoanalysis, a process that she herself underwent with a disciple of Sigmund Freud. She took her first analytic patients in 1919. In 1932 she began her American career with an appointment at the Chicago Institute for Psychoanalysis, soon moving on to New York, where she taught and built her own practice. In 1941 she and several other analysts organized the American Association for the Advancement of Psychoanalysis, through which she edited the *American Journal of Psychoanalysis*, and the American Institute for Psychoanalysis, a teaching institution in which Horney served as dean.

Horney emphasized sociocultural factors in neuroses. Rejecting Freud's phallocentricism, she insisted on the positive and fulfilling nature of motherhood, suggesting that men might envy this experience.

See also Health Professionals and Paraprofessionals; Social Workers.

References Jack L. Rubins, *Karen Horney: Gentle Rebel of Psychoanalysis* (1978); Barbara Sicherman et al., eds., *Notable American Women: The Modern Period* (1980); Jennifer S. Uglow, comp. and ed., *International Dictionary of Women's Biography* (1985).

Hosmer, Harriet Goodhue (1830–1908)

This sculptor, a native of Massachusetts, was privately educated. Her teachers encouraged her to consider sculpture as a profession. She studied technique with a sculptor and anatomy with a physician before traveling to Rome for lessons with the English sculptor John Gibson, who both taught her and helped her to secure commissions.

Hosmer was the first, and considered by many to be the best, of the professional women sculptors of the mid-nineteenth century. With well-placed and affluent patrons on both sides of the Atlantic, she established an international reputation, made a good living selling her work, and enjoyed herself in the bargain.

See also Artists.

References Cornelia Crow Carr, *Harriet Hosmer, Letters and Memories* (1912); Edward T. James et al., eds., *Notable American Women II* (1971); Dolly Sherwood, *Harriet Hosmer: American Sculptor, 1830–1908* (1991); Jennifer S. Uglow, comp. and ed., *International Dictionary of Women's Biography* (1985).

Hours Laws

See Protective Legislation.

Househusband

This term for the male equivalent of *housewife* encompasses a very small cohort. Although occasionally a married couple reverses the traditional pattern, with the husband keeping house and tending children while the wife supports the family, the arrangement is usually short-term.

See also Child Care; Housekeeping.

Housekeeping

Housekeeping in most American homes is unpaid work, uncounted in the gross national product, and accordingly under- or unvalued. Throughout American history, women, whether or not they work for wages or otherwise contribute to the family income, have done and continue to do most of the housework. The highest estimate for men's share of housework is 1 to 1½ hours a day. Housewives who hold down paid jobs do about 35 hours of housework a week; housewives without paid jobs about 50. Men with employed wives spend about 10 minutes more a day on housework than men whose wives are full-time housewives. Men with small children add another 10 minutes a day, for a grand total of under 11 hours a week. But men out of the labor force are stepping up their share of household labor.

The housewife's relationship to the workplace is contingent upon many variables, most particularly the uncertainty of the marital situation. Divorce and separation are now common and the economic consequences for the wife are substantial, often forcing her into the labor market as a displaced homemaker without necessary skills or appropriate experience.

See also Cooperative Housekeeping; Displaced Homemakers; Displaced Homemakers' Self-Sufficiency Assistance Act; Househusband; Second Shift.

References Barbara B. Bergmann, *The Economic Emergence of Women* (1986); Ruth Schwartz Cowan, *More Work for Mother* (1983); Ann Oakley, *Woman's Work: The Housewife, Past and Present* (1976); Juliet B. Schor, *The Overworked American: The Unexpected Decline of Leisure* (1992).

Huerta, Dolores (b. 1930)

In the late 1950s Huerta joined a grass-roots advocacy group, working with Cesar Chavez. In 1962 this pregnant mother of six became an organizer for the United Farm Workers, where she eventually rose to vice-president.

See also Union Organizers; United Farm Workers.

References James J. Kenneally, "Women in the United States and Trade Unionism," in Norbert C. Soldon, ed., *The World of Women's Trade Unionism: Comparative Historical Essays* (1985);

Angela Howard Zophy and Frances M. Kavenik, eds. *Handbook of American Women's History* (1990).

Hull House

This early settlement house, founded in Chicago by Jane Addams, was the site of extraordinary ferment for improved conditions for women. The brilliant women who lived there in the Progressive Era reinforced, helped, and taught each other and the young college women and men who flocked there. Their influence extended throughout the country into every segment of reform. Among them were Alice Hamilton, Julia Lathrop, Sophonisba Breckinridge, Gertrude Barnum, Edith and Grace Abbott, Florence Kelley, Mary Eliza McDowell, Mary Kenney O'Sullivan, Ellen Gates Starr, and Alzina Parsons Stevens. Countless other reformers, including Margaret Dreier Robins, visited Hull House frequently and cooperated with its residents.

Hull House founder Jane Addams

See also Abbott, Edith; Abbott, Grace; Barnum, Gertrude; Breckinridge, Sophonisba Preston; Hamilton, Alice; Kelley, Florence; McDowell, Mary Eliza; O'Sullivan, Mary Kenney; Progressive Era; Robins, Margaret Dreier; Settlement Houses; Social Workers; Starr, Ellen Gates; Stevens, Alzina Parsons.

References Rivka Shpak Lissak, *Pluralism and Progressives, Hull House and the New Immigrants, 1890–1919* (1989).

Human Resources Managers

As in the late nineteenth century businesses became more complex, hiring moved out of the hands of foremen and bosses to a separate department. The new field of "employment management," increasingly known after World War I as "personnel management," attracted women. Women's reputation for sensitivity, nurturing, tact, and expertise in social work made them attractive in this field, despite the revulsion at the idea that women might exercise a degree of control over men's working lives.

Personnel management developed out of psychology, vocational guidance, and welfare work—all fields that interested women. But many women in personnel earned their jobs by internal promotion from clerical work. Some women reformers and feminists saw in this work the opportunity for improving the lot of women employees. Some of them embraced scientific management as a means to judge workers on the basis of aptitudes and productivity, thus benefiting women employees by rewarding them on the basis of merit.

By the 1920s many personnel offices had stratified, often with higher-paid men in charge and women working for less money, responsible for specific functions like employment, training, recreation, and health.

Now known as human resources management, the field has developed specialties like benefits, training, employee development, and staff reduction. Women in corporations still gravitate toward this area. It offers rich opportunities for service, but as a staff rather than a line job, it seldom leads to the topmost echelons.

See also Benefits; Clerical Workers; Gilson, Mary Barnett; Glass Ceiling; Herrick, Elinore Morehouse; Line Jobs; Psychologists and Psychiatrists; Scientific Management; Social Workers; Staff Jobs; Vocational Guidance; Welfare Work.

Human Rights Commissions

The individual states have variously named agencies to which workers of both genders may bring complaints of work-related discrimination.

See also Equal Employment Opportunity Commission; Grievances; Sex Discrimination; Sexual Harassment.

Hunt, Harriot Kezia (1805–1857)

Hunt may have been the first woman to practice medicine in the United States. She and her sister Sarah went into practice in 1835, after two years studying and working with an English couple named Mott who had successfully treated Sarah for an illness that had resisted the harsh regimen of conventionally trained local physicians. The two sisters trained themselves, relying on common sense and a belief that good nursing, proper diet, cleanliness, and rest would solve many health problems. As their practice grew they became increasingly impressed by the importance of mental health. Although they were uncredentialed and thus barred from hospitals, the sisters' practice nonetheless boomed, primarily among women and children. This practice provided them with an independent income. Sarah withdrew from the partnership after her marriage in 1840, but Harriot continued, expanding her work into health education and social reform.

When in 1847 she learned that Elizabeth Blackwell had been enrolled in the Medical College at Geneva, New York, she sought permission to attend lectures at the Harvard Medical School and was rejected. Her practice brought her into intimate contact with working women's lives—the abuses suffered, the restrictions endured, the indignities of their inferior status—and led to her involvement in the women's rights movement, for which she traveled widely, seeking always to broaden women's employment opportunities. She did much to prepare the way for the women who entered the medical profession in the 1850s and 1860s.

See also Blackwell, Elizabeth; Physicians.

References Harriot Hunt, *Glances and Glimpses* (1856); Edward T. James et al., eds., *Notable American Women II* (1971); Jennifer S. Uglow, comp. and ed., *International Dictionary of Women's Biography* (1985).

Hutchins, Grace (1885–1969)

This labor researcher, a native of Boston, was educated in private preparatory schools and at Bryn Mawr, from which she graduated in 1907. Later she studied labor problems at the New York School of Philanthropy and education at Teachers College, Columbia. A lifelong idealist, she spent four years, from 1912–1916, as a missionary in China, and at least five years in the 1920s as an employee of a Christian pacifist organization. In 1927 she joined the Communist party.

The greater number of her working years, from 1929 to 1967, however, she gave to the Labor Research Association, which she formed with Anna Rochester, her friend and companion, and Robert W. Dunn. The association provided information to labor organizations and publications. Always concerned with the health and welfare of workers, especially women and children, Hutchins published *Women Who Work* in 1933; it focused on efforts to improve working conditions for women.

See also Communist Party.

Reference Barbara Sicherman et al., eds., *Notable American Women: The Modern Period* (1980).

Hyde, Ida Henrietta (1857–1945)

This scientist, a native of Iowa, earned her baccalaureate degree from Cornell in 1891. A pioneer in physiological science, she was repeatedly required to overcome prejudices against women who sought a professional career in science. In 1896 she was the first woman to receive an earned (rather than an honorary) Ph.D. from the University of Heidelberg. Upon her return to the United States, she was allowed to do research in the laboratories of the Harvard Medical School—another first. In 1898 she began her long professorial career at the University of Kansas, where she established a stellar reputation as a teacher, while continuing to be a productive researcher. She earned yet another first: her election to the American Physiological Society—until 1914 the only woman so honored. In addition to her scholarly pursuits, she interested herself in women's issues, supporting the suffrage movement and particularly helping women seeking academic careers.

See also Academic Women; Science, Mathematics, and Science-Based Professions.

Reference Edward T. James et al., eds., *Notable American Women II* (1971).

Ickes, Anna Wilmarth Thompson (1873–1935)

This social reformer and legislator, a native of Chicago, was educated in private preparatory schools in the United States and abroad and at the University of Chicago, which she attended for three years. In 1897 she married one of its history instructors, James Westfall Thompson; in this marriage, which ended in divorce in 1909, she bore a son and adopted a daughter. In 1911 she married the lawyer Harold Ickes; in this marriage she bore one son and adopted another.

Like her mother before her, Ickes strongly supported the Women's Trade Union League, furnishing bail for strikers and walking picket lines. She also worked politically, for a few years for the Progressive party, then for the Republican party—though she could not bring herself to support Warren G. Harding. In 1924 she won election to a post on the board of trustees of the University of Illinois, where she served until 1929. In 1928, she ran successfully for the state legislature, her husband acting as her campaign manager. She repeated that success in 1930 and 1932.

In the 1932 election, however, Harold Ickes endorsed the Democratic presidential candidate, Franklin Delano Roosevelt, who in 1933 appointed Ickes Secretary of the Interior. For a time Anna Ickes pursued her own independent Republican course, continuing her work as a legislator even while she acted as a cabinet wife in the Democratic administration in Washington. As the complexities of that situation mounted, she decided not to run again in 1934, but instead to devote herself to a long-standing interest, the American Indian. In 1935, while pursuing that interest, she was fatally injured in an automobile accident in New Mexico.

See also Government Workers; Women's Trade Union League.
Reference Edward T. James et al., eds., *Notable American Women II* (1971).

Immigrant Women

The contribution of immigrant women to the labor force varied according to their cultural, ethnic, and social backgrounds, as did their adaptation to American life. Common to their experience, however, is the necessity for most of them to earn wages. Up through the early twentieth century the shortage of servants in the United States pulled many into domestic service (especially the Irish and Asians). Similarly, in the nineteenth and twentieth centuries immigrant women have provided a source of cheap labor for many industries, especially in textiles and garment-making, cigar-making, and agriculture (e.g., the Japanese in California). Immigrants or children of immigrants became union organizers, marched in picket lines, and supported their families by sweated labor at home or in factories and mills. Rose Pesotta, herself a foreign-born organizer of the Progressive Era for the International Ladies' Garment Workers' Union, noted in one instance (strikes in Cleveland factories) that the predominantly female employees included representatives from every Balkan and central-European nation.

Even in the 1990s many immigrant women wind up doing domestic work or toiling in sweat factories, where their ignorance of English and their isolation renders them liable to exploitation and vulnerable to low wages and denial of benefits. The Network for the Rights of Immigrant Women, an organization of New York–based groups, and other organizations are providing brochures in different languages to help immigrant women understand their rights.

See also Benefits; Domestic Servants; Factory Workers; International Ladies' Garment Workers' Union; Pesotta, Rose; Progressive Era; Strikes; Sweatshops; Union Organizers.

References Miriam Cohen, *Workshop to Office: Two Generations of Italian Women in New York City, 1900–1950* (1992); Hasia A. Diner, *Erin's Daughters: Irish Immigrant Women in the Nineteenth Century* (1983); Louise Lamphere, *From Working Daughters to Working Mothers: Immigrant Women in a New England Industrial Community* (1987); Sydney Stahl Weinberg, *The World of Our Mothers* (1988).

Indentured Servants

Because in the seventeenth and eighteenth centuries the American colonies needed women's productive and reproductive labor, European women, like men, could "buy" their passage to America with a promise of their labor for a fixed period of time, usually four to seven years. Organizations kidnapped others in Europe and sold them as servants here. And the British government banished still others, usually prostitutes or convicts, to work in the colonies for the Crown or to be sold as servants. Buyers separated wives from husbands, children from parents.

African women were similarly indentured, particularly before the slave trade got into full swing. So were children of poor women, and these poor women themselves.

Colonial America forbade indentured servants to marry without the permission of their masters and treated them as immoral and sexually available. Yet, since her master owned her labor for the length of her indenture, a woman who became pregnant and presumably less productive could be punished by whipping, fines, and an extension of her service. (Sometimes not only did she herself have to labor for more years, but the labor of her baby for the first 21 years of life was arrogated to the owner.) If her master had fathered her child, the extension of the woman's service was owed not to him but to the town.

Hard-worked, abused, sexually harassed, and deprived of free choice, some indentured servants tried to escape, at the risk of fines, whipping, branding, and extension of their indentures. Colonial law, however, differentiated indentured servants from slaves by specifying minimum amounts of food and clothing for them, forbidding beatings, and permitting them to sue their masters for violating these rights. And, in time, most indentured servants completed their contracts and "earned" their freedom.

See also Colonial America; Prostitutes; Slavery.

References Mimi Abramovitz, *Regulating the Lives of Women: Social Welfare Policy from Colonial Times to the Present* (1988); Philip S. Foner, *Women and the American Labor Movement: From Colonial Times to the Eve of World War I* (1979).

Individual Retirement Accounts (IRA)

These accounts permit all employed women (and men) to defer taxes on some of their savings for retirement. IRA funds may not be withdrawn until age 59½, at which point earnings may be less and taxes levied at a lower rate. Self-employed individuals have the same opportunity to secure retirement funds through "Keogh" accounts, which are similar in purpose and design to IRAs.

Reference Barbara A. Burnett, *Every Woman's Legal Guide* (1983).

Industrial Workers of the World (IWW)

Popularly known as the Wobblies, the IWW was founded in 1905 by radical elements in the union movement to wage a more militant struggle on behalf of the working class and to emancipate its members from "wage slavery." Its *Manifesto* proclaimed the class struggle as its principal tenet and recognized "the irrepressible conflict between the capitalists and the working class." It assumed that the problems of women were inseparable from those of the working class. In practice the IWW advocated militant strikes and industrial unions. Mary Harris ("Mother") Jones signed the *Manifesto* and, with 11 other women, acted as delegate to the IWW's founding convention. Among the other notable women associated with the IWW are Elizabeth Gurley Flynn, Kate Richards O'Hare, Lucy Gonzalez Parsons, Emma Goldman, and Rose Harriet Pastor Stokes.

The Wobblies made a genuine effort to attract women (and also, uniquely, Chinese, Mexican, and Japanese) members and give them equal duties and privileges in the organization. Initiation fees and dues were kept low to attract underpaid women workers; women were employed as organizers and union officials; and male workers were exhorted to welcome and encourage women as fellow victims of capitalist exploitation being forced to work out of necessity. However, some problems remained for IWW women, particularly the issue of women continuing to work after marriage, leaving their homes and children. The organization also debated the eligibility of wives of workers for membership and the right of wives of striking husbands to march on the picket lines and attend strike meetings.

Its socialist and revolutionary ideology and its involvement in many bloody strikes made the IWW a target for repressive measures. Strikes after the United States entered World War I led to its suppression and the arrest of its entire leadership.

See also American Federation of Labor; Anarchism; Communist Party; Congress of Industrial Organizations; Flynn, Elizabeth Gurley; Goldman, Emma; Jones, Marry Harris; Knights of Labor; Mesabi Range Strike; Parsons, Lucy Gonzalez; Socialist Party; Stokes, Rose Harriet Pastor; Strikes; Unions; World War I.

References Philip S. Foner, *Women and the American Labor Movement: From the First Trade Unions to the Present* (1982); Carol Hymowitz and Michaele Weissman, *A History of Women in America* (1980); Annie Huber Tripp, *The I.W.W. and the Paterson Silk Strike of 1913* (1987).

Injunctions

These court orders require persons or organizations to refrain from performing specified acts. Early in the twentieth century injunctions were freely used by judges against such union activities as striking and picketing, typically on the grounds that such activities can lead to violence.

See also Lockouts; Norris-LaGuardia Act; Strikes; Unions; Yellow-Dog Contract.

Inman, Elizabeth Murray (1726–1785)

Inman exemplified that rarity in colonial America, an independent and successful businesswoman. Located in Boston, she sold millinery, cloth, and sewing supplies and taught young ladies needlework. At a time when the common law kept married women from owning property, making a will, or entering into contracts, Inman protected her own legal identity and her rights to manage her own property and business enterprises by prenuptial agreements with the last two of her three husbands. Once financially secure, she used her resources to assist other women (including her nieces) to become self-supporting.

See also Colonial America; Coverture; Entrepreneurs.

Reference Mary Beth Norton, "A Cherished Spirit of Independence: The Life of an Eighteenth-Century Boston Businesswoman," in Carol Ruth Berkin and Mary Beth Norton, *Women of America: A History* (1979).

Institute for Women's Policy Research

Founded in 1987, this organization explores many women's issues, including economic equity, employment, and work and family.

Intercollegiate Bureau of Occupations

This early–twentieth-century organization, presided over by Mary van Kleeck, aimed to help women find work in fields other than teaching.

See also Employment Agencies; Van Kleeck, Mary Abby.

International Alliance: An Association of Executive and Professional Women (ITA)

Founded in 1980, ITA affiliates local networks of 6,000 executive and professional women in support of their professional development.

See also Networking.

International Congresses of Working Women

See Women's International Labor Conferences.

International Ladies' Garment Workers' Union (ILGWU)

This union, formed in 1900, attracted more than the normal proportion of women, largely because the garment industry employed so many women. But the leadership was overwhelmingly male, even after the 1909 Uprising of the 20,000, sparked by women, brought thousands of new women members to the union. In 1913 this leadership agreed to a code that reserved all higher-paying jobs for men, even though women constituted half the membership. In the 1930s ILGWU strikes lowered hours and increased membership. But the imbalance between a mostly female membership and a mostly male leadership continued; on her retirement in the 1940s Rose Pesotta commented: "Ten years in office had made it clear to me that a lone woman vice president could not adequately represent the women who now made up 85 percent of the International's membership of 305,000." In the early 1990s, with a membership about 80 percent female, ILGWU counts only four women among its 20 vice-presidents.

See also American Federation of Labor; Brookwood Labor College; Cohn, Fannia Mary; Marot, Helen; Miller, Frieda Segekle; Pesotta, Rose; Schneiderman, Rose; Strikes; Taylor, Rebecca; Unions; Uprising of the 20,000; Wolfson, Theresa.

References Susan Ware, *Holding Their Own: American Women in the 1930s* (1982); Angela Howard Zophy and Frances M. Kavenik, eds., *Handbook of American Women's History* (1990).

Inventors

Women, for so long shut out from studies that prepared men to actualize their ideas, nonetheless have contributed many inventions. Throughout American history some women have somehow broken through the restrictions of training, experience, and societal disapproval with their inventions. In 1809 Mary Kies won the first patent issued to a woman in the United States with her method of weaving straw. In 1991 the Inventors Hall of Fame elected its first woman, Nobel laureate Gertrude Ellon, honored for her anticancer drugs.

Since inventors get ideas only after they recognize needs, women in early America invented most (but not all) of their devices for clothes or domestic life or nursing. As their menfolk departed during the Civil War, they broadened their scope to include farm machines—not to mention Mary Jane Montgomery's improved planking of iron- or steel-armored war vessels to discourage barnacles. As women's horizons expanded with their move into the work force and public life, so expanded their inventions. Thus Margaret Knight (1838–1914), who began her career as a child mill worker, first invented a shuttle-restraining device; when she went to work about 1867 for a paper bag factory, she invented the now ubiquitous "satchel-bottomed" paper bag. The sculptor Harriet Hosmer invented a product closely resembling marble. In the late nineteenth century Mary Walton developed a method for deflecting smokestack emissions into water tanks and flushing them into city sewers.

An International Ladies' Garment Workers' Union member is a cutter in the garment industry.

In the twentieth century women inventors have often worked for companies that then owned their patents—like Marjorie Joyner, who in 1928 while in the employ of Sarah Breedlove McWilliams Walker invented a permanent-wave machine that would, she wrote in her patent application, "wave the hair of both white and colored people."

In the 1990s, faced with a declining share of patents in the world market, the United States is trying to encourage young people—girls and boys alike—to invent. Girls can take as role models Ruth Handler, inventor of the Barbie doll and the first breast prosthesis for mastectomy patients, and Dr. Stephanie Kwolek, who made possible the development of a fiber used for radial tires, airplanes, space vehicles, and bulletproof vests. But as late as 1988 only 5.6 percent of patents went to women.

See also Hosmer, Harriet Goodhue; Masters, Sybilla; Walker, Sarah Breedlove McWilliams.

References Anne L. Macdonald, *Feminine Ingenuity: Women and Invention in America* (1992); Jennifer S. Uglow, comp. and ed., *International Dictionary of Women's Biography* (1985); Ethlie A. Vare and Greg Ptacek, *Mothers of Invention* (1989).

Jacobi, Mary Corinna Putnam (1842–1906)

This physician obtained her M.D. degree from Women's (then Female) Medical College of Philadelphia in 1864. In 1866 she went to France for additional medical training, succeeding against substantial odds in obtaining admission to the Ecole de Médecine, where she passed her examination with high honors and won a bronze medal for her graduating thesis. Possessing formal medical training that equaled or excelled that of most American doctors, she returned to New York in 1871 and soon established her preeminence as a woman physician. Her marriage in 1873 to Abraham Jacobi, another physician, was firm and lasting. The two strong personalities managed to combine successful careers with the production of three children, of whom only one (a daughter) survived.

For many years Jacobi worked as attending and consulting physician at the New York Infirmary and in 1886 opened a children's ward there. She also maintained a longtime association with Mount Sinai Hospital after inaugurating what turned into a permanent pediatric dispensary. And beginning in 1893 Jacobi was visiting physician at St. Mark's Hospital. She also published more than a hundred scientific articles; her paper "The Question of Rest for Women during Menstruation" won the Harvard Boylston Prize in 1876. She belonged to such medical societies as the New York Pathological Society, the New York Neurological Society, the Therapeutical Society of New York, the Medical Society of the County of New York, and the New York Academy of Medicine. (Only the Obstetrical Society found her unworthy of membership.)

Concerned about the problems women encountered in obtaining a first-rate medical education, Dr. Jacobi founded the Association for the Advancement of the Medical Education of Women (later the Women's Medical Association of New York City) in 1872, and for many years taught at the Women's Medical College of the New York Infirmary for Women and Children. She extended her concern to women in other work, helping to found the Working Women's Society. She also strove to protect the environment and campaigned for women's suffrage.

See also Physicians; Working Women's Society.

References Edward T. James et al., eds., *Notable American Women II* (1971); Ruth Putnam, ed., *Life and Letters of Mary Putnam Jacobi* (1925); Jennifer S. Uglow, comp. and ed., *International Dictionary of Women's Biography* (1985); Women's Medical Association of New York City, *Mary Putnam Jacobi, M.D.: A Pathfinder in Medicine* (1925).

Jane Clubs

Mary Kenney O'Sullivan led this cooperative low-cost boarding arrangement for young working women, in part to ensure that women on strike would not have to give in because they had no place to live or no food. In 1891 Jane Addams, for whom the clubs were named, assisted in starting the first one, which survived until 1938.

See also Boarding; O'Sullivan, Mary Kenney; Strikes.

Reference Angela Howard Zophy and Frances M. Kavenik, eds., *Handbook of American Women's History* (1990).

Japanese Americans

Of the few Japanese women immigrants in the nineteenth century, about a third worked for pay, usually as agricultural or domestic laborers or as prostitutes. A 1907 agreement between Japan and the

United States barred the entry of unskilled men, but permitted the entry of male immigrants' wives—often, until 1920, "picture brides" who had never met their husbands-to-be. About a quarter of them went to work, usually in agriculture and domestic service; only gradually and much later did they diversify into sales, manufacturing, clerical, professional, and managerial jobs.

The typical Japanese immigrant woman, much like her European counterpart on the East Coast, entered upon a life of unremitting toil. Forced by economic necessity to work, she often toiled with her husband in the operation of labor camps or on farms (as sharecroppers or cash tenants). In urban areas, women would help in their husbands' small businesses or find work in a cannery or as domestic servants. In any case their working and living conditions were often primitive.

During World War II the discrimination always exercised economically against Japanese Americans, despite their hard work and good educations, erupted into hysteria. The United States imprisoned almost all ethnic Japanese, including American citizens, moving them to "permanent relocation camps" in the interior, paying them a pittance to cook, farm, teach, and provide medical care, then as labor shortages grew, allowing some to leave for domestic, agricultural, or factory jobs. Some left to become students, and some, including a hundred women, to join the U.S. Army. The end of the war set the other two-thirds free to try to put their lives back together and (usually unsuccessfully) to reclaim their property. The experience moved more Japanese women into the paid labor force: by 1950, 42 percent of them, mostly in domestic service and manufacturing.

The postwar period saw a relaxation in immigration restrictions, but, except for the Japanese war brides of American soldiers, no surge in immigration. Japanese-American women, many of them well-educated, made real occupational gains. Almost 60 percent of them had joined the labor force by 1960. Despite persistent racism, their educations enable many in the late twentieth century to hold managerial and professional jobs. Indeed, in 1980 they earned higher median incomes than all European-American women (but not as much as comparably educated European-American women, or as men) and enjoyed the lowest unemployment rates and lowest poverty rates for female-maintained households of all racial-ethnic groups.

See also Agricultural Workers; Domestic Servants; Prostitutes; World War II.

References Teresa Amott and Julie Matthaei, *Race, Gender, and Work: A Multicultural Economic History of Women in the United States* (1991); Roger Daniels, *Asian America: Chinese and Japanese in the United States since 1950* (1988); Evelyn Nakano Glenn, *Issei, Nisei, War Bride: Three Generations of Japanese American Women in Domestic Service* (1986); Yuji Ichioka, *The Issei: The World of the First Generation Japanese Immigrants, 1885–1924* (1988).

Jarrell, Helen Ira (1896–1973)

This educator and union leader, a native Georgian, prepared herself to teach at the Atlanta Normal School. Later she took a bachelor's and a master's degree at Oglethorpe University.

Jarrell, who never married, devoted her long career in education to the Atlanta Public Schools, as a teacher, as a union leader, and as a principal, and eventually a superintendent of schools (1944–1960). As a union leader for the Atlanta Public School Teachers' Association (American Federation of Labor) she campaigned for the election of a mayor and a board of education friendly to her union's causes. As an administrator—the first woman superintendent in Atlanta and one of the few women in charge of big-city schools—she exercised adeptly the political skills honed in her union work, winning the support of her teachers by lowering class sizes and raising salaries. She oversaw a huge building program, won financial independence for the schools from city hall, and promoted programs for gifted and handicapped students.

Jarrell's firm control eventually led to charges of dictatorship. She ignored pleas from the African-American community for equal opportunities for their children, even delaying integration after the U.S. Supreme Court ordered it in 1954. She lost control of her board. In 1960 she retired, but for the next seven years she directed curriculum development for the state.

See also American Federation of Labor; Teachers; Unions.

Jeanes Teachers

Beginning in 1908 these black women, primarily supervisors, traveled from county to county to help other teachers in black rural schools to organize classes in domestic science, gardening, and carpentry. The first Jeanes teacher was Virginia E. Randolph. By 1913, 120 Jeanes teachers were working in 11 states. The program was funded by a gift of $1 million from the Quaker heiress Anna Jeanes. The Jeanes fund operated until 1937, when it merged into the Southern Education Foundation.

See also Teachers.

Jemison, Mae Carol (b. 1956)

A chemical engineer and physician, in 1992 Dr. Jemison became the first African-American woman to go into space. (*New York Times*, 13 September 1992) Jemison earned her medical degree at Cornell University Medical College in New York. After several years as a Peace Corps doctor in Africa, private practice, and graduate work in engineering at Stanford, she was accepted into the astronaut program in 1987.

See also Engineers; Physicians; Space.

Job Sharing

Under this arrangement two or more part-time employees share one position,

ensuring among themselves that the job gets done. Ideally job-sharers have parity with full-time positions in salaries and benefits. But the system may cause benefit problems and it reduces the pay and probably the career expectations of employees. Employees who contemplate job sharing or other forms of part-time work may change their minds when they examine the cuts they face in total compensation, with benefits comprising up to 60 percent of that total. Nonetheless job sharers are better off than other part-time workers in terms of job security, compensation, and better opportunities for advancement.

The plan may particularly help women with heavy family responsibilities, who can thus guarantee that skilled, informed partners can assume their tasks in their absence. Other women choose this arrangement to devote more time to education, an avocation, or pleasure. Job sharing has also helped people cope with burn-out.

Employers get the talents of two for the price of one employee. Often the arrangement enables them to keep employees whom they might otherwise lose. It may also provide an effective means of training, when one sharer is older and more experienced than the other.

Obviously the success of job sharing depends on good communication between the sharers. The program should be voluntary, with its terms clearly defined, an evaluation process established, and provision for hiring a new employee in case one sharer leaves. So far the system has been used most successfully in the public sector and among professionals.

See also Benefits; Bridge Job; Compensation; Flextime; Part-Time Workers.

References Catalyst, *Flexible Work Arrangements: Establishing Options for Managers and Professionals* (1989); Felice N. Schwartz with Jean Zimmerman, *Breaking with Tradition: Women and Work, the New Facts of Life* (1992); Vivienne Monty, "Work Sharing and Job Sharing: Whose Priorities Prevail?" in Barbara D. Warme, Katherina L. P. Lundy, and Larry A. Lundy, eds., *Working Part-Time: Risks and Opportunities* (1992);

Working Woman editors with Gay Bryant, *The Working Woman Report* (1984).

Job Training Partnership Act (JTPA)

This act was passed in 1982 to replace the Comprehensive Employment and Training Act (CETA); it provides funds to state and local governments to establish job-training programs for low-income persons suffering from some employment disability, e.g., displaced homemakers, school dropouts, or people with limited language proficiency. It is administered through Private Industry Councils and the Department of Labor. In 1991 JTPA was amended by the Nontraditional Employment for Women (NEW) Act to require states and localities to set goals to increase the number of women trained for nontraditional jobs.

Over half of those served are women (typically displaced homemakers and teenage mothers). But the program has been criticized as preparing women for low-paying female-stereotyped jobs (clerical work, health care) and thus ineffective in enabling single women supporting children to leave Aid to Families with Dependent Children. In 1992 it was serving only 5 percent of its eligible population. Critics remark particularly on JTPA's failure to provide longer-term classroom training, essential particularly for women of low educational attainment, whereas CETA offered courses in English as a second language and courses toward the completion of the General Educational Development (GED) certificate. JTPA is funded at a third of the level of CETA, restricts support services (like child care and transportation), and emphasizes a quick fix. Under JTPA, many women who need training cannot afford programs lengthy enough to prepare them to support themselves and their dependents. JTPA, critics say, has a built-in disadvantage for women, in that it offers more on-the-job training (usually required for traditionally male jobs) and less classroom training and work experience (usually required for traditionally female jobs).

See also Aid to Families with Dependent Children; Displaced Homemakers; Nontraditional Occupations.

References Marta Escutia and Margarita M. Prieto, *Hispanics in the Workforce, Part II: Hispanic Women* (1988); Ms. Foundation for Women and the Center for Policy Alternatives, *Women's Voices: A Policy Guide* (1992); Jo Sanders, *Staying Poor: How the Job Training Partnership Act Fails Women* (1988).

Johnson v. Transportation Agency of Santa Clara (1987)

In this affirmative action case the U.S. Supreme Court ruled on preferential treatment of women for the first time. The male plaintiff was passed over for a road dispatcher job in favor of a female employee; he sued the county for sex discrimination, alleging that its affirmative action goal (voluntarily adopted) of increasing the percentage of women in its employ violated Title VII of the Civil Rights Act of 1964. A female employee, Diane Joyce, got the job even though she had scored slightly lower on her interview and thus seemed slightly less qualified than Johnson. Both were qualified for the position, and Joyce was appointed in conformity with the agency's plan of increasing the number of women in its employ. The court took notice of the statistical evidence that in the pertinent category of jobs there were no women and held against Johnson, allowing preferential treatment of the woman employee because of a "manifest imbalance" in the agency's work force.

See also Affirmative Action; Civil Rights Act of 1964; Sex Discrimination.

Reference Susan Gluck Mezey, *In Pursuit of Equality: Women, Public Policy and the Federal Courts* (1992).

Jones, Mary Harris, aka "Mother Jones" (1830–1930)

A redoubtable, almost mythic figure in American labor history, Mother Jones devoted her long life to the cause of the economically and socially deprived. Without fixed abode, she moved about the country wherever there was depression, industrial unrest, or strikes. She seemed unconcerned about her own safety at a time when labor strife was particularly bloody, and marched fearlessly into many a troubled region to encourage the workers, to organize them, to educate them, and to bring their cause before the bar of public opinion and the councils of government. She was identified with the cause of coal miners particularly and participated in many of their strikes. But her concern extended to all workers in trouble.

Her sense of the dramatic was awesome. In one instance, during the strikes of 1900 and 1902, she directed nationwide attention to the plight of the anthracite miners by leading the strikers' wives armed with brooms and mops against scabs and routing them. In another, she led the "March of the Mill Children"

Mary Harris Jones

(May 1903) from the textile mills of the Philadelphia area to see President Theodore Roosevelt at Oyster Bay, New York, to enlist his support for child labor legislation. On more than one occasion she obtained employment in a factory or mill to collect information about child labor conditions from personal observation. She was also one of the leaders in the Lawrence (MA) Textile Strike of 1912.

Mother Jones's confrontational style inevitably brought her face to face with company guards, police, and the courts. In West Virginia her involvement in a coal mine strike (1912–1913) led to her conviction by a state military court of conspiracy to commit murder and a 20-year prison sentence. She never served the sentence, however; the West Virginia governor pardoned her, urged on by a nationwide storm of protest in labor circles and the threat of a U.S. Senate investigation. In 1913–1914 she joined striking coal miners in Colorado: there she was repeatedly locked up by the mine operators, escorted off company property, and threatened with physical violence. Outraged by the Ludlow Massacre of 1914, Mother Jones again carried the case of the workers to both the public and the government in Washington.

The world in which she moved was in ideological ferment: anarchism, socialism, trade unionism, and class loyalty. Mother Jones herself professed no consistent philosophy, except an uncomplicated sense of a class struggle. She worked with union leaders and was one of the organizers of the Industrial Workers of the World in 1905. But her individualism often made her an uneasy partner in a team effort. She made brief forays into politics: helping to found the Social Democratic Party in 1898, campaigning for the Democratic ticket in the coal mine region of Indiana in 1916, addressing the 1924 convention of the Farmer-Labor Party. But her place in history was made as a labor organizer and agitator.

See also Anarchism; Industrial Workers of the World; Lawrence, Massachusetts, Textile Strike; Ludlow Massacre; Scab; Strikes; Unions.

References Edward T. James et al., eds., *Notable American Women II* (1971); Mary Harris Jones, *Autobiography of Mother Jones* (1972); Edward M. Steel, ed., *The Correspondence of Mother Jones* (1985).

Jordan, Barbara (b. 1936)

This attorney was the first African-American congresswoman from the deep South. After a career in the Texas state senate, she entered the U.S. House of Representatives in 1972. Since beginning teaching at the University of Texas at Austin in 1979, she has remained a spokesperson for civil rights, the underprivileged, and the environment.

See also Attorneys; Government Workers.

Reference *Handbook of American Women's History*, ed. Angela Howard Zophy and Frances M. Kavenik (1990).

Barbara Jordan

Journalists

Women involved themselves in printing and publishing in the eighteenth century, with 17 women publishing newspapers in colonial America. In the nineteenth century women broadened their scope to include sitting in the congressional press gallery (until they were barred) and editing magazines—like Sarah Josepha Buell Hale's *Godey's Lady's Book*. On newspapers they did everything they were allowed, many as sob sisters, stunt reporters, advisers to the lovelorn, and beauty columnists. By 1900 the census counted 2,193 women among 30,098 journalists. Some of these women attained fame, like the adventurous Nellie Bly (1865–1922), the "muckraker" Ida Tarbell (1857–1944), the advice-columnist Dorothy Dix (1861–1951), and the black lynch-fighter Ida Wells-Barnett (1862–1931). They also pushed the door ajar for women in journalism—though painfully and slowly. Despite the twentieth-century attainments of stars like Rheta Dorr (1866–1948), Anne O'Hare McCormick, newsphotographer Margaret Bourke-White (1904–1971), war correspondent Marguerite Higgins (1920–1966), and foreign correspondent Georgie Anne Geyer, it has taken the lawsuits of women journalists like those in the 1970s at *Newsweek*, *Time*, the *New York Times*, and the National Broadcasting Company to gain a modicum of justice and opportunity for women journalists.

With the advent of radio and television, women journalists have undergone the same difficult process of breaking into the business almost one woman at a time. Only gradually did some overcome the objection that women's voices are not grave or heavy enough to report serious news and the later insistence that the public would accept women as reporters only if they are pretty. At first women were confined to reporting the weather or reporting on "soft" news like fashions, interior decorating, and consumer interests. Pauline Fredericks moved from newspaper reporting in the 1930s to radio to television, from interviewing politicians' wives and literally doing their makeup to full-time staff television journalism from 1948 to 1975; she was unique in her era. In 1947 Dorothy Fuldheim became the first (and for a long time the only) television news anchorwoman, a career that she triumphantly carried on into her mid-80s. Not until 1971 did the networks grant a woman—Barbara Walters—the position of anchor, and then only over the heated protests of her male colleagues. Christine Craft alleged that she was fired because she was "too old, too ugly, and not deferential to men." A flick through the dial in the 1990s suggests that standards haven't changed much.

See also Ayer, Harriet Hubbard; Colonial America; Fern, Fannie; Gilder, Jeannette Leonard; Greeley-Smith, Nixola; Hale, Sarah Josepha Buell; Hawes, Elizabeth; Henry, Alice; Herrick, Elinore Morehouse; Hobby, Oveta Culp; Lane, Gertrude Battles; Livermore, Mary Ashton Rice; McDowell, Anne Elizabeth; Printers; Shadd, Mary Ann; Strong, Anna Louise; Tarbell, Ida Minerva; Thompson, Dorothy; Troup, Augusta Lewis; Vorse, Mary Heaton; Walters, Barbara.

References Barbara Belford, *Brilliant Bylines: A Biographical Anthology of Notable Newspaperwomen in America* (1986); Christine Craft, *Too Old, Too Ugly and Not Deferential to Men: An Anchorwoman's Courageous Battle against Sex Discrimination* (1988); Julia Edwards, *Women of the World: The Great Foreign Correspondents* (1988); Linda Ellerbee, *"And So It Goes": Adventures in Television* (1987); Georgie Anne Geyer, *Buying the Night Flight: The Autobiography of a Woman Foreign Correspondent* (1983); George H. Hill, Lorraine Raglin, and Chas Floyd Johnson, *Black Women in Television: An Illustrated History and Bibliography* (1990); David H. Hosley and Gayle K. Yamada, *Hard News: Women in Broadcast Journalism* (1987); Joan McCullough, *First of All* (1980); Kay Mills, *A Place in the News: From the Women's Pages to the Front Page* (1990); Nan Robertson, *The Girls in the Balcony: Women, Men, and the New York Times* (1992); Ishbel Ross, *Ladies of the Press* (1974); Marlene Sanders and Marcia Rock, *Waiting for Prime Time: The Women of Television News* (1990); Liz Trotta, *Fighting for Air: In the Trenches with Television News* (1991).

Just Cause

As a protection against wrongful discharge most union contracts and other employment agreements seek to replace the practice of employment at will with procedures to ensure that there is "just cause" to fire an employee. "Just cause" is generally understood to mean: (a) that the condition of the employer's business is such that certain positions must be eliminated, and/or (b) that the employee's performance on the job has been below established and understood standards, and/or (c) that the employee has violated reasonable rules of workplace conduct. Procedurally, "just cause" requires "due process," i.e., impartial consideration of evidence and rights of appeal (in labor cases, usually arbitration).

See also At-Will Employment.

Reference Lewis L. Maltby, *A State of Emergency in the American Workplace* (1990).

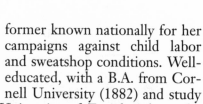

Kehew, Mary Morton Kimball (1859–1918)

A reformer in the field of women's employment, Kehew directed and presided over the Women's Educational and Industrial Union of Boston for many years. In that position she successfully promoted legislation to improve the lot of the state's working women. To ensure the vigorous enforcement of such laws she served on numerous commissions. She also actively participated in the work of many of the humanitarian organizations that made up the reform movement in Massachusetts during the Progressive Era, like the Tyler Street Day Nursery, the Milk and Baby Hygiene Association, and the Massachusetts Association for Promoting the Interests of the Blind.

She energetically supported the cause of trade unionism for women at a time when women were not welcomed by the male-dominated labor movement. Late in the nineteenth century she and Mary Kenney O'Sullivan founded the Union for Industrial Progress, whose purpose was to promote trade unionism among women; by 1901 her efforts had led to the organization of Boston unions among women workers in such fields as bookbinding, laundries, tobacco manufacture, and the garment trade. In 1903 she was elected the first president of the national Women's Trade Union League.

See also Bookbinders; O'Sullivan, Mary Kenney; Progressive Era; Unions; Women's Educational and Industrial Union; Women's Trade Union League.

References Edward T. James et al., eds., *Notable American Women II* (1971); Jennifer S. Uglow, comp. and ed., *International Dictionary of Women's Biography* (1985).

Kelley, Florence (1859–1932)

Kelley was the long-time secretary of the Consumers' League and a social reformer known nationally for her campaigns against child labor and sweatshop conditions. Well-educated, with a B.A. from Cornell University (1882) and study at the University of Zurich (where she was converted to socialism), she settled in Chicago, residing at Hull House. There she investigated working conditions in the garment industry and living conditions in city slums. Her reports helped to pass an Illinois factory act that limited hours of work for women, prohibited child labor, and attempted to control tenement sweatshops; the governor of Illinois appointed her chief factory inspector to administer the new law. The problems of enforcement that she encountered led her to take a law degree in 1894 at Northwestern University. In 1899 she became general secretary of the newly formed national Consumers' League, a position she used for the rest of her life to bring pressure on manufacturers to improve working conditions.

In the course of a lifetime devoted to social reform Kelley roused public concern for the plight of working women and children and fought to protect them legally. She helped to enact minimum wage laws in nine states (by 1913), the Keatings-Owen Child Labor Act of 1916, and the Sheppard-Towner Maternity and Infancy Act of 1921. She participated in forming the New York Child Labor Committee in 1902 and the National Child Labor Committee in 1904.

Her interests were broad, including the National Association for the Advancement of Colored People, the Women's International League for Peace and Freedom, the International Socialist Society, and the Socialist party. Although a staunch supporter of women's suffrage, she argued against the proposed Equal Rights Amendment for fear that its passage would jeopardize protective legislation for women.

See also Consumers' League; Equal Rights Amendment; Factory Workers; Hull House; Minimum Wage; Protective Legislation; Sheppard-Towner Act; Socialist Party; Sweatshops.

References Dorothy Rose Blumberg, *Florence Kelley: The Making of a Social Pioneer* (1966); Josephine Goldmark, *Impatient Crusader: Florence Kelley's Life Story* (1953); Edward T. James et al., eds., *Notable American Women II* (1971); Jennifer S. Uglow, comp. and ed., *International Dictionary of Women's Biography* (1985).

Kellor, Frances (1873–1952)

This reformer and labor arbitrator, raised in Michigan, worked from her girlhood, earning her education in law at Cornell and sociology at the University of Chicago. Reform-minded women's groups supported much of her study, which convinced her of the link between environment and crime. She focused her research on women criminals, unemployed women, and southern black migrants, coming to believe that governments could resolve their problems by establishing special educational programs, labor organizations, employment agencies, and vocational training programs. Her later extensive work in New York State for immigrants rested on the same premise. In 1906 she called together concerned women and men to organize the National League for the Protection of Colored Women, for which she served as executive secretary. From 1926–1952 Kellor directed the American Arbitration Association, which she had helped to found, trying to find ways to resolve industrial and international problems.

See also Employment Agencies; Vocational Education.

References Mary E. Dreier, *Margaret Dreier Robins: Her Life, Letters, and Work* (1950); William Joseph Maxwell, "Frances Kellor in the Progressive Era: A Case Study in the Professionalization of Reform" (1968); Barbara Sicherman et al., eds., *Notable American Women: The Modern Period* (1980).

Kennedy, Kate (1827–1890)

This teacher and advocate of equal pay for women grew up in Ireland, immigrating to the United States in 1849. She worked in the garment industry of New York for a time, while preparing herself to teach. In 1856 she moved with her family to California, where she pursued a teaching career, mostly in San Francisco, both as teacher and as administrator.

Her own experience of receiving the lower salary of a primary school principal while working as a grammar school principal led to her fight for equal pay for equal work, an endeavor supported by the community. In 1874 her efforts and those of her supporters won state legislation requiring that women public school teachers with the same qualifications as similarly employed males receive the same compensation.

Kennedy worked for labor reform, helped strikers, and joined the Knights of Labor. But she interested herself particularly in Henry George's single tax. In 1887 the board of education, allegedly for political reasons, demoted her; when she refused to accept the transfer, they fired her. She fought back and won, in a suit that established the basis for teacher tenure in California.

See also Knights of Labor; Teachers.

Reference Edward T. James et al., eds., *Notable American Women II* (1971).

Kenney, Mary

See O'Sullivan, Mary Kenney.

Keogh Accounts

See Individual Retirement Accounts.

King, Billie-Jean (b. 1943)

King, a superstar and promoter of women's tennis as a major sport, set many a record. A serve-and-volley player, she won 20 titles at Wimbledon and others worldwide. To mitigate the sharp differences in pay between male and female players, she worked to form the Women's Tennis Association in 1973, so that women could negotiate as a group. In 1975 she established the World Team Tennis

League and the Women's Professional Softball League. She has also written several books on tennis and with her husband, Larry King, cofounded the magazine *WomanSport*.

See also Sports.

References Joan McCullough, *First of All* (1980); Jennifer S. Uglow, comp. and ed., *International Dictionary of Women's Biography* (1985); Angela Howard Zophy and Frances M. Kavenik, eds., *Handbook of American Women's History* (1990).

King, Florence

Holder of a degree in mechanical and electrical engineering, this suffragist and patent attorney was the first woman to win a case in the U.S. Supreme Court. She also founded the Woman's Association of Commerce in 1918.

See also Attorneys; Engineers; Woman's Association of Commerce.

Reference Anne L. Macdonald, *Feminine Ingenuity: Women and Invention in America* (1992).

Kingsbury, Susan Myra (1870–1949)

This social researcher and educator, a Californian, graduated from the College of the Pacific in 1890. She took her graduate work at Stanford and Columbia, earning her doctorate in history in 1905 and following it with a year in England. But soon she turned to social research: as director of the research department of the Women's Educational and Industrial Union and economics professor at Simmons College she undertook studies of working women and children in American industries.

In 1915 Kingsbury went to Bryn Mawr College as professor of social economy and director of graduate study in social work. In this capacity she established a rigorous training program that included field experience and research. In 1921 she participated in the planning of the Bryn Mawr Summer School for Women in Industry and was its first director. She continued to publish scholarly articles and books on the legal and economic status of women, and worked in such professional organizations as the American Association of Schools of Social Work (which she helped found), the American Economic Association, and the American Sociological Society.

See also Bryn Mawr Summer School for Women Workers; Social Workers; Women's Educational and Industrial Union.

Reference Edward T. James et al., eds., *Notable American Women II* (1971).

Kirkpatrick, Jeanne J. (b. 1926)

A scholar with a Ph.D. in political science from Columbia (1968) and a political activist, Kirkpatrick was named U.S. Ambassador to the United Nations by Ronald Reagan, a position she held until June 1985. After she resigned because of disagreements on policy issues with many of the president's advisors, she returned to her faculty position at Georgetown University.

See also Academic Women; Government Workers.

Reference Judith Freeman Clark, *Almanac of American Women in the 20th Century* (1987).

Knights of Labor (KOL) (1869–1900)

This loose organization, with a membership of both reformers and laborers, was notable for its acceptance of workers of color, women workers, and even housewives. It advocated equal pay for women as early as 1878 and in 1879 accepted women as members. By 1886 it had enrolled almost 50,000 women. Black women formed locals of laundresses, chambermaids, housekeepers, and agricultural workers within it. Women members participated at all levels. In 1885 its General Assembly took note of the growing number of female members by appointing a committee to investigate working conditions for women; in 1886 the Assembly created a Department of Women's Work to be headed by a general investigator, a position first held by Leonora Marie Kearney Barry.

Membership in the Knights of Labor peaked in 1886 and declined thereafter, as the Knights lost members to the trade unions. As women workers, too, moved to the unions, KOL abandoned efforts to organize them. Nonetheless it left a legacy of trained female labor leaders and evidence of women's will to improve conditions. In a statement that reflected the stereotypes of his time, KOL's president remarked after one strike: "Women are the best men in the order."

See also American Federation of Labor; Barry, Leonora Marie Kearney; Congress of Industrial Organizations; Rodgers, Elizabeth Flynn; Stevens, Alzina Parsons; Strikes; Unions.

References Teresa Amott and Julie Matthaei, *Race, Gender, and Work: A Multicultural Economic History of Women in the United States* (1991); Mary H. Blewett, *Men, Women, and Work: Class, Gender, and Protest in the New England Shoe Industry, 1780–1910* (1988); Leon Fink, *Workingmen's Democracy: The Knights of Labor and American Politics* (1983); James J. Kenneally, "Women in the United States and Trade Unionism," in Norbert C. Soldon, ed., *The World of Women's Trade Unionism* (1985); Alice Kessler-Harris, *Out To Work: A History of Wage-Earning Women in the United States* (1982).

Korean Americans

The greatest number of working-class Koreans came to the United States after 1965. Most of these went into business for themselves in basic service enterprises, typically operated by a husband, wife, and assorted relatives and often in ghetto areas because space in more desirable locations was unavailable or unaffordable. Their workday is long (sometimes as much as 14–16 hours) and the wife is also expected to fulfill the traditional wifely duties in the home. In the 1980s an increasing number of Korean women were going outside the family to earn wages, usually in low-status, blue-collar occupations like domestic service. The job outside the home often increases the woman's burdens because of the traditional division of household labor and the husband's traditional authority.

See also Blue-Collar Workers; Domestic Servants.

Reference Diana Yu, *The Winds of Change* (1991).

Kreps, Juanita Morris (b. 1921)

This economist was the first woman director of the New York Stock Exchange and the first female Secretary of Commerce, appointed in 1977. A Kentuckian, she worked her way through Berea College and earned her Ph.D. in economics at Duke University. In 1944 she married economist Clifton Kreps, with whom she has three children. After several other teaching appointments, she returned to Duke in 1958, working her way up to professor in 1967 and vice-president in 1973. She has focused her research on women's employment, publishing her findings in several books, including *Sex in the Marketplace: American Women at Work* (1971) and *Sex, Age and Work* (1975).

See also Government Workers; Siebert, Muriel F.

References References Joan McCullough, *First of All* (1980); Jennifer S. Uglow, comp. and ed., *International Dictionary of Women's Biography* (1985); Angela Howard Zophy and Frances M. Kavenik, eds., *Handbook of American Women's History* (1990).

Labor Colleges
See Workers' Education.

Labor Force
See Work Force.

Labor Legislation
At the time of the Revolutionary War and for some time thereafter the law affecting workers and conditions of employment was based on two English common law doctrines: at-will employment, which left the employer free from any restraints in hiring and firing, and criminal conspiracy, which effectively outlawed labor organizing. The conspiracy doctrine has been superseded by legislation, passed first in the states and then at the federal level, recognizing labor's right to organize and bargain collectively. A range of labor legislation enacted over the years has limited the employers' freedom in setting terms and conditions of employment. Laws now exist to protect workers from hazardous jobs, to set minimum wages and maximum hours, to ban discrimination (including sex discrimination), to eliminate gender inequities in compensation, to protect mothers in their job rights, and to shield workers from unfair labor practices.

The New Deal saw the enactment of legislation that still, at the end of this century, governs management-union relationships: the Wagner Act of 1935 and the Taft-Hartley Act of 1947, as subsequently amended by the Landrum-Griffin Act of 1959 and the Health Care Amendments of 1974. This legislation established the National Labor Relations Board to resolve disputes between labor and management. It shields employees against unfair labor practices and requires their employers to bargain with unions chosen by a majority of the employees. Individual workers enjoy a right to assist and join unions, or to refuse. Strikers remain protected, unless they accept permanent jobs elsewhere. Unions have a duty to represent each of their workers fairly.

But the legislation governing contemporary relations between employer and employee generally excludes government jobs, agricultural workers, persons in domestic service who work in their employers' homes, employees' spouses and children, and agents of the employers. The exclusion of agricultural workers and domestics holds particular significance for women.

Remnants of the at-will employment doctrine still remain and raise serious questions about the rights of workers versus an employer's right to inquire (as a condition of employment) into such matters as life-style, smoking habits, drug use, sexual orientation, and medical history. Legislation and court decisions are just beginning to deal with these and similar issues.

See also Agricultural Workers; At-Will Employment; Boycotts; Civil Rights; Compensation; Criminal Conspiracy; Domestic Servants; Fair Labor Standards Act; Government Workers; Injunctions; Minimum Wage; National Industrial Recovery Act; New Deal; Norris-LaGuardia Act; Sex Discrimination; Strikes; Taft-Hartley Act; Unions; Wagner Act.

References Michael Evan Gold, *An Introduction to Labor Law* (1989); Susan Ware, *Holding Their Own: American Women in the 1930s* (1982).

Labor Management Relations Act
See Taft-Hartley Act.

Labor-Management Reporting and Disclosure Act (1959)
See Taft-Hartley Act.

Ladies Industry Association

This militant effort to organize the sewing women of New York City began in 1845 and lasted only a few months.

See also International Ladies' Garment Workers' Union; Shirt Sewers' Cooperative Union; Triangle Shirtwaist Fire; United Tailoresses Society of New York; Uprising of the 20,000.

Landrum-Griffin Act (1959)

See Taft-Hartley Act.

Lane, Gertrude Battles (1874–1941)

This editor and publishing company executive, a native of Maine, took a stenographic course after graduation from her private high school. After several dead-end jobs in publishing and writing, in 1903 Lane joined the editorial staff of the *Woman's Home Companion*. By 1912 she was the editor-in-chief, a position she held for 29 years. During her tenure the magazine advocated the necessity of home economics training for housewives, urged the importance of proper education for women seeking a business career, and inaugurated a "Better Babies Bureau" that offered advice on maternity and infant care. Widely admired for her ability and judgment, Lane at one time was called "the best man in the business" by the male chairman of the board of Crowell Publishing Company; her salary in 1940 had reached $52,000.

Lane never married: her taste, she said, was better than her opportunities.

See also Business and Industry; Home Economists; Journalists.

Reference Edward T. James et al., eds., *Notable American Women II* (1971).

Lanham Act (1943)

The Lanham Act allocated federal funds to provide child care centers for some women in the defense industries of World War II.

See also Child Care; World War II.

Latina Americans

See Hispanic Americans.

Law Enforcement

Women's involvement in police work began in 1845 when, at the urging of women's reform groups, New York City hired matrons in local jails; by 1900 most large cities employed them. The Progressive Era expanded women's presence and duties. In 1905 the Portland, Oregon, police department appointed Lola Baldwin to protect children. In 1910 Alice Stebbins Wells of the Los Angeles police spearheaded efforts for the employment of women in the field, organizing the International Association of Policewomen in 1915.

Until the late 1960s, however, most police departments assigned women only to counseling and protecting women and children. Since then women police officers have significantly increased their numbers and the breadth of their responsibilities. Penny Harrington, for example, joined the police force of Portland, Oregon, in 1964 and became chief of police in 1985. In 1990 Mayor Kathryn Whitmire appointed Elizabeth M. Watson Houston's chief of police, the first woman to head the police force of a major American city.

In 1992 the federal Bureau of Justice statistics showed 53,577 women law enforcement officers, about 10 percent of the total. But this figure does not include federal officers or special police (those responsible exclusively for the enforcement of laws on wildlife conservation, liquor, parks, airports, transit systems, and college and university campuses).

See also Bona Fide Occupational Qualification; Government Workers; Nontraditional Occupations; Progressive Era; Sex Discrimination; Sexual Harassment; Tests.

References Judith Freeman Clark, *Almanac of American Women in the 20th Century* (1987); Tamar Hosansky and Pat Sparling, *Working Vice: The Gritty True Story of Lt. Lucie J. Duvall* (1992); Paula Ries and Anne J. Stone, eds., *The American Woman, 1992–93: A Status Report* (1992); Angela Howard Zophy and Frances M. Kavenik, eds., *Handbook of American Women's History* (1990).

Lawrence, Massachusetts, Textile Strike

See Bread and Roses Strike.

League for Equal Opportunity for Women

This group of professional women of the Progressive Era vigorously opposed protective legislation for women.

See also Progressive Era; Protective Legislation.

Reference Mary E. Dreier, *Margaret Dreier Robins: Her Life, Letters, and Work* (1950).

Lee, Ann (1736–1784)

In her twenties, this English-born religious leader joined a group of former Quakers who danced, sang, shouted, and shook in worship. In 1762 she married blacksmith Abraham Standerin; the deaths in infancy of all four of the children she subsequently bore brought her to a nervous breakdown and convinced her that co-habitation was the source of all evil. About 1770 Lee assumed a position of leadership in the United Society of Believers in Christ's Second Appearing, called Shakers for their manner of worship. With other Shakers she was persecuted and jailed. After their release the Shakers felt a call to the New World. Lee, now "Mother Ann," sailed for America with eight others. Eventually they settled near Albany, New York, in the first of some 19 Shaker colonies, where their hard work and orderly lives brought them prosperity for a long period. Since they practiced celibacy as a central tenet of their religion, they multiplied only by the reception of new members.

Lee, regarded by her followers as part of the godhead, spoke out against slavery and war; she advocated neatness, economy, and charity to the poor. The Shakers were remarkable in their insistence on equal privileges for both genders and all races.

See also Religion.

Reference Edward T. James et al., eds., *Notable American Women II* (1971); Jennifer S. Uglow, comp. and ed., *International Dictionary of Women's Biography* (1985).

Leisure

The American worker in the 1990s typically enjoys less leisure than in 1948. Hours at paid work have risen in the past 20 years regardless of gender, marital status, children, and economic class. In the early 1990s workers report a decline in leisure time of as much as a third since the early 1970s. The average employed woman is on the job 305 hours more a year than in 1969. Between the demands of the workplace and those of the home, she has little personal time.

The movement of so many wives and mothers, married or single, into the workplace has required them to spend almost all their time fulfilling responsibilities either for their paid jobs or for housekeeping, child care, and more and more often, parental care. According to some estimates, when a woman takes a paying job her schedule expands by at least 20 hours a week; average estimates of the time employed mothers spend in paid work and household work range from 65 to 89 hours a week.

See also Compensation; Housekeeping; Moonlighting; Productivity.

Reference Juliet B. Schor, *The Overworked American: The Unexpected Decline of Leisure* (1992).

Lesbians

See Sexual Preference.

Lewis, Edmonia (1843?–1911?)

Daughter of a black father and a Native American mother, Lewis was the first minority artist to win international fame and popularity. Born in upstate New York and raised by her mother's tribe, she studied for three years at Oberlin College and later with the sculptor Edmund Brackett, as well as in Italy. Though she gradually moved toward a neoclassical style, she based some of her most moving work on her heritage as a minority member and a woman.

See also Artists.

Reference Edward T. James et al., eds., *Notable American Women II* (1971); Jennifer S. Uglow, comp. and ed., *International Dictionary of Women's Biography* (1985).

Librarians

In the latter part of the nineteenth century, libraries began to spring up across the country, often thanks to the volunteer efforts of a community's women. At that time librarianship was one of the few fields open to unmarried educated women. As their numbers increased from 20 percent of all librarians in 1870 to 82 percent in 1970, it became a profession in which women greatly outnumber men. But even in the early 1990s more men than women work in technical libraries and occupy top-level administrative and executive positions in large libraries. This disparity in pay and position concerns women's groups within the American Library Association. Since the 1960s affirmative action procedures have been providing greater opportunities for advancement for women making a career in library work.

Professional training for librarians began with Melvil Dewey at Columbia University. He faced many difficulties, including disquiet at his willingness to admit women to the School of Library Economy, which opened in 1887; in 1889 this school was transferred to Albany, where it did little but focus on routine and technical procedures. A protégée of Dewey, Katharine Lucinda Sharp, went on to establish a library school at the University of Illinois. Other women also contributed to the development of the profession. Alice Sarah Tyler, the first professionally trained librarian at the Cleveland Public Library, received her professional certificate in 1895 at the age of 36 and in 1913 became director (later dean) of the Library School at Western Reserve University in Cleveland. In 1929 Beatrice Winser became librarian of the Newark Public Library and a vigorous advocate of the open-shelves system to enable all the people to reach all the books they could read. Lutie Eugenia Stearns, without any professional training, extended Wisconsin's library system to remote parts of the state and set up traveling libraries.

Training of black librarians began in 1905 with an apprenticeship class in the Louisville Free Public Library, which also served black librarians from other southern cities. In 1925 the Hampton Library School opened, the only black library school to grant a bachelor's degree, but it had to close for lack of funds in 1939. The Atlanta University School of Library Service, founded in 1941, offers a master's degree in library science. Its first dean was Eliza Atkins Gleason (b. 1909), who earned her Ph.D. in library science from the University of Chicago. Virginia Lacy Jones (1912–1984), also with a Ph.D. in library science from the University of Chicago, followed Gleason as dean at Atlanta; she distinguished herself by fund-raising, by upgrading library services to black communities and schools, and by setting up continuing education programs for black librarians.

See also Affirmative Action.

References Kathleen M. Heim, ed., *The Status of Women in Librarianship* (1983); Carolyn Kenedy, *Pay Equity: An Action Manual for Library Workers* (1989); Angela Howard Zophy and Frances M. Kavenik, eds., *Handbook of American Women's History* (1990).

Line Jobs

These positions, unlike staff jobs, contribute directly to the central mission of the organization. In private industry, they are often in sales-marketing, production, or high-level finance departments, all directly concerned with profit-making. From these line jobs come promotions into the highest ranks. Career counselors often urge on ambitious women the importance of finding line jobs.

See also Staff Jobs.

Reference Jennie Farley, ed., *The Woman in Management: Career and Family Issues* (1983).

Livermore, Mary Ashton Rice (1820–1905)

This journalist and lecturer typified many "housewives" of her day in that she not only worked for pay as a teacher and governess before her marriage but also worked to supplement the family income during her marriage by writing and by helping manage her husband's business.

She also exemplifies a woman whose energies and abilities could be limited but not suppressed by the society into which she was born.

After her education in Boston's Hancock School and Miss Martha Whiting's Female Seminary, she taught, first at the seminary, then as governess to a southern family, and then as head of a private coeducational school in Massachusetts. In 1845 she married Daniel Park Livermore, a young Universalist minister, with whom she lived happily, bearing three daughters. Her writing during this period concentrated on religious subjects and the evils of alcohol.

A move to Chicago in 1857 made her husband editor of the *New Covenant*, a Universalist monthly, with Mary Livermore the associate editor. She also volunteered in charitable work, and with the onset of the Civil War she focused her energies on all-out volunteerism for the Sanitary Commission, hiring a housekeeper and a governess to care for her family.

The experience converted her to women's suffrage, which she saw as necessary to combat poverty, drunkenness, and prostitution. Accordingly the family moved to a Boston suburb and Mary Livermore became editor of the *Woman's Journal* and an ardent suffragist. There her abilities attracted the attention of a promoter who invited her to undertake a career as a professional lecturer. Beguiled by the opportunity of propagandizing for her ideas, she appeared for 23 years on the lecture circuit, delivering on average three lectures a week, and earning thousands of dollars and the eponym "Queen of the Platform"—all this with her husband's strong support. In this role she promoted both temperance and women's rights. She retired in 1895.

See also Civil War; Journalists; Prostitutes; Teachers.

References Edward T. James et al., eds., *Notable American Women II* (1971); Mary Ashton Rice Livermore, *My Story of the War* (1887); Mary Ashton Rice Livermore, *Story of My Life* (1897).

Living Wage
See Family Wage.

Lockouts
In the past employers have used this ploy of shutting down a plant temporarily to strengthen their bargaining positions or to fight off unions. Section 7 of the Wagner Act now forbids the lockout as a tactic to prevent unionization. Employers, however, still may use the lockout as a bargaining device.

See also Collective Bargaining; Injunctions; Strikes; Unions; Wagner Act; Yellow-Dog Contract.

Reference Michael Yates, , *Labor Law Handbook* (1987).

Lockwood, Belva Ann Bennett McNall (1830–1917)
Lockwood was the first woman attorney admitted to practice before the U.S. Supreme Court (1879). Educated in the country schools of upper New York State, she had to leave school and begin teaching at 15. At 19 she married a farmer and sawmill operator, Uriah McNall, but five years later he died, leaving her with a four-year-old daughter. For the next few years she combined further study with teaching, earning her B.S. in 1857. As she continued her teaching career, she encouraged the girls under her tutelage to participate in gymnastics and public speaking.

In 1866 she moved to Washington, D.C., where she soon opened her own coeducational school. When she married the minister and dentist Ezekiel Lockwood two years later, he took over its supervision. Meanwhile Belva Lockwood applied to law school after law school, finally securing admission to the new National University Law School in 1871; when she completed the course two years later, she had to persuade President Ulysses Grant to intervene so that she could receive her degree. The bar of the District of Columbia admitted her at once. The refusal of the federal Court of Claims and the Supreme Court to let her practice before them set her to lobbying singlehandedly the Congress, which passed a bill in 1879 granting women qualified to practice law the right to pursue legal affairs before the highest federal courts of the country. That year both the Supreme Court and the Court of Claims admitted Lockwood.

A lifelong supporter of women's rights, Lockwood fought for women's suffrage, for New York state legislation giving women government employees equal pay for equal work (1872), and for liberalization of the property rights of married women in the District of Columbia. She mentored hundreds of women who wanted to be attorneys.

In 1884 and again in 1888 she ran as the National Equal Rights party's candidate for president on a platform of equal rights for all, the regulation of the liquor traffic, uniform marriage and divorce laws, and universal peace. During her later career she built a reputation as a lecturer, not only earning lecture fees on her tours but also gathering business

Belva Lockwood

for her lucrative law practice, which her daughter managed.

See also Attorneys.

Reference Edward T. James et al., eds., *Notable American Women II* (1971).

Lothrop, Alice Louise Higgins (1870–1920)

Lothrop was general secretary of the Associated Charities of Boston from 1903–1913, a period during which social work was being professionalized. A native of Massachusetts, she was educated in private schools and briefly at the New York School of Philanthropy. In 1898 she joined the staff of the Associated Charities, working her way up to district secretary and then to general secretary.

She pioneered in developing medical social work, conceptualizing it broadly to include not only facilitating communications between physicians and patients but also promoting reform legislation and research in areas affecting patients, like housing, labor, and recreation. She efficiently organized disaster relief, as for the San Francisco fire of 1906, and broadened the scope of the Associated Charities in respect to social reform and legislation, public health, and interagency cooperation.

See also Social Workers.

Reference Edward T. James et al., eds., *Notable American Women II* (1971).

Lowell, Josephine Shaw (1843–1905)

This charitable worker and reformer, brought up in New York and educated there and abroad, was widowed at 20, her husband killed in the Civil War, leaving her with an infant daughter. She at once devoted herself to the Freedmen's Relief Association and other charities. After years of service she set forth in *Public Relief and Private Charity* (1884) her belief that charity should aim not primarily to relieve suffering but to make the recipient a productive member of society.

In 1890 she decided to devote herself to labor problems. That year she helped to found the Consumers' League of New York, over which she presided for six years. She supported the Homestead Strike of 1892, and during the depression of 1893–1894 tried to provide work relief for New York's unemployed. In 1894, she helped start the Woman's Municipal League, and in 1895, the Civil Service Reform Association of New York State. By such means she pushed toward the development of the "preventive social work" of the Progressive Era.

See also Civil War; Consumers' League; O'Reilly, Leonora; Progressive Era; Social Workers; Woman's Municipal League.

References Edward T. James et al., eds., *Notable American Women II* (1971); William Rhinelander Stewart, *The Philanthropic Work of Josephine Shaw Lowell* (1911); Jennifer S. Uglow, comp. and ed., *International Dictionary of Women's Biography* (1985).

Lowell Female Industrial Reform and Mutual Aid Society
See Lowell Girls.

Lowell Female Labor Reform Association
See Bagley, Sarah G.; Lowell Girls.

Lowell Girls
In the early nineteenth century employers were seeking women to work in their factories. Since most married women preferred to work at home and society decreed that they should, employers turned to young, white, native-born, middle-class, single women, whom they tried to recruit by offering sheltered living in strictly supervised boarding houses. For a while the system worked well. The "Lowell girls" (so-called because of the many textile mills in Lowell, Massachusetts), proud of their work and zestful for knowledge and culture, enjoyed the respect of the society and undiminished opportunities for marriage.

The Lowell mill owners understood that it was good business to recruit and maintain a dependable, disciplined work force. The hundreds of young, single women coming from rural communities to earn better wages in the mills were provided not only with jobs and income, but also with a sisterhood of workers away from home. To ensure respectability and reassure parents back home, the mill owners imposed curfews and dress codes, provided boarding houses and dormitories with house mothers, and enforced strict rules of behavior. (The Rodgers and Hammerstein musical *Carousel* was somewhat romantically based on the lives of the Lowell Girls).

But problems soon arose: in the mid-1830s abortive strikes occurred. In 1844 the Lowell Girls organized the Lowell Female Labor Reform Association, later known as the Lowell Female Industrial Reform and Mutual Aid Society, to fight for shorter hours and against pay cuts. Competition eventually caused factory owners to eliminate supervised boarding houses, pay less, demand longer hours and higher productivity, and deskill the work. Irish immigrant women desperate enough to accept worse conditions and lower wages replaced native-born farm daughters.

See also Bagley, Sarah G.; Boarding; Factory Workers; Farley, Harriet; Harvey Girls; Mercer Girls; Robinson, Harriet Jane Hanson; Strikes; Waltham System.

References Mimi Abramovitz, *Regulating the Lives of Women: Social Welfare Policy from Colonial Times to the Present* (1988); Thomas Dublin, *Farm and Factory: The Mill Experience and Women's Lives in New England, 1830–1860* (1982); Philip S. Foner, ed., *The Factory Girls* (1977); Harriet H. Robinson, *Loom and Spindle; or Life among the Early Mill Girls* (1898).

Lozier, Clemence Sophia Harned (1813–1888)
This maverick crusading physician was educated in her native New Jersey. About 1830 she married carpenter and builder Abraham Witton Lozier; only one of their children survived infancy, and her husband fell sick soon after their marriage. For 11 years Lozier supported her family with a girls' school she established

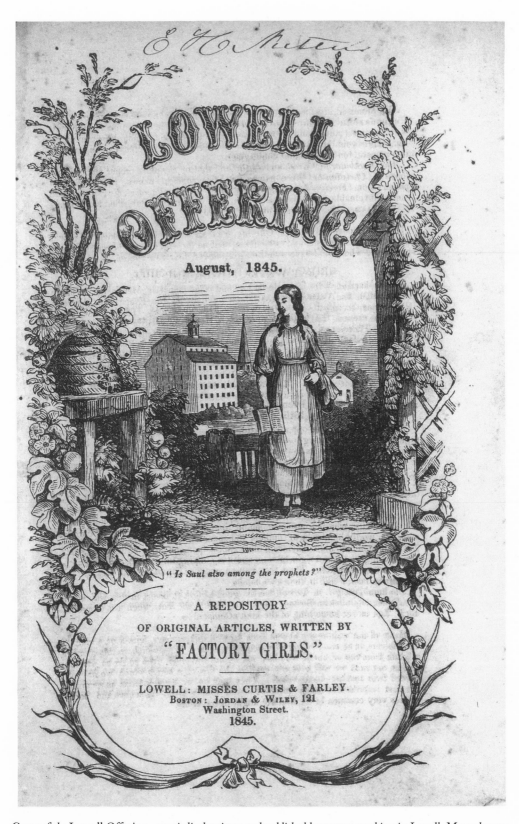

Cover of the Lowell Offering, *a periodical written and published by women working in Lowell, Massachusetts*

in her home. Her husband died in 1837. In 1844 she remarried, unhappily, and somewhere along the line she and her second husband separated.

During these years she had been reading medical books and lecturing on physiology and hygiene. In 1849 she entered medical school; as soon as she graduated in 1853 she set up a practice, specializing in obstetrics and surgery. She offered her women patients lectures and a library where they could educate themselves on medical subjects. In 1863 she successfully lobbied the legislature to charter the New York Medical College and Hospital for Women. She served there for more than 20 years. Ardently advocating women's rights in particular and human rights in general, she also worked diligently for the National Workingwomen's League.

See also Physicians.

Reference Edward T. James et al., eds., *Notable American Women II* (1971).

Ludlow Massacre (April 1914)

One of the more notorious incidents of violence in the history of American labor, the Ludlow Massacre occurred as the climax of a coal strike in Colorado when armed guards and militia overran the tent city in which miners and their families lived, setting fires and shooting hapless women and children.

Reference Howard M. Gitelman, *Legacy of the Ludlow Massacre* (1988).

Lynn, Massachusetts, Shoe Strike of 1860

In this strike male leaders fatefully rejected an alliance between the new women factory workers and the women who worked at home, choosing instead to concentrate on a family wage for men, and thereby splitting the women factory workers from the women home workers.

See also Factory Workers; Family Wage; Strikes.

Women march during the 1860 shoemakers strike in Lynn, Massachusetts.

Reference Mary H. Blewett, *Men, Women, and Work: Class, Gender, and Protest in the New England Shoe Industry, 1780–1910* (1988).

Lyon, Mary (1797–1849)

This educator founded Mount Holyoke Seminary, now Mount Holyoke College. As a young farm woman she alternated teaching and attending schools, and in 1824 she opened a girls' school in western Massachusetts. For several years she continued to combine study and teaching in her own school and elsewhere. After a trip in the summer of 1833 in which she visited schools and colleges in New York State, she focused on founding a residential seminary for "adult female youth in the common walks of life." She raised much of the money herself and watched over the construction. Chartered in 1836, Mount Holyoke Seminary opened the next year, with 80 students 17 and older. Until her death Lyon labored there, as principal, teacher, and for some time supervisor of the domestic work system that the students engaged in.

See also Academic Women.

References Fidelia Fisk, *Recollections of Mary Lyon* (1866); Beth Bradford Gilchrist, *The Life of Mary Lyon* (1910); Marion Lansing, ed., *Mary Lyon through Her Letters* (1937).

Lytle, Lutie (ca. 1871–?)

Lytle, possibly the first black accredited as an attorney, was admitted to the Tennessee Bar in 1897.

See also Attorneys.

Reference Angela Howard Zophy and Frances M. Kavenik, eds., *Handbook of American Women's History* (1990).

McClintock, Barbara (1902–1992)

McClintock, a genetic scientist, graduated from Cornell University with a B.A. (1923), M.A. (1925), and her Ph.D. in cytology (1927). A productive scholar, she won a National Research Council fellowship in 1931 and a Guggenheim in 1933. In 1939 she was elected vice-president of the Genetics Society of America. McClintock taught for a time on the faculty at Cornell and the University of Missouri but was disenchanted by the prejudice against academic women that she encountered. In 1941 she moved to the Cold Spring Harbor Laboratory on Long Island to continue her research in genetics. In 1944 she was elected president of the Genetics Society of America and a member of the National Academy of Science, the third woman so honored in its history.

McClintock's discovery of movable genetic elements in 1951 was initially dismissed as nonsense by her colleagues, but her findings were eventually vindicated with the help of molecular biology. Praise and recognition followed: the Kimber Genetics Award in 1967, the National Medal of Science in 1970, the Albert Lasker Award and Israel's Wolf Foundation Prize in 1981, and a MacArthur Foundation grant in 1981 that provided a lifetime annuity of $60,000. Her Nobel Prize came in 1983.

See also Academic Women; Science, Mathematics, and Science-Based Professions.
Reference Judith Freeman Clark, *Almanac of American Women in the 20th Century* (1987).

McCormick, Ruth Hanna (1880–1944)

This self-described "working politician" and supporter of progressive causes, particularly the welfare of women and children, was the first woman nominated by a major party for the Senate and the first to manage a nomination campaign. A native of Ohio, she was educated in private schools.

She gained practical experience in politics by accompanying her father, Mark Hanna, when he managed William McKinley's presidential campaign.

In 1924 she became Republican national committeewoman from Illinois and in 1928 she won election to the House of Representatives. She lost her 1930 bid for the Senate, her last attempt at national office. Thereafter she published newspapers; owned a radio station, a dairy farm, and a ranch; and founded a girls' school. In 1939 she comanaged Thomas E. Dewey's try for the Republican nomination.

See also Government Workers.
Reference Edward T. James et al., eds., *Notable American Women III* (1971); Kristie Miller, *Ruth Hanna McCormick: A Life in Politics* (1992).

McCreery, Maria Maud Leonard (1883–1938)

From an early commitment to political action in the cause of women's suffrage, this Wisconsin union organizer shifted her interests to labor, peace, and socialism. A native of Wisconsin, she was educated in local schools. In 1902 she married Rex McCreery; her only child died in infancy. She volunteered in the Milwaukee railroad strikes of 1918–1922, and in the late 1920s became an organizer for the Amalgamated Clothing Workers of America, as well as a reporter for the *Milwaukee Leader,* and a worker for the Stenographers, Typewriters, Bookkeepers, and Assistants Union of the American Federation of Labor (AFL). In the mid-1930s she concentrated on helping Federal Labor Union #18545 (AFL) to organize the Kohler plumbing-ware company, until she fell sick. Even then she pieced together a living organizing for unions and teaching for the University of Wisconsin's School of Workers.

See also American Federation of Labor; Union Organizers.
Reference Edward T. James et al., eds., *Notable American Women II* (1971).

McDowell, Anne Elizabeth (1826–1901)

In 1855 this journalist, a native of Delaware, founded the *Woman's Advocate*, produced entirely by women and devoted to bettering the lot of women workers. McDowell focused not on political but on economic rights for women. After the *Advocate's* demise in 1860(?), she edited women's departments in Philadelphia newspapers, formed a sickness and death benefit organization for employees of Wanamaker's department store, and set up a library for women employees.

See also Journalists.
Reference Edward T. James et al., eds., *Notable American Women II* (1971).

McDowell, Mary Eliza (1854–1936)

The Pullman strike of 1894 shocked this settlement house worker into investigating the causes of labor unrest, a study which led to her directing the University of Chicago settlement house near the stockyards and meat-packing plants. She helped establish the first women's union in the yards and, alone among the district's public figures, stood with the strikers in 1904. Though the strike failed, it encouraged a federal investigation of the yards. McDowell went on to help found the Women's Trade Union League, to lobby Congress successfully for an appropriation to finance a study of women in industry (ultimately produced in 1911), to work for legislation limiting hours for women and children, and to help establish the Women's Bureau in the Department of Labor. After 1919 she interested herself particularly in race relations.

See also Settlement Houses; Strikes; Unions; Women's Bureau; Women's Trade Union League.
References Caroline M. Hill, comp., *Mary McDowell and Municipal Housekeeping* (1938); Edward

T. James et al., eds., *Notable American Women II* (1971); Howard E. Wilson, *Mary McDowell, Neighbor* (1928).

McGee, Anita Newcomb (1864–1940)

This physician was educated in Washington, D.C., and abroad. In 1888 she married geologist and anthropologist William John McGee; they had three children, one of whom died in infancy. After her marriage she continued her studies, taking her M.D. degree in 1892 and following it with a postgraduate course in gynecology at Johns Hopkins. She practiced only briefly.

But McGee's combination of medical training, organizational skills, and association with the Daughters of the American Revolution got her appointed Acting Assistant Surgeon General in the Spanish-American War. Despite a turf fight with the American Red Cross, she distinguished herself in the struggle to found the Army Nurse Corps. For the rest of her life she tried to help the women in the Corps. In 1898–1899 she organized the Society of Spanish-American War Nurses, over which she presided for six years.

See also Army Nurse Corps; Military Women; Nurses; Physicians.
Reference Edward T. James et al., eds., *Notable American Women II* (1971).

McLaren, Louise Leonard (1885–1968)

This labor educator, a native of Pennsylvania, graduated from Vassar in 1907. Twenty years later she took a master's degree in economics from Columbia. After a few years of teaching, she found her vocation in 1914 as industrial secretary for the Young Women's Christian Association. Her work in the South led her to found and for 17 years (1927–1944) promote and direct the Southern Summer School for Women Workers in Industry, a residential school distinguished for its emphasis on economics and industrial history. She then worked for various nonprofit organizations, finishing her career as teacher and researcher with the American Labor Education Service.

See also* Southern Summer School for Women Workers in Industry; Workers' Education; Young Women's Christian Association.

Reference Barbara Sicherman et al., eds., *Notable American Women: The Modern Period* (1980).

McPherson, Aimée Semple (1890–1944)

This conservative, itinerant evangelist and founder of the International Church of the Foursquare Gospel grew up in Canada, where she was converted at 17 at a Pentecostal revival. In 1908 she married the revivalist Robert James Semple and they traveled around conducting revivals. He died in 1910 in China, a month before their daughter's birth. She married again, unhappily, in 1912, one Harold Stewart McPherson, a bookkeeper, and later bore a son. In 1915 she left her husband and took the children to Canada.

That year McPherson resumed a life as a revivalist, preaching a fundamentalist religion, interpreting the Bible literally, and practicing faith healing. Her career brought her fame and fortune, with more than a dash of notoriety. She was much assisted by her own charisma, beauty, and bent for the dramatic—and her mother's joining her to help with her children and her career. McPherson established magazines, summer camps, Bible conferences, a radio station, and a Bible college. A quarrel with her mother and estrangement from her daughter darkened the last part of her life; she died in 1944 from an overdose of sleeping pills, an event medical officials ruled accidental.

See also Religion.

Reference Edward T. James et al., eds., *Notable American Women II* (1971); Jennifer S. Uglow, comp. and ed., *International Dictionary of Women's Biography* (1985).

Magill, Helen (1853–1944)

Magill held the first Ph.D. ever awarded to an American woman, earned from Boston University in 1877, 15 years after the first American doctoral degree was awarded. She went on to study four more years at Cambridge University in England. On her return to the United States she organized and directed the Howard Collegiate Institute for young women, but four years later, in 1887, she resigned because of a conflict with her board. She taught at a short-lived women's annex to Princeton and then in a Brooklyn high school. Her promising career had petered out.

In 1890 she married Andrew Dickson White, the first president of Cornell University and later ambassador to Russia and Germany; they had two children.

See also Academic Women; Dykes, Eva B.; Mossell, Sadie Tanner; Simpson, Georgiana.

References Lynn D. Gordon, *Gender and Higher Education in the Progressive Era* (1990); Barbara Miller Solomon, *In the Company of Educated Women* (1985).

Mahoney, Mary Eliza (1845–1926)

This first black trained nurse, a native of Massachusetts, received her diploma from the New England Hospital for Women and Children in 1879. As a private-duty nurse she built a considerable reputation around Boston. She strongly supported the National Association of Colored Graduate Nurses and the cause of women's suffrage.

See also Nurses.

Reference Edward T. James et al., eds., *Notable American Women II* (1971).

Malkiel, Theresa Serber (1874–1949)

This Jewish immigrant garment worker and trade union organizer wrote a novel, *The Diary of a Shirtwaist Striker* (1910), the story of a middle-class woman whose experiences as a striker convert her to socialism. The novel includes descriptions of the Triangle Shirtwaist Fire and the Uprising of the 20,000.

See also Strikes; Triangle Shirtwaist Fire; Union Organizers; Uprising of the 20,000; Writers and Publishers.

Reference Angela Howard Zophy and Frances M. Kavenik, eds., *Handbook of American Women's History* (1990).

Malone, Annie
See Turnbo-Malone, Annie Minerva.

Management and Technical Assistance 7(J) Program

See Small Business Administration.

Managers

Business education has been only one route by which women have become managers. Entrepreneurs have developed their own businesses. Clerical work has brought women by the millions into offices, and some have moved up into lower, middle, and in a handful of cases, upper management. College graduates in liberal arts curricula have taken jobs in publishing or as "girl Fridays" in corporations from which they occasionally managed to wangle upward mobility. As banks, insurance companies, and investment firms sized up women as potential customers, they began to appoint women heads of "women's departments." "Employment management," known after World War I as "personnel management" and later still as "human relations management," attracted women, who were sometimes hired as managers there because of the gender's touted sensitivity and empathy. And with the women's movement of the 1960s and 1970s, court cases and legislation opened new opportunities.

Since then women have gained ground in management, particularly in fields like banking and insurance. But in all fields women managers encounter "glass ceilings" and "brick walls" that shut them away from top posts and the more lucrative sides of the business—not to mention the "sticky floors" that prevent their rising at all. Sometimes fancy titles for women managers conceal lack of real power. More often women are shunted into visible customer-service positions that do not directly affect the bottom line.

Some theorists believe that women exhibit different managerial styles than men: less authoritarian and confrontational, more tactful, relying more on cooperation than on coercion. Some feminists claim that women managers listen more carefully, care more about their subordinates and co-workers, and respect differences. In the early 1990s some companies, confronted with the demographic probability of more women managers, are trying to learn to profit from these different skills and approaches.

See also Business and Industry; Clerical Workers; Entrepreneurs; Follett, Mary Parker; Gilbreth, Lillian Evelyn Moller; Girl Fridays; Glass Ceiling; Herrick, Elinore Morehouse; Human Resources Managers; Line Jobs; Scientific Management; Staff Jobs; Sticky Floor; Transformational Leadership; Women's Movement.

References Catalyst, *Building an Effective Corporate Women's Group* (1988); Sally Helgasen, *Female Advantage: Women's Ways of Leadership* (1990); J. Hunsaker and P. Hunsaker, *Strategies and Skills for Managerial Women* (1992); Rosabeth Moss Kanter, *Men and Women of the Corporation* (1977); Rosabeth Moss Kanter, *When Giants Learn To Dance: Mastering the Challenge of Strategy, Management and Careers in the 1990s* (1989); M. F. Karsten, *Gender Issues in Management* (1992); Judith A. Leavitt, *American Women Managers and Administrators: A Selective Biographical Dictionary of Twentieth-Century Leaders in Business, Education, and Government* (1985); Judith A. Leavitt and Paul Wasserman, *Women in Administration and Management: An Information Sourcebook* (1988); Felice N. Schwartz with Jean Zimmerman, *Breaking with Tradition: Women and Work, the New Facts of Life* (1992).

Manhattan Trade School for Girls

Opened in 1902 under the direction of Mary Raphael Schenck Woolman, this institution offered working-class women vocational training.

See also Vocational Education; Woolman, Mary Raphael Schenck.

Mann Act (1910)

This act of Congress was passed to combat prostitution and white slavery by making it illegal to transport women across state boundaries for immoral purposes.

See also Prostitutes; White Slavery.

Mansfield, Arabella (1846–1911)

In 1869 this professor became the first woman in the United States admitted to the bar. She never practiced; instead she built her career as a historian and college administrator.

See also Academic Women; Attorneys.

Reference Edward T. James et al., eds., *Notable American Women III* (1971).

Manufactory
See Factory Workers.

Marginal Workers
In 1990, 30 percent of all job-holders were marginal, a term that encompasses part-time, temporary, or contract workers. Although jobs like these meet the needs of some women, most of them result from employer needs to reduce the work force and even more to circumvent paying benefits. This trend particularly affects women workers.

See also Benefits; Contingent Work Force; Contract Labor; Part-Time Workers; Temporary Workers.

References Richard S. Belous, *The Contingent Economy: The Growth of the Contemporary, Part-Time and Subcontracted Workforce* (1989); Nine to Five, National Association of Working Women, "Profile of Working Women" (1990).

Marot, Helen (1865–1940)
In 1897 this Philadelphia-born social investigator and labor reformer organized a small library of resources on social and economic problems and in 1899 published a *Handbook of Labor Literature*. At the same time she began to investigate Philadelphia custom tailoring trades for the U.S. Industrial Commission; what she uncovered made her an activist for women and children workers. In 1902 her investigation of child labor in New York City culminated in a report, coauthored by Florence Kelley and Josephine Goldmark, that furnished the rationale for New York's Compulsory Education Act of 1903.

In 1906 she began a seven-year stint as the executive secretary of the Women's Trade Union League (WTUL) of New York, a period brilliant with accomplish-

ment. Besides expanding the scope of the WTUL, she broke new ground in one area of women's work after another, helping to organize the Bookkeepers, Stenographers and Accountants Union of New York, and with Kelley and Goldmark gathering information for the Brandeis Brief in *Muller v. Oregon*. In 1909–1910 she directed the WTUL's vital support for the Uprising of the 20,000 that enabled today's International Ladies' Garment Workers' Union and enormously expanded the unionization of women workers. She resigned her WTUL post in 1913 partly to encourage the movement of working-class women into its leadership.

Marot then reverted to writing and editing. In *American Labor Unions* (1914) she advocated a socialist reconstruction of society. She worked on the board of the *Masses* and the staff of the *Dial*. Her *Creative Impulse in Industry* (1918) envisaged a more rational reorganization of industry, labor relations, and education.

Marot's career combined activism, investigative research, and theoretical analysis. She made an enormous difference to working women.

See also Goldmark, Josephine Clara; International Ladies' Garment Workers' Union; Kelley, Florence; *Muller v. Oregon*; Socialist Party; Uprising of the 20,000; Women's Trade Union League.

Reference Edward T. James et al., eds., *Notable American Women III* (1971).

Marriage Bars
See Married Women's Employment.

Married Women's Employment
Should married women work for wages outside the home regardless of economic necessity? As women moved in sizable numbers out of their homes and into the public sphere, this question was ferociously debated. Opponents argued from a traditional view of women's role in society: married women had a moral responsibility to home and family; only cruel necessity could give married women the right to work for wages outside the home.

On the other hand, feminists argued that only through outside employment could married women emancipate themselves from dependence upon their husbands, raise their family's standard of living, and break free of their home-bound isolation.

The debate heated up during World War I and immediately after, partly because the war opened unprecedented employment opportunites for women, both married and single. During the Great Depression many argued against the employment of married women in a desperate effort to spread out the few jobs available. The debate flared up again in the aftermath of World War II, as government and employers who, during the war, had preached to women their duty to work now adjured them to go home and surrender their jobs to male veterans. In the 1960s and 1970s with the women's movement the old arguments were rehashed, possibly for the last time, as women expressed their psychological needs for significant work and for assuming their share of the responsibility for the financial well-being of their families.

In point of fact, up through the Great Depression, overt restrictions against married women's employment prevailed in many kinds of work, particularly teaching and clerical work. Blue-collar married women faced less formal but almost as formidable barriers, erected by the opposition of the male trade union movement and social sanctions. In the Great Depression the National Economy Act of 1933 provided that, if personnel cutbacks were necessary in the federal government, wives were to be dismissed if their husbands also held government jobs, even if the wife had seniority or held a more important position than her spouse. Even Frances Perkins, Secretary of Labor during the Depression, advised married women to give up working in favor of unemployed men. These marriage bars punished women not only by refusing them jobs, but also by reinforcing the prejudice against promoting unmarried women on the theory that they would leave when they married—as indeed marriage bars often forced them to.

Until 1940, proportionally few married women worked for pay. For every decade since 1940, their percentage in the labor force has increased by about 10 percentage points. Older married women (over 35) at first entered in greater numbers, only to be followed by younger married women in the late 1960s and 1970s. In 1988, 56.7 percent of married women with resident husbands worked, compared with 67.7 percent of never-married women and with 46.2 percent of widowed, divorced, or separated women. In 1989 nearly 30 million wives were in the labor force. Married women in fact display lower rates of unemployment than other women.

In most quarters the question of married women's employment has now become moot. What remains of the debate has shifted to whether or not mothers of young children should be in the workplace, but in the face of the actualities even that discussion has been muted: the proportion of working women with young children has increased fivefold since 1948. In any case opponents of the gainful employment of wives and mothers become considerably less ardent when discussing the problems of welfare recipients.

See also Aid to Families with Dependent Children; Blue-Collar Workers; Clerical Workers; Gender Gap; Great Depression; Government Workers; Mothers' Employment; Mothers' Pensions; National Association of Working Women; Perkins, Frances; Teachers; Unions; Wives; Women's Industrial Conference; Women's Movement; World War II.

References Catalyst, *Corporations and Two-Career Families: Directions for the Future* (1981); Claudia Goldin, *Understanding the Gender Gap: An Economic History of American Women* (1990); Maurine Weiner Greenwald, "Working-Class Feminism and the Family Wage Ideal: The Seattle Debate on Married Women's Right To Work, 1914–1920" (1989), 118–149; Paula Ries and Anne J. Stone, eds., *The American Woman, 1992–93: A Status Report* (1992); Juliet B. Schor, *The Overworked Ameri-*

can: The Unexpected Decline of Leisure (1992); Cynthia Taeuber, comp. and ed., *Statistical Handbook on Women in America* (1991).

Married Women's Property Acts

Under the common law that Americans inherited from Great Britain, a married woman's earnings as well as her property became her husband's. Indeed married women enjoyed no legal identity of their own. The law assumed that husband and wife were one, and he was that one.

But colonial courts did recognize (rarely used) prenuptial agreements. More significantly, some states allowed some married women, especially widows and deserted wives, to conduct business, if only to keep them off the public rolls. The scarcity of women in colonial America prompted the granting of some limited legal rights: dower rights, the ability of some women to sign contracts, the right of some women to be consulted about the sale of property.

Affairs changed in the nineteenth century, in large part because men as fathers and brothers were interested in protecting their own rights in their female relatives' property. Moreover, husbands in financial difficulties experienced the disadvantage of having the debt collector seize all the family property, since wives could hold nothing in their own names. In 1839 states began to enact laws recognizing married women's right to control their own property. Mississippi was the first of these, motivated by a desire to protect the rights of women to dispose of slaves they had brought to the marriage. Michigan, New York, and Pennsylvania enacted married women's property legislation in the 1840s, and other states followed suit, often propelled by the demands of women's rights activists like Elizabeth Cady Stanton and Susan B. Anthony.

The years 1869–1887 showed a significant change in attitude toward women, in one degree or another recognizing women as possessing a legal identity separate from their husbands'. Thirty-three states and the District of Columbia gave women the power to control their own earnings. Thirty states provided for a separate estate for women. Louisiana, Texas, New Mexico, Arizona, and California became community property states, with both spouses holding equal shares in the family property.

In their *History of Women's Suffrage*, Susan B. Anthony and Ida H. Harper wrote of women's rights in 1900: "The wife now may own and control her separate property in three-fourths of the states, and in the other fourth only one Northern State is included. In every State a married woman may make a will, but can dispose only of her separate property. In about two-thirds of the states she possesses her earnings. In the great majority she may make contracts and bring suit."

Yet in 1920 women's property rights fell far short of their husbands'. Bits of surviving common law in some states allowed husbands to control their wives' wages and limited a woman's inheritance from an intestate husband to a third of his estate. In 1930, 17 states denied women equal rights in the sale of real estate. In community property states husbands had the power to manage the jointly held property. In 1940, 12 states still did not permit a wife to contract.

Even in the early 1990s, with no uniform marital property act in force, women's property rights differ significantly from state to state. Even the nine community property states differ among themselves. A woman moving from one state to another in our mobile society may easily fail to understand the legal disabilities imposed upon her until death or divorce jolts her into awareness.

See also Colonial America; Coverture; Ward, Hortense Sparks Malsch.

References Carl N. Degler, *At Odds: Women and the Family in America from the Revolution to the Present* (1980); Sara M. Evans, *Born for Liberty: A History of Women in America* (1989); Rita J. Simon and Gloria Danziger, *Women's Movements in America* (1991); Angela Howard Zophy and Frances M. Kavenik, eds., *Handbook of American Women's History* (1990).

Martin, Anne Henrietta (1875–1951)

This woman suffragist and feminist was the first woman to run for the United States Senate. A native of Nevada, she graduated from the University of Nevada in 1894 and earned a second baccalaureate degree from Stanford in 1896 and a master's in history in 1897. She then established the history department at Nevada, heading it for four years.

Several years abroad led to a commitment to women's suffrage, to which she devoted herself on her return to the United States. She ran as an independent candidate for a Nevada senatorial seat in 1918 and 1920; she polled only 20 percent of the vote but opened a new possibility for women.

Martin spent her later years as a volunteer for the Women's International League for Peace and Freedom, urging women to challenge men's control of the culture. She wrote extensively. For most of her life she urged above all the importance of women's equal participation in politics.

See also Government Workers.
References Anne Bail Howard, *The Long Campaign: A Biography of Anne Martin* (1985); Barbara Sicherman et al., eds., *Notable American Women: The Modern Period* (1980).

Martinez, Maria Montoya (1881–1980)

This Native-American Pueblo potter was known for her distinctive, elegant, black pots adapted from ancient crafts.

See also Artists.
Reference Angela Howard Zophy and Frances M. Kavenik, eds., *Handbook of American Women's History* (1990).

Mason, Lucy Randolph (1882–1959)

This labor reformer, descended from two first families of Virginia, was brought up to social responsibility. Denied a college education by poverty, she taught herself stenography and typing and for ten years worked as a stenographer in Richmond. In 1914 she began work as industrial secretary of the Richmond Young Women's Christian Association and served as its general secretary from 1923–1932, focusing particularly on industrial reforms to help working women, especially blacks.

In 1932 she moved to New York to direct the Consumers' League. After five years there, she returned to her native South in largely self-defined work for the Congress of Industrial Organizations (CIO), particularly in the drive to organize the textile workers. Her understanding of the region and her own relationship to it inspired her to present herself not as an organizer but as an interpreter and troubleshooter. Her gender, her ladylike appearance and demeanor, and her ancestry enabled her to do what others could not and attracted the support of community leaders. She not only negotiated for workers in strikes but also publicized civil rights' violations, undoubtedly helped by her personal friendship with Eleanor Roosevelt.

Mason was eventually frustrated, though, by the southern employers' backlash against organized labor. She concentrated less on troubleshooting and more on public relations, political action, civil liberties, and labor legislation. She retired from the CIO in 1953.

See also Bellanca, Dorothy Jacobs; Congress of Industrial Organizations; Consumers' League; Roosevelt, Anna Eleanor; Strikes; Union Organizers; Unions; Young Women's Christian Association.
References Lucy R. Mason, *To Win These Rights: A Personal Story of the CIO in the South* (1970); John A. Salmond, *Miss Lucy of the CIO: The Life and Times of Lucy Randolph Mason, 1882–1959* (1988); Barbara Sicherman et al., eds., *Notable American Women: The Modern Period* (1980).

Masters, Sybilla (?–1720)

Possibly the first woman American inventor, Masters secured patents in England and in Pennsylvania for two inventions: one to pulverize maize, and the other for a new way to work and stain straw, work palmetto leaves, and trim hats. Her husband, Thomas, put the first to practice in a Pennsylvania mill, and Masters herself employed the second at the West India Hat and Bonnet Shop in London.

See also Inventors.

Reference Edward T. James et al., eds., *Notable American Women II* (1971).

Maternity Leave

Maternity leave is the period of time allowed a woman worker in which to prepare for, give birth to, and bond with her baby before returning to her job. Title VII of the Civil Rights Act of 1964 considerably increased the availability of maternity leave.

In many other developed countries, mothers and sometimes fathers receive extended paid maternity or paternity leave, but in the United States the period is almost always uncompensated, although the company usually continues the woman's health insurance. In 1989 about 3 percent of full-time employees in firms with more than 100 workers enjoyed paid maternity leaves and about 37 percent unpaid leaves; in 1990, 2 percent of full-time employees in smaller firms had paid maternity leaves and 17 percent unpaid leaves. In the early 1990s five states offer, as an alternative to paid leave, temporary disability insurance programs jointly paid for by employers and employees, providing up to two-thirds of regular wages to employees unable to work because of non–job-related disabilities.

The same arguments have centered around maternity leave as around the idea of the "mommy track" or the provision of child care by the employer. Employers have alleged that they cannot afford maternity leaves and still remain competitive. They sometimes fear that a valued employee may not return after maternity leave. Some feminists believe that maternity leaves, especially if paid, would render women less attractive as employees.

The experience of the American military, which does grant paid maternity leave, is that even though most of the women in our armed forces are of childbearing age, and even counting maternity leave, servicewomen lose less time from work than servicemen.

See also *California Federal Savings and Loan v. Guerra*; Child Care; Civil Rights Act of 1964; Family and Medical Leave Act; Family Leave; *General Electric v. Gilbert*; Health Insurance; Mommy Track; *Nashville Gas Co. v. Satty*; Pregnancy; Pregnancy Discrimination Act of 1978.

References Joyce Gelb and Marian Lief Palley, *Women and Public Policies* (1982); Shiela B. Kamerman and Alfred J. Kahn, *Maternity Policies and Working Women* (1985); Nine to Five, National Association of Working Women, "Profile of Working Women" (1990); *Pregnancy and Employment* (1987); Dorothy Schneider and Carl J. Schneider, *Sound Off!* (1992).

Mathematics

See Science, Mathematics, and Science-Based Professions.

Matthews, Victoria Earle (1861–1907)

This social worker and reformer, daughter of a slave and her master, devoted herself, after years of club work, to helping young black working women avoid prostitution. In 1896 she toured the South to investigate red-light districts and the "employment agencies" that too often exploited young women going North to work. She founded the White Rose Industrial Association, where she taught a class in black history and established a library of books by and about blacks.

See also Employment Agencies; Prostitutes; Social Workers; White Rose; White Slavery.

Reference Edward T. James et al., eds., *Notable American Women II* (1971).

Mayer, Maria Gertrude Goeppert (1906–1972)

Mayer, the first woman to win a Nobel Prize for theoretical physics, was born and educated in Germany, earning her Ph.D. at Göttingen in 1930. That year she married American chemist Joseph E. Mayer and immigrated to the United States.

Despite her brilliant doctoral dissertation, nepotism rules at the successive universities that hired her husband kept her from employment there. But she continued her research in theoretical physical chemistry, which in time led to important publications on the lattice theory of crystals and on molecular physics and solid-state theory. She also developed the theory of double-beta decay. With her husband she produced a classic textbook on statistical mathematics. During World War II she participated in the Manhattan Project to produce the atomic bomb.

In 1946 the University of Chicago ventured so far as to appoint both Mayers to their faculty—Maria Mayer, however, without salary, though the university allowed her to earn a half-time salary at a nearby laboratory. In collaboration with Edward Teller she began work on a theory of the origin of the elements, work which led her to a shell theory of the nucleus; in 1955 she published *Elementary Theory of Nuclear Shell Structure* with German physicist Hans D. Jensen. In 1959 the University of California in San Diego offered both the Mayers full professorships, with salaries for each. Although soon thereafter she was assaulted by a severe stroke, Mayer continued to write and do research, publishing important articles during the 1960s. In 1963 she shared the Nobel Prize for physics with Eugene Wigner and Hans Jensen.

See also Academic Women; Nepotism; Science, Mathematics, and Science-Based Professions; World War II.

Reference Barbara Sicherman et al., eds., *Notable American Women: The Modern Period* (1980).

Mead, Margaret (1901–1978)

Mead, the first woman to earn a Ph.D. in anthropology, gained worldwide recognition for studies of human behavior and generational change. Her research led her to believe that modes of behavior as expressed in gender differences and adolescent turmoil were culturally rather than genetically patterned. In such books as *Coming of Age in Samoa* (1928) and *Sex and Temperament* (1935) she addressed a lay as well as a scholarly audience, and she applied anthropological techniques to analyzing contemporary American culture. Her extensive publications and activities on behalf of many causes (nutrition, for example) brought her awards and honors, including the presidency of the American Association for the Advancement of Science in 1979 and the establishment of the Margaret Mead Chair of Anthropology at the American Museum of Natural History in 1976. Her last book, *Culture and Commitment: A Study of the Generation Gap* (1978), related contemporary issues to her previous studies of tensions between generations.

See also Academic Women.

Margaret Mead

References Mary Catherine Bateson, *With a Daughter's Eye: A Memoir of Margaret Mead and Gregory Bateson* (1984); Margaret Mead, *Blackberry Winter (1973)*; Barbara Sicherman et al., eds., *Notable American Women: The Modern Period* (1980); Jennifer S. Uglow, ed., *International Dictionary of Women's Biography* (1985).

Media

See Cinema; Comediennes; Communications; Journalists; Theater.

Men-Only Clubs

The exclusion of women from men-only organizations with business agendas, such as Rotary and Jaycees (Junior Chamber of Commerce), where contacts and deals can be made in a convivial club setting, became an issue as more and more women entered the business and professional world in the 1960s and 1970s. The restrictive policy was defended by men-only clubs as an exercise of their constitutional right of free assembly and association; they further denied that laws against sex discrimination applied to them as private associations with a right to choose their own associates. These arguments have been rejected by the courts, which have upheld the overriding objective of eliminating sex discrimination in at least those organizations that have a business agenda. In the early 1990s the U.S. Supreme Court has not banned all men-only clubs, and it is not entirely clear which private clubs are subject to nondiscrimination laws and which are not.

See also Board of Directors of Rotary International v. Rotary Club of Duarte; Business and Industry; Networking; *Roberts v. United States Jaycees*; Sex Discrimination.

Reference Susan Gluck Mezey, *In Pursuit of Equality: Women, Public Policy and the Federal Courts* (1992).

Mentors

Mentoring is a process by which a senior or influential worker teaches, helps, and protects a junior. With the rise of the women's movement in the 1960s and 1970s, women workers, especially those in management and the professions, sought mentors who would oversee their careers and help them anticipate and resolve problems.

See also Networking; Queen Bee.

References Nancy W. Collins, *Professional Women and Their Mentors* (1983); Agnes K. Missirian, *The Corporate Connection: Why Executive Women Need Mentors To Reach the Top* (1982).

Mercer Girls

Because of the famed respectability of the Lowell Girls, more than 100 of them were recruited in the 1860s by Asa Mercer to move to Seattle, Washington, where marriageable women were scarce. They were known as Mercer Girls.

See also Harvey Girls; Lowell Girls.

Reference Lynn Y. Weiner, *From Working Girl to Working Mother: The Female Labor Force in the United States, 1820–1980* (1985).

Meritor Savings Bank v. Vinson (1986)

In this case Michelle Vinson charged that her supervisor in the bank had made sexual advances and that when she refused them she was fired. The U.S. Supreme Court ruled that sexual harassment on the job was a form of discrimination prohibited by Title VII of the Civil Rights Act of 1964, thus opening avenues of redress for women who had been struggling against harassment for years. But the justices also indicated that in such instances courts may accept evidence regarding women's personal attire, manner, and sexual activities.

See also Civil Rights Act of 1964; Sex Discrimination; Sexual Harassment.

Reference Susan Gluck Mezey, *In Pursuit of Equality: Women, Public Policy and the Federal Courts* (1992).

Mesabi Range Strike

The Mesabi Range in Minnesota was a rich source of iron ore. Discovered in 1890, it soon was covered with mines employing thousands of men, mostly immigrants with their families. In 1916 dissatisfaction with wages and working conditions led to a strike. The wives and children of the striking miners marched with the men, participating in their demonstrations and often walking the picket line. They demonstrated great courage and steadfastness in the face of violence and thuggery. Assisting the strikers were Elizabeth Gurley Flynn of the Industrial Workers of the World and Mary Heaton Vorse, who reported the strike for several magazines (including the *Masses*) and newspapers.

See also Flynn, Elizabeth Gurley; Industrial Workers of the World; Strikes; Vorse, Mary Heaton.

Reference Dee Garrison, *Mary Heaton Vorse* (1989).

Mexican Americans
See Hispanic Americans.

Midwives
The fortunes of midwives in the United States have risen and fallen as they have competed with physicians and as women and men have battled for control over the birthing process. In colonial America and for decades thereafter midwives were neighborhood women without formal training but with much practical experience, and lore passed from woman to woman. Many of them extended their practices beyond obstetrics, and people were as apt to resort to them as to doctors, or to both. After all, they were operating in a society where most doctors knew little and where housewives kept recipes for remedies along with their recipes for food. During the birthing process the laboring mother was usually surrounded by women relatives and friends, most of whom had assisted in more births than young doctors.

The midwife debate was particularly vigorous in the early twentieth century, when the country was increasingly concerned over high rates of infant and maternal mortality. In 1900 approximately 50 percent of all reported births were still attended by midwives; by 1930 this figure had dropped to 15 percent, most of these in the South. This shift occurred partly because of the eagerness of physicians to pick up this lucrative practice and partly because of the spread of hospitals. In their competition with midwives doctors held a great advantage because they could administer anesthetics, especially after the development of twilight sleep about 1915. Rural communities continued to suffer from lack of adequate medical facilities, and midwives were encouraged to move out from the cities. Most midwives, however, were unable to move about freely because most were married.

Intermittent efforts to professionalize midwifery and to regulate its practice have been exerted, often with opposition from the mainline medical profession. In the Progressive Era several successful programs were developed for the training and supervision of midwives. Thus, in 1911 the first and only municipally funded midwifery school was founded in New York City as a branch of Bellevue Hospital; lack of students forced it to close its doors in 1935. In 1925 the Frontier Nursing Service, staffed by nurse-midwives, was established by Mary Breckinridge; and in 1955 the American College of Midwifery opened.

In the women's movement of the 1960s and 1970s many women made vigorous efforts to reclaim their control over the birthing process. Demand for midwives who would assist in home births rose, and women, many of them nurses, sought training. By 1980 the number of midwives certified by the American College of Midwives was on the increase, to a total of about 2,500. Hospitals, concerned that they were losing patients because of womens' dislike of the cold and indifferent treatment afforded prospective mothers, instituted comfortable and attractive birthing rooms and hired midwives to work under the supervision of or in cooperation with physicians. But in 1990 some experts estimate that midwives attend no more than about 1 percent of births in the United States. Legislation regulating midwifery varies widely from state to state, reflecting divergent views of where midwives stand in the hierarchy of medical practice.

See also Colonial America; Health Professionals and Paraprofessionals; Physicians; Pinkham, Lydia Estes; Progressive Era; Women's Movement.

References Jeanne Achterberg, *Woman as Healer* (1991); Judith Freeman Clark, *Almanac of American Women in the 20th Century* (1987); Jane B. Donegan, *Women and Men Midwives: Medicine, Morality, and Misogyny in Early America* (1978); Barbara Ehrenreich and Deidre English, *Witches, Midwives, and Nurses: A History of Women Healers* (1973); Alice Kessler-Harris, *Out To Work* (1982); Judith Walzer Leavitt, *Brought to Bed: Childbearing in America. 1750 to 1950* (1986); Judy Barrett Litoff, *American Midwives, 1860 to the Present* (1978); Dorothy Schneider and Carl J. Schneider, *American Women in the Progressive Era* (1993); Laurel Thatcher Ulrich, *A Midwife's Tale: The Life of Martha Ballard, Based on Her Diary, 1785–1812* (1990).

Migrant Laborers

Agriculture's shift during the course of American history from family farms to factory farms has occasioned the use of migrant laborers who move, usually in sizable groups, often including whole families, from region to region to pick the crops as they ripen. These pickers have always included disproportionate numbers of African Americans, Mexicans, and Mexican Americans forced to work at these poorly paid tasks. Large-scale Mexican immigration for this purpose began during World War I and continues into the 1990s. These low-status, unpredictable, insecure, boring, seasonal jobs also attract a proportion of near-unemployables.

Migrant workers are often hired by crew bosses, who find the jobs for their crews and may also transmit orders to them, assign tasks to individuals, and collect pay for them. The crew boss may serve as contractor, recruiter, transporter, camp manager, work supervisor,

meal provider, policeman, and banker. His power often tempts him to exploit his workers.

Housing for migrant laborers and education for their children (many of whom have labored alongside their parents in the fields), have occasioned many problems, as farmers, needing their labor for only a few weeks a year, hesitated to build decent housing, and the continuous shifting of the migrant families around the country moved their children from one school to another, or none.

See also Contract Labor; United Farm Workers.

References Teresa Amott and Julie Matthaei, *Race, Gender, and Work: A Multicultural Economic History of Women in the United States* (1991); Dorothy Healey and Maurice Isserman, *Dorothy Healey Remembers: A Life in the American Communist Party* (1990); Dorothy Nelkin, *On the Season: Aspects of the Migrant Labor System* (1970).

Military Women

In America's early wars wives and children sometimes accompanied soldiers, a situation tolerated by the military establishment partly because it needed the women's labor for washing and nursing. Inevitably some wives participated in the fighting: spying, guarding prisoners, rallying troops. After the Revolutionary War Congress rewarded the services rendered by Margaret "Molly" Corbin with a military pension and other veterans' benefits. In the Civil War one woman, Sally Louisa Tompkins, was commissioned an officer in the Confederate Army, in recognition of her conduct of a private hospital. The Union Army surgeon Dr. Mary Edwards Walker was the first woman to receive the Congressional Medal of Honor. Up until World War I, which introduced physical examinations, other women disguised themselves as men to enlist: Deborah Sampson (1760–1827) served in the Continental Army in 1782 as Robert Shurtleff.

The Civil War evoked the superb organizational skills of Dorothea Dix and Clara Barton to alleviate the suffering of the sick and wounded. But not until 1901 with the creation of the Army Nurse Corps did the military formally incorporate women. World War I brought the enlistment of women, mostly as clerks, in the Navy and Marine Corps. Occupational and physical therapists also served; so did telephone operators, who were finally acknowledged as veterans in 1979.

World War II created such urgent womanpower needs that each of the services established an auxiliary: the Women's Army Auxiliary Corps (WAAC), the Navy's Women Accepted for Volunteer Emergency Service (WAVES), the Woman Marines, and the Coast Guard's SPARS (from the motto "Semper Paratus"). Including nurses, some 350,000 women volunteered for these services. In addition women served as Women's Airforce Service Pilots (WASPs) in the often dangerous work of towing targets and ferrying planes; they finally earned recognition as veterans in 1979. Some 375,000 women served in the military in World War II. In 1948 the women's corps became permanent.

The 1970s, which opened so many new opportunities for American women, did not spare the military. Four Army women, one Air Force woman, and one Navy woman were promoted into the highest echelons (general or admiral) in 1970, and in 1973 Jeanne Holm earned her second star. In 1976 the military academies began to admit women. In 1978 the women's corps were integrated into the military establishment. In 1979 Coast Guard Lieutenant (jg) Beverly Kelley became the first woman captain of a U.S. military vessel. The decade of the 1970s also saw military women resorting to the courts to establish their right to equal benefits and equal opportunity. In the early 1990s women constitute about 11 percent of the armed forces, and about 4 percent of the veterans (about 1.2 million women veterans).

Although law has barred military women from service on ships and airplanes on combat missions, practice has increasingly placed both enlisted women and officers in critical positions that necessitate their presence in missile silos, on missile firing sites, fueling combat planes in the air, tending combat ships, and transporting troops into battle. Many career military women have urged that they be allowed on combat ships and planes, though few believe it practical for them to fight as infantry soldiers. The Gulf War of 1990–1991, which for the first time widely publicized military women, roused the public mostly to praise and to approve, not to protest their participation.

The trend of the 1970s and 1980s toward integrating them even more fully into combat operations may well continue. The Presidential Commission on the Assignment of Women in the Armed Forces in 1992 recommended, however, that women be excluded from combat aircraft positions, the reinstatement of the law (repealed in 1991) barring Air Force and Navy women from flying combat planes, the enactment of a new law excluding Army women from combat aircraft positions, and the enactment of a law excluding women from land combat. On the other hand the commission advocated opening combat ships except submarines and amphibious vessels to women.

The Defense Advisory Council on Women in the Services (DACOWITS), a group of 50 prominent civilian women and men appointed by the president of the United States, oversees the well-being of and acts as advocate for women in the military services. It was established in 1951 to inform the public of recruiting needs, reassure parents about the supervision of young women in the military, inform young women about career opportunities, and raise the prestige of military women among the public. Over the years it has now and then functioned as an investigating agency, uncovering egregious examples of sexual harassment. Some of its members regularly visit military establishments to get a better sense of the problems of servicewomen.

DACOWITS has also taken positions on the issue of women in combat. In 1992,

World War I recruiting poster

for instance, the council commented on the report of the Presidential Commission on the Assignment of Women in the Armed Forces. DACOWITS agreed on such points as rejecting quotas or goals for women's representation in the military, endorsing separate physical fitness standards for women and men, and approving gender-neutral physical standards for military jobs that require extraordinary muscular strength or cardiovascular capacity. On other points DACOWITS disagreed, wishing to extend women's service on naval vessels to submarines and amphibious vessels and opposing the commission's recommendation that one parent in a dual-service couple be forced to leave military service. (*Minerva's Bulletin Board*, Winter 1992)

In 1993 women were authorized to fly combat planes, and the Navy increased women's seagoing assignments.

Women veterans, despite their legal entitlement, have long experienced difficulties in getting care at veterans' hospitals, usually set up to deal exclusively with men. The Women Veterans Health Program Act of 1992 requires the expansion of services for women, including breast examinations and mammographies, Pap smears and reproductive health services, management of menopause, and postservice treatment for women who suffered sexual abuse while in the military. The act does not cover prenatal care, abortions, and infertility, unless the veteran suffers complications or is at risk for a reason related to military service.

See also Army Nurse Corps; Barton, Clara; Civil War; Dix, Dorothea Lynde; *Frontiero v. Richardson*; Hobby, Oveta Culp; Passing; *Rostker v. Goldberg*; Sexual Harassment; Sexual Preference; Veterans' Preference; Walker, Mary Edwards; World War I; World War II.

References Rhonda Cornum, *She Went to War* (1992); Jeanne Holm, *Women in the Military* (1982); Joan McCullough, *First of All* (1980); Paula Ries and Anne J. Stone, eds., *The American Woman, 1992–93: A Status Report* (1992); Dorothy Schneider and Carl J. Schneider, *Into the Breach: American Women Overseas in World War I* (1991); Dorothy Schneider and Carl J. Schneider, *Sound Off! American Military Women Speak Out* (1992); Christine L. Williams, *Gender Differences at Work* (1989).

Miller, Frieda Segekle (1889–1973)

This labor reformer adopted a gradualist approach to labor difficulties, relying on law and mediation. After graduating from college she studied labor economics and political science for four years at the University of Chicago, then launched her career in labor relations. She worked for the Women's Trade Union League from 1917 to 1923. She then undertook employment as a factory inspector for the International Ladies' Garment Workers' Union, and in 1929 for New York's labor department's Division of Women in Industry. She consistently advocated higher wages for women.

After a stint with the League of Nations' International Labor Organization (ILO) and their Advisory Committee on Women Workers, in 1938 she became New York's industrial commissioner, where she organized a state unemployment insurance system. In that capacity she concentrated on reemployment, revamping the employment service.

In 1944 Miller was appointed director of the Women's Bureau (WB), where she focused on the postwar reemployment of women. In 1945 she created the Labor Advisory Committee of the Women's Bureau, inviting trade union women to come to the WB, and organizing conferences of union leaders and representatives of national women's groups to discuss postwar problems. Throughout her tenure she emphasized equal pay and equal access for women, shifting the focus of the WB away from protective legislation. She resigned in 1952, but continued to work for the ILO.

See also Government Workers; International Ladies' Garment Workers' Union; Protective Legislation; Unions; Women's Bureau; Women's Trade Union League.

Reference Barbara Sicherman et al., eds., *Notable American Women: The Modern Period* (1980).

Minimum Wage

Like several other forms of protective legislation, minimum wage laws at first applied only to women and children, thus avoiding much potential opposition. The first was enacted in Massachusetts in 1912, at the behest of social feminists. In the next eight years 14 other states passed such laws. A second wave followed in the

1930s, culminating in a provision in the federal Fair Labor Standards Act (1938) for a minimum wage regardless of sex.

In the early 1990s, with the federal minimum wage at $4.25 an hour, almost 65 percent of minimum wage earners are women, though women comprise only 46 percent of the labor force. Eighty percent of women living alone who work at or below the minimum wage are living below the poverty level. If a woman works full-time for a year, her minimum-wage job will pay her $8,840, below the poverty line of $9,190 for a family of two. Only about half a dozen states have set their minimum wage above the federal standard.

See also *Adkins v. Children's Hospital;* Edson, Katherine Philips; Evans, Elizabeth Gardiner Glendower; Fair Labor Standards Act; Nestor, Agnes; Protective Legislation; Social Feminists; Training Wage; *West Coast Hotel Co. v. Parrish.*

References Jenny Morris, *Women Workers and the Sweated Trades: The Origins of Minimum Wage Legislation* (1986); Angela Howard Zophy and Frances M. Kavenik, eds., *Handbook of American Women's History* (1990).

Mitchell, Lucy Sprague (1878–1967)

In her Chicago childhood, this educator educated herself, using her wealthy father's sizable library. In her late teens Jane Addams influenced her and Alice Freeman Palmer adopted her as a protégée, inviting the young girl to live with the Palmer family and attend Radcliffe, where she majored in philosophy. After graduate study at Harvard, in 1906 she was appointed dean of women and assistant professor of English at the University of California at Berkeley. Sprague used her position as dean to enlarge educational and social opportunities for women, strengthening women's campus organizations and encouraging students to study and work in the larger community.

In 1912 she married Wesley Clair Mitchell, a fellow faculty member, and they moved to New York City. There, persuaded of the value of public education in dealing with social problems, Lucy Mitchell studied with John Dewey and worked with other educators, testing public school children and teaching in an experimental play school.

In 1916, with her husband and Harriet Johnson, Mitchell cofounded the Bureau of Educational Experiments, later to become the Bank Street College of Education, to experiment and do research in progressive education. Her own four children, two natural and two adopted, became pupils there. Mitchell herself directed the cooperative bureau's institutional growth and helped to institute innovative educational methods based on detailed observation of children's mental, emotional, and physical development. There too she helped to originate teacher-training and writing programs, programs that she later extended through public school workshops. In 1931 she founded the Cooperative School for Teachers with her colleagues.

Mitchell wrote prolifically, some books for adults and more for children. Her Writers Workshop, founded in 1938, intended to help writers of children's books understand children's development and interests, uses children's linguistic patterns, and centers their stories on children's own experiences.

See also Palmer, Alice Freeman; Teachers; Writers and Publishers.

References Joyce Antler, *Lucy Sprague Mitchell: The Making of a Modern Woman* (1987); Barbara Sicherman et al., eds., *Notable American Women: The Modern Period* (1980).

Mitchell, Maria (1818–1889)

This astronomer, a native of Massachusetts, after a rather sketchy education opened her own school for girls at age 17. From 1836–1856 she held the position of librarian of the new Nantucket (MA) Atheneum, where she rigorously educated herself, spending her evenings in her father's observatory and assisting him in stellar research. In 1847 she discovered a new comet, which was named for her; and in 1848 she became the first woman member of the American Academy for the Advancement of Science of

Boston; the record reveals no other woman until 1943. In 1850 the American Association for the Advancement of Science elected Mitchell a member.

Her accomplishments and international reputation led to her appointment as one of Vassar's first faculty in 1865. There she trained the first generation of women astronomers and encouraged hundreds of other women to pursue careers in science and medicine; 25 of her students won recognition in *Who's Who in America*. In 1869 her election broke the barrier against women in the American Philosophical Society.

She worked consistently to help women advance, particularly in the sciences. At Vassar she battled for equal pay for women faculty and fought against the rules of deportment with which the college at first tried to regulate women. In 1873 she helped to found the Association for the Advancement of Women, over which she presided for two years; these moderate feminists provided opportunities for professional women and social service workers to discuss women's work and problems.

See also Academic Women; Professional Women; Science, Mathematics, and Science-Based Professions.

References Edward T. James et al., eds., *Notable American Women II* (1971); Phebe Mitchell Kendall, *Maria Mitchell: Life, Letters, and Journals* (1896); Jennifer S. Uglow, comp. and ed., *International Dictionary of Women's Biography* (1985); Helen Wright, *Sweeper in the Sky* (1949).

Mommy Track

This career path has developed to reconcile the biological fact that women have babies and the social fact that they work outside the home for pay. It allows them extended maternity leave, perhaps for years, and/or a reduced work load while their children are young and their family responsibilities heavy, without endangering their jobs.

The concept has attracted much criticism, especially from feminists who fear that its widespread acceptance would, as Barbara Presley Noble warned, "establish a gender-based caste system designed to keep women barefoot, pregnant and at the edge of the fast track." (*New York Times*, 23 February 1992) Some have argued that it would discourage corporations from hiring women, by making them more expensive to employ than men. Others believe that women on the mommy track would have to settle for lower-status and lower-paid work. As Felice Schwartz of Catalyst has pointed out, the term *mommy track* demeans women as workers.

Others counter that with so many employees having to assume the care of frail, older relatives, men as well as women may need such consideration from their employers. The increasing value that many men place on family life may prompt similar requests from them.

In any case, some executives recognize that demographic shifts in the work force necessitate that corporations recruit women and offer them real opportunities for advancement. Schwartz has pointed out that these real opportunities must include consideration of family life, with provision not only for maternity leave but also for alternative arrangements like flextime, job sharing, and part-time work during the years of peak family responsibilities, without loss of status and with the chance to move back onto the fast track when family responsibilities lessen. Workers who take leaves or choose to work part-time because of family responsibility also need to be allowed compensatory time to make partner or get tenure.

See also Catalyst; Child Care; Elder Care; Family Leave; Flextime; Job Sharing; Maternity Leave; Part-Time Workers.

Reference Felice N. Schwartz with Jean Zimmerman, *Breaking with Tradition: Women and Work, the New Facts of Life* (1992).

Moonlighting

Moonlighting is the practice of holding more than one job at a time. In the late twentieth century, the practice has increased even more sharply among women workers than among men, usually for financial reasons. In 1989 the Bureau of Labor Statistics reported 3.1 million women working two or more jobs, almost five times the 1970 number. In 1990 more than 40 percent of moonlighters were women. Whereas 80 percent of men who moonlight work full-time on at least one job, 40 percent of women who moonlight hold more than one part-time job. These women work on average 50 hours a week but as part-timers seldom enjoy the benefits or rate of pay of full-timers.

See also Benefits; Catalyst; Compensation; Leisure; Maternity Leave; Part-Time Workers.

References Nine to Five, National Association of Working Women, "Profile of Working Women" (1990); Paula Ries and Anne J. Stone, eds., *The American Woman, 1992–93: A Status Report* (1992); Felice N. Schwartz with Jean Zimmerman, *Breaking with Tradition: Women and Work, the New Facts of Life* (1992); Barbara D. Warme, Katherina L. P. Lundy, and Larry A. Lundy, *Working Part-Time* (1992).

Moreno, Luisa (n.d.)

A Communist, this Guatemala-born labor activist led a pecan-workers' strike in the 1930s, mobilized Latinas against police brutality, and organized the first National Congress of Spanish-Speaking People. She later organized cannery workers, cotton workers, and beet workers. In the 1950s she was deported to Mexico.

See also Communist Party; Hispanic Americans; Union Organizers.

Reference Teresa Amott and Julie Matthaei, *Race, Gender, and Work: A Multicultural Economic History of Women in the United States* (1991).

Morgan, Julia (1872–1957)

This pioneering woman architect grew up in California, wanted to be an architect, and entered the University of California at Berkeley's College of Engineering as its first woman student. Graduating in 1894, she soon went on to the École des Beaux Arts in Paris, where she obtained her degree in 1902, the first woman in its architectural section.

Back in California, Morgan extended her record of "first woman" by being granted an architect's license there. Her work on two buildings at the University of California earned her the admiration of the philanthropist Phoebe Apperson Hearst, who gave her commissions and may have encouraged her to open her own office in San Francisco in 1904. With Hearst's help work flowed in, particularly after Morgan rebuilt the Fairmont Hotel after the earthquake of 1906. Her range was wide: she built residences, stores, churches, offices, and academic buildings.

In 1919 Hearst's son, William Randolph Hearst, commissioned Morgan to design San Simeon, integrating into it sections of European monasteries and castles. Additionally he gave her so much other work that she had to enlarge her staff to 35. Meanwhile other commissions continued to pour in, even during the Great Depression. With the difficulties of obtaining materials during World War II, Morgan gradually decreased her work, retiring in 1946.

Her work combined elegance with functionalism. She made imaginative use of cement, particularly for the Spanish Revival style that became her favorite. Her early residential designs helped to develop the Bay area shingle style. Her stylistic innovations, her prolific achievements, and her thoroughness combined to make her an important influence on the development of architecture in her time—an influence that she extended by acting as mentor, benefactor, employer, and role model to other women architects.

See also Architects.

References Sara H. Boutelle, *Julia Morgan, Architect* (1988); Barbara Sicherman et al., eds., *Notable American Women: The Modern Period* (1980); Ginger Wadsworth, *Julia Morgan, Architect of Dreams* (1990).

Moskowitz, Belle Lindener Israels (1877–1933)

This behind-the-throne politician trained as a welfare worker at Teachers College,

Columbia. She then worked in a New York City settlement house. In 1903 she married a colleague, who died in 1911, leaving her with three children. In 1914 she married another colleague, Dr. Henry Moskowitz. From 1914 to 1916 she headed the labor department of the Dress and Waists Manufacturers' Association, adjusting labor disputes. In 1918 to forward the causes in which she was interested she campaigned for Alfred E. Smith for governor, for whom she laid out a plan for a makeover of the state government. Never personally ambitious, Moskowitz became Smith's trusted advisor during his several terms as governor, exercising considerable influence in the conduct of his administration.

See also Government Workers; Settlement Houses.

References Edward T. James et al., eds., *Notable American Women II* (1971); Robert McHenry, ed., *Liberty's Women* (1980); Elisabeth I. Perry, *Belle Moskowitz: Feminine Politcs and the Exercise of Power in the Age of Alfred E. Smith* (1987).

Mossell, Sadie Tanner (n.d.)

In 1921 Mossell earned her Ph.D. from the University of Pennsylvania, one of the first three blacks to hold the doctorate.

See also Academic Women; Dykes, Eva B.; Magill, Helen; Simpson, Georgiana.

Mothers' Employment

American politicians and the population generally have traditionally doubted that mothers of families, particularly mothers of young children, should work for pay, though they have tolerated the practice with considerable ease when the mothers have been poor and/or black. Indeed some politicians now argue that mothers of young children *ought* to work for pay rather than rely on welfare to support their children.

In any case the question has become moot as more and more mothers have entered the work force: in 1950 only 12 percent of mothers with preschool children were in the labor force, but in 1985 more than half were working or looking for work. In 1990, 65 percent of mothers with children under 18 were in the labor force, more than three times the number in 1960, and 56 percent of women with children under six worked for pay. Before their babies' first birthdays, 51 percent of new mothers were back in the work force. The fastest growing segment of the work force in the early 1990s is married mothers with children under two years.

See also Child Care; Entrepreneurs; Family Leave; Married Women's Employment; Mommy Track; Mothers' Pensions; Pregnancy Discrimination Act of 1978.

References Nine to Five, National Association of Working Women, "Profile of Working Women" (1990); Paula Ries and Anne J. Stone, eds., *The American Woman, 1992–93: A Status Report* (1992).

Mothers' Pensions

Prompted by concern for the well-being of children, Progressive Era reformers campaigned for pensions for single-parent mothers to enable them to stay home to raise their children rather than having to work to support them. Beginning in 1911, soon after the historic White House Conference on Children of 1909, state after state enacted laws providing mothers' pensions; by 1921, 40 of the 48 states had such laws, though actual distribution of the pensions lagged seriously.

To qualify, women had to show themselves "deserving" and "fit" to raise children. This provision automatically excluded unmarried mothers, state laws usually excluded wives abandoned by their husbands, and minority women were hardly considered, so most of the relatively few actual recipients were white widows—and even they had to mind their manners, or the social workers who regularly visited them might disqualify them for such offenses as smoking, not going to church, or taking in a male boarder. What's more, their benefits ran lower than the amount a woman could earn or what it took to support a family. In short, the program sent more mothers into the work force than it kept out. But by 1921 the Census Bureau estimated that about 121,000 children in 45,000 families benefited from this support. By 1935 state-supported mothers' pensions had given way to the federal program Aid to Families with Dependent Children.

The undergirding principles of mothers' pensions, that children need their mothers at home (particularly their single-parent mothers) and that government has an interest in providing children with good homes, are still being challenged by opponents of aid to dependent children and advocates of workfare.

See also Aid to Families with Dependent Children; Child Care; Progressive Era; Social Security Act of 1935; Workfare.
References Mimi Abramovitz, *Regulating the Lives of Women: Social Welfare Policy from Colonial Times to the Present* (1988); Lynn K. Weiner, *From Working Girl to Working Mother: The Female Labor Force in the United States, 1820–1980* (1985).

Mourning Dove (ca. 1888–1936)
Christine Quintasket, who took this pen name, was the first Native-American woman to publish a novel. *Cogewea*, the draft of which she finished about 1915, finally appeared in 1927.
See also Writers and Publishers.
Reference Jay Miller, ed., *Mourning Dove: A Salishan Autobiography* (1990).

Movies
See Cinema.

Ms. Foundation for Women (MFW)
Founded in 1972, the foundation strives to improve the status of women and girls. Among other projects, it assists community-based self-help groups of women working on economic development. It also sponsors an annual Take Our Daughters to Work Day.
See also Steinem, Gloria.

La Mujer Obrera (The Working Woman)
This contemporary group of Hispanic-American garment workers cooperates with the International Ladies' Garment Workers' Union to improve working conditions in sweatshops.
See also Hispanic Americans; International Ladies' Garment Workers' Union; Sweatshops.

Muller v. Oregon (1908)
This landmark U.S. Supreme Court decision affirmed the right of government to limit the workday for women workers. Basing his case on the research of Josephine Goldmark and Helen Marot, Louis Brandeis argued that a workday longer than ten hours would endanger a woman's reproductive and mothering abilities. Brandeis presented the court with 113 pages of evidence (the Brandeis Brief) showing the bad effects of long hours on the health and morale of women workers, deleterious not only for the workers but also for future generations.

The decision in *Muller* became a precedent to sustain many kinds of protective legislation for women. It assumed that women may be denied certain rights to employment in their own interests and in the interest of the nation; and this legitimized the exclusion of women from certain kinds of jobs and opportunities.

In the early 1990s many advocates of women's rights criticize the court's decision because it justified restrictive legislation directed exclusively at women, depriving them of equal opportunities to work because of their "differences." The special treatment versus equal treatment controversy continues. *Muller* has of course been significantly modified by subsequent legislation and court cases.

See also Eight-Hour Day; *Goesaert v. Cleary*; Goldmark, Josephine Clara; Marot, Helen; Pregnancy Discrimination Act; Protective Legislation; *UAW v. Johnson Controls*; *Radice v. New York*.
References Mimi Abramovitz, *Regulating the Lives of Women: Social Welfare Policy from Colonial Times to the Present* (1988); Karen J. Maschke, *Litigation, Courts, and Women Workers* (1989); Susan Gluck Mezey, *In Pursuit of Equality: Women, Public Policy and the Federal Courts* (1992); Deborah L. Rhode, *Justice and Gender: Sex Discrimination and the Law* (1989); Marlene Stein Wortman, ed., *Women in American Law* (1985).

Murray, Judith Sargent (1751–1820)

Murray, a native of Massachusetts, was exceptionally well-educated for her day. In her writing Murray questioned the status that society assigned women and called for more education for them. In a series of essays appearing in the last decade of the eighteenth century, she argued that women should be competent in more than marriage and should be educated accordingly. She did not, however, suggest that woman's proper place could be anywhere but in the home.

References Vena B. Field, *Constantia: A Study of the Life and Works of Judith Sargent Murray* (1931); Edward T. James et al., eds., *Notable American Women II* (1971).

Musicians

In the early nineteenth century here and there American women gained employment as musicians at the harpsichord, the piano, and the organ (especially as church organists), though even earlier some of them had taught their instruments privately. Sophie Henriette Hewitt Ostinelli (1799?–1846) taught music and occasionally sang, accompanied choruses and soloists, played piano concerti, and also gained repute in Boston as an organist.

By mid-century a few women could build careers as keyboard performers or singers: the New York Philharmonic Society first employed a woman pianist in 1856. The child prodigy Teresa Carreno (1854–1917), a native of Venezuela who became an American citizen, won international fame both as a vocalist and as a pianist. Her rival, another prodigy, was Julia Rive-King (1857–1937), perhaps a finer musician. Pianist and lecturer Amy Fay (1844–1928) became mentor and role model for thousands of aspiring women musicians when in 1881 she published *Music Study in Germany*, which went through 20 printings: she praised her German training and German willingness to accept women as pupils, but she advised American women to study in the United States. At the turn of the century women pianists and piano students decidedly outnumbered men, but men dominated the concert stage, as at the end of the twentieth century they still do.

Among the strings the harp was for some reason early considered appropriate for "ladies," an association that still survives. By 1876 violinist Camilla Urso (1842–1902) was ranked among the major virtuosi of her instrument, but she found the life so arduous that she discouraged other women from following in her steps. At the turn of the century women violin teachers and performers had gained common acceptance.

In short, although many American women in the nineteenth century studied music, although many taught, only in the twentieth century have significant numbers become professional instrumentalists. They made some gains between 1870 and 1920, only to be rejected again until the late 1960s. Although discrimination against the employment of women in musical organizations officially ended in 1903 when the musicians' union joined the American Federation of Labor and perforce had to admit women, only a few women harpists were hired by major orchestras. The reluctance of bands and orchestras to employ women until relatively recently confined all women instrumentalists but those with great talent, energy, and luck to teaching to support themselves.

From the 1870s on, all-women chamber-music groups, bands, and even orchestras appeared here and there. The professionals among them played where they could—often in German-American music halls or beer gardens. The most prominent was the Fadette Women's Orchestra of Boston, founded in 1888 and conducted by violinist Caroline B. Nichols; in its 32-year existence it toured the United States and Canada, playing symphonies, overtures, selections from grand opera, and popular songs, sometimes by audience request. Until the musicians' union interfered, the Fadette orchestra accompanied silent films in a New York theater. The women's orchestra ended during World War II. But in the 1990s significant numbers of women play in all sections of most symphony orchestras.

Professional singing was a field more open to women. Even in the nineteenth century good numbers of women sang professionally in concerts, vaudeville, operas, and musical comedy, and even more have flourished in the twentieth century. Notable among them was Emma Azalia Smith Hackley, who trained and encouraged many black singers in both European and African-American music.

By 1900 only two American women, Caroline Nichols and light-opera conductor Emma Steiner, had made their reputations as conductors. In 1924 Ethel Liginska (1886–1970), a noted pianist with a flair for publicity, took up conducting. She founded a new Boston Philharmonic men's orchestra, toured with the Boston Women's Symphony, and in 1932 started a National Women's Symphony in New York, composing and sometimes conducting operas in the interstices of her orchestral career. Antonia Brico (b. 1902), the first American graduate of the master school of conducting of the Berlin State Academy of Music, established herself in Europe before her American debut in 1933. Finding few opportunities for employment and maintaining the conscious intention of proving that women can play as well as men, she, too, formed her own orchestra—the New York Women's Symphony—in 1935. But for most of her career Brico was frustrated by the united opposition of orchestra boards, managers, and orchestra members to women conductors. In the latter half of the twentieth century Sarah Caldwell, founder of the Opera Company of Boston and the first woman to conduct at the Metropolitan Opera, has forged new paths as a conductor. Liza Redfield became the first conductor of musical comedy on Broadway in 1960.

In the difficult field of composing, women faced even greater odds, finding little or no opportunity (even in church music), no patronage, and no support for their long and expensive educations. Although even in colonial America a woman occasionally composed songs that found an audience, Amy Marcy Cheney Beach (1867–1944) was the first outstanding woman composer in America. A society woman whose husband encouraged her, largely self-taught, Beach experimented with many forms, including symphonies and grand opera, and toured internationally presenting her own compositions. The first outstanding black woman composer was Florence Beatrice Smith Price (1888–1953), who won Wanamaker Foundation Awards for a symphony and a piano sonata; Price often referred to her ethnic musical heritage by using its characteristic rhythms and melodies in her works. The numbers of women composers increased markedly beginning in the mid–1880s, but not the performances of their works. Only in the mid–1970s did women's representation in performance begin to increase—slightly.

In the history of jazz, women songwriters and composers appear from the latter part of the nineteenth century—exslave Mammy Lou, for instance—playing jazz, recording, leading bands, writing, arranging, producing albums, managing groups, giving concerts. The best-known women in jazz have been either vocalists, like Ma Rainey (1886–1939), Bessie Smith (1898–1937), and Billie Holliday (1915–1959); or pianists, like Lil Hardin Armstrong (1900–1971) and Mary Lou Williams (1910–1981)—both also composers. But the black blues singers both established notable reputations of their own and influenced the course of American music. Jazz also spawned all-women bands, from the Colored Female Brass Band of the late 1880s to the Swing Era's International Sweethearts of Rhythm and Ina Ray Hutton and her Melodears.

Women have now in the late twentieth century established themselves in both classical and popular music, though even yet few flourish as composers or conductors, and women's groups still struggle for survival and record contracts.

See also American Federation of Labor; Caldwell, Sarah; Hackley, Emma Azalia Smith; Mentors.

References Christine Ammer, *Unsung: A History of Women in American Music* (1980); Gene Claghorn, *Women Composers and Hymnists: A Concise Biographical Dictionary* (1984); Aaron I. Cohen, *International Encyclopedia of Women Composers* (1987); Linda Dahl, *Stormy Weather: The Music and Lives of Jazzwomen* (1984); Gillian G. Gaar, *She's a Rebel: The History of Women in Rock and Roll* (c. 1992); Mildred D. Green, *Black Women Composers* (1983); D. Antoinette Handy, *Black Women in American Bands and Orchestras* (1981); Diane P. Jezic, *Women Composers* (1988); Jane W. LePage, *Women Composers, Conductors, and Musicians of the Twentieth Century* (1980); Loretta Lynn and George Vecsey, *Loretta Lynn: Coal Miner's Daughter* (1985); Joan McCullough, *First of All* (1980); Karin Pendle, ed., *Women and Music: A History* (1991); Judith Tick, *American Women Composers before 1870* (1989); Elizabeth Wurtzel, "Popular Music" (1992).

Nashville Gas Co. v. Satty (1977)

The U.S. Supreme Court held that the gas company's policy of requiring its pregnant employees to take leave but denying them accumulated seniority upon return violated Title VII of the Civil Rights Act of 1964.

See also Civil Rights Act of 1964; Pregnancy; Pregnancy Discrimination Act.

Reference Susan Gluck Mezey, *In Pursuit of Equality: Women, Public Policy and the Federal Courts* (1992).

Nathan, Maud (1862–1946)

At 17 this native New Yorker married a cousin, the wealthy broker Frederick Nathan; their only child died young. Nathan engaged in many charitable activities. She presided over the New York Consumers' League from 1897–1917, years during which her passionate advocacy of fair labor conditions markedly improved the situation of department store workers and helped to abolish piecework. Frustrations at lobbying without the power of the vote propelled her into the cause of women's suffrage, an issue on which she violently disagreed with her sister, Annie Nathan Meyer (1867–1951), a founder of Barnard College.

See also Consumers' League; Kelley, Florence; Lowell, Josephine Shaw; Pieceworkers.

References Agnes Nestor, *Woman's Labor Leader: The Autobiography of Agnes Nestor* (1954).

National Association for Women in Careers

Founded in 1981, this 1,500-member organization supports the professional development of women in various segments of the work force.

National Association of Commissions for Women (NACW)

Founded in 1970, this organization affiliates state, city, and county commissions that focus on the status of women, including their economic status.

National Association of Working Women

This organization was founded in 1932 to combat the movement against the employment of married women, a movement that flourished particularly during the Great Depression, often on the grounds that these workers were taking jobs away from "men who needed them."

See also Great Depression; Married Women's Employment.

Reference Lynn Y. Weiner, *From Working Girl to Working Mother: The Female Labor Force in the United States, 1820–1980* (1985).

National Center for Policy Alternatives, Women's Economic Justice Center

This organization, which seeks to create sound state policies, focuses on the issues of economically disadvantaged women, including economic development, economic equity, economic self-sufficiency, and family and medical leaves.

National Center for Women and Retirement Research

This organization researches and prepares educational materials on retirement benefits and other issues of older women.

See also Age Discrimination Acts; Older Women.

National Commission for Women's Equality

Founded in 1984, this 200-member organization of leaders concerns itself with a variety of issues confronting Jewish women, including economic equity.

National Commission on Working Women

See Wider Opportunities for Women.

National Committee for Equal Pay

In 1952 a coalition of civic groups, women's organizations, labor, and employer organizations formed this group. They were motivated by falling wage rates for women's jobs relative to their World War II highs and to men's wages.

Reference Alice Kessler-Harris, *Out To Work* (1982).

National Committee on Household Employment

This organization was founded in 1964 to upgrade the status of black domestic workers by establishing training programs, to increase public awareness of the importance of their work, and to improve their working conditions. The driving spirit behind its organization was the National Council of Negro Women, supported by various national women's organizations and the Women's Bureau. In 1971 it spun off the Household Technicians of America, which shifted from an emphasis on training unskilled houseworkers to organizing low-paid workers to support specific legislation, such as the inclusion of domestic workers under the minimum wage provisions of the Fair Labor Standards Act.

See also Domestic Servants; Fair Labor Standards Act; Minimum Wage; Women's Bureau.

Reference Phyllis Palmer, "Housework and Domestic Labor," in Karen Brodkin Sacks and Dorothy Remy, eds., *My Troubles Are Going To Have Trouble with Me: Everyday Trials and Triumphs of Women Workers* (1984).

National Committee on Pay Equity (NCPE)

Founded in 1979, the individuals and 120 organizations in NCPE educate the public about pay inequities between genders and among races.

See also Comparable Worth; Gender Gap; Pay Equity.

National Congress of Neighborhood Women

Founded in 1975, this nonmembership organization unites women in the lower economic brackets to deal with various issues, including improving their economic status.

National Council for Research on Women

Founded in 1981, this national association affiliates 70 centers and organizations concerned with women's issues, and encourages, conducts, and disseminates research on many issues, including economic inequities.

National Council of Career Women

Founded in 1975, this 355-member organization aims to support the professional development of women in business and the professions.

National Education Association (NEA)

This organization, formed in 1857 as the National Teachers' Association, began as a group of educational leaders, mostly school administrators. It did not formally recognize the presence of women within the teaching profession until 1866, when women fought to replace the term "gentlemen" as applied to members with "persons." Though in 1870 it granted women the right to hold office, it was dominated by a small, male elite, mainly professors or college presidents, who thought of themselves as "philosopher kings" and strongly supported centralization and professionalism.

From 1899 until 1907 women teachers, led by Margaret Haley of the Chicago Teachers' Federation, staged a rebellion within NEA in the interests of teacher unions and better school financing. The hierarchy of NEA quelled the rebellion by the now-familiar techniques of paying lip service to the women's demands and giving women token positions; the rebellious teachers benefited little, but the school administrators within the organization benefited greatly. In 1910 Haley managed the successful campaign for the presidency of NEA of Ella Flagg Young, one of the few women who had worked her way into a superintendency. In 1912 under Young's leadership the classroom teachers got their own department within NEA, and in 1916, after the founding of the American Federation of Teachers (AFT), NEA began actively to recruit teachers. The superintendents in power in NEA persuaded and pressured their teachers into membership, using World War I hysteria to make it their professional duty.

In the interwar years NEA's Charles Williams created the first long-term educational lobby in Washington, working for a cabinet position in education and a national bill for funding education. The Great Depression with its heavier teaching loads, enlarged classes, pay cuts, deterioration of school programs, and school closings prompted both NEA and AFT to demand more funds for education and more attention to children's needs, particularly from the federal government.

After World War II, NEA with AFT confronted the crisis presented by school overpopulation, the shortage of teachers, and, though to a lesser extent than AFT, the threats to educators of the Communist scare. Although by the 1950s NEA rendered lip service against racism, many of its own state organizations were segregated into white and black associations, and NEA took no firm stand on school integration; not until 1961 did it mildly endorse the U.S. Supreme Court's 1954 desegregation decision in *Brown v. Board of Education*. In 1966 NEA finally took the black American Teachers Association into its fold, agreeing to integrate NEA's state associations. In 1967 NEA elected Elizabeth Koontz as its first black president.

NEA at first denounced the teachers' strikes of the 1960s and AFT's involvement. But with AFT's successes, NEA tried to compete in the push for collective bargaining by launching a membership drive in urban areas, unifying its membership, and widening its insurance packages for members. With its strong lobby in Washington, NEA could also boast of the National Defense Education Act of 1958 (to encourage scientific education), the Manpower and Development Training Act of 1962 (to strengthen vocational education), and a whole spate of education acts in Lyndon Johnson's presidency, including a major commitment to federal aid to education, long sought by both NEA and AFT. In short, NEA felt more comfortable with lobbying than with collective bargaining.

Rather than collective bargaining NEA tried such ploys as "professional day" strikes, where teachers would call in sick for a day, and sanctions, whereby the organization would urge teachers not to take jobs in sanctioned districts or states. Ultimately, though, NEA had no choice but to adopt the weapons of labor and to compete with AFT to represent teachers at the bargaining table. This necessity forced NEA to accelerate its integration program in the late 1960s, and to infiltrate teachers into its old hierarchy of school administrators.

NEA has nonetheless preserved its emphasis on state and national political power. In 1979 it triumphed in the creation of a federal department of education. Although collective bargaining has blurred the differences between NEA and AFT, NEA still boasts that it is the "professional" organization, while AFT accuses NEA of being administrator-ridden. NEA has strongly opposed demands for accountability: performance evaluations, testing, and merit pay. Oddly enough, however, NEA and AFT have nearly switched roles politically, with NEA taking more progressive positions on social issues and AFT seeking conservative solutions to educational problems.

See also American Federation of Teachers; American Association of Colored Teachers; Great Depression; Haley, Margaret Angela; Strikes; Teachers; Unions; Young, Ella Flagg.

Reference Marjorie Murphy, *Blackboard Unions: The AFT and the NEA, 1900–1980* (1990).

National Federation of Business and Professional Women's Clubs, Inc. of the U.S.A. (BPW/USA)

See Business and Professional Women's Clubs.

National Industrial Recovery Act (1933) (NIRA or NRA)

This early New Deal program was designed to bring about cooperation between government and industry by means of fair practice codes. Codes for individual industries were drawn up and administered by the National Recovery Administration (NRA). The act also established minimum wages and maximum hours for all major industries, along with provisions to regulate production and marketing and to discourage price-fixing. Section 7(a), known as Labor's Bill of Rights, guaranteed workers' rights to organize, to join unions of their own choosing, and to bargain collectively. NIRA stimulated union organizing and a rash of strikes because of alleged or actual code violations.

It helped some working women by fixing minimum wages higher than those they had been receiving, but it exempted almost half of all employed women: those employed as domestics, independent laundresses, independent seamstresses, telephone company employees, and workers in agriculture, in insurance, in public service, in professional service, and most clerical workers. The codes also differentiated on the bases of race and gender.

NIRA was declared unconstitutional in the Schechter Poultry case (1935) on the grounds that the federal government lacked the power to regulate companies not engaged in interstate commerce; the code, which fixed wages and hours, was therefore an invalid exercise of federal power; and the code system itself was an unconstitutional delegation of legislative power by Congress.

See also Clerical Workers; Great Depression; Minimum Wage; New Deal; Strikes; Unions; Wagner Act.

References Mimi Abramovitz, *Regulating the Lives of Women: Social Welfare Policy from Colonial Times to the Present* (1988); Robert E. Doherty, *Industrial and Labor Relations Terms* (1989); Michael Evan Gold, *An Introduction to Labor Law* (1989).

National Labor Relations Act (NLRA) (1935)

See Wagner Act.

National Labor Relations Board

See Wagner Act.

National Labor Union (NLU)

In 1868 this organization, representing a coalition of reformers and trade unionists, supported the eight-hour day for women, equal pay, unions for all working women, the opening of all trades and professions to women, and women's suffrage. But in 1869 resentment flared when Susan B. Anthony, representing the Working Women's Association, encouraged women to surmount the barriers that male typographers had placed against admitting women to the trade, even if to do so they had to become scabs, taking jobs when the male typographers went on strike. The NLU expelled Anthony and despite the efforts of some women members began to oppose women's rights. But until its demise in 1873, the NLU continued to endorse equal pay and welcome women delegates.

See also Scab; Strikes; Unions; Working Women's Association.

References Mary H. Blewett, *Men, Women, and Work: Class, Gender, and Protest in the New England Shoe Industry, 1780–1910* (1988); James J. Kenneally, "Women in the United States and Trade Unionism," in Norbert C. Soldon, ed., *The World of Women's Trade Unionism* (1985).

National League of Women Workers

This organization, founded in 1897, consisted of 100 clubs of 14,000 members by 1914; most of them were factory workers. Within it groups dedicated to self-government and self-support joined in activities designed to develop character. Some clubs offered savings and loan programs, insurance plans, and industrial training. Others helped their members enjoy inexpensive vacations. Often these groups were sponsored by the Young Women's Christian Association, churches, and boarding homes, but working women organized others on their own.

See also Young Women's Christian Association.

Reference Lynn Y. Weiner, *From Working Girl to Working Mother: The Female Labor Force in the United States, 1820–1980* (1985).

National Organization for Women (NOW)

Founded in 1966 to move governments to combat gender discrimination and fight for women's rights, this largely middle-class group has broadened its concerns to include women's issues like the right to abortion, lesbian rights, and the Equal Rights Amendment. But NOW still works on many issues of specific concern to women in the workplace: sex discrimination, maternity leaves, Social Security benefits, tax deductions for child- and home-care expenses for working parents, child-care centers, and equal job training opportunities and allowances for women in poverty. Its Women's Economic Rights Project helps women to seek economic equality. The Legal Defense and Education Fund, associated with NOW, participates in litigation of cases involving the rights of women in the workplace, either as counsel or by filing an amicus brief. It also supports nonlitigation activity: research, writing, education, and supplying expertise to government agencies.

See also Child Care; Equal Rights Amendment; Friedan, Betty; Maternity Leave; Sex Discrimination; Women's Equity Action League.

National Teachers' Association

See National Education Association.

National Youth Administration (NYA)

See New Deal.

Native Americans

The American Indian peoples who migrated to the Americas from Asia over 30,000 years ago had, by colonial times, developed distinctly different life-styles and societal organizations, in which the roles of women varied markedly. Some tribes afforded a high degree of sexual equality. But all divided labor by gender, though the allocation varied from tribe to tribe.

By the early twentieth century, the sorry history of European-American treatment of Native Americans all too often left them confined to reservations, geographically and culturally, destroyed as societies and as individuals, dependent on the authority and disbursements of the United States government. Even the best intentioned within that government were determined to change Native Americans, imbuing them with white value systems, even as they denied them economic opportunity. Fourteen percent of Native American women worked for pay; about half of them worked in agriculture, ranching, and fishing, a fourth in manufacturing, and another fourth in domestic or

An Arapaho, Freckled Face, photographed in the late 1890s

personal service. Only 2 percent worked as professionals—mostly teachers.

In World War II many Native Americans left their reservations. Native American women gradually moved away from agricultural work toward clerical, service, and professional jobs, doubling their labor force participation from 1950 to 1970, up to 35 percent. Subsequently, on and off the reservations, Native Americans have experienced high rates of unemployment. Although their women's labor force participation has been rising, to 48 percent in 1980, all too many of them can find only part-time jobs: in 1980, almost two-thirds of employed Native American women held part-time jobs. Most of the few female professionals and technicians are confined to traditionally women's jobs.

See also Part-Time Workers; Unemployment.

References Teresa Amott and Julie Matthaei, *Race, Gender, and Work: A Multicultural Economic History of Women in the United States* (1991); Gretchen M. Bataille, ed., *Native American Women: A Biographical Dictionary* (1992); H. Ferguson, *A Study of the Characteristics of American Indian Professional Women in Oklahoma* (1985); Jay Miller, ed., *Mourning Dove: A Salishan Autobiography* (1990).

Navy Nurse Corps
See Army Nurse Corps.

Nepotism
Nepotism policies prohibited appointments (typically in universities, colleges, and research institutes) of members of the same family. The policy was explained as a protection against favoritism, but its practical effect was discriminatory: it relegated women, usually wives, to marginal positions or denied them employment opportunities entirely. Academic institutions got around these policies by "emergency" hiring, which confined wives to one-year appointments and denied them opportunities for promotion, raises, and benefits. Nepotism rules are now voided as contrary to the principles of equal opportu-

nity incorporated in the Civil Rights Act of 1964.

See also Academic Women; Benefits; Civil Rights Act of 1964; Cori, Gerty; Mayer, Maria Gertrude Goeppert.

Nestor, Agnes (1880–1948)
This trade union leader, schooled only through the eighth grade, rose from girlhood work in a cotton mill and as a glovemaker to national prominence in the labor movement. At 18 she led a successful strike, thereafter committing her life to organizing women workers. Throughout most of her life she held high office in the International Glove Workers Union. Through the Women's Trade Union League she organized unions in the stockyard and garment industries and among waitresses, dressmakers, milliners, nurses, and teachers. Her lobbying helped to enact first the ten-hour and then the eight-hour day. Rendering outstanding service on a succession of public commissions, she also fought against child labor and for minimum wages for women, a public employment service, and a Women's Bureau in the Department of Labor.

See also Minimum Wage; Strikes; Union Organizers; Unions; Women's Bureau; Women's Trade Union League.

References Edward T. James et al., eds., *Notable American Women II* (1971); Agnes Nestor, *Woman's Labor Leader: The Autobiography of Agnes Nestor* (1954).

Networking
Women, so long segregated and excluded from public activity, have always naturally turned to each other for support and mutual help. But with the women's movement of the 1960s and 1970s and the entry into competition in a man's world, more women began consciously "networking," emulating the "old boys' networks" that had long assisted men. That is, they exchange information about available jobs and techniques for handling problems and passes. They introduce themselves and each other to friends of friends, particularly those in

influential positions. They recommend and mentor each other.

See also Business and Industry; Men-Only Clubs; Mentors; Networking Project for Disabled Women and Girls.

Networking Project for Disabled Women and Girls

Founded in 1984, this project of the Young Women's Christian Association tries to increase the career aspirations of disabled girls by linking them with successful disabled role models.

See also Mentors; Networking; Rehabilitation Act; Young Women's Christian Association.

New Century Guild for Working Women

This Philadelphia organization grew out of low-cost evening classes originated in 1882 under the leadership of Eliza Sproat Turner. The guild provided not only classes in both domestic and marketable skills, but also a library, a dining room, a gymnasium, a recreational center, and a publication, the *Working Woman's Journal*, written from the employees' viewpoint. Though its classes were taken over in 1892 by the Drexel Institute, the guild continues to function in the late twentieth century.

Reference Edward T. James et al., eds., *Notable American Women III* (1971).

New Deal

In President Franklin D. Roosevelt's inaugural address he promised a "new deal" for the American people and thus provided a name for the domestic reform program introduced by his administration. Included in its first phase (1933–1934) was the National Industrial Recovery Act (NIRA), which spearheaded the recovery program, seeking to revive the economy by industrywide codes regulating prices and production, guarantees of labor's right to organize and bargain collectively, public works, aid to farmers, and relief for the unemployed; but in 1935 the Supreme Court declared NIRA unconsti-

tutional. The second phase (1934–1941) was notable for the passage of the Social Security Act of 1935, designed as a safety net for the working population, and a body of labor legislation to establish and protect employees' rights to bargain collectively and their rights as individual workers.

Women workers participated in labor's gains, and such prominent women as Frances Perkins and Rose Pesotta were actively involved. Black women, however, benefited less since agriculture and domestic service, in which many of them were engaged, were exempted from most New Deal legislation. Some of the New Deal programs, like the Civilian Conservation Corps (CCC), excluded women. But the National Youth Administration (NYA) helped students, about half of them women, stay in school.

On the other hand, other New Deal agencies concentrated on men. The short-lived Civil Works Administration (CWA) employed 4,000,000 workers in public works projects, only 300,000 of them women. The statistics are muddy for the Federal Emergency Relief Administration (FERA), an agency that funded state relief programs, but it is certain that of the workers aided by these programs, only a small percentage were women: Abramovwitz sets the figure at 12 percent. FERA did make a stab at helping young unemployed women who were wandering from city to city. Kenneally states that during 1934–1935 FERA served 50,000 unemployed women in 70 residence schools and educational camps with 750 teachers. Unlike their CCC brothers, these women received neither pay nor vocational training, but they did get some education.

The Work Projects Administration (WPA), originally established as the Works Progress Administration, put millions of unemployed to work on such civic projects as constructing schools. For most of the life of this agency, about 12 percent of these were women (of whom a tiny minority were black), although women comprised 25 percent of the total labor force. Fearful of being criticized for employing too many women, agency administrators also wanted to discourage women's "eagerness" to become the family breadwinners. This policy shut out women with able-bodied husbands, even though those husbands were unemployed. Women also lacked appropriate work experience: since the Great Depression had forced so many of them into the work force for the first time or for reentry after a long absence, they needed more training. WPA did train women in such nontraditional occupations as welding and shipbuilding, but it assigned more than half its women workers to sewing. Black women fared even worse, most of them being confined to domestic service. During the Great Depression some 36,000 people taught for the WPA, often out-of-work professionals. Their own experiences in having to apply for relief caused many of them to identify with workers generally. WPA teachers worked in adult education courses in urban and rural literacy work and for unions in workers' education.

The long-range effect of the New Deal was to establish precedents for governmental intervention in the labor market and governmental responsibility for the well-being of citizens.

See also Agricultural Workers; Domestic Servants; Fair Labor Standards Act; Great Depression; Labor Legislation; National Industrial Recovery Act; Nontraditional Occupations; Perkins, Frances; Pesotta, Rose; Social Security Act; Unions; Wagner Act; Woodward, Ellen Sullivan; Workers' Education.

References Mimi Abramovitz, *Regulating the Lives of Women: Social Welfare Policy from Colonial Times to the Present* (1988); James J. Kenneally, "Women in the United States and Trade Unionism," in Norbert C. Soldon, ed., *The World of Women's Trade Unionism* (1985); Marjorie Murphy, *Blackboard Unions: The AFT and the NEA, 1900–1980* (1990); Arthur Schlesinger, Jr., *The Age of Roosevelt* (1959); Susan Ware, *Holding Their Own: American Women in the 1930s* (1982).

New England Labor Reform League
See New England Workingmen's Association.

New England Workingmen's Association (1844–1848)
This early organization coordinating local unions arose in part to respond to the needs of women mill workers. Because so many of its members were women, in 1846 it changed its name to the New England Labor Reform League.
See also Unions.

New York Working Woman's Protective Union
See Working Woman's Protective Union.

New York Working Women's Association
See Working Women's Association.

Nine to Five, National Association of Working Women
This organization, founded in Boston in 1973, has dedicated itself to obtaining rights and respect for office workers. It counsels them on their legal rights and on-the-job problems; operates a survival hotline; lobbies to win new national policies on child care, family leave, and other provisions to help working families; bargains for gains in pay equity, health and safety protections, career advancement, and back pay and pay equity raises; exposes abuses of electronic monitoring and health problems associated with office automation; and issues regular reports on matters of concern to its members. With the Service Employees' International Union in 1981, Nine to Five founded a new, woman-led union for office workers. Particularly notable are its efforts to transform both the image and content of unions to better serve the needs of women workers.
See also Clerical Workers; Coalition of Labor Union Women; Electronic Monitoring; Pay Equity; Unions.
Reference Ruth Milkman, ed., *Women, Work and Protest* (1985).

Ninety-Nines (1929)
Amelia Earhart was the first president of this first women pilots' organization, which still functions in support of the in-

terests of women in aviation. It was named after the number of original members. The organization provided many pilots for the Women's Airforce Service Pilots (WASP) of World War II.

See also Earhart, Amelia Mary; Military Women; Pilots; World War II.

Reference Joan McCullough, *First of All* (1980).

Nontraditional Employment for Women (NEW) Act
See Job Training Partnership Act.

Nontraditional Occupations

The idea that gender predetermines fitness for particular kinds of occupations is not specific to any time or place; throughout American history woman's role in the labor force has been construed according to prevailing social views of the nature of the female. Employers, unions, and society generally have resisted women's entry into the professions and many of the trades. Since male-dominated jobs are almost universally better-paid, of higher status, and considered peculiarly appropriate for men, male workers have also resisted. Their resentment takes many forms, from sexual harassment to interfering with women's performance of their duties.

The U.S. Department of Labor defines as "nontraditional" for women those jobs that have a large proportion of male workers and few or no females. The National Commission on Working Women, supported by Wider Opportunities for Women, more precisely defines them as jobs in which more than three-quarters of the workers are men.

In colonial America a handful of extraordinary women can be identified working in business and trade and other jobs that society labeled "for men only." By 1900 at least a few women worked in almost every job category the census listed, and so many women had qualified as physicians as to create a backlash against them from their male colleagues. Only

with the women's movement of the 1960s and 1970s, however, was the relegation of women to occupations "appropriate" to their gender seriously challenged.

In the last quarter of the twentieth century an increasing number of women have taken degrees in nontraditional fields. Since there is a close correlation between fields of study and occupational goals, this shift indicates a perception of expanded job opportunities as well as easier access to graduate schools, now required by law. And in the 1970s, 1980s, and 1990s women have been entering nontraditional occupations in larger numbers than before, stepping up their representation in nontraditional fields like medicine and the law, and to a lesser extent architecture, science, and engineering. They have also been seeking entry into such high-paying (as compared with traditional "women's

Marie Klundt, a system protection specialist with a Colorado power company, monitors transmissions lines.

jobs") technical and skilled-craft fields as telephone installation, truck driving, machine-tool work, construction labor, local transit driving, and law enforcement. But they remain a minority in most despite affirmative action programs: in 1991 women still constituted only 6 percent of craft workers. Moreover, women moving into these fields have to work very hard to "prove themselves," have to endure covert and overt hostility, and often have to fight for job opportunities, promotions, and raises.

The *Directory of Non-traditional Training and Employment Programs Serving Women*, published by the U.S. Department of Labor, lists, state by state, programs for jobs from basic computer skills to carpentry to sheet metal work.

See also Affirmative Action; Apprentices; Blue-Collar Workers; Colonial America; Construction Workers; Engineers; Job Training Partnership Act; Law Enforcement; Military Women, *Occupational Outlook Handbook*; Occupational Segregation; Physicians; Progressive Era; Sexual Harassment; Suitable Occupations; Trades; Unions; Wider Opportunities for Women.

References Connecticut Permanent Commission on the Status of Women, "Non Traditional Jobs for Women" (1991); Mariam K. Chamberlain, *Women in Academe: Progress and Prospects* (1991); *Directory of Non-traditional Training and Employment Programs Serving Women* (1991).

Norris-LaGuardia Act (1932)

This act was designed to enable labor organizations to engage in boycotts, picketing, and strikes. It forbade federal courts to issue injunctions in cases growing out of labor disputes; it also stipulated that yellow dog contracts were unenforceable in federal courts. Although it was an important step in the struggle of unions for recognition as the workers' legitimate representatives, it did not meet all of labor's needs and wants. It left state courts free to order injunctions, both federal and state courts free to hold unions liable in civil suits, employers free to discharge workers in sympathy with unions, and employers without any legal obligation to bargain with unions.

See also Boycotts; Injunctions; Labor Management Relations Act; Strikes; Unions; Wagner Act; Yellow-Dog Contract.

Reference Michael Evan Gold, *An Introduction to Labor Law* (1989).

Norton, Mary Teresa Hopkins (1875–1959)

This congresswoman, a native of New Jersey, learned secretarial skills in her youth at Packard Business College in New York City and worked as a secretary. In 1909 she married businessman Robert Francis Norton; their only child died in infancy.

In grief Norton turned to volunteer work. Her fund-raising efforts for a Jersey City church day-care center introduced her to political boss Frank Hague, who started her on her political career. From 1921 to 1944 she headed New Jersey's Democratic State Committee. Election in 1923 to the Hudson County Board of Freeholders, where she successfully advocated the building of a maternity hospital, led to candidacy in 1924 for the U.S. House of Representatives. She was the first woman Democrat elected to Congress on her own (her husband not having preceded her) and later the first woman to chair a congressional committee.

As chair of the House Labor Committee from 1937 to 1947, she fought long, hard, and ultimately successfully for the Fair Labor Standards Act. For many years she protected New Deal labor legislation. Ahead of her time she introduced—but could not get passed—legislation to combat racial discrimination in employment. Throughout her career she advocated working women's rights, including equal pay for equal work. Her belief in protective legislation caused her to oppose the Equal Rights Amendment, and her religion caused her to oppose the birth control movement. She retired from Congress in 1951.

See also Equal Rights Amendment; Fair Labor Standards Act; New Deal; Protective Legislation.

Reference Notable American Women: The Modern Period.

Nurses

Nursing has long been associated with woman's traditional role as nurturer and caretaker. The Civil War, with its gaping lack of provision for caring for the sick and wounded, inspired American women to establish nursing as a profession. Formal training began in the second half of the nineteenth century in nursing schools usually affiliated with hospitals, where nurses did most of the work as slaveys for the doctors. After graduation they might continue to work there as head nurses, or take their chances freelancing on private duty, dependent on doctors' recommendations for their placement. In 1873 reform-minded women organized nurses' training schools at Bellevue Hospital in New York, Massachusetts General Hospital in Boston, and Connecticut Hospital in New Haven, but graduates of such programs were the exception for many years. In 1880 the census counted 13,000 women who nursed for hire, of whom only about 560 had graduated from hospital courses.

During the Progressive Era hospitals proliferated, creating more demand for nurses and better training for them. Women like Lillian Wald, interested in the welfare of the poor, developed school nursing, visiting nursing, public health nursing, and industrial nursing, all of which afforded the nurse much greater independence and called for the exercise of her own judgment and her assumption of great responsibility.

As a major part of professionalization, nurses have upgraded requirements. In the 1920s the landmark Goldmark Report led to baccalaureate degrees in nursing, despite the opposition of some hospitals and doctors. After World War II, hospital diploma schools moved toward baccalaureate degrees, and collegiate and university nursing programs multiplied. In the late twentieth century nurses constantly refresh their skills and learn new ones, and many of them specialize. They have broadened their field to include nurse anesthetists (some of whom were already practicing by World War I) and nurse practitioners.

Only after the medical debacle of the Spanish-American War did the military admit its need of professional nurses and establish Navy and Army Nurse Corps in the early twentieth century. Nurses were not awarded full status as officers until after World War II. But military nursing, where perforce nurses have performed more procedures and exercised more authority than in many civilian jobs, has helped to give the profession status and raise its standards.

Perennial shortages of nurses have afflicted hospitals and patients and in the last quarter of the twentieth century are prompting men to move into the field, especially as pay rises, benefits increase, and nurses get more control and responsibility. For years men have made up a stable 4 or 5 percent of all registered nurses, but in 1992 they constituted about 10 percent of student nurses. (*New York Times*, 29 November 1992) Nurses are receiving higher compensation than ever before, and many of them may take their pick of jobs: those who choose can travel the country, finding work easily wherever they go. But in many hospitals they are also carrying heavy workloads and performing nonnursing tasks, including housekeeping chores and clerical work, because of inadequate staffing levels. Some of them complain that their tight schedules leave them without enough time for patient care and others that they are pushed into assignments for which they do not feel qualified. (*New York Times*, 10 January 1993)

Nurses today are on-the-spot caretakers, experts in sophisticated techniques, educators and ombudswomen for patients, and interpreters of doctors' dicta. With doctors and patients, they will increasingly confront the dilemmas imposed by the ability of modern medicine to keep bodies breathing and our societal inability to agree about when life begins and ends.

See also Army Nurse Corps; Bickerdyke, Mary Ann Ball; Civil War; Compensation; Goldmark, Josephine Clara; Health Professionals and Paraprofessionals; McGee, Anita Newcomb; Mahoney, Mary Eliza; Nutting, Mary Adelaide; Palmer, Sophia French; Richards, Linda; Thoms, Adah B. Samuels; Wald, Lillian; World War I; World War II; Zakrzewska, Marie Elizabeth.

References Barbara Melosh, "Every Woman Is a Nurse: Work and Gender in the Emergence of Nursing," in Ruth J. Abram, ed., *"Send Us a Lady Physician": Women Doctors in America, 1835-1920* (1985); Karen Buhler-Wilkerson, *False Dawn: The Rise and Decline of Public Health Nursing, 1900–1935* (1990); Vern L. Bullough, et al., eds., *American Nursing: A Biographical Dictionary* (1989); Vern Bullough and Bonnie Bullough, *The Care of the Sick: The Emergence of Modern Nursing* (1978); Philip A. Kalisch and Beatrice J. Kalisch, *The Advance of American Nursing* (1978); Barbara Melosh, *The Physician's Hand: Work Culture and Conflict in American Nursing* (1983); Susan M. Reverby, *Ordered To Care: The Dilemma of American Nursing, 1859-1945* (1987).

Nutting, Mary Adelaide (1858–1948)

This leader in nursing education graduated in 1891 in the first class from Johns Hopkins Training School for Nurses. In 1894 she became its principal, raising standards and improving working conditions. In 1907 she moved to Teachers College, Columbia University, as professor in institutional management and head of a new department of household administration with a division of hospital economics. The first nurse appointed to a university chair, she built a department that trained the leaders who developed the country's training schools and public health nursing services. As an officer of the American Society of Superintendents of Training Schools for Nurses of the United States and Canada (later the National League for Nursing Education) she helped establish the *American Journal of Nursing* in 1900, move nursing education within universities, and professionalize nursing. In 1912 she wrote a landmark monograph, *Educational Status of Nursing*.

See also Nurses.

Reference Edward T. James et al., eds., *Notable American Women II* (1971).

Oakley, Annie (1860–1926)

This "Girl of the Western Plains," a sharpshooter and Wild West performer who as a girl discovered her natural talent for shooting, at 16 married the professional marksman Frank Butler. For five years she toured with him, while he taught her to read and coached her in marksmanship and stagecraft. In 1885 when Oakley was hired by the Buffalo Bill rodeo, Butler became her manager. Her performances were spectacular: shattering glass balls in midair, standing on a galloping horse and shooting the flames from a revolving wheel of candles, flipping playing cards and perforating them with bullets as they fell. She gained fame both in the United States and in Europe, to the point of making Buffalo Bill Cody jealous. In 1901 a train wreck ended her career with the Wild West show. For a while she played Western heroines on stage and then gave demonstrations and lessons in trapshooting with her husband. In 1922 an automobile accident partially paralyzed her.

See also Cowgirls.

References Walter Havighurst, *Annie Oakley of the Wild West* (1992); Edward T. James et al., eds., *Notable American Women II* (1971); Jennifer S. Uglow, comp. and ed., *International Dictionary of Women's Biography* (1985).

Occupational Outlook Handbook

This publication, issued regularly by the Bureau of Labor Statistics of the U.S. Department of Labor, lists job titles and explains the nature of the work and its duties, training requirements, and salary range. It also projects employment prospects. Useful supplements to this work include the *Directory of Non-traditional Training and Employment Programs Serving Women,* published by the U.S. Department of Labor; *Jobs for the Future,* jointly published by the Business and

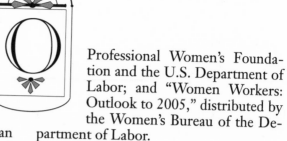

Professional Women's Foundation and the U.S. Department of Labor; and "Women Workers: Outlook to 2005," distributed by the Women's Bureau of the Department of Labor.

Occupational Safety and Health Act of 1970 (OSHA)

This act created the Occupational Safety and Health Administration to reduce workplace hazards, improve safety and health programs, provide research in occupational safety and health, establish responsibilities and rights for employers and employees, maintain a reporting and record-keeping system of job-related injuries and illnesses, train safety and health personnel, and develop mandatory safety and health standards. It covers all employers except federal, state, and local governments, but exempts self-employed persons, farms that employ only immediate family members, and working conditions regulated by other federal agencies. The act also instructs federal agency heads to provide safe and healthful working conditions, consistent with those set by OSHA for the private sector.

OSHA sets occupational health standards for the private sector and, to a lesser degree, for the public sector; the Environmental Protection Agency (EPA) regulates the health of farm workers and indirectly regulates other chemical exposures. OSHA requires that employers label hazardous-chemical containers, train workers who handle them, and make available Material Safety Data Sheets to inform the employees of the risks involved.

The act also created the National Institute of Occupational Safety and Health (NIOSH) to conduct studies and investigations of health hazards. NIOSH, however, has no legal enforcement power.

See also Fetal Protection Policies; Health Hazards.

References Randy Rabinowitz, *Is Your Job Making You Sick?: A CLUW Handbook on Workplace Hazards* (n.d.); U.S. Department of Labor, "All about OSHA" (1991).

Occupational Segregation

The designation of certain occupations as predominantly "male" or "female" (men's work and women's work) has characterized American society from its beginnings. The exclusion of women from certain kinds of employment has been justified in terms of their weaker physique, their lack of training, their bent for nurturing rather than for competition, and their higher spiritual abhorrence of the rough trades. Others have argued that women are by nature or by socialization prone to care more about people than about things, more about families than about work, and therefore are less committed to their work than their male colleagues. Economists have chimed in that women are less willing to invest in "human capital" such as education, training, and continuity of employment—in effect women offer less in the work force and deserve less compensation.

On the other hand, given the chance, whether by war, economic expansion, necessity, or changes in public policy (like affirmative action), women have surged into the available openings in the workplace and performed efficiently. Afforded real opportunities for mobility and power, women have responded with commitment and dedication.

During the 1970s and 1980s government, schools, and businesses developed programs to encourage women to enter nontraditional professions (science, law, management) and trades (welding, carpentry, truck driving) and affirmative-action programs to encourage employers to hire them. In the 1970s occupational segregation slightly decreased, as women moved in significant numbers into accounting, engineering, law, and sales management.

But resegregation also occurred: with more women in a given profession or trade, female ghettos developed within it, where women hold positions of lower status and visibility, fewer opportunities for promotion, less access to centers of power, and lower pay than their male colleagues. For example, in the early 1990s women constitute 99 percent of dental assistants versus 9 percent of dentists; 94 percent of nurses versus 18 percent of physicians; 76 percent of legal assistants versus 22 percent of attorneys; 88 percent of data entry keyers versus 32 percent of computer systems analysts. In the higher paying blue-collar jobs, women comprise only 8 percent of precision production, craft, and repair workers.

In 1990 more than two-thirds of all employed women worked as domestics, teachers, waitresses, and nurses, or in protective services, or in wholesale and retail trade. Forty-six percent of all women who worked for wages were concentrated in 12 occupations, sometimes called female ghettos: secretaries and receptionists, typists, retail clerks, data entry keyers, food servers, bookkeepers, nurses and nurses' aides, teachers, household workers, childcare workers, sewing machine operators, and hairdressers.

In the last quarter of the twentieth century, despite continuing stratifications by sex, the lines separating men's and women's work are being challenged and redrawn. The wage disparity between male and female occupations remains despite the Equal Pay Act's requirement of "equal pay for equal work" and the prohibition against sex discrimination in Title VII of the Civil Rights Act of 1964. The struggle for equality shifted in the 1980s to efforts to require equal pay for work of comparable worth.

Women workers' responses to job segregation and its underlying assumptions about the differences between men and women have varied over time and from place to place. And women workers themselves react differently according to their particular career expectations, work culture (often a product of their ethnic or racial background), family situation, and workplace experiences. Occupational segregation becomes a visible and salient issue for most women when the boundary between men's and women's jobs is demonstrably arbitrary as, for example, when shortly before World War II the Philco manufacturing company reclassified over a thousand men's jobs, assigning them to women without raising the women's pay to the male level. Situations such as this undermine the concept of separate spheres, radicalize women, and open up access to nontraditional occupations.

See also Affirmative Action; Attorneys; Blue-Collar Workers; Civil Rights Act of 1964; Civil War; Comparable Worth; Construction Workers; Engineers; Equal Pay Act; Feminization; Gender Gap; Glass Ceiling; Job Training Partnership Act; Nontraditional Occupations; Nurses; Physicians; Separate Spheres; Shoemakers; Sticky Floor; Suitable Occupations; Teachers; Trades; Velvet Ghettos; World War II.

References Ava Baron, *Work Engendered* (1991); Martha Blaxall, ed., *Women and the Workplace: The Implications of Occupational Segregation* (1976); Jerry A. Jacobs, *Revolving Doors: Sex Segregation and Women's Careers* (1989); Judith S. McIlwee and J. Gregg Robinson, *Women in Engineering: Gender, Power, and Workplace Culture* (1992); Susan Gluck Mezey, *In Pursuit of Equality: Women, Public Policy and the Federal Courts* (1992); Nine to Five, National Association of Working Women,"Profile of Working Women" (1990); Paula Ries and Anne J. Stone, eds., *The American Woman, 1992–93 : A Status Report* (1992); Christine L. Williams, *Gender Differences at Work: Women and Men in Nontraditional Occupations* (1989); Leslie Wolfe, ed., *Women, Work, and School: Occupational Segregation and the Role of Education* (1991).

Occupational Therapy
See Health Professionals and Paraprofessionals; Slagle, Eleanor Clarke.

O'Connor, Sandra Day (b. 1930)
The first woman member of the U.S. Supreme Court, O'Connor desegregated the court when she was appointed in 1981 by President Reagan. O'Connor's elevation was not greeted enthusiastically by all women's groups, some of whom

Sandra Day O'Connor

thought her too liberal on abortion, family issues, and the Equal Rights Amendment, while others thought her record on those and related matters too conservative. She graduated from Stanford University law school in 1952 and opened her own law office in 1959 in Maryvale, Arizona. Before her appointment to the Supreme Court, O'Connor served in various elective and appointive positions in Arizona; at the time of her appointment she was sitting on the Arizona Court of Appeals. She is married and has three sons.

See also Attorneys; Equal Rights Amendment; Government Workers.

References Judith Freeman Clark, *Almanac of American Women in the 20th Century* (1987); Jennifer S. Uglow, comp. and ed., *International Dictionary of Women's Biography* (1985).

O'Day, Caroline Love Goodwin (ca. 1869–1943)
This congresswoman began her working life as an artist and illustrator. In 1916 she moved into social welfare work, volunteering for the Consumers' League

and the Women's Trade Union League among other organizations. Her work for the Democratic party led in 1934 to her election to Congress on a platform of "Higher standards for wage earners, adequate relief at lowest cost to the taxpayer, a power program of benefit to the consumer, a sound fiscal policy, friendly foreign relations and wider opportunity for women in government." (*New York Times*, 7 November 1934) She served until 1942, supporting the major New Deal measures, including the Fair Labor Standards Act of 1938.

See also Artists; Consumers' League; Fair Labor Standards Act; Government Workers; New Deal; Women's Trade Union League.

Reference Edward T. James et al., eds., *Notable American Women II* (1971).

Office of Federal Contract Compliance Programs (OFCCP)

This agency is charged with enforcing the executive order that bars the federal government from buying goods and services from firms that discriminate against women and minorities. OFCCP's strategy of enforcement has been to require federal contractors with more than 15 employees to formulate an affirmative, action plan setting numerical goals for the employment of minority workers, accompanied by a timetable. OFCCP is supposed to monitor the fulfillment of plans it has accepted. The agency needs strengthening, since in practice it has been only moderately effective in reducing discrimination against protected groups.

See also Affirmative Action; Equal Employment Opportunity Commission; Executive Order 11246.

References Barbara B. Bergmann, *The Economic Emergence of Women* (1986); Michael Yates, *Labor Law Handbook* (1987).

Old Age Insurance Program

Like other provisions of the Social Security Act of 1935, this program reflected the ethic of its time, when men were generally supposed to be entitled to or to need jobs, and women not. To build a re-

tirement fund from which retired workers over 62 might draw, it imposed a tax on both employers and employees. It originally called for benefits to wives and children of covered men, but not to husbands and children of covered women, and it excluded occupations in which women workers predominated. Since wages determined benefits, women, disadvantaged both by being overwhelmingly confined to lower paid jobs and by moving in and out of the labor force in response to family needs, received lower benefits. Women workers who had paid their dues to the state by having babies suffered because that labor had reduced their time spent in wage earning. Moreover, the flat percentage payment required from active workers made the Social Security tax regressive, and consequently more painful for the many women bunched in low-paid occupations.

Changing ethics, the women's movement of the 1960s and 1970s, and court cases remedied some of these inequities. Most of those that remain stem from the ambiguity in the Social Security system itself as a cross between an insurance and a welfare scheme, and from the ambiguity in women's roles in modern society, with their uneasy balance between productive and reproductive labor. The act, for most of its history, has favored traditional one-earner married couples who manage to survive together past the earning spouse's retirement age, though that pattern is gradually changing as women workers earn, on their own, pensions higher than those to which they may be entitled as wives or widows.

The program has so far survived criticism that it imposes no needs test, financial crises, and raids on its reserves by government managers. With the graying of America in the late twentieth century, the tax required to support it (originally minimal) has become onerous for workers, who fear that its funds may be depleted before they themselves can reap its benefits.

Nonetheless the Old Age Insurance

Program, generally referred to as "Social Security," continues to make the difference between impoverishment and independence to millions of retired women as well as retired men, and the difference between penury and a relatively comfortable old age to millions of others.

See also Aid to Families with Dependent Children; Social Security Act; Unemployment Insurance Program.

Reference Mimi Abramovitz, *Regulating the Lives of Women: Social Welfare Policy from Colonial Times to the Present* (1988).

Older Women

In 1990 more than 3.4 million people aged 65 and older, over 41 percent of them women, were in the work force. Fourteen percent of women 65–69 and 4 percent of women 70 and older worked.

Though age discrimination is illegal, statistics show that older workers face many disadvantages. Almost two-thirds of those over 65 work in the low-paid trade and service industries. Employers often hesitate to invest in training them. Many older women workers belong to the contingent work force; many do part-time or temporary work. Their insecurity is increased by the trend toward early retirement (usually before 65) as a means of reducing payrolls. Older workers are more likely to be laid off; when they are, they experience longer periods of unemployment, and many, especially women, leave the work force discouraged. Nonetheless, older women workers are disadvantaged more through pay and job status than through unemployment, at least partly because most of them are located in less cyclically prone industries.

When employers rehire retirees, they typically pay them less than the retirees formerly earned and give them few or no benefits, even when they do the same work as before. Low-level workers often return at entry-level pay, despite their years of experience. Retirees, however, often willingly accept such conditions of employment, partly to supplement their incomes, but also partly to give their lives focus and companionship.

The gender gap in wages is higher among older workers: in the early 1990s women over 45 average only about 61 percent of men's wages, against the 72 percent of men's wages that women average overall. Fewer women than men are covered by pensions, and those who are receive smaller payments, partly because of shorter job tenure but mainly because of occupational segregation.

See also Age Discrimination Acts; Benefits; Bridge Job; Contingent Work Force; Gender Gap; Occupational Segregation; Part-Time Workers; Pensions; Retirement Equity Act; Temporary Workers; Unemployment.

References Peter B. Doeringer, ed., *Bridges to Retirement: Older Workers in a Changing Labor Market* (1990); Nine to Five, National Association of Working Women, "Social Insecurity: The Economic Marginalization of Older Female Workers" (1987); Lonnie Golden, "Employment and the Marginalization of Older Workers in the United States," in Barbara D. Warme, Katherina L. P. Lundy, and Larry A. Lundy, eds., *Working Part-Time: Risks and Opportunities* (1992).

O'Reilly, Leonora (1870–1927)

At 11 this labor leader began work in a collar factory. Thanks to her mother, who despite her own sweated labor and near destitution took her to labor and radical meetings, O'Reilly began organizing at 16. While working a ten-hour day as a shirtwaist maker she started the Working Women's Society, which put together the information that inspired Josephine Shaw Lowell to found the Consumers' League. O'Reilly moved into union work, spoke frequently before reform groups, and widened her circle of friends among upper-class reformers, who, in 1897, supported her for a year of study and reform work. With their support she studied at Pratt Institute to qualify as a secondary school sewing teacher, graduating in 1900. From 1902–1909 she taught at the Manhattan Trade School for Girls; all her life she preached the importance of vocational education.

With the founding of the Women's Trade Union League (WTUL) in 1903,

O'Reilly joined its board, and recruited Mary Dreier and Margaret Dreier Robins. In 1909 Robins gave O'Reilly a lifetime annuity to enable her to devote all of her time to the WTUL, to their mutual advantage—despite O'Reilly's difficulties and doubts about working with the WTUL's upper-class reformers of the "mink brigade." The League called on her expertise as a worker and union member to support strikes, organize women, and educate workers for union leadership. Ill health forced her retirement in 1914. O'Reilly was also a founder of the National Association for the Advancement of Colored People, a delegate to two International Congresses of Women, and an instructor on the theory of the labor movement at the New School for Social Research in 1925–1926.

See also Consumers' League; Lowell, Josephine Shaw; Robins, Margaret Dreier; Strikes; Unions; Vocational Education; Women's Trade Union League; Working Women's Society.

Reference Edward T. James et al., eds., *Notable American Women II* (1971).

OSHA
See Occupational Safety and Health Act.

O'Sullivan, Mary Kenney (1864–1943)
This labor organizer and factory inspector began her working life in printing and bookbinding. As a bookbinder in Chicago, she joined and soon became a leader in the Women's Federal Union #2703 of the American Federation of Labor (AFL), the city's only stable group of organized women. With Jane Addams' aid she organized a union of women bookbinders and the Jane Clubs for working girls. In 1892 Samuel Gompers appointed her the first woman organizer for the American Federation of Labor, which bared its lack of commitment to women workers by refusing to reappoint her in 1893. With the help of Hull House she carried on, lobbying for a state factory law that regulated the employment of women and children, under the terms of which she was appointed a deputy to Chief Inspector Florence Kelley.

Her marriage in 1894 to labor editor Jack O'Sullivan moved her to Boston, where she organized and acted as executive secretary for the Union for Industrial Progress to study factory conditions. Supported by Mary Morton Kehew and the Women's Educational and Industrial Union, she organized the rubber makers and women laundry and garment workers. Though after her husband's death in 1902 she had to struggle to support their four children, she kept on with her work in the labor movement. In 1903 she was a principal founder of the Women's Trade Union League, in which she was an important officer in the early years. Against the orders of the AFL she supported the Bread and Roses Strike. In 1914 she became a factory inspector for the Massachusetts Department of Labor and Industries, a post she did not relinquish until 1934.

See also American Federation of Labor; Bookbinders; Bread and Roses Strike; Hull House; Jane Clubs; Kehew, Mary Morton Kimball; Kelley, Florence; Printers; Unions; Women's Educational and Industrial Union; Women's Trade Union League.

Reference Edward T. James et al., eds., *Notable American Women II* (1971).

Outworkers
See Pieceworkers.

Overtime
American wage earners in the 1990s work many hours of overtime (beyond their regularly scheduled workday or workweek), partly because they need the extra money, but also because benefits make it less expensive for employers to pay extra for overtime than to hire more workers.

See also Benefits.

Reference Juliet B. Schor, *The Overworked American: The Unexpected Decline of Leisure* (1992).

Packard, Sophia B. (1824–1891)

This native of Massachusetts and founder of Spelman College spent the first years of her career in teaching, business, and paid church work. In 1877 she cofounded the Woman's American Baptist Home Mission Society. As its corresponding secretary she discovered Georgia's need for a school for black women and girls, persuaded the society to endorse it, and with her lifelong companion Harriet E. Giles (1833–1909) set off in 1881 to establish a school in a church basement.

Getting students was no problem. Getting money was. But she raised enough with help from the Baptists and John D. Rockefeller to buy property formerly occupied by Union Army troops; she named the school Spelman Seminary in honor of Mrs. Rockefeller and her parents. The seminary moved into these quarters in 1883, with a teacher training program, a model school, and industrial and boarding departments. Its rapid growth forced Packard to spend much of her energy raising money. In ten years the seminary had 464 students and 34 faculty members. After Packard's death Giles succeeded her as president. The seminary became Spelman College in 1924 and in 1929 affiliated with Morehouse College and Atlanta University.

See also Academic Women.

References Edward T. James et al., eds., *Notable American Women III* (1971); Florence M. Read, *The Story of Spelman College* (1961).

Palmer, Alice Elvira Freeman (1855–1902)

In her relatively short life, Palmer exercised a major influence on women's education. As a young woman she persuaded her parents to pay for her education at the University of Michigan by promising not to marry until she had repaid them and had helped her brother and sisters through the educations of their choice. In any event, she paid her own way for her last two undergraduate years and her graduate work by teaching and educational administration. In 1879 she accepted an offer to become head of the history department at Wellesley College, continuing work toward a doctorate during the summers.

As president of Wellesley, a responsibility she undertook at the age of 27, Freeman transformed the institution from a boarding school into a college. She systematically involved the faculty in the governance of the college. She sophisticated the curriculum, raised admission standards, and established a system of 15 feeder preparatory schools.

Freeman strengthened Wellesley's ties to the community and to other academic institutions. Off campus she helped organize college alumnae across the nation into what is now the American Association of University Women. After she resigned in 1887 and married Harvard philosophy professor George Herbert Palmer, she continued her academic activities, mostly as a volunteer: serving on the Wellesley board of trustees, acting as the University of Chicago's first dean of women, working to transform the Harvard Annex into Radcliffe College, helping to modernize this oldest private school for girls in New England as a trustee of Bradford Academy, and upgrading Massachusetts' normal schools as a member of the Massachusetts State Board of Education. Additionally she acted as role model and mentor for many young women, including Lucy Sprague Mitchell and African-American Charlotte Hawkins Brown, later founder of Palmer Memorial Institute, a school for girls in North Carolina.

See also Academic Women; American Association of University Women; Mitchell, Lucy Sprague.

References Edward T. James et al., eds., *Notable American Women III* (1971); George Herbert Palmer, *The Life of Alice Freeman Palmer* (1908).

Palmer, Sophia French (1853–1920)

This nurse and administrator, after graduating from the Boston Training School for Nurses in 1878, spent several years in private nursing. In 1889 she founded the nursing school at Garfield Memorial Hospital in Washington, D.C., of which she became administrator. From 1896–1900 she superintended the Rochester City Hospital and Training School. During these years she also helped edit the *Trained Nurse and Hospital Review* and cofounded the American Society of Superintendents of Training Schools for Nurses and the Nurses' Associated Alumnae of the United States and Canada (later the American Nurses' Association). In 1900 she became editor-in-chief of the new *American Journal of Nursing*, promoting reforms in nursing education and campaigning for state supervision of nursing schools and state registration of nurses.

See also Nurses.

Reference Edward T. James et al., eds., *Notable American Women III* (1971).

Parental Leave

See Family and Medical Leave Act; Family Leave; Maternity Leave.

Parker, Julia Sarsfield O'Connor (1890–1972)

This union organizer, a native of Massachusetts, went to work as a telephone operator in 1908, immediately after her high school graduation. In 1912 she joined the telephone operators' union, initiating a lifelong career in the labor movement. She sustained it after she married reporter Charles Austin Parker in 1925 and even after the birth of her two daughters, in 1926 and 1928.

She devoted the years from 1912 until 1938 to the Telephone Operators' Union of the International Brotherhood of Electrical Workers (IBEW). Her participation in the Women's Trade Union League (WTUL), on whose national board she served from 1917 to 1926, broadened her outlook even while she complained of their insufficient attention to field organizing. In the Telephone Operators' Union she rose rapidly, and when in 1918 IBEW reluctantly granted the union its own autonomous department, she became its president. During her tenure she led two strikes: the one in 1919 won many gains for union members; that of 1923, lacking the support of the operators, failed catastrophically.

In the second half of her career, from 1939 until 1957, Parker worked as an organizer for the American Federation of Labor, working in the South and then in Boston.

See also American Federation of Labor; Strikes; Telephone Operators' Department of the International Brotherhood of Electrical Workers; Union Organizers; Unions; Women's Trade Union League.

Reference Barbara Sicherman et al., eds., *Notable American Women: The Modern Period* (1980).

Parsons, Lucy Gonzalez (1852–1942)

This Chicana organizer devoted her life to the cause of labor, among many other activities helping to found the Industrial Workers of the World (IWW), and in 1913 demanding an eight-hour day.

See also Industrial Workers of the World.

Reference Angela Howard Zophy and Frances M. Kavenik, eds., *Handbook of American Women's History* (1990).

Part-Time Workers

Historically, American women have frequently sought part-time work, which allowed them to supplement the family income while also housekeeping and nurturing the family. Women still opt for part-time work for reasons that vary with life cycles: time to study, to meet family responsibilities, to enjoy leisure, to ease into retirement, to supplement retirement incomes. In the late twentieth century women in management and the professions have developed variations on part-time work, such as job sharing, to assist them during their childbearing and child-nurturing years.

On the other hand, the trend of the 1980s and 1990s toward hiring part-time workers, often in order to avoid the payment of benefits, has shut many women, both skilled and unskilled, out of the full-time labor market. Indeed the increase in part-time employment in the late 1980s and early 1990s stems almost entirely from workers who cannot find full-time jobs. In 1990, 4.9 million people, more than half of them women, worked part-time involuntarily. The mounting numbers of women who work two part-time jobs testify to the involuntary nature of much part-time work.

In 1990, 27 percent of all women workers were part-timers, compared to fewer than 12 percent of male workers. Part-time workers averaged only $4.83 an hour, compared with $7.83 an hour for full-timers; much of this gap results from the high concentration of part-time workers in sectors where all workers are poorly paid.

Protective legislation often does not apply to part-timers. Unions, though they have fought to curb the expansion of part-time work, have historically shown little interest in part-time workers; only in the late 1980s and early 1990s have they begun to understand the numbers and importance of these workers and to try to recruit and protect them. Employers seldom reward these workers for work experience, granting seniority rights only to full-timers. Many part-timers receive fewer benefits than full-timers, or none at all. The Employment Retirement Income Security Act (ERISA), however, requires companies with existing pension plans to extend that benefit to employees who work more than 1,000 hours a year. And an occasional company voluntarily experiments with benefits for part-timers. The Starbucks Coffee Company, for example,

has decided that paying benefits costs less than accepting inordinately high turnover and having to recruit constantly: after 90 days at Starbucks, all employees, including part-timers, qualify for medical, dental, and vision benefits, sick leave, and vacation, and for other benefits after longer employment. (*New York Times,* 16 August 1992)

In general, the trend toward part-time work is promoted by the employers' efforts to avoid high benefit costs, particularly for health insurance, and their need for cost minimization (including the reduction of overtime), higher productivity from less fatigued workers, reduced absenteeism, labor market flexibility, and labor market predictability.

The growth in part-time work has supported and perhaps even increased occupational segregation. Certainly it has decreased job satisfaction, earnings, and career progression. Though the practice threatens unskilled women most, it affects even professional women, especially in higher education, where colleges and universities resort to part-timers to avoid tenure problems, increase curricular flexibility, and hold down labor costs.

See also Benefits; Bridge Jobs; Contingent Work Force; Employment Retirement Income Security Act; Job Sharing; Marginal Workers; Occupational Segregation; Older Women; Overtime; Unions.

References Teresa Amott and Julie Matthaei, *Race, Gender, and Work: A Multicultural Economic History of Women in the United States* (1991); Richard S. Belous, *The Contingent Economy: The Growth of the Contemporary, Part-Time and Subcontracted Workforce* (1989); Charlene Canape, *The Part-Time Solution: The New Strategy for Managing Your Career while Managing Motherhood* (1991); Nine to Five, National Association of Working Women, "Working at the Margins: Part-Time and Temporary Workers in the United States" (1986); Barbara D. Warme, Katherina L. P. Lundy, and Larry A. Lundy, eds., *Working Part-Time: Risks and Opportunities* (1992).

Passing

To avoid their economic and political disadvantages as females, or for adventure, a few women throughout American history have masqueraded as men, earning men's wages, voting before the 19th Amendment, or going to war.

See also Military Women.

Reference Teresa Amott and Julie Matthaei, *Race, Gender, and Work: A Multicultural Economic History of Women in the United States* (1991).

Pattern Bargaining

In this system unions negotiate for a standard set of terms for workers throughout an industry.

See also Unions.

Reference Barbara Kingsolver, *Holding the Line: Women in the Great Arizona Mine Strike of 1983* (1989).

Pay Equity

The phrase "Equal pay for equal work," held out as a goal for women workers, may imply either the same pay for the same job or the same pay for different jobs of comparable worth. As a group, American women workers have never come close to either. But they have improved their situation somewhat. In the 1990s overall they average 72 percent of men's wages. (*New York Times*, 18 October 1992) Individually some women receive the same pay as their male peers. And women in the late twentieth century have a legal basis to sue for equity.

Change has been prompted in part by the fear that women paid lower wages might replace male workers. Some economists have urged that discrimination in the pay envelope might so lower women's morale that they would not sustain high levels of productivity, might discourage women from working when society needed their labor, or might depress the standard of living because women could not afford to consume much. But most importantly, through legislation and court cases, women have fought to close the gender gap.

See also Civil Rights Act of 1964; Comparable Worth; Equal Pay Act; Gender Gap; President's Commission on the Status of Women; *Schultz v. Wheaton Glass Co.*

References Barbara B. Bergmann, *The Economic Emergence of Women* (1986); Rita Mae Kelly and Jane Bayes, eds. *Comparable Worth, Pay Equity, and Public Policy* (1988); Carolyn Kenedy, *Pay Equity: An Action Manual for Library Workers* (1989); Alice Kessler-Harris, *A Woman's Wage: Historical Meanings and Social Consequences* (1990); National Committee on Pay Equity, *Pay Equity in the Public Sector: 1979–1989* (1989).

Peabody, Elizabeth Palmer (1804–1894)

This educational reformer began teaching in her teens in her mother's school in Salem, Massachusetts. For years she eked out a living running her own school, teaching for Bronson Alcott, tutoring, writing textbooks, operating a bookstore, and publishing Transcendentalist books and the *Dial*. Meanwhile she challenged the attention of people like William Ellery Channing, Ralph Waldo Emerson, Jones Very, Margaret Fuller, and Nathaniel Hawthorne. Devoted to the ideal of Christian-Transcendentalist education, Peabody wrote and lectured from 1850 to 1884, particularly as an advocate of the kindergarten movement. In 1860 she organized the first formal kindergarten in the United States.

See also Teachers.

References Edward T. James et al., eds. *Notable American Women III* (1971); Jennifer S. Uglow, comp. and ed., *International Dictionary of Women's Biography* (1985).

Peale, Anna Claypoole (1791–1878), Margaretta Angelica (1795–1882), and Sarah Miriam (1800–1885)

These three artists, who grew up in Philadelphia, were the daughters of the portrait painter James Peale and nieces of the artist Charles Willson Peale. They began their life work by assisting their father with the finely detailed backgrounds of his paintings.

As her father's eyesight deteriorated, Anna took over painting miniatures, a genre in which she established her own reputation, earning high prices for her portraits. In 1824 she was elected to the Pennsylvania Academy of the Fine Arts, where she exhibited regularly until her retirement in 1842.

Margaretta, though she gained a considerable reputation for painting fruit, worked mostly as an amateur. Sarah earned an artistic success beyond that of any previous American woman. Primarily a portraitist in oils, she began her independent work at 18. By 1822 she was well established, traveling to seek patrons, mostly between Baltimore and Philadelphia. She too was elected to the academy in 1824. When her father died in 1831, she moved to Baltimore and to fame as the city's favorite portrait painter. St. Louis stole her away in 1846, and she lived there for 32 years. As she aged she turned from portraits to still lifes.

See also Artists.

References Edward T. James et al., eds. *Notable American Women III* (1971); Joan King, *Sarah M. Peale: America's First Woman Artist* (1987).

Pensions

Historically, women either have not received the same benefits upon retirement as men, or have been required to make higher payments into pension plans than men in order to qualify for the same retirement benefits. This common practice has been held to be sex-based discrimination: in 1978 the U.S. Supreme Court in *Los Angeles v. Manhart* held that a pension plan that required women to pay more than men to participate was a violation of the Civil Rights Act of 1964.

Because women may drop out of the labor force more frequently, two features of pensions may affect women workers more than men: early vesting (putting the employee in possession of the pension funds) and portability (the employee's power to carry pension rights from one employer to another).

The Employment Retirement Income Security Act of 1974 limited some pension abuses. But the proportion of all workers with employer- or union-sponsored pension plans fell during the 1980s, and concern rose as companies closed down operations, fired unvested workers on the brink of retirement, or invaded pension funds for other purposes.

In 1990 only 23 percent of all women, compared to 46 percent of men, received pension benefits at retirement. Women's average pension income was only 60 percent that of men, and Social Security (Old Age Insurance Program) payments received by retired women were only 76 percent of men's. In 1991 the government proposed changes to move toward portable pensions. Individual employed women (and men) may now save for their retirement by funding an Individual Retirement Account (IRA) or, if self-employed, a Keogh account.

See also Benefits; Civil Rights Act of 1964; Employment Retirement Income Security Act; Individual Retirement Accounts ; Old Age Insurance Program; Older Women; Retirement Equity Act; Unions.

References Barbara A. Burnett, ed., *Every Woman's Legal Guide* (1983); Nine to Five, National Association of Working Women, "Profile of Working Women" (1990).

People v. Charles Schweinler Press

In this 1913 case the New York State Court of Appeals upheld a state law barring night work for women.

See also Protective Legislation.

Reference Lynn Y. Weiner, *From Working Girl to Working Mother: The Female Labor Force in the United States, 1820–1980* (1985).

Perkins, Frances (1880–1965)

Perkins, the first woman cabinet member, served in the Roosevelt administration as Secretary of Labor from 1933 to 1945. She brought extensive experience as a labor reformer to that position. As a young teacher she met poor people and was exposed to labor unions in her Chicago settlement house work. Her move east in 1907 led to graduate study and the secretariat of the New York Consumers' League. Impassioned by witnessing the Triangle Shirtwaist fire, she went to work for the Committee on Safety of the City of New York, lobbying new labor measures through the legislature and exposing employers who were endangering workers. Through such experiences she learned the art of political compromise, becoming "a half-loaf girl; take what you can get now and try for more later."

Perkins married in 1913. For a period she did volunteer work, some of it political, but soon her husband's mental illnesses and frequent institutionalization necessitated her earning a living. She accepted Alfred E. Smith's appointment as the first woman member of the New York State Industrial Commission (later the Industrial Board) and the highest paid state employee in the nation. On Smith's advice she joined the Democratic party; for the next 30 years she worked for social legislation in the party platform, particularly legislation affecting women. In her work she concentrated on workmen's compensation, arbitration, and child labor. She rose to the chair of the Industrial Board and later Industrial Commissioner of the State of New York under both

Frances Perkins

Smith and Franklin D. Roosevelt, a position in which she advocated the 48-hour week, a minimum-wage law, and protective legislation for women.

She responded to the Great Depression by working with (then Governor) Roosevelt on measures like state unemployment insurance, regional solutions to joblessness, and relief. When Roosevelt was elected president, Perkins hesitated about accepting the appointment as Secretary of Labor, on the grounds of family responsibilities and her belief that the appointment should go to a woman trade unionist.

A woman of remarkable courage, as secretary she won the respect and support of organized labor, though her impatience with militant unionists and her efforts to unite the American Federation of Labor and the Congress of Industrial Organizations drew fire from labor leaders. Despite a right-wing effort to impeach her, she courageously confronted employers reluctant to bargain in good faith. She helped draft New Deal labor legislation and persuaded Roosevelt to take the country into the International Labor Organization. She strengthened the Department of Labor, upgrading and expanding its work and ridding it of racketeers. In World War II she opposed the forced conscription of labor and fought to uphold labor standards against the pressures of total war.

She resigned her office in 1945, but served under Truman on the Civil Service Commission, augmenting her income by writing and public speaking. From 1957 until her death she taught at Cornell University's School of Industrial and Labor Relations.

See also American Federation of Labor; Congress of Industrial Organizations; Consumers' League; Government Workers; Great Depression; Labor Legislation; Minimum Wage; New Deal; Protective Legislation; Settlement Houses; Triangle Shirtwaist Fire; Unions; World War II.

References Lillian Holmen Mohr, *Frances Perkins: "That Woman in FDR's Cabinet!"* (1979); Barbara Sicherman et al., eds., *Notable American Women: The Modern Period* (1980); Jennifer S. Uglow, comp. and ed., *International Dictionary of Women's Biography* (1985).

Permanent Commissions on the Status of Women

Several states have instituted these commissions, designed to help and protect women in many aspects of their lives. The commissions provide vocational information and advice on protection in cases of sex discrimination or sexual harassment.

See also Apprentices; Nontraditional Occupations; Sex Discrimination; Sexual Harassment.

Personnel Managers

See Human Resources Managers.

Pesotta, Rose (1896–1965)

Pesotta was a labor organizer and the first woman vice-president of the International Ladies' Garment Workers' Union (ILGWU). Born in the Ukraine, she came to the United States at the age of 17 and like so many Jewish immigrant women found a job in the garment industry, joining Local 25 of ILGWU. She was drawn to anarchism and never lost faith in its tenets, but she committed her life's work to the labor movement as the most likely way to improve conditions for the working class; her anarchist sympathies led her to the defense of Sacco and Vanzetti after their conviction. In the middle 1920s she attended the Bryn Mawr Summer School for Women Workers and the Brookwood Labor College. During the Great Depression she was an indefatigible organizer for ILGWU, successful all over the country despite antiunion hostility and ethnic and religious opposition. Throughout her career, Pesotta was acutely aware of the connections among the workplace, the home, and the community. A worker herself, she understood, as much of the leadership did not, the impact of the double workday for women, one on the job and the other at home.

In 1934 she was elected a vice-president of ILGWU, a position she held for three terms. Uneasy with her situation as the token woman in the union's leadership, she constantly fought to increase the power of women in an organization whose rank-and-file membership was more than three-fourths female. She resigned her position in 1944, advising ILGWU president David Dubinsky to throw the practice of a token woman on the board "out of the window."

See also Anarchism; Brookwood Labor College; Bryn Mawr Summer School for Women Workers; Great Depression; International Ladies' Garment Workers' Union; Unions.

References Edward T. James et al., eds., *Notable American Women III* (1971); Rose Pesotta, *Bread upon the Waters* (1987).

Petition Campaigns

In the nineteenth century working women, forbidden by law to bargain collectively, used petitions to try to improve their condition. Factory workers failed in their 1840s petition campaign for a ten-hour day. In the 1860s sewing women sent petitions to government agencies in an effort to rid the industry of the middlemen subcontractors who cut their wages and often cheated them. In 1896 women deprived by the Civil War of marriageable males even petitioned the government for housing—or, alternatively, "good and kind husbands and suitable homes."

See also Civil War; Cooperative Industries; Factory Workers.

Reference Alice Kessler-Harris, *Out To Work: A History of Wage-Earning Women in the United States* (1982).

Phillips v. Martin Marietta Corporation (1971)

In this case, the first based on Title VII of the Civil Rights Act of 1964 to reach the U.S. Supreme Court, Ida Phillips sued Martin Marietta for discriminating against her on the basis of sex when it refused to hire her because she had preschool children. The court held for the plaintiff, primarily because the company happily hired men with preschool children.

See also Civil Rights Act of 1964; Sex Discrimination.

References Susan Gluck Mezey, *In Pursuit of Equality: Women, Public Policy and the Federal Courts* (1992); Rita J. Simon and Gloria Danziger, *Women's Movements in America* (1991).

Photographers

From its creation in the 1830s the field of photography attracted some women. The number of professional women photographers, however, swelled with the technical advances from 1880 to 1909 and the efforts of the industry to create a market for cameras among women. By 1900 more than 3,500 women worked as professional photographers. Many specialized in portraits, working out of their homes. In the twentieth century women like Frances Benjamin Johnston (1864–1952), portraitist Gertrude Kasebier (1852–1934), Jessie Tarbox Beals (1870–1942), and news-and-documentary photographer Margaret Bourke-White (1904–1971) opened all areas of professional photography to women.

See also Beals, Jessie Tarbox.

References C. Jane Gover, *The Positive Image* (1988); Constance Sullivan, comp., *Women Photographers* (1990); Jennifer S. Uglow, comp. and ed., *International Dictionary of Women's Biography* (1985).

Phillis Wheatley Home

This Chicago establishment was founded in 1908 to help the black working wo-

Eighteenth-century poet Phillis Wheatley

men flooding into the city during the Great Migration, as blacks fled economic oppression in the South. The Phillis Wheatley home, like the White Rose Mission and several social-service organizations, offered such services as social clubs, an employment agency, and a residence for young working women.

See also Employment Agencies; White Rose Mission.

Reference Mimi Abramovitz, *Regulating the Lives of Women: Social Welfare Policy from Colonial Times to the Present* (1988).

Physicians

Medicine has always presented something of an anomaly in American history, since from the time of colonial America women bore so much of the responsibility for tending the sick and wounded, yet men monopolized the profession of physician. Understandably, therefore, women challenged this male domination early, thereby attacking the traditional division of labor between male and female, the separate spheres. Medicine was also an intensely competitive field, in which practitioners of eclectic medicine, homeopathy, and osteopathy vied for patients with graduates of "regular" medical colleges and all of them with the local midwife with a sideline in herbs. On the other hand, medicine was not a prestigious profession, and nineteenth-century society conceptualized women as pure, virtuous, and nurturing, natural healers who might elevate the profession, bringing to it "the leaven of tender humanity that women represent."

Before the Civil War, American women experienced extreme difficulty in getting formal training in medicine. (But as late as 1875 most states imposed no legal restrictions on anyone who wanted to practice medicine.) Early American medical schools refused women admission until the mid-nineteenth century. A handful of American women trained in Europe. Soon after Elizabeth Blackwell became the first woman to earn a medical degree from an American institution in 1849, medical colleges for women were founded in Philadelphia, Boston, and New York. But, excluded from hospitals, women could obtain no clinical experience until Blackwell and Marie Elizabeth Zakrzewska founded the New York Infirmary in 1857. By 1859 about 300 American women were licensed as physicians.

The Civil War brought progress, despite a continuing debate over whether women were physiologically equipped to become good doctors. Zakrzewska's New England Hospital provided, for its day, excellent care for women patients and excellent training for women physicians. Mary Harris Thompson, who earned her medical degree in 1863 and two years later founded the Chicago Hospital for Women and Children, was the country's first woman surgeon. In 1864 Rebecca Lee became the first black woman to receive a medical degree—though she may have qualified as a nurse or midwife; African-American Susan Smith McKinney Steward (1848–1919) earned her M.D. in 1870.

By the last decade of the nineteenth century, women's hospitals in New York, Philadelphia, Boston, Chicago, San Francisco, and Minneapolis employed female doctors and women's medical colleges opened in New York, Chicago, and Baltimore. But Blackwell, Zakrzewska, and Mary Putnam Jacobi all agreed that women should be trained with their male peers in coeducational medical schools.

In 1869 the University of Michigan, a land-grant institution open regardless of gender to citizens of the state, founded the first coeducational medical school—though it ran identical duplicate courses on "embarrassing" subjects for women and men. Boston, Syracuse, and Buffalo followed suit before 1880 and other institutions thereafter. The American Medical Association admitted women as members in 1876. New York's Mount Sinai Hospital gave a woman doctor the first regular staff appointment. In 1893 Johns Hopkins became the first eastern university to grant medical degrees to women. Women pressed in where they could: by 1900, 42 percent of Tufts Medical School graduates were women.

The overpopulation of physicians by the turn of the century created a predictable backlash against women (some 7,000 doctors in 1900) and a decrease in their numbers. The Flexner Report (1910) effectively eliminated several women's medical colleges because they did not meet the standards of Johns Hopkins. The numbers of women students in medical schools declined as women's medical colleges closed and coeducational colleges severely limited the quotas for women students, down to 5 percent in 1925. In 1920 less than 10 percent of general hospitals accepted women interns. The percentage of women doctors declined from 6 percent in 1910 to 5 percent in 1920 and 4.4 percent in 1930. At Boston University, where almost 30 percent of the graduating classes from 1898–1918 were women, not one woman graduated in the class of 1939. Women's influence on medicine also decreased as doctors competed with midwives in assisting at births. Fortunately for the country, some women physicians, like Dr. S. Josephine Baker (1873–1945), instead of struggling with the difficulties of setting up a private practice, directed their energies to public health work, instituting school health programs and educating the public.

In World War I the American military refused to employ women physicians, except now and then as civilians under contract, with less pay than male medical officers and no comparable authority; the women doctors who insisted on serving in that war usually either worked for another Allied military or served in hospitals organized, staffed, and paid for by women. World War II created a shortage of physicians, and women doctors were not only commissioned in the military but also in demand among civilians. Medical schools short of male students recruited women, and hospitals opened internships to them. Of course, after the war the trend reversed. Medical schools reimposed quotas and hospitals denied women internships. Even in 1960 the New York Obstetrical Society would not admit women physicians.

Not until the late 1970s did women represent as many as 10 percent of physicians. The women's movement of the 1960s and 1970s changed the face of the profession. In 1989 women earned a third of all medical degrees awarded and, as Blackwell, Zakrzewska, and Jacobi had hoped, received their medical education in coeducational institutions. (The Women's Medical College of Pennsylvania, the last surviving medical college for women only, went coed in 1969.) And in 1990 women constituted almost a fifth of physicians—more than 100,000. Even in 1991, though, women physicians earned on the average only a little more than half what men physicians earned. On medical school faculties in 1992 women were sparse at the top ranks: 9.5 percent of women faculty were full professors (compared with about a third of male faculty). Of 126 medical school deans, one was a woman.

In 1991 Dr. Bernadine P. Healy became the first woman director of the National Institutes of Health, pledging herself to encourage research on women's health problems, many of which, like heart attacks and breast cancer, have been egregiously underfunded.

See also Blackwell, Elizabeth; Civil War; Colonial America; Hamilton, Alice; Health Professionals and Paraprofessionals; Hunt, Harriot Kezia; Jacobi, Mary Corinna Putnam; Jamison, Mae Carol; Lozier, Clemence Sophia; McGee, Amy Newcomb; Pinkham, Lydia; Preston, Ann; Professional Women; Psychologists and Psychiatrists; Separate Spheres; Shaw, Anna Howard; Walker, Mary Edwards; World War I; World War II; Zakrzewska, Marie Elizabeth.

References Ruth Abram, *Send Us a Lady Physician: Women Doctors in America, 1835–1920* (1985); Joyce Antler, *The Educated Woman and Professionalization: The Struggle for a New Feminine Identity, 1890–1920* (1987); Penina Migdal Glazer and Miriam Slater, *Unequal Colleagues* (1987); Barbara J. Harris, *Beyond Her Sphere: Women and the Professions in American History* (1978); Joan McCullough,

First of All (1980); Paula Ries and Anne J. Stone, eds., *The American Woman, 1992–93: A Status Report* (1992); Pamela Wilson, ed., *Salaried and Professional Women: Relevant Statistics* (1992).

Pickers
See Migrant Laborers.

Pieceworkers
When in the early nineteenth century production began to move out of the house into the marketplace, working-class families in effect lost part of the productive labor on which they had depended. Earlier wife and husband had worked together to support the family; now the ethic, insisting that women's place was in the home, cast the burden of support on the husband alone. But, since few working-class men earned enough to support their families, many wives were driven to help out as best they could, whether by taking in washing, boarders, or piecework from the factories—work, that is, for which they were paid by the piece, not by the hour. They might sew, or bind shoes, or braid straw hats.

At the same time, the loss of men in the Revolutionary War and the male migration westward increased the number of single and widowed women who had to support themselves. They outnumbered married women in the labor force of this "putting-out" (or "given-out work" or "outwork" or "home work" or "domestic") system.

This work often paid even less than factory work, partly because women dominated it. It often required women to rent the necessary machines and to provide their own "findings," like thread. In the late nineteenth and early twentieth centuries it led to a system by which mothers and their young (sometimes as young as two- or three-year-old) children sweated in "outside shops" (their homes) throughout the daylight hours for pennies, sewing, making artificial flowers, or picking nuts from their shells.

But when during the Great Depression the National Industrial Recovery Act (NIRA) tried to abolish piecework in the home, an outcry forced the administration to exempt the handicapped and those who cared for invalids. In any case the U.S. Supreme Court shortly declared NIRA unconstitutional. In 1949, however, industrial home work became illegal, remaining so until the Reagan administration legalized it again.

Ironically, even in the early 1990s, women seek such work, because it enables them to earn money at home while they care for their children. The system is capable of exploiting women or of helping them solve their economic problems, depending on how well they are paid. All too often pieceworkers in the home pay their own overhead, work long hours for low rates, and seldom receive benefits.

The term "piecework" also sometimes applies to factory production wherein workers are paid by work accomplished, not by time spent. In the early twentieth century Frederick Winslow Taylor's philosophy of scientific management encouraged piece rates. During the 1920s unions fought to abolish this system, only to resort to it again in the Great Depression, negotiating rates per piece and putting a guaranteed minimum-wage floor under them.

See also Benefits; Factory Workers; Female Society of Lynn and Vicinity for the Protection and Promotion of Female Industry; Great Depression; Home Workers; Minimum Wage; Nathan, Maud; National Industrial Recovery Act; Scientific Management; Unions.

References Mimi Abramovitz, *Regulating the Lives of Women: Social Welfare Policy from Colonial Times to the Present* (1988); Teresa Amott and Julie Matthaei, *Race, Gender, and Work: A Multicultural Economic History of Women in the United States* (1991); Eileen Boris and Cynthia R. Daniels, eds., *Homework: Historical and Contemporary Perspectives on Paid Labor at Home* (1989).

Pilots

In the earliest years of aviation Mary H. "Carlotta" Myers did research with her husband on lighter-than-air craft; she made her first ascension in 1880. The decade that began in 1910 saw women among the pioneers of the burgeoning field of aviation. Women barnstormed; one of them, Katherine Stinson, in 1913 became the first woman to fly airmail. The same year Georgia "Tiny" Thompson Broadwick became the first woman to parachute from an airplane; her jumps eventually prompted the army's first order for parachutes. Blanche Stuart Scott, first woman to drive alone across the United States, soloed in 1910. Harriet Quimby qualified for a pilot's license in 1911, the first American woman so certified; a year later she flew across the English Channel, the first woman ever to do so. A handful of American women flew in World War I.

Laura Ingalls was the first woman to fly coast to coast across the United States, in 1930. Amelia Earhart, the first person to fly solo from Hawaii to California, vanished in 1937 in an attempt to be first to circumnavigate the earth at the equator. In World War II, under the leadership of Jacqueline Cochran, Women's Airforce Service Pilots (WASPs) delivered aircraft and towed targets; toward the end of the war, with too many pilots on their hands, the military summarily dismissed the WASPs and refused to recognize them as veterans, a recognition they won only in 1979.

Yet not until the 1970s did women get top jobs as commercial pilots. In 1973 Frontier Airlines hired Emily Howell Warner as a first officer, and six months later American Airlines hired Bonnie Tiburzi, the first woman pilot for a major airline. In 1986 American Airlines by chance assigned the first all-female crew. By 1992 almost a thousand women were flying for major lines.

See also Cochran, Jacqueline; Coleman, Bessie; Earhart, Amelia Mary; Military Women; Ninety-Nines; Quimby, Harriet; World War I; World War II.

References Kathleen Brooks-Pazmany, *United States Women in Aviation 1919–1929* (1991); Jean

Ruth Law served as a pilot during World War I.

H. Cole, *Women Pilots of World War II* (1992); Deborah G. Douglas, *United States Women in Aviation, 1940–1985* (1991); Henry M. Holden, *Ladybirds: The Untold Story of Women Pilots in America* (1991); Joan McCullough, *First of All* (1980); Claudia M. Oakes, *United States Women in Aviation, 1930–1939* (1991); Sally Van Wagenen Keil, *Those Wonderful Women in Their Flying Machines* (1990).

Pin Money

Many employers and union men have claimed that women work only to earn "pin money," that is, to purchase frivolities, and therefore do not need compensation adequate for their own support, let alone that of their dependents.

See also Compensation; Gender Gap; Married Women's Employment; Unions; Women's Wages.

Pinckney, Eliza Lucas (1722–1793)

At age 17, this agricultural pioneer took charge of her father's three South Carolina plantations. Talented in administration, she began experimenting in 1738 with the cultivation of indigo, a textile dye that subsequently made the fortunes of many other planters. When in 1744 she married a wealthy planter, she assumed for years the traditional roles of plantation mistress, wife, and mother of four children. But at her husband's death in 1758 she again undertook the responsibilities of plantation management.

See also Agricultural Workers; Farmers.

References Edward T. James et al., eds., *Notable American Women III* (1971); Elise Pinckney, *The Letterbook of Eliza Lucas Pinckney, 1739–1762* (1972); Harriet Horry Ravenel, *Eliza Pinckney* (1967); Constance B. Schulz, "Eliza Lucas Pinckney, 1722–1793," in G. J. Barker-Benfield and Catherine Clinton, *Portraits of American Women* (1991); Jennifer S. Uglow, comp. and ed., *International Dictionary of Women's Biography* (1985).

Pink-Collar Workers

This term applies to women clerical and secretarial workers, suggesting that, unlike blue-collar workers, they do little physical labor, and that, unlike white-collar workers, they exercise little authority.

See also Blue-Collar Workers; Clerical Workers; White-Collar Workers.

Pinkham, Lydia Estes (1819–1883)

This entrepreneur started her career as a schoolteacher, leaving the workplace when she married Isaac Pinkham; she then bore five children. Over the years, while her husband dreamed of making a fortune in real estate, the family slid into destitution.

The Pinkham sons came to the rescue with a suggestion that they market the botanical home remedies with which their mother had nursed family and neighbors. Pinkham cooked up a batch of the brew she had devised to treat "female complaints," with 18 percent alcohol as a "solvent and preservative," and in 1875 the family put Lydia E. Pinkham's Vegetable Compound on the market.

The Pinkham boys, especially Daniel, anticipated twentieth-century marketing devices. But it was their mother's picture that they put on the label, and she who wrote the advertising copy, which expounded on the evils of fashion and the lot of the working girl as well as touting the compound and displaying the testimonials of satisfied customers—including leaders of the Women's Christian Temperance Union. She also conducted an advice service, prescribing by mail for the woes and ills of the many women who responded to her often-repeated assertion that only a woman could understand a woman's problems. Fortunately for them she recommended good diet, exercise, and cleanliness. She also offered them information about sex and reproduction in a booklet she wrote, information much needed among women in that era.

When Pinkham died, her face was at least as well-known as that of any nineteenth-century woman, and her company was grossing about $300,000 annually. The company survived, reaching its zenith in the 1920s.

See also Entrepreneurs; Health Professionals and Paraprofessionals; Midwives; Physicians.

References Edward T. James et al., eds., *Notable American Women III* (1971); Jennifer S. Uglow, comp. and ed., *International Dictionary of Women's Biography* (1985).

Plantation System

This phrase, drawn from the days of slavery, is now sometimes used as a metaphor for the treatment of workers by a paternalistic employer who sets up a system that keeps his workers dependent on him and who may resort to capriciousness and personal abuse of workers who displease him.

See also Slavery.

Reference Karen Brodkin Sacks, *Caring by the Hour: Women, Work, and Organizing at Duke Medical Center* (1988).

Police

See Government Workers; Law Enforcement.

Politicians

See Government Workers.

Pregnancy

Pregnant women and women who might become pregnant have long been at a disadvantage in the workplace. In the past in some occupations pregnancy was cause for immediate termination of employment. Pregnant servicewomen, for example, faced automatic discharge until 1975, when the prospect of substantial litigation induced the Pentagon to change its policy. And for many years pregnancy was considered completely inappropriate for schoolteachers, probably on the grounds that their innocent charges had to be protected from such palpable evidence of sexual activity. Pregnant workers were also liable to other disabilities such as mandatory leave without pay, denial of use of sick leave during the birthing period and immediately after, and exclusion from a company's health plan.

Some have argued that restrictions on the work of pregnant women are justified on the assumption that pregnancy is a condition that renders women unfit to work and therefore restrictions are not discriminatory but necessary to protect their health. This view has led in the past to mandatory maternity-leave policies that forced women to stop work, often very early in their pregnancy and without an assured job to come back to. Two 1974 U.S. Supreme Court cases, *Cleveland Board of Education v. LaFleur* and *Turner v. Department of Employment Security*, struck down such restrictions, the court ruling that they were based on an assumption of physical incompetency that was arbitrary and thus violated due process.

Another category of restrictions deals with benefits, disability compensation, and other employment rights. Policies that exclude pregnant women from such benefits have been challenged in the courts with mixed and sometimes confusing results. The passage of the Pregnancy Discrimination Act in 1978 was an effort to end the confusion and promote equality of treatment. Issues remain, however, including the controversial question of whether pregnancy is just another disability or whether pregnancy is sufficiently unique to justify special treatment.

In the early 1990s government policy and that of employers toward pregnant workers is still in a state of some confusion because of conflicting goals and standards. The outstanding issue currently among feminists as well as among employers and within governments is whether working women are better served by equal treatment or by preferential treatment.

See also Benefits; *California Federal Savings and Loan v. Guerra*; Fetal Protection Policies; *General Electric v. Gilbert*; *Nashville Gas Co. v. Satty*; Pregnancy Discrimination Act; Sex Discrimination.

References Barbara B. Bergmann, *The Economic Emergence of Women* (1986); Susan Gluck Mezey, *In Pursuit of Equality: Women, Public Policy and the Federal Courts* (1992).

Pregnancy Discrimination Act (PDA) of 1978

This act overrides *General Electric v. Gilbert* and amends Title VII of the Civil Rights Act of 1964 by expanding the definition of sex discrimination. PDA prohibits discrimination against women employees because of pregnancy, childbirth, or related medical conditions. Women unable to work because of pregnancy must be treated the same as other temporarily disabled workers. Applicable to all institutions with 15 or more employees, PDA covers all areas of employment, including hiring, promotion, firing, and seniority rights, as well as benefits like sick leave and health insurance. Employers may exempt elective abortions from medical coverage, except if the life of the mother is threatened or if medical complications have resulted from abortion, but they must provide disability and sick-leave benefits to women recovering from abortions.

Still problematic are employers' policies that limit job opportunities for pregnant workers and/or for women who may become pregnant. Women's rights organizations do not agree among themselves as to whether women who may become pregnant ought to be excluded from jobs that might threaten the fetus.

The situation grows more complicated as modern technology introduces new risks for pregnant workers: in 1992, for example, International Business Machines (IBM) found that two chemicals widely used in manufacturing semiconductor chips significantly increase the risk of miscarriage. (*New York Times*, 12 October 1992) In 1991 the U.S. Supreme Court in *UAW v. Johnson Controls* held that sex-specific fetal protection policies were illegal under the Civil Rights Act of 1964 as amended by PDA: under this ruling the company could not bar fertile or pregnant women from such jobs unless it also refused them to fertile men.

Problems remain, however, as individual states attempt to provide special treatment for pregnant workers despite the PDA goal of equal treatment. Title VII and PDA require only that men and women be treated equally, which leaves employers free to deny their female workers benefits not available to male workers. Equality of treatment, therefore, can produce difficulties for workers who are pregnant or subject to pregnancy-related disabilities. This situation has given rise to preferential treatment legislation in many states, requiring employers to provide leaves for pregnant workers, reasonable guarantees of reinstatement, and protection of benefits. The U.S. Supreme Court has had difficulty in addressing the issue of preferential treatment in any consistent way; this difficulty underlines the lack of a national policy on workplace pregnancy and suggests that the equal treatment/special treatment debate will continue for some time.

See also Benefits; *California Federal Savings and Loan v. Guerra;* Civil Rights Act of 1964; Equal Employment Opportunity Commission; Fetal Protection Policies; *General Electric v. Gilbert;* Health Insurance; Maternity Leave; *Nashville Gas Co. v. Satty;* Pregnancy; Protective Legislation; Sex Discrimination; *UAW v. Johnson Controls.*

References Barbara A. Burnett, ed., *Every Woman's Legal Guide* (1983); Joyce Gelb and Marian Lief Palley, *Women and Public Policies* (1982); Karen J. Maschke, *Litigation, Courts, and Women Workers* (1989).

President's Commission on the Status of Women (PCSW) (1961)

This commission was created by President Kennedy, at the behest of Eleanor Roosevelt, to review progress in such areas as discrimination in private and public employment, protective laws, and government hiring. Its report established beyond doubt the existence of discrimination detrimental not only to women but to the nation as a whole. This middle-of-the-road report rejected the Equal Rights Amendment and recommended increased minimum wages, paid maternity leaves, and equal opportunity. It was influential primarily in awakening the public to the existence of sex discrimination, laying a foundation for remedial legislation, and giving the women's movement a substantial boost.

See also Equal Rights Amendment; Maternity Leave; Minimum Wage; Sex Discrimination;

White House Conference on the Emergency Needs of Women.

References Claudia Goldin, *Understanding the Gender Gap: An Economic History of American Women* (1990); Cynthia E. Harrison, *On Account of Sex: The Politics of Women's Issues, 1945–1968* (1988); Alice Kessler-Harris, *Out To Work* (1982), James J. Kenneally, "Women in the United States and Trade Unionism," in Norbert C. Soldon, ed., *The World of Women's Trade Unionism* (1985).

Preston, Ann (1813–1872)

This Quaker physician founded the Women's Hospital in Philadelphia in 1861. In 1866 she became the first woman dean of a medical school, the Women's Medical College of Pennsylvania.

See also Physicians.

Reference Jennifer S. Uglow, comp. and ed., *International Dictionary of Women's Biography* (1985); Angela Howard Zophy and Frances M. Kavenik, eds., *Handbook of American Women's History* (1990).

Price Waterhouse v. Hopkins (1989)

In this historic U.S. Supreme Court case, Ann Hopkins, a candidate for partnership in the accounting firm of Price Waterhouse, sued when she was passed over, successfully alleging that the partners discriminated against her by using sexual stereotyping in evaluating her qualifications. The court noted that "it takes no special training to discern sex stereotyping in a description of an aggressive female employee as requiring 'a course in charm school.'" The court held that if a woman charging sex discrimination under Title VII of the Civil Rights Act of 1964 presents direct evidence that illegal sex stereotyping motivated a denial of promotion, the burden is on the employer to prove that the promotion would have been denied even if sex stereotyping had not been a factor.

See also Civil Rights Act of 1964; Sex Discrimination.

References Susan Gluck Mezey, *In Pursuit of Equality: Women, Public Policy and the Federal Courts* (1992); Paula J. Ries and Anne J. Stone, eds., *The American Woman, 1992–93: A Status Report* (1992).

Printers

In colonial America and well into the nineteenth century the employment of women in the printing trade, typically wives and female relatives, was common and well-regarded. The many instances of women in the printing trade in the late eighteenth and early nineteenth century reflect the nature of the trade—a household industry in which the women of the family and the children were naturally called upon to help.

It was also customary for a wife to continue the business after the death of her husband. Martha Draper, for example, succeeded her husband as proprietor of the *Boston News Letter* in 1774. Jane Franklin of Rhode Island, after the death of her husband in 1735, ran the business as official printer for the colony and published pamphlets, assisted by her two daughters. Jane Aitken carried on her father's business in the early nineteenth century and was well-known in Philadelphia for the excellence of her work, which included Thompson's translations of the Bible in four volumes. Anne Timothy succeeded her husband as printer to the state of South Carolina. Anne Catherine Hoof Green (c. 1720–1775), the official printer for the province of Maryland for eight years, assisted her husband until he died in 1767, when the youngest of her six (of 14) surviving children was seven years old. Thereafter she ran and expanded the business until her own death.

See also Aitken, Jane; Bookbinders; Colonial America; O'Sullivan, Mary Kenney; Stevens, Alzina Parsons; Timothy, Elizabeth; Troup, Augusta Lewis; Wives.

Reference Isaiah Thomas, *The History of Printing in America* (1970).

Privacy Rights

See Civil Rights; Genetic Discrimination.

Producer Cooperatives

See Cooperative Industries.

Productivity

Between 1948 and 1990 American workers almost doubled their productivity. Since about 1970 the rate has been rising steadily at just over 1 percent a year.

Reference Juliet B. Schor, *The Overworked American: The Unexpected Decline of Leisure* (1992).

Professional Women

Barriers to women entering the professions have gradually eroded to the point that today women legally have equal access to colleges and universities and professional degrees, and the number of women qualifying for the professional fields has increased. Among traditionally male-dominated, high-status fields, the legal profession has the most women, followed by medicine, with architecture, dentistry, and engineering lagging behind. Women are also increasingly prominent in the communications professions as television and radio commentators, syndicated newspaper columnists, and war correspondents.

But greater access to high-level professional positions has not eliminated problems of sex discrimination, particularly where evaluations of professional competence and qualifications are concerned, as, for example, tenure decisions in academia or partnerships in law or accounting firms. Decisions on such issues involve standards that cannot easily be objectified (if at all) and judgments by peers and colleagues. The courts have generally been reluctant to substitute their judgment for the professional judgment of professors and deans, law and accounting partners, and corporate committees and administrators. Although discrimination at this level is difficult to establish, women are going to court and courts are increasingly willing to hear their cases and hold their employers accountable to the ban on sex discrimination in Title VII of the Civil Rights Act of 1964.

See also Academic Women; Accountants and Bookkeepers; Architects; Attorneys; Civil Rights Act of 1964; Engineers; Health Professionals and Paraprofessionals; Physicians; *Price Waterhouse v. Hopkins;* Psychologists and Psychiatrists; Religion; Sex Discrimination; Teachers.

References Penina Migdal Glazer and Miriam Slater, *Unequal Colleagues* (1987); Barbara J. Harris, *Beyond Her Sphere: Women and the Professions in American History* (1978); Susan Gluck Mezey, *In Pursuit of Equality: Women, Public Policy and the Federal Courts* (1992).

Professors
See Academic Women.

Progressive Era (1890–1920)

The Progressive Era breathed optimism and hope for the elimination of society's ills. A good many Americans fervently believed that they could so mold their own lives and their society as to achieve real progress for their children. The women among them undertook the job of public housekeeping, which forbade sweeping problems under the rug. Millions of volunteer and paid women fought for social reform and for women's suffrage. In the spirit of the period they based their efforts on careful research and investigation; with the information thus collected they identified problems and constructed solutions. The huge and sophisticated network of women's clubs lobbied for new laws to enforce these solutions. Lacking the vote, women reformers relied heavily on education and persuasion.

These years stand out for the numbers of women entering the workplace and for the numerous efforts to improve the workplace for them. European women were immigrating into the country in large numbers, and many of them had to work to support themselves and contribute to their families, whether in domestic service, in factories, or on farms. Black women were leaving the rural and urban South to flood into northern and midwestern cities in search of economic opportunity. European-American women were surging into the rapidly multiplying jobs in clerical work. Women from all these ethnic groups were surmounting the barriers to traditionally male professions and founding new female-dominated professions like social work and home economics.

Reformers, widely supported by women's clubs, successfully fought through protective legislation designed to improve the lot of these working women. They successfully lobbied for a Women's Bureau in the U.S. Department of Labor to further the interests of women in paid work. Directly and indirectly they supported strikes and boycotts through such groups as the Women's Trade Union League and the Consumers' League. In these and many other ways women outside the labor force united to improve the lot of women who worked for pay and to reinforce the efforts that women in the workplace were making to unionize and bargain collectively.

See also Boycotts; Clerical Workers; Consumers' League; Domestic Servants; Factory Workers; Home Economists; Protective Legislation; Social Feminists; Social Workers; Strikes; Unions; Women's Bureau; Women's Trade Union League.

Prostitutes

Although prostitution existed in America from colonial days, it was not generally criminalized until the early twentieth century. It has always been driven by economic factors—far more so than by forced prostitution (white slavery): despite its obvious degradations and dangers, it has often represented the best economic choice for some women. In 1858 Dr. William Sanger surveyed 2,000 prostitutes, finding that half of them had been domestic servants, and a quarter had worked in the needle trades; as prostitutes they earned much more, but their life expectancy in this oldest profession was four years.

What with the industrialization, westward expansion, and wars of the years between 1850 and 1900, the demand for prostitutes swelled. The census of 1870 identified prostitution as an occupational category. Chinese prostitution, for example, had become a highly organized institution as early as 1854: women were kidnapped, enticed, or bought in China for brothels in San Francisco and elsewhere, where they were often kept prisoners, sometimes literally in cages, the keys to which their owners rented out. In 1870, out of 3,536 adult Chinese women in California, 2,157 were listed as prostitutes.

Reformers fought the spread of prostitution with legislation like the Mann Act (1910) and drives to close down red-light districts. As some of these efforts succeeded and brothels dwindled in number, streetwalking increased and new forms of prostitution surfaced in massage parlors and call girl operations, to the greater endangerment of women. Prostitutes and madams more and more lost control of their work to pimps. This sad history has repeated itself from the Progressive Era on; in the 1990s American cities run a revolving door into and out of their jails for prostitutes, but almost never penalize the men who patronize them and seldom the men who profit by their earnings.

In the early 1990s, as in the past, prostitution supports a network of pimps, taxi drivers, hotel bellboys, organized crime, lawyers, physicians, liquor and drug dealers, law enforcement officers, landlords, and real estate speculators, few of whom wish to reduce it. Women experience its dangers, including sickness, superannuation, and violent death, and men share largely in its profits.

See also Domestic Servants; Mann Act; Matthews, Victoria Earle; Progressive Era; Purple Cross Society; Travelers' Aid; White Rose Mission; White Slavery.

References Frederique Delacoste and Priscilla Alexander, eds., *Sex Work: Writings by Women in the Sex Industry* (1991); Lucie Cheng Hirata, "Chinese Immigrant Women in Nineteenth-Century California," in Carol Ruth Berkin and Mary Beth Norton, *Women of America: A History* (1979); Barbara Meil Hobson, *Uneasy Virtue: The Politics of Prostitution and the American Reform Tradition* (1987); Ruth Rosen, *The Lost Sisterhood: Prostitution in America, 1919–1981* (1982).

Protective Legislation

Laws designed to protect working women against exploitation originated in the struggle, initiated in the early nineteenth century and intensifying during the Progressive Era, to protect workers of both genders by providing safe and clean working conditions, minimizing health hazards, putting a floor under wages, shortening hours, and compensating workers injured on the job. Special laws to protect women in the workplace came into being because women (along with children) were employed primarily in poorly paid jobs under horrendous working conditions but also because it proved politically more feasible to push through laws applicable only to women than laws for all workers. The opposition to initiating such laws sometimes caused reformers to seek first laws applying only to women, arguing, notably in *Muller v. Oregon*, that society had an interest in preserving women's ability to reproduce and to mother.

The process and the argument eventually resulted in *some* laws that applied only to women or regulated women's work more stringently than men's. Reform groups like the Women's Trade Union League and the Consumers' League, discouraged by the difficulties they experienced in unionizing women, sometimes chose instead to lobby through protective legislation for them. Male union workers, frightened by the bugbear of competition from women, supported these efforts, sometimes in the belief that such laws would dissuade employers from hiring women. Businessmen who opposed governmental interference necessarily opposed protective laws. The National Women's Party, which advocated equality for women, also resisted them. Feminists argued that legislation intended for young, inexperienced workers unduly restricted older married women and single careerists.

But most reformers in the Progressive Era viewed legislation protecting women workers as not only necessary but enlightened, and thus hailed *Muller v. Oregon*. The rationale for *Muller* and other cases sustaining legislation applicable only to women was that women differ from men in important ways that require special treatment in the workplace. The Civil Rights Act of 1964 (Title VII), however, makes all protective legislation suspect; and many modern feminists condemn legislation purporting to give women workers special protection as simply devices to exclude women from competing with men in certain occupations.

HOURS LAWS

As early as 1842 Lowell, Massachusetts, factory operatives had demanded a ten-hour day. Seven states enacted general hours statutes between 1847 and 1855, but they usually only forbade compelling workers to labor for longer hours. By 1867 the ten-hour movement excluded men; in 1874 Massachusetts enacted a ten-hour law for women in manufacturing only. Illinois' eight-hour law for women of 1893 was struck down by the state supreme court on the grounds that it interfered with the employer's freedom of contract and denied women equal protection under the law. But in 1908 the U.S. Supreme Court in *Muller v. Oregon* upheld a law limiting hours for women. Between 1909 and 1917, 41 states enacted or revised hours laws for women in industry and in some cases for women in stores. Efforts between 1890 and 1904 to forbid night work for women were usually blocked by court injunctions, but by 1928 ten states had outlawed women's night employment in at least two industries.

Legislation restricting the number of hours women may work has been consistently upheld by the U.S. Supreme Court on grounds that the restrictions were not arbitrary. A 1920s study by the Women's Bureau suggested that limitation of hours did not disadvantage women competitively, but disbarment from night work did.

WAGES LAWS

In 1910, prompted in part by concern that women's low wages led to urban prostitution, the Consumers' League and other groups pressed for minimum-wage laws. Massachusetts enacted the first in 1912; by 1917, 17 states had legislated women's wages. In the 1920s court rulings doomed minimum-wage laws applicable only to women. In 1937, however, the U.S. Supreme Court in *West Coast Hotel Co. v. Parrish* upheld the constitutionality of a minimum-wage statute of the state of Washington, thus overruling earlier decisions and laying the basis for the court to sustain the broad protections provided in the Fair Labor Standards Act of 1938.

EQUAL EMPLOYMENT OPPORTUNITY COMMISSION (EEOC)

The validity of state protective laws became an issue for EEOC when Title VII of the Civil Rights Act of 1964 became effective, because such laws might in fact be a subterfuge for discrimination against women. In 1967 EEOC issued guidelines stating that it would consider the validity of state laws on a case-by-case basis. Women's rights groups were split on the issue: the National Organization for Women argued that protective legislation was inherently discriminatory; other women's organizations argued for such laws. The question was resolved with the concept of "bona fide occupational qualification."

In the early 1990s, Americans, including labor union members, still argue about whether "protective" laws have really protected women or instead have protected them out of all they are entitled to. Opponents believe that protective legislation applicable only to women has shut them out of certain higher paid occupations, shunted them into low-level jobs, reduced their earnings, made employers reluctant to hire them, perpetuated stereotypes, evidenced society's tendency to treat women as helpless children unable to protect themselves, de-

nied them the right to contract freely, and pitted women workers against men workers. Supporters point to improved conditions for working women created by these laws. This division of opinion constitutes a major barrier to an Equal Rights Amendment. For some feminists in the early 1990s, protective legislation applicable only to women is incorrect because it stresses the *special* nature of women, thus undercutting the principle of *equality*. Since the 1970s the debate over protective legislation has revolved around such issues as employed mothers, maternity leave, and special treatment for pregnant workers.

Ironically enough in view of all this disagreement, protective legislation has often failed to cover such large groups of women workers as agricultural workers, domestics, office workers, and professionals.

See also Adkins v. Children's Hospital; Bona Fide Occupational Qualification; Civil Rights Act of 1964; Consumers' League; Edson, Katherine Philips; Eight-Hour Day; Equal Rights Amendment; Fair Labor Standards Act; Fetal Protection Policies; *Goesaert v. Cleary*; Maternity Leave; Minimum Wage; *Muller v. Oregon*; National Organization for Women; *People v. Charles Schweinler Press*, Pregnancy Discrimination Act; Progressive Era; Prostitutes; *Radice v. New York*; Separate Spheres; *UAW v. Johnson Controls*; Unions; *West Coast Hotel Co. v. Parrish*; Women's Bureau; Women's Trade Union League.

References Mimi Abramovitz, *Regulating the Lives of Women: Social Welfare Policy from Colonial Times to the Present* (1988); Steve Fox, *Toxic Work: Women Workers at GTE Lenkurt* (1991); Alice Kessler-Harris, *Out To Work: A History of Wage-Earning Women in the United States* (1982); Susan Lehrer, *Origins of Protective Labor Legislation for Women, 1905–1925* (1987); Karen J. Maschke, *Litigation, Courts, and Women Workers* (1989); Susan Gluck Mezey, *In Pursuit of Equality: Women, Public Policy, and the Federal Courts* (1992); William E. Pepper and Florynce R. Kennedy, *Sex Discrimination in Employment* (1981); Rita J. Simon and Gloria Danziger, *Women's Movements in America* (1991).

Psychologists and Psychiatrists

The study of psychology developed rapidly in the late nineteenth and early twentieth centuries. This discipline immediately appealed to women. Ironically enough, the difficulties they encountered in educating themselves in the field and in finding academic jobs helped to open the discipline to the many women who study and practice it in the 1990s. Women like Wellesley's Mary Calkins (1863–1930) and Vassar's Margaret Washburn (1871–1939) often found their academic homes at women's colleges, which accordingly became noted for the excellence of their psychological training. Their graduates went on in increasing numbers to the best graduate schools and to careers in psychology, psychoanalysis, and psychiatry.

Both psychology and psychiatry (which focuses on disorders of the mind and the personality) in their early days reflected a gender bias, assuming males as the norm and focusing on males in most of their studies. This bias was challenged early on by psychoanalysts Helene Deutsch (1884–1982) and Karen Horney (1885–1952) and by many feminist scholars. Virginia Satir (1914–1989) changed psychotherapy by her emphasis on family therapy.

Many women have studied psychology to prepare themselves for social work, vocational guidance, and human relations management; others have become counselors, psychoanalysts, psychotherapists, psychologists, and psychiatrists. As early as 1921, a fifth of all psychologists were women. In 1989, according to the Bureau of the Census, women earned 56.1 percent of the doctorates in psychology, and 54 percent of the 210,000 employed psychologists were women. In 1993 the 73,263 members of the American Psychological Association included 30,625 women, and the 28,080 members of the American Psychiatric Association included 10,035 women.

See also Health Professionals and Paraprofessionals; Human Resources Managers; Physicians; Professional Women; Social Workers; Vocational Guidance.

References Edward T. James et al., eds., *Notable American Women II* and *III* (1971); Sharon Hartman Strom, *Beyond the Typewriter: Gender, Class, and the Origins of Modern American Office Work, 1900–1930* (1992); Angela Howard Zophy and Frances M. Kavenik, eds., *Handbook of American Women's History* (1990).

Public Relations
See Communications.

Publishers
See Writers and Publishers.

Puerto Ricans
See Hispanic Americans.

Purple Cross Society
Established in 1905 by Anna Perry Bunell, this organization aimed at providing moral and financial support for working girls. Efforts like these were often aimed at keeping women out of prostitution.

See also Prostitutes.

Reference Judith Freeman Clark, *Almanac of American Women in the 20th Century* (1987).

Putting-Out System
See Pieceworkers.

Queen Bee

This derogatory term applies to a woman who attributes her success in business or a profession solely to her own efforts and qualifications. She gives no credit to the women's movement, announces that she prefers the company and conversation of men, argues that she made it in a man's world and so could anyone else with equal power, energy, ambition, and self-discipline, and takes little interest in helping other women.

See also Mentors.

Quimby, Harriet (1875–1912)

In 1911 Quimby, a journalist and drama critic, became the first American licensed female pilot. The following year she flew the English Channel; she was the first woman to pilot a plane across it. Quimby was killed in an accident while flying in a Boston-Harvard aviation meet on 1 July 1912.

See also Journalists; Pilots.

References Judith Freeman Clark, *Almanac of American Women in the 20th Century* (1987); Angela Howard Zophy and Frances M. Kavenik, eds., *Handbook of American Women's History* (1990).

Quintasket, Christine

See Mourning Dove.

Radical Women

Founded in 1967, this organization of left-wing feminists strives for reform in many areas, including affirmative action and working women.

See also Affirmative Action.

Radice v. New York

In this 1924 case the U.S. Supreme Court upheld a New York law prohibiting employment of waitresses in large cities at night, on the grounds that "night work . . . seriously affected the health of women, . . . threatened and impaired their peculiar and maternal functions and . . . exposed them to the dangers and menaces incident to night life."

Radice accepted statutory classifications based on gender differences that seemed to require special treatment for women in the workplace. In fact, however, the New York night-work law was full of exceptions that had no apparent relationship either to women's health and morals or to the public welfare. The *Radice* decision, although ostensibly benefiting women workers, had the effect of restricting their opportunities to choose jobs. This sort of dilemma led Alice Paul and the National Woman's Party to introduce the Equal Rights Amendment. The Civil Rights Act of 1964 nullified the sex discrimination embodied in *Radice*.

See also Civil Rights Act of 1964; Equal Rights Amendment; *Muller v. Oregon;* Protective Legislation; Sex Discrimination.

References Dorothy M. Brown, *Setting a Course: American Women in the 1920s* (1987); Susan Gluck Mezey, *In Pursuit of Equality: Women, Public Policy and the Federal Courts* (1992); Marlene Stein Wortman, ed., *Women in American Law: From Colonial Times to the New Deal* (1985).

Rankin, Jeannette Pickering (1880–1973)

Rankin, a native of Montana elected to the House of Representatives in 1916 and the first woman to serve in Congress, immediately showed her political courage and principle by voting against the entry of the United States into World War I. Rankin had gained the political experience that made her candidacy successful in the women's suffrage campaign. Her pacifism continued throughout her lifetime. In 1941, again serving in the House, she alone voted against entry into World War II. Only ill health deterred her from running yet once more in 1968 (at the age of 88) in order to oppose the Vietnam war more effectively. During her congressional career Rankin also sponsored protective legislation for women and children.

See also Government Workers; Protective Legislation; World War I; World War II.

References Kevin Giles, *Flight of the Dove: The Story of Jeannette Rankin* (1980); Ted Harris, *Jeanette Rankin: Suffragist, First Woman Elected to Congress, and Pacifist* (n.d.); Barbara Sicherman et al., eds., *Notable American Women: The Modern Period* (1980); Jennifer S. Uglow, comp. and ed., *International Dictionary of Women's Biography* (1985).

Jeannette Rankin

Ray, Dixy Lee (b. 1914)

A scientist who earned her Ph.D. from Stanford in 1945, Dixy Lee Ray is best known for her often stormy career in the public service: as consultant and then assistant to the director of the National Science Foundation (1960–1963); as commissioner and then head of the Atomic Energy Commission (1972–1975); and as governor of Washington State (1975–1979). After losing her bid for reelection in 1980, she continued her interest in public issues (especially environmental ones), speaking and consulting.

See also Government Workers; Science, Mathematics, and Science-Based Professions.

Reference Judith Freeman Clark, *Almanac of American Women in the 20th Century* (1987).

Real Estate

Women have entered this field in large numbers, usually either as owners of their own businesses or as independent contractors who depend on commissions that they divide with the companies with whom they contract in return for office space and advertising. Many of these companies are marginal, especially in the down cycles of this boom-and-bust business. Most women concentrate on residential sales, especially in urban areas, where men dominate the commercial, construction, and multiple-family housing fields.

See also Entrepreneurs.

Refugee Women in Development

Founded in 1981, this organization helps Third World Women in the United States toward social and economic independence.

Regan, Agnes Gertrude (1869–1943)

This Roman Catholic social welfare leader, a native of California trained in the San Francisco Normal School, worked for more than 30 years in the school system of that city as teacher, principal, and member of the Board of Education. She moved into social service in 1920 as the first executive secretary of the National Council of Catholic Women, a post she held until her death. In that capacity she encouraged Catholic women to support religious vacation schools, aid immigrants, study the needs of Catholic working girls, and support social legislation. To these duties she added the responsibilities of an instructor in 1922; and in 1925 she added those of the assistant director of the new National Catholic Service School for Women (later the National Catholic School of Social Service), affiliated with the Catholic University.

See also Academic Women; Social Workers; Teachers.

Reference Edward T. James et al., eds., *Notable American Women III* (1971).

Rehabilitation Act of 1973

This complicated statute in general forbids the federal government, companies and agencies with federal contracts, and recipients of federal grants to discriminate against otherwise qualified individuals with handicaps who can perform the essential functions of a job with reasonable accommodation (access to the workplace, assistance for the deaf or blind, etc.).

See also Americans with Disabilities Act; Networking Project for Disabled Women and Girls.

Reference *Working Woman* editors with Gay Bryant, *The Working Woman Report: Succeeding in Business in the 80s* (1984).

Religion

Although women have provided major support for churches throughout American history, most denominations have long refused to ordain them; even in the 1990s resistance continues strong in Roman Catholic and fundamentalist churches.

But in the first half of the nineteenth century a few determined women succeeded in entering the country's then most prestigious profession, the ministry. In 1853 a Congregational church ordained Antoinette Louisa Brown Blackwell, and in 1863 the Universalist denomination ordained Olympia Brown. Anna Howard Shaw was still confronted by arduous difficulties in ordination in the 1870s. Yet in this period Protestant mission boards began to send single women to India and China, women who like most missionary wives of their time focused on establishing girls' schools.

Meanwhile Roman Catholic nuns had to struggle against the patriarchal authority of both the Vatican and local bishops in the United States in their effort to develop lifestyles and modes of service appropriate to this country. Often the objects of suspicion and calumny, the nuns changed their image by their service in the Civil War, where they constituted about a fifth of all nurses. They went on to respond creatively to all kinds of needs, from women's colleges to succor for the sick and oppressed. In the twentieth century many of them have shifted the locus of religious life from the cloister to the contemporary world.

Since the 1950s most mainstream Protestant denominations have accepted women as ministers. Certainly demographic factors have helped women who wanted to be ministers; without them theological seminaries would have had to downsize dramatically or close their doors altogether. In March 1978 the National Council of Churches reported that the number of Protestant women ministers had risen to 10,470 in 1977, and that in some major divinity schools 50 percent of the students were women. The various denominations have liberalized their positions at different rates. The Episcopal Church, for example, began to ordain women in 1975, and in 1988 it appointed its first woman bishop. By 1992 it had ordained 1,100 women, and its Episcopal Clergy Couples Association had about 150 couples of married priests. (*New York Times*, 29 November 1992)

Similarly the 1970s saw women moving into the rabbinate. Sally J. Preisand was the first American woman rabbi. In 1979 a special commission of the Conservative branch of Judaism recommended that qualified women be ordained as rabbis.

Like most fundamentalist churches, the Roman Catholic church has intransigently refused ordination to women, despite the many calls for women priests from lay people and among the professed religious. The numbers of nuns have plummeted, from a high of 176,341 in 1968 to 99,337 in 1992—in part as a result of the determination of the sisters to resist patriarchal authority when it interfered with what they perceived as their religious duty: in 1968, 400 of the 450 Sisters of the Immaculate Heart of Mary chose to leave their community and form a lay group rather than allow Cardinal McIntyre to overrule their chapter decisions.

In 1991 only 481 women signed up for the novitiate at the approximately 530 religious orders in the United States. As a group nuns have grown older, from a median age of 45 in 1968 to 65 in 1992. Many women now entering the novitiate are markedly older than the recent high school graduates recruited in 1968; many already have advanced degrees and significant work and life experience. Far from being young, quiet, and docile, they bring to the religious life well-considered opinions and familiarity with other modes of life. Some orders are actively recruiting these older women, who have so much to offer and who are broadening the range of service nuns offer the wider community. Their independence, their impatience with the denial of priesthood to women, and their disappointment at the church's failure to diversify religious communities racially exert a new force within the Roman Catholic church. (*New York Times*, 27 December 1992) But they still function within a tradition: as James Kenneally remarks, from the colonial era onward "... many Catholic women of the past, like their contemporaries today, have not been inhibited by the traditions of a male-dominated church." Some among them believe that lay groups of women will form to do the work the church prohibits for religious women, like the Sisters for Christian Community with its lay membership comprised mostly of former nuns.

In the early 1990s feminist theologians have found their voices in Judaism and in most denominations of Christianity. Many of them protest the male-centered, patriarchal conceptions of traditional religions.

Women in religious institutions face the same kinds of problems as women in other parts of the workplace: glass ceilings, sexual harassment, and sex discrimination. Some churches prefer to call as their pastors far less qualified men, or men with acknowledged problems with alcohol or womanizing rather than employ a woman.

See also Blackwell, Antoinette Louisa Brown; Brown, Olympia; Eddy, Mary Baker; Glass Ceiling; Lee, Ann; McPherson, Aimée Semple; Professional Women; Religious Network for Equality for Women; Seton, Elizabeth Ann Bayley; Sex Discrimination; Sexual Harassment; Shaw, Anna Howard; Woman's Commonwealth; Young Women's Christian Association.

References Elisabeth Behr-Sigel, *The Ministry of Women in the Church* (1990); Judith Freeman Clark, *Almanac of American Women in the 20th Century* (1987); Mary Donovan, *Women Priests in the Episcopal Church* (1988); Martha L. Ice, *Clergy Women and Their Worldviews* (1987); James J. Kenneally, *The History of American Catholic Women* (1990); Karen Kennelly, ed., *American Catholic Women: A Historical Exploration* (1989); Ruth A. Wallace, *They Call Her Pastor: A New Role for Catholic Women* (1992).

Religious Network for Equality for Women

This ecumenical association of 40 religious organizations strives to improve justice for women, especially by eliminating legal and economic inequities.

See also Religion.

Research Science

See Science, Mathematics, and Science-Based Professions.

Restrooms

The unavailability of bathroom facilities almost automatically becomes an issue whenever women seek or gain entry into a nontraditional occupation. Employer after employer stumbles over this "problem," dubiously mulling over its difficulties and sometimes suggesting that it cannot be solved. Prestigious corporations, their "Executive Restrooms" designed for men only, often relegate women executives to the much less luxurious facilities provided for female secretaries and clerks. The military cites the cost problems created when women's presence on ships, maneuvers, field exercises, or aircraft must be accommodated. The numerous women subway workers in New York complain about the shortage of restroom facilities they can use. At the highest reaches of government female United States senators, ever since Hattie Wyatt Caraway became the first in 1931, have had to use a public lavatory while their male counterparts retired to an exclusive restroom labeled "For Senators Only." Only when the election of 1992 tripled the number of female senators (to six) was a ladies' restroom provided, reportedly with two washbasins and two stalls. And, at long last, in 1993 the U.S. Supreme Court is creating a restroom for women lawyers appearing before the court. Don't ask what Sandra Day O'Connor does. (*New York Times*, 10 January 1993)

See also Nontraditional Occupations.

Reference Patricia Hilliard, "Hero Rides Discrimination Out on a Rail," *New Directions for Women*, (1992).

Retirement Equity Act (1984)

The purpose of this legislation is to make it easier for women to earn pension rights under private pension plans.

See also Age Discrimination Acts; Older Women; Pensions.

Reference Judith Freeman Clark, *Almanac of American Women in the 20th Century* (1987).

Rhoads Dress

Patented during World War I by New York couturière May Rhoads, this costume combined a neat, ladylike overdress with bloomer overalls. The employee arriving at work could unbutton the outer skirted smock, toss it in her locker, and be ready for the job. After the war Rhoads converted her dress, so that a woman could do her housework in black satin breeches topped with a black satin waist and had only to slip on a tailored overslip to go out. Rhoads presided over the Better Dress Club for Better Business Women.

See also Dress for Success.

Reference Anne L. Macdonald, *Feminine Ingenuity: Women and Invention in America* (1992).

Richards, Ellen Henrietta Swallow (1842–1911)

This chemist and pioneer in domestic science, possibly the first woman admitted to a "scientific school," in 1873 received an M.A. from Vassar and a B.S. from the Massachusetts Institute of Technology (MIT); her next two years of study at MIT resulted in no degree, reportedly because the institution refused to award its first D.S. in chemistry to a woman.

She and her husband, Robert Hallowell Richards, a sympathetic and supportive fellow scientist, worked together, but Ellen Richards also devoted her energies to the scientific education of women, establishing a Woman's Laboratory at MIT, organizing a science section for Anna Eliot Ticknor's correspondence school for women, and through the Association of Collegiate Alumnae (now the American Association of University Women) working to improve physical education in colleges and broaden opportunities for women in graduate education. Simultaneously, through the MIT Woman's Laboratory, she consulted for industry and government on such problems as spontaneous combustion of oil and food contamination. In 1884 MIT appointed her instructor in sanitary chemistry, a post she held until her death.

From about 1890 on she concentrated on the home economics movement. Convinced of the importance of family to civilization, she hoped that this movement would make the home more comfortable and healthful and easier to keep. With the funding of Pauline Agassiz Shaw, she opened the widely imitated New England Kitchen in Boston, demonstrating cookery and selling scientifically prepared foods to provide maximum nutrition at the least cost, a scheme that failed, in large part because the immigrants to whom she wanted to cater didn't like her Yankee cooking. The kitchen's offshoots, though, like school lunches, not only flourished but drew wide attention to the importance of healthful food.

Richards's work also led to the institution of departments of home economics in colleges and universities. When professionals in this new discipline organized the American Home Economics Association, they elected her president; in that position she founded the *Journal of Home Economics*. She wrote ten books on applying science to daily life.

See also Academic Women; American Association of University Women; Home Economists; Science, Mathematics, and Science-Based Professions.

References Robert Clarke, *Ellen Swallow: The Woman Who Founded Ecology* (1973); Edward T. James et al., eds., *Notable American Women III* (1971); Robert H. Richards, *Robert Hallowell Richards, His Mark* (1936); Jennifer S. Uglow, comp. and ed., *International Dictionary of Women's Biography* (1985).

Richards, Linda (1841–1930)

This nursing educator, who received the earliest American diploma in nursing, keenly felt the necessity for training for nurses. She devoted the early part of her career, from 1873 to 1885, to developing regular classroom instruction and winning the support of the medical community for it, first at the Boston Training School (later the Massachusetts General Hospital School of Nursing) and then at the Boston City Hospital. After five years of similar work in Japan, despite qualms about the objectives of the newly formed nursing organizations, she improved training schools and established new ones in hospitals and institutions for the insane from New England to Michigan; she continued such work until she reached the age of 70.

See also Nurses.

References Edward T. James et al., eds., *Notable American Women III* (1971); Linda Richards, *Reminiscences of Linda Richards* (1911).

Richmond, Mary Ellen (1861–1928)

This central figure in the development of professional social work learned her job by observation and by association with outstanding colleagues at the Baltimore Charity Organization Society, of which she became general secretary in 1891. As she became convinced of the necessity of scientifically conducted social study of each case, she felt the need for professional workers and schools in which to train them. In 1900 she moved to the secretariat of the Philadelphia Society for Organizing Charity, which she thoroughly overhauled; that experience led to the writing of *The Good Neighbor in the Modern City* (1907), outlining a city's social needs and the means of meeting them. In 1909 she moved again, this time to the influential directorship of the Charity Organization Department of the new Russell Sage Foundation, where she directed research on social problems and improved methodology, wrote, and conducted institutes for caseworkers and supervisors.

Her opposition to public relief for families, to widows' and old age pensions, and to centralized fund soliciting raised the hackles of her colleagues in the social work community. But she significantly influenced many schools of social work and the pattern of graduate social work education, with its combination of classroom instruction and hands-on experience.

See also Social Workers.

Reference Edward T. James et al., eds., *Notable American Women III* (1971).

Roberts, Lillian (b. 1928)

A labor union organizer, Lillian Roberts grew up in the black ghetto of Chicago, was forced to leave the University of Illinois for lack of money to pay room and board, and at age 18 secured a job as nurses' aide at the University of Chicago Lying-In Clinic. She subsequently became an active unionist in the American Federation of State, County, and Municipal Employees (AFSCME), surmounting obstacles of gender, race, and class to become director of organization in New York City's 100,000-member District Council 37 of AFSCME.

See also Union Organizers.

Reference Susan Reverby, "From Aide to Organizer: The Oral History of Lillian Roberts," in Carol Ruth Berkin and Mary Beth Norton, *Women of America: A History* (1979).

Roberts v. United States Jaycees (1984)

The issue in this U.S. Supreme Court case was whether the Minnesota Human Rights Act (which banned discrimination on the basis of sex, etc.) was applicable to the Jaycees (Junior Chamber of Commerce), whose membership was restricted to men. The local Minneapolis and St. Paul chapters began admitting women as early as 1974; the national organization objected and threatened to revoke the local charters and sued to enjoin enforcement of the Minnesota Human Rights Act. The court held that the application of the ban on sex discrimination did not deprive the Jaycees of any First Amendment rights to free association and assembly, thus legitimizing the admission of women to what had been a men-only club.

See also *Board of Directors of Rotary International v. Rotary Club of Duarte*; Business and Industry; Men-Only Clubs; Networking; Sex Discrimination.

Reference Susan Gluck Mezey, *In Pursuit of Equality: Women, Public Policy and the Federal Courts* (1992).

Robins, Margaret Dreier (1868–1945)

This outstanding labor reformer of the Progressive Era spent many years and much of her fortune trying to improve the lot of working women. Born in Brooklyn into a family that taught her to think of their wealth as imposing a responsibility to society, she chaired the Women's Municipal League in 1903–1904 and joined social worker Frances Kellor to lobby through a bill regulating employment agencies in New York.

In 1905 she married settlement worker Raymond Robins. She and her husband, each independently wealthy, chose to live in a Chicago cold-water flat, involving themselves with the settlement house workers then transforming that city and with its labor leaders. From 1907–1922 Robins presided over the Women's Trade Union League (WTUL), to which she had been recruited by Leonora O'Reilly. Her personal charm, gentle tact, and modest willingness to perform any needed task attracted loyal members, enabled the WTUL to function with its unlikely alliance of upper-class and working-class women, and even wrung a degree of support for working women from the American Federation of Labor.

See also American Federation of Labor; Employment Agencies; Kellor, Frances; O'Reilly, Leonora; Progressive Era; Settlement Houses; Women's Trade Union League.

References Mary E. Dreier, *Margaret Dreier Robins: Her Life, Letters, and Work* (1950); Edward T. James et al., eds., *Notable American Women III* (1971); Elizabeth Anne Payne, *Reform, Labor, and Feminism: Margaret Dreier Robins and the Women's*

Margaret Dreier Robins

Trade Union League (1988); Jennifer S. Uglow, comp. and ed., *International Dictionary of Women's Biography* (1985).

Robinson, Harriet Jane Hanson (1825–1911)

This "Lowell girl" who went to work at age 11 led other child workers out to join striking adults. As an adult she and her editor/columnist husband took up the causes of slavery and women's suffrage.

See also Lowell Girls; Strikes.

References Edward T. James et al., eds., *Notable American Women III* (1971); Harriet H. Robinson, *Loom and Spindle* (1898).

Robinson v. Jacksonville Shipyards, Inc., et al. (1991)

In this landmark sexual harassment case, the issue was whether Lois Robinson's rights under Title VII of the Civil Rights Act of 1964 were violated by (a) the display of pornographic pictures of nude women at her workplace, and (b) comments and observations of a sexual nature from her male co-workers. The U.S. Court for the Middle District of Florida found for Robinson and held the company and two senior managers liable for having violated Robinson's right to work in an environment free from sex discrimination and harassment.

See also Civil Rights Act of 1964; Sex Discrimination; Sexual Harassment.

References Susan Gluck Mezey, *In Pursuit of Equality: Women, Public Policy and the Federal Courts* (1992); National Organization for Women Legal Defense and Education Fund, "Legal Program Case Docket and Other Professional Activities" (1992).

Rodgers, Elizabeth Flynn (1847–1939)

This labor leader, in 1881 head of an all-woman unit of the Knights of Labor in Chicago, by 1886 had become president of all the Chicago units, the first woman to hold such an office—though she refused to stand for national treasurer on the grounds that her ten children kept her too busy. With the decline of the

Knights of Labor after 1887, she left the movement. She later built a second career by organizing the Women's Catholic Order of Foresters, a fraternal life insurance society, over which she presided until 1908.

See also Entrepreneurs; Knights of Labor.

Reference Edward T. James et al., eds., *Notable American Women III* (1971).

Roebling, Emily (1844–1903)

Roebling grew up in the Hudson Valley of upstate New York. In 1865 she married Washington Roebling, the chief engineer of the Brooklyn Bridge, and bore one child. For the 14 years of the construction of the Brooklyn Bridge, with her husband an invalid for most of them, Emily Roebling acted as his amanuensis, his agent in receiving his subordinates and issuing orders, his reporter and communicator on visits to the bridge, and the peacemaker between the engineers and the politicians in charge of the project. In the process she learned a great deal about engineering. Some contemporaries indeed credited her with being the de facto chief engineer of the Brooklyn Bridge. Probably no one will ever know exactly how much expertise she acquired and how much authority she exercised. In later life she took a law degree.

See also Attorneys; Engineers.

Reference David McCullough, *The Great Bridge* (1972).

Roosevelt, Anna Eleanor (1884–1962)

This social reformer was born into a wealthy dysfunctional family in New York and educated privately in the United States and abroad; yet, through her own efforts and her extensive work with women reformers of the Progressive Era, she learned to empathize with people whose experiences differed markedly from her own. As the wife of the governor of New York and the president of the United States and in her own right as teacher,

journalist, lecturer, U.S. delegate to the United Nations (UN), and shaper of the UN's Universal Declaration of Human Rights, she used her compassion, her money, her influence, and her opportunities to help people all over the world. For tens of thousands she acted directly as an ombudsperson; for millions of women she remains a role model.

See also Progressive Era.

References Blanche Wiesen Cook, *Eleanor Roosevelt: 1884–1933* (1992); Tamara K. Hareven, *Eleanor Roosevelt: An American Conscience* (1968); Joseph Lash, *Eleanor: The Years Alone* (1971); Joseph Lash, *Eleanor and Franklin* (1972); Eleanor Roosevelt, *Autobiography* (1961); Eleanor Roosevelt, *This I Remember* (1949); Eleanor Roosevelt, *This Is My Story* (1937); Barbara Sicherman et al., eds., *Notable American Women: The Modern Period*; Jennifer S. Uglow, comp. and ed., *International Dictionary of Women's Biography* (1985).

Rosie the Riveter

See World War II.

Rostker v. Goldberg (1981)

The issue in this case (brought by a man) was whether the exclusion of women from the military registration and draft violated the equal protection clause of the constitution. The U.S. Supreme Court upheld the sex-based classification, prompting Eleanor Smeal, president of the National Organization for Women, to complain that the court's ruling was discriminatory and "upholds the myth of this country that all men are better than all women."

See also Military Women; National Organization for Women; Sex Discrimination.

References Judith Freeman Clark, *Almanac of American Women in the 20th Century* (1987); Susan Gluck Mezey, *In Pursuit of Equality: Women, Public Policy and the Federal Courts* (1992).

Russell Sage Foundation

See Van Kleeck, Mary Abby

Sabin, Florence Rena (1871–1953)

Possibly the most famous woman scientist of her generation, this physician and public health worker entered the Johns Hopkins Medical School in 1896 after her graduation from Smith College. She was kept on at Hopkins first as a research fellow and then as its first woman faculty member. She attained the rank of full professor, but the chair of her department was denied her. In 1925 she accepted appointment to a research position at the Rockefeller Institute for Medical Research, the first woman appointed a full member of that institution. An outstanding teacher, she was widely respected in scientific circles for her work on the lymphatic system. After a remarkable career as teacher and researcher, she moved to Colorado, where she became a vital force in a crusade for public health reform.

See also Academic Women; Science, Mathematics, and Science-Based Professions.

References Penina Migdal Glazer and Miriam Slater, *Unequal Colleagues* (1987); Barbara Sicherman et al., eds., *Notable American Women: The Modern Period* (1980); Jennifer S. Uglow, comp. and ed., *International Dictionary of Women's Biography* (1985).

Florence Rena Sabin

St. Denis, Ruth (1879–1968)

This great dancer and foremother of modern dance, a native of New Jersey, showed an early proclivity for playacting and dancing. In 1894 she began her professional career under the aegis of Augustin Daly, working both as a dancer and as an actress. In 1904 an advertisement awoke an interest in the Orient that she transmuted into her distinctive dance style. A European tour enhanced her success and promoted an American tour as a solo dancer.

In 1914 dancer Ted Shawn sought her out as a teacher; they married the same year, and the next year they founded their company and school, Denishawn, in Los Angeles, enrolling such talented dancers as Martha Graham and Doris Humphrey. Though St. Denis often resented Denishawn as cramping her independence and experimentation, she used it to popularize dance in America. The Great Depression ended the company and its founders separated. After an eclipse of several years, St. Denis refueled her career with a position as dance director of Adelphi College and an acclaimed revival of her great Oriental dance "Radha" at Jacob's Pillow. She continued her work in California for another 20 years, triumphing in 1964 in a golden wedding celebration concert with Shawn, with whom she had remained friendly.

See also Dancers; Graham, Martha; Great Depression.

References Ruth St. Denis, *An Unfinished Life*

Rose Schneiderman speaks in New York in 1913 at a rally of the Women's Trade Union League.

(1939); Barbara Sicherman et al., eds., *Notable American Women: The Modern Period* (1980); Walter Terry, *Miss Ruth: The"More Living Life"of Ruth St. Denis* (1969); Jennifer S. Uglow, comp. and ed., *International Dictionary of Women's Biography* (1985).

Sandwich Generation

People who carry responsibilities for both their aging parents and their children are sandwiched between the two. These duties fall particularly heavily on working women.

See also Elder Care.

Scab

This derogatory term is applied to a worker who replaces a striking worker: a strikebreaker hired by an employer to maintain production and undermine the strikers' morale.

See also Strikes.

Schneiderman, Rose (1882–1972)

This union organizer, who started work at 13 as a department store cash girl, began her union career in 1903 by organizing the cap factory where she worked. After 1907 she concentrated her energies on the Women's Trade Union League (WTUL), becoming a full-time organizer for it in 1910. She participated actively in the organizing drives of the International Ladies' Garment Workers' Union from 1909–1914 and helped to lead the Uprising of the 20,000.

Despite her doubts about the wealthy women "allies" of the WTUL, she found them more sympathetic to the cause of women workers than union men. From 1918 until 1949 she presided over the New York WTUL, and from 1926 to 1950 over the national organization, promoting workers' education and lobbying for protective legislation. As a friend of Franklin and Eleanor Roosevelt, she influenced their views on labor relations. In 1933 President Roosevelt appointed her as the only woman member of the labor advisory board of the National Recovery Administration, where she concentrated on the development of codes for industries that employed many women. From 1937 to 1943 she served as secretary of the New York State Department of Labor but resigned in disgust because she found too little to do.

See also International Ladies' Garment Workers' Union; National Industrial Recovery Act; Protective Legislation; Roosevelt, Anna Eleanor; Union Organizers; Unions; Uprising of the 20,000; Women's Trade Union League; Workers' Education.

References Gary E. Endelman, *Solidarity Forever: Rose Schneiderman and the Women's Trade Union League* (n.d.); Barbara Sicherman et al., eds., *Notable American Women: The Modern Period* (1980).

School for Active Workers in the Labor Movement (1914)

This Chicago school was founded by the Women's Trade Union League to train women for leadership positions in trade unions. The program consisted of four months of academic work and eight months of field work. The school graduated a new generation of women activists, many of whom became full-time paid union organizers.

See also Union Organizers; Unions; Women's Trade Union League; Workers' Education.

References Philip S. Foner, *Women and the American Labor Movement* (1982); Joyce L. Kornbluh and Mary Frederickson, eds., *Sisterhood and Solidarity: Workers' Education for Women* (1984).

Schultz v. Wheaton Glass Company (1970)

In this, the first case involving the Equal Pay Act, the appellate court (Third Circuit) held that the term "equal work" did not mean "identical" but simply "substantially equal." The court ruled that the company's pay schedule was in fact so designed that it benefited male selector-packers and discriminated against their female counterparts—that in fact the work both did was "substantially equal." Instead of relying on the company's job descriptions the court used its own judgment in ascertaining the equality of the work performed and rejected the company's argument that the men deserved a higher wage because they occasionally did extra work not assigned to the women.

See also Comparable Worth; Equal Pay Act; Pay Equity; Sex Discrimination.

Reference Susan Gluck Mezey, *In Pursuit of Equality: Women, Public Policy and the Federal Courts* (1992).

Science, Mathematics, and Science-Based Professions

Women in the sciences, particularly the hard sciences, have experienced, in intensified form, the general prejudice and discrimination against academic women. Even if they could enroll as students, they were seldom hired as faculty. Brilliant women like Ellen Swallow Richards, who enrolled in the Massachusetts Institute of Technology in 1870 (perhaps the first woman ever accepted at a scientific institution), were denied the degrees they earned and/or shunted into irregular positions or low-status fields.

In their early years, women scientists had the best chance of employment at women's colleges in the East or in the home economics departments of the state-supported land-grant universities of the Midwest and West. Not until after 1920 (when almost half of American college students were women) did significant opportunities open for them elsewhere in academia, and then usually at the lowest levels and the less prestigious institutions. Industry was equally unwelcoming. Before 1920 a lot of highly trained women scientists were unemployed or worked outside their fields.

It took the desperation and manpower shortages of World War I to open opportunities in industry to women scientists. At that time money became available from industry and philanthropy for modern laboratories and research institutes. In research, women scientists found career opportunities not easily available to them in medical practice. The laboratory directors and industrial capitalists who were funding research were concerned primarily with recruiting scientists of merit with little regard for gender. For a time women were successful in obtaining places for themselves in biological and medical research, but they soon found themselves in a hierarchy that was increasingly male in the top-level positions. A few notable women, possessed of unusual stamina and ability, were able to make it to the top in the first half of the twentieth century, among them Florence Sabin and Alice Hamilton. The National Academy of Science elected Sabin its first woman member in 1925, and Margaret Washburn its second in 1931.

Nonetheless, during the 1920s women's doctorates in science peaked at about 12 percent. But then, with the Great Depression and the aftermath of World War II, they dwindled to less than 7 percent in the 1950s. The percentages rose slowly during the 1960s and precipitously during the 1970s, from 9 percent in 1970 to 21 percent in 1979. The expanding economy of the 1960s and 1970s and the development of a strong women's movement opened new opportunities; the number of women who entered graduate and professional programs increased markedly; and their graduates moved into traditionally male fields. In 1988 women constituted 33 percent of computer and mathematical scientists. But on average women scientists' careers are shorter than those of men of the same age, and women scientists more often work part-time.

Near the end of the twentieth century American women scientists are increasingly found among the ranks of important prize winners and recognized contributors to scholarship. But in the sciences as elsewhere in the workplace women still encounter many barriers. Women scientists experience unemployment and underemployment far more often than men. Women scientists are more likely to be employed in the academy, men in industry. Zuckerman observes three patterns: (1) persisting differences between men and women scientists on average, in performance and attainments, usually in the direction of comparative disadvantage for women; (2) growing convergence, especially among younger scientists, between men and women in access to resources, research performance, and rewards; and (3) growing divergence between men and women of the same professional age in publications and some other career attainments.

See also Academic Women; Cori, Gerty; Great Depression; Hamilton, Alice; Home Economists; McClintock, Barbara; Mayer, Maria Gertrude Goeppert; Mitchell, Maria; Physicians; Professional Women; Psychologists and Psychiatrists; Ray, Dixy Lee; Richards, Ellen Henrietta Swallow; Sabin, Florence Rena; Unemployment; Women's Movement; World War I; World War II; Yalow, Rosalyn S.

References Pnina Abir-Am and Dorinda Outram, eds., *Uneasy Careers and Intimate Lives: Women in Science, 1789–1979* (1992); Beatriz C. Clewell and Bernice Anderson, *Women of Color in Science, Mathematics, and Engineering* (1991); Penina Migdal Glazer and Miriam Slater, *Unequal Colleagues* (1987); Violet B. Haas and Carolyn C. Perrucci, eds., *Women in Scientific and Engineering Professions* (1984); Barbara J. Harris, *Beyond Her Sphere: Women and the Professions in American History* (1978); Judith S. McIlwee and J. Gregg Robinson, *Women in Engineering* (1992); Lynn M. Osen, *Women in Mathematics* (1974); Londa Schiebinger, *The Mind Has No Sex? Women in the Origins of Modern Science* (1989); Paula Studios, *Women of Computer History: Forgotten Heroines* (1990); Paula Studios and Christopher Zenger, *Women in the Electronic Industry* (1989); Edna Yost, *Women of Modern Science* (1984); Harriet Zuckerman, Jonathan R. Cole, and John T. Bruer, eds., *The Outer Circle: Women in the Scientific Community* (1991).

Scientific Management

This system, originated in the 1880s by Frederick Winslow Taylor for the factory, applied by William Henry Leffingwell to the office, and sophisticated by Frank and Lillian Gilbreth early in the twentieth century, aims for the highest worker efficiency, intending to get the best product in the shortest time with the least effort. Scientific managers search for the best arrangement of the workplace, analyze tasks and break them down into their component parts, and make time and motion studies in an effort to determine the optimal workplace.

Under scientific management, wages are fixed according to a rational formula. Workers are given rest periods, limited working hours, proper tools, and a safe environment to protect their efficiency.

In the wrong hands, administered without regard to human comfort and individual rights, the system results in deskilling jobs, assigning them to the lowest paid workers possible, and decreasing the worker's control. It may deepen the tedium of the job and lends itself to speedups that tax workers by setting quotas beyond what they can accomplish without great stress.

But in the early days its emphasis on assigning workers to jobs for which they were suited and judging them on the basis of aptitudes and productivity made scientific management attractive to some reformers and feminists concerned with bettering the lot of women employees.

See also Gilbreth, Lillian Evelyn Moller; Speed-Up.

References Margery W. Davies, *Woman's Place Is at the Typewriter: Office Work and Office Workers, 1870–1930* (1983); Sharon Hartman Strom, *Beyond the Typewriter: Gender, Class, and the Origins of Modern American Office Work, 1900–1930* (1992).

SCORE

See Small Business Administration.

Second Shift

This term refers to the hours most women who work for pay must toil after they return home, with child and/or elder care and housekeeping.

See also Child Care; Elder Care; Housekeeping.

Reference Arlie Hochschild with Anne Machung, *The Second Shift: Working Parents and the Revolution at Home* (1989).

Self-Employment

See Entrepreneurs; Self-Employment Learning Project.

Self-Employment Learning Project

This Aspen Institute group sponsors research and evaluation. It aims to produce new information and encourage dialogue in the field of self-employment and microenterprise. Participants include the Women's Self-Employment Project of Chicago; the Good Faith Fund of Pine Bluff, Arkansas; the North Carolina Rural Economic Development Center of Raleigh; the MICRO project of Tucson, Arizona; and the Institute for Social and Economic Development of Iowa City, Iowa.

See also Entrepreneurs.
Reference *Equal Means* (1992).

Sellins, Fannie Mooney (1870–1919)

This union organizer made a reputation in 1909–1911 by gathering nationwide support for locked-out garment workers in St. Louis. In 1913 she began work in West Virginia, where she was jailed for defying an injunction against aiding striking miners' families evicted from their homes by mine owners, an offense for which she was not pardoned until 1916. She remained a target, particularly after she recruited to the United Mine Workers black workers brought in as scabs. She was shot and killed by deputy sheriffs in Pennsylvania.

See also Injunctions; Scab; Strikes; Union Organizers.
Reference Angela Howard Zophy and Frances M. Kavenik, eds., *Handbook of American Women's History* (1990).

Seneca Falls Convention (1884)

This historic convention on behalf of women's rights was held in Seneca Falls, New York. It produced a declaration that demanded not only the right to vote but also an end to men's privileged position in employment opportunities and wages.

Reference Aileen Kraditor, *Up from the Pedestal* (1970).

Separate Spheres

This concept, based on the physical differences between men and women, dominated thinking about gender roles throughout much of the nineteenth cen-

tury. According to this ideology women's proper sphere of activity is in the home and family, as wives and mothers. It has historically been used to legitimize sex-based laws, encouraging legislatures to enact and courts to uphold laws that treat women differently from men, a stubborn obstacle to women's obtaining equal rights in the workplace. The point was baldly stated in *Bradwell v. Illinois* (1873): ". . . the civil law, as well as nature herself, has always recognized a wide difference in the respective spheres and destinies of man and woman. Man is, or should be, woman's protector and defender. The natural and proper timidity and delicacy which belongs to the female sex evidently unfits it for many of the occupations of civil life." The separate spheres ideology has also served to justify protective legislation as well as to restrict women's employment opportunities. In the women's movements of the Progressive Era and the 1960s and 1970s the concept was vigorously attacked.

See also Nontraditional Occupations; Occupational Segregation; Progressive Era; Protective Legislation; Sex Discrimination; Velvet Ghettos; Women's Movement.
Reference Susan Gluck Mezey, *In Pursuit of Equality: Women, Public Policy and the Federal Courts* (1992).

Servants

See Domestic Servants.

Service Corps of Retired Executives (SCORE)

See Small Business Administration.

Service Sector

In the 1980s, as the United States lost jobs in agriculture and manufacturing, service sector jobs—an encompassing term for jobs that produce no goods, from psychiatrist to waitress—to some extent replaced them. Unfortunately most of these jobs tend to be low-paid and offer little upward mobility; many are part-time or temporary. By 1990 women constituted more than half the employees in the service sector; the service industry employed 45 percent of all women workers.

See also Part-Time Workers; Temporary Workers.

Reference Paula Ries and Anne J. Stone, eds., *The American Woman, 1992–93: A Status Report* (1992).

Servicewomen
See Military Women.

Seton, Elizabeth Ann Bayley (1774–1821)
This founder of the first American Roman Catholic parochial school, the first American Roman Catholic orphanage, and the first American Roman Catholic order of nuns was also the first native-born American to be canonized.

See also Religion.

Reference Jennifer S. Uglow, comp. and ed., *International Dictionary of Women's Biography* (1985); Angela Howard Zophy and Frances M. Kavenik, eds., *Handbook of American Women's History* (1990).

Settlement Houses
Beginning in the 1890s middle-class idealists, mostly women, founded settlement houses in urban working-class neighborhoods to assist immigrants. Among countless other projects, settlement house residents defended the workers' right to organize, strike, and bargain collectively. Some of these women reformers established and officered unions. They helped to organize the Women's Trade Union League and to enact protective legislation. They also offered clubs, boarding houses, employment services, and educational programs for working women.

See also Employment Agencies; Hull House; Jane Clubs; Protective Legislation; White Rose Mission; Women's Trade Union League.

References Allen F. Davis, *Spearheads for Reform: The Social Settlements and the Progressive Movement 1890–1914* (1967); James J. Kenneally, "Women in the United States and Trade Unionism," in Norbert C. Soldon, ed., *The World of Women's Trade Unionism* (1985); Dorothy Schneider and Carl J. Schneider, *American Women in the Progressive Era* (1993).

Sex Discrimination
The American economic system has historically discriminated against women on the basis of their gender. Employers long argued that women workers do not need the money they earn, since they are or should be supported by men. Male workers have feared women as competitors, whose entrance into a particular occupation would tend to lower its pay. When the nation has needed an expanded work force, as in the world wars, society has called on women to do their patriotic duty of going into the workplace and afterward tried to send them back to the kitchen, tongue-lashing those among them reluctant to sacrifice their earning power. In depressions it has attacked women for preempting "men's jobs."

In the twentieth century women workers and their advocates have reduced—but certainly not eliminated—sex discrimination through legislation and the courts. During the Progressive Era reformers responded to the inequities imposed on women workers by attempting to unionize them, by offering them workers' education, and by lobbying for protective legislation.

The passage of the Equal Pay Act of 1963 and the Civil Rights Act of 1964 launched an even more forceful attack on sex discrimination. In the 1970s the federal courts developed a new approach to questions involving a differential treatment of men and women, departing from the separate spheres doctrine that treated men and women as inherently and legally different. In the 1971 *Reed v. Reed* case, the U.S. Supreme Court for the first time invalidated a state law on the grounds that it discriminated against women; and in 1973 in *Frontiero v. Richardson* the court held that a military regulation violated Frontiero's constitutional right of equality. In subsequent cases the court has moved toward a stricter scrutiny of sex-based

Elizabeth Seton

classifications, requiring that the use of gender as a classifying device not be arbitrary or based on cultural biases. Although sex-specific laws are presumptively un-constitutional, controversy over legislation designed to protect women from hazardous working conditions continues.

Women facing discrimination in the

workplace also have found relief in state laws and agencies. Thus, for example, in 1976 the Kentucky Commission on Human Rights ordered two coal mines in Kentucky to hire women as miners and to pay $29,000 to two women who had been denied employment. State laws fill in some of the gaps left by federal legislation, often applying to smaller employers not covered by federal laws. State laws also provide different statutes of limitations and in some states are better enforced than federal regulations.

In the latter half of the twentieth century the definition of sex discrimination has broadened. It now includes sexual harassment.

See also Affirmative Action; Bona Fide Occupational Qualification; Civil Rights Act of 1964; Comparable Worth; *Dothard v. Rawlinson;* Equal Pay Act; *Frontiero v. Richardson; General Electric v. Gilbert;* Glass Ceiling; *Johnson v. Transportation Agency of Santa Clara; Meritor Savings Bank v. Vinson; Phillips v. Martin Marietta Corporation; Price Waterhouse v. Hopkins;* Progressive Era; Protective Legislation; *Radice v. New York; Rostker v. Goldberg; Schultz v. Wheaton Glass Company;* Separate Spheres; Sexual Harassment; Workers' Education.

References Judith Freeman Clark, *Almanac of American Women in the 20th Century* (1987); Christine Craft, *Too Old, Too Ugly and Not Deferential to Men: An Anchorwoman's Courageous Battle against Sex Discrimination* (1988); Jennie Farley, ed., *Sex Discrimination in Higher Education: Strategies for Equality* (1981); Barbara A. Gutek, *Sex and the Workplace* (1985); William E. Pepper and Florynce R. Kennedy, *Sex Discrimination in Employment* (1981).

Sex Segregation
See Occupational Segregation.

Sexual Harassment
Sexual harassment is unwanted sexual behavior at work, creating a situation in which a woman's job (or her raise or her promotion) may be in jeopardy. Under Title VII of the Civil Rights Act of 1964, the courts have recognized two types of

sexual harassment: (1) The "quid pro quo" claim arises when a supervisor demands sexual favors as a condition or term of employment; (2) The "hostile work environment" claim arises when the workplace becomes intimidating or offensive because of the unwelcome behavior of a sexual nature on the part of *anyone* in the workplace, and the employer fails to remedy the situation.

Title VII aims to protect working women from sex discrimination in the "terms, conditions and privileges of employment." But in 1986 the U.S. Supreme Court extended the definition of sex discrimination when it held in *Meritor Savings Bank v. Vinson* that sexual harassment on the job was a form of discrimination and therefore illegal. Up to that time, federal courts had viewed advances made by one employee to another (whistles, off-color jokes, persistent requests for favors, etc.) as "personal" conduct and not employment-related; additionally, courts were reluctant to hold employers liable for such actions on the part of their employees. *Meritor* established that conduct that creates a hostile environment for women workers constitutes discrimination even if the woman is not promised or denied anything connected with her job. Since then women have been redefining sexual harassment through other court cases: in 1991, for instance, welder Lois Robinson won a ruling that putting up pictures of nude women in the workplace

"I FINALLY GOT HIS HANDS OFF MY BODY... NOW IF ONLY I COULD GET HIS HANDS OFF MY PROMOTION."

constitutes sexual harassment. In 1992 a federal district judge in Minnesota first allowed female iron mine workers to claim class action status for their sexual harassment case.

Congress (in the wake of the Clarence Thomas–Anita Hill disputes) amended the Civil Rights Act of 1964 by the Civil Rights Act of 1991, enabling employees who suffered personal injury from sexual harassment on the job to sue for limited compensatory damages. Many states have also made sexual harassment illegal under their antidiscrimination laws; some states have no statutes at all. Where such laws exist, enforcement ranges from nonexistent to rigorous.

The law about sexual harassment is still evolving. Court cases on various circuits are often inconsistent. Important questions of employer liability for the behavior of employees continue to arise, as do the problems that complainants face in establishing their credibility. Nonetheless, the litigation and controversy surrounding charges of sexual harassment have focused attention on a wide variety of offensive actions that have plagued women in the workplace.

Sexual harassment typically is most overt where women are moving into such previously all-male occupations as fire fighting, police work, the military, the skilled trades, and surgery. Although it seems to occur most severely in nontraditional jobs, it is pervasive in every workplace.

Historically, women have been reluctant to come forward after experiencing harassment, out of embarrassment or out of fear of the male involved or his brothers-under-the-skin. A 1985 survey revealed that 50 percent of respondents believed that complaining would not change anything and another 50 percent said they feared they would be blamed. Respondents also reported fear of retaliation. While no one knows exactly how many cases of harassment are suffered in silence, the Legal Defense Fund estimates that only about 6 percent of victims file complaints with enforcement agencies. Another student of the problem reports that the formal complaint rate in companies is 1.4 per thousand. The number of women experiencing sexual harassment on the job appears to be high: in a *Newsweek* survey (October 1991) 21 percent of those surveyed reported personal incidents and 45 percent reported knowledge of others who had been sexually harassed.

Any company or institution can make enormous strides toward reducing sexual harassment by plainly showing top management's opposition to the practice. Here is one instance where the trickledown theory clearly works. Management can demonstrate this opposition by building the elimination of sexual harassment into the reward structure. This practice, coupled with widespread publicity, training, role modeling of professional behavior by top management, and responsible investigations of charges of sexual harassment will drastically alter employees' behavior. In 1991 Maine enacted sophisticated legislation requiring employers to provide sexual harassment education and training. Other states are following suit.

See also Civil Rights Act of 1964; Equal Employment Opportunity Commission; *Franklin v. Gwinett County School District; Meritor Savings Bank v. Vinson;* Nontraditional Occupations; *Robinson v. Jacksonville Shipyards;* Sex Discrimination; Trades.

References Ellen Bravo and Ellen Cassidy, *The 9 to 5 Guide to Combating Sexual Harassment* (1992); Barbara A. Burnett, ed., *Everywoman's Legal Guide* (1983); Coalition of Labor Union Women *News* (1992); Martin Eskenazi and David Gallen, *Sexual Harassment: Know Your Rights* (1992); Barbara A. Gutek, *Sex and the Workplace* (1985); Catherine A. MacKinnon, *Sexual Harassment of Working Women* (1979); Susan Gluck Mezey, *In Pursuit of Equality: Women, Public Policy and the Federal Courts* (1992); National Organization for Women Legal Defense & Education Fund, "Legal Resource Kit: Employment—Sex Discrimination and Sexual Harassment" (1992); *The 1988 Working Woman Sexual Harassment Survey* (1988); Michele Paludi and Richard B. Barickman, *Academic and Workplace Sexual Harassment: A Resource Manual* (1991); William Petrocelli and Barbara Kate Repa, *Sexual Harassment on the Job*

(1992); Paula Ries and Anne J. Stone, eds., *The American Woman, 1992–93: A Status Report* (1992); Amber Coverdale Sumrall and Dessa Taylor, eds., *Sexual Harassment: Women Speak Out* (1992).

Sexual Preference

In the early 1990s no federal law protects lesbians from discrimination in the workplace, although some states and municipalities have laws to prohibit discrimination on the basis of sexual orientation. If a male employer or supervisor refers to women employees as lesbians *in hopes of forcing them or other women to quit*, his behavior may constitute sexual discrimination under Title VII of the Civil Rights Act of 1964.

At the federal level the military by its own regulations has always barred homosexuals from its ranks and upon discovery has dismissed them from the service. These antigay and antilesbian regulations, although consistently sustained by the courts, have come under increasing attack, and President Bill Clinton promised in his campaign to remove them, arguing that sexual orientation is no predictor of performance, the only rational standard. Nobody knows how many lesbians and gays are actually in the military, but the service record of those known has usually been good.

See also Civil Rights Act of 1964; Military Women; Sex Discrimination; Sexual Harassment.

Reference National Organization for Women Legal Defense and Education Fund, "Legal Resource Kit: Employment—Sex Discrimination and Sexual Harassment" (1992).

Seymour, Mary Foot (1846–1893)

This self-taught stenographer and entrepreneur recognized in the invention of efficient typewriters the possibility of a new occupation for women. Seizing the moment, she opened in 1879 the Union School of Stenography, and later the Union Stenographic Company with 25 typists, and an employment agency for stenographers and typists. In 1889 she founded the bimonthly *Business Woman's Journal*, published by the Mary F. Seymour Publishing Company, all of whose officers were women; when it did well she started the *American Woman's Journal* (of which the earlier publication became a department), with columns on occupations for women, reliable investments, and insurance.

See also Business and Industry; Clerical Workers; Employment Agencies; Entrepreneurs; Gibbs, Katharine.

Shadd, Mary Ann (1823–1893)

This courageous and principled journalist and attorney was the first black woman editor of a weekly newspaper.

See also Attorneys; Journalists.

Reference Angela Howard Zophy and Frances M. Kavenik, eds., *Handbook of American Women's History* (1990).

Sharecropping

See Tenant Farmers.

Shaw, Anna Howard (1847–1919)

This minister, physician, and lecturer, prominent in the women's suffrage movement, was brought from her native England to the United States when she was a three-year-old child. At 12 she and a younger brother had to assume major responsibility for their semi-invalid mother and their younger siblings on a homestead claim in Michigan, while her father and older brothers lived in relative comfort in Massachusetts. The experience left her with a low opinion of men and a belief that whatever they did she could do at least as well.

At 15 she began to teach. A couple of years later she started to prepare herself to preach, studying elocution and debating, and giving her first sermon in 1870 under the aegis of a movement within the Methodist church to license women ministers. In 1871 she was licensed as a preacher. Rejected by her horrified Universalist family, she sought more education at Albion College and in 1876 at the Boston University divinity school, earning her own way until a woman's organization came to her aid. After her graduation she accepted calls to two small churches. Denied ordination by one brand of Methodists, she was finally ordained by another in 1880, the first woman minister of the Methodist Protestant Church.

Three years later, feeling the need of another challenge and eager to do more for women, she enrolled in Boston University's medical school and initiated a long career as a lecturer on temperance and women's suffrage. But by the time she graduated in 1886 she had concluded that only enfranchisement could significantly help women.

A brilliant orator but a woefully inadequate organizer, she devoted herself to the cause of women's suffrage (and, peripherally, temperance), supporting herself with a career as lecturer. She lived to hear that the Congress had passed the 19thAmendment, but not long enough to know that it was ratified.

See also Homesteaders; Physicians; Religion.
References Edward T. James et al., eds., *Notable American Women III* (1971); Wil A. Linkugel and Martha Solomon, *Anna Howard Shaw: Suffrage Orator and Social Reformer* (1990); Anna Howard Shaw with Elizabeth Jordan, *The Story of a Pioneer* (1915).

Sheppard-Towner Act (1921)

The product of the lobbying efforts of a number of women's organizations, the Sheppard-Towner Act provided states with federal funds to establish prenatal and child health-care clinics that would train mothers and pregnant women in personal hygiene and scientific child care. This effort by child-welfare reformers, social feminists, nurses, and social workers was undercut at the 1930 Conference on the Health and Protection of Children, when male medical professionals denigrated the training and skills of the women running the community health clinics. The Sheppard-Towner Act also provided the states with federal funds to train and regulate midwives.

See also Midwives; Nurses; Social Feminists; Social Workers.
References Marlene Stein Wortman, ed., *Women in American Law* (1985); Angela Howard Zophy and Frances M. Kavenik, eds., *Handbook of American Women's History* (1990).

Sherman Anti-Trust Act (1890)
See Clayton Anti-Trust Act.

Shirt Sewers' Cooperative Union
See Cooperative Industries.

Shirtwaist Makers Strike (1909)
See Uprising of the 20,000.

Shoemakers

This industry furnished "outwork" in their homes to many women in the late eighteenth century, first as helpers to their menfolk, who received the pay for the women's work, and then, about 1810, as independent laborers, often for goods rather than cash. In the 1850s mechanization, division of labor, and centralization required the employment of women on factory premises (though manufacturers rented some machines to outworkers) but sharply reduced the number and proportion of women in the industry. In 1860 women and men in Massachusetts and New Hampshire struck with little success for better wages and decentralized production; during the strike married women outworkers discovered the differences between their interests and those of the usually single women factory workers.

In the aftermath of the Civil War, with more single women forced to earn their own living due to the war, manufacturers tried to save labor costs by relying more heavily on machinery and on women workers, whom they paid less than men, and by employing workers only during busy seasons, creating a floating population. During this period, despite the difficulties of juggling the roles of "lady stitchers" and union girls, women formed a number of labor organizations, notably lodges of the Daughters of St. Crispin and assemblies of the Knights of Labor (KOL), and engaged in a number of labor actions.

In the late nineteenth century the mostly native North American women shoemakers differed from the mostly immigrant women of the garment and textile industries in the shoemakers' *relatively* high wages, their access to skilled work, and their experience in labor organizations and actions. This status was threatened, though, as manufacturers moved their plants to the countryside of northern New England and New York to avoid paying high wages and employed immigrants. In the depression of the 1890s, women and men joined together in the new Boot and Shoe Workers' Union (BSWU), on whose board Mary A. Nason represented women workers. But in 1903 a split within the BSWU over a stitchers' strike caused a loss of membership to the Women's Trade Union League and to trade unions of the American Federation of Labor. At the same time gender solidarity among women shoeworkers was assaulted by ethnic and gender shifts within the work force, changes in the gender segregation of occupations within the industry, and new protective legislation limiting the hours of factory women. Women lost their monopoly over stitching, and immigrant men often replaced native-born women.

See also American Federation of Labor; Daughters of St. Crispin; Factory Workers; Female Society of Lynn and Vicinity for the Protection and Promotion of Female Industry; Knights of Labor; Pieceworkers; Protective Legislation; Society of Shoebinders; Strikes; Unions; Women's Trade Union League.

Reference Mary H. Blewett, *Men, Women, and Work: Class, Gender, and Protest in the New England Shoe Industry, 1780–1910* (1988).

Shop Stewards

These workers, elected by their fellow union members, inform their co-workers about the union and present workers' grievances to management.

See also Unions.

Short-Time Compensation

Several states, including California and New York, have plans for short-time compensation. In these plans employers agree to reduce full-time hours instead of laying off workers. The state unemployment compensation funds compensate workers for lost work time and employers continue to provide full benefits.

See also Benefits; Contingent Work Force; Part-Time Workers; Temporary Workers; Work Sharing.

Reference Nine to Five, National Association of Working Women, "Working at the Margins: Part-Time and Temporary Workers in the United States" (1986).

Siebert, Muriel F. (n.d.)

In 1967 Siebert became the first woman permitted to buy a seat on the New York Stock Exchange (NYSE). (Julia Walsh and Phyllis Peterson had become the first female members of the American

Muriel Siebert

Stock Exchange in 1965.) Siebert's efforts on behalf of Wall Street's women were honored by the 1992 Veuve Clicquot Business Woman of the Year award. In 1992 almost 50 women owned seats on the NYSE. (*New York Times*, 5 July 1992)

See also Business and Industry; Kreps, Juanita Morris.

References Anne B. Fisher, *Wall Street Women: Women in Power on the Street Today* (1990); Barbara J. Harris, *Beyond Her Sphere: Women and the Professions in American History* (1978).

Simms, Daisy Florence (1873–1923)

This leader in the Young Women's Christian Association (YWCA) began her career in that organization during her student days at DePauw University. After graduation she gained wide experience in various YWCA posts from Michigan to Maine. In 1909 Grace H. Dodge appointed her director of the YWCA's new industrial department. There she soon concluded that improved working conditions had to precede efforts at religious conversion.

At the same time she was participating in research that persuaded YWCA leaders to commit the organization to study social and industrial problems pertaining to the welfare of working women. Simms accordingly inaugurated self-governing industrial clubs in laundries, mills, factories, and stores, free to create their own agenda within broad limits. Her influence throughout her lifelong career committed the YWCA more and more to the social gospel and the welfare of working women.

See also Young Women's Christian Association.

References Edward T. James et al., eds., *Notable American Women III* (1971); Richard Roberts, *Florence Simms: A Biography* (1926).

Simms, Ruth Hanna McCormick

See McCormick, Ruth Hanna.

Simpson, Georgiana (n.d.)

In 1921 Simpson earned her Ph.D. from the University of Chicago, one of the first three black women to receive the doctorate.

See also Academic Women; Dykes, Eva B.; Magill, Helen; Mossell, Sadie Tanner.

Sitdown Strikes

See Strikes.

Slagle, Eleanor Clarke (1871–1942)

This leader in occupational therapy (OT) entered the field in her late thirties as a member of the first class studying "invalid occupation" at the Chicago School of Civics and Philanthropy. After seven years of organizing OT programs and training programs for therapists and superintending OT for the Illinois Department of Public Welfare, in 1922 she became director of occupational therapy for the New York State Hospital Commission. In her 20 years in that position she proved that OT could work in a state hospital system and raised professional standards for therapists. In 1917 she cofounded the National Society for the Promotion of Occupational Therapy, later renamed the American Occupational Therapy Association, for which she acted as executive secretary from 1922 to 1937, working to develop standards and registration for therapists and to make the association a counseling organization to provide information and assistance for the establishment of OT programs.

See also Health Professionals and Paraprofessionals.

Reference Edward T. James et al., eds., *Notable American Women III* (1971).

Slavery

Almost all of the approximately half a million Africans who entered the American colonies or the United States before the Emancipation Proclamation of 1863 came involuntarily, as slaves. Some had been prisoners of tribal wars, some sold by tribal chiefs to black slave merchants, and some kidnapped by white slavers. The women—as the trade grew, about a third of all slaves—were expected to work the fields and bear children. In the earliest days their owners usually treated them like indentured servants, freeing them after several years. But by 1639, 20 years after the first load of slaves was sold at Jamestown, colonists had begun to hold them for life—and black women slaves instantly rose above white women servants in value.

From the moment of their captivity or sale in Africa, the slaves endured brutally harsh treatment. The terrible, crowded, often chained journey across the ocean taught them what to expect for the rest of their lives. Sexual harassment and attacks increased the suffering of the women. Crews tortured children before their mothers' eyes. Many a slave woman, if she survived the trip at all, landed insane.

Arrival in the new country brought no surcease. The system of slavery rested on the assumption that blacks were inferiors, scarcely or not at all human, mere producers of labor rather than human beings. Before the nineteenth century northern states used significant numbers of slaves: in mid-eighteenth-century New York, for instance, slaves comprised a fifth of the population. But most slaves lived in the South, where the plantation system depended on their labor.

There women slaves labored, without rights, under threat of force. Some were trained to spin and sew. Some cared for white children or worked as domestic servants in the master's house. But many more worked in the fields, hoeing, plowing, shoveling, felling trees, splitting rails, doing "men's work." Their masters hired them out to build roads and railroads, to mine ore, to lumber. Their masters regarded breeding as one more form of labor to be extracted from black women. In short, their masters exercised absolute power over their bodies, to force them to work, to beat them, to impregnate them, to kill them. No law, only economic motives, stood between the slave and death. Every law stood between her and freedom.

Every black woman born or brought into this system knew that life would be especially hard for her. For besides working just as hard as a black male, often at the same job, she had her work in the slave quarters—the traditional "woman's work" of cooking and sewing and cleaning and spinning and child care—for those children she was allowed to keep, but whom she could not protect from sadistic treatment and a life like her own. She could fight back only by subterfuge: slowdowns, destruction of crops and equipment, the secret use of contraceptives and abortive herbs, arson, poisoning "Massa," or maiming herself, or suicide. Or, for a lucky few, running away. Or organizing suicidal slave uprisings. Only one of the most horrible wars in human history could change her condition—the Civil War, or the War Between the States, of 1861–1865, when Union soldiers were finally able to enforce Abraham Lincoln's Emancipation Proclamation.

See also Black Americans; Civil War; Housekeeping; Indentured Servants; Second Shift; Wives.

References Mimi Abramovitz, *Regulating the Lives of Women: Social Welfare Policy from Colonial Times to the Present* (1988); Alice Kessler-Harris, *Out To Work* (1982); Deborah Gray White, *Ar'n't I a Woman? Female Slaves in the Plantation South* (1984).

Slowdown

This term applies to the practice of employees' reducing the rate of production as a form of covert protest.

See also Strikes.

Small Business Administration (SBA)

This federal agency created in 1953 provides information and services to small business entrepreneurs. Its Service Corps of Retired Executives (SCORE), established in the 1960s, numbers 13,000 volunteers, both active and retired, who counsel people engaged in small businesses. SBA's Management and Technical Assistance 7(J) Program offers management and technical aid to small business clients, specifically socially and economically disadvantaged persons, businesses operating in areas of low income or high unemployment, and firms owned by low-income individuals. Its Small Business Development Centers provide training and counseling.

SBA's Office of Women's Business Ownership (OWBO), established in 1979, developed a Women's Network for Entrepreneurial Training to match successful women entrepreneurs (mentors) with women business owners whose companies were ready to grow (protegées); mentors served for a year. OWBO also offered women entrepreneurs prebusiness workshops, "Access to Capital" conferences; technical and financial information; a national data base; procurement conferences on how to sell to the federal government; exporting conferences; and long-term training and counseling centers set up in partnership with private companies. By 1992 OWBO had been discontinued.

SBA guarantees up to 90 percent of certain loans made by private lenders and offers lender incentives for loans of less than $50,000. In 1992 SBA offered no preferential loan programs for women-owned businesses.

See also Entrepreneurs; Mentors.

Smith, Charlotte (n.d.)

This nineteenth-century labor organizer helped to found the Women's National Labor League (1882) for women clerks employed by the federal government, which affiliated with the Knights of Labor in 1883.

See also Government Workers; Knights of Labor; Union Organizers.

Reference Philip S. Foner, *Women and the American Labor Movement* (1979 and 1982).

Smith, Sophia (1796–1870)

Founder of Smith College, a native of Massachusetts, Smith lived a quiet life with her birth family and inherited their fortune. On her pastor's suggestion, she left her money to establish a women's college, a plan that she approved and incorporated in her will, hoping that "by the higher and more thoroughly Christian education of women, what are called their 'wrongs' will be redressed, their wages will be adjusted, [and] their weight of influence in reforming the evils of society will be greatly increased."

See also Academic Women.

Reference Edward T. James et al., eds., *Notable American Women III* (1971).

Smith, Zilpha Drew (1852?–1926)

This early social worker became registrar in 1879, and later general secretary, of Boston's new Associated Charities. She successfully recruited many volunteers, who, she believed, should imbue the poor with their middle-class values, thus rehabilitating them. She encouraged paid agents and volunteers to exchange information and established training classes for them. In 1903 she became associate director for the new Boston School for Social Workers, jointly sponsored by Harvard University and Simmons College, a post she held until her retirement in 1915.

See also Social Workers.

Reference Edward T. James et al., eds., *Notable American Women III* (1971).

Smith Vocational Education Act (1917)

This law enabled school systems to add a vocational education component to junior high schools, which were expanding in response to working-class demands for more education. Workers eagerly supported vocational high schools but suspected that the introduction of vocational education into junior high schools implied tracking and class-oriented education.

See also Vocational Education.

Reference Marjorie Murphy, *Blackboard Unions: The AFT and the NEA, 1900–1980* (1990).

Smith-Hughes Act (1917)

See Clerical Workers; Home Economists.

Smith-Lever Act (1914)
See Home Economists.

Social Feminists
During the Progressive Era (1890–1920) large numbers of middle- and upper-class women banded together in various organizations to clean up society and to help and defend women and children. They enjoyed notable success not only in securing the vote for women but also in ending child labor, establishing libraries, improving schools, and bettering conditions for women workers.

See also Consumers' League; Domestic Feminists; Progressive Era; Protective Legislation; Shirt Sewers' Cooperative Union; Travelers' Aid; Woman's Union for Christian Work; Women's Educational and Industrial Union; Women's Protection Union; Women's Trade Union League; Working Woman's Protective Union; Working Women's Association; Working Women's League.

References William L. O'Neill, *Everyone Was Brave: The Decline and Fall of Feminism in America* (1969);

Social Security Act of 1935
This landmark legislation (and its subsequent amendments), born of the Great Depression and the New Deal, recognized the inability of the market economy to consistently provide enough jobs. In several innovative programs, it increased the economic security of American citizens. The most controversial of these, Aid to Families with Dependent Children, tries to ensure good homes for children without parents, or with a single parent. Unemployment insurance taxes employers to fund employees between jobs. The Old Age Insurance Program taxes both employers and employees to provide supplementary pensions to retired workers.

In 1989 Gwendolyn King became the first black to head the Social Security Administration.

See also Aid to Families with Dependent Children; Great Depression; New Deal; Old Age Insurance Program; Pensions; Unemployment Insurance Program.

Reference Mimi Abramovitz, *Regulating the Lives of Women: Social Welfare Policy from Colonial Times to the Present* (1988).

Social Workers
The profession of social worker stems from the volunteer work of lay and church-related charitable women's societies of the early nineteenth century and from society's assignment of nurturing tasks to women. In the Progressive Era (1890–1920), settlement house workers and others devoted to ameliorating conditions for the poor discovered the necessity of full-time experts. Traditionally social workers have been women, but in the second half of the twentieth century more men have entered the profession.

The profession has relied upon more and more schooling to raise its standards, with an effort to require the degree of Master of Social Work. Increasingly social workers have been expected to master counseling skills for both individuals and whole families. To set and maintain standards for the profession, in 1921 social workers established the American Association of Social Workers, which cooperates with more specialized associations within the field, like the American Association of Hospital Social Workers, the American Association of Visiting Teachers, and the American Association of Psychiatric Social Workers.

The emergence of psychiatric social work as a subfield of social work dates from the end of World War I, when the treatment of shell-shocked soldiers became a national concern. Resourceful women like Mary Cromwell Jarrett, who founded the Smith College School for Social Work in 1919, and Bertha C. Reynolds pioneered to build a new female profession whose main focus would be medical social work, in which psychological and psychiatric concepts of human behavior would be incorporated into the training of social workers. This innovative focus on personality disorder caused some dissension and animosity from other types of social workers. And the medical hierarchy (both in hospitals and universities) was prepared to accept psychiatric social workers only as subordinates. Despite its failure to secure equal treatment with physicians, psychiatric social work, like all other forms of social work, has become a paid profession open to educated women.

See also Abbott, Edith; Abbott, Grace; Breckinridge, Sophonisba Preston; Hamilton, Gordon; Health Professionals and Paraprofessionals; Lothrop, Alice Louise Higgins; Lowell, Josephine Shaw; Matthews, Victoria Earle; O'Day, Caroline Love Goodwin; Progressive Era; Regan, Agnes Gertrude; Richmond, Mary Ellen; Settlement Houses; Smith, Zilpha Drew; Woerishoffer, Emma Carola.

References Dorothy M. Brown, *Setting a Course: American Women in the 1920s* (1987); Penina Migdal Glazer and Miriam Slater, *Unequal Colleagues* (1987); Susan Vandiver, "A History of Women in Social Work," in *Women's Issues and Social Work Practice*, ed. Elaine Norman and Arlene Mancuso (1980).

Socialist Party of America

This party was founded in July 1901 at a convention in which eight women delegates participated. In the years immediately following, women constituted 10 percent of the party's membership and 6–10 percent of delegates at the party's conventions. It was the first political organization to welcome women. Although its platform demanded "equal civil and political rights for men and women," and the party accepted women as members in good standing, nothing was said or done about women's having a distinct role to play in the party's activities.

Within the party it was an article of faith that the introduction of a socialist society, in which private ownership of the means of production would be abolished and workers would share in the profits of their labor, would necessarily eliminate discrimination against women. The dominant labor movement, embodied in the American Federation of Labor, openly opposed the socialists, whom they viewed as radically un-American. The Socialist party, however, was committed to parliamentary politics and sought to displace capitalism peacefully. It thus differentiated itself from the Industrial Workers of the World, which disdained electoral victories and sought to achieve its ends by means of direct confrontation with capitalist exploitation, i.e., strikes, displays of militancy, and worker solidarity.

The formation of the Socialist party, although it gave considerable impetus to the work of left-wing reformers and labor organizers, failed to meet the expectations of the more radical women socialists, who demanded greater effort towards unionizing working women, a larger share in union leadership, and greater militancy in demanding equal pay and better working conditions.

Despite the conservatism of most American unions and the inability of the Socialist/Marxist parties to gain mass worker support at the polls, socialist and Marxist concepts continue to inform the thinking of some labor reformers and activists. Essentially what remains today is the proposition that no amount of labor law reform or legal procedures will create a just society or eliminate exploitation; that the capitalist system, which depends upon private ownership of the workplace and profit-making, must eventually be replaced by worker control of production, which will make a free and just society possible. Legal and legislative reform are thus a necessary but not a sufficient means to meet the needs of workers.

See also American Federation of Labor; Bloor, Ella Reeve; Communist Party; Goldman, Emma; Industrial Workers of the World; Stokes, Rose Harriet Pastor; Strikes; Unions.

References Mari Jo Buhle, *Women and American Socialism, 1870–1920* (1981); Philip S. Foner, *Women and the American Labor Movement* (1979 and 1982); Carol Hymowitz and Michaele Weissman, *A History of Women in America* (1980); Michael Yates, *Labor Law Handbook* (1987).

Society of Shoebinders

Women "outworkers" formed this organization in 1831 to get higher wages and a uniform wage scale for shoebinding. The short-lived society claimed to represent more than 225 shoebinders.

See also Female Society of Lynn and Vicinity for the Protection and Promotion of Female Industry; Pieceworkers; Shoemakers.

Reference Mary H. Blewett, *Men, Women, and Work: Class, Gender, and Protest in the New England Shoe Industry, 1780–1910* (1988).

Southern Council on Women and Children in Industry

This organization, which was functioning in the 1930s, advocated child labor laws and shorter working hours for women.

Reference John A. Salmond, *Miss Lucy of the CIO: The Life and Times of Lucy Randolph Mason, 1882–1959* (1988).

Southern Summer School for Women Workers in Industry (1927–1951)

This school was organized in Atlanta, Georgia, by Lois McDonald and Louise Leonard McLaren, both former industrial secretaries for the Young Women's Christian Association. It offered short courses, normally in the summer, for women industrial workers, mostly tobacco or textile workers, often union representatives. The residential sessions stressed social and political issues. These courses helped students to understand the impact of industrialization on their lives; living in a cooperative community with the faculty empowered them and enabled them to express themselves.

During the 1930s McLaren struggled to reconcile organized labor, to which the school was moving closer, and the middle-class women's organizations who had long provided the school's support. From 1938 on, the school enrolled men as well as women, but remained primarily a woman's organization. The boom times of World War II left workers little leisure for residential sessions, so the school turned to community seminars and training sessions. After the war it declined, as more unions chose to run their own workers' education programs.

Early graduates of the Southern School, as well as women trained by the Young Women's Christian Association and the Women's Trade Union League, became a natural base for the Congress of Industrial Organizations' drives to organize Southern women workers during the 1930s and 1940s.

See also Barker, Mary Cornelia; Bryn Mawr Summer School for Women Workers; Congress of Industrial Organizations; Unions; Women's Trade Union League; Workers' Education; World War II; Young Women's Christian Association.

References Dorothy M. Brown, *Setting a Course: American Women in the 1920s* (1987); Judith Freeman Clark, *Almanac of American Women in the 20th Century* (1987); Mary E. Frederickson, " 'A Place To Speak Our Minds': The Southern School for Women Workers" (1981); John A. Salmond, *Miss Lucy of the CIO: The Life and Times of Lucy Randolph Mason, 1882–1959* (1988).

Space

Women have increased their representation in aerospace engineering from 1.8 percent of all aerospace engineers in 1970 to 8.1 percent in 1990.

Although the U.S. space program paid token tribute to the possibility of women in space from its inception, it took almost a quarter of a century to put a woman into space. Jerrie Cobb, a pilot, was the first women to be selected for astronaut training, in February 1960. In July 1962, she testified before a House of Representatives committee that of 25 women who had applied for the space program 13 had qualified as astronauts. Cobb attributed the failure of the National Aeronautics and Space Administration (NASA) to use any of these women to sex discrimination. Finally, in 1978, NASA named six women astronauts for the space shuttle flights scheduled for the 1980s: Anna L. Fisher, M.D.; Shannon W. Lucid, M.D.; Judith A. Resnik, Ph.D. in electrical engineering; Sally K. Ride, Ph.D. in physics; Margaret R. Seddon, M.D.; and Kathryn D. Sullivan, Ph.D. in geology.

Dr. Ride became the first American woman to enter space as a member of the crew of the space shuttle *Challenger* on its seventh flight in June 1983. Dr. Resnick became the second when she flew as a member of the crew of space shuttle *Discovery* on its maiden flight in August 1984. In October 1984 Ride made her second flight along with Kathryn Sullivan, the first American woman to make a space walk. And in November 1984 Dr. Fisher became the third American woman (and the first mother) to fly into space, also on the space shuttle *Discovery*. In 1985 the remaining two of the original six astronauts had their turns, Dr. Seddon in April and Dr. Lucid in June.

The first black woman astronaut was Dr. Mae Carol Jemison, a physician and chemical engineer who orbited into space on 12 September 1992, as a member of the shuttle *Endeavor*'s seven-member crew. On the same flight were N. Jan Davis (Ph.D. in mechanical engineering) and her husband, the first married couple assigned to the same space flight. Ordinarily married couples are not assigned to the same flight, but these two, married after the crew was made up, were permitted to remain, since it would have been inefficient and uneconomical to replace one of them at such a late hour.

Two women died when the *Challenger* exploded shortly after blast-off in January 1986: Dr. Resnick, making her second flight, and Christa McAuliffe, Teacher in Space Participant.

By the early 1990s, 15 American women astronauts had flown into space, nine of them with Ph.D.s in a scientific field, five with medical degrees, and one a pilot with a B.S. in aerospace engineering. At the end of 1992 the corps of 92 astronauts included 16 women, of whom Jemison is the only black. (*New York Times*, 13 September 1992)

See also Jemison, Mae Carol; Sex Discrimination.

Reference Judith Freeman Clark, *Almanac of American Women in the 20th Century* (1987).

Speed-Up

This term applies to employers' efforts to force employees to work faster, whether by setting production quotas higher or by running assembly lines faster.

See also Scientific Management; Stretch-Out.

Sports

Women's progress in sports was impeded in the nineteenth century by the myth of women's delicacy and fragile health and fears that their participation in sports might damage their reproductive potential. Nonetheless a women's baseball team, the Dolly Vardens of Philadelphia, appeared on the scene in 1867, shocking their fans with their uniforms of red calico dresses that stopped above their ankles. Wellesley introduced crew in 1875. With the emergence of the New Woman in the late nineteenth century, women engaged in bicycling, croquet, and tennis as well as more vigorous sports. Fay Fuller climbed Mount Rainier in 1890—in skirts. In 1896 a women's six-day bicycle race was held in Madison Square Garden. Margaret Abbott won the Women's International Golf Match in Paris in 1900, for an unofficial Olympic gold medal.

The twentieth century has seen the emergence of professional athletes, early on in tennis and swimming and later in almost every sport. In 1926 Gertrude Ederle became the first woman to swim the English Channel.

Twentieth-century institutional reluctance, especially by coeducational schools and universities, to spend money on women's athletic programs has persisted despite Title IX of the Education Amendments Act of 1972, which requires institutions receiving federal monies not to discriminate against women. Though this regulation has not been much honored, it has forced many schools to give women at least some training and opportunity for participation. In their own educational institutions and within the National Collegiate Athletic Association, sportswomen in the late twentieth century continue to press for gender equity.

Outstanding role models like Mildred Ella (Babe) Didrikson Zaharias (1911–1956) have also helped, as have the girls and young women who have gone to court to force schools to allow them to participate in various sports. So have the pioneering women who have broken

The University of Colorado Buffs play against the University of Wyoming

the barriers into nontraditional sports competitions and jobs, like Bernice Gera, who from 1967–1972 fought through the courts for the right to a job as a minor-league umpire, only to be faced with death threats; Melissa Ladtke, a *Sports Illustrated* sportswriter, who in 1978 won a case before a federal district court forcing the New York Yankees management to permit her to interview players in the locker room after a game; Christine Wren, who umpired in a minor league in 1975; Ann Meyers, who in 1979 signed a three-year contract with the New Jersey Gems of the Women's Professional Basketball League; Lynette Woodard, who in 1985 signed with the Harlem Globetrotters; and Pam Postema, who in 1988 became the first woman to umpire in the major leagues. (*New Directions for Women*, Fall 1992)

See also Cowgirls; Education Amendments Act; Gibson, Althea; King, Billie-Jean.

References Judith Freeman Clark, *Almanac of American Women in the 20th Century* (1987); Rachel daSilva, ed., *Leading Out: Women Climbers Reaching for the Top* (1992); Marianna Davis, *American Women in Olympic Track and Field* (1992); Joan McCullough, *First of All* (1980); Pam Postema and Gene Wojciechowski, *You've Got To Have Balls To Make It in This League: My Life as an Umpire* (1992); Ruth M. Sparhawk, et al., eds., *American Women in Sport: 1887–1987* (1989).

Staff Jobs

These positions, unlike line jobs, contribute only indirectly to the purpose of the organization, and the people in them do not have policy decision-making authority. In private industry staff jobs are in accounting, personnel, public relations, advertising, research, consumer affairs, customer relations, data processing, human resources management, office administration, and legal departments. Cutbacks take their first toll in staff jobs.

See also Human Resources Managers; Line Jobs.

Reference Jennie Farley, ed., *The Woman in Management: Career and Family Issues* (1983).

Starr, Ellen Gates (1859–1940)

From 1889 until 1920 this settlement house worker lived at Hull House, which she cofounded. Dedicated to art, she came to realize that creativity and aesthetic response could not flourish in a society dominated by sweatshops, low wages, and long hours. Thereafter she militantly supported strikes, organizing mass meetings, speaking, relieving the strikers, marching in picket lines, even getting arrested—though a jury found it impossible to convict this 100-pound lady of interfering with a police officer in the performance of his duty. In 1920 she converted to Roman Catholicism and turned to writing and speaking about Catholic art and worship.

See also Hull House; Settlement Houses; Strikes; Sweatshops.

Reference Edward T. James et al., eds., *Notable American Women III* (1971).

Steinem, Gloria (b. 1934)

Best known for launching *Ms.* magazine in 1977 (with Patricia Carbine), Steinem is an active and imaginative champion of women's rights. With Betty Friedan she helped organize the Women's Strike for Equality held in August 1970. She cofounded the National Women's Political Caucus, the Women's Action Alliance, and the Ms. Foundation for Women. She is a key supporter of the Equal Rights Amendment.

See also Equal Rights Amendment; Ms. Foundation for Women.

References Judith Freeman Clark, *Almanac of American Women in the 20th Century* (1987); Jennifer S. Uglow, comp. and ed., *International Dictionary of Women's Biography* (1985).

Stevens, Alzina Parsons (1849–1900)

This labor leader began her career in the printing trades in Chicago, where in 1877 she organized and presided over Working Woman's Union #1—the first president of a women's labor group. When she moved to Toledo, she joined the Knights of Labor and helped organize the Joan of Arc Assembly for women, of which she became the first master workman or president. In 1890 she rose to district master workman, and attended Knights of Labor national conventions from 1888 through 1890. As the Knights of Labor declined, Stevens shifted to the American Federation of Labor, organizing several new unions in Chicago (where she then lived at Hull House) and walking picket lines. From 1893–1897 she worked as assistant factory inspector for Illinois under Florence Kelley, lobbying with Kelley for a better state child labor law. In 1899 she was appointed the first probation officer of the new Cook County Juvenile Court.

See also American Federation of Labor; Hull House; Kelley, Florence; Knights of Labor; Troup, Augusta Lewis; Union Organizers.

Reference Edward T. James et al., eds., *Notable American Women III* (1971).

Stewart, Maria W. Miller (1803–1879)

This free black teacher and activist on behalf of black working women made history in a speech to the African-American Female Intelligence Society in Boston (1832), urging these women to unite and create better employment opportunities for themselves.

Reference Philip S. Foner, *Women and the American Labor Movement* (1979 and 1982).

Sticky Floor

Researcher Catherine White Berheide coined this term to suggest the difficulty that workers encounter in earning promotions out of low-level jobs of the sort in which many women are trapped. As Berheide points out, far more women have to worry about the sticky floor than those fast-track executives who bump their heads against the glass ceiling.

See also Glass Ceiling.

Stockbrokers

See Business and Industry; Kreps, Juanita Morris; Siebert, Muriel F.

Stokes, Rose Harriet Pastor (1879–1933)

This socialist and communist labor leader and writer, born in Poland, immigrated to the United States from England at age 11, immediately going to work in a cigar factory. When her family moved to New York in 1903, she became an assistant editor on the Yiddish *Daily News*, went to interview the wealthy James Graham Phelps Stokes, and married him. They then devoted themselves to Socialist party work, Rose Stokes working especially with urban working women. In 1916 she wrote a play about a woman labor leader, *The Woman Who Wouldn't*. Despite many contretemps with the police, she continued to walk picket lines until she fell ill in 1930.

See also Socialist Party.

References Edward T. James et al., eds., *Notable American Women III* (1971); Arthur Zipser and Pearl Zipser, *Fire and Grace: The Life of Rose Pastor Stokes* (1990).

Stoop Labor

This term is applied to the backbreaking labor necessary to tend and harvest delicate plants.

See also Agricultural Workers; Migrant Laborers.

Reference Tricia Knoll, *Becoming Americans: Asian Sojourners, Immigrants, and Refugees in the Western United States* (1982).

Stretch-Out

This is a term for increasing work loads, often by raising production quotas.

See also Speed-Up.

Reference Jacquelyn Dowd Hall et al., *Like a Family: The Making of a Southern Cotton Mill World* (1987).

Strikes

Strikes are work stoppages by means of which workers seek to force their employers to negotiate, to recognize their unions, or to meet their demands. These work stoppages may take different forms. "Wildcat strikes" are conducted by workers without approval of their own unions. In "sitdown strikes," popular during the 1930s and 1940s, workers in effect occupied factories, staying near their machines or assembly lines but refusing to work. In "slowdown strikes" the workers do not cease production but slow it down to the point of nonprofitability.

Although American women workers have lagged far behind their male counterparts in unionization and despite the frequently unwelcoming attitudes of unions toward them, women have participated in many labor stoppages throughout their history: strikes supporting male workers, both male and female workers, and women workers alone. Women's strikes date from the earliest days of manufacturing. In 1828, 300–400 workers walked out of a New Hampshire cotton mill in possibly the first all-woman strike. Not only such workers as the Lowell girls, who lived and worked together, struck but even the women who sewed shoes at home alone. Throughout the labor history of the United States women workers have repeatedly emerged as militant and courageous leaders in their own strikes or those dominated by women workers, like the Uprising of the 20,000.

The participation of women, whether workers or family members of strikers, has often been crucial to the success of strikes of male workers or of both female and male workers. The inventive leader of mine strikes, Mary Harris Jones, always relied on the miners' womenfolk, who, she said, she never had to teach how to fight. Often women have displaced men on the picket lines, as in the Bread and Roses Strike of 1912, on the demonstrably false theory that the police would not beat them up. In the nationwide railroad strike of 1877, the wives and children of the striking railroad men in every community took an active part in the "disturbances." In the terrible Ludlow Massacre employers directed most of their violence against women and children.

The involvement of women in strikes continues into the last part of the twentieth century, particularly as more women unionize and as groups of women workers who formerly never considered using work stoppages, like teachers, clerical workers, and journalists, adopt this means of protest.

The right of labor to unionize and strike was not fully protected legally until the Wagner Act of the New Deal.

See also Arizona Mine Strike; Boycotts; Bread and Roses Strike; Clerical Workers; El Paso Laundry Worker's Union (AFL) Strike; Elizabethton, Tennessee, Strike; Flint Auto Workers' Strike; Gastonia, North Carolina, Strike; General Textile Strike; Injunctions; Jones, Mary Harris; Journalists; Lockouts; Lowell Girls; Ludlow Massacre; Lynn (Massachusetts) Shoe Strike; Mesabi Range Strike; Moreno, Luisa; Nestor, Agnes; New Deal; Norris-LaGuardia Act; Parker, Julia Sarsfield O'Connor; Robinson, Harriet Jane Hanson; Starr, Ellen Gates; Stokes, Rose Harriet Pastor; Teachers; Unions; United Tailoresses Society of New York; Uprising of the 20,000; Wagner Act; Washerwoman's Strike; Women's Trade Union League; Yellow-Dog Contract.

References Sarah Eisenstein, *Give Us Bread but Give Us Roses: Working Women's Consciousness in the United States, 1890 to the First World War* (1983); Robert L. Friedheim, *The Seattle General Strike* (1964); Steve Golin, *The Fragile Bridge: Paterson Silk Strike, 1913* (1988); James J. Kenneally, "Women in the United States and Trade Unionism," in Norbert C. Soldon, ed., *The World of Women's Trade Unionism* (1985); Alice Kessler-Harris, *Out To Work* (1982); Barbara Kingsolver, *Holding the Line: Women in the Great Arizona Mine Strike of 1983* (1989); Theresa Serber Malkiel, *Diary of a Shirtwaist Striker* (1990); Nan Robertson, *The Girls in the Balcony: Women, Men, and the New York Times* (1992).

Strong, Anna Louise (1885–1970)

This radical journalist, who earned her doctorate in philosophy in 1908, began her career in child welfare and civic betterment. By 1912 she considered herself a socialist, opposing war and capitalism. Her support of the Seattle General Strike of 1919 made her even more notorious, a reputation that grew with her move to Russia in 1921. As an internationally renowned journalist she focused on Russia and China, devoting herself to popularizing the thought of Lenin, Stalin, and Mao Tse-tung for the masses. Tensions between the USSR and the United States led to her expulsion from Russia in 1949, and in 1958 she moved to

Woolworth workers strike during the 1940s.

China permanently. She returned to the United States in 1969 to work against the war in Vietnam.

See also Journalists.

References Robert L. Friedheim, *The Seattle General Strike* (1964); Barbara Sicherman et al., eds., *Notable American Women: The Modern Period* (1980); Jennifer S. Uglow, comp. and ed., *International Dictionary of Women's Biography* (1985).

Suitable Occupations

For most of American history women who out of inclination or necessity sought paid work have had relatively few occupational choices, since many occupations have not been considered "suitable" for women. In general, the most suitable (and the lowest paid) jobs have always been those utilizing the so-called womanly virtues of nurturing, mothering, teaching, and nursing.

The designation of certain jobs as unladylike or otherwise unsuitable for women is a matter of social convention. That convention, seeming at any given period so rigid, has proved extremely flexible over the years, yielding frequently to the need for more workers in wartime or to the lower wages that women have been willing to accept. Jobs once considered a male preserve have become feminized: for example, bank telling and clerical work in offices are now considered preeminently women's work, a change from the turn of the century. Women are now moving more and more into work once dominated by men, nontraditional occupations.

See also Clerical Workers; Gender Gap; Nontraditional Occupations; Occupational Segregation; Separate Spheres; Velvet Ghettos.

Reference Barbara R. Bergmann, *The Economic Emergence of Women* (1986).

Swartz, Maud O'Farrell (1879–1937)

This Irish-born labor leader, educated as a governess, became a proofreader soon after her 1901 immigration to America. In 1912 Rose Schneiderman recruited her as a worker for the Women's Trade Union League (WTUL). A year at their training school prepared her to be the secretary of the New York WTUL from 1917 to 1921, and in 1922 their "compensation adviser" for women seeking workmen's compensation. She succeeded Margaret Dreier Robins in 1922 as president of the national WTUL, a position she held until 1926. From 1919 until 1923 she was active in the International Congress of Working Women. In 1931 she was appointed secretary of the New York State Department of Labor, where she expanded their activities among women workers.

See also Government Workers; Robins, Margaret Dreier; Schneiderman, Rose; Women's International Labor Conferences; Women's Trade Union League.

Reference Edward T. James et al., eds., *Notable American Women III* (1971).

Sweatshops

Factories set up in dangerous, dirty, ill-lighted, and ill-ventilated buildings are often called sweatshops. Here laborers are "sweated," overworked, and underpaid. The term is associated with nineteenth-century factories, conditions that prompted the reforms of the Progressive Era, but it also applies to workplaces today that violate laws governing wages, hours, and working conditions, and employ workers, often illegal immigrants, who fear to complain.

See also Progressive Era; Triangle Shirtwaist Fire.

Taft-Hartley Act
(Labor Management Relations Act of 1947)

This act, later amended by the Landrum-Griffin Act, empowered the National Labor Relations Board and the courts to stop unfair labor practices and to compensate their victims.

Enacted over the veto of President Truman in 1947, the Taft-Hartley Act reflected growing popular hostility to unions, stimulated by rising inflation and an outbreak of strikes after World War II. As unions sought to make up for what they had lost during the war, management demanded more restrictive labor legislation. The Taft-Hartley Act outlawed such controversial union tactics as secondary boycotts (of companies that do business with a boycotted establishment), the closed shop (in which all employees are required to join the union), and jurisdictional strikes (between different unions for control of a specific workplace). It also provided for an 80-day cooling-off period to facilitate negotiation of a labor dispute, a provision that in practice has seldom succeeded.

The Landrum-Griffin Act, officially known as the Labor-Management Reporting and Disclosure Act of 1959, extended some of Taft-Hartley's restrictions on labor activities and gave the government certain rights to regulate the internal affairs of unions to protect the rank-and-file membership against corrupt leadership.

See also Boycotts; Labor Legislation; Norris-LaGuardia Act; Strikes; Unions; Wagner Act.

Reference Robert E. Doherty, *Industrial and Labor Relations Terms* (1989); Michael Yates, *Labor Law Handbook* (1987).

Tallchief, Maria (b. 1925)

Tallchief was the first Native American prima ballerina. Born in Oklahoma, she studied with Bronislava Nijinska in California. She has danced with the Ballet Russe de Monte Carlo, with the Paris Opera Ballet, as prima ballerina with the New York City Ballet, and with the American Ballet Theater. She has also served with the Chicago City Ballet as artistic director.

See also Dancers.

Reference Angela Howard Zophy and Frances M. Kavenik, eds., *Handbook of American Women's History* (1990).

Tarbell, Ida Minerva (1857–1944)

Tarbell, a highly successful journalist, won her greatest fame through her influential muckraking articles, particularly her study of the Standard Oil Company (1904). A

Ida Minerva Tarbell

257

native Pennsylvanian, she graduated from Allegheny College in 1880 and taught for two years. She then took a job with the *Chautauquan* for eight years, writing material to supplement Chautauqua's home study courses. In 1891 she left to go to France, freelancing with magazine articles. The next year S. S. McClure recruited her to write for his new magazine and in 1894 persuaded her to join his staff in New York, beginning her work there with a series of articles on Napoleon that made her reputation. After another series on Lincoln, McClure assigned Tarbell to investigate the Standard Oil Trust, which she passionately attacked.

In 1906 Tarbell left *McClure's* to jointly purchase and edit the *American Magazine*, in which she published a series of articles against the protective tariff. Despite her reputation as a muckraker, Tarbell admired businessmen, studied factories experimenting with industrial relations and employee welfare, and warmly advocated scientific management and Henry Ford's paternalism. After the sale of the *American Magazine* in 1915, Tarbell joined the Chautauqua circuit as a lecturer, keeping at it, with wartime interruptions, until 1932, and accepting freelance assignments.

Tarbell's girlhood prayer to be spared marriage was answered. Ironically, she moved from her youthful feminist commitment to the belief that "women had a business assigned by nature and society which was of more importance than public life."

See also Journalists; Scientific Management.

References Edward T. James et al., eds., *Notable American Women III* (1971); Ida M. Tarbell, *All in the Day's Work* (1985); Ida Tarbell, *The Business of Being a Woman* (1912); Jennifer S. Uglow, comp. and ed., *International Dictionary of Women's Biography* (1985).

Taylor, Lucy Beaman Hobbs (1833–1910)

Taylor was the first American woman to earn a dental degree. Rejected by the Ohio College of Dental Surgery because of her gender, she served an apprentice-ship and practiced dentistry for three years. Only then, in 1865, did the Ohio College admit her, granting her a degree four months later. After her marriage in 1867, she taught her husband dentistry, and over the next 20 years they built an extensive practice.

See also Apprentices; Health Professionals and Paraprofessionals.

Reference Edward T. James et al., eds., *Notable American Women III* (1971).

Taylor, Rebecca (?–1980)

Although Taylor achieved some success in the 1930s in her work for the International Ladies' Garment Workers' Union in San Antonio, Texas, she failed in her efforts to persuade the union to draw its organizers from among the Mexican-American women who constituted most of the work force.

See also International Ladies' Garment Workers' Union; Union Organizers.

Reference Angela Howard Zophy and Frances M. Kavenik, eds., *Handbook of American Women's History* (1990).

Teachers

From the dames' schools of colonial America that taught children their ABCs to contemporary graduate schools, American women have taught. Level by level, women of all ethnic groups have moved upward within the profession, despite society's resistance to higher education for women. Emergency labor shortages, women's missionary spirit, the significantly lower salaries paid to women, and societal assumptions about the association between teaching and nurturing gradually feminized the elementary level of the profession, and women's high performance and persistence slowly won them places in the higher reaches. Up until the end of the nineteenth century, when clerical work opened for women, teaching was a forced choice for many.

At one time most teachers were the children of farmers; in the late twentieth century elementary and high school teachers are still recruited primarily from manual laboring and clerical families. Blacks are better represented than in other professions.

By the 1830s women had begun to replace men in teaching. After all, it was cheaper to hire women. Catharine Beecher opened a training school for teachers in 1830. By the time of the Civil War, about a quarter of all teachers were women. With the war, those figures surged—partly because of the manpower shortage and partly because towns paid women only 30 to 50 percent of what they paid comparable men. After that war, thousands of white women went south to teach freed slaves and provided their own replacements by training black women. Others instructed Native American children, often with an eye to "Americanizing" and Christianizing them. With the multiplication of public schools, demand for teachers rocketed, and for European-

American and black women teaching became almost uniquely an open profession, highly respectable though notoriously ill-paid. At the turn of the century three-fourths of teachers were women. But in the cities women teachers usually reported to male school administrators and in the country to school committees of local men.

In the early twentieth century the militancy of women like Harriet Rodman eventually established the rights of women teachers to marry and bear children and to escape the rigid behavioral constraints imposed upon them by many communities. The Great Depression decreased opportunities for teachers, as for other professional women. The percentage of women teachers fell from 85 percent in 1920 to 78 percent in 1940.

In the latter half of the twentieth century the powerful teachers' unions, the

A turn-of-the-century history class at Tuskegee Institute in Tuskegee, Alabama

American Federation of Teachers and the National Education Association, have raised teachers' pay and reduced their hours, the size of their classes, and their community obligations. Teachers' strikes, once unthinkable (because of their potential damage to students' educations), have become commonplace.

But they have not resolved the power struggle existing between teachers, mostly women, and administrators, mostly men. At the heart of this struggle have been the issues of centralization and professionalization. In the late nineteenth and early twentieth centuries administrators fought to take into their own hands the authority traditionally reserved to local communities, particularly the authority to hire and fire teachers. Administrators' arguments for more professionalization reflected a shift in expectation for teachers, from virtuous deportment to "intellectual achievement," which the administrators defined as passing courses in colleges of education—thereby barring from public school teaching many gifted people who cannot stomach these courses. Tensions between teachers and administrators have also obstructed the adoption of systems of merit pay, since teachers do not trust administrators to evaluate them fairly.

In the early 1960s only 100 out of a total 16,000 school superintendents were women. In the 1990s women still struggle to obtain the more lucrative administrative jobs at all levels of education.

See also Academic Women; Adams, Annette A.; American Association of Colored Teachers; American Federation of Teachers; Barker, Mary Cornelia; Beecher, Catharine Esther; Bethune, Mary McLeod; Clerical Workers; Colonial America; Great Depression; Haley, Margaret Angela; Jarrell, Helen Ira; Jeanes Teachers; Kennedy, Kate; Married Women's Employment; Mitchell, Lucy Sprague; National Education Association; New Deal; Peabody, Elizabeth Palmer; Professional Women; Regan, Agnes Gertrude; Strikes; Wheelock, Lucy; Willard, Emma Hart; Young, Ella Flagg.

References Barbara J. Harris, *Beyond Her Sphere: Women and the Professions in American History* (1978); Marjorie Murphy, *Blackboard Unions* (1990); Rita J. Simon and Gloria Danziger, *Women's Movements in America* (1991).

Telecommuting
The possibility of working at home, at least part of the time, with links to the workplace provided by telephone, facsimile machines, and computers, offers opportunities for women with family responsibilities. Such an arrangement is sometimes called flexplace.

See also Home Workers.

Telephone Operators' Department of the International Brotherhood of Electrical Workers (TOD)
Telephone operators, almost all young women, began efforts to unionize against the paternalism of their employers in Boston in 1912. Other unions sprang up in the Far West and the South. In 1919 after years of agitating for equal rights for union women, telephone operators established TOD, in effect the first national trade union controlled and officered by women. TOD's locals spread across the United States. But the movement collapsed in the 1923 New England telephone strike.

See also Parker, Julia Sarsfield O'Connor; Unions.

Reference Stephen H. Norwood, *Labor's Flaming Youth: Telephone Operators and Worker Militancy, 1878–1923* (1990).

Television
See Comediennes; Journalists.

Temporary Workers
As employers in the late twentieth century strive to cut labor costs, they often turn to temporary workers. Some use this tactic to prevent unionization. They can also lay off temporary workers more easily. On the other hand, some workers prefer temporary jobs. Women often opt for them as a strategy to juggle paid work and child or dependent care, or as a response to their husbands' loss of employment. These combined forces made the temporary help agencies in the mid-1980s the fastest growing industry in the economy: these

agencies specialize in contracting out the services of their on-call employees, sometimes day-to-day and sometimes for longer periods of time.

Temporary workers earn less per hour than permanent full-time workers, seldom are rewarded for experience, and usually receive few or no benefits. The Tax Equity and Fiscal Responsibility Act of 1982 (TEFRA) requires that if the employee is working for an agency customer with a pension plan, the leasing company or temporary help agency provide pension benefits after the employee has completed 12 months or 1,500 hours of substantially full-time service. A 1985 law permitted the federal government to hire "temporary" workers for up to four years without providing benefits.

About 6.5 million people worked as temporaries in 1989, more than 60 percent of them women. Their hourly earnings averaged only 65 percent of those of permanent staff, yet 44 percent of them were their families' primary breadwinners. Fewer than a quarter received health insurance coverage. The great majority were employed less than 35 hours a week.

See also Benefits; Bridge Job; Contingent Work Force; Older Women; Part-Time Workers; Pensions.

Reference Heidi Hartman and June Lapidus, *Temporary Work* (1989).

Tenant Farmers

People who cannot afford to own their own land may rent it from the owners. Despite hard and continuous labor, few can manage to get ahead enough to buy their own land, and most remain permanently in debt to their landlords. Though many European Americans in the southeastern United States eke out a miserable living in this way, blacks, Mexicans, and Mexican Americans have historically been overrepresented among tenant farmers. Landowners have preferred to rent their lands to families with wives strong enough to work in the field and with many children who could labor alongside their parents.

See also Agricultural Workers.

References Teresa Amott and Julie Matthaei, *Race, Gender, and Work: A Multicultural Economic History of Women in the United States* (1991); Margaret Jarman Hagood, *Mothers of the South: Portraiture of the White Tenant Farm Woman* (1939).

Tests

The use of tests and similar requirements for employment has been disallowed by the courts if such tests and conditions are not clearly and closely related to the duties of the job, and if it can be established that they exclude a disproportionate number of women or minorities. For example: height and weight requirements for police and fire departments must be validated as strictly relevant for the job and not a covert method to eliminate women applicants.

See also Bona Fide Occupational Qualification; Disparate Impact; *Griggs v. Duke Power Company*; Law Enforcement.

Reference Barbara B. Bergmann, *The Economic Emergence of Women* (1986).

Theater

Actresses in the early days of the United States had to face the condemnation of Puritan morality. Women like dramatist and actress Olive Logan (1839–1909) fought to dispel their ill-repute. By 1900 more than 6,000 women were working in the profession, many of them earning the respect and admiration of their audiences. In the twentieth century with the publicity-fed popularity of the movies and later of television, the acting profession has attracted hundreds of thousands of aspirants, most of whom fail to make a living at it. Even the most successful of them have to confront the culture's emphasis on youth (particularly for women), which often denies them employment as they age.

Success in other professions in the theater has proved at least as difficult. With notable exceptions like the great Shakespearean Margaret Webster (1905–1972), a cofounder of the American Repertory Theatre, relatively few women have suc-

Playwright Clare Boothe Luce

ceeded as directors or producers. Similarly only a few women authors have had plays presented on Broadway: among them Zona Gale (1874–1928), who broke the barrier with her play *Miss Lulu Bett* in 1920; Susan Glaspell (1882–1948) of the innovative Provincetown Players; Lorraine Hansberry (1930–1965), author of *A Raisin in the Sun* and the first black woman playwright whose work appeared on Broadway; and the remarkable Lillian Hellman (1905–1984).

See also Cinema; Comediennes; Vorse, Mary Heaton.

References Alice M. Robinson, et al., eds., *Notable Women in the American Theater* (1989); Angela Howard Zophy and Frances M. Kavenik, eds., *Handbook of American Women's History* (1990).

Thomas, Martha Carey (1857–1935)

This distinguished educator as a young woman had to battle her father's prejudices against higher education for women to earn an A.B. from Cornell and, after study at Johns Hopkins and Leipzig, a Ph.D. *summa cum laude* from the University of Zurich. When she learned that Bryn Mawr was to open in 1885 as a college for women, she applied for its presidency; instead the trustees (including her father) appointed her dean and professor of English. By 1892 she had taken over the responsibilities of the presidency, though she was not given the title until two years later. She served as president until 1922, combining that function with the deanship until 1908.

Thomas shaped Bryn Mawr with her insistence on admission and curricular standards as high as those of the most prestigious men's colleges. She prescribed courses of study, rather than allowing students free electives. She instituted graduate studies. Her autocratic methods complicated retention of talented faculty; hard-pressed, she suppressed her contempt for the process and accepted faculty self-government in 1915. Her egalitarian views on women's capabilities were not reflected in her opinions on race, and during her tenure Jewish instructors and black students found no cordial welcome.

Her activities on behalf of women, however, extended off-campus. In 1885 she helped to found the Bryn Mawr School for Girls, with a college preparatory course. She led the fight for the admission of women to the Johns Hopkins University Medical School. She led college women's suffrage work. After the passage of the 19th amendment she associated herself with the National Woman's Party, which first introduced an Equal Rights Amendment. She vigorously opposed protective legislation for women. Above all Thomas insisted on the importance of women entering the work force, in all occupations. In her eyes a career was at least as viable a possibility for women as marriage. She enthusiastically supported the Bryn Mawr Summer School for Women in Industry.

See also Academic Women; Bryn Mawr Summer School for Women Workers; Equal Rights Amendment; Protective Legislation.

References Edith Finch, *Carey Thomas of Bryn Mawr* (1947), Edward T. James et al., eds., *Notable American Women III* (1971); Jennifer S. Uglow, comp. and ed., *International Dictionary of Women's Biography* (1985).

Thompson, Dorothy (1893–1961)

This highly successful journalist built her career on reporting international affairs. A New York State native, she graduated from Syracuse University in 1914 and then spent several years working for women's suffrage. She began her career in journalism in Europe with stories carried by the International News Service and worked her way up to Central European bureau chief for the *Philadelphia Public Ledger* and the *New York Evening Post*, stationed in Berlin. Fascinated by European affairs, Thompson based her journalism on a long residence and a wide acquaintance in Europe during the 1920s and 1930s, crossing the Atlantic at intervals for American lecture tours. Eventually as a columnist for the *New York Herald Tribune* and later for the Bell syndicate and as a magazine writer she won widespread fame.

Thompson exercised great influence, particularly in urging the United States to enter World War II. In 1946 she dismayed many of her admirers by suddenly switching from strong support to opposition to Zionism.

Both her marriages, the second to novelist Sinclair Lewis, ended in divorce. Michael Lewis was her only child. She developed intense friendships with women and experimented with a lesbian relationship.

See also Journalists; World War II.

References Marion K. Sanders, *Dorothy Thompson: A Legend in Her Time* (1973); Vincent Sheean, *Dorothy and Red* (1963); Barbara Sicherman et al., eds., *Notable American Women: The Modern Period* (1980); Jennifer S. Uglow, comp. and ed., *International Dictionary of Women's Biography* (1985).

Thoms, Adah B. Samuels (ca. 1863–1943)

This black nursing pioneer graduated from the Woman's Infirmary and School of Therapeutic Massage and from the school of nursing at the Lincoln Hospital and Home, both in New York City. In 1906, a year after her graduation, she was appointed assistant director of nurses at Lincoln, staying there for 19 years, her race alone precluding her permanent appointment as head of the training school, though she often served in that capacity temporarily. She worked to broaden educational and career opportunities for black nurses, primarily through the National Association of Colored Graduate Nurses (later merged with the American Nurses Association), which she cofounded in 1908 and over which she presided from 1916 to 1923.

See also Nurses.

Reference Edward T. James et al., eds., *Notable American Women III* (1971).

Thorne, Florence Calvert (1877–1973)

This labor researcher and editor, a native of Missouri, obtained her college education at Oberlin and the University of Chicago, earning a Ph.B. in history and political science in 1909. Her study of economics led to a meeting with Samuel Gompers, president of the American Federation of Labor (AFL), who in 1911 offered her a research job and later the assistant editorship of the *American Federationist*. For 40 years thereafter she served the AFL, at first as Gompers's editorial aide and then as research director. Indeed Thorne founded the research department by setting up a system to collect and report unemployment figures, figures at that time available nowhere else. Her research contributed to the development of social security and unemployment benefits and to child labor regulation. During both world wars she served on governmental committees and agencies. She retired from the AFL in 1953.

See also American Federation of Labor; Social Security Act.

Reference Barbara Sicherman et al., eds., *Notable American Women: The Modern Period* (1971).

Timothy, Elizabeth (?–1757)

This Dutch-born printer was the first American woman to publish a newspaper—the weekly *South Carolina Gazette*.

See also Printers.

Reference Isaiah Thomas, *The History of Printing in America* (1970).

Title VII

See Civil Rights Act of 1964.

Title IX

See Education Amendments Act.

Trades

A relatively few women have surmounted barriers to enter the trades traditionally reserved for men, in jobs that pay much more than those of the women's occupational ghettos. Some 400 trades, from aircraft mechanic to woodworker, from baker to telephone services installer, require apprenticeships, which generally do not welcome women. Women's underrepresentation in the trades contributes to their seeming like outsiders to their male co-workers.

In the 1980s and early 1990s as the United States has lost its industries because of leveraged buyouts and foreign competition, blue-collar jobs have dwindled. Consequently women in the trades confront new difficulties, since many of them have not accumulated enough seniority to be kept on.

Nonetheless the future holds some promise. Since the 1970s approximately 4,000 women have worked in mines in the United States. Although in 1991 women constituted less than 9 percent of the construction work force, the industry projects a need of 270,000 new entrants each year during the decade; the United States Census Bureau forecasts that 42 percent of them will be women. The Intermodal Surface Transportation Efficiency Act (ISTEA) makes $10 million a year available to organizations that help women enter the trades. Funding can go toward training, recruitment, and support services for women and minorities working on state highways and bridges.

Despite the rejection and often blatant sexual harassment that they have to endure, successful women in the trades claim that their presence sometimes changes the workplace for the better, showing men the advantages of asking for help and figuring out easier ways to accomplish tasks, defusing quarrels and substituting calm for confrontation, heightening the satisfaction employees take in their work, and fighting for better working conditions.

See also Apprentices; Arizona Mine Strike; Blue-Collar Workers; Construction Workers; Manhattan Trade School for Girls; Nontraditional Occupations; *Occupational Outlook Handbook*; Sexual Harassment; Vocational Education.

References Kipp Dawson, *Women Miners and the UMWA: 1973–1983* (1992); Kay Deaux and Joseph C. Ullman, *Women of Steel* (1983); Elaine P. Enarson, *Woods-Working Women: Sexual Integration in the U.S. Forest Service* (1984); Patricia W. Lunneborg, *Women Changing Work* (1990); Molly Martin, ed., *Hard-Hatted Women: Stories of Struggle and Success in the Trades* (1988); Herbert H. Meyer and Mary D. Lee, *Women in Traditionally Male Jobs: The Experience in Ten Public Utility Companies* (1978); Joyce Slaton Mitchell, *The Work Book: A Guide to Skilled Jobs* (1979); Larry J. Ricci, *High-Paying Blue Collar Jobs for Women* (1981); Jean Reith Schroedel, *Alone in a Crowd: Women in the Trades Tell Their Stories* (1985); Carroll W. Wilkinson, *Women in Nontraditional Occupations* (1991); Women's Enterprises of Boston, *Earning a Breadwinner's Wage: Nontraditional Jobs for Women on AFDC* (1978).

Training School for Women Organizers (1914)

Founded by the Women's Trade Union League with the cooperation of Northwestern University and the University of Chicago, this first full-time labor school in the United States was for many years the only one that combined academic work and practicums. The school trained union members in the skills necessary for trade union organization. When it closed in 1926, it had trained 44 women in 17 trades, 32 of whom became active union organizers.

See also Nestor, Agnes; Union Organizers; Unions; Women's Trade Union League; Workers' Education.

References Dorothy M. Brown, *Setting a Course: American Women in the 1920s* (1987); Joyce L. Kornbluh and Mary Frederickson, eds., *Sisterhood and Solidarity: Workers' Education for Women* (1984).

Training Wage

This term applies to a lower minimum wage paid to 16–19-year-olds in their first jobs.

See also Minimum Wage.

Transformational Leadership

Professor Judy B. Rosener of the University of California at Irvine applies this term to a female style of management that is interactive and relies on charisma, interpersonal skills, or personal contacts.

See also Managers.

Reference Paula Ries and Anne J. Stone, eds., *The American Woman, 1992–93: A Status Report* (1992).

Transient Workers

See Women Adrift.

Travelers' Aid

Founded in 1851 to furnish relief to poor immigrants and travelers passing through St. Louis to settle in the West, the organization had narrowed its goal by 1866 to the protection of young women moving to the cities to find work. Other organizations, notably the Young Women's Christian Association, joined in the effort. Working together these organizations in the Travelers' Aid movement set up referral services for housing and employment in city railroad stations and distributed similar information to rural clergy to be passed on to young women moving to the cities. Some organizations also provided women's hotels and transient homes. About 1900 Grace Hoadley Dodge led a drive to unify the Travelers' Aid organizations, and in 1917 the National Travelers' Aid Society was formed.

See also Prostitutes; Social Feminists; White Slavery; Young Women's Christian Association.

Reference Lynn Y. Weiner, *From Working Girl to Working Mother: The Female Labor Force in the United States, 1820–1980* (1985).

Triangle Shirtwaist Fire

In 1911 a fire in the ten-story Triangle Shirtwaist building in New York City killed 143 garment workers, mostly young immigrant women. Like many other garment industry factories, the building was a

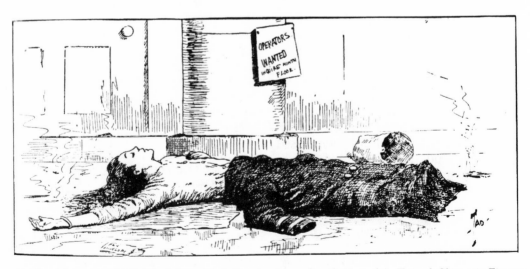

An editorial cartoon published in the New York Evening Journal *at the time of the Triangle Shirtwaist Fire was captioned, "This is one of a hundred—is anyone to be punished for this?"*

catastrophe waiting to happen, with doors locked to prevent the workers from wasting time and flammable materials scattered everywhere. Many of the women, with the flames at their backs or on their skirts, jumped to their deaths. This horror evoked public sympathy and support for industrial regulation.

See also Factory Workers; Uprising of the 20,000.

References Teresa Amott and Julie Matthaei, *Race, Gender, and Work: A Multicultural Economic History of Women in the United States* (1991); Theresa Serber Malkiel, *Diary of a Shirtwaist Striker* (1990); Leon Stein, *The Triangle Fire* (1962).

Troup, Augusta Lewis (1848–1920)

This union organizer and journalist began her career as a reporter for the *New York Sun* and as a freelance magazine writer. She learned typesetting and, in the course of her reporting for the *New York World*, met many artists and reformers. She resigned, apparently in protest against the *World*'s treatment of women typesetters, and then worked for small printing firms and reform periodicals that treated women workers fairly. In 1868 she cofounded the New York Working Women's Association and the Women's Typographical Union #1, over which she presided. Both groups experienced difficulties, the former because of internal policy disagreements, and the latter because of the opposition of employers and of male union leaders worried that women workers would threaten union pay scales. Nonetheless Lewis (later Troup) was elected to a one-year term as corresponding secretary of the International Typographical Union (ITU). Although in 1878 the Women's Typographical Union ceased functioning and the ITU voted not to charter any more women's locals, the ITU soon thereafter admitted women to membership in its other locals.

See also Journalists; Printers; Stevens, Alzina Parsons; Union Organizers; Unions; Working Women's Association.

Reference Edward T. James et al., eds., *Notable American Women III* (1971).

Turnbo-Malone, Annie Minerva (1869–1957)

This black entrepreneur, a native of Illinois educated in the public schools there, accumulated her fortune by manufacturing hair-care products and establishing a system of franchised agent-operators. Her talent in advertising and management helped her build the business she launched in 1900 to a national enterprise by 1910. But she lived modestly and devoted her profits to charities.

For Turnbo-Malone, husbands and business did not consort well. She divorced her first husband for attempting to interfere with her company. Aaron Malone, her second, sued for divorce in 1927, demanding half of her business; the out-of-court settlement left her in sole control.

She actively encouraged women in business, especially through her "Poro College," which taught her techniques. She personally supervised her recruits, encouraging them to invest in real estate. Worldwide she created jobs for some 75,000 women.

See also Entrepreneurs; Walker, Sarah Breedlove.

Reference Barbara Sicherman et al., eds., *Notable American Women: The Modern Period* (1980).

Two-Paycheck Couples

The rising number of women in the work force means that in the late twentieth century more and more couples are bringing home two paychecks—in 1988, about 25 million. About 18 percent of women in such couples earn more than their husbands.

See also Married Women's Employment; Wives.

References Susan McRae, *Cross-Class Families: A Study of Wives' Occupational Superiority* (1986); Alice Nakamura and Masso Nakamura, *Second Paycheck: An Analysis of the Employment and Earning of Wives Compared with Unmarried Women and Men* (1985); Felice N. Schwartz with Jean Zimmerman, *Breaking with Tradition: Women and Work, the New Facts of Life* (1992); Cynthia M. Taeuber, comp. and ed. *Statistical Handbook on Women in America* (1991).

UAW v. Johnson Controls (1991)
Johnson Controls, an auto battery manufacturer, barred fertile women employees from jobs with high lead exposure, which might damage a developing fetus, requiring women employees under 70 who wanted such (high-paying) jobs to produce medical proof of sterilization or infertility. The company imposed no such requirement on men employees. The U.S. Supreme Court ruled against the company.

See also Fetal Protection Policies; Health Hazards; Pregnancy Discrimination Act.

References Lin Nelson, "Women's Occupational Health and Workplace Politics," *Environmental Action* (1992); Randy Rabinowitz, *Is Your Job Making You Sick?: A CLUW Handbook on Workplace Hazards* (n.d.).

Underemployment
From 1970–1990 the proportion of the work force who could not work as many hours as they would have liked more than doubled. Paradoxically, underemployment and hours of overtime for employed wage-earners have risen together. The cost of benefits encourages employers to ask for more hours from fewer full-time workers and to use part-time workers, independent contractors, and consultants, to whom they need not pay benefits. The decline in manufacturing jobs and the proliferation of jobs in the service industries accelerate this trend.

See also Benefits; Contingent Work Force; Overtime; Part-Time Workers; Temporary Workers.

References Juliet B. Schor, *The Overworked American: The Unexpected Decline of Leisure* (1992); Pamela Wilson, ed. *Salaried and Professional Women: Relevant Statistics* (1992).

Unemployment
Economists debate whether without government intervention it is possible for the American system to produce enough jobs for full employment, or at least for a toler-ably low rate of unemployment. In the latter half of the twentieth century, the rate of unemployment even during periods of business expansion like those of 1969, 1973, 1979, and 1987 has crept steadily up, from 3.4 percent in 1969 to 6.7 percent in 1991.

See also Displaced Workers; Underemployment; Unemployment Insurance Program.

Unemployment Insurance Program
Until the New Deal, unemployed workers had to rely on whatever assistance they could extract from their labor union– or employer-sponsored benefit plans (both rare), their towns, charity, or their own resources. The federal Social Security Act of 1935 taxed employers to establish a fund on which the unemployed could draw to tide them over to the next job.

Like other parts of the Social Security Act, the Unemployment Insurance Program was devised primarily to meet the needs of male workers, in part because of the old myth that most women work only for pin money. Historically, as the program has been administered by the individual states, each state with its own regulations, it has fallen short of its aims, in that many jobless persons have not qualified for it. Women in particular have been underrepresented on its rolls. For one thing, they may have in-and-out work records, often occasioned by shifts in family needs. They may have worked in one of the "female" uncovered occupations. They may have difficulty in proving their availability for any "suitable" job, as when family responsibilities prevent them from leaving home at certain hours. They may be able to work only part-time, or to find only part-time jobs. They may have quit previous jobs "voluntarily" to relocate with their husbands or to care for an aged relative.

See also Aid to Families with Dependent Children; Benefits; New Deal; Old Age Insurance Program; Part-Time Workers; Pin Money; Social Security Act.

Reference Mimi Abramovitz, *Regulating the Lives of Women: Social Welfare Policy from Colonial Times to the Present* (1988).

Uniform Guidelines on Employee Selection Procedures (UGESP)

These guidelines have been developed by the Equal Employment Opportunity Commission, the Department of Justice, and the Department of Labor to clarify the federal position with regard to prohibiting discrimination in employment practices. They include a broad definition of affirmative action as well as procedures involved in affirmative action. The *Federal Register* gives the latest version of these guidelines.

See also Affirmative Action; Equal Employment Opportunity Commission.

Reference Kathanne W. Greene, *Affirmative Action and Principles of Justice* (1989).

Union Organizers

Until the Women's Trade Union League (WTUL) founded its School for Active Workers in the Labor Movement in 1914, unions hired few women as full-time, paid organizers. Before then almost all women organizers supported themselves by continuing to work in their own trade, giving of their time out of concern for their colleagues. Later, more and more women found it possible to become full-time organizers, many of them trained in WTUL schools.

See also Barnum, Gertrude; Barry, Leonora Marie Kearney; Bellanca, Dorothy Jacobs; Bloor, Ella Reeve; Christman, Elisabeth; Dickason, Gladys Marie; Huerta, Dolores; Jones, Mary Harris; McCreery, Maria Maud Leonard; Malkiel, Theresa Serber; Marot, Helen; Mason, Lucy Randolph; Moreno, Luisa; Nestor, Agnes; O'Sullivan, Mary Kenney; Parker, Julia Sarsfield O'Connor; Pesotta, Rose; Roberts, Lillian; Schneiderman, Rose; School for Active Workers in the Labor Movement; Sellins, Fannie Mooney; Smith, Charlotte; Stevens, Alzina Parsons; Taylor, Rebecca; Unions; Valesh, Eva Macdonald; Women's Trade Union League; Workers' Education; Younger, Maud.

Reference Philip S. Foner, *Women and the American Labor Movement* (1979 and 1982).

Unions

In labor or trade unions workers combine to better their wages and working conditions by collective bargaining, electing their own representatives to negotiate with their employers, with the strike as their ultimate sanction. They may be either craft unions, enrolling all the members skilled in a given craft, or industrial unions, combining all the workers in a given industry, whatever jobs they do.

Unions began to develop in the United States in the 1830s. The New Deal legislation of the 1930s, like that creating the National Labor Relations Board, strengthened unions, but the Taft-Hartley Act of 1947 and the Landrum-Griffin Act of 1959 restricted them. As in the later part of the twentieth century the United States economy has shifted toward services, union membership and power, historically concentrated in manufacturing and the trades, have declined.

Unions have often argued that women workers are difficult to organize. In support of this theory they have sometimes alleged that women do not see themselves as permanent members of the labor force. Feminists have feared that women's socialization against confrontation and for obedience to authority have ill prepared them for union activity. Even the Women's Trade Union League found organizing women workers so difficult that it eventually diverted most of its energies to protective legislation and education. Moreover, easily replaceable workers at the bottom of the labor hierarchy, in unskilled or deskilled "women's jobs," confront the greatest difficulty in unionizing. It's all too easy for an employer to do without them. And employers, eager to preserve the pool of cheap labor, have resorted to all sorts of ruses and concessions to divide women employees from their brothers and prevent them from unionizing.

History and the long record of women who have sustained their own strikes and aggressively supported men's strikes suggest, however, that a major deterrent to organizing women has been the reluctance of male union members to admit them, allow them to function as union officers in proportion to their numbers, and support their strikes or their rights. Union men fearful of losing their own jobs to women have accused activist women workers of "losing their femininity" and have struck to prevent women's hiring. Mixed-gender unions have as a rule called for equal pay for women only when women's low wages threatened male jobs.

Black women were excluded from union membership for many decades. Before the Civil War no black women were recruited into membership by any trade union or cooperative association of white women. After the Civil War the black washerwomen of Jackson, Mississippi, took collective action to raise their wages—a historic first.

Nonetheless women have joined in unions ever since the 1820s, almost as long as they have been in the workplace, and long before the United States legalized collective bargaining. Their participation increased after the Civil War, as women united in trade unions for better wages and conditions, appealing to the public to prevent price reductions and turning their organizations to self-help projects. But after the disintegration of the Knights of Labor that began in 1886, women unionists dropped off, so that by 1900 only about 2.2 percent of union members were women—at the very time when women's participation in the labor force was soaring. Even in 1920, at the end of the reforming Progressive Era, only 6.7 percent of women workers belonged to unions. The American Federation of Labor (AFL) and its affiliates,

despite random (and often grudging) efforts to organize women and noble disclaimers of gender discrimination, usually turned its back on women workers or actively sought to get rid of them altogether.

When the Congress of Industrial Organizations (CIO) split off from the AFL in the late 1930s, the CIO solicited and supported women workers. Its success spurred the AFL to a new interest in women. By 1940, 800,000 women were organized in unions, a tripling of the 1930 figure. By 1945, with the World War II increase in the female labor force, women's union memberships had soared to over three million, with some increase in union solicitude for women. By then both the AFL and the CIO advocated equal pay and federally assisted day-care centers and attacked the Equal Rights Amendment as destructive of protective legislation. At that point almost all AFL and CIO unions had integrated women; many unions worked closely with the Women's Bureau in negotiating for equal pay, seniority rights, and promotion; and women were beginning to get important posts in unions.

But male union members often lagged behind their leadership, resenting women workers and circumventing equal pay provisions. After World War II union interest in women's issues declined, despite the concern of national leaders. Even the International Ladies' Garment Workers' Union signed discriminatory contracts. But when the AFL and the CIO united in 1957, the situation for women workers improved. In the 1970s the AFL-CIO responded to increasing feminism among women wage earners and in society generally by strengthening its commitment to women, even endorsing the Equal Rights Amendment.

In the latter part of the twentieth century, with their rapid loss of male membership, unions have been courting those sections of the economy in which women workers are concentrated, and women have been responding affirmatively. In the mid-1980s unions or associations represented over 40 percent of the 7.7 million women workers in the public sector. Women teachers no longer refuse to consider strikes for fear of harming their students; the National Education Association (NEA) with its largely female membership is the biggest professional organization in the world and a powerful union, and the American Federation of Teachers vies with the NEA for women members. Women clerical workers, particularly in the public sector, no longer automatically identify their interests with those of their employers. A majority of women no longer consider themselves temporary workers. The Coalition of Labor Union Women and Nine to Five have encouraged women to unionize and unions to put women into leadership positions and negotiate on women's issues. At the same time men's unions, in their desperate search for new members to replace those they have lost, now seek out women, and women recruits outnumber men.

In 1990, 22 percent of male and 15 percent of female employees were unionized. Although proportions of union members in both the male and female labor forces dropped between 1983 and 1990, in actual numbers women union members increased by 300,000, so that in 1990 more than a third of all union members were women. Black women workers were leading the way, with 23 percent of them unionized, compared to only 14 percent of white women. Unions of public workers were growing faster than any others. And unionized women earned on average 30 percent more than non-unionized women. But unions still lagged in electing or appointing women to top posts: in 1990 Karen Ignagni and Peg Seminario became the second and third women to head departments of the AFL-CIO.

See also American Federation of Labor; American Federation of Teachers; Anderson, Mary; Bagley, Sarah G.; Barker, Mary Cornelia; Borchardt, Selma Munter; Cannery and Agricultural Workers Industrial Union; Clayton Anti-Trust Act; Clerical Workers; Closed Shop; Coalition of Labor Union Women; Cohn, Fannia Mary; Collective Bargaining; Collins, Jennie; Congress of Industrial Organizations; Criminal Conspiracy; Daughters of St. Crispin; Edson, Katherine Philips; Equal Rights Amendment; Evans, Elizabeth Gardiner Glendower; Female Society of Lynn and Vicinity for the Protection and Promotion of Female Industry; Flynn, Elizabeth Gurley; Gillespie, Mabel Edna; Haley, Margaret Angela; Hawes, Elizabeth; Henrotin, Ellen Martin; Henry, Alice; Herrick, Elinore Morehouse; Huerta, Dolores; Hutchins, Grace; Ickes, Anna Wilmarth Thompson; Injunction; Industrial Workers of the World; Injunction;International Ladies' Garment Workers' Union; Jarrell, Helen Ira; Jones, Mary Harris; Kehew, Mary Morton Kimball; Kelley, Florence; Kellor, Frances; Kennedy, Kate; Knights of Labor; La Mujer Obrera; Ladies Industry Association; Lowell Girls; McDowell, Mary Eliza; McLaren, Louise Leonard; Marot, Helen; Miller, Frieda Segekle; Nathan, Maud; National Education Association; National Labor Union; Nestor , Agnes ; New Deal ; New England Workingmen's Association; Nine to Five; Norris-LaGuardia Act; Norton, Mary Teresa Hopkins; O'Reilly, Leonora; O'Sullivan, Mary Kenney; Parker, Julia Sarsfield O'Connor; Perkins, Frances; Pesotta, Rose; Progressive Era; Protective Legislation; Robins, Margaret Dreier; Rodgers, Elizabeth Flynn; Schneiderman, Rose; Shop Stewards; Simms, Daisy Florence; Stevens, Alzina Parsons; Strikes; Swartz, Maud O'Farrell; Taft-Hartley Act; Taylor, Rebecca; Teachers; Telephone Operators' Department of the International Brotherhood of Electrical Workers; Temporary Workers; Thorne, Florence Calvert; Troup, Augusta Lewis; Union Organizers; United Auto Workers' (UAW) Women's Department; United Farm Workers; United Office and Professional Workers of America; United Tailoresses Society of New York; Uprising of the 20,000; Van Kleeck, Mary Abby; Vorse, Mary Heaton; Ward, Hortense Sparks Malsch; Woerishoffer, Emma Carola; Wolfson, Theresa; Women's Bureau; Women's Protection Union; Women's Trade Union League; Younger, Maud.

References Mary H. Blewett, *Men, Women, and Work: Class, Gender, and Protest in the New England Shoe Industry, 1780–1910* (1988); Judith Freeman Clark, *Almanac of American Women in the 20th Century* (1987); Dorothy Sue Cobble, *Dishing It Out: Waitresses and Their Unions in the Twentieth Century* (1991); Cynthia B. Costello, *"We're Worth It!": Women and Collective Action in the Insurance Workplace* (1991); Nancy Shrom Dye, *As Equals and as Sisters: Feminism, Unionism, and the Women's Trade Union League of New York* (1980); Sarah Eisenstein, *Give Us Bread but Give Us Roses: Working Women's Consciousness in the United States, 1890 to the First World War* (1983); Philip S. Foner, *Women and the American Labor Movement* (1979,

1982); James J. Kenneally, "Women in the United States and Trade Unionism," in Norbert C. Soldon, ed., *The World of Women's Trade Unionism* (1985); Ruth Milkman, ed., *Women, Work and Protest: A Century of U.S. Women's Labor History* (1985); Marjorie Murphy, *Blackboard Unions: The AFT and the NEA, 1900–1980* (1990); Judith O'Sullivan and Rosemary Gallick, *Workers and Allies: Female Participation in the American Trade Union Movement, 1824–1976* (n.d.); Paula Ries and Anne J. Stone, eds., *The American Woman, 1992–93: A Status Report* (1992); Meredith Tax, *The Rising of the Women: Feminist Solidarity and Class Conflict, 1880–1917* (1980).

United Auto Workers' (UAW) Women's Department

After the Flint auto workers' strike, the UAW established its Women's Department in 1937; it has built a good record of service. The UAW was the first major union to reject protective legislation for women. In 1970 it announced its support for the right to abortion, day-care centers, and the Equal Rights Amendment.

See also Equal Rights Amendment; Flint Auto Workers' Strike; Protective Legislation.

References Carol Groneman and Mary Beth Norton, eds., *"To Toil the Livelong Day": America's Women at Work, 1780–1980*; Gerda Lerner, ed., *The Female Experience: An American Documentary* (1977); Ruth Milkman, ed., *Women, Work and Protest* (1985); Angela Howard Zophy and Frances M. Kavenik, eds., *Handbook of American Women's History* (1990).

United Farm Workers (UFW)

In the mid-1960s this organization emerged from the amalgamation of already existing labor groups. Under the leadership of Cesar Chavez, La Causa, a union of low-paid, unskilled women and men workers—many of them black, Hispanic American, and Asian American— has attracted an almost religious devotion. Employing such devices as the pilgrimage and the consumer boycott, in 1966 the UFW and Schenley Industries negotiated the first contract that farmworkers ever had. Successive contracts with other growers followed. The UFW has sup-

ported its members with social services, fighting for health and safety measures, substituting union hiring halls for the exploitative system of labor contractors, opposing heavy use of child labor, and advocating social equality for all poor and working people, regardless of race or gender. By such means it has maintained its membership and held to its image as a grassroots movement.

Women have earned important places in La Causa by their dedication and efficiency: Dolores Huerta as its first elected vice-president, Jessie Lopez de la Cruz as the first woman to organize workers in the field, Marie Sabadado as director of its medical plan, and Helen Chavez as head of its credit union.

See also Boycotts; De la Cruz, Jessie Lopez; Huerta, Dolores; Migrant Laborers; Unions.

References Ellen Cantarow, with Susan Gushee O'Malley and Sharon Hartman Strom, *Moving the Mountain: Women Working for Social Change* (1980); Tricia Knoll, *Becoming Americans: Asian Sojourners, Immigrants, and Refugees in the Western United States* (1982); Angela Howard Zophy and Frances M. Kavenik, eds., *Handbook of American Women's History* (1990).

United Office and Professional Workers of America (UOPWA)

This leftist organization, established in 1937, was a relatively early attempt to organize clerical workers. The Great Depression had lowered wages and worsened working conditions for clerical workers. Briefly, UOPWA strikes succeeded, but in 1950 the Congress of Industrial Organizations expelled the office workers' union, which soon ceased to exist.

See also Clerical Workers; Congress of Industrial Organizations.

Reference Ruth Milkman, ed., *Women, Work and Protest* (1985).

United States Employment Service (USES)

This agency, founded in 1919, helps states to establish and maintain a system of local public employment offices, responsible for providing job seekers with job placement and other employment services and for providing employers with recruitment services. It offers job seekers guidance, counseling, and testing referral. USES also administers the Work Incentive Program (WIN) for persons receiving Aid to Families with Dependent Children.

See also Aid to Families with Dependent Children; Bureau of Vocational Information; Employment Agencies.

Reference Leonard P. Adam, *The Public Employment Service in Transition, 1933–1968: Evolution of a Placement Service into a Manpower Agency* (1969).

United Tailoresses Society of New York

The members of this organization, founded in 1825, were among the first American white women workers to strike independently. In 1831 they struck for five weeks, demanding higher wages. The strike failed and the organization dissolved.

See also Strikes; Unions.

Uprising of the 20,000 (1909)

The low wages, filthy working conditions, long hours, and economic harassment (fines and charges for needles, seats, and electricity) inflicted on women in the garment trades about the turn of the century finally drove them to strike. In an energizing speech Clara Lemlich overcame the apathy of male union leaders with a call to the workers to strike, taking the Jewish oath, "If I turn traitor to the cause I now pledge, may this hand wither from the arm I now raise." Twenty thousand of them, mostly Jewish women, joined by Jewish men, Italian women, and native-born American women, walked out; within a week 30,000 had struck. With the efficient support of the Women's Trade Union League and other allies and the high physical and moral courage of the strikers, they held out against police brutality and outrageous court judgments, and the strike spread to Philadelphia.

Although the strikers won agreements from many of the smaller employers early on, they failed to get recognition or contracts from such large employers as the Triangle Shirtwaist Company. The strikes did, however, raise union membership, particularly that of the International Ladies' Garment Workers' Union.

See also International Ladies' Garment Workers' Union; Marot, Helen; Perkins, Frances; Schneiderman, Rose; Strikes; Triangle Shirtwaist Fire; Unions; Woerishoffer, Emma Carola; Women's Trade Union League.

References Charles Bernheimer, *The Shirtwaist Strike* (1910); Dorothy Schneider and Carl J. Schneider, *Women in the Progressive Era* (1993).

Urban Institute Program of Policy Research on Women and Families

The institute researches and publishes reports on women's issues, including pay equity.

See also Pay Equity.

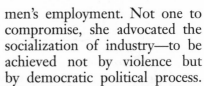

Valesh, Eva MacDonald (n.d.)

Valesh, commissioned an organizer in the American Federation of Labor (AFL) in 1900, unionized women in the Bureau of Engraving and Printing. For ten years she edited the AFL journal but resigned when the organization refused to put her name on the masthead. She warned male union officials that only by treating women workers as allies, rather than a source of danger, could they win higher wages or shorter hours.

See also American Federation of Labor; Family Wage; Unions.

Reference James J. Kenneally, "Women in the United States and Trade Unionism," in Norbert C. Soldon, ed., *The World of Women's Trade Unionism* (1985).

Van Kleeck, Mary Abby (1883–1972)

This social reformer began her career with research on New York City factory women and tenement child labor for the College Settlements Association and the Russell Sage Foundation. Her work led the foundation to establish a research department of industrial studies in 1910; she directed the department (except for war service in 1918–1919) until 1948. As an expert on women's employment, in World War I she undertook the direction of the women's branch of the army's Ordnance Department, where she drafted standards for the employment of women in war industries. Near war's end she accepted an appointment as director of the Department of Labor's new Women in Industry Service, the forerunner of the Women's Bureau.

Back at Russell Sage, van Kleeck broadened the work of her department, particularly on experiments in employer-employee relations, unemployment statistics, and the causes of worker dissatisfaction, with special regard to wo-men's employment. Not one to compromise, she advocated the socialization of industry—to be achieved not by violence but by democratic political process. From 1928–1948 she involved herself extensively in international affairs, with special interest in the Soviet Union.

See also Unemployment; Women's Bureau; World War I.

Reference Barbara Sicherman et al., eds., *Notable American Women: The Modern Period* (1980).

Van Vorst, Marie Louise (1867–1936)

This writer and reformer collaborated at the beginning of the twentieth century with her widowed sister-in-law Bessie Van Vorst on a landmark book on the plight of women laborers, *The Woman Who Toils: Being the Experiences of Two Ladies as Factory Girls*. The authors based it on their experiences in several factories, where they dressed, worked, and lived as workers.

Reference Edward T. James et al., eds., *Notable American Women III* (1971).

Velvet Ghettos

As women move in significant numbers into nontraditional occupations, breaking the barriers of occupational segregation, resegregation may occur, confining women to "velvet ghettos" in jobs attractive and well-paid compared to those held by most women, but of lower status, power, and compensation than those dominated by their male colleagues.

See also Gender Gap; Glass Ceiling; Nontraditional Occupations; Occupational Segregation; Sticky Floor.

Reference Carolyn G. Cline, *The Velvet Ghetto* (1986).

Veterans' Preference

Former military personnel are given preferential treatment in applications for civil service jobs with the federal government and most state governments. Typically this amounts to the addition of five to ten points to the veteran's score on a civil service exam. This preferential system has been criticized as discriminating against women because of the smaller numbers of women veterans. In *Personnel Administrator of Massachusetts v. Feeney* (1979) the U.S. Supreme Court agreed that veterans' preference generally had an unintended adverse impact on women; nonetheless it upheld the Massachusetts law because its purpose was not to discriminate but to prefer veterans regardless of gender.

See also Military Women.

References Susan Gluck Mezey, *In Pursuit of Equality: Women, Public Policy and the Federal Courts* (1992); Susan Deller Ross and Ann Barcher, *The Rights of Women* (1984).

Video Display Terminals
See Health Hazards.

Vinson v. Meritor Savings Bank (1986)
See Meritor Savings Bank v. Vinson.

Vocational Education
The workplace has historically excluded women from high-paying "men's jobs" by denying them the necessary training or apprenticeships, an obstacle that survives today in industries like construction and services like firefighting. In the past the argument loomed that women entered the labor force too briefly to justify the training; moreover, any kind of education might keep women from marrying. Advocates of vocational education for women in the Progressive Era weaseled: vocational education would make them better wives, mothers, household managers, and—most important of all—consumers. It might also provide a form of insurance for those among them who would be widowed, deserted, or childless. And, in an effort to reassure men that women would not threaten their jobs, programs of vocational education emphasized traditional "women's jobs."

In consideration of the growth in women's employment and the economic differences between male and female workers, Congress amended the Vocational Education Act in 1976 to eliminate sex discrimination and sex stereotyping in federally assisted vocational education programs. The objective was to give women in low-paying, dead-end jobs access to training programs that would prepare them for entry into the work force and narrow the gender gap.

Community colleges, state vocational technical high schools, state technical colleges, and community organizations offer adult education courses that may help women improve their chances for employment or entry into apprenticeship programs.

See also Apprentices; Gender Gap; Manhattan Trade School for Girls; *Occupational Outlook Handbook*; Progressive Era; Sex Discrimination; Smith Vocational Education Act; Woolman, Mary Raphael Schenck.

References Barbara A. Burnett, ed., *Every Woman's Legal Guide* (1983); Connecticut Permanent Commission on the Status of Women, *Women in Apprenticeships: Steps to Building a Career* (1989).

Vocational Guidance
The vocational guidance movement of the late nineteenth and early twentieth centuries was propelled by reformers who wanted to help workers find jobs for which they were suited, rather than assigning them on the basis of their family connections, race, sex, or appearance. Settlement house workers wanted to help the working poor by providing vocational education and employment counseling. Educators wanted to expand high school offerings to keep children in school longer. Feminists wanted to develop occupations for women, a desire that they implemented in part by starting employment agencies like the Bureau of Vocational Information.

See also Apprentices; Bureau of Vocational Information; Employment Agencies; Follett, Mary Parker; *Occupational Outlook Handbook*; Scientific Management; Settlement Houses; Vocational Education.

Reference Sharon Hartman Strom, *Beyond the Typewriter: Gender, Class, and the Origins of Modern American Office Work, 1900–1930* (1992).

Vorse, Mary Heaton (1874–1966)

This writer and champion of labor grew up privileged, usually spending her summers in Massachusetts and winters in Europe, where she was educated. In 1898 she married Albert White Vorse, explorer and writer, and subsequently bore two children. In 1907 the Vorses bought a house in Provincetown, where she was to become a central figure in the colony of artists and writers she attracted there and in the Provincetown Players, a group she helped to found.

Vorse published her first book in 1908. When her husband died in 1910, she began to write to support herself, often writing about children. Her observations of the miserable lives of workers' children led to her involvement in the Bread and Roses Strike of 1912, where she worked with Elizabeth Gurley Flynn. In 1912 she married the radical journalist Joseph O'Brien, with whom she had another son. This second husband died in 1915. Vorse married again in 1920, this time a radical cartoonist, Robert Minor, whom she divorced in 1922.

Meanwhile Vorse built a career as a journalist, reporting on the 1915 International Congress of Women at The Hague and the aftermath of World War I, particularly in Russia. She reported on all the great labor struggles from 1912 through the Chrysler Strike of 1950, publishing books and articles. In 1937 she was wounded in the steel strike in Muncie, Indiana, and again soon thereafter on a women's picket line in Youngstown. But Vorse believed that to be pro-labor was not necessarily to be blindly pro-union, in 1952 denouncing the corrupt longshoremen's union and applauding a series of wildcat strikes.

In her old age Vorse continued to write, turning more often to fiction and humor. This prolific woman lived in many worlds—literary, theatrical, radical, and labor.

See also Bread and Roses Strike; Flynn, Elizabeth Gurley; Journalists; Strikes; Theater; Union Organizers; Unions; World War I; Writers and Publishers.

References Dee Garrison, *Mary Heaton Vorse: The Life of an American Insurgent* (1989); Barbara Sicherman et al., eds., *Notable American Women: The Modern Period* (1980).

Wage Discrimination

The difference in earnings between groups that is unaccounted for by the differences in such attributes as job experience, education, performance, and tenure with employer constitutes wage discrimination. In other words, wage discrimination is a contributory cause of the gender gap.

See also Comparable Worth; Equal Pay Act; Fair Labor Standards Act; Gender Gap.

References Claudia Goldin, *Understanding the Gender Gap: An Economic History of American Women* (1990); Karen J. Maschke, *Litigation, Courts, and Women Workers* (1989).

Wage Laws

See Protective Legislation.

Wagner Act

Popularly known as the Wagner Act, the National Labor Relations Act of 1935 (NLRA) was an important piece of President Franklin Roosevelt's New Deal and the cornerstone of all subsequent labor legislation. Excluding domestic servants and farm workers, the Wagner Act affirmed labor's right to organize and bargain collectively; it required private employers to deal with unions and prohibited discrimination against union members. Responsibility for administration of the act is vested in the National Labor Relations Board (NLRB), which has the power to determine proper bargaining units, to adjudicate disputes between employers and employees, and to prosecute unfair labor practices cases.

See also Domestic Servants; Herrick, Elinore Morehouse; Labor Legislation; New Deal; Norris-LaGuardia Act; Taft-Hartley Act; Unions.

References Ellen Cantarow with Susan Gushee O'Malley and Sharon Hartman Strom, *Moving the Mountain: Women Working for Social Change* (1980); Robert E. Doherty, *Industrial and Labor Relations Terms* (1989); Michael Evan Gold, *An Introduction to Labor Law* (1989).

Waitresses

See Food Services; Harvey Girls.

Wald, Lillian (1867–1940)

This nurse, settlement house leader, and social reformer not only thought creatively and acted on her ideas but persuaded others to support and implement them. In 1893, as a graduate nurse enrolled in the Woman's Medical College in New York, she agreed to organize home nursing classes for immigrant families. This experience led her to establish the Henry Street Visiting Nurses Service, which by 1913 employed 92 nurses in the first public health nursing service. She originated the first school nursing program by lending the services of Henry Street's Lina L. Rogers to the New York City Board of Health. She introduced industrial nursing by suggesting a nursing program for their industrial policyholders to the Metropolitan Life Insurance Company. At her instance the American Red Cross set up the Town and Country Nursing Service. In 1904 with Florence Kelley and others she founded the National Child Labor Committee as part of a continuing effort to outlaw child labor. In 1905 she proposed a Children's Bureau to Theodore Roosevelt, a suggestion that resulted in its establishment in the Department of Labor in 1912.

See also Kelley, Florence; Nurses; Settlement Houses.

References Doris G. Daniels, *Always a Sister: The Feminism of Lillian D. Wald* (1990); R. L. Duffus, *Lillian Wald, Neighbor and Crusader* (1938); Edward T. James et al., eds., *Notable American Women III* (1971); Jennifer S. Uglow, comp. and ed., *International Dictionary of Women's Biography* (1985).

Walker, Mary Edwards (1832–1919)

This physician, a native of upstate New York, graduated from Syracuse Medical

College in 1855. With her husband Albert Walker, whom she married that year, she practiced medicine for several years, but she divorced him in 1869. During the Civil War, she volunteered and eventually with much effort was commissioned an assistant surgeon. Despite many a contretemps with her superiors, colleagues, and patients, she won a decoration for her war work. She devoted much of her life to dress reform, adopting bloomers in the 1850s, men's uniforms during the war, and men's civilian dress in her later life.

See also Civil War; Physicians.

References Edward T. James et al., eds., *Notable American Women III* (1971); Jennifer S. Uglow, comp. and ed., *International Dictionary of Women's Biography* (1985).

Walker, Sarah Breedlove McWilliams (1867–1919)

This black entrepreneur made a million dollars from her beauty products business. A native of Louisiana, she married at 14. When her husband died in 1887, she took in washing to support her daughter A'Lelia and herself. In 1905 she concocted a formula to treat the hair of black women and changed the direction of her life, moving to Denver, marrying newspaperman Charles J. Walker, peddling her discovery door-to-door, and recruiting agent-operators, whom she taught her method of treating hair. A year later with her headquarters established in Denver she began to travel throughout the South and East, lecturing and demonstrating. The Madame C. J. Walker Manufacturing Company employed some 3,000 people in its heyday and inspired many imitators. Before the days of beauty salons, her "Walker Agents" gave home hair treatments.

Walker not only contributed generously to charities herself but also encouraged her agents in philanthropic work.

See also Entrepreneurs; Turnbo-Malone, Annie Minerva.

References A'Lelia Perry Bundles, *Madam C. J. Walker* (1991); Edward T. James et al., eds., *Notable American Women III* (1971); Jennifer S.

Uglow, comp. and ed., *International Dictionary of Women's Biography* (1985).

Walters, Barbara (b. 1929)

A television star, Barbara Walters is known best for her interviews with famous people and for her 1976 record-breaking $1 million per year contract with ABC-TV to coanchor the evening news with Harry Reasoner. Born in Boston, raised in Florida and New York City, Walters completed her education at Sarah Lawrence College. From the mid-1950s she worked in television, booking interviews and assuming increasing responsibility, seizing opportunities to appear before the camera. In 1964 she began to appear regularly on the National Broadcasting Company's *Today* show. In 1971 she became its coanchor—the first woman network anchor. Ambitious, hard-working, and skillful at building her career, she also got her own show, "Not for Women Only." In 1976 she moved to the American Broadcasting Company, at a much-touted annual salary of $1 million. Walters commented that it was a lot of money, but not as much as that of her male colleagues. In her subsequent career, she has moved away from reporting toward television specials and interviews.

Walters has married three times and has an adopted daughter. She is known for her hard work, her skill in booking interviewees, and her careful preparation for interviews.

See also Journalists.

References Jennifer S. Uglow, comp. and ed., *International Dictionary of Women's Biography* (1985); Jerry Oppenheimer, *Barbara Walters: An Unauthorized Biography* (1990).

Waltham System

This system tightly regulated young women who worked in the mills of Waltham, Massachusetts, in the early nineteenth century. Employers prescribed not only their working but also their living conditions: they must live in factory lodgings and attend church. They were fired for immoral conduct, bad language, disrespect, attending dance classes, or any other cause at which their overseers took umbrage.

See also Factory Workers; Harvey Girls; Lowell Girls; Mercer Girls.

References Teresa Amott and Julie Matthaei, *Race, Gender, and Work: A Multicultural Economic History of Women in the United States* (1991); Lynn Y. Weiner, *From Working Girl to Working Mother: The Female Labor Force in the United States, 1820–1980* (1985).

Ward, Hortense Sparks Malsch (1872–1944)

In 1912 this Texas attorney and reformer campaigned for a married woman's property act. She wrote and successfully lobbied for a Texas bill on this score and fought for workmen's compensation, a 54-hour week for women in industry, a woman's division in the state department of labor, and the right of married women to serve as officers of corporations.

See also Attorneys; Married Women's Property Acts.

Reference Edward T. James et al., eds., *Notable American Women III* (1971).

Warren, Mercy Otis (1728–1814)

Warren was a political writer, dramatist, poet, and historian of the American Revolution.

References Marianne B. Geiger, "Mercy Otis Warren," in G. J. Barker-Benfield and Catherine Clinton, *Portraits of American Women* I (1991); Linda Kerber, *Women of the Republic: Intellect and Ideology in Revolutionary America* (1980).

Washerwoman's Strike (1881)

In 1880 black laundresses organized within their church. The next year 3,000 of them went on strike for higher wages. Authorities used arrests, fines, license fees, and higher rents to break the strike, which lasted for several weeks.

See also Collar Laundry Union of Troy, New York; El Paso Laundry Workers' Union Strike; Strikes.

Reference Philip S. Foner, *Women and the American Labor Movement* (1979).

Welfare Secretaries

See Human Resources Managers; Welfare Work.

Welfare Work

In the nineteenth century some employers provided such services for employees as bathhouses, company housing, company stores, libraries, and lunchrooms. Late in the century employers added such programs as savings, loan, and insurance plans; medical departments; and recreational activities. Companies with a large proportion of women employees often instituted highly paternalistic programs.

Sometimes companies with welfare programs employed women as "welfare secretaries"; as early as 1904 the Young Women's Christian Association offered courses for welfare secretaries—forerunners of human resources managers.

See also Benefits; Harvey Girls; Human Resources Managers; Lowell Girls; Mercer Girls; Waltham System; Young Women's Christian Association.

Wells-Barnett, Ida Bell (1862–1931)

This black journalist and lecturer investigated and denounced lynchings throughout her life. A Mississippi-born daughter of slaves, she was educated at a freedmen's high school and industrial school. At 14, upon her parents' death, she assumed responsibility for her siblings, teaching and continuing her own education at Fisk University. Still in her teens, she sued the Chesapeake and Ohio Railroad for relegating her to a segregated car. Her criticism of the inadequate black schools cost her job. Thereupon she bought a part interest in the *Memphis Free Speech* and turned to journalism.

In 1892 she used its pages to analyze the cause of the lynching of three of her friends: not chivalry toward white women, she said, but economic competition prompted it. She urged Memphis blacks to leave the city for the West. While she was on a trip to the North a white mob destroyed her newspaper offices. Wells then undertook a lecture tour, founding antilynching societies and black women's clubs as she went.

In 1895 Wells married black attorney Ferdinand Lee Barnett; they had four children. In her new home in Chicago she organized and presided over a black women's club and founded the Negro Fellowship League for black men recently arrived from the South, maintaining a social center, reading rooms, dormitory, and employment agency for them. From 1913 to 1916 she served as probation officer for the Chicago municipal court. She also worked with white women in the suffrage and women's movements. With Jane Addams she blocked the segregation of the Chicago school system.

Over the years she investigated lynchings and other forms of mob violence against blacks, speaking out when no one else dared.

See also Journalists.

References Edward T. James et al., eds., *Notable American Women III* (1971); Jennifer S. Uglow, comp. and ed., *International Dictionary of Women's Biography* (1985); Ida B. Wells, *Crusade for Justice* (1970).

West Coast Hotel Co. v. Parrish (1937)

In this landmark case the U.S. Supreme Court upheld the constitutionality of a state of Washington minimum wage law, rejecting a freedom of contract defense. The court thus reversed its decision in *Adkins v. Children's Hospital* and laid the basis for subsequent decisions sustaining such labor legislation as the Fair Labor Standards Act.

See also Adkins v. Children's Hospital; Fair Labor Standards Act; Minimum Wage; *Muller v. Oregon;* Protective Legislation.

Reference Alice Kessler-Harris, *A Woman's Wage* (1990).

Wheeler, Candace Thurber (1827–1923)

This pioneer in American textile design and interior decoration, with a wide acquaintance among artists, started the Society of Decorative Art of New York City in 1877 to provide an outlet for women's handicrafts. The next year Wheeler cofounded the Woman's Ex-

change to market all kinds of articles produced by women. After a period of working with Louis Comfort Tiffany in an interior decorating firm, Wheeler established her own all-woman Associated Artists in 1883 to design fabrics. She served on the advisory council of the Woman's Art School of Cooper Union, lectured at the New York Institute for Artist-Artisans, and directed the exhibit of women's work in the applied arts at the Chicago World's Columbian Exposition of 1893. Wheeler opened doors for women in American design, textiles, and interior decoration.

See also Artists; Cooper Union; Entrepreneurs.

References Edward T. James et al., eds., *Notable American Women III* (1971); Madeleine B. Stern, *We the Women* (1962); Jennifer S. Uglow, comp. and ed., *International Dictionary of Women's Biography* (1985).

Wheelock, Lucy (1857–1946)

Wheelock specialized in kindergarten education. After ten years of teaching kindergarten, she took charge of the new training course for kindergarten teachers at Chauncy Hall in Boston. By then a leader in the nationwide kindergarten movement, she established Wheelock College in 1896.

See also Academic Women; Teachers.

Whistle-Blowing

When an employee perceives her employer's demands, policies, or practices as wrong, she confronts an ethical and moral dilemma: is it her responsibility to speak out, even if she may consequently lose her job? The cost exacted may be high. Employees who report violations of laws or dangers to public health and safety to those in authority are known as whistle-blowers. Under the "at-will employment" doctrine the whistle-blower would be vulnerable to retaliatory dismissal. Limitations on employers' freedom to discipline and discharge whistle-blowers have been enacted by Congress and most states since the Civil Rights Act of 1964, but the terms and scope of the protection afforded by this legislation vary from one jurisdiction to another. At the federal level, for example, an employee who reports a dangerous situation on the work site to the Occupational Safety and Health Administration (OSHA) and requests an inspection is legally entitled to protection; similarly, most federal environmental protection statutes try to provide safeguards for whistle-blowers.

In 1970 in the course of her work as a chemist for Polaroid, African-American Caroline Hunter discovered that the company was making identification passes for use in South Africa and organized a protest, challenging her, own employer. Polaroid retaliated by firing her, and Hunter alleged that they also harassed her and her family.

Teresa Fischette was luckier. She fought Continental Airlines for her right not to wear makeup and lost her job. But when she went public, the airline rehired her.

In 1985 research scientist Margot O'Toole blew the whistle on the Massachusetts Institute of Technology when she could not duplicate results of experiments conducted by the head of her laboratory and could not persuade him to retract. O'Toole suffered professional isolation, negative recommendations, and accusations of mental instability for five years before she was vindicated and the paper was retracted. (*Radcliffe News*, Winter 1993)

When the safeguards provided by law fail to satisfy or are ineffective, employees may seek redress by going public, telling their story to the media and hoping that public opinion will compel remedial action by employers and/or the relevant government agency.

See also Academic Women; At-Will Employment; Civil Rights; Civil Rights Act of 1964; Just Cause.

Reference Wayne N. Outten with Noah A. Kinigstein, *The Rights of Employees* (1983).

White-Collar Workers

This term designates salaried managerial, professional, and technical workers whose work does not usually involve manual labor and who are often expected to dress with some degree of formality.

See also Blue-Collar Workers; Dress for Success; Pink-Collar Workers.

White House Conference on Children (1909)

This landmark conference officially asserted that children are entitled to good homes and that government must provide the money for them when the parent(s) cannot. Society, President Theodore Roosevelt said at the conference, has an interest in ensuring the welfare of children, so that they can become productive and enlightened citizens. But, officials made clear, government would aid only the children of "worthy" parents—a category that in practice often excluded working mothers.

See also Aid to Families with Dependent Children; Mothers' Pensions.

Reference Mimi Abramovitz, *Regulating the Lives of Women: Social Welfare Policy from Colonial Times to the Present* (1988).

White House Conference on the Emergency Needs of Women (1933)

This conference acknowledged governmental neglect of the problems of the 4,000,000 unemployed women of the Great Depression.

See also Great Depression; New Deal; President's Commission on the Status of Women.

Reference Mimi Abramovitz, *Regulating the Lives of Women: Social Welfare Policy from Colonial Times to the Present* (1988).

White Rose Mission

This institution was founded by Victoria Earle Matthews in 1897 in New York City as the White Rose Industrial Association. It worked effectively to protect black women domestics from exploitation, particularly by rogue employment agencies and white slavers. This protection was necessitated by the many unscrupulous people who preyed on the women trying to escape the economic desperation in the South in the Great Migration of the late nineteenth and early twentieth centuries. The association opened a home for new arrivals in the North, training them in domestic skills, and stationed agents to meet them at the piers in Norfolk, Virginia, and New York. Gradually the mission also assumed the characteristics of a settlement house.

See also Employment Agencies; Matthews, Victoria Earle; Settlement Houses; White Slavery.

Reference Mimi Abramovitz, *Regulating the Lives of Women: Social Welfare Policy from Colonial Times to the Present* (1988).

White Slavery

In the nineteenth and early twentieth centuries this term denoted the practice of seducing or forcing women into prostitution and keeping them there against their wills. Although its proportions were exaggerated, the practice did exist on an international scale. Poor Chinese families sometimes sold their daughters to rings who imported them into the United States, where the tongs (Chinese secret societies) saw to it that the women could not escape. Women in middle Europe on their way to the United States might find themselves inadvertently lodging in a house of ill repute.

Native-born white American women feared white slavery out of proportion to the threat it offered them. Most at risk were recent immigrants with no knowledge of English and black women traveling north in hopes of economic opportunity. Pimps offered them help on trains or paid their fare in return for the promise of purportedly respectable work. Lodging house owners betrayed them. Employment agencies deceived them about the kind of work they were accepting.

Social agencies and reformers, particularly women's groups, responded with vigorous efforts to prevent enslavement and to rescue the victims. For a time Travelers' Aid focused on protecting single women moving to the cities to find work. The Young Women's Christian Association supplied information about decent jobs and lodgings. Black organizations provided advice and respectable lodgings for the northward hegira. Jewish women employed a worker on Ellis Island to help women traveling alone. Chicago settlement house workers got lists of immigrant women taking trains from New York and met them at the Chicago station.

Economic motivation nonetheless always operated far more powerfully than human conspiracy in inviting or driving women into prostitution. For many women, despite its danger, degradation, and short life expectancy, prostitution simply represented the best job they could get.

See also Employment Agencies; Mann Act; Prostitutes; Travelers' Aid; White Rose Mission; Young Women's Christian Association.

References Edward J. Bristow, *Prostitution and Prejudice: The Jewish Fight against White Slavery 1870–1939* (1983); Frederick K. Grittner, *White Slavery: Myth, Ideology, and American Law* (1990); Ruth Rosen, *The Lost Sisterhood: Prostitution in America, 1919–1981* (1982).

Wider Opportunities for Women (WOW)

Founded in 1964, this organization tries to expand women's employment. It offers information, training, and advocacy; sponsors a nationwide Women's Work Force Network of 350 women's employment programs and advocates; evaluates and advises on policies affecting working women; assists women's employment programs; and supports the National Commission on Working Women, which concerns itself particularly with women in low-paying, low-status jobs.

Wildcat Strikes

See Strikes.

Willard, Emma Hart (1787–1870)

This educator's politically liberal father widened her horizons and encouraged her to think of other roles for women than that of farm wife. In 1802 at 15 she enrolled in the Berlin (Connecticut) Academy; two years later she began to teach, while also attending classes in Hartford.

In 1809 she married Dr. John Willard, a supporter of women's education; she bore him one child and mothered four others from his two earlier marriages. When financial need pressed him in 1814, she opened the Middlebury Female Seminary in their Vermont home. When Middlebury College refused to admit her, she taught herself to keep ahead of her students and to prove that women could learn the same materials as men.

This venture emboldened her to press for a state-aided school for girls in New York in 1819; her brief for it, *An Address to the Public: Particularly to the Members of the Legislature of New-York, Proposing a Plan for Improving Female Education*, did not affect the legislature, but attracted the attention of James Monroe, John Adams, and Thomas Jefferson. And in 1821, five years before the first public high schools for girls opened in New York and Boston, she opened the Troy (New York) Female Seminary, partially funded by a city tax. There she held to high standards, instituting science courses more rigorous than those at many men's colleges, but she also believed in instructing girls in household management and child rearing. Her students, many of whom became teachers, spread her influence nationwide.

After her retirement from the seminary in 1838, despite a disastrous second marriage that ended in a divorce granted by the legislature, Willard worked at improving the common schools and helping to form educational societies.

See also Academic Women.
References Edward T. James et al., eds., *Notable American Women III* (1971); Alma Lutz, *Emma Willard: Pioneer Educator of American Women* (1984); Jennifer S. Uglow, comp. and ed., *International Dictionary of Women's Biography* (1985).

Willard, Frances Elizabeth Caroline (1839–1898)

Willard, best known for her temperance work, was also the country's first woman college president. A New York State native who grew up in the Wisconsin Territory, she graduated from the Evanston, Illinois, North Western Female College. She taught for several years. To earn money for a two-year trip abroad she wrote newspaper articles.

In 1870 she was appointed president of the new Methodist Evanston College for Ladies, but a year later she was demoted to dean of women and professor, as Northwestern University assumed responsibility for the college's academic work. She resigned in 1874 and devoted the rest of her life to a spectacular success with the Women's Christian Temperance Union, which she used as a vehicle to promote women's causes. In 1889 she published her autobiography, *Glimpses of Fifty Years*.

See also Academic Women.
References Ruth Bordin, *Frances Willard* (1986); Edward T. James et al., eds., *Notable American Women III* (1971); Jennifer S. Uglow, comp. and ed., *International Dictionary of Women's Biography* (1985).

Wives

Being a wife has traditionally been one way—a societally approved way—by which an American woman could earn a living. At periods when sparse new settlements needed women's productive and reproductive labor, leaders and traders have devised schemes to recruit wives. The early colonial period, the settlement of the West, and Asian immigration, for example, all prompted such arrangements where women were enlisted to travel to sparsely populated areas singly or in groups to marry men they did not know.

In the seventeenth century several of the colonies promised acreages to European women, but backed off when the new landowners refused to marry. Sometimes enticement turned into coercion: sea captains might transport from Europe women looking for husbands and exchange them for tobacco—or they might kidnap Englishwomen to sell as wives.

Even in more usual situations, though, the colonial ethic and colonial law strongly directed women to marry: in effect the women were to earn their living by homemaking. Colonial society, needing population growth and eager to keep the poor rolls down, did everything in its power to encourage marriage. In many towns laws forbade single people to live alone. Deserting husbands were legally required to get back home and resume supporting their wives; if they didn't, their wives could remarry within three years. Laws inspired by the same desire to keep her off public relief allowed a widow to run her husband's business and ensured her of inheriting at least a third of his household goods and a lifetime interest in at least a third of his real estate.

See also Colonial America; Married Women's Employment; Mercer Girls; Married Women's Property Acts; Prostitutes.

Reference Mimi Abramovitz, *Regulating the Lives of Women: Social Welfare Policy from Colonial Times to the Present* (1988).

Woerishoffer, Emma Carola (1885–1911)

After graduating from Bryn Mawr, this social worker and philanthropist went to live in New York's Greenwich House (a settlement house). There she became active in labor organizations, anonymously funding campaigns for reform legislation. In 1909 she worked incognito in several different laundries to observe and share the experiences under which women labored. During the Uprising of the 20,000, she furnished money for the strikers and later contributed $10,000 to inaugurate a strike fund for the Women's Trade Union League. Convinced of the necessity of government regulation, she undertook work for the New York Department of Labor; in the course of her duties she was killed in an automobile accident. She became an icon for the settlement workers of her day.

See also Settlement Houses; Strikes; Uprising of the 20,000; Women's Trade Union League.

References Carola Woerishoffer: Her Life and Work (1912); Edward T. James et al., eds., *Notable American Women III* (1971).

Wolfson, Theresa (1897–1972)

This labor economist and educator, a native of Brooklyn, earned her A.B. from Adelphi in 1917; later she pursued graduate studies in economics, earning a master's from Columbia in 1923 and a Ph.D. from the Brookings Institution in 1926. In 1920 she married medical student Iago Galdston; they had two children but were divorced in 1935. In 1938 Wolfson married Brooklyn College professor Austin Bigelow Wood.

A high achiever all her life, Wolfson devoted her early adult years to a combination of study and work for such organizations as the National Child Labor Committee, the International Ladies' Garment Workers' Union, and the Consumer's League. After she finished her doctorate she taught at Brooklyn College from 1928 until she retired in 1967. All these years she advocated trade unionism, despite the many attacks on it. She urged its expansion through broader participation by women and unskilled workers. To that end she taught in the workers' education movement.

See also Academic Women; Consumers' League; International Ladies' Garment Workers' Union; Workers' Education.

Reference Barbara Sicherman et al., eds., *Notable American Women: The Modern Period* (1980).

Woman's Association of Commerce

Founded in 1918 by Florence King, this federation of businesswomen's clubs and professional leagues aimed to encourage women in their professional lives.

See also King, Florence .

Reference Anne L. Macdonald, *Feminine Ingenuity: Women and Invention in America* (1992).

Woman's Board of Trade

In 1907 Charlotte Smith organized this board in Boston to advance the industrial and commercial interests of Massachusetts women.

See also Women's National Industrial League.

Reference Anne L. Macdonald, *Feminine Ingenuity: Women and Invention in America* (1992).

Woman's Commonwealth (Sanctified Sisters, True Church Colony) (ca. 1867–1983)

This utopian community of celibate Christian women in Washington, D.C. flourished under the leadership of Martha White McWhittier. Members refused financial support of male relatives (including their estranged husbands), supporting their community by hard work and inherited property. After McWhittier died in 1904, few women applied for membership, though the organization did not dissolve until 1983.

See also Religion.

Reference Angela Howard Zophy and Frances M. Kavenik, eds., *Handbook of American Women's History* (1990).

Woman's Medical College of Pennsylvania (1850)

The longest lived of the several women's schools founded to train women as physicians when they were so often refused entry into men's medical schools or denied practical experience, this institution went coeducational in 1969, becoming the Medical College of Pennsylvania.

Woman's Movement

See Women's Movement.

Woman's Municipal League

Josephine Shaw Lowell organized this league in 1894 in New York City to interest women in civic affairs. Its legislative committee studied such problems as employment agencies, lobbying for new legislation on the basis of their research, and overseeing its administration.

See also Employment Agencies; Lowell, Josephine Shaw.

References Mary E. Dreier, *Margaret Dreier Robins: Her Life, Letters, and Work* (1950); Edward T. James et al., eds., *Notable American Women III* (1971).

Woman's Record

See Haley, Margaret Angela.

Woman's Union for Christian Work

Founded in 1869 by middle-class women of Lynn, Massachusetts, this organization befriended and tried to protect transient women factory workers (a "floating population") by opening a recreational room with reading materials and lessons in the arts and crafts and keeping a list of decent boarding houses.

See also Shoemakers; Social Feminists; Tran-

Reference Mary H. Blewett, *Men, Women, and Work: Class, Gender, and Protest in the New England Shoe Industry, 1780–1910* (1988).

Woman's Wage

See Women's Wages.

Women Achieving Greater Economic Status (WAGE$)

Founded in 1987, this for-profit organization studies businesses whose customers are mostly women to ascertain women's numbers and status within these businesses.

Women Adrift

This term, like "homeless women" and "working girls," was applied in the nineteenth and early twentieth centuries to working women who lived apart from their families. Many of them had moved from farms and small towns into cities. From the antebellum period until 1900 their numbers increased rapidly, so that by the turn of the century they constituted a third of the urban female labor force.

Some of these women were more adrift than others. Self-supporting nineteenth-century women factory workers (a "floating population") frequently had to move from town to town in response to the demand for seasonal work in such industries as shoemaking. In a society that prescribed marriage for all women, they often faced suspicion about their moral respectability, particularly because they often worked alongside men.

See also Factory Workers; Migrant Laborers; Woman's Union for Christian Work; Women's Educational and Industrial Union; Working Girls.

References Mary H. Blewett, *Men, Women, and Work: Class, Gender, and Protest in the New England Shoe Industry, 1780–1910* (1988); Joanne J. Meyerwitz, *Women Adrift: Independent Wage Earners in Chicago, 1880–1930* (1987); Lynn Y. Weiner, *From Working Girl to Working Mother: The Female Labor Force in the United States, 1820–1980* (1985).

Women Employed (WE)

Founded in 1973, this 1,500-member organization advises and supports women in the work force and those seeking work. Its research and education division, Women Employed Institute, promotes economic equity for women.

Women Employed Institute

Founded in 1978, this organization develops model programs to improve women's economic status, monitors federal agencies responsible for enforcing equal opportunity laws, and works to help women enter nontraditional jobs.

See also Nontraditional Occupations.

Women for Racial and Economic Equality (WREE)

Founded in 1975, this 1,600-member organization of multiracial and multinational blue-collar women promotes economic equality for women among its other efforts.

See also Blue-Collar Workers.

Women in Community Service (WICS)

Founded in 1964, WICS uses its staff of 150 to coordinate the efforts of Church Women United, the National Council of Catholic Women, the National Council of Jewish Women, the National Council of Negro Women, and American GI Forum Women to serve their communities, particularly through support for young women in their working lives.

Women in Crisis (WIC)

Founded in 1979, this organization concerns itself with helping women in crisis in various aspects of their lives, including their work.

Women in Industry Service (WIS)

See Women's Bureau.

Women in Transition (WIT)

Founded in 1971, this organization with a staff of 18 serves women in difficulties in various ways, including career workshops and career groups for women entering or reentering the work force.

Women's Bureau, United States Department of Labor (WB)

A 1920 successor to the Labor Department's Women in Industry Service of World War I, the bureau operated on the fringes of the Labor Department in its early days, because it envisioned its task as fighting on behalf of women workers. Consequently the bureau leaned heavily on the support of women's organizations. Until well after World War II, relying mainly on groups like the Women's Trade Union League, the Consumer's League, and the League of Women Voters, the WB focused on protective legislation. In the 1940s the WB sought to extend New Deal social benefits to domestic and agricultural workers. In the 1950s it began to concentrate more on utilizing womanpower for national economic well-being than on protecting women and to look for means of encouraging women to work. But in the 1960s and 1970s, the WB supported law after law moving women workers toward equality. In 1970 it endorsed the Equal Rights Amendment, finally abandoning its long-standing opposition, which had been based on a perceived need for special protective legislation for women.

See also Anderson, Mary; Consumers' League; Equal Rights Amendment; McDowell, Mary

Eliza; Miller, Frieda Segekle; Nestor, Agnes; New Deal; Protective Legislation; Van Kleeck, Mary Abby; Women's Trade Union League.

Reference Alice Kessler-Harris, *Out To Work* (1982).

Women's Business Ownership Act of 1988

See Small Business Administration.

Women's Charter

This proposed international treaty, originated about 1935, was designed to effect a compromise between advocates of the Equal Rights Amendment and social feminist proponents of special protective legislation for women. The Joint Conference Group of Women in the United States could not develop a text acceptable to both sides and finally abandoned the attempt.

See also Equal Rights Amendment; Protective Legislation; Social Feminists.

Reference John A. Salmond, *Miss Lucy of the CIO: The Life and Times of Lucy Randolph Mason, 1882–1959* (1988).

Women's Computer Literacy Center (WCLC)

This for-profit organization offers courses in computer literacy to women only.

Women's Educational and Industrial Union (WEIU)

Middle-class women founded this organization in Boston in 1877 in response to the problems faced by the increasing number of women adrift—young women migrating to the city from New England's rural areas. WEIU began by providing legal aid and counsel on employment, protecting women's legal rights, and redressing complaints about salary disputes, to which a range of cultural and educational programs was later added. The initial schools for domestic servants and waitresses failed dismally, since they were designed from the employers' rather than the workers' viewpoint and overlooked the workers' concern for higher wages. Discouraged in these efforts to help the poorest women, the WEIU turned to a constituency a rung higher on the job status ladder, with classes for department store clerks that employers loved. But real success came as the WEIU focused on college students' vocational aspirations by creating an appointment bureau.

Under the leadership of Mary Morton Kehew the union became active in many reform movements launched in Boston during the Progressive Era, including support for trade unionism among women workers. The investigations and reports of its research department, founded in 1905 and directed for many years by Susan M. Kingsbury, enabled the WEIU to successfully promote legislation to protect women workers' health and safety and to improve their economic conditions. In the 1990s WEIU includes a career resource room, career counseling, and placement services among its many other services to women.

See also Employment Agencies; Kehew, Mary Morton Kimball; Kingsbury, Susan Myra.; O'Sullivan, Mary Kenney; Progressive Era; Social Feminists; Unions; Women Adrift; Woolman, Mary Raphael Schenck.

Reference Alice Kessler-Harris, *Out To Work* (1982).

Women's Equity Action League (WEAL)

This organization, founded in 1968, had a primary constituency of professional and executive women. It was distinguished by the excellence of its research on a range of issues, including the status of women in the military. It also lobbied, testified before Congress, and filed *amicus* briefs in court cases. Notably between 1964 and 1972, with other women's groups it persuaded all state legislatures to enact prohibitions against sex discrimination in employment. WEAL disbanded in the late 1980s for lack of funds.

See also Sex Discrimination.

References Joyce Gelb and Marian Lief Palley, *Women and Public Policies* (1982), Alice Kessler-Harris, *Out To Work* (1982).

Women's Industrial Conference

At this 1923 conference sponsored by the U.S. Department of Labor and the Women's Bureau, critics deplored the employment of married women, but a few feminists argued for all women's right to work.

See also Married Women's Employment; Women's Bureau.

Reference Lynn Y. Weiner, *From Working Girl to Working Mother: The Female Labor Force in the United States, 1820–1980* (1985).

Women's International Labor Conferences (1919–1923)

Organized by the Women's Trade Union League and held in Washington, D.C., the 1919 conference drew women from 11 nations. They studied the eight-hour day, child labor, unemployment, and maternity care and elected Margaret Dreier Robins president and Maud Swartz secretary-treasurer. The deep divisions among European union supporters (Socialists, Christians, and Communists) impeded progress; so did the misinformation rife in Europe about American labor practices. European working women regarded American middle-class women who wanted to help working women with suspicion. Nevertheless the 1921 Congress founded the International Federation of Working Women. But in 1923 profound philosophical differences caused a split, with American delegates refusing to be reduced to a woman's department of the International Federation of Trade Unions, with no autonomy.

See also Robins, Margaret Dreier; Swartz, Maud O'Farrell; Unions; Women's Trade Union League.

References Dorothy M. Brown, *Setting a Course: American Women in the 1920s* (1987); Mary E. Dreier, *Margaret Dreier Robins: Her Life, Letters, and Work* (1950).

Women's Legal Defense Fund (WLDF)

Founded in 1971, this 1,800-member organization uses litigation and legal coun-

seling to win equal rights for women in many areas, including employment.

Women's Movement

This term is associated particularly with two periods: the Progressive Era and the 1960s and 1970s. From 1890 to 1920, women in larger and more organized numbers actively engaged in public affairs, including women's suffrage, improvement of working conditions for women, the abolition of child labor, encouragement of women's labor organizations and strikes, and settlement house work. These women, predominantly middle-class and white, provided a critical source of support for women workers in their efforts to unionize and resist male domination of the workplace; they provided models of forceful and politically savvy leadership.

In the 1960s and after, the women's movement was reinvigorated by the publication of Betty Freidan's *The Feminine Mystique*. "Women's liberation" encouraged and led to, among other things, the entry of women into nontraditional occupations, the drive for equality of opportunity and pay for women, and vigorous efforts to eliminate sex discrimination and sexual harassment from the workplace.

The women's movement as a whole impacted almost all American women. Whether or not they called themselves feminists or "women's libbers," millions of women felt and expressed the need for greater freedom and opportunity. The movement frightened some women who saw it as putting them in even riskier situations than those to which they were accustomed and threatened a lot of men who found it difficult to accept the possibility of a gain for women without a corresponding loss for men. But just as it was with the women's suffrage movement before it had changed attitudes and actualities, so it was with this new women's movement. By no means has it created an ideal world of true equality. But, significantly, the Women's Voices poll of 1992, sponsored by the Ms. Foundation for Women and the Center for Policy Alternatives—a poll that oversampled poor women, black women, and Latinas—found that 69 percent of women believe that the women's movement has improved women's lives, and 77 percent believe that women's lives have improved since 1965.

The years since 1960 have seen the publication of the report of the President's Commission on the Status of Women; the passage of many laws to help women in the workplace, like the Equal Pay Act and Title VII of the Civil Rights Act of 1964; and judicial decisions in which women have won back pay and promotion on the basis of discrimination against them because of their gender. Hundreds of organizations are now in place to promote the welfare of women in the workplace and enlarge their opportunities, both general and specific, both governmental (like the state commissions on the status of women) and private.

See also Civil Rights Act of 1964; Equal Pay Act; Ms. Foundation for Women; Nontraditional Occupations; President's Commission on the Status of Women; Progressive Era; Settlement Houses; Sex Discrimination; Sexual Harassment; Strikes.

References Rochelle Gatlin, *American Women since 1945* (1987).

Women's National Industrial League

In 1888 Charlotte Smith, champion of the rights of working women, founded this alternative organization for women excluded by unions. It never achieved national significance.

See also Unions; Woman's Board of Trade.

Reference Anne L. Macdonald, *Feminine Ingenuity: Women and Invention in America* (1992).

Women's Prison Association (WPA)

Founded in 1986, this service agency with 50 local groups does work for women prisoners, including helping them with employment aid when they leave prison.

Women's Protection Union

Organized during the Civil War by middle-class reformers and seamstresses, this organization provided legal aid to wage-earning women for 30 years.

See also Civil War; Social Feminists.

Reference Alice Kessler-Harris, *Women Have Always Worked: A Historical Overview* (1981).

Women's Protective Union

This union for women boarding house workers, founded about 1891 in Butte, Montana, later expanded to include women restaurant workers, hotel and hospital maids, custodians, movie candy sellers, car hops, cocktail waitresses, and tamale factory workers. In 1973, at the behest of the Hotel and Restaurant Employees International Union, it joined with another union to form the Culinary and Miscellaneous Workers Union, Local 457, admitting men for the first time.

See also Boarding; Food Services.

Reference Angela Howard Zophy and Frances M. Kavenik, eds., *Handbook of American Women's History* (1990).

Women's Research and Education Institute

Established in 1977, this organization provides information, research, and policy analysis on women's issues to members of Congress, especially the Congressional Caucus for Women's Issues. It also acts as a national information source and clearing house.

See also Congressional Caucus for Women's Issues.

Reference Paula Ries and Anne J. Stone, eds., *The American Woman, 1992–93: A Status Report* (1992).

Women's Rights Project

See American Civil Liberties Union.

Women's Trade Union League (WTUL)

This organization of white middle- and upper-class "allies" and immigrant factory worker "members," founded in

1903, was perhaps the most successful of all women's organizations in involving women of several economic classes. At first WTUL concentrated on encouraging women to unionize, educating them as union leaders, and supporting their strikes (most spectacularly the Uprising of the 20,000). But by 1913 its leaders had plumbed the depths of male unions' (especially the American Federation of Labor's) resistance to women workers and learned the difficulties of organizing women workers, many of whom spoke no English, thought of themselves as temporarily in the labor force, and were passively acculturated. Accordingly the WTUL turned its major efforts toward passing women's suffrage and protective legislation.

Its glory days ended about 1920. The WTUL, however, continued important educational work, like the Bryn Mawr Summer School and other training schools for labor leaders, in cooperation with various universities. It also continued to promote unionization of women workers and to support strikes.

In 1950, hopeful of the seemingly increasing commitment to women among unions, the WTUL dissolved. Although the task it had undertaken was unfinished, the organization had accomplished miracles. For almost half a century it had publicized the cause of women workers. It had lobbied effectively for governmental protection for women through legislation and by the establishment of the Women's Bureau. It had helped to raise women's membership and active participation in unions dramatically. It had assisted many thousands of strikers. It had trained thousands of reformers and women workers for union and governmental office. Above all it had enabled them to know, work with, and support one another's efforts.

See also American Federation of Labor; Bryn Mawr Summer School for Women Workers; Christman, Elisabeth; Henrotin, Ellen Martin; Henry, Alice; Ickes, Anna Wilmarth Thompson; Kehew, Mary Morton Kimball; McDowell, Mary Eliza; Marot, Helen; Miller, Frieda Segekle; Nestor, Agnes; O'Reilly, Leonora; O'Sullivan, Mary Kenney; Parker, Julia Sarsfield O'Connor; Protective Legislation; Robins, Margaret Dreier; Schneiderman, Rose; School for Active Workers in the Labor Movement; Strikes; Swartz, Maud O'Farrell; Training School for Women Organizers; Unions; Uprising of the 20,000; Woerishoffer, Emma Carola; Women's Bureau; Workers' Education.

References Nancy Shrom Dye, *As Equals and as Sisters: Feminism, Unionism, and the Women's Trade Union League of New York* (1980); Gary E. Endelman, *Solidarity Forever: Rose Schneiderman and the Women's Trade Union League* (n.d.); James J. Kenneally, "Women in the United States and Trade Unionism," in Norbert C. Soldon, ed., *The World of Women's Trade Unionism: Comparative Historical Essays* (1985).

Women's Wages

As the American woman moved into the workplace, the idea persisted that she belonged at home, that she worked only for "pin money," that her wages belonged to the family and merely supplemented those of a male primary wage earner. Until the third quarter of the nineteenth century, the law reinforced these ideas, making her wages the property of her husband or father. Wage scales were built on these concepts, not on the value of her production, her skills, or her real need. Women workers averaged little more than half what men earned. Low wages for women were approved by society as a means of social control and enjoyed by employers as a means of reducing costs. So much the worse for the many women wage earners forced by necessity to support themselves and their dependents. When about 1912 state minimum wages for women began to be enacted, they usually provided only enough for the barest necessities.

In the 1990s, women continue to earn only about 72 percent of men's wages. Correspondingly more and more women are moonlighting. As the use of consultants, contract employees, part-timers, and temporary workers increases with employers' efforts to escape the necessity of paying benefits, (particularly health insurance), women piece together a living at the expense of long hours and low hourly pay. Differences in men's and women's qualification such as education, skills, and time on the job account for less than half of the difference between their earnings. Women can increase their wages somewhat if they can get full-time jobs, if they join unions, if they can make their way into traditionally male jobs, and/or if they can obtain college degrees. But the rewards they receive by these means do not equal those of men: for instance, it takes four years of college to pull a woman's earning power up to that of a man with a high school education. In 1992 black women still earned on average $.42 less an hour than white women.

See also Benefits; Comparable Worth; Fair Labor Standards Act; Family Wage; Gender Gap; Health Insurance; Moonlighting; Minimum Wage; Part-Time Workers; Pin Money; Temporary Workers; Unions; Wage Discrimination.
Reference Alice Kessler-Harris, *A Woman's Wage: Historical Meanings and Social Consequences* (1990).

Women's World Banking (WWB)

This nonprofit financial institution, founded in the Netherlands in 1979, promotes and encourages direct participation by women and their families in the full use of the economy. It focuses on women who have not generally had access to the services of established financial institutions. Local WWB affiliates in 37 countries help women entrepreneurs gain access to capital, credit, management, and technical assistance. In some cases WWB guarantees 50 percent of loans obtained elsewhere, with the local chapter guaranteeing an additional 25 percent; for smaller loans the local affiliates themselves provide the money. WWB's repayment rate runs at 99 percent.

See also Entrepreneurs.

Woodbury, Helen Laura Sumner (1876–1933)

This labor historian and government official committed herself to the rights of labor and social justice as a student at Wellesley and at the University of Wisconsin, where she studied and collaborated with John R. Commons. She made her career as a freelance scholar, an investigator with the Children's Bureau, and a staff member of the Brookings Institution. Her pioneer research and writing are incorporated in 12 volumes and many articles on American labor history, labor problems, and the labor of women and children.

See also Academic Women; Government Workers.
Reference Edward T. James et al., eds., *Notable American Women III* (1971).

Woodward, Ellen Sullivan (1887–1971)

Woodward, who as a young matron served as campaign manager for her husband, succeeded him in the Mississippi legislature after his death. From 1929–1933 she served on the State Board of Development as director of civic development and then as executive director. Mary Dewson, impressed by Woodward's work in Roosevelt's 1932 presidential campaign, recommended her for appointment to the Work Projects Administration (WPA), where in 1933 she took charge of emergency relief programs for women. As the second highest ranking woman in the federal government (after Frances Perkins), Woodward advocated equal pay for equal work and emergency programs to train women for gainful employment. Her support of traditional family values caused her to emphasize programs promoting traditional occupations for women. In 1936 she also began to direct WPA cultural programs for workers in the arts.

In 1938 she moved to the Social Security Board, where she fought to expand social security for women and dependent children, opening new job opportunities for women, and extending unemployment insurance coverage for women. In 1946 Truman appointed her director of the Office of Inter-agency and International Relations of the Federal Security

Administration. She retired in 1954, but continued her work in women's organizations, particularly the Business and Professional Women's Clubs.

See also Business and Professional Women's Clubs; Dewson, Mary Williams; Government Workers; New Deal; Perkins, Frances; Unemployment Insurance Program.

Reference Barbara Sicherman et al., eds., *Notable American Women: The Modern Period* (1980).

Woolman, Mary Raphael Schenck (1860–1940)

This home economist and textile specialist took half time off from Teachers College, Columbia University, to organize and direct the Manhattan Trade School for Girls. From 1902 to 1910, when the school was integrated into the public system, she expanded its training from the needle trades to other vocational programs. From 1912 to 1914, Woolman headed the home economics department at Simmons College and presided over the Women's Educational and Industrial Union of Boston, an arrangement that allowed her to offer Simmons' students practical experience in vocational education. Throughout her career she helped modify methods of instruction and broadened the scope of vocational education.

See also Academic Women; Home Economists; Manhattan Trade School for Girls; Vocational Education; Women's Educational and Industrial Union.

Reference Edward T. James et al., eds., *Notable American Women III* (1971).

Work: A Story of Experience (1873)

This autobiographical novel by Louisa May Alcott describes the protagonist's experiences in jobs that Alcott had personally held.

See also Writers and Publishers.

Work Culture

This term is sometimes used to describe the social ties and sense of common interests that workers develop in the process of dealing with management's demands and efforts to socialize workers to its views of work and production. These informal strategies of resistance create bonds that transcend differences of age, ethnic background, marital status, race, and religion. But these ties and strategies are easily broken as differences among workers prove more powerful than their common interests; where solidarity is maintained, however, the work culture can be a powerful agency for change.

Reference Louise Lamphere, "On the Shop Floor: Multi-ethnic Unity against the Conglomerate," in Karen Brodkin Sacks and Dorothy Remy, eds., *My Troubles Are Going To Have Trouble with Me: Everyday Trials and Triumphs of Women Workers* (1984).

Work Force

In 1990, 56 million American women were in the work force, with their numbers growing rapidly. More than 67 percent of women 16 to 64 worked for pay. Those figures include 73 percent of women 20–34, a figure expected to rise to 84 percent by the year 2000. Fifty-eight percent of women in the labor force were single, divorced, widowed, separated, or married to men who earned less than $15,000.

See also Heads of Household.

Reference Nine to Five, National Association of Working Women, "Profile of Working Women" (1990).

Work Incentive Program (WIN)

See Aid to Families with Dependent Children.

Work Projects Administration (WPA)

See New Deal.

Work Projects Administration (WPA) Teachers

See New Deal; Teachers.

Work Sharing

This emergency measure calls for a temporary, across-the-board reduction in the hours of full-time workers. Work-sharing plans have required workers to learn a number of skills, with extra pay for each acquired skill. Their increased flexibility raises productivity and helps employers keep skilled employees. Unions sometimes introduce work-sharing proposals to avoid layoffs, spreading the available work among more employees who work for reduced time and lower compensation. In some states work-sharing employees may receive short-time compensation from government to supplement their reduced wages. Women and minorities have been disproportionately represented in work sharing.

See also Short-Time Compensation; Unions.

References Vivienne Monty, "Work Sharing and Job Sharing: Whose Priorities Prevail?" in Barbara D. Warme, Katherina L. P. Lundy, and Larry A. Lundy, eds., *Working Part-Time: Risks and Opportunities* (1992); *Working Woman* editors with Gay Bryant, *The Working Woman Report: Succeeding in Business in the 80s* (1984).

Workers' Education

This movement, originated by union leaders and reformers, aimed to train women labor leaders and to equip workers with the mental discipline, confidence, and knowledge necessary to meet the problems of the machine age. The movement began before World War I and gained momentum in the 1920s. Probably the first workers' school of more than local significance was the Rand School for Social Science, founded by socialists in 1906 in New York. The Women's Trade Union League established several schools to train women union organizers, among them the first residential workers' education program in the country, which opened in Chicago in 1913.

But pride of place goes to Local 25 of the International Ladies' Garment Workers' Union, which set up an education department in 1915, with Juliet Stuart Poyntz as director. The department organized night classes where young immigrant waistmakers could learn English and supplement their education with courses in the social sciences. It also arranged weekly outings; later it established the union's first vacation center, Unity House in the Catskills, and subsequently a larger center in the Poconos. The example set by Local 25 was emulated by other unions and provided a significant training ground for union leaders.

The workers' education sponsored and provided by the Young Women's Christian Association, the Women's Trade Union League, and the various labor colleges prepared a generation of women knowledgeable about the principles of industrywide union organization. When in the late 1930s the Congress of Industrial Organizations made serious efforts at organizing women, it found a natural base among just such women.

See also Brookwood Labor College; Bryn Mawr Summer School for Women Workers; Congress of Industrial Organizations; Gillespie, Mabel Edna; Henry, Alice; International Ladies' Garment Workers' Union; Kingsbury, Susan Myra; McLaren, Louise Leonard; Pesotta, Rose; School for Active Workers in the Labor Movement; Southern Summer School for Women Workers in Industry; Training School for Women Organizers; Union Organizers; Unions; Wolfson, Theresa; Women's Trade Union League; Young Women's Christian Association.

References Joyce L. Kornbluh and Mary Frederickson, eds., *Sisterhood and Solidarity: Workers' Education for Women* (1984); Rose Pesotta, *Bread upon the Waters* (1987).

Workfare

This effort to lighten the burden of public assistance mandates work from some recipients of welfare. Welfare recipients may be required to perform unpaid work in the public sector, or their welfare payments may be reduced as their earnings increase.

See also Family Support Act; Aid to Families with Dependent Children.

Workhouses (Almshouses or Poorhouses)

In colonial America towns established workhouses as a form of "indoor relief," an alternative to the "outdoor relief" that aided the poor in their own homes with no compensating labor from them. "Deserving" poor women, those who conformed to community standards of marriage and willingness to work, were more likely to receive outdoor relief, while "undeserving" women were more frequently consigned to workhouses to labor there for their own support, or were farmed or contracted out.

In the early nineteenth century, towns increasingly turned away from outdoor relief and workhouses proliferated, supported as far as possible by the labor of the inmates. As reformers came to envisage them, these residences would inculcate the Puritan work ethic, teaching inmates work habits that they had previously failed to learn (or why, the authorities reasoned, would they be in a workhouse?). But of course many workhouses simply warehoused people, whether insane, retarded, disabled, rebellious against the community ethic, or simply unlucky.

See also Apprentices; Colonial America; Farming Out; Indentured Servants; Slavery.

Reference Mimi Abramovitz, *Regulating the Lives of Women: Social Welfare Policy from Colonial Times to the Present* (1988).

Working Girls' Clubs (1885–1897)

The first of these, the Working Girls' Society, was founded in New York in 1885 with the help of Grace Hoadley Dodge. Based on the domestic code that insisted on the centrality of women's role in the family, these societies tried to keep women from prostitution by in effect providing them with an alternative family. Working-class women, screened for gentility and morals, met with speakers and teachers in lectures, classes, and social events designed for uplift. As the teachers lauded home roles for women rather than trade unionism, middle-class virtues were supposed to trickle down.

See also Prostitutes.

Reference Alice Kessler-Harris, *Women Have Always Worked: A Historical Overview* (1981).

Working Mothers
See Mothers' Employment

Working Poor

In the early 1990s many working people, the majority of them women, are poor. While prices increased almost 89 percent from 1978 to 1990, wages increased only 65 percent. More than half of the new jobs created between 1980 and 1990 paid less than the poverty level for a family of four. Almost 11 million full-time workers in 1990 had no health insurance.

See also Health Insurance.

Reference Nine to Five, National Association of Working Women, "Profile of Working Women" (1990).

Working Woman's Protective Union (WWPU) (1863–1894)

This organization stemmed from a joint meeting of middle-class women in benevolent societies and working women called by the editor of the *New York Sun*. Sewing women bitterly revealed the extremes of their poverty and proposed a self-governed Workingwomen's Union democratically open to all workers. The benevolent society representatives used their clout to transform this proposal into the WWPU, which, significantly, excluded domestic servants and reduced working women to an advisory capacity in its governance. The middle-class women who consequently ran the organization focused on legal services for workers victimized by employers, an employment agency, and the expansion of job opportunities for women. By such means they hoped to protect working women against prostitution. But their services were significant: by 1890 they had collected $41,000 for 12,000 women through court action. Similar organizations were established in several cities, including Philadelphia, Indianapolis, Chicago, and St. Louis.

See also Employment Agencies; Prostitutes.

References Alice Kessler-Harris, *Out to Work* (1982); Lynn Y. Weiner, *From Working Girl to Working Mother: The Female Labor Force in the United States, 1820–1980* (1985).

Working Women's Association (WWA)

This organization, founded in New York in 1868 by Susan B. Anthony, Elizabeth Cady Stanton, and Augusta Lewis Troup, proposed to negotiate for its members with their employers. The founders divided over policy issues. Should the association support women's suffrage? Should it hold to the principle of union loyalty, even at the cost of sacrificing wider employment opportunities for women?

The suffragists, mostly middle-class women who did not work for pay, insisted on the primacy of the ballot, while the working women emphasized economic issues. Anthony blundered in 1869 when New York's book printers struck: she urged employers to train women who would then act as scabs and allowed such women to work on her own paper during the strike. At this blatant abrogation of union principles, the wage-earning members deserted the WWA, leaving Anthony to use it as an instrument in the suffrage campaign.

See also National Labor Union; Scab; Strikes; Troup, Augusta Lewis; Unions.

References Philip S. Foner, *Women and the American Labor Movement* (1979 and 1982); Alice Kessler-Harris, *Out To Work* (1982).

Working Women's League

Mrs. Elizabeth L. Daniels organized this Boston league in 1869. She believed that highly skilled working women should help organize and protect the less skilled.

Reference Mary H. Blewett, *Men, Women, and Work: Class, Gender, and Protest in the New England Shoe Industry, 1780–1910* (1988).

Working Women's Society (WWS)

This New York organization was established in 1886 by garment workers and cash girls in protest against harsh working conditions. WWS was a prime mover in the founding of the Consumer's League and was itself later absorbed into the Women's Trade Union League.

See also Consumers' League; O'Reilly, Leonora; Women's Trade Union League.

Reference Lynn Y. Weiner, *From Working Girl to Working Mother: The Female Labor Force in the United States, 1820–1980* (1985).

Workmen's Compensation

When a worker is injured or contracts an occupationally associated disease on the job, state laws may provide for her compensation by her employer for her medical expenses, incapacity to work, and/or vocational rehabilitation.

Reference Michael Yates, *Labor Law Handbook* (1987).

World War I (1914–1918)

Even before the United States entered World War I, in 1917, wartime necessities and the shortage of men created new employment opportunities for women. Jobs traditionally identified as "men's work" were filled by women; this action challenged the view that women were incapable of performing certain kinds of work. The changes in women's job opportunities were only temporary. Thus the figures for women's employment remained fairly stable from 1910 to 1940, and the average woman worker was young, single, and poor. One permanent result, however, was an increased interest in protective legislation for working women.

These years saw the first wartime experience of the Army and Navy Nurse Corps. For the first time the military formally incorporated a sizable group of women clerks into the Navy and Marine Corps. And from 1914–1918 some 25,000 American women went overseas as volunteers or as employees of the military, newspapers, relief organizations, or organizations dedicated to the comfort and entertainment of servicemen.

See also Army Nurse Corps; Military Women; Protective Legislation; Rhoads Dress; World War II.

References Maureen Weiner Greenwald, *Women, War and Work: The Impact of World War I on Women Workers in the United States* (1980); Jeanne Holm, *Women in the Military* (1982); Carol Hymowitz and Michaele Weissman, *A History of Women in America* (1980); Juanita M. Kreps, ed., *Women and the American Economy: A Look to the 1980s* (1976); Dorothy Schneider and Carl J. Schneider, *Into the Breach: American Women Overseas in World War I* (1991).

World War II (1941–1945)

World War II altered the job discrimination against women, especially married women workers, characteristic of the Great Depression. The nation trumpeted its need for its secondary labor force. Suddenly the ideal woman touted by the government on posters and in the women's magazines became a female who was backing up her man at the front by moving into the workplace—or into the military. Women were no longer too weak to rivet, to do construction work, or to build boats and airplanes. The media sang the praises of "Rosie the Riveter."

Women work on a car during World War I.

Female participation in the workplace shot up markedly as a result of the unprecedented need for new workers and new production. Six million women went to work during the war. Women of all ages and classes responded to the government's call to enter the job market as a matter of patriotic duty. More than three out of four of the new women workers were married and more than 60 percent were over 35. "The number of women in the labor force increased by 50 percent compared to prewar years, and the number of working wives doubled. Women's union membership quadrupled," wrote Judith Clark. And women defense workers earned 40 percent more than in civilian jobs. By the end of the war 36 percent of all women were employed, as contrasted with some 25 percent in 1940.

Although most women struggled with combining home and workplace responsibilities as best they could, some industries instituted support systems for them—notably the Kaiser Shipyard, which not only installed a paradigmatic child-care center that could if necessary keep children overnight and accepted sick children, but also provided hot meals for women coming off their shifts to carry home. All that stopped immediately when the war ended.

The military competed with industry for women's services. All branches organized auxiliary women's corps, and Jacqueline Cochran formed the civilian Women's Airforce Service Pilots (WASPs), which ferried planes and towed practice targets for the military.

At war's end the propaganda machine that had urged women into the work force informed them that duty now demanded that they leave their jobs and return home. Some industries simply closed down completely. Many women were fired or quit: their rate of dismissal was 75 percent higher than men's. Women wage earners numbered about 600,000 fewer in November 1946, than in September 1945. Of those that remained, many,

Women Airforce Service Pilots (WASPs) flew B-17s during World War II.

bumped from their lucrative wartime jobs by returning male veterans, had to take jobs at lower pay.

But turning the clock back did not prove easy. Although between September 1945 and November 1946, 2.25 million women voluntarily left their jobs and another million were laid off, in the same period 2.75 million women were hired; by 1947 female employment had regained its wartime levels. Women's participation in the workplace continued to grow after the war, particularly among older women and married women. But no longer could they get the wartime wages they had earned for "men's jobs."

See also Army Nurse Corps; Child Care; Cochran, Jacqueline; Great Depression; Military Women; World War I.

References Karen Anderson, *Wartime Women: Sex Roles, Family Relations and the Status of Women during World War II* (1981); Judith Freeman Clark, *Almanac of American Women in the 20th Century* (1987); Sherna Berger Gluck, *Rosie the Riveter Revisited: Women, the War, and Social Change* (1987); Barbara J. Harris, *Beyond Her Sphere: Women and the Professions in American History* (1978); Susan M. Hartmann, *The Home Front* and Beyond: American Women in the 1940s (1982); Jeanne Holm, Women in the Military (1982); Maureen Honey, Creating Rosie the Riveter: Class, Gender and Propaganda during World War II (1984); James J. Kenneally, "Women in the United States and Trade Unionism," in Norbert C. Soldon, ed., The World of Women's Trade Unionism: Comparative Historical Essays (1985); Juanita M. Kreps, ed., Women and the American Economy: A Look to the 1980s (1976); Ruth Milkman, Gender at Work: The Dynamics of Job Segregation by Sex during World War II (1987); Marc Scott Miller, The Irony of Victory: World War II and Lowell, Massachusetts (1988); U.S. Department of Labor, Women's Bureau, Changes in Women's Employment during the War (1943).

WPA
See New Deal.

Writers and Publishers

Despite being hampered in colonial America and the early years of the United States by lack of education, throughout our history American women have written for pay in almost all genres. Several factors have propelled them in this direction. If in fact women excel men in verbal facility, they enjoy natural talent. Their family roles have cast them as communicators, writers of diaries and letters, and accustomed them to expressing themselves on paper. Women's involvement in printing from colonial days sometimes occasioned their writing. Most importantly, for a long time writing was one of the few occupations open to middle- and upper-class women. The profession did not require advanced education, financial outlay, or leaving home. Women authors could conceal their gender with pseudonyms and need not appear in public workplaces to ply their trade.

At any rate, women show up impressively in the history of American writing. Of course, few (except journalists) have been able to earn a living by writing—a condition shared by the opposite sex. Louisa May Alcott (1832–1888) was an outstanding exception, thanks to her incessant work and the popularity of *Little Women*. At no period has financial reward been commensurate with literary merit. Harriett Beecher Stowe (1811–1896) made enough with her novels, biographies, children's stories, and essays to support her family comfortably and pay for their homes. Emily Dickinson (1830–1886) never earned a penny with her poems.

American women have engaged successfully in every kind of writing, from hackwork and ghosting to distinguished literature. In the late nineteenth and early twentieth centuries historical novelists and sentimental optimists, chief among them the creator of Pollyanna, Eleanor Hodgman Porter (1868–1920), flourished in the mass market. But Ellen Glasgow (1873–1945) and Willa Cather (1873–1947) wrote accurately and realistically about their own social and geographical segments of the United States. In 1921 Edith Wharton (1862–1937) won the first Pulitzer Prize awarded to a woman. In 1938 Pearl Buck (1892–1973) became the first woman to win the Nobel Prize in literature.

Women writers, of course, have not been exempt from the common fate of women: their family responsibilities have often held them back, as several of them, like African-American Toni Morrison (b. 1931), have eloquently told us. But, unprofitable as freelance writing is for most of its practitioners, it presents fewer barriers of gender and age than many another. In the twentieth century, it has offered at least as equitable opportunities for women as any other profession, and more than most.

A number of American women have significantly forwarded the careers of writers. Poet Amy Lowell (1874–1925), editors Harriet Monroe (1860–1936) of *Poetry* and Margaret Anderson (1886–1973) of *The Little Review*, and iconoclast Gertrude Stein (1874–1946) promoted the welfare of European and American writers. Sylvia Woodbridge Beach (1887–1962) offered authors aid, comfort, refuge, and even publication at her Parisian bookshop, Shakespeare and Company.

Marian Griswold Nevins MacDowell (1857–1956) created the MacDowell Colony as a refuge for artists—whether musicians, painters, or writers.

The book publishing industry annually absorbs many bright, qualified women college graduates, who work hard on the editorial side of the house for low pay; some rise to better-paying, more responsible, even powerful positions. Relatively few women are in the sales force, from which promotion to the highest executive positions is more likely to follow. But women have attained important and remunerative positions in selling subsidiary rights. And the large number of women editors assures that women exercise influence over what is published.

The women's movement of the 1970s and the new legislation of the period forbidding sex discrimination encouraged and enabled women in magazine publishing to bring suits against the discrimination that had kept them glued to a sticky floor: the women of *Newsweek* led off. In that decade women moved into the editorship of a number of magazines—particularly women's magazines.

See also Bookbinders; Colonial America; Hale, Sarah Josepha Buell; Hawes, Elizabeth; Journalists; Malkiel, Teresa Serber; Mitchell, Lucy Sprague; Mourning Dove; Printers; Sex Discrimination; Sticky Floor; Theater; Van Vorst, Marie Louise; Vorse, Mary Heaton; Warren, Mercy Otis; *Work: A Story of Experience.*

References Virginia Blain et al., *The Feminist Companion to Literature in English* (1990); Elizabeth Brown-Guillory, *Their Place on the Stage: Black Women Playwrights in America* (1990); Barbara Christian, *Black Women Novelists, The Development of a Tradition, 1892–1976* (1985); Margo Culley, ed., *A Day at a Time: The Diary Literature of American Women from 1764 to the Present* (1985); Langdon Lynne Faust, ed., *American Women Writers* (1983); Dexter Fisher, *The Third Woman:*

Minority Women Writers of the United States (1980); Amy Ling, *Between Worlds: Women Writers of Chinese Ancestry* (1990); Patricia Maida, *Mother of Detective Fiction: The Life and Works of Anna Katharine Green* (1989); Lina Mainiero and Langdon L. Faust, eds., *American Women Writers* (1982); Judith Olauson, *The American Woman Playwright* (1981); Marlene Sanders and Marcia Rock, *Waiting for Prime Time: The Women of Television News* (1990); Donna C. Stanton and Jeanine F. Plottel, eds., *The Female Autograph* (1987); Cheryl Walker; *The Nightingale's Burden: Women Poets and American Culture before 1900* (1983).

Pulitzer Prize and Nobel Prize–winning author Pearl Buck

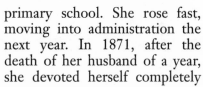

Yalow, Rosalyn S. (b. 1921)

The second woman to receive the Nobel Prize in physiology or medicine, Rosalyn Yalow pioneered in radioimmunoassay (RIA) techniques. After receiving her Ph.D. in physics from the University of Illinois (where she met her husband) in 1945, she began her research career at the Veterans' Administration Hospital in the Bronx, where in 1973 she became the director of the Solomon A. Berson Research Laboratory. She was also on the research faculty of the Mount Sinai School of Medicine, where in 1974 she was named Distinguished Service Professor. Among many honors and awards, two stand out: the Albert Lasker Prize for Basic Medical Research in 1976, the first awarded to a woman, and the Nobel Prize in 1977. In her Nobel Prize address she deplored discrimination against women.

See also Academic Women; Science, Mathematics, and Science-Based Professions.

References Judith Freeman Clark, *Almanac of American Women in the 20th Century* (1987); Jennifer S. Uglow, comp. and ed., *International Dictionary of Women's Biography* (1985).

Yellow Dog Contract

This is an agreement, now illegal, between employer and employee whereby an applicant for a job agrees not to be a union member while employed.

See also Closed Shop; Injunctions; Lockouts; Norris-LaGuardia Act; Unions.

Young, Ella Flagg (1845–1918)

Young, the first woman to head a major school system in the United States and the first woman president of the National Education Association, worked in Chicago schools for more than 50 years. A native of upstate New York, she graduated from the Chicago Normal School at 17 and began her career by teaching in a primary school. She rose fast, moving into administration the next year. In 1871, after the death of her husband of a year, she devoted herself completely to her career.

In 1899, distressed by threats to the teachers' councils she had helped organize to increase teacher participation in administrative decisions, she resigned as assistant superintendent of the Chicago schools and accepted an appointment on the faculty of the University of Chicago, where she received her doctorate in 1900. There, too, she collaborated with John Dewey. She left the university in 1904 to become principal of the Chicago Normal School. In 1909 she accepted the position of superintendent of the Chicago schools, where she significantly revised the curriculum. After many battles with the Board of Education, she ended her tenure there in 1915.

Young always advocated more thorough training for teachers, more teacher influence on school policy, and the use of schools as instruments of society.

See also Academic Women; National Education Association; Teachers.

Reference Edward T. James et al., eds., *Notable American Women III* (1980).

Young Women's Christian Association (YWCA)

From its founding the YWCA has contributed imaginatively and significantly to the welfare of women who work for pay. The organization has distinguished itself not only by its sensitivity to needs of all sorts, but also by its ability to recognize and respond to change.

Founded as a local organization in Boston in 1866, it proposed to assist young women and girls moving to the city. By 1900 almost 600 local organizations existed, which affiliated into a loose national association in 1906. But even before then, in 1904, its first national industrial secretary, Daisy Florence Simms, had begun to develop autonomous industrial departments within the local YWCAs, with programs geared to the needs of young working-class women, providing a national network for spreading trade unionism and advocacy for labor legislation for women.

In the early twentieth century the YWCA recognized the need to bridge the gap between club women and working women. From 1906–1910 an international commission compiled information about possible service the YWCA could render to women in industry, and the international organization in 1910 and 1911 committed itself to this cause, condemning inadequate wages, calling for protective legislation, and extending YWCA work into factories and shops. Florence Simms organized affiliated but independent industrial clubs free to write their own agenda; besides offering working women religion, education, and recreation, they collaborated with the Consumers' League and the Women's Trade Union League for protective legislation and support of the Women's Bureau of the Department of Labor. In World War I the YWCA took responsibility for the working women entering war industries, and after the war appointed an Industrial Commission to cooperate with European labor leaders in achieving acceptable labor standards for women internationally. Simms persuaded the YWCA to adopt the 16-point social creed of the Federal Council of Churches of Christ in 1919, advocating such causes as the abolition of child labor, minimum wage legislation, collective bargaining, and the rights of labor to organize. In 1922 the National Assembly of Industrial Girls became the first constituent group to operate as part of the National Convention, assuming full participation in the policy-making affairs of the YWCA. Two years later business and professional women's clubs received similar status. Thus, perhaps uniquely,

working women could participate regularly in the decision-making process of this organization.

Individually, the YWCA has helped women of all ages, ethnic groups, and races find work, both by teaching them skills and by operating employment agencies; in 1967 it undertook projects to teach low-income youth how to make it in the business world, and in 1969 it launched a special initiative for women reentering the labor force. It has offered working women housing, recreational facilities, and decent places to meet people when they have moved into new locations: in 1918 it responded to the request of the United States Ordnance Department to serve a million and a half women working in war plants. It has improved working women's health, giving courses in everything from sex education to aerobics and mastectomy rehabilitation. It has supported the union activities of working women and educated them about economics and unions by its involvement with the Bryn Mawr Summer School and the Southern Summer School for Women Workers in Industry. It has concerned itself with the well-being of working women off as well as on the job, counseling them about their personal problems and relationships.

For women in the marketplace as a group, the YWCA has lobbied for protective legislation: in 1920 it agreed to work for an eight-hour day and the right of labor to organize, and in 1932 for unemployment insurance and greater economic opportunities for black Americans. It has helped organize formal support networks: in 1919 the Business and Professional Women's Clubs and in 1949 the National Employed Women's Coordinating Assembly.

The YWCA has coordinated its efforts for working women with those of private and public agencies, in 1930 at the request of the Emergency Committee for Employment assuming special responsibility for white-collar women, and in 1965 opening the first resident training center of the Job Corps. It has followed American women overseas in wartime, and into factories and bakeries and stores, where it has offered classes for them.

The YWCA has studded its record of assistance to working women with firsts: in 1870, the first instruction in typing for women; in 1889 the first domestic science courses for mistress and servant; in 1893 the first school to train women in careers for practical nursing; in 1908 the first industrial federation of clubs to train girls in self-government; in 1912 the first summer conference exclusively for factory women; and in 1978 the first voluntary agency to receive a Department of Commerce grant, with which it formed a network to publicize jobs for women in local public works projects.

See also Bryn Mawr Summer School for Women Workers; Business and Professional Women's Clubs; Consumers' League; Employment Agencies; McLaren, Louise Leonard; Mason, Lucy Randolph; Minimum Wage; National League of Women Workers; Networking Project for Disabled Women and Girls; Protective Legislation; Simms, Daisy Florence; Southern Summer School for Women Workers in Industry; Unemployment Insurance Program; Unions; Welfare Work; White-Collar Workers; White Slavery; Women's Bureau; Women's Trade Union League; World War I.

References John A. Salmond, *Miss Lucy of the CIO: The Life and Times of Lucy Randolph Mason, 1882–1959* (1988); Annabel M. Stewart, *The Industrial Work of the Y.W.C.A.* (1937).

Younger, Maud (1870–1936)

This suffragist and labor reformer, born wealthy, embraced the cause of labor as a result of five years' residency at New York's College Settlement. To understand working women's lives, she worked as a waitress in a series of restaurants in New York and California. In San Francisco she organized and officiated in a waitress's union. In 1911 she lobbied actively for a state eight-hour day for women. The next year, back east, she vigorously supported the International Ladies' Garment Workers' White Goods Strike and helped the Women's Trade Union League (WTUL) secure protective legislation for women in Washington, D.C. After several years devoted to women's suffrage, she resumed her involvement in labor reform through the WTUL, the Consumers' League, and the advisory council of the Women's Bureau. But in 1923 her belief in the Equal Rights Amendment, to which she devoted the rest of her life, caused her to part company with all three groups.

See also Consumers' League; Equal Rights Amendment; International Ladies' Garment Workers' Union; Protective Legislation; Settlement Houses; Strikes; Unions; Women's Bureau; Women's Trade Union League.

Reference Edward T. James et al., eds., *Notable American Women III* (1971).

Zakrzewska, Marie Elizabeth (1829–1902)

This physician and major contributor to the success of women in medicine in America was born in Germany and came to the United States in the mistaken belief that the country offered good opportunities for women physicians. They did not await her, but she developed them for other women.

In her girlhood, despite her father's insistence that she leave school and learn housewifery, she read medical works, inspired by her midwife mother. She trained as a midwife and in 1851 became chief midwife and professor at the Charité Hospital school for midwives, but hospital politics soon forced her resignation.

In 1852 she immigrated to the United States; she and two sisters supported themselves for a time by knitting. Soon Dr. Elizabeth Blackwell adopted her as a protégée and got her admitted to the Cleveland Medical College. When she graduated in 1856 the strong prejudice against women physicians prevented her from so much as renting rooms, so she had to settle for an office in Blackwell's back parlor. The next year she and Drs. Elizabeth and Emily Blackwell opened the New York Infirmary for Women and Children, the first American hospital staffed by women. Zakrzewska was resident physician and general manager.

In 1859, having put the new institution on a firm footing, she moved on to found another hospital under the aegis of the New England Female Medical College in Boston but resigned out of dissatisfaction with the school's low standards and financial instability. In 1862, with the support of some faculty and trustees of that institution, she founded the New England Hospital for Women and Children, staffed entirely by women, to provide women with medical aid from competent women doctors, to provide educated women with an opportunity for practical study in medicine, and to train nurses. With the encouragement and help of activists in women's rights, it flourished and still functions. Although Zakrzewska soon passed on her job of resident physician to younger women, she continued to serve as attending physician until 1887 when she then became advisory physician, overseeing the hospital's growth and development, insisting on standards of excellence. She retired in 1899.

See also Blackwell, Elizabeth; Midwives; Nurses; Physicians.

References Edward T. James et al., eds., *Notable American Women III* (1980); Agnes C. Vietor, ed., *A Woman's Quest: The Life of Marie E. Zakrzewska, M.D.* (1972); Marie Elizabeth Zakrzewska, *A Practical Illustration of "Woman's Right To Labor,"* ed. Caroline H. Dall (1860).

Chronology

1714 Elizabeth Short, the first woman bookbinder of record, binds 2,000 copies of the Saybrook Platform printed by her husband Peter.

1715 Sybilla Masters obtains a patent in London for her invention of a device for cleaning and curing Indian corn.

1775– The American Revolution creates
1783 more demand for products (like cloth) that American women make at home. Women travel with their soldier husbands, serving as laundresses and cooks. Deborah Samson disguises herself as a man and serves as a soldier.

1809 The first U.S. patent is issued to a woman, Mary Kies, for her method of weaving straw.

1825 The United Tailoresses Society of New York is formed.

1828 Women textile workers in Dover, New Hampshire, strike unsuccessfully against a wage cut and for a ten-hour workday law.

The first American day nursery is established for the children of working women.

1831 The United Tailoresses Society of New York strikes.

Women workers found a shortlived Society of Shoebinders.

1832 Maria W. Stewart, a black activist, delivers the first public speech by a native-born American woman.

1833 Women in the shoebinding industry found the shortlived Female Society of Lynn (Massachusetts) and Vicinity for the Protection and Promotion of Female Industry, to demand pay equality with men.

Oberlin becomes the first coeducational college in the United States, and the first to grant undergraduate degrees to women.

1836 Mary Lyon founds Mount Holyoke Seminary.

1837– Depression.
1839

1837 After being denied the right to speak at male-dominated abolition meetings, women hold the first national American Women's Anti-slavery Society convention.

1839 States begin to enact laws recognizing married women's right to control their own property.

1844 The Lowell Female Labor Reform Association is founded by Sarah

Bagley to fight for shorter hours and against pay cuts.

1844 The New England Workingmen's Association is founded; in 1846 its name is changed to the New England Labor Reform League in response to the growing numbers of women members.

1845 At the insistence of women's reform groups, New York City hires matrons for local jails, an example soon followed by other large cities.

1847 Maria Mitchell, pioneer woman astronomer, discovers a new comet.

1848 The first Women's Rights Convention is held at Seneca Falls, New York.

1848– Medical colleges for women are
1870 established: the New England Female Medical College (1848); the Woman's Medical College of Pennsylvania (1850); the New York Medical College and Hospital for Women (1863); the Woman's Medical College of the New York Infirmary (1868); the Woman's Medical College of Chicago (1870).

1849 Elizabeth Blackwell becomes the first woman to earn a medical degree in the United States.

1851 The Travelers' Aid Society is founded; by 1866 its primary mission is narrowed to the protection of young women moving to cities in search of work.

1853 Antoinette Louisa Brown Blackwell is ordained by a Congregational Church, the first American woman minister.

1855 Anne McDowell founds the *Woman's Advocate* to promote the economic

rights of women workers and improve their working conditions.

Dr. Emeline Roberts Jones, America's first woman dentist, apprentices to her dentist husband.

1856 The New York Philharmonic Society hires a woman pianist.

1857 The National Teachers' Association is founded, the forerunner of the National Education Association.

The New York Infirmary for Women and Children is opened, the first American hospital staffed by women.

1860 Lynn, Massachusetts, shoe workers strike.

Elizabeth Palmer Peabody organizes the first formal kindergarten in the United States.

1861– The Civil War opens new job
1865 opportunities for civilian women. Perhaps 400 women disguise themselves as men to serve in both the Union and the Confederate armies. Clara Barton and other women supply the armies with food, clothing, and medical supplies and minister to the sick and wounded. Dr. Mary Walker is commissioned as a lieutenant in the medical corps, the first woman doctor in the United States Army.

1862 The Homesteading Act is passed; it allows single women to homestead and own land.

The New England Hospital for Women and Children is opened.

1863 The Universalists ordain Olympia Brown, the first woman minister ordained by a denomination.

The Working Woman's Protective Union is founded.

1864 Rebecca Lee becomes the first black woman to earn a medical degree.

The Collar Laundry Union of Troy, New York, is founded.

1866　The first organization to be called the Young Women's Christian Association is founded in Boston.

1867　The Woman's Commonwealth (The Sanctified Sisters, the True Church Colony) is founded; it endures until 1983.

The Dolly Vardens of Philadelphia, a women's baseball team, make their debut.

1868　The Working Women's Association is founded in New York.

The Daughters of St. Crispin, the first national women's trade union, is founded in Massachusetts after a strike by male and female shoemakers.

1869　Myra Bradwell becomes the first woman to seek admission to the bar; in 1890 the Illinois bar finally admits her.

Arabella Mansfield becomes the first American woman admitted to the bar.

The Working Women's League is founded in Boston.

The Knights of Labor, a labor organization notable for its acceptance of women and black workers, is founded. It functions until about 1900.

The Cooper Union, a free training school for men and women workers, is founded in New York City.

The Woman's Union for Christian Work is founded in Lynn, Massachusetts.

The University of Michigan admits women to medical study, the first co-educational institution to do so.

1870　Frances Willard becomes the first woman college president.

1872　The Association for the Advancement of the Medical Education of Women is founded by Dr. Mary Corinna Putnam Jacobi.

Charlotte E. Ray becomes the first black woman admitted to the bar.

1873　Depression.

The National Labor Union, representing both reformers and trade unionists supporting better working conditions for women, ceases to function.

Mary Baker Eddy publishes the first edition of *Science and Health*.

Lydia E. Pinkham's Vegetable Compound goes on the market.

Linda Richards receives the first diploma of the first American nursing school, at the New England Hospital for Women and Children in Boston.

1877　The Society of Decorative Arts of New York City is founded by Candace Thurber Wheeler, the first of a series of organizations to open doors for women artisans and decorators.

The Women's Educational and Industrial Union is founded in Boston.

Helen Magill earns from Boston University the first Ph.D. ever awarded an American woman.

1879　Belva Ann Lockwood becomes the first woman lawyer admitted to practice before the U.S. Supreme Court.

Harvard Annex, later to become Radcliffe College, is founded.

Mary Eliza Mahoney, the first black trained nurse, receives her diploma from the New England Hospital for Women and Children.

The Union School of Stenography is founded by Mary Foot Seymour.

1881 Black workers organize the Washerwoman's Strike in Atlanta.

Louise Blanchard Bethune, the first professional American woman architect, sets up practice in Buffalo, New York.

Sophia Packard founds Spelman Seminary, later Spelman College.

1882 The New Century Guild for Working Women is founded in Philadelphia.

1883 Susan Hayhurst, America's first woman pharmacist, already a physician, earns her degree from the Philadelphia College of Pharmacy.

1885 The Working Girls' Society is founded in New York; it is the first of many working girls' clubs.

1886 Police and working men battle in the Haymarket Riot in Chicago after a demonstration for an eight-hour workday.

The American Federation of Labor is founded; for many years it was to provide only intermittent and grudging support for women workers.

The Working Women's Society is founded in New York by garment workers.

The Equity Club is founded for women students and alumnae of the University of Michigan Law School, the first organization to provide a network for women attorneys.

The Knights of Labor create a Department of Women's Work, headed by a general investigator, a position first held by Leonora Marie Kearney Barry.

1888 The Women's National Industrial League is founded.

1889 Hull House is founded by Jane Addams.

The first factory inspection law is enacted in Pennsylvania, with the lobbying help of many women's groups.

1890– The Progressive Era sees many
1920 reforms, particularly in business and industry. In this period the first major American women's movement crests, as women organize for protective legislation and better wages for women workers, the elimination of child labor and sweat shops, women's suffrage, and civic betterment.

1890 Law schools begin admitting women students.

The Sherman Anti-Trust Act is passed.

1891 Mary E. Kenney becomes the first woman organizer appointed in the American Federation of Labor.

The Consumers' League is founded to improve working conditions for women in department stores.

1891 The Women's Protective Union is founded for boarding house operators.

1893– Depression. Unemployment reaches
1894 40 percent of the work force in Chicago and New York.

1894 The Woman's Municipal League is founded.

1896 A women's six-day bicycle race is held in Madison Square Garden.

1897 The National League of Women Workers is founded to mainly support factory workers.

The Nurses Associated Alumnae of the United States and Canada is founded.

The White Rose Mission is founded in New York City to protect black women domestics from exploitation, particularly by rogue employment bureaus and white slavers.

Lutie Lytle is admitted to the Tennessee Bar, perhaps the first black accredited as an attorney.

1898 Charlotte Perkins Gilman publishes *Women and Economics.*

1898– The Spanish-American War
1901 occasions the recruitment of 1,200 women nurses by Dr. Anita Newcomb McGee to serve in the Army under civilian contract.

1900 The International Ladies' Garment Workers' Union is organized.

Annie Turnbo-Malone launches her hair-care products business.

1901 The Socialist party is organized.

The U.S. Army Nurse Corps is established.

1902 The Manhattan Trade School for Girls opens.

The first school strike occurs in Chicago.

1903 The National League for Nursing Education is founded to raise standards and to professionalize nursing.

The *Buffalo Inquirer and Courier* hires Jessie Tarbox Beals as the world's first woman staff photographer.

The Women's Trade Union League is founded to support unionizing women workers, train them for union work, and agitate for better working conditions. It functions until 1950.

Mignon Nicholson becomes the first woman veterinarian, graduating from McKillip College.

1904 Mary McLeod Bethune founds a school for girls that later becomes Bethune-Cookman College.

1905 The Industrial Workers of the World (IWW) is founded.

Sarah Breedlove Walker launches her hair-products business.

1907 The Woman's Board of Trade is organized in Boston.

Kate Barnard, as Commissioner of Charities and Corrections in Oklahoma, becomes the first woman elected to major state office in the United States.

1908 The U.S. Navy Nurse Corps is established.

The National Association of Colored Graduate Nurses is founded; eventually it merges with the American Nurses Association.

Muller v. Oregon is argued before the U.S. Supreme Court, which upholds the constitutionality of a state law limiting the hours women may work.

Mary Baker Eddy founds the *Christian Science Monitor.*

1909– "Uprising of the 20,000" garment and
1910 waist-makers in New York City generates widespread support and attention.

1909 A White House Conference on Children is held.

The American Home Economics Association is founded.

The National Trade and Professional School for Women and Girls is established by Nannie Burroughs in Washington, D.C.

The country's first university school of nursing is established at the University of Minnesota.

1910 The first woman police officer is appointed under civil service regulations in Los Angeles.

The Mann Act is passed, to combat prostitution by making it a crime to transport women across state lines for immoral purposes.

1910–
1911 A strike against Hart, Schaffner & Marx involves many women workers.

1911 The first mothers' pension law is enacted by Missouri.

The Triangle Shirtwaist Factory fire in New York kills 143 workers, almost all women.

The first and only municipally funded school for midwives opens as a branch of Bellevue Hospital; it functions until 1935.

Harriet Quimby is licensed as the first American woman pilot; in 1912 she becomes the first woman to fly across the English Channel.

Intercollegiate Bureau of Occupations, later the Bureau of Vocational Information, is founded.

1912 Fifteen women employees of the *Ladies' Home Journal* are dismissed for dancing the turkey-trot during their lunch hour.

The "Bread and Roses" strike attracts national attention, particularly because of police attacks on women and children.

The Children's Bureau is established in the Department of Labor.

The first minimum-wage law is enacted, in Massachusetts.

1913 The case of *People v. Charles Schweinler Press* in New York upholds a law barring night work for women.

Katherine Stinson becomes the first woman to fly air mail and Georgia "Tiny" Thompson Broadwick the first woman to parachute from an airplane.

1914–
1918 About 25,000 American women go overseas in response to the needs created by World War I. These include about 10,000 nurses, but also relief workers, canteen workers, journalists, photographers, pilots, entertainers, clerks, telephone operators, and occupational and physical therapists. In the United States women by the millions volunteer in nutrition and relief efforts, many adding war work to their women's suffrage work. Particularly after the United States enters in 1917, the war necessitates the recruitment of thousands of women into the workforce to do "men's jobs."

1914 The Training School for Women Organizers is founded under the aegis of the Women's Trade Union League; it functions until 1926.

In the Ludlow Massacre during the Colorado miners' strike, miners' tents are set afire with their wives and children inside; women and children are shot as they flee.

The Smith-Lever Act provides support for home economics education.

The Clayton Anti-Trust Act attempts to give unions legal protection by exempting them from the provisions of the Sherman Anti-Trust Act.

1915 ILGWU Local 25 organizes an education department for its members, the first of its kind in the country.

1916 The American Federation of Teachers, the first national teachers' union, is founded by rank-and-file teachers.

The first woman (Jeannette Rankin) is elected to the House of Representatives.

The Cambridge School of Architecture and Landscape Architecture, the first architectural school for women, is founded.

1917 The American Women's Hospital Service is created by the American Women's National Medical Association to facilitate the participation of female doctors overseas during World War I.

The United States recruits women for the first time into the Naval Reserve. Eighteen-year-old Loretta Walsh becomes the first female petty officer in the U.S. Navy.

The wartime federal Women in Industry Service Bureau is established, the forerunner of the Women's Bureau of the U.S. Department of Labor.

Mary Florence Lathrop becomes the first woman admitted to the American Bar Association.

Puerto Ricans are granted U.S. citizenship, facilitating the immigration of Puerto Rican workers.

The Smith Vocational Education Act is passed, providing support for programs in junior high schools.

The Smith-Hughes Act is passed, providing support for vocational educational programs in high schools.

1918 The United States recruits women for the first time into the Marine Corps. Opha May Johnson becomes the first woman member of the Marine Corps Reserve.

The Woman's Association of Commerce is founded.

1919 Mary Evelyn Beatrice Longman, sculptor, becomes the first woman elected to the National Academy of Design.

The National Federation of Business and Professional Women's Clubs is founded.

Brenda Vineyard Runyon opens the country's first all-woman bank.

Civil service examinations for federal government jobs are opened to women as well as men.

The Telephone Operators Department of the International Brotherhood of Electrical Workers is established, the first national union controlled and officered by women; it

collapses in 1923 in the New England telephone strike.

Zonta International is founded to improve the status of business and professional women.

A union of women laundry workers, mostly Chicanas, strikes in El Paso, Texas.

Edith Clarke receives the first electrical engineering degree that MIT ever granted a woman.

1919– Women's International Labor
1923 Conferences are held.

1920 Alice Paul proposes the Equal Rights Amendment, which since has been approved by Congress but never ratified.

The Women's Bureau is established in the U.S. Department of Labor.

The 19th Amendment is ratified providing for women's suffrage.

Marie Luhring is elected to the American Society of Automotive Engineers.

1921 The Sheppard-Towner Maternity and Infancy Act is passed.

Mrs. Samuel Gompers criticizes married women who work out of choice, not necessity, for taking jobs away from men.

Brookwood Labor College is founded by Fannia Mary Cohn; it functions until 1937.

Bryn Mawr Summer School for Women Workers is founded. It functions until 1938.

Eva B. Dykes earns her Ph.D. from Radcliffe; Sadie Tanner Mossell earns hers from the University of Pennsylvania; Georgiana Simpson earns hers from the University of Chicago—the first three black women to hold the doctorate.

1922 The Government Printing Office agrees to pay women the same as men for equal work.

1923 In *Adkins v. Children's Hospital* the U.S. Supreme Court holds unconstitutional a law setting a minimum wage for women working in the District of Columbia.

1924 Nellie Tayloe Ross succeeds her husband as governor of Wyoming, to become the first woman governor.

In *Radice v. New York* the U.S. Supreme Court upholds a New York law prohibiting employment of waitresses at night in large cities.

1925 The Frontier Nursing Service is founded in Kentucky by Mary Breckinridge.

1927 The Southern School for Women Workers in Industry is founded in Atlanta by two former YWCA workers. It functions until 1951.

1929– The stock market crash and the onset
1939 of the Great Depression brings years of suffering to workers across the United States.

1929 Women workers initiate a strike in a textile mill in Elizabethton, Tennessee, which spreads throughout the south.

Women workers participate in the Gastonia, North Carolina, textile workers' strike, despite violence and the death of a female striker (Ella May Wiggins).

The Ninety-Nines, the first women pilots' association, is founded.

1930 The first woman flight attendant, Ellen Church, is hired.

Mary Harris "Mother" Jones (b. 1830), a fabled labor organizer and agitator, dies.

Congresswoman Ruth Hanna McCormick becomes the first woman nominated for the U.S. Senate by a major political party; her bid fails.

1932 The National Association of Working Women is founded to support the employment of married women.

Amelia Earhart becomes the first woman to fly the Atlantic alone and the first pilot to cross by air more than once.

The enactment of the Norris-LaGuardia Act enables labor organizations to engage legally in boycotts, picketing, and strikes.

1933– The New Deal, a term designating
1941 the domestic programs of President Franklin Delano Roosevelt, attempts to reform the economy and counteract the Great Depression.

1933 Frances Perkins is appointed Secretary of Labor, the first woman in a cabinet position.

A White House Conference on the Emergency Needs of Women is held.

The National Industrial Recovery Act is passed, an early New Deal effort to regulate business and revive the economy.

Women become eligible to be appointed postmistresses.

1934 A textile strike involves plants throughout much of the southeast, the largest single labor conflict in U.S. history.

Rose Pesotta becomes the first woman vice-president of the International Ladies' Garment Workers' Union.

1935 The U.S. Supreme Court in the *Schechter Poultry Case* invalidates the codes promulgated under the National Industrial Recovery Act (1933) as an unconstitutional delegation of legislative power.

The Social Security Act is enacted. It includes not only the old age insurance program but also Aid to Families with Dependent Children to assist families headed by single mothers or mothers deserted by their husbands.

The National Labor Relations Act (Wagner Act) is passed, regulating relations between employers and unions, and affirming the right of employees to organize and bargain.

1937 In the Flint Auto Workers' Strike women workers' participation contributes to the union victory and the creation by the United Auto Workers' union of its Women's Department.

In *West Coast Hotel Co. v. Parrish* the U.S. Supreme Court upholds the constitutionality of the Washington State minimum-wage law.

The United Office and Professional Workers of America is created.

Clerical workers employed by the Efficient Letter Company strike.

1938 The Fair Labor Standards Act is passed, setting for the first time national standards of pay, hours, and working age for both men and women and protecting labor's right to organize and bargain collectively.

Formation of the Congress of Industrial Organizations promotes the acceptance of women into unions.

The Wharton School first admits women.

1939 World War II erupts in Europe, causing the United States to gear up its war industries.

1940 The number of women organized into unions reaches 800,000, an increase of 300 percent from 1930.

1941– When the Japanese attack Pearl
1945 Harbor on 7 December 1941, the United States enters World War II. This "total war" affects the lives of almost all U.S. women, sending millions into the work force, and thousands into the military.

1942 Congress authorizes the establishment of the Women's Auxiliary Army Corp (WAAC), which

in 1943 becomes the Women's Army Corps (WAC); the Navy Women's Reserves, better known as the Women Accepted for Volunteer Emergency Service (WAVES); the Marine Corps Women's Reserve; and the Coast Guard Women's Reserve, known as SPARS, an acronym for Semper Paratus—Always Ready. Women's Airforce Service Pilots (WASPs) are hired as civilians.

1943 The Lanham Act is passed, providing child-care centers for women defense workers in wartime.

Oveta Culp Hobby is sworn in as first director of the Women's Army Corps.

1947 The Labor Management Relations Act (Taft-Hartley) is passed to regulate further employer-union relations.

Gerty Cori becomes the first American woman to receive a Nobel Prize for medicine and physiology.

1948 The Women's Armed Services Act is passed, establishing a permanent place for women in the armed forces.

In *Goesaert v. Cleary* the U.S. Supreme Court upholds a Michigan law barring women from being licensed as bartenders unless they are related to male bar owners.

1952 The National Committee for Equal Pay is founded.

The number of women working outside the home reaches one-third of all women over age 14, about 20 million.

1953 The Small Business Administration is created with several departments concerned with women in business.

The first regular army commission for a woman is awarded to Lt. Fae Adams.

Oveta Culp Hobby becomes Secretary of Health, Education, and Welfare, the second woman cabinet member.

Jacquelyn Cochran breaks the sound barrier.

Clare Boothe Luce is appointed ambassador to Italy, the first woman to represent the United States to a major foreign power.

1955 The American College of Midwifery is opened.

The AFL and the CIO merge into a single union, somewhat improving the situation of women wage earners; AFL-CIO supports the Equal Rights Amendment.

1957 Sarah Caldwell founds and directs the Opera Company of Boston.

1958 Mary Gindhard Roebling becomes the first woman stock exchange director.

1960 The second major wave of the women's movement begins to swell, as women organize to improve their status before the law and in the workplace and to open many new opportunities to women. The publication of Betty Friedan's *The Feminine Mystique* in 1963 gives the movement impetus.

1961 The President's Commission on the Status of Women is called to review progress in eliminating discrimination against working women.

1962 Catalyst, an organization to foster women's career development, is founded.

1963 The Equal Pay Act, requiring equal pay for men and women performing essentially the same work, is passed.

The Harvard Graduate School of Business Administration first admits women.

Theoretical physicist Maria Mayer wins a Nobel Prize.

1964 The Civil Rights Act is passed, Title VII of which bans sex discrimination in the workplace, and creates the Equal Employment Opportunity Commission as the agency of enforcement.

The National Committee on Household Employment is founded to upgrade the status of black domestic workers.

The Wider Opportunities for Women (WOW) organization is founded to expand women's employment.

The Women in Community Service organization is founded.

1965– The number of dual-salary families
1970 equals the number of families with only one wage earner.

1965 The United Farm Workers is formed.

Patricia Roberts Harris is appointed ambassador to Luxembourg, the first African-American woman ambassador.

1966 The National Organization for Women (NOW) is founded.

1967 The Age Discrimination in Employment Act is passed.

Pickets protest against the *New York Times* classified advertising office for running separate male and female help-wanted ads.

Muriel F. Siebert becomes the first woman to buy a seat on the New York Stock Exchange.

1968 The Women's Equity Action League (WEAL) is established. It functions until the late 1980s.

Shirley Chisholm is elected to the U.S. House of Representatives, the first black woman to serve in the Congress.

1969 In *Cheatwood v. South Central Bell Telephone Co.* the U.S. Supreme Court requires the employer to consider an applicant's individual competency and not rely upon assumptions as to the capabilities of her gender.

1970 The National Association of Commissions for Women is founded.

The Occupational Safety and Health Act (OSHA) is passed.

In *Schultz v. Wheaton Glass Company*, the first case involving the Equal Pay Act, the court held that the term "equal work" did not mean "identical" but simply "substantially equal."

1971 The Women's Legal Defense Fund is founded.

The U.S. Civil Service Commission stops designating federal jobs as "for men" or "for women."

EEOC charges American Telephone & Telegraph (AT&T) with discrimination against women, blacks, and Hispanics, calling the company "the largest oppressor of women workers in the United States."

In *Griggs v. Duke Power Co.* the U.S. Supreme Court finds that the company's tests and educational requirements are unrelated to the jobs and have a disparate impact on women and minorities.

In *Phillips v. Martin Marietta Corporation* the U.S. Supreme Court finds the company guilty of sex discrimination when it refused to hire women with preschool children.

Barbara Walters becomes the first television network newswoman co-anchor.

1972 The Center for Women Policy Studies is founded to provide technical expertise on women's issues.

The Education Amendments Act is passed, Title IX of which prohibits discrimination against women in educational institutions receiving federal funds.

The Women's Rights Project is founded as an agency of the American Civil Liberties Union.

The Equal Rights Amendment, having passed both houses of Congress, goes to the states for ratification, where it fails.

Women editorial writers at *Newsweek* file job discrimination charges with EEOC.

The Federal Bureau of Investigation swears in its first women agents.

Shirley Chisholm announces her candidacy for the Democratic party's nomination for the presidency.

The Ms. Foundation for Women is established.

1973 In *Frontiero v. Richardson*, the U.S. Supreme Court requires the military services to provide the same family benefits to servicewomen as to servicemen.

The Rehabilitation Act is passed to prohibit discrimination against handicapped workers able to meet other job qualifications.

The Nine to Five Assocation of Working Women is founded in Boston.

AT&T agrees to a multimillion dollar award to women and minority employees as compensation for past discriminatory hiring and promotion practices, and to an affirmative-action program to improve conditions for its women workers.

Women employees of the *New York Times* bring suit over sex discrimination in salaries and assignments; five years later it is settled out of court.

1974 The Comprehensive Employment and Training Act (CETA) is passed.

The Employee Retirement Income Security Act (ERISA) is passed to protect workers' pensions.

The Equal Credit Opportunity Act is passed, banning discrimination against women applying for credit.

The Coalition of Labor Union Women is founded.

In *Corning Glass Works v. Brennan* the U.S. Supreme Court finds that the company violated the Equal Pay Act by paying women employees working day shifts less than men employees working at night at the same jobs.

Ella Grasso is elected governor of Connecticut, the first woman governor not preceded by her husband.

1975 The National Congress of Neighborhood Women is founded.

The National Council of Career Women is founded.

Military practice requiring the automatic discharge of pregnant servicewomen or women with dependent children is discontinued.

1976 Department of Defense service academies admit the first female cadets, as required by law.

The Organization of Pan Asian American Women (Panasia) is founded.

Sarah Caldwell debuts as the first woman conductor at the Metropolitan Opera in New York.

In *General Electric v. Gilbert* the U.S. Supreme Court rules that denial of benefits for pregnancy-related disability and illness is not discrimination based on sex.

1977 The American Woman's Economic Development Corporation (AWED) is created to assist entrepreneurial women.

Physicist Dr. Rosalyn Yalow receives a Nobel Prize.

The Congressional Caucus for Women's Issues is established in the House of Representatives.

The Women's Research and Education Institute is established.

In *Dothard v. Rawlinson* the U.S. Supreme Court upholds Alabama's exclusion of women from positions as guards who work in close physical proximity to male inmates but disqualifies height and weight requirements for these positions.

Ms. magazine is launched.

Patricia Roberts Harris is appointed Secretary of Housing and Urban Development, the first African-American woman in a president's cabinet.

Economist Juanita Kreps becomes the first woman director of the New York Stock Exchange.

In *Nashville Gas Co. v. Satty* the U.S. Supreme Court requires the employer to acknowledge the accumulated seniority of an employee returning from maternity leave.

1978 The Coalition of Labor Union Women is founded to promote understanding of the needs of working women and their families.

In *Board of Trustees of Keene State College v. Sweeney* the Court finds the college guilty of sex discrimination in failing to promote women.

The military services begin denying servicewomen in essential jobs the option of resigning because of pregnancy.

The Pregnancy Discrimination Act is passed, expanding the definition of sexual discrimination.

1979 The National Committee on Pay Equity is founded.

The American Society of Professional and Executive Women is founded to serve the interests of career women.

The Women in Crisis organization is founded.

Women's World Banking is founded with local affiliates in the United States.

AFL/CIO reserves two seats for women on its executive council of 35 members.

Graduation classes at all the service academies and the Coast Guard Academy include women for the first time.

A job discrimination case against Ford Motor Co. is settled with Ford agreeing to provide over $20 million for special training programs and to open more jobs for women.

In *Kunda v. Muhlenberg College* the court finds for the plaintiff in a tenure case on the basis of sex discrimination.

Coalition of Labor Union Women president Joyce Miller becomes the first woman member of the executive council of the AFL/CIO.

Coast Guard Lieutenant (jg) Beverly Kelley becomes the first woman captain of a U.S. military vessel.

1981 The National Association for Women in Careers is founded.

Sandra Day O'Connor becomes the first woman to sit on the Supreme Court of the United States.

1982 The union sues the state in *AFSCME v. Washington*, charging that the state of Washington was discriminating against its women employees by paying them less than their male counterparts for comparable work. The state settles with the union in 1986.

The Alliance of Minority Women for Business and Political Development is founded.

The Job Training Partnership Act is passed to replace the Comprehensive Employment and Training Act.

The Equal Rights Amendment fails three states short of ratification.

Ways to keep women from working outside the home are discussed by the Family Forum, an organization supported by the Free Congress and Research and Education Foundation and the Moral Majority.

1983 A *New York Times* survey (4 December 1983) reports that 26 percent of women surveyed say that motherhood is the "best part" of being a woman, compared to 53 percent answering in 1970.

Women miners and the wives of miners participate in the Arizona Mine Strike, a year-and-a-half strike in the copper mines.

Genetic scientist Barbara McClintock wins a Nobel Prize.

Dr. Sally Ride becomes the first American woman to enter space.

1984 The National Commission for Women's Equality is founded to deal with issues of concern to Jewish women.

Democrat Geraldine Ferraro becomes the first woman to run for vice-president as a candidate of a major political party.

The Retirement Equity Act makes it easier for women to earn pension rights under private pension plans.

In *Roberts v. United States Jaycees* the U.S. Supreme Court holds that the Junior Chamber of Commerce cannot maintain its status as a "men-only" club.

Networking Project for Disabled Women and Girls is founded by the YWCA.

In *Hishon v. King & Spalding* the U.S. Supreme Court makes the law partnership decision subject to the requirements of Title VII of the Civil Rights Act of 1964.

The Carl D. Perkins Vocational Act authorizes the largest allotment of money ever designated for women's training programs.

1986 In *Meritor Savings Bank v. Vinson* the U.S. Supreme Court expands the definition of sexual discrimination to include sexual harassment on the job.

The Women's Prison Association is founded.

In *County of Washington v. Gunther* the U.S. Supreme Court upholds the right of women to sue over sex-based wage disparity without meeting an equal work standard.

1987 The Woman's Workshop is founded.

In *Board of Directors of Rotary International v. Rotary Club of Duarte* the U.S. Supreme Court holds that Rotary International's exclusion of women is discriminatory.

In *California Federal Savings and Loan v. Guerra* the court upholds a California law requiring employers to grant women disability leave for pregnancy and childbirth.

Wilma Mankiller becomes the first woman head of the Cherokee Nation.

In *Johnson v. Transportation Agency of Santa Clara* the U.S. Supreme Court upholds an affirmative-action program to correct past discrimination.

1988 The Women's Business Ownership Act is passed; it is discontinued in 1992.

The Family Support Act of 1988 aims to move people off Aid to Families with Dependent Children through education, training, and employment.

1989 The *Price Waterhouse v. Hopkins* case on sex stereotyping and denial of promotion places the burden of proof on the employer.

Ileana Ros-Lehtinen becomes the first Cuban American ever elected to Congress; Julia Chang Bloch becomes the first American ambassador of Asian descent; and Antonia Novello becoames the first woman and the first Hispanic American appointed Surgeon General.

1990 The Displaced Homemakers Self-Sufficiency Assistance Act is passed, providing support for training programs for unprepared women entering the labor market later in life.

Elizabeth M. Watson is appointed chief of police in Houston, Texas, the first woman to hold that office in a major American city.

Americans with Disabilities Act is passed, extending many of the protections of the Civil Rights Act of 1964 to persons with physical disabilities and outlawing discrimination against them in the workplace.

The Community Reinvestment Act requires lenders to give equal treatment to businesses owned by women and minorities.

The State Department signs a consent decree agreeing to recompense in some degree women denied appointments and honors because they were female.

1991 The Civil Rights Act of 1991 is passed, following the Clarence Thomas–Anita Hill hearing; it establishes conditions under which an employee may sue for damages in sexual harassment cases.

Dr. Bernadine P. Healy becomes the first woman director of the National Institutes of Health.

In *UAW v. Johnson Controls* the U.S. Supreme Court rules against an employer who barred women from jobs dangerous to a developing fetus.

Patricia F. Saiki takes office as head of the Small Business Administration, the first Asian American in that position; Sharon Pratt Dixon is elected the first woman mayor of Washington, D.C.; and Unita Blackwell, mayor of a town of only 300 people, becomes the first woman to preside over the National Association of Black Mayors.

In *Robinson v. Jacksonville Shipyards, Inc., et. al.* the court holds that forcing a woman to work in a hostile environment constitutes sex discrimination.

1992 In *Franklin v. Gwinett County School District* the U.S. Supreme Court rules that students and employees of educational institutions may sue for damages in cases of sexual harassment.

Dr. Mae Carol Jemison becomes the first African-American woman to go into space.

1993 The Family and Medical Leave Act requires employers of more than 50 people to grant unpaid leaves of 12 weeks a year for family obligations and personal illnesses.

Bibliography

Aaron, Henry J., and Cameran M. Lougy. *The Comparable Worth Controversy.* Washington, DC: Brookings Institute, 1986.

Abarbanel, Karen, and Connie McClung Siegel. *Women's Work Book.* New York: Praeger, 1975.

Abbott, Edith. *Women in Industry.* New York: Source Book Press, [1910] 1970.

Abel, Emily K., and Margaret K. Nelson, eds. *Circles of Care: Work and Identity in Women's Lives.* Albany: State University of New York Press, 1990.

Abir-Am, Pnina, and Dorinda Outram, eds. *Uneasy Careers and Intimate Lives: Women in Science, 1789–1979.* New Brunswick, NJ: Rutgers University Press, 1992.

Abram, Ruth, ed. *"Send Us a Lady Physician": Women Doctors in America, 1835–1920.* New York: Norton, 1985.

Abramovitz, Mimi. *Regulating the Lives of Women: Social Welfare Policy from Colonial Times to the Present.* Boston: South End Press, 1988.

Achterberg, Jeanne. *Woman as Healer.* Boston: Shambhala, 1991.

Acker, Ally. *Reel Women: Pioneers of the Cinema, 1896 to the Present.* New York: Continuum, 1991.

Acosta-Belen, Edna, ed. *The Puerto Rican Woman: Perspectives on Culture, History, and Society.* New York: Praeger, 1986.

Adair, Christy. *Women and Dance: Sylphs and Sirens.* New York: New York University Press, 1992.

Adam, Leonard P. *The Public Employment Service in Transition, 1933–1968: Evolution of a Placement Service into a Manpower Agency.* Ithaca, NY: ILR Press, 1969.

Adams, Jane. *Women on Top: Success Patterns and Personal Growth.* New York: Berkley, 1981.

Adelman, Clifford. *Women at Thirtysomething: Paradoxes of Attainment.* Washington, DC: U.S. Department of Education, 1991.

Agassi, Judith Buber. *Women on the Job: The Attitudes of Women to Their Work.* Lexington, MA: Lexington Books, 1979.

Aisenberg, Nadya, and Mona Harrington. *Women of Academe: Outsiders in the Sacred Grove.* Amherst: University of Massachusetts Press, 1988.

Alland, Alexander, Sr. *Jessie Tarbox Beals, First Woman News Photographer.* New York: Camera/Graphic Press, 1978.

Allison, Charlete J., et al. *Winds of Change: Women in Northwest Commercial Fishing.* Seattle: University of Washington Press, 1989.

Ames, Azel. *Sex in Industry.* Boston: J. R. Osgood, 1875.

Ammer, Christine. *Unsung: A History of Women in American Music.* Westport, CT: Greenwood Press, 1980.

Bibliography

Amott, Teresa, and Julie Matthaei. *Race, Gender, and Work: A Multicultural Economic History of Women in the United States.* Boston: South End Press, 1991.

Amsden, Alice H., ed. *The Economics of Women and Work.* New York: St. Martin's, 1980.

Anderson, Dorothy May. *Women, Design and the Cambridge School.* West Lafayette, IN: PDA, 1980.

Anderson, Karen. *Wartime Women: Sex Roles, Family Relations and the Status of Women during World War II.* Westport, CT: Greenwood Press, 1981.

Anderson, Mary. *Woman at Work: The Autobiography of Mary Anderson as Told by Mary N. Winslow.* Minneapolis: University of Minnesota Press, 1951.

Andre, Rae. *Homemakers, The Forgotten Workers.* Chicago: University of Chicago Press, 1981.

Andrews, John B. *History of Women in Trade Unions: 1825 through the Knights of Labor,* vol. 10 of the *Report on Conditions of Woman and Child Wage-Earners in the United States,* 19 vols., U.S. Document 645, 61st Congress, 2d session. Washington, DC, 1911.

Anthology of Contemporary African-American Women Artists, introd. Lesley King-Hammond. New York: Midmarch Arts-WAN, 1992.

Anthony, Susan B., and Ida Husted Harper, eds. *The History of Woman Suffrage.* 6 vols. Rochester, NY, 1902.

Anthony, Susan B. *Out of the Kitchen into the War: Woman's Winning Role in the Nation's Drama.* New York: Stephen Daye, 1943.

Antler, Joyce. *The Educated Woman and Professionalization: The Struggle for a New Feminine Identity, 1890–1920.* New York: Garland, 1987.

———. *Lucy Sprague Mitchell: The Making of a Modern Woman.* New Haven, CT: Yale University Press, 1987.

Apple, Rima D., ed. *Women, Health and Medicine in America: A Historical Handbook.* Hamden, CT: Garland, 1990.

Arber, Sara, and Nigel Gilbert, eds. *Women and Working Lives: Divisions and Change.* New York: St. Martin's, 1992.

Ash, Mary Kay. *Mary Kay: The Success Story of America's Most Dynamic Businesswoman.* New York: Harper Collins, 1987.

Ashmore, Ruth. *The Business Girl: In Every Phase of Her Life.* Philadelphia: Ladies' Home Journal Library, 1895.

Astin, Helen S., and Carole Leland. *Women of Influence, Women of Vision: A Cross-Generational Study of Leaders and Social Change.* San Francisco: Jossey-Bass, 1991.

Ayer, Margaret Hubbard, and Isabella Taves. *The Three Lives of Harriet Hubbard Ayer.* 1957.

Babcock, Barbara A., and Nancy J. Parezo. *Daughters of the Desert: Women Anthropologists and the Native American Southwest, 1880–1980.* Albuquerque: University of New Mexico Press, 1988.

Baer, Judith A. *Women in American Law: The Struggle toward Equality from the New Deal to the Present.* New York: Holmes and Meier, 1991.

Baker, C. Edwin, et al. *Liberty at Work: Expanding the Rights of Employees in America.* New York: ACLU, 1988.

Baker, Elizabeth Faulkner. *Technology and Women's Work.* New York: Columbia University Press, 1964.

Baker, Nina Brown. *Cyclone in Calico.* 1952.

Baker, Orrin C. *Travelers' Aid Society in America: Protection from Danger and Prevention of Crime for Travelers, Especially Young Women, Girls, and Boys Traveling Alone.* New York: Funk and Wagnalls, 1917.

Balser, Diane. *Sisterhood and Solidarity: Feminism and Labor in Modern Times.* Boston: South End Press, 1987.

Banner, Lois. *Women in Modern America.* New York: Harcourt Brace Jovanovich, 1974.

Bannister, Robert C. *Jessie Bernard: The Making of a Feminist.* New Brunswick, NJ: Rutgers University Press, 1992.

Barber, James D., and Barbara Kellerman, eds. *Women Leaders in American Politics.* Englewood Cliffs, NJ: Prentice-Hall, 1986.

Barker-Benfield, G. J., and Catherine Clinton. *Portraits of American Women.* 2 vols. New York: St. Martin's, 1991.

Barnett, R., L. Biener, and G. Baruch, eds. *Gender and Stress.* New York: Free Press, 1987.

Baron, Ava, ed. *Work Engendered: Toward a New History of American Labor.* Ithaca, NY: Cornell University Press, 1991.

Barton, William E. *Life of Clara Barton.* 2 vols. Boston: Houghton Mifflin, 1922.

Bataille, Gretchen M., ed. *Native American Women: A Biographical Dictionary.* Hamden, CT: Garland, 1992.

Bateson, Mary Catherine. *With a Daughter's Eye: A Memoir of Margaret Mead and Gregory Bateson.* New York: Morrow, 1984.

Baxandall, Rosalyn. *Words on Fire: The Life & Writing of Elizabeth Gurley Flynn.* New Brunswick, NJ: Rutgers University Press, 1987.

Baxandall, Rosalyn, Linda Gordon, and Susan Reverby. *America's Working Women: A Documentary History—1600 to the Present.* New York: Vintage Books, 1976.

Beach, Betty. *Integrating Work and Family Life: The Home-Working Family.* Albany, NY: State University of New York Press, 1989.

Beam, Lura. *He Called Them by the Lightning: A Teacher's Odyssey in the Negro South, 1908–1919.* New York: Bobbs-Merrill, 1967.

Beasley, Maurine H. *The First Women Washington Correspondents.* St. Louis: Washington University Press, 1976.

Beckett, Wendy. *Contemporary Women Artists.* Englewood, NJ: Universe, 1988.

Beechey, Veronica, and Tessa Perkins. *A Matter of Hours: Women, Part-Time Work and the Labour Market.* Minneapolis: University of Minnesota Press, 1987.

Behr-Sigel, Elisabeth. *The Ministry of Women in the Church.* Torrance, CA: Oakwood, 1990.

Belford, Barbara. *Brilliant Bylines: A Biographical Anthology of Notable Newspaperwomen in America.* New York: Columbia University Press, 1986.

Belous, Richard S. *The Contingent Economy: The Growth of the Contemporary, Part-Time and Subcontracted Workforce.* Washington, DC: National Planning Association, 1989.

Beneria, Lourdes, and Catharine R. Stimpson, eds. *Women, Households, and the Economy.* New Brunswick, NJ: Rutgers University Press, 1979.

Bennion, Sherilyn C. *Equal to the Occasion: Women Editors of the Nineteenth-Century West.* Reno: University of Nevada Press, 1990.

Benson, Mary Sumner. *Women in Eighteenth Century America.* New York: Columbia University Press, 1966.

Benson, Susan Porter. *Counter Cultures: Saleswomen, Managers, and Customers in American Department Stores, 1890–1940.* Urbana: University of Illinois Press, 1986.

Berg, Barbara J. *The Remembered Gate: Origins of American Feminism: The Woman and the City 1800–1860.* Oxford: Oxford University Press, 1978.

Bergmann, Barbara B. *The Economic Emergence of Women.* New York: Basic Books, 1986.

Berkin, Carol Ruth, *Within the Conjurer's Circle: Women in Colonial America.* Morristown, NJ: General Learning Press, 1974.

Berkin, Carol Ruth, and Mary Beth Norton. *Women of America: A History.* Boston: Houghton Mifflin, 1979.

Berman, Avis. *Rebels on Eighth Street: Juliana Force and the Whitney Museum of American Art.* New York: Atheneum, 1990.

Bernard, Jessie. *Academic Women.* New York: Meridian, [1964] 1974.

Bernheimer, Charles. *The Shirtwaist Strike.* New York: University Settlement Series, 1910.

Bernstein, Irving. *The Lean Years: A History of the American Worker, 1920–1933.* Baltimore: Penguin Books, 1966.

———. *The Turbulent Years: A History of the American Worker, 1933–1941.* Boston: Houghton Mifflin, 1970.

Bianchi, Suzanne M., and Daphne Spain. *American Women in Transition.* New York: Russell Sage, 1986.

Binkin, Martin, and Shirley J. Bach. *Women and the Military.* Washington, DC: Brookings Institute, 1977.

Bird, Caroline. *Enterprising Women.* New York: Norton, 1976.

———. *The Two-Paycheck Marriage.* New York: Pocketbooks, 1980.

Blackwell, Elizabeth. *Pioneer Work in Opening the Medical Profession to Women.* [1895] 1914.

Blain, Virginia, et al. *The Feminist Companion to Literature in English: Women Writers from the Middle Ages to the Present.* New Haven, CT: Yale University Press, 1990.

Blair, Gwenda. *Almost Golden: Jessica Savitch and the Selling of Television News.* New York: Avon, 1989.

Blau, Francine D., and Marianne A. Ferber. *The Economics of Women, Men, and Work.* Englewood Cliffs. NJ: Prentice-Hall, 1986.

Blaxall, Martha, ed. *Women and the Workplace: The Implications of Occupational Segregation.* Chicago: University of Chicago Press, 1976.

Blea, Irene I. *La Chicana and the Intersection of Race, Class, and Gender.* New York: Praeger, 1992.

Blewett, Mary H. *Men, Women, and Work: Class, Gender, and Protest in the New England Shoe Industry, 1780–1910.* Urbana: University of Illinois Press, 1988.

———. *We Will Rise in Our Might: Workingwomen's Voices from Nineteenth-Century New England.* Ithaca, NY: Cornell University Press, 1991.

Bloor, Ella R. *We Are Many: An Autobiography.* New York: International, 1940.

Blumberg, Dorothy Rose. *Florence Kelley: The Making of a Social Pioneer.* New York: Augustus M. Kelley, 1966.

Bodnar, John E. *Worker's World: Kinship, Community, and Protest in an Industrial Society, 1900–1940.* Baltimore: Johns Hopkins University Press, 1982.

Bodnar, John E., Roger Simon, and Michael P. Weber. *Lives of Their Own: Blacks, Italians, and Poles in Pittsburgh, 1900–1960.* Urbana: University of Illinois Press, 1982.

Bohan, Janis S., ed. *Seldom Seen, Rarely Heard: Women's Place in Psychology.* Boulder, CO: Westview Press, 1992.

Boone, Gladys. *The Women's Trade Union Leagues in Great Britain and the U.S.* 1942.

Bordin, Ruth. *Frances Willard: A Biography.* Chapel Hill: University of North Carolina Press, 1986.

Boris, Eileen, and Cynthia R. Daniels, eds. *Homework: Historical and Contemporary Perspectives on Paid Labor at Home.* Chicago: University of Illinois Press, 1989.

Bose, Christine, and Glenna Spitze, eds. *Ingredients for Women's Employment Policy.* Albany, NY: State University of New York Press, 1987.

Bosworth, Louise Marion. *The Living Wage of Women Workers.* Philadelphia: American Academy of Political and Social Science, 1911.

Boutelle, Sara H. *Julia Morgan: Architect.* New York: Abbeville Press, 1988.

Boydston, Jeanne. *Housework, Wages, and the Ideology of Labor in the Early Republic.* New York: Oxford University Press, 1990.

Brater, Enoch, ed. *Feminine Focus: The New Women Playwrights.* New York: Oxford University Press, 1989.

Bravo, Ellen, and Ellen Cassidy. *The 9 to 5 Guide to Combating Sexual Harassment.* New York: John Wiley and Sons, 1992.

Breckinridge, Sophonisba P. *Women in the Twentieth Century.* New York: McGraw Hill, 1933.

Bristow, Edward J. *Prostitution and Prejudice: The Jewish Fight against White Slavery, 1870–1939.* New York: Schocken, 1983.

Brooks, Thomas R. *Toil and Trouble: A History of American Labor*. New York: Delta, [1964] 1971.

Brooks-Pazmany, Kathleen. *United States Women in Aviation 1919–1929*. Washington, DC: Smithsonian Institute, 1991.

Brown, Clair, and Joseph A. Pechman, eds. *Gender in the Workplace*. Washington, DC: Brookings Institute, 1987.

Brown, Dorothy M. *Setting a Course: American Women in the 1920s*. Boston: Twayne, 1987.

Brown-Guillory, Elizabeth. *Their Place on the Stage: Black Women Playwrights in America*. Westport, CT: Greenwood Press, 1990.

Buhle, Mari Jo. *Women and American Socialism, 1870–1920*. Urbana: University of Illinois Press, 1981.

Buhler-Wilkerson, Karen. *False Dawn: The Rise and Decline of Public Health Nursing, 1900–1935*. Hamden, CT: Garland, 1990.

Buhler-Wilkerson, Karen, ed. *Nursing and the Public's Health: An Anthology of Sources*. New York: Garland, 1989.

Bullough, Vern, and Bonnie Bullough. *The Care of the Sick: The Emergence of Modern Nursing*. New York: Prodist, 1978.

Bullough, Vern L., Olga Church, and Alice P. Stein, eds. *American Nursing: A Biographical Dictionary*. 2 vols. Hamden, CT: Garland 1989.

Bundles, A'Lelia Perry. *Madam C. J. Walker*. New York: Chelsea House, 1991.

Burbash, Jack. *Unions and Telephones: The Story of the Communications Workers of America*. New York: Harpers, 1952.

Burek, Deborah M., ed. *Encyclopedia of Associations*. 3 vols. 27th ed. New York: Gale Research, 1993.

Burnett, Barbara A., ed. *Every Woman's Legal Guide: Protecting Your Rights at Home, in the Workplace, in the Marketplace*. New York: Doubleday, 1983.

Burnett, Jane, ed., Julie Cotterill, Annette Kennerley, Phoebe Nathan, and Jeanne Wilding. *The Common Thread: Writings of Working-Class Women*, London: Mandorin, 1990.

Buss, Fran Leeper. *Dignity: Lower Income Women Tell of Their Lives and Struggles*. Ann Arbor: University of Michigan Press, 1985.

Butler, Elizabeth Beardsley. *Saleswomen in Mercantile Stores*. New York: Russell Sage, 1913.

———. *Women and the Trades*. New York: Arno Press, [1911] 1969.

Byerly, Victoria. *Hard Times Cotton Mill Girls: Personal Histories of Womanhood and Poverty in the South*. Ithaca, NY: ILR Press, 1987.

Camarillo, Albert. *Chicanos in a Changing Society: From Mexican Pueblos to American Barrios in Santa Barbara and Southern California, 1848–1930*. Cambridge: Harvard University Press, 1979.

Campbell, D'Ann. *Women at War with America: Private Lives in a Patriotic Era*. Cambridge: Harvard University Press, 1984.

Canape, Charlene. *The Part-Time Solution: The New Strategy for Managing Your Career while Managing Motherhood*. New York: HarperCollins, 1991.

Candee, Helen Churchill. *How Women May Earn a Living*. New York: Macmillan, 1900.

Cantarow, Ellen, with Susan Gushee O'Malley and Sharon Hartman Strom. *Moving the Mountain: Women Working for Social Change*. Old Westbury, NY: Feminist Press, and New York: McGraw-Hill, 1980.

Cantor, Milton, and Bruce Laurie, eds. *Class, Sex, and the Woman Worker*. Westport, CT: Greenwood Press, 1977.

Caplow, Theodore, et al. *Middletown Families: Fifty Years of Change and Continuity*. Minneapolis: University of Minnesota Press, 1982.

Carola Woerishoffer: Her Life and Work. Bryn Mawr, PA: Class of 1907 of Bryn Mawr College, 1912.

Carp, F. M., ed. *Lives of Career Women: Approaches to Work, Marriage and Children*. New York: Plenum Press, 1991.

Carpenter, Jesse Thomas. *Competition and Collective Bargaining in the Needle Trades, 1910–1967.* Ithaca, NY: ILR Press, 1972.

Carr, Cornelia Crow. *Harriet Hosmer: Letters and Memories.* 1912.

Carter, Ruth, and Gill Kirkup. *Women in Engineering.* New York: New York University Press, 1990.

Casey, Eileen L. *Maternity Leave: The Working Woman's Practical Guide to Combining Pregnancy, Motherhood and Career.* Shelburne, VT: Green Mountain Pub., 1992.

Catalyst. *Beyond the Transition: The Two-Gender Workforce and Corporate Policy.* New York, 1984.

———. *Building an Effective Corporate Women's Group.* New York, 1988.

———. *Corporate Child Care Options.* New York, 1987.

———. *Corporations and Two-Career Families: Directions for the Future.* New York, 1981.

———. *Flexible Work Arrangements: Establishing Options for Managers and Professionals.* New York, 1989.

———. *Report on a National Study of Parental Leaves.* New York, 1986.

———. *Women in Corporate Management: Results of a Catalyst Survey.* New York, 1990.

———. *Work and Family Seminars: Corporations Respond to Employees' Needs.* New York, 1984.

Cazden, Elizabeth. *Antoinette Brown Blackwell: A Biography.* New York: Feminist Press, 1983.

Center for the American Woman and Politics Staff, comp. *Women in Public Office: A Biographical Directory and Statistical Analysis.* Metuchen, NJ: Scarecrow Press, 1978.

Center for Creative Leaderhip Staff, et al. *Breaking the Glass Ceiling: Can Women Reach the Top of America's Largest Corporations?* Redding, MA: Addison-Wesley, 1987.

Center for Information Management, American Veterinary Medicine Association. "Economic Report on Veterinarians and Veterinary Medicine." 1993.

Chafe, William. *The American Woman: Her Changing Social, Economic and Political Roles, 1920–1970.* New York: Oxford University Press, 1972.

———. *The Paradox of Change: American Women in the 20th Century.* New York: Oxford University Press, 1992.

———. *Woman and Equality: Changing Patterns in American Culture.* Oxford: Oxford University Press, 1978.

Chamberlain, Mariam K. *Women in Academe: Progress and Prospects.* New York: Russell Sage, 1991.

Chastain, Sherry. *Winning the Salary Game: Salary Negotiations for Women.* New York: John Wiley, 1980.

Chavkin, Wendy, ed. *Double Exposure: Women's Health Hazards on the Job and at Home.* New York: Monthly Review Press, 1984.

Cheng, Lucie, and Edna Bonacich, eds. *Labor Immigration under Capitalism: Asian Workers in the United States before World War II.* Berkeley: University of California Press, 1984.

Chiarmonte, Paula. *Women Artists in the United States: Guide on the Fine and Decorative Arts, 1750–1986.* New York: Macmillan, 1990.

Child Care Action Campaign. *Not Too Small To Care.* New York, 1992.

Christian, Barbara. *Black Women Novelists: The Development of a Tradition, 1892–1976.* Westport, CT: Greenwood Press, 1985.

Church, Ella Rodman. *Money-Making for Ladies.* New York: Harper, 1882.

Claghorn, Gene. *Women Composers and Hymnists: A Concise Biographical Dictionary.* Metuchen, NJ: Scarecrow Press, 1984.

Clark, Alice. *Working Life of Women in the Seventeenth Century.* New York: Augustus Kelley, [1919] 1967.

Clark, Judith Freeman. *Almanac of American Women in the 20th Century*. New York: Prentice-Hall, 1987.

Clarke, Robert. *Ellen Swallow: The Woman Who Founded Ecology*. New York: Follett, 1973.

Clayton, Susan D., and Faye J. Crosby. *Justice, Gender, and Affirmative Action*. Ann Arbor: University of Michigan Press, 1992.

Clewell, Beatriz C., and Bernice Anderson. *Women of Color in Science, Mathematics, and Engineering: A Review of the Literature*. Washington, DC: Center for Women Policy Studies, 1991.

Cline, Carolyn Garrett, et al. *The Velvet Ghetto: The Impact of the Increasing Percentage of Women in Public Relations and Business Communication*. San Francisco: International Association for Business Communication Foundation, 1986.

Clinton, Catherine. *The Other Civil War: American Women in the Nineteenth Century*. New York: Hill and Wang, 1984.

Coalition of Labor Union Women. *News* (January/February 1992).

Cobble, Dorothy Sue. *Dishing It Out: Waitresses and Their Unions in the Twentieth Century*. Chicago: University of Illinois Press, 1991.

Cochran, Jacqueline. *The Stars at Noon*. Boston: Little, Brown, 1954.

Cochran, Jacqueline, and Maryann Bucknum Brinley. *Jackie Cochran: An Autobiography*. New York: Bantam Books, 1987.

Cockburn, Cynthia. *In the Way of Women: Men's Resistance to Sex Equality in Organizations*. Ithaca, NY: ILR Press, 1991.

Cockcroft, James. *Outlaws in the Promised Land: Mexican Immigrant Workers and America's Future*. New York: Grove Press, 1986.

Coffee, Robert, and Richard Scase. *Women in Charge: The Experiences of Female Entrepreneurs*. New York: Unwin Hyman, 1985.

Cohen, Aaron I. *International Encyclopedia of Women Composers*. 2 vols. 2d ed. New York: Books and Music USA, 1987.

Cohen, Miriam. *Workshop to Office: Two Generations of Italian Women in New York City, 1900–1950*. Ithaca, NY: Cornell University Press, 1992.

Cohen, Ricki Carole Myers. "Fannia Cohn and the International Ladies' Garment Workers' Union." Ph.D. dissertation, University of Southern California, 1976.

Cohen, Rose, *Out of the Shadow*. New York: George Doran, 1918.

Colatosti, Camille, and Elissa Karg. *Stopping Sexual Harassment: A Handbook for Union and Workplace Activists*. Detroit: Labor Notes, 1992.

Cole, Doris. *From Tipi to Skyscraper: A History of Women in Architecture*. Boston: MIT Press, 1978.

Cole, Jean H. *Women Pilots of World War II*. Salt Lake City: University of Utah Press, 1992.

Cole, Jonathan R. *Fair Science: Women in the Scientific Community*. New York: Columbia University Press, 1987.

Collins, Nancy W. *Professional Women and Their Mentors: A Practical Guide to Mentoring for the Woman Who Wants To Get Ahead*. Englewood Cliffs, NJ: Prentice-Hall, 1983.

Commander, Lydia Kingsmill. *The American Idea*. New York: Arno Press, [1907] 1972.

Connecticut Permanent Commission on the Status of Women. *Women in Apprenticeships: Steps to Building a Career*. Hartford, CT, 1989.

———. *Non Traditional Jobs for Women: A Resource Guide*. 4th ed. Hartford, CT, 1991.

Consumer's League of New York. *Behind the Scenes in a Restaurant*. New York, 1916.

Conway, Jill K. *The First Generation of American Women Graduates*. New York: Garland Pub., 1987.

Cook, Alice H. *Comparable Worth: The Problem and States' Approaches to Wage Equity*. Honolulu: University of Hawaii Press, 1983.

———. *The Working Mother: A Survey of Problems and Programs in Nine Counties.* 2d ed. Ithaca, NY: ILR Press, 1978.

Cook, Blanche Wiesen. *Eleanor Roosevelt: 1884–1933.* New York: Viking, 1992.

Cooper, Courtney Ryley. *Annie Oakley: Woman at Arms.* 1927.

Cooper, Patricia. *Once a Cigar Maker: Men, Women and Work Culture in American Cigar Factories, 1900–1919.* Urbana: University of Illinois Press, 1987.

Cornum, Rhonda, as told to Peter Copeland. *She Went to War: The Rhonda Cornum Story.* Novato, CA: Presidio, 1992.

Costello, Cynthia B. *"We're Worth It!": Women and Collective Action in the Insurance Workplace.* Urbana: University of Illinois Press, 1991.

Cote, Charlotte. *Olympia Brown: The Battle for Equality.* Racine, WI: Mother Courage, 1989.

Cott, Nancy F., *The Bonds of Womanhood: Women's Sphere in New England, 1780–1835.* New Haven, CT: Yale University Press, 1977.

Cott, Nancy F., and Elizabeth H. Peck, eds. *A Heritage of Her Own: Toward a New Social History of American Women.* New York: Simon and Schuster, 1979.

Cowan, Ruth Schwartz. *More Work for Mother: The Ironies of Household Technology from the Open Hearth to the Microwave.* New York: Basic Books, 1983.

Craft, Christine. *Too Old, Too Ugly and Not Deferential to Men: An Anchorwoman's Courageous Battle against Sex Discrimination.* Rocklin, CA: Prima Pub., 1988.

Crites, Laura L., and Winifred J. Hepperle. *Women, the Courts and Equality.* New York: Russell Sage, 1987.

Crow, Martha F. *The American Country Girl.* New York: Arno Press, [1915] 1974.

Culley, Margo, ed. *A Day at a Time: The Diary Literature of American Women from 1764 to the Present.* New York: Feminist Press, 1985.

Cuney-Hare, Maud. *Negro Musicians and Their Music.* 1936.

Dahl, Linda. *Stormy Weather: The Music and Lives of a Century of Jazzwomen.* New York: Pantheon Books, 1984.

Dalrymple, Candace. *Sexual Distinctions in the Law: Early Maximum Hour Decisions of the United States Supreme Court, 1905–1917.* Hamden, CT: Garland Pub., 1987.

Daniels, Doris G. *Always a Sister: The Feminism of Lillian D. Wald.* New York: Feminist Press, 1990.

Daniels, Roger. *Asian America: Chinese and Japanese in the United States since 1950.* Seattle: University of Washington Press, 1988.

DaSilva, Rachel, ed. *Leading Out: Women Climbers Reaching for the Top.* Seattle: Seal Press, 1992.

Davenport, M. Marguerite. *Azalia.* 1947.

Davidson, Marilyn J., and Cary L. Cooper, eds. *Stress and the Woman Manager.* New York: St. Martin's, 1983.

———. *Women and Information Technology.* New York: John Wiley, 1987.

Davies, Margery W. *Woman's Place Is at the Typewriter: Office Work and Office Workers, 1870–1930.* Philadelphia: Temple University Press, 1983.

Davis, Allen F. *Spearheads for Reform: The Social Settlements and the Progressive Movement 1890–1914.* New York: Oxford University Press, 1967.

Davis, K., M. Leijenaar, and J. Oldersma. *The Gender of Power.* Newbury Park, CA: Russell Sage, 1991.

Davis, Marianna. *American Women in Olympic Track and Field: A Complete Illustrated Reference.* Jefferson, NC: McFarland, 1992.

———. *Contributions of Black Women to America.* Columbia, SC: Kendfay Press, 1982.

Dawson, Kipp. *Women Miners and the UMWA: 1973–1983.* Occasional Paper #11. New York: Center for Labor-Management Policy Studies, the Graduate

School and University Center of the City University of New York, 1992.

Deacon, Desley. *Managing Gender: The State, the New Middle Class and Women Workers, 1830–1930.* New York: Oxford University Press, 1990.

Deaux, Kay, and Joseph C. Ullman. *Women of Steel: Female Blue Collar Workers in the Basic Steel Industry.* Westport, CT: Greenwood Press, 1983.

Degler, Carl N. *At Odds: Women and the Family in America from the Revolution to the Present.* New York: Oxford University Press, 1980.

Delacoste, Frederique, and Priscilla Alexander, eds. *Sex Work: Writings by Women in the Sex Industry.* Pittsburgh: Cleis Press, 1991.

DeMille, Agnes. *Dance to the Piper.* Boston: Atlantic Monthly Press, 1952.

Dennis, Peggy. *The Autobiography of an American Communist: A Personal View of a Political Life, 1925–1975.* Berkeley, CA: Lawrence Hall, 1977.

DeSole, Gloria, and Leonore Hoffman, eds. *Rocking the Boat: Academic Women and Academic Processes.* New York: Modern Language Association, 1981.

Desti, Mary. *The Untold Story: The Life of Isadora Duncan, 1921–1927.* New York: Da Capo, [1929] 1989.

DeVault, Ileen A. *Sons and Daughters of Labor: Class and Clerical Work in Turn-of-the-Century Pittsburgh.* Ithaca, NY: Cornell University Press, 1990.

Dex, Shirley, and Lois Shaw. *British and American Women at Work.* New York: Macmillan, 1986.

Dexter, Elizabeth A. *Career Women of America, 1776–1840.* Francestown, NH: Marshall Jones Co., 1950.

———. *Colonial Women of Affairs: Women in Business and Professions in America before 1776.* 2d ed., rev. Clifton, NJ: Augustus Kelley, 1972.

Dickey, Adam H. *Memoirs of Mary Baker Eddy.* 1927.

Diner, Hasia A. *Erin's Daughters: Irish Immigrant Women in the Nineteenth*

Century. Baltimore: Johns Hopkins University Press, 1983.

Directory of Non-Traditional Training and Employment Programs Serving Women. Washington, DC: U.S. Department of Labor, Women's Bureau, 1991.

Displaced Homemakers Network Staff and Institute for Women's Policy Research Staff. *Low Wage Jobs and Workers: Trends and Options for Change.* Washington, DC: Institute for Women's Policy Research, 1989.

Dodge, Grace H., Thomas Hunter, Mrs. Mary J. Lincoln, S. S. Palmer Packard, Mrs. A. M. Palmer, Helen M. Winslow, et al. *What Women Can Earn: Occupations of Women and Their Compensation.* New York: Fredrick A. Stokes, 1898.

Doeringer, Peter B., ed. *Bridges to Retirement: Older Workers in a Changing Labor Market.* Ithaca, NY: ILR Press, 1990.

Doherty, Robert E. *Industrial and Labor Relations Terms: A Glossary.* Ithaca, NY: ILR Press, 1989.

Donahoe, Myrna C. *Resolving Discriminatory Practices against Minorities and Women in Steel and Auto—Los Angeles, California, 1936–1982.* Los Angeles: University of California, Institute of Industrial Relations, 1991.

Donegan, Jane B. *Women and Men Midwives: Medicine, Morality, and Misogyny in Early America.* Westport, CT: Greenwood Press, 1978.

Donovan, Mary. *Women Priests in the Episcopal Church.* Cincinnati, OH: The Forward Movement, 1988.

Dorr, Rheta Childe. *A Woman of Fifty.* New York: Arno Press, [1924] 1980.

———. *What Eight Million Women Want.* New York: Kraus Reprint Co., [1910] 1971.

Douglas, Deborah G. *United States Women in Aviation, 1940–1985.* Washington, DC: Smithsonian Institute, 1991.

Doumato, Lamia. *Architecture and Women: A Bibliography Documenting Women Architects, Landscape Architects, Designers, Architectural*

Critics and Writers, and Women in Related Fields Working in the United States. New York: Garland Pub., 1988.

Drachman, Virginia G. *Women Lawyers and the Origins of Professional Community in America: The Letters of the Equity Club, 1886 to 1890.* Ann Arbor: University of Michigan Press, 1992.

Draper, Theodore. *The Roots of American Communism.* New York: Octagon Books, 1957.

Dreier, Mary E. *Margaret Dreier Robins: Her Life, Letters, and Work.* New York: Island Press, 1950.

Drinnon, Richard. *Rebel in Paradise: A Biography of Emma Goldman.* Chicago: University of Chicago Press, 1961.

Drum, Sue, and H. Ellen Whiteley. *Women in Veterinary Medicine.* Ames: Iowa State University Press, 1992.

Dublin, Thomas. *Farm and Factory: The Mill Experience and Women's Lives in New England, 1830–1860.* New York: Columbia University Press, 1982.

———. *Women at Work: The Transformation of Work and Community in Lowell, Massachusetts, 1826–1860.* New York: Columbia University Press, 1979.

Dubofsky, Melvyn, and Stephen Burwood, eds. *Women and Minorities during the Great Depression: Selected Articles on Gender, Race, and Ethnicity.* Hamden, CT: Garland Press, 1990.

Dudden, Faye E. *Serving Women: Household Service in Nineteenth-Century America.* Middletown, CT: Wesleyan University Press, 1983.

Duffus, R. L. *Lillian Wald, Neighbor and Crusader.* New York: Macmillan, 1938.

Duffy, Susan, comp. *Shirley Chisholm: A Bibliography.* Metuchen, NJ: Scarecrow Press, 1988.

Duke, C., and B. Sitterly. *A Woman's Place: Management.* Englewood Cliffs, NJ: Prentice-Hall, 1988.

Duncan, Isadora. *My Life.* New York: Liveright, 1972.

Dunfee, Susan N. *Beyond Servanthood: Christianity and the Liberation of Women.* Lanham, MD: University Press of America, 1989.

Dunford, Penny. *A Biographical Dictionary of Women Artists in Europe and America since 1850.* Philadelphia: University of Pennsylvania Press, 1990.

Dusky, L., and B. Zeitz. *The Best Companies for Women.* New York: Simon & Schuster, 1988.

Dye, Nancy Shrom. *As Equals and as Sisters: Feminism, Unionism, and the Women's Trade Union League of New York.* Columbia: University of Missouri Press, 1980.

Dzieck, Billie Wright, and Linda Weiner. *The Lecherous Professor: Sexual Harassment on Campus.* Urbana: University of Illinois Press, 1990.

Earhart, Amelia. *The Fun of It.* 1932.

———. *Last Flight.* 1937.

Easton, Susan. *Equal to the Task: How Working Women Are Managing in Corporate America.* New York: Seaview Books, 1982.

Edson, Sakre. *Pushing the Limits: The Female Administrative Aspirant.* Albany: State University of New York Press, 1988.

Edwards, Julia. *Women of the World: The Great Foreign Correspondents.* Boston: Houghton Mifflin, 1988.

Edwards, Richard C. *Contested Terrain: The Transformation of the Workplace in the Twentieth Century.* New York: Basic Books, 1979.

Ehrenreich, Barbara, and Deidre English. *Witches, Midwives, and Nurses: A History of Women Healers.* Old Westbury, NY: Feminist Press, 1973.

Eisenstein, Sarah. *Give Us Bread but Give Us Roses: Working Women's Consciousness in the United States, 1890 to the First World War.* London: Routledge & Kegan Paul, 1983.

Elder, Glen, Jr. *Children of the Great Depression: Social Change and Life Experience.* Chicago: University of Chicago Press, 1974.

Ellerbee, Linda. *"And So It Goes": Adventures in Television.* New York: Berkley Books, 1987.

Elwood-Akers, Virginia. *Women War Correspondents in the Vietnam War, 1961–1975.* Metuchen, NJ: Scarecrow Press, 1988.

Enarson, Elaine P. *Woods-Working Women: Sexual Integration in the U.S. Forest Service.* Tuscaloosa: University of Alabama Press, 1984.

Endelman, Gary E. *Solidarity Forever: Rose Schneiderman and the Women's Trade Union League.* Salem, NH: Ayer, n.d.

England, Paula. *Comparable Worth: Theories and Evidence.* Hawthorne, NY: Aldine de Gruyter, 1992.

Entrikin, Isabelle Webb. *Sarah Josepha Hale and "Godey's Lady's Book."* 1946.

Epstein, Cynthia F. *Woman's Place: Options and Limits in Professional Careers.* Berkeley: University of California Press, 1970.

Epstein, Richard A. *Forbidden Grounds: The Case against Employment Discrimination Laws.* Cambridge: Harvard University Press, 1992.

Epstein, T. Scarlett, et al., eds. *Women, Work and Family.* New York: St. Martin's, 1986.

Equal Means (Spring 1992).

Escutia, Marta, and Margarita M. Prieto. *Hispanics in the Workforce, Part II: Hispanic Women.* Washington, DC: Policy Analysis Center, Office of Research, Advocacy, and Legislation, National Council of La Raza, 1988.

Eskenazi, Martin, and David Gallen. *Sexual Harassment: Know Your Rights.* New York: Carroll and Graf, 1992.

Evans, Sara M. *Born for Liberty: A History of Women in America.* New York: Free Press, 1989.

Ewen, Elizabeth. *Immigrant Women in the Land of Dollars: Life and Culture on the Lower East Side, 1890–1925.* New York: Monthly Review Press, 1985.

Ewen, Lynda Ann. *Which Side Are You On?* Chicago: Vanguard Books, 1979.

Fader, Shirley Sloan. *From Kitchen to Career: How Any Woman Can Skip Low-Level Jobs and Start in the Middle or at the Top.* New York: Stein and Day, 1977.

———. *Successfully Ever After.* New York: McGraw-Hill, 1982.

Falinski, E., D. Friedman, and C. Hernandez. *The Corporate Reference Guide to Work-Family Programs.* New York: Families and Work Institute, 1992.

Farley, Jennie, ed. *Sex Discrimination in Higher Education: Strategies for Equality.* Ithaca, NY: ILR Press, 1981.

———. *The Woman in Management: Career and Family Issues.* Ithaca, NY: ILR Press, 1983.

———. *Women Workers in Fifteen Countries: Essays in Honor of Alice Hanson Cook.* Ithaca, NY: ILR Press, 1985.

Farley, Lin. *Sexual Shakedown.* New York: Warner Books, 1978.

Faust, Langdon Lynne, ed. *American Women Writers.* 2 vols. New York: Frederick Ungar, 1983.

Ferber, Edna. *Personality Plus: Some Experiences of Edna McChesney and Her Son Jock.* New York: Frederick A. Stokes, 1914.

Ferber, Marianne A. *Women and Work, Paid and Unpaid: A Selected, Annotated Bibliography.* Hamden, CT: Garland, 1987.

Ferber, Marianne A., and Brigid O'Farrell, eds. *Work and Family: Policies for a Changing Work Force.* Washington, DC: National Academy Press, 1991.

Ferguson, H. *A Study of the Characteristics of American Indian Professional Women in Oklahoma.* Columbus: Ohio State University Press, 1985.

Fernandez, John P. *Managing a Diverse Work Force: Regaining the Competitive Edge.* New York: Free Press, 1991.

Ferris, Helen. *Girls Clubs: Their Organization and Management: A Manual for Workers.* New York: E. P. Dutton, 1918.

Fiedorek, Mary B., and Diana Lewis Jewell. *Executive Style: Looking It, Living It.* Piscataway, NJ: New Century, 1983.

Field, Vena B. *Constantia: A Study of the Life and Works of Judith Sargent Murray.* 1931.

Fields, Daisy B. *A Woman's Guide to Moving Up in Business and Government.* New York: Prentice-Hall, 1983.

Finch, Edith. *Carey Thomas of Bryn Mawr.* 1947.

Fine, Lisa M. *The Souls of the Skyscraper: Female Clerical Workers in Chicago, 1870–1930.* Philadelphia: Temple University Press, 1990.

Fink, Gary, ed. *Biographical Dictionary of American Labor Leaders.* Westport, CT: Greenwood Press, 1974.

Fink, Leon. *Workingmen's Democracy: The Knights of Labor and American Politics.* Urbana: University of Illinois Press, 1983.

Finley, Ruth E. *The Lady of Godey's.* 1931.

Fisher, Anne B. *Wall Street Women: Women in Power on the Street Today.* New York: Knopf, 1990.

Fisher, Dexter. *The Third Woman: Minority Women Writers of the United States.* New York: Houghton Mifflin, 1980.

Fisk, Fidelia. *Recollections of Mary Lyon.* 1866.

Flynn, Elizabeth Gurley. *I Speak My Own Piece: Autobiography of "the Rebel Girl."* New York: Masses and Mainstream, 1955.

Foner, Philip S., ed. *The Factory Girls: A Collection of Writings on Life and Struggles in the New England Factories of the 1840s by the Factory Girls Themselves, and the Story, in Their Own Words, of the First Trade Unions of Women Workers in the United States.* Urbana: University of Illinois Press, 1977.

———. *Women and the American Labor Movement: From Colonial Times to the Eve of World War I.* New York: Free Press, 1979.

———. *Women and the American Labor Movement: From the First Trade Unions to the Present.* New York: Free Press, 1982.

Foster, James C. *The Union Politic: The CIO Political Action Committee.* Columbia: University of Missouri Press, 1975.

Foster, John O. *The Life and Labors of Mrs. Maggie Newton Van Cott, the First Lady Licensed To Preach in the Methodist Episcopal Church in the United States.* Hamden, CT: Garland Press, 1988.

Foster-Dixon, Gwendolyn, and Wheeler Dixon. "Women Who Made the Movies." 1991. Videotape.

Fox, Steve. *Toxic Work: Women Workers at GTE Lenkurt.* Philadelphia: Temple University Press, 1991.

Frankenhauser, M., et al., eds. *Women, Work, and Health.* New York: Plenum, 1991.

Frederickson, Mary E. "'A Place To Speak Our Minds': The Southern School for Women Workers." Ph.D. dissertation, University of North Carolina, 1981.

Freeman, S. J. M. *Managing Lives.* Amherst: University of Massachusetts Press, 1990.

French, Emily. *Emily: The Diary of a Hard-Worked Woman,* ed. Janet LeCompte. Lincoln: University of Nebraska Press, 1987.

Friedheim, Robert L. *The Seattle General Strike.* Seattle: University of Washington Press, 1964.

Friedlander, Judith, Blanche Wiesen Cook, Alice Kessler-Harris, and Caroll Smith-Rosenberg, eds. *Women in Culture and Politics: A Century of Change.* Bloomington: Indiana University Press, 1986.

Frug, Mary J. *Women and the Law.* Westbury, NY: Foundation Press, 1992.

Fuchs, Victor R. *Women's Quest for Economic Equality.* Cambridge: Harvard University Press, 1988.

Gaar, Gillian G. *She's a Rebel: The History of Women in Rock and Roll.* Seattle: Seal Press, c. 1992.

Gabin, Nancy F. *Feminism in the Labor Movement: Women and the United Auto Workers, 1935–1975.* Ithaca, NY: Cornell University Press, 1990.

Gacs, Uta D., et al., eds. *Women Anthropologists: Selected Biographies.* Urbana: University of Illinois Press, 1989.

Galinski, Ellen, and William H. Hooks. *The New Extended Family: Day Care That Works.* Boston: Houghton Mifflin, 1972.

Garcia, Mario T. *Desert Immigrants: The Mexicans of El Paso, 1880–1920.* New Haven, CT: Yale University Press, 1981.

Garland, Anne White. *Women Activists: Challenging the Abuse of Power.* New York: Feminist Press, 1988.

Garrison, Dee. *Mary Heaton Vorse: The Life of an American Insurgent.* Philadelphia: Temple University Press, 1989.

Gatlin, Rochelle. *American Women since 1945.* Jackson: University Press of Mississippi, 1987.

Gelb, Joyce, and Marian Lief Palley. *Women and Public Policies.* Princeton, NJ: Princeton University Press, 1982.

Gelfman, Judith S. *Women in Television News.* New York: Columbia University Press, 1976.

Gerdts, William H. *Women Artists of America 1707–1964.* 1965.

Gerstel, Naomi, and Harriet E. Gross, eds. *Families and Work.* Philadelphia: Temple University Press, 1987.

Geyer, Georgie Anne. *Buying the Night Flight: The Autobiography of a Woman Foreign Correspondent.* New York: Dell, 1983.

Giddings, Paula. *When and Where I Enter: The Impact of Black Women on Race and Sex in America.* Toronto: Bantam Books, 1984.

Gilbreth, Frank, Jr. *Time Out for Happiness.* 1970.

Gilchrist, Beth Bradford. *The Life of Mary Lyon.* 1910.

Gilden, K. B. *Between the Hills and the Sea.* Garden City, NY: Doubleday, 1971.

Giles, Kevin. *Flight of the Dove: The Story of Jeannette Rankin.* Beaverton, OR: Touchstone Oregon, 1980.

Gilman, Charlotte Perkins. *The Living of Charlotte Perkins Gilman.* 1935.

Gilman, Glenn. *Human Relations in the Industrial Southeast: A Study of the Textile Industry.* Chapel Hill: University of North Carolina Press, 1956.

Gilson, E., and S. Kane. *Unnecessary Choices: The Hidden Life of the Executive Woman.* New York: William Morrow, 1987.

Gitelman, Howard M. *Legacy of the Ludlow Massacre: A Chapter in American Industrial Relations.* Philadelphia: University of Pennsylvania Press, 1988.

Glazer, Penina Midgal, and Miriam Slater. *Unequal Colleagues: The Entrance of Women into the Professions, 1880–1940.* New Brunswick, NJ: Rutgers University Press, 1987.

Glenn, Evelyn Nakano. *Issei, Nisei, War Bride: Three Generations of Japanese American Women in Domestic Service.* Philadelphia: Temple University Press, 1986.

Glenn, Susan A. *Daughters of the Shtetl: Life and Labor in the Immigrant Generation.* Ithaca, NY: Cornell University Press, 1990.

Gluck, Sherna Berger. *Rosie the Riveter Revisited: Women, the War, and Social Change.* Boston: Twayne Pub., 1987.

Gold, Michael Evan. *A Dialogue on Comparable Worth.* Ithaca, NY: ILR Press, 1983.

———. *An Introduction to Labor Law.* Ithaca, NY: ILR Press, 1989.

Goldin, Claudia. *Understanding the Gender Gap: An Economic History of American Women.* New York: Oxford University Press, 1990.

Goldman, Emma. *Living My Life.* 2 vols. New York: Dover, [1931] 1970.

Goldmark, Josephine. *Impatient Crusader: Florence Kelley's Life Story.* Urbana, Ill: University of Illinois Press, 1953.

Golin, Steve. *The Fragile Bridge: Paterson Silk Strike, 1913.* Philadelphia: Temple University Press, 1988.

Gordon, Lynn D. *Gender and Higher Education in the Progressive Era.* New Haven, CT: Yale University Press, 1990.

Gover, C. Jane. *The Positive Image: Women Photographers in Turn-of-the-Century America.* Albany, NY: State University of New York Press, 1988.

Graham, Martha. *Blood Memory.* New York: Doubleday, 1991.

Green, James, ed. *Workers' Struggles, Past and Present: A "Radical America" Reader.* Philadelphia: Temple University Press, 1983.

Green, Mildred D. *Black Women Composers: A Genesis*. New York: Macmillan, 1983.

Greene, Kathanne W. *Affirmative Action and Principles of Justice*. Westport, CT: Greenwood Press, 1989.

Greenwald, Carol S. *Women in Management*. Scarsdale, NY: Work in America Institute, 1980.

Greenwald, Maurine Weiner. *Women, War and Work: The Impact of World War I on Women Workers in the United States*. Westport, CT: Greenwood Press, 1980.

———. "Working-Class Feminism and the Family Wage Ideal: The Seattle Debate on Married Women's Right To Work, 1914–1920." *The Journal of American History* 76 (June 1989): 118–149.

Griffith, Barbara S. "The Crisis of American Labor: Operation Dixie and the Defeat of the CIO." Ph.D. dissertation, Duke University, 1986.

Grittner, Frederick K. *White Slavery: Myth, Ideology, and American Law*. New York: Garland Press, 1990.

Groneman, Carol, and Mary Beth Norton, eds. *"To Toil the Livelong Day": America's Women at Work, 1780–1980*. Ithaca, NY: Cornell University Press, 1987.

Gustafson, S. B., and D. Magnusson, eds. *Female Life Careers: A Pattern Approach*. Hillsdale, NJ: Erlbaum 1991.

Gutek, Barbara A. *Sex and the Workplace*. San Francisco: Jossey-Bass, 1985.

Gutek, Barbara A., and L. Larwood. *Women's Career Development*. Newbury Park, CA: Russell Sage, 1987.

Haas, Violet B., and Carolyn C. Perrucci, eds. *Women in Scientific and Engineering Professions*. Ann Arbor: University of Michigan Press, 1984.

Hagan, Oliver, Carol Rivchun, and Donald Sexton., eds. *Women-Owned Businesses*. New York: Praeger, 1989.

Hagood, Margaret Jarman. *Mothers of the South: Portraiture of the White Tenant Farm Woman*. Chapel Hill: University of North Carolina Press, 1939.

Hale, Mary M., and Rita Mae Kelly, eds. *Gender, Bureaucracy, and Democracy: Careers and Equal Opportunity in the Public Sector*. Westport, CT: Greenwood Press, 1989.

Hall, Jacquelyn Dowd, James Leloudis, Robert Korstad, Mary Murphy, Lu Ann Jones, and Christopher B. Daly. *Like a Family: The Making of a Southern Cotton Mill World*. Chapel Hill: University of North Carolina Press, 1987.

Hamilton, Alice. *Exploring the Dangerous Trades*. Boston: Northwestern University Press, [1943] 1985.

Handy, D. Antoinette. *Black Women in American Bands and Orchestras*. Metuchen, NJ: Scarecrow Press, 1981.

Hapke, Laura. *Tales of the Working Girl: Wage-Earning Women in American Literature, 1890–1925*. New York: Twayne Pub., 1992.

Hareven, Tamara K., *Eleanor Roosevelt: An American Conscience*. New York: Quadrangles, 1968.

Hareven, Tamara K. and Ralph Langenbach. *Amoskeag: Life and Work in an American Factory City*. New York: Pantheon Books, 1978.

Harlan, Anne, and Carol Weiss. *Moving Up: Women in Managerial Careers*. Wellesley, MA: Wellesley College Center for Research on Women, 1981.

Harlan, Sharon I., and Ronnie J. Steinberg, eds. *Job Training for Women: The Promise and Limits of Public Policies*. Philadelphia: Temple University Press, 1990.

Harragan, Betty Lehan. *Games Mother Never Taught You*. New York: Warner Books, 1978.

Harris, Ann S. *Women Artists, Fifteen Fifty to Nineteen Fifty*. New York: Knopf, 1977.

Harris, Barbara J. *Beyond Her Sphere: Women and the Professions in American History*. Westport, CT: Greenwood Press, 1978.

Harris, Ted. *Jeannette Rankin: Suffragist, First Woman Elected to Congress, and Pacifist*. Salem, NH: Ayer, n.d.

Harris, William. *The Harder We Run: Black Workers since the Civil War*. New York: Oxford University Press, 1982.

Harrison, Cynthia E. *On Account of Sex: The Politics of Women's Issues, 1945–1968*. Berkeley: University of California Press, 1988.

Hartmann, Heidi. *Women's Work: Economic Trends and Policy Issues*. Washington, DC: Institute for Women's Policy Research, 1988.

Hartmann, Heidi, and June Lapidus. *Temporary Work*. Washington, DC: Institute for Women's Policy Research, 1989.

Hartmann, Susan M. *From Margin to Mainstream: American Women and Politics since 1960*. New York: Knopf, 1989.

———. *The Home Front and Beyond: American Women in the 1940s*. Boston: Twayne, 1982.

Harveson, Mae E. *Catharine Esther Beecher, Pioneer Educator*. Salem, NH: Ayer, [1932] 1969.

Haslett, B., F. Geis, and M. Carter. *The Organizational Woman: Power and Paradox*. Norwood, NJ: Ablex, 1992.

Havighurst, Walter. *Annie Oakley of the Wild West*. Lincoln: University of Nebraska Press, 1992.

Hayden, Dolores. *The Grand Domestic Revolution: A History of Feminist Designs for American Homes, Neighborhoods, and Cities*. Cambridge: MIT Press, 1981.

Hazou, Winnie. *The Social and Legal Status of Women: A Global Perspective*. New York: Praeger, 1990.

Healey, Dorothy, and Maurice Isserman. *Dorothy Healey Remembers: A Life in the American Communist Party*. New York: Oxford University Press, 1990.

Heck-Rabi, Louise. *Women Filmmakers: A Critical Reception*. Metuchen, NJ: Scarecrow Press, 1984.

Heiler, Rita. *The Women of Summer: Bryn Mawr Summer School for Women Workers, 1921–1938*. 1985. Film.

Heim, Kathleen M., ed. *The Status of Women in Librarianship: Historical, Sociological, and Economic Issues*. New York: Neal-Schuman, 1983.

Helgasen, Sally. *Female Advantage: Women's Ways of Leadership*. New York: Doubleday, 1990.

Heller, Nancy G. *Women Artists: An Illustrated History*. New York: Abbeville Press, 1987.

Hendee, Elizabeth Russell. *The Growth and Development of the Young Women's Christian Association*. New York: Women's Press, 1930.

Henry, Alice. *The Trade Union Woman*. New York: D. Appleton, 1915.

Hewlett, Sylvia A. *A Lesser Life: The Myth of Women's Liberation in America*. New York: Warner Books, 1989.

Hill, Caroline M., comp. *Mary McDowell and Municipal Housekeeping*. 1938.

Hill, George H., Lorraine Raglin, and Chas Floyd Johnson. *Black Women in Television: An Illustrated History and Bibliography*. Hamden, CT: Garland Press, 1990.

Hill, Joseph A. *Women in Gainful Occupations, 1870 to 1920*. Census Monographs 9. Washington, DC: Government Printing Office, 1929.

Hill, M. Anne, and Mark R. Killingsworth, eds. *Comparable Worth: Analyses and Evidence*. Ithaca, NY: ILR Press, 1989.

Hilliard, Patricia. "Hero Rides Discrimination Out on a Rail." *New Directions for Women* (January/February 1992).

Hine, Darlene Clark, ed. *Black Women in America: An Historical Encyclopedia*, 2 vols. Brooklyn, NY: Carlson, 1993.

Hitchings, Catherine F. *Universalist and Unitarian Women Ministers*. Boston: UUHS, 1985.

Hobson, Barbara Meil. *Uneasy Virtue: The Politics of Prostitution and the American Reform Tradition*. New York: Basic Books, 1987.

Hochschild, Arlie, with Anne Machung. *The Second Shift: Working Parents and the*

Revolution at Home. New York: Viking Penguin, 1989.

Hoerle, Helen C., and Florence B. Saltzberg. *The Girl and the Job.* New York: Henry Holt, 1919.

Hoff, Joan. *Law, Gender, and Injustice: A Legal History of U.S. Women.* New York: New York University Press, 1991.

Holden, Henry M. *Ladybirds: The Untold Story of Women Pilots in America.* Seattle, WA: Black Hawk Press, 1991.

Holm, Jeanne. *Women in the Military: An Unfinished Revolution.* Novato, CA: Presidio, 1982.

Holt, Rackham. *Mary McLeod Bethune: A Biography.* New York: Doubleday, 1964.

Honey, Maureen. *Creating Rosie the Riveter: Class, Gender and Propaganda during World War II.* Amherst: University of Massachusetts Press, 1984.

Hooks, Janet M. *Women's Occupations through Seven Decades.* Women's Bureau Bulletin #218. Washington, DC: Zenger, [1947] 1976.

Hosansky, Tamar, and Pat Sparling. *Working Vice: The Gritty True Story of Lt. Lucie J. Duvall—A Courageous Cop Who Dared To Make a Difference.* New York: Harper Collins, 1992.

Hosley, David H., and Gayle K. Yamada. *Hard News: Women in Broadcast Journalism.* Westport, CT: Greenwood Press, 1987.

Hot, Louis B., and J. David Dalke. *The Sexes at Work: Improving Work Relationships between Men and Women.* Englewood Cliffs, NJ: Prentice-Hall, 1983.

Howard, Anne Bail. *The Long Campaign: A Biography of Anne Martin.* Reno: University of Nevada Press, 1985.

Howe, Louise Kapp. *Pink Collar Workers: Inside the World of Women's Work.* New York: G. P. Putnam's Sons, 1977.

Hoyt, Michael, and Charles J. Press, eds. *Liberty at Work: Expanding the Rights of Employees in America.* New York: ACLU, 1988.

Hudson Institute. *Opportunity 2000: Creative Affirmative Action Strategies for a Changing Workforce.* Washington, DC: U.S. Department of Labor, Employment Standards Administration, September 1988.

Hunsaker, J., and P. Hunsaker. *Strategies and Skills for Managerial Women.* Cincinnati, OH: South-Western, 1992.

Hunt, Harriot. *Glances and Glimpses.* 1856.

Hutner, Frances C. *Equal Pay for Comparable Worth: The Working Woman's Issue of the Eighties.* Westport, CT: Greenwood Press, 1986.

Hymowitz, Carol, and Michaele Weissman. *A History of Women in America.* New York: Bantam Books, 1980.

I Dream a World: Portraits of Black Women Who Changed America. New York: Stewart, Tabori & Chang, 1989.

Ice, Martha L. *Clergy Women and Their Worldviews: Calling for a New Age.* Westbrook, CT: Greenwood Press, 1987.

Ichioka, Yuji. *The Issei: The World of the First Generation Japanese Immigrants, 1885–1924.* New York: Free Press, 1988.

Institute for Women's Policy Research. *Research in Brief: The Wage Gap: Women and Men's Earnings.* Washington, DC, n.d.

Irwin, Inez. *Angels and Amazons: A Hundred Years of American Women.* Salem, NH: Ayer, [1934] 1974.

Jacobs, Jerry A. *Revolving Doors: Sex Segregation and Women's Careers.* Stanford, CA: Stanford University Press, 1989.

Jacobson, Aileen. *Women in Charge: Dilemmas of Women in Authority.* New York: Van Nostrand Reinhold, 1985.

James, Edward T., Janet Wilson James, and Paul S. Boyer, eds. *Notable American Women 1607–1950: A Biographical Dictionary.* 3 vols. Cambridge: Harvard University Press, 1971.

Jaynes, Gerald David. *Branches without Roots: Genesis of the Black Working Class in the American South: 1862–1882.* New York: Oxford University Press, 1986.

Jensen, Joan M. *Loosening the Bonds: Mid-Atlantic Farm Women, 1750–1850.* New Haven, CT: Yale University Press, 1986.

———. *With These Hands: Women Working on the Land.* Old Westbury, NY: Feminist Press, 1981.

Jensen, Joan M., and Sue Davidson, eds. *A Needle, a Bobbin, a Strike: Women Needleworkers in America.* Philadelphia: Temple University Press, 1984.

Jewell, Donald O., ed. *Women and Management: An Expanding Role.* Atlanta: Georgia State University Business Press, 1977.

Jezic, Diane P. *Women Composers: The Lost Tradition Found.* New York: Feminist Press, 1988.

Jones, Jacqueline. *Labor of Love, Labor of Sorrow: Black Women, Work and the Family from Slavery to the Present.* New York: Basic Books, 1985.

Jones, Mary Harris. *Autobiography of Mother Jones,* ed. Mary Field Parton. Chicago: Illinois Labor Historical Society, [1925] 1972.

Josephson, Hannah. *The Golden Threads: New England's Mill Girls and Magnates.* New York: Duell, Sloan and Pearce, 1949.

Kahn-Hut, Rachel, Arlene Kaplan Daniels, and Richard Colvard, eds. *Women and Work: Problems and Perspectives.* New York: Oxford University Press, 1982.

Kaledin, Eugenia. *Mothers and More: American Women in the 1950s.* New York: Macmillan, 1985.

Kalisch, Philip A., and Beatrice J. Kalisch. *The Advance of American Nursing.* Boston: Little, Brown, 1978.

Kamerman, Sheila B., and Alfred J. Kahn. *Maternity Policies and Working Women.* New York: Columbia University Press, 1985.

———. *The Responsive Workplace: Employers and a Changing Labor Force.* New York: Columbia University Press, 1987.

Kandel, Thelma. *What Women Earn.* New York: Simon and Schuster, 1981.

Kanter, Rosabeth Moss. *Men and Women of the Corporation.* New York: Basic Books, 1977.

———. *When Giants Learn To Dance: Mastering the Challenge of Strategy, Management and Careers in the 1990s.* New York: Simon & Schuster, 1989.

Kaplan, Glenn. *The Big Time.* New York: Congdon and Weed, 1982.

Karsten, M. F. *Gender Issues in Management.* Madison, WI: Margaret Foegen Karsten, 1992.

Katzman, David. *Seven Days a Week: Women and Domestic Service in Industrializing America.* New York: Oxford University Press, 1978.

Kelley, Mary, ed. *Woman's Being, Woman's Place: Female Identity and Vocation in American History.* Boston: G. K. Hall, 1979.

Kelly, Rita Mae, and Jane Bayes, eds., *Comparable Worth, Pay Equity, and Public Policy.* Westport, CT: Greenwood Press, 1988.

Kendall, Elaine. *Peculiar Institutions: An Informal History of the Seven Sister Colleges.* New York: G. P. Putnam's Sons, 1975–1976.

Kendall, Phebe Mitchell. *Maria Mitchell: Life, Letters, and Journals.* 1896.

Kenedy, Carolyn. *Pay Equity: An Action Manual for Library Workers.* Chicago: American Library Association, 1989.

Kenen, Regina H. *Reproductive Hazards in the Workplace: Mending Jobs, Managing Pregnancies.* Binghamton, NY: Haworth Press, 1992.

Kenneally, James J. *The History of American Catholic Women.* New York: Crossroad, 1990.

———. "Women in the United States and Trade Unionism," in Norbert C. Soldon, ed., *The World of Women's Trade Unionism: Comparative Historical Essays.* Westport, CT: Greenwood Press, 1985.

Kennedy, Susan Estabrook. *If All We Did Was To Weep at Home: A History of White Working Class Women in America.* Bloomington: Indiana University Press, 1977.

Kennelly, Karen, ed. *American Catholic Women: A Historical Exploration.* New York: Macmillan, 1989.

Kerber, Linda K. *Women of the Republic: Intellect and Ideology in Revolutionary America*. 2 vols. Chapel Hill: University of North Carolina Press for the Institute of Early American History and Culture at Williamsburg, 1980.

Kerber, Linda K., and Jane S. DeHart. *Women's America: Refocusing the Past*. 3d ed. New York: Oxford University Press, 1989.

Kesselman, Amy. *Fleeting Opportunities: Women Shipyard Workers in Portland and Vancouver during World War II and Reconversion*. Albany: State University of New York Press, 1990.

Kessler-Harris, Alice. *Out To Work: A History of Wage-Earning Women in the United States*. Oxford: Oxford University Press, 1982.

———. *A Woman's Wage: Historical Meanings and Social Consequences*. Lexington, KY: University Press of Kentucky, 1990.

———. *Women Have Always Worked: A Historical Overview*. New York: Feminist Press, 1981.

King, Joan. *Sarah M. Peale: America's First Woman Artist*. Boston: Branden, 1987.

Kingsolver, Barbara. *Holding the Line: Women in the Great Arizona Mine Strike of 1983*. Ithaca, NY: ILR Press, 1989.

Kirkpatrick, Jeanne. *The New Presidential Elite: Men and Women in National Politics*. New York: Russell Sage, 1976.

Klatch, Rebecca E. *Women of the New Right*. Philadelphia: Temple University Press, 1987.

Klein, Abbie Gordon. *The Debate over Child Care, 1969–1990*. Albany: State University of New York Press, 1992.

Kleinberg, Susan. "Technology's Stepdaughters: The Impact of Industrialization upon Working Class Women, Pittsburgh, 1865–1890." Ph.D. dissertation, University of Pittsburgh, 1973.

Klejment, Anne, and Alice Klejment. *Dorothy Day and the Catholic Worker: A Bibliography and Index*. Hamden, CT: Garland, 1986.

Knoll, Tricia. *Becoming Americans: Asian Sojourners, Immigrants, and Refugees in the Western United States*. Portland, OR: Coast to Coast Books, 1982.

Koehler, Lyle. *A Search for Power: The "Weaker Sex" in Seventeenth-Century New England*. Urbana: University of Illinois Press, 1980.

Kornbluh, Joyce L., and Mary Frederickson, eds. *Sisterhood and Solidarity: Workers' Education for Women*. Philadelphia: Temple University Press, 1984.

Koziara, Karen S., et al., eds. *Working Women: Past, Present, Future*. Washington, DC: Bureau of National Affairs, 1987.

Kraditor, Aileen. *Up from the Pedestal*. Chicago: Quadrangle Books, 1970.

Krannich, Ronald L., and Caryl Rae Krannich. *The Complete Guide to Public Employment*. Manassas, VA: Impact, 1986.

Kreps, Juanita M. *Sex in the Marketplace: American Women at Work*. Baltimore: Johns Hopkins University Press, 1971.

Kreps, Juanita M., ed. *Women and the American Economy: A Look to the 1980s*. Englewood, NJ: Prentice-Hall, 1976.

Krimerman, Len, and Frank Lindenfeld, eds. *When Workers Decide: Workplace Democracy Takes Root in America*. Philadelphia: New Society, 1991.

Lamphere, Louise. *From Working Daughters to Working Mothers: Immigrant Women in a New England Industrial Community*. Ithaca, NY: Cornell University Press, 1987.

Lansing, Marion, ed. *Mary Lyon through Her Letters*. 1937.

Larwood, Laurie, and Marion M. Wood. *Women in Management*. Lexington, MA: Lexington Books, 1977.

Lash, Joseph. *Eleanor: The Years Alone*. New York: W. W. Norton, 1971.

———. *Eleanor and Franklin*. New York: W. W. Norton, 1972.

LaTeef, Nelda. *Working Women for the 21st Century*. Charlotte, VT: Williamson, 1992.

Laughlin, Clara E. *The Work-a-Day Girl*. New York: Fleming H. Revell, 1913.

Leacock, Eleanor, and Helen I. Safa. *Women's Work: Development and the Division of Labor by Gender.* Westport, CT: Bergin and Garvey, 1986.

Leavitt, Judith A. *American Women Managers and Administrators: A Selective Biographical Dictionary of Twentieth-Century Leaders in Business, Education, and Government.* Westport, CT: Greenwood Press, 1985.

Leavitt, Judith A., and Paul Wasserman. *Women in Administration and Management: An Information Sourcebook.* Phoenix, AZ: Oryx Press, 1988.

Leavitt, Judith Walzer. *Brought to Bed: Childbearing in America. 1750 to 1950.* New York: Oxford University Press, 1986.

Lee, Roy F. *The Setting for Black Business Development: A Study in Sociology and Political Economy.* Ithaca, NY: ILR Press, 1973.

Lehrer, Susan. *Origins of Protective Labor Legislation for Women, 1905–1925.* Albany: State University of New York Press, 1987.

Lemons, J. Stanley. *The Woman Citizen: Social Feminism in the 1920s.* Urbana: University of Illinois Press, 1973.

LePage, Jane W. *Women Composers, Conductors, and Musicians of the Twentieth Century: Selected Biographies.* Metuchen, NJ: Scarecrow Press, 1980.

Lerner, Gerda. *Black Women in White America: A Documentary History.* New York: Vintage Books, 1973.

———. *The Majority Finds Its Past: Placing Women in History.* New York: Oxford University Press, 1979.

———. *The Woman in American History.* Menlo Park, CA: Addison-Wesley, 1971.

Lerner, Gerda, ed. *The Female Experience: An American Documentary.* Indianapolis: Bobbs-Merrill Education, 1977.

Lerner, Jacqueline V., and Nancy L. Galambos. *Employed Mothers and Their Children.* Hamden, CT: Garland, 1991.

LeVeness, Frank P., and Jane P. Sweeney, eds. *Women Leaders in Contemporary U.S. Politics.* Boulder, CO: Lynne Rienner, 1987.

Levenstein, Harvey A. *Revolution at the Table: The Transformation of the American Diet.* New York: Oxford University Press, 1988.

Levine, Louis. *The Women's Garment Workers.* New York: Arno Press, [1924] 1969.

Levine, Susan. *Labor's True Woman: Carpet Weavers, Industrialization and Labor Reform in the Gilded Age.* Philadelphia: Temple University Press, 1984.

Lewenson, Sandra Beth. *Taking Charge: Nursing, Suffrage, and Feminism in America, 1873–1920.* Hamden, CT: Garland, 1993.

Lewis, Sinclair. *The Job: An American Novel.* New York: Grosset & Dunlap, 1917.

Lichtendorf, Susan S., and Phyliss L. Gillis. *The New Pregnancy: The Active Woman's Guide to Work, Legal Rights, Health Care, Travel, Sports, Dress, Sex, and Emotional Well-Being.* New York: Random House, 1979.

Lilienthal, Meta Stern. *From Fireside to Factory.* New York: Macmillan, 1910.

Lim, Shirley Geok-Lin, and Mayumi Tsuktakawa, eds. *The Forbidden Stitch: An Asian American Women's Anthology.* Corvallis, OR: Calyx Press, 1988.

Lindgren, H. Elaine. *Land in Her Own Name: Women as Homesteaders in North Dakota.* Fargo: North Dakota Institute for Regional Studies, 1991.

Lindsey, Almont. *The Pullman Strike: The Story of a Unique Experiment and of a Great Labor Upheaval.* Chicago: University of Chicago Press, 1943.

Ling, Amy. *Between Worlds: Women Writers of Chinese Ancestry.* New York: Pergamon, 1990.

Link, Arthur S. *Wilson II: The New Freedom.* Princeton, NJ: Princeton University Press, 1956.

Linkugel, Wil A., and Martha Solomon. *Anna Howard Shaw: Suffrage Orator and Social Reformer.* Westport, CT: Greenwood Press, 1990.

Lissak, Rivka Shpak. *Pluralism and Progressives, Hull House and the New*

Immigrants, 1890–1919. Chicago: University of Chicago Press, 1989.

Litoff, Judy Barrett. *American Midwives, 1860 to the Present.* Westport, CT: Greenwood Press, 1978.

Livermore, Mary Ashton Rice. *My Story of the War.* 1887.

———. *Story of My Life.* 1897.

Livernash, E. Robert, ed. *Comparable Worth: Issues and Alternatives.* 2d ed. Washington, DC: Equal Employment Advisory Council, 1984.

Lobsenz, Johanna. *The Older Woman in Industry.* New York: Arno Press, [1929] 1974.

Lopate, Carol. *Women in Medicine.* Baltimore: Johns Hopkins University Press, 1968.

Lotze, Barbara, intro. *Making Contributions: An Historical Overview of Women's Role in Physics.* College Park, MD: American Association of Physics Teachers, 1984.

Lovejoy, Esther Pohl. *Certain Samaritans.* New York: Macmillan, 1933.

Lunneborg, Patricia W. *Women Changing Work.* Westport, CT: Greenwood Press, 1990.

Lutz, Alma. *Emma Willard: Pioneer Educator of American Women.* Westport, CT: Greenwood Press, [1964] 1984.

Lynd, Robert S., and Helen Merell Lynd. *Middletown in Transition.* New York: Harcourt Brace, 1937.

Lynn, Loretta, and George Vecsey. *Loretta Lynn: Coal Miner's Daughter.* Chicago: Contemporary Books, 1985.

McBroom, Patricia A. *The Third Sex: The New Professional Woman.* New York: William Morrow, 1986.

McCann, Nancy Dodd, and Thomas A. McGinn. *Harassed: 100 Women Define Inappropriate Behavior in the Workplace.* Homewood, IL: Business One Irwin, 1992.

McCullough, David. *The Great Bridge.* New York: Simon and Schuster, 1972.

McCullough, Joan. *First of All: Significant "Firsts" by American Women.* New York: Holt, Rinehart and Winston, 1980.

Macdonald, Anne L. *Feminine Ingenuity: Women and Invention in America.* New York: Ballantine Books, 1992.

Macdougall, Allan Ross. *Isadora: A Revolutionary in Art and Love.* 1960.

McGovern, James R. "The American Woman's Pre-World War I Freedom in Manners and Morals," *Journal of American History* LV (September 1968).

McHenry, Robert, ed. *Liberty's Women.* Springfield, MA: G. and C. Merriam Co., 1980.

McIlwee, Judith S., and J. Gregg Robinson. *Women in Engineering: Gender, Power, and Workplace Culture.* Albany: State University of New York Press, 1992.

MacKenzie, Susan T. *Noise and Office Work.* Ithaca, NY: ILR Press, 1975.

MacKinnon, Catherine A. *Sexual Harassment of Working Women: A Case of Sex Discrimination.* New Haven, CT: Yale University Press, 1979.

McKissack, Patricia, and Frederick McKissack. *Madam C. J. Walker: Self-Made Millionaire.* Hillside, NJ: Enslow, 1992.

MacLean, Annie Marion. *Wage-Earning Women.* New York: Macmillan, 1910.

———. *Women Workers and Society.* Chicago: A. C. McClurg, 1916.

McRae, Susan. *Cross-Class Families: A Study of Wives' Occupational Superiority.* New York: Oxford University Press, 1986.

Maida, Patricia. *Mother of Detective Fiction: The Life and Works of Anna Katharine Green.* Bowling Green, OH: Bowling Green University Press, 1989.

Mainiero, Lina, and Langdon L. Faust, eds. *American Women Writers: A Critical Reference Guide.* 4 vols. New York: Continuum, 1982.

Majors, Monroe A. *Noted Negro Women.* New York: Gordon Press, 1972.

Malkiel, Theresa Serber. *Diary of a Shirtwaist Striker*. Ithaca, NY: ILR Press, 1990.

Mallier, A. T., and M. J. Rosser. *Women and the Economy: A Comparative Study of Britain and the United States*. New York: St. Martin's, 1986.

Maltby, Lewis L. *A State of Emergency in the American Workplace*. Washington, DC: ACLU, 1990.

Mansbridge, Jane. *Why We Lost the ERA*. Chicago: University of Chicago Press, 1986.

Margolis, Maxine. *Mothers and Such: Views of American Women and Why They Changed*. Berkeley: University of California Press, 1984.

Marshall, F. Ray. *Labor in the South*. Cambridge: Harvard University Press, 1967.

Marshall, Helen E. *Dorothea Dix: Forgotten Samaritan*. 1937.

Marshall, Nancy T., and Pam Vredevelt. *Women Who Compete*. Tarrytown, NY: Revell, 1988.

Martin, Linda, and Kerry Segrave. *Women in Comedy*. Secaucus, NJ: Citadel Press, 1986.

Martin, Molly, ed. *Hard-Hatted Women: Stories of Struggle and Success in the Trades*. Seattle, WA: Seal Press Feminist, 1988.

Maschke, Karen J. *Litigation, Courts, and Women Workers*. New York: Praeger, 1989.

Mason, Lucy R. *To Win These Rights: A Personal Story of the CIO in the South*. Westport, CT: Greenwood Press, [1952] 1970.

Massey, Mary E. *Bonnet Brigades*. New York: Knopf, 1966.

Matson, Molly, ed. *An Independent Woman: The Autobiography of Edith Guerrier*. Amherst, MA: University of Massachusetts Press, 1991.

Matthaei, Julie. *An Economic History of Women in America: Women's Work, the Sexual Division of Labor, and the Development of Capitalism*. New York: Schocken Books, 1982.

Matthews, Glenna. *"Just a Housewife": The Rise and Fall of Domesticity in America*. New York: Oxford University Press, 1987.

Matthews, Lillian. *Women in Trade Unions in San Francisco*. Berkeley: University of California Press, 1913.

Mattis, Mary C. *Flexible Work Arrangements for Managers and Professionals: Findings from a Catalyst Study*. New York: Catalyst, 1990.

Maxwell, William Joseph. "Frances Kellor in the Progressive Era: A Case Study in the Professionalization of Reform." Ph.D. dissertation, Teachers College, Columbia University, 1968.

Mazzei, George. *The New Office Etiquette*. New York: Poseidon Press, 1983.

Mead, Margaret. *Blackberry Winter*. New York: Touchstone-Clarion, 1973.

Medsger, Betty. *Women at Work: A Photographic Documentary*. New York: Sheed and Ward, 1975.

Meier, August, and Elliot Rudwick. *From Plantation to Ghetto*. 3d ed. New York: Hill and Wang, 1976.

Melendy, H. Brett. *Asians in America: Filipinos, Koreans, and East Indians*. Boston: Twayne, 1977.

Melosh, Barbara. *The Physician's Hand: Work Culture and Conflict in American Nursing*. Philadelphia: Temple University Press, 1983.

Meyer, Annie Nathan, ed. *Woman's Work in America*. New York: Arno Press, [1891] 1972.

Meyer, Herbert H., and Mary D. Lee. *Women in Traditionally Male Jobs: The Experience in Ten Public Utility Companies*. Washington, DC: U.S. Government Printing Office, 1978.

Meyerowitz, Theresa Berstein. *William Berstein Myerowitz*. Philadelphia: Art Alliance Press, 1986

Meyerwitz, Joanne J. *Women Adrift: Independent Wage Earners in Chicago, 1880–1930*. Chicago: University of Chicago Press, 1987.

Mezey, Susan Gluck. *In Pursuit of Equality: Women, Public Policy and the Federal Courts.* New York: St. Martin's, 1992.

Milkman, Ruth. *Gender at Work: The Dynamics of Job Segregation by Sex during World War II.* Urbana: University of Illinois Press, 1987.

Milkman, Ruth, ed. *Women, Work and Protest: A Century of U.S. Women's Labor History.* Boston: Routledge & Kegan Paul, 1985.

Miller, Jay, ed. *Mourning Dove: A Salishan Autobiography.* Lincoln: University of Nebraska Press, 1990.

Miller, Kristie. *Ruth Hanna McCormick: A Life in Politics.* Albuquerque: University of New Mexico Press, 1992.

Miller, Marc Scott. *The Irony of Victory: World War II and Lowell, Massachusetts.* Urbana: University of Illinois Press, 1988.

Miller, Marc Scott, ed. *Working Lives: The "Southern Exposure" History of Labor in the South.* New York: Pantheon, 1980.

Mills, Kay. *A Place in the News: From the Women's Pages to the Front Page.* New York: Columbia University Press, 1990.

Milwid, Beth. *Working with Men: Women in the Workplace Talk about Sexuality, Success, and Their Male Co-Workers.* New York: Berkeley Books, 1992.

Missirian, Agnes K. *The Corporate Connection: Why Executive Women Need Mentors To Reach the Top.* Englewood Cliffs, NJ: Spectrum/Prentice-Hall, 1982.

Mitchell, Joyce Slaton. *The Work Book: A Guide to Skilled Jobs.* 1979.

Mohr, Lillian Holmen. *Frances Perkins: "That Woman in FDR's Cabinet!"* Croton-on-Hudson, NY: North River Press, 1979.

Moldow, Gloria. *Women Doctors in Gilded-Age Washington: Race, Gender, and Professionalization.* Urbana: University of Illinois Press, 1987.

Molloy, John T. *The Woman's Dress for Success Book.* New York: Warner Books, 1978.

Moore, Dahlia. *Labor Market Segmentation and Its Implications: Inequality, Deprivation and Entitlement.* Hamden, CT: Garland, 1992.

Morrall, Patricia A. *The Directory of Women Entrepreneurs: A National Sourcebook.* Rev. ed. Atlanta: Wind River Georgia, 1990.

Morris. *Women in Computing.* Stoneham, MA: Butterworth-Heinemann, 1990.

Morris, Celia. *Storming the State House: Running for Governor with Ann Richards and Dianne Feinstein.* New York: Scribner's, 1992.

Morris, Jenny. *Women Workers and the Sweated Trades: The Origins of Minimum Wage Legislation.* Brookfield, VT: Ashgate, 1986.

Morrison, A., R. White, and E. Van Velsor. *Breaking the Glass Ceiling.* Greensboro, NC: Center for Creative Leadership, 1987.

Morrissey, Muriel Earhart. *Courage Is the Price.* 1963.

Morrone, Wenda Wardell. *Pregnant while You Work.* New York: Macmillan, 1984.

Ms. Foundation for Women and the Center for Policy Alternatives. *Women's Voices: A Policy Guide.* New York, 1992.

———. *Women's Voices: A Polling Report.* New York, 1992.

Mulford, Carolyn. *Elizabeth Dole: Public Servant.* Hillside, NJ: Enslow, 1992.

Mulroy, Elizabeth A., ed. *Women as Single Parents: Confronting Institutional Barriers in the Courts, the Workplace, and the Housing Market.* Westport, CT: Auburn House, 1988.

Murphy, Marjorie. *Blackboard Unions: The AFT and the NEA, 1900–1980.* Ithaca, NY: Cornell University Press, 1990.

Murphy, Teresa Anne. *Ten Hours' Labor: Religion, Reform, and Gender in Early New England.* Ithaca, NY: Cornell University Press, 1992.

Nakamura, Alice, and Masso Nakamura. *Second Paycheck: An Analysis of the Employment and Earning of Wives Compared with Unmarried Women and Men.* San Diego, CA: Academic Press, 1985.

Nash, June. *We Eat the Mines, the Mines Eat Us.* New York: Columbia University Press, 1979.

Nathan, Maud. *The Story of an Epoch-Making Movement.* Garden City, NY: Doubleday, Page & Co., 1926.

National Committee on Pay Equity. *Pay Equity in the Public Sector: 1979–1989.* Washington, DC, 1989.

———. *Work and Wages: Facts on Women and People of Color in the Workforce.* Washington, DC, n.d.

National Council for Research on Women. *Sexual Harassment: Research and Resources.* Rev. ed. New York, 1992.

———. *Women in Academe.* New York, 1991.

National Directory of Women-Owned Business Firms. Washington, DC: Business Research Services, 1990.

National Organization for Women (NOW) Legal Defense & Education Fund. "Fetal-Protection Policy Fact Sheet." New York, 1992.

———. "Legal Program Case Docket and Other Professional Activities." New York, 1992.

———. "Legal Resource Kit: Employment—Pay Equity/Comparable Worth." New York, 1988, 1989.

———. "Legal Resource Kit: Employment—Sex Discrimination and Sexual Harassment." New York, 1992.

———. "Legal Resource Kit: Pregnancy and Parental Leave." New York, 1992.

Navaretta, Cynthia. *Guide to Women's Art Organizations and Directory for the Arts.* Rev. ed. New York: Midmarch Arts-WAN, 1982.

Neff, Wanda. *Victorian Working Women.* London: Allen & Unwin, 1929.

Nelkin, Dorothy. *On the Season: Aspects of the Migrant Labor System.* Ithaca, NY: ILR Press, 1970.

Nelson, Albert J. *Emerging Influentials in State Legislatures: Women, Blacks, and Hispanics.* Westport, CT: Greenwood, 1991.

Nelson, Lin. "Women's Occupational Health and Workplace Politics." *Environmental Action* (Summer 1992).

Nestor, Agnes. *Woman's Labor Leader: The Autobiography of Agnes Nestor.* Rockford, IL: Bellevue Books, 1954.

Nicholas, Susan Cary, Alice M. Price, and Rachel Rubin. *Rights and Wrongs: Women's Struggle for Legal Equality.* 2d ed. New York: Feminist Press, 1986.

Nielsen, Georgia Panter. *From Sky Girl to Flight Attendant: Women and the Making of a Union.* Ithaca, NY: ILR Press, 1982.

Nieva, Veronica F., and Barbara A. Gutek. *Women and Work: A Psychological Perspective.* New York: Praeger, 1981.

Nine to Five, National Association of Working Women. "Profile of Working Women." New York, 1990.

———. "Social Insecurity: The Economic Marginalization of Older Female Workers." Cleveland, OH, 1987.

———. "Stories of Mistrust and Manipulation: The Electronic Monitoring of the American Workforce." Cleveland, OH, 1990.

———. "White Collar Displacement: Job Erosion in the Service Sector." Cleveland, OH, 1989.

———. "Working at the Margins: Part-Time and Temporary Workers in the United States." New York, 1986.

The 1988 Working Woman Sexual Harassment Survey. 1988.

Norton, Mary Beth. *Liberty's Daughters: The Revolutionary Experience of American Women, 1750–1800.* Boston: Little, Brown, 1980.

Norwood, Stephen H. *Labor's Flaming Youth: Telephone Operators and Worker Militancy, 1878–1923.* Urbana, IL: University of Illinois Press, 1990.

NWO: A Directory of National Women's Organizations. New York: National Council for Research on Women, 1992.

Nye, Francis Ivan, and Lois Wlapis Hoffman, eds. *The Employed Mother in*

America. Chicago: Rand McNally, 1963.

Oakes, Claudia M. *United States Women in Aviation, 1930–1939*. Washington, DC: Smithsonian Institution, 1991.

Oakley, Ann. *Woman's Work: The Housewife, Past and Present*. New York: Vintage Books, [1974] 1976.

Occupational Outlook Handbook. Washington, DC: U.S. Department of Labor, 1988–1989.

O'Connor, Karen. *Women's Organizations' Use of the Courts*. Lexington, MA: D. C. Heath, 1980.

Ogden, Annegret S. *The Great American Housewife: From Helpmate to Wage Earner, 1776–1986*. Westport, CT: Greenwood Press, 1986.

Olauson, Judith. *The American Woman Playwright: A View of Criticism and Characterization*. Troy, NY: Whitston Pub., 1981.

Olds, Sally Wendkos. *The Working Parent's Survival Guide*. New York: Bantam Books, 1983.

O'Neill, William L. *Everyone Was Brave: The Decline and Fall of Feminism in America*. Chicago: Quadrangle Books, 1969.

Opfell, Olga S. *The Lady Laureates: Women Who Have Won the Nobel Prize*. 2d ed. Metuchen, NJ: Scarecrow Press, 1978.

Oppenheimer, Jerry. *Barbara Walters: An Unauthorized Biography*. New York: St. Martin's, 1990.

Oppenheimer, Valerie Kincaide. *The Female Labor Force in the United States*. Berkeley, CA: Institute of International Studies, 1970.

Organization for Economic Cooperation and Development (OECD) Staff. *Enterprising Women: Local Initiatives for Job Creation*. Washington, DC, 1991.

Osen, Lynn M. *Women in Mathematics*. Cambridge, MA: MIT Press, 1974.

Osterud, Nancy Grey. *Bonds of Community: The Lives of Farm Women in Nineteenth-Century New York*. Ithaca, NY: Cornell University Press, 1991.

O'Sullivan, Judith, and Rosemary Gallick. *Workers and Allies: Female Participation in the American Trade Union Movement, 1824–1976*. Washington, DC: Smithsonian Institution, n.d.

Ott, Mary, and Nancy A. Reese, eds. *Women in Engineering: Beyond Recruitment*. Ithaca, NY: Cornell University Press, 1975.

Outten, Wayne N., with Noah A. Kinigstein. *The Rights of Employees: The Basic ACLU Guide to an Employee's Rights*. New York: Bantam Books, 1983.

Palley, Marian Lief, and Howard A. Palley. "The Thomas Appointment: Defeats and Victories for Women," in *PS: Political Science and Politics* XXV (September 1992): 481–495.

Palmer, George Herbert. *The Life of Alice Freeman Palmer*. 1908.

Palmquist, Peter E., ed. *Camera Fiends and Kodak Girls: Fifty Selections by and about Women in Photography, 1840–1930*. New York: Midmarch Arts-WAN, 1989.

Paludi, Michele, and Richard B. Barickman. *Academic and Workplace Sexual Harassment: A Resource Manual*. Albany: State University of New York Press, 1991.

Paton, Lucy A. *Elizabeth Cary Agassiz: A Biography*. Salem, NH: Ayer, [1919] 1974.

Paules, Greta Foff. *Dishing It Out: Power and Resistance among Waitresses in a New Jersey Restaurant*. Philadelphia: Temple University Press, 1991.

Payne, Elizabeth Anne. *Reform, Labor, and Feminism: Margaret Dreier Robins and the Women's Trade Union League*. Urbana: University of Illinois Press, 1988.

Peare, Catherine Owens. *Mary McLeod Bethune*. New York: Vanguard, 1951.

Pendle, Karin, ed. *Women and Music: A History*. Bloomington: Indiana University Press, 1991.

Pepitone-Rockwell, Fran, ed. *Dual-Career Couples*. Beverly Hills, CA: Sage, 1980.

Pepper, William E., and Florynce R. Kennedy. *Sex Discrimination in Employment*. Charlottesville, VA: Michie, 1981.

Perl, Teri. *Math Equals: Biographies of Women Mathematicians.* Menlo Park, CA: Addison-Wesley, 1978.

Perry, Elizabeth I. *Belle Moskowitz: Feminine Politics and the Exercise of Power in the Age of Alfred E. Smith.* New York: Oxford University Press, 1987.

Perry, Lorinda. *Millinery as a Trade for Women.* New York: Longman, 1916.

Pesotta, Rose. *Bread upon the Waters,* ed. John Nicholas Beffel. Ithaca, NY: ILR Press, 1987.

Peterson, Richard R. *Women, Work, and Divorce.* Albany: State University of New York Press, 1989.

Petrocelli, William, and Barbara Kate Repa. *Sexual Harassment on the Job.* Berkeley, CA: Nolo Press, 1992.

Pinchbeck, Ivy. *Women Workers and the Industrial Revolution: 1750–1850.* New York: Augustus Kelley, [1930] 1969.

Pinckney, Elise. *The Letterbook of Eliza Lucas Pinckney, 1739–1762.* Chapel Hill: University of North Carolina Press, 1972.

Placksin, Sally. *American Women in Jazz, 1900 to the Present: Their Words, Lives, and Music.* New York: Seaview, 1982.

Pleck, Joseph H. *Working Wives/Working Husbands.* Beverly Hills, CA: Russell Sage, 1985.

Poling-Kempes, Lesley. *The Harvey Girls: Women Who Opened the West.* New York: Paragon House, 1989.

Posner, Judith. *The Feminine Mistake: Women, Work, and Identity.* New York: Warner Books, 1992.

Postema, Pam, and Gene Wojciechowski. *You've Got To Have Balls To Make It in This League: My Life as an Umpire.* New York: Simon and Schuster, 1992.

Powell, Garny N. *Women and Men in Management.* Newbury Park, CA: Russell Sage, 1988.

Pregnancy and Employment: The Complete Handbook of Discrimination, Maternity Leave, and Health and Safety. Washington, DC: Bureau of National Affairs, 1987.

Prelinger, Catherine M., ed. *Episcopal Women: Gender, Spirituality and Commitment in an American Mainline Denomination.* New York: Oxford University Press, 1992.

Pryor, Elizabeth B. *Clara Barton, Professional Angel.* Philadelphia: University of Pennsylvania Press, 1987.

Putnam, Ruth, ed. *Life and Letters of Mary Putnam Jacobi.* 1925.

Quart, Barbara X. *Women Directors: The Emergence of a New Cinema.* Westport, CT: Greenwood Press, 1989.

Quintasket, Christine. *Mourning Dove: A Salishan Autobiography,* ed. Jay Miller. Lincoln: University of Nebraska Press, 1990.

Quiroz, Julia Teresa, and Regina Tosca. *For My Children: Mexican American Women, Work, and Welfare.* Washington, DC: Policy Analysis Center, Office of Research, Advocacy, and Legislation, National Council of La Raza, 1992.

Rabinowitz, Randy. *Is Your Job Making You Sick?: A CLUW Handbook on Workplace Hazards,* prepared for the Coalition of Labor Union Women, n.d.

Ramos, M. *A Study of Black Women in Management.* Amherst: University of Massachusetts Press, 1981.

Ratner, Ronnie Steinberg, ed. *Equal Employment Policy for Women.* Philadelphia: Temple University Press, 1980.

Ravenel, Harriet Horry. *Eliza Pinckney.* Spartanburg, SC: Reprint Co., [1896] 1967.

Read, Florence M. *The Story of Spelman College.* 1961.

Remick, Helen, ed. *Comparable Worth: Issues and Alternatives: Technical Possibilities and Political Realities.* Philadelphia: Temple University Press, 1984.

Reskin, Barbara F., ed. *Sex Segregation in the Workplace: Trends, Explanations, Remedies.* Washington, DC: National Academy Press, 1984.

Reskin, Barbara F., and Heidi Hartmann, eds. *Women's Work, Men's Work: Sex Segregation on the Job.* Washington, DC: National Academy Press, 1986.

Reuben, Elaine, and Leonore Hoffman, eds. *Unladylike and Unprofessional: Academic Women and Academic Unions*. New York: Modern Language Association, 1975.

Reverby, Susan M. *Ordered To Care: The Dilemma of American Nursing, 1859–1945*. Cambridge: Cambridge University Press, 1987.

Rhode, Deborah L. *Justice and Gender: Sex Discrimination and the Law*. Cambridge: Harvard University Press, 1989.

Ricci, Larry J. *High-Paying Blue Collar Jobs for Women*. New York: Ballantine Books, 1981.

Riccucci, Norma M. *Women, Minorities and Unions in the Public Sector*. Westport, CT: Greenwood Press, 1990.

Richards, Linda. *Reminiscences of Linda Richards: America's First Trained Nurse*. Boston: Whitcomb and Barrows, 1911.

Richards, Robert H. *Robert Hallowell Richards, His Mark*. 1936.

Richardson, Dorothy. *The Long Day: The Story of a New York Working Girl*. Charlottesville: University Press of Virginia, [1905] 1990.

Ries, Paula, and Anne J. Stone, eds. *The American Woman, 1992–93: A Status Report*. New York: Norton, 1992.

Riley, Glenda. *Inventing the American Woman: A Perspective on Women's History*. Arlington Heights, IL: Harlan Davidson, 1986.

Rix, Sara E., ed., for the Women's Research and Education Institute. *The American Woman: 1988–89: A Status Report*. New York: Norton, 1988.

Rizzo, A., and C. Mendez. *The Integration of Women in Management*. New York: Quorum Books, 1990.

Roberts, Mary. *American Nursing: History and Interpretation*. New York: Macmillan, 1954.

Roberts, Richard. *Florence Simms: A Biography*. 1926.

Robertson, Janet. *The Magnificent Mountain Women: Adventures in the Colorado Rockies*. Lincoln: University of Nebraska Press, 1991.

Robertson, Nan. *The Girls in the Balcony: Women, Men, and the* New York Times. New York: Random House, 1992.

Robinson, Alice M., et al., eds. *Notable Women in the American Theater: A Biographical Dictionary*. Westport, CT: Greenwood Press, 1989.

Robinson, Harriet H. *Loom and Spindle; or Life among the Early Mill Girls with a Sketch of the Lowell Offering and Some of Its Contributors*. New York: Thomas Y. Crowell, 1898.

Rodgers, Daniel T. *The Work Ethic in Industrial America, 1850–1920*. Chicago: University of Chicago Press, [1974] 1978.

Rodgers, Harrell R., Jr. *Poor Women, Poor Families: The Economic Plight of America's Female-Headed Households*. Rev. ed. Armonk, NY: M. E. Sharpe, 1990.

Rohrlich, Jay B. *Work and Love: The Crucial Balance*. New York: Summit Books, 1980.

Roosevelt, Eleanor. *Autobiography*. New York: Harper & Row, 1961.

———. *This I Remember*. New York: Harper and Brothers, 1949.

———. *This Is My Story*. New York: Garden City, 1937.

Rose, Suzanna, and Laurie Larwood, eds. *Women's Careers: Pathways and Pitfalls*. New York: Praeger, 1988.

Rosen, Ellen J. *Bitter Choices: Blue Collar Women in and out of Work*. Chicago: University of Chicago Press, 1987.

Rosen, Ruth. *The Lost Sisterhood: Prostitution in America, 1919–1981*. Baltimore: Johns Hopkins University Press, 1982.

Ross, Ishbel. *Angel of the Battlefield*. New York: Harper and Brothers, 1958.

———. *Child of Destiny*. 1944.

———. *Ladies of the Press: The Story of Women in Journalism by an Insider*. Salem, NH: Ayer, [1936] 1974.

Ross, Susan Deller, and Ann Barcher. *The Rights of Women: The Basic ACLU Guide to a Woman's Rights*. Rev. ed. New York: Bantam Books, 1984.

Rotella, Elyce. *From Home to Office: U.S. Women at Work, 1870–1930*. Ann Arbor: University of Michigan Research Press, 1981.

Rothman, Sheila M. *Woman's Proper Place: A History of Changing Ideals and Practices, 1870 to the Present*. New York: Basic Books, 1978.

Rubins, Jack L. *Karen Horney: Gentle Rebel of Psychoanalysis*. 1978.

Rubinstein, Charlotte S. *American Women Artists: From Early Indian Times to the Present*. New York: Avon, 1982.

———. *American Women Sculptors: A History of Women Working in Three Dimensions*. New York: G. K. Hall, 1990.

Ruiz, Vicki L. *Cannery Women, Cannery Lives: Mexican Women, Unionization, and the California Food Processing Industry*. Albuquerque: University of New Mexico Press, 1987.

Rupp, Leila J. *Mobilizing Women for War: German and American Propaganda, 1939–1945*. Princeton, NJ: Princeton University Press, 1978.

Rury, John L. *Education and Women's Work: Female Schooling and the Division of Labor in Rural America, 1870–1930*. Albany: State University of New York Press, 1991.

Ryan, Mary P. *Womanhood in America from Colonial Times to the Present*. New York: New Viewpoints, 1975.

———. *Women in Public: Between Banners and Ballots, 1825–1880*. Baltimore: Johns Hopkins University Press, 1990.

Sacks, Karen Brodkin, *Caring by the Hour: Women, Work, and Organizing at Duke Medical Center*. Urbana: University of Illinois Press, 1988.

Sacks, Karen Brodkin, and Dorothy Remy, eds. *My Troubles Are Going To Have Trouble with Me: Everyday Trials and Triumphs of Women Workers*. New Brunswick, NJ: Rutgers University Press, 1984.

St. Denis, Ruth. *An Unfinished Life*. 1939.

Salem, Dorothy C., ed. *African-American Women: A Biographical Dictionary*, Hamden, CT: Garland, 1993.

Salmond, John A. *Miss Lucy of the CIO: The Life and Times of Lucy Randolph Mason, 1882–1959*. Athens: University of Georgia Press, 1988.

Sanders, Jo. *Staying Poor: How the Job Training Partnership Act Fails Women*. Metuchen, NJ: Scarecrow Press, 1988.

Sanders, Marion K. *Dorothy Thompson: A Legend in Her Time*. New York: Avon, 1973.

Sanders, Marlene, and Marcia Rock. *Waiting for Prime Time: The Women of Television News*. New York: Harper Collins, 1990.

Schaffer, Robert. "Women and the Communist Party USA, 1930–1940." *Socialist Review* 46 (May/June 1974).

Scharf, Louis. *To Work and To Wed: Female Employment and the Great Depression*. Westport, CT: Greenwood Press, 1980.

Scharnau, Ralph. "Elizabeth Morgan, Crusader for Labor Reform," *Labor History* 14 (Winter 1973): 340–371.

Schiebinger, Londa. *The Mind Has No Sex? Women in the Origins of Modern Science*. Cambridge: Harvard University Press, 1989.

Schilpp, Madeon G., and Sharon M. Murphy. *Great Women of the Press*. Carbondale, IL: Southern Illinois University Press, 1983.

Schlesinger, Arthur, Jr. *The Age of Roosevelt*. New York: Houghton Mifflin, 1959.

Schneider, Dorothy, and Carl J. Schneider. *Into the Breach: American Women Overseas in World War I*. New York: Viking, 1991.

———. *Sound Off!: American Military Women Speak Out*. New York: E. P. Dutton, 1989; Paragon House, 1992.

———. *American Women in the Progressive Era*. New York: Facts on File, 1993.

Schneider, Florence Hemley. *Patterns of Workers' Education: The Story of the Bryn Mawr Summer School*. 1941.

Schneider, Ilya I. *Isadora Duncan: The Russian Years*. New York: Da Capo, 1981.

Schneiderman, Rose, with Lucy Goldthwaite. *All for One*. New York: Paul S. Eriksson, 1967.

Schor, Juliet B. *The Overworked American: The Unexpected Decline of Leisure*. New York: Basic Books, 1992.

Schroedel, Jean Reith. *Alone in a Crowd: Women in the Trades Tell Their Stories*. Philadelphia: Temple University Press, 1985.

Schwartz, Felice N., with Jean Zimmerman. *Breaking with Tradition: Women and Work, the New Facts of Life*. New York: Warner Books, 1992.

Sears, Elizabeth. "Business Women and Women in Business," *Harper's Monthly* 134 (January 1917).

Sekaran, U., and F. Long, eds. *Womanpower: Managing in Times of Demographic Turbulence*. Newbury Park, CA: Russell Sage, 1992.

Sementilli-Dann, Lisa, et al. *Family and Medical Leave: Strategies for Success*. Washington, DC: Center for Policy Alternatives, 1992.

Shaw, Anna Howard, with Elizabeth Jordan. *The Story of a Pioneer*. 1915.

Shaw, Lois B., ed. *Midlife Women at Work: A Fifteen-Year Perspective*. New York: Free Press, 1985.

Sheehan, Vincent. *Dorothy and Red*. 1963.

Sheldon, F. E. *Souvenir History of the Strike of the Ladies Waist Makers Union*. New York, 1910.

Shelton, Beth Anne. *Women, Men, and Time: Gender Differences in Paid Work, Housework and Lesiure*. Westport, CT: Greenwood Press, 1992.

Shelton, Cynthia J. *The Mills of Manayunk, Industrialization and Social Conflict in the Philadelphia Region, 1787–1837*. Baltimore: Johns Hopkins University Press, 1986.

Sherman, Claire R., and Adele M. Holcomb, eds. *Women as Interpreters of the Visual Arts, 1820–1979*. Westport, CT: Greenwood Press, 1981.

Sherwood, Dolly. *Harriet Hosmer, American Sculptor, 1830–1908*. Columbia: University of Missouri Press, 1991.

Shields, Laurie. *Displaced Homemakers: Organizing for a New Life*. New York: McGraw-Hill, 1981.

Sicherman, Barbara. *Alice Hamilton: A Life in Letters*. Cambridge: Harvard University Press, 1984.

Sicherman, Barbara, Carol Hurd Green, Ilene Kantrov, and Harriette Walker, eds., *Notable American Women: The Modern Period: A Biographical Dictionary*. Cambridge: Harvard University Press, 1980.

Silverstein, Pam, and Jozetta H. Srb. *Flexitime: Where, When, and How?* Ithaca, NY: ILR Press, 1979.

Simeone, A. *Academic Women: Working towards Equality*. Hadley, MA: Bergin and Garvey, 1987.

Simon, Rita J., and Gloria Danziger. *Women's Movements in America*. New York: Praeger, 1991.

Sinclair, Andrew. *The Emancipation of American Women*. New York: Harper and Row, 1965.

Sivers, Bonnie. *Count Your Change: A Woman's Guide to Sudden Financial Change*. New York: Arbor House, 1983.

Sklar, Kathryn Kish. *Catharine Beecher: A Study in American Domesticity*. New Haven: Yale University Press, 1973.

Smith, Hilda Worthington. *Women Workers at the Bryn Mawr Summer School*. 1929.

Smith, Jessie Carney, ed. *Notable Black American Women*. Detroit: Gale Research, 1992.

Smith, John M. *Women and Doctors*. New York: Atlantic Monthly Press, 1992.

Smith, Ralph, ed. *The Subtle Revolution: Women at Work*. Washington, DC: Urban Institute, 1980.

Smuts, Robert. *Women and Work in America*. New York: Columbia University Press, 1959.

Sochen, June. *Herstory: A Woman's View of American History*. New York: Alfred, 1974.

Sokoloff, Natalie J. *Between Money and Love: The Dialectics of Women's Home and Market Work*. New York: Praeger, 1981.

Solomon, Barbara Miller. *In the Company of Educated Women*. New Haven, CT: Yale University Press, 1985.

Southport Institute for Policy Analysis. *Caring Too Much? American Women and the Nation's Caregiving Crisis*. Southport, CT, 1990.

Sowell, Thomas. *Ethnic America: A History*. New York: Basic Books, 1981.

Sparhawk, Ruth M., et al., eds. *American Women in Sport: 1887–1987*. Metuchen, NJ: Scarecrow Press, 1989.

Sparkes, Boyden, and Samuel T. Moore. *Hetty Green: A Woman Who Loved Money*. 1930. Reprinted as *The Witch of Wall Street: Hetty Green*. Cutchogue, NY: Bucca Ree Press, 1992.

Spruill, Julia Cherry. *Women's Life and Work in the Southern Colonies*. New York: Norton, 1972.

Stadum, Beverly. *Poor Women and Their Families: Hard Working Charity Cases, 1900–1930*. Albany: State University of New York Press, 1992.

Stansell, Christine. *City of Women: Sex and Class in New York, 1789–1860*. Urbana: University of Illinois Press, 1987.

Stansfield, Roger. *The Great Depression*. New York: Harper and Row, 1982.

Stanton, Donna C., and Jeanine F. Plottel, eds. *The Female Autograph: Theory and Practice of Autobiography from the Tenth to the Twentieth Century*. Chicago: University of Chicago Press, 1987.

Statham, Anne, Eleanor M. Miller, and Hans O. Mauksch, eds. *The Worth of Women's Work: A Qualitative Synthesis*. Albany: State University of New York Press, 1987.

Stead, Betty A. *Women in Management*. 2d ed. New York: Prentice-Hall, 1985.

Steegmuller, Frances, ed. *Your Isadora: The Love Story of Isadora Duncan and Gordon Craig*. New York: N.Y. Public Library, 1974.

Steel, Edward M., ed. *The Correspondence of Mother Jones*. Pittsburgh: University of Pittsburgh Press, 1985.

Stein, Leon. *The Triangle Fire*. Philadelphia: J. B. Lippincott, 1962.

Steinfels, Margaret O'Brien. *"Who's Minding the Children?" The History and Politics of Day Care in America*. New York: Simon and Schuster, 1973.

Stephenson, Charles, and Robert Asher, eds. *Life and Labor: Dimensions of American Working-Class History*. Albany: State University of New York Press, 1986.

Sterling, Dorothy. *We Are Your Sisters: Black Women in the Nineteenth Century*. New York: Norton, 1984.

Stern, Madeleine B. *We the Women*. 1962.

Sterne, Emma Gelders. *Mary McLeod Bethune*. 1957.

Stewart, Annabel M. *The Industrial Work of the Y.W.C.A.* New York: Woman's Press, 1937.

Stewart, Elinore Pruitt. *Letters of a Woman Homesteader*. Boston: Houghton Mifflin, [1913] 1988.

Stewart, William Rhinelander. *The Philanthropic Work of Josephine Shaw Lowell*. New York: Patterson Smith, [1911] 1974.

Stolz, Barbara A. *Still Struggling: A Portrait of Low-Income Women in the 1980s*. New York: Free Press, 1985.

Strom, Sharon Hartman. *Beyond the Typewriter: Gender, Class, and the Origins of Modern American Office Work, 1900–1930*. Urbana: University of Illinois Press, 1992.

Studios, Paula. *Women of Computer History: Forgotten Heroines*. Wilmington, DE: World Information Institution, 1990.

Studios, Paula, and Christopher Zenger. *Women in the Electronic Industry*. Wilmington, DE: World Information Institution, 1989.

Stumberg, Robert, Janice Steinschneider, and George Elser. *State Legislative Sourcebook on Family and Medical Leave*. Washington, DC: Center for Policy Alternatives, 1990.

Sullivan, Constance, comp. *Women Photographers*. New York: Abrams, 1990.

Sumner, Helen L. *History of Women in Industry in the United States*. Vol. 9 of *Report on Conditions of Woman and Child Wage-Earners in the United States*. Washington, DC, 1911.

Sumrall, Amber Coverdale, and Dessa Taylor, eds. *Sexual Harassment: Women Speak Out*. Freedom, CA: Crossing Press, 1992.

Swartout, Annie Fern. *Missie*. 1947.

Taeuber, Cynthia, comp. and ed. *Statistical Handbook on Women in America*. Phoenix, AZ: Oryx Press, 1991.

Taft, Philip, ed. *American Labor: From Conspiracy to Collective Bargaining*. New York: Arno Press and *New York Times*, 1971.

Tarbell, Ida. *All in the Day's Work: An Autobiography*. Boston: G. K. Hall, [1939] 1985.

———. *The Business of Being a Woman*. 1912.

Tax, Meredith. *The Rising of the Women: Feminist Solidarity and Class Conflict, 1880–1917*. New York: Monthly Review Press, 1980.

———. *Rivington Street*. New York: William Morrow, 1982.

Taylor, Charlotte. *Women and the Business Game: Strategies for Successful Ownership*. New York: Venture Concepts Press, 1980.

Tentler, Leslie Woodcock. *Wage-Earning Women: Industrial Work and Family Life in the United States, 1900–1930*. Oxford: Oxford University Press, 1979.

Terry, Walter. *Miss Ruth: The "More Living Life" of Ruth St. Denis*. New York: Dodd. 1969.

Tharp, Twyla. *Push Comes to Shove: An Autobiography*. New York: Bantam Books, 1992.

Thomas, Isaiah. *The History of Printing in America*, ed. Marcus A. McCorison. New York: Weathervane Books, 1970.

Thomas, R. Roosevelt, Jr. *Beyond Race and Gender: Unleashing the Power of Your Total Work Force by Managing Diversity*. New York: Amacom (American Management Association), 1991.

Tick, Judith. *American Women Composers before 1870*. Rochester, NY: University of Rochester Press, 1989.

Tilly, Louise A., and Patricia Gurin, eds. *Women, Politics, and Change*. New York: Russell Sage, 1990.

Tilly, Louise A., and Joan W. Scott. *Women, Work, and Family*. New York: Holt, Rinehart and Winston, 1978.

Todd, Janet, ed. *Women and Film*. New York: Holmes and Meier, 1988.

———. *Gender and Literary Voice*. New York: Holmes and Meier, 1981.

Treiman, D. J., and H. I. Hartmann. *Women, Work and Wages: Equal Pay for Jobs of Equal Value*. Washington, DC: National Academy Press, 1981.

Tripp, Annie Huber. *The I.W.W. and the Paterson Silk Strike of 1913*. Urbana, IL: University of Illinois Press, 1987.

Trotta, Liz. *Fighting for Air: In the Trenches with Television News*. New York: Simon and Schuster, 1991.

Tucker, Cynthia G. *Prophetic Sisterhood: Liberal Women Ministers of the Frontier, 1880–1930*. Boston: Beacon Press, 1990.

Tufts, Eleanor. *American Women Artists, 1830–1930*. New York: Garland, 1987.

Turbin, Carole. *Working Women of Collar City: Gender, Class, and Community in Troy, 1864–86*. Urbana: University of Illinois Press, 1992.

Tuve, Jeannette E. *First Lady of the Law: Florence Ellinwood Allen*. Lanham, MD, 1985.

Uglow, Jennifer S., comp. and ed. *International Dictionary of Women's Biography*. New York: Continuum, 1985.

Ulrich, Laurel Thatcher. *Good Wives: Image and Reality in the Lives of Women in Northern New England, 1650–1750*. New York: Alfred Knopf, 1982.

———. *A Midwife's Tale: The Life of Martha Ballard, Based on Her Diary, 1785–1812*. New York: Alfred Knopf, 1990.

U.S. Bureau of the Census. *Statistical Abstract of the United States, 1991.* 111th ed. Washington, DC, 1991.

U.S. Bureau of Labor, Women's Bureau. *Time of Change: 1983 Handbook on Women Workers.* Washington, DC: Government Printing Office, 1983.

U.S. Department of Commerce and Labor, Bureau of the Census. *Statistics of Women at Work.* Washington, DC: Government Printing Office, 1907.

U.S. Department of Labor. *Self-Employment Programs for Unemployed Workers.* Washington, DC, 1992.

———. "All about OSHA." Washington, DC, 1991.

———. *Work and Family Patterns of American Women.* Washington, DC: Government Printing Office, 1990.

U.S. Department of Labor, Women's Bureau. *Changes in Women's Employment during the War.* Washington, DC: Government Printing Office, 1943.

———. *Women and Office Automation: Issues for the Decade Ahead.* Washington, DC: Government Printing Office, 1985.

U.S. President's Commission on the Status of Women. *American Women.* Washington, DC: Government Printing Office, 1981.

Unterbrink, Mary. *Funny Women: American Comediennes, 1860–1985.* Jefferson, NC: McFarland, 1987.

Van Horn, Susan Householder. *Women, Work, and Fertility, 1900–1986.* New York: New York University Press, 1988.

van Kleeck, Mary. *Artificial Flower Makers.* New York: Russell Sage, 1913.

Van Vorst, Mrs. John, and Marie Van Vorst. *The Woman Who Toils, Being the Experiences of Two Gentlewomen as Factory Girls.* New York: Doubleday, Pate, 1903.

Van Wagenen Keil, Sally. *Those Wonderful Women in Their Flying Machines: The Unknown Heroines of World War II.* Rev. ed. New York: Four Directions, 1990.

Vandiver, Susan. "A History of Women in Social Work," in *Women's Issues and Social Work Practice,* ed. Elaine Norman and

Arlene Mancuso. Itasca, IL: Peacock, 1980.

Vare, Ethlie A., and Gregg Ptacek. *Mothers of Invention: From the Bra to the Bomb, Forgotten Women and Their Unforgettable Ideas.* New York: Morrow, 1989.

Vicinus, Martha. *Independent Women: Work and Community for Single Women, 1850–1920.* Chicago: University of Chicago Press, 1988.

Victor, Agnes C., ed. *A Woman's Quest: The Life of Marie E. Zakrzewska, M.D.* Salem, NH: Ayer, [1924] 1972.

Vorse, Mary Heaton. *Strike!* New York: Horace Liveright, 1930.

Wadsworth, Ginger. *Julia Morgan, Architect of Dreams.* Minneapolis, MN: Lerner, 1990.

Wagner, Lilya. *Women War Correspondents in World War II.* Westport, CT: Greenwood Press, 1989.

The Waitresses' Handbook: A Guide to the Legal Rights of Waitresses and Other Restaurant Workers. Washington, DC: Women's Legal Defense Fund, 1986.

Walker, Cheryl. *The Nightingale's Burden: Women Poets and American Culture before 1900.* Bloomington: University of Indiana Press, 1983.

Wallace, Phyllis A. *Black Women in the Labor Force.* Cambridge, MA: MIT Press, 1980.

Wallace, Ruth A. *They Call Her Pastor: A New Role for Catholic Women.* Albany: State University of New York Press, 1992.

Waller, Susan. *Women Artists in the Modern Era: A Documentary History.* Metuchen, NJ: Scarecrow Press, 1991.

Wandersee, Winifred D. *On the Move: American Women in the 1970s.* Boston: Twayne, 1988.

———. *Women's Work and Family Values, 1920–1940.* Cambridge: Harvard University Press, 1981.

Ware, Susan. *Beyond Suffrage: Women in the New Deal.* Cambridge: Harvard University Press, 1981.

———. *Holding Their Own: American Women in the 1930s.* Boston: Twayne, 1982.

———. *Modern American Women: A Documentary History.* Belmont, CA: Wadsworth, 1989.

———. *Partner and I: Molly Dewson, Feminism, and New Deal Politics.* New Haven, CT: Yale University Press, 1987.

Waring, Marilyn. *If Women Counted: A New Feminist Economics.* New York: Harper & Row, 1988.

Warme, Barbara D., Katherina L. P. Lundy, and Larry A. Lundy, eds. *Working Part-Time: Risks and Opportunities.* Westport, CT: Praeger, 1992.

Warren, Joyce W. *Fanny Fern: An Independent Woman.* New Brunswick, NJ: Rutgers University Press, 1992.

Watkins, Kathleen Pullan, and Lucius Durant, Jr. *Day Care: A Source Book.* 2d ed. Hamden, CT: Garland Pub., 1992.

Weatherford, Doris. *American Women and World War II.* New York: Facts on File, 1990.

Weaver, E. W. *Profitable Vocations for Girls.* New York: A. S. Barnes, 1916.

Weddington, Sarah Ragle. *A Question of Choice.* New York: Putnam's, 1992.

Weinberg, Sydney Stahl. *The World of Our Mothers.* Chapel Hill: University of North Carolina Press, 1988.

Weiner, Lynn Y. *From Working Girl to Working Mother: The Female Labor Force in the United States, 1820–1980.* Chapel Hill: University of North Carolina Press, 1985.

Weisberg, D. Kelly, ed. *Women and the Law: The Social Historical Perspective.* Cambridge, MA: Schenkman, 1982.

Welch, Mary Scott. *Networking.* New York: Warner Books, 1981.

Wells, Ida B. *Crusade for Justice: The Autobiography of Ida B. Wells,* ed. Alfreda M. Duster. Chicago: University of Chicago Press, 1970.

Wertheimer, Barbara Mayer, ed. *Labor Education for Women Workers.* Philadelphia: Temple University Press, 1981.

———. *We Were There: The Story of Working Women in America.* New York: Pantheon Books, 1977.

Westwood, Sallie. *All Day, Every Day: Factory and Family in the Making of Women's Lives.* Urbana: University of Illinois Press, 1985.

Wheatley, Meg, and Marcie Hirsch Schorr. *Managing Your Maternity Leave.* Boston: Houghton Mifflin, 1983.

White, Deborah Gray, *Ar'n't I a Woman? Female Slaves in the Plantation South.* New York: W. W. Norton, 1984.

Wilbur, Sibyl. *The Life of Mary Baker Eddy.* c. 1907.

Wilder. Denise. *Issues in Education and Training for Women Workers.* Washington, DC: National Institution for Work and Learning, 1980.

Wiler, Paul. "The Wages of Sex: The Uses and Limits of Comparable Worth." *Harvard Law Review* 99 (June 1986): 1728–1807.

Wilkinson, Carroll W. *Women in Nontraditional Occupations: References and Resources.* New York: Macmillan, 1991.

Willard, Frances E. *Women in the Pulpit.* Washington, DC: Zenger, [1889] 1976.

Willborn, Steven L. *A Comparable Worth Primer.* Lexington, MA: Lexington Books, 1986.

———. *A Secretary and a Cook: Challenging Women's Wages in the Courts of the United States and Great Britain.* Ithaca, NY: ILR Press, 1989.

Williams, Blanche Colton. *Clara Barton: Daughter of Destiny.* 1941.

Williams, Christine L. *Gender Differences at Work: Women and Men in Nontraditional Occupations.* Berkeley: University of California Press, 1989.

Wilson, Howard E. *Mary McDowell, Neighbor.* 1928.

Wilson, Margaret G. *The American Woman in Transition: The Urban Influence, 1870–1920.* Westport, CT: Greenwood Press, 1979.

Wilson, Michael. *Salt of the Earth*. Old Westbury, NY: Feminist Press, 1978.

Wilson, Pamela, ed. *Salaried and Professional Women: Relevant Statistics*. New York: Department for Professional Employees, AFL-CIO, 1992.

With Just Care: Unionization of American Journalism. Lanham, MD: University Press of America, 1992.

Witt, Stephanie L. *The Pursuit of Race and Gender Equity in American Academe*. New York: Praeger, 1990.

Wolf, Naomi. *The Beauty Myth: How Images of Beauty Are Used against Women*. New York: Doubleday Anchor, 1991.

Wolfe, Leslie, ed. *Women, Work, and School: Occupational Segregation and the Role of Education*. Boulder, CO: Westview Press, 1991.

Woloch, Nancy. *Women and the American Experience*. New York: Alfred Knopf, 1984.

Women and Work in the 80s: Perspectives from the 30s and 40s. Berkeley: University of California, Center for the Study, Education and Advancement of Women, 1981.

Women in Blue-Collar Jobs. Ford Foundation Conference Report, 1976.

Women in Congress, 1917–1990. Washington, DC: Office of the Historian, U.S. House of Representatives, Government Printing Office, 1991.

"Women-Owned Businesses: Special Problems and Access to Credit." Hearing before the Subcommittee on Exports, Tax Policy, and Special Problems of the Committee on Small Business. House of Representatives, 101st Congress, 2d session, Goldsboro, NC, 12 March 1990. Serial No. 101-49. Washington, DC: Government Printing Office, 1990.

Women's Enterprises of Boston. *Earning a Breadwinner's Wage: Nontraditional Jobs for Women on AFDC*. Cambridge, MA: World Guild, 1978.

Women's Legal Defense Fund Staff. *Expanding Employment Opportunities for Women: A Blueprint for the Future*. Washington, DC, 1989.

Women's Medical Association of New York City. *Mary Putnam Jacobi, M.D.: A Pathfinder in Medicine*. New York, 1925.

Woods, Robert A., and Albert J. Kennedy, eds. *Young Working Girls: A Summary of Evidence from Two Thousand Social Workers*. Boston: Houghton Mifflin, 1913.

Woody, Bette. *Black Women in the Workplace: Impacts of Structural Change in the Economy*. Westport, CT: Greenwood Press, 1992.

Work and Family Patterns of American Women. Washington, DC: Government Printing Office, March 1990.

Working Woman editors with Gay Bryant. *The Working Woman Report: Succeeding in Business in the 80s*. New York: Simon and Schuster, 1984.

Working Woman's Guide to Her Job Rights. Washington, DC: Government Printing Office, 1988.

Wortman, Marlene Stein, ed. *Women in American Law: From Colonial Times to the New Deal*. New York: Holmes and Meier, 1985.

Wright, Barbara Drygulski et al., eds. *Women, Work, and Technology: Transformations*. Ann Arbor: University of Michigan Press, 1987.

Wright, Helen. *Sweeper in the Sky*. 1949.

Wroth, Lawrence C. *The Colonial Printer*. Charlottesville: University Press of Virginia, [1938] 1964.

Wurtzel, Elizabeth. "Popular Music." *New Yorker* (29 June 1992).

Yates, Michael. *Labor Law Handbook*. Boston: South End Press, 1987.

Yost, Edna. *Frank and Lillian Gilbreth: Partners for Life*. 1949.

———. *Women of Modern Science*. Westport, CT: Greenwood Press, [1959] 1984.

Yu, Diana. *The Winds of Change: Korean Women in America*. Silver Spring, MD: Women's Institute Press, 1991.

Zandy, Janet, ed. *Calling Home: Working-Class Women's Writings*. New Brunswick, NJ: Rutgers University Press, 1992.

Zavella, Patricia. *Women's Work and Chicano Families: Cannery Workers of the Santa Clara Valley*. Ithaca, NY: Cornell University Press, 1987.

Zigler, Edward P., and Meryl Frank, eds. *The Parental Leave Crisis: Toward a National Policy*. New Haven, CT: Yale University Press, 1988.

Zipser, Arthur, and Pearl Zipser. *Fire and Grace: The Life of Rose Pastor Stokes.* Atlanta: University of Georgia Press, 1990.

Zophy, Angela Howard, and Frances M. Kavenik, eds. *Handbook of American Women's History*. Hamden, CT: Garland, 1990.

Zuckerman, Harriet, Jonathan R. Cole, and John T. Bruer, eds. *The Outer Circle: Women in the Scientific Community*. New York: Norton, 1991.

Illustration Credits

ii Printed by permission of the Norman Rockwell Family Trust copyright 1943 by the Norman Rockwell Family Trust.

vii From a photograph by Diana McNees.

8 U.S. Department of Agriculture.

14 UPI/Bettmann.

23 From *History of Woman Suffrage*, Vol. II, edited by Elizabeth C. Stanton, Susan B. Anthony, and Matilda J. Gage (New York: Rand, McNally, 1894).

24 The Schlesinger Library, Radcliffe College.

28 Moorland-Spingarn Research Center, Howard University.

42 Photograph by Donald Woodman, courtesy Judy Chicago.

46 U.S. House of Representatives.

47 Library of Congress.

53 State Historical Society of Wisconsin WHi(t57)41.

65 Photograph by O. T. Davis; Colorado Historical Society.

67 Herbert Mingdoll/The Joffrey Ballet.

71 Library of Congress.

72 Photograph by Charles Van Schaick; State Historical Society of Wisconsin WHi(V22)137.

74 Photograph by Frances Benjamin Johnson; Library of Congress.

77 Colorado Historical Society.

78 Church History Division of the First Church of Christ, Scientist, in Boston, Massachusetts.

94 Photograph by Earl Dotter; courtesy Association of Flight Attendants.

95 Brown Brothers.

103 International Tennis Hall of Fame, Newport, Rhode Island.

104 Library of Congress.

107 Chicago Historical Society DN 3882.

110 Library of Congress.

112 Courtesy the Guerrilla Girls.

125 The Nobel Foundation.

133 Cara Metz/ILGWU.

139 Colorado Historical Society.

140 U.S. House of Representatives.

152 Photograph by C. M. Bell. Sophia Smith Collection, Smith College.

154 Lowell Historical Society, Lowell, Massachusetts.

155 Library of Congress.

156 Copyright by *Washington Post*; Reprinted by permission of the D.C. Public Library.

171 Poster Collection, Hoover Institution Archives, Stanford University.

185 Photograph by Frank A. Rinehart; Southwest Museum, Los Angeles 22994.

189 Courtesy Public Service Company of Colorado.

195   National Geographic Society.
204   National Archives.
206   Library of Congress.
210   National Archives 86-G-9F-38.
223   Sophia Smith Collection, Smith College.
229   Courtesy Department of Special Collections, University of Florida.
231   Colorado Historical Society.
232   Brown Brothers.
238   Library of Congress.
239   Carol Simpson Productions.
243   Courtesy Muriel Siebert.
251   Photograph by Jay Quadracci, Boulder *Daily Camera*; Courtesy University of Colorado Athletic Media Relations.
255   Library of Congress.
257   Library of Congress.
259   Library of Congress.
262   Library of Congress.
265   From *The Triangle Fire* by Leon Stein (Philadelphia, PA: Lippincott, 1962).
296   National Archives.
297   U.S. Army Air Force Photo, U.S. Air Force Museum—Research Division, Wright Patterson Air Force Base.
299   Library of Congress.

Index

Abbott, Edith, 1, 125
Abbott, Grace, 1, 125
Academic women, 1–4
Accountants, 3–4
Ace, Jane, 57
Acquired Immune Deficiency Syndrome (AIDS), 49
Adams, Annette A., 4
Addams, Jane, 104, 125, 135, 280
Adkins v. Children's Hospital, 4
AFDC. *See* Aid to Families with Dependent Children
Affirmative action, 2, 4–5
AFL-CIO. *See* American Federation of Labor
AFL-CIO Standing Committee on Salaried and Professional Women, 5
African Americans. *See* Black Americans
AFSCME v. State of Washington, 5
Agassiz, Elizabeth Cabot Cary, 5–6
Age Discrimination Acts, 6–7
Agricultural workers, 7, 169
Aid to Families with Dependent Children, 7–9, 89, 177
AIDS (Acquired Immune Deficiency Syndrome), 49
Airline stewardesses. *See* Flight attendants
Aitken, Jane, 9, 214
Alcott, Louisa May, 292, 298
Allen, Gracie, 57
Alliance of Minority Women for Business and Political Development, 9
Almshouses, 293–294
Amalgamated Clothing Workers of America (ACWA) 26, 69, 157
American Association of Black Women Entrepreneurs, 9–10

American Association of Colored Teachers (AACT), 10
American Association of University Women (AAUW), 10, 37, 227
American Civil Liberties Union (ACLU), 10, 49, 86
American Federation of Labor (AFL) 10–11, 34, 37, 53, 60–61, 136, 178, 198, 200, 204, 229, 243, 248, 263, 269, 273. *See also* Unions
American Federation of Teachers (AFT), 10, 11–12, 21, 34, 114, 183, 260, 270
American Labor party, 26
American Labor Unions, 161
American Library Association (ALA), 150
American Missionary Association (AMA), 12
American Red Cross, 17, 22–23, 114, 158
American Society of Civil Engineers, 22
American Society of Professional and Executive Women, 12
American Teachers' Association. *See* American Association of Colored Teachers
American Women's Economic Development Corporation (AWED), 13
American Women's Educational Association (AWEA), 13
American Women's Hospital Service (AWHS), 13
Americans with Disabilities Act of 1990 (ADA), 13
Anarchism, 14, 106
Anderson, Marian, 14, 113
Anderson, Mary, 14
Anthony, Susan B., 163, 184, 295
Apprentices, 15
Architects, 15–16, 27, 175

Arden, Elizabeth, 83
Arizona Mine Strike of 1983, 16
Army Nurse Corps, 17, 158, 191
Artists, 17–18
Arzner, Dorothy, 47
Asian Americans. *See* Chinese Americans;
  Filipina Americans; Japanese Americans;
  Korean Americans
Assertiveness, 18
Attorneys, 18–19
At-will employment, 19
Authors. *See* Writers and publishers
AWED. *See* American Women's Economic
  Development Corporation
Ayer, Harriet Hubbard, 19

Bagley, Sarah G., 21
Baldwin, Ruth Ann, 47
Baldwin, Tammy, 108
Bambace, Angela, 21
Barker, Mary Cornelia, 21
Barnard, Kate, 21
Barney, Nora Stanton Blatch, 21–22, 81
Barnum, Gertrude, 22, 125
Barry, Leonora Marie Kearney, 22, 145
Barton, Clara, 22–23, 51, 169
Beach, Amy Marcy Cheney, 179
Beals, Jessie Tarbox, 23–25, 206
Beaux, Cecilia, 17
Beech, Olive Ann Mellor, 83
Beecher, Catharine Esther, 13, 15, 25, 259
Bellanca, Dorothy Jacobs, 26
Benefits, 26–27
Bernays, Doris Fleischman, 27
Bethune, Louise Blanchard, 15, 27
Bethune, Mary McLeod, 27–29, 31
Bethune-Cookman College, 29
Bickerdyke, Mary Ann Ball, 29–30
Biological clock, 30
Blache, Alice Guy, 30, 47
Black Americans, 30–31, 244–245
Black Business Women's News, 9
Blackwell, Antoinette Louisa Brown, 32, 37
Blackwell, Elizabeth, 32, 125, 206–208
Blackwell, Emily, 32
Blatch, Harriot Stanton, 22
Bloor, Ella Reeve, 32–33, 59
Blue-collar workers, 33
Bly, Nellie, 140
*Board of Directors of Rotary International v.
  Rotary Club of Duarte*, 33
Board of National Popular Education, 25
*Board of Trustees of Keene State College v.
  Sweeney*, 33
Boarding, 33–34

Bona Fide Occupational Qualification
  (BFOQ), 6–7, 34
Bookbinders, 34
Bookkeepers. *See* Accountants; Clerical
  workers
Borchardt, Selma Munter, 34–35
Bourke-White, Margaret, 140, 206
Boycotts, 35. *See also* Strikes
Bradwell, Myra Colby, 35
Brandeis Brief. *See Muller v. Oregon*
Bread and Roses Strike (Lawrence,
  Massachusetts, Textile Strike), 35–36,
  95, 159, 198, 254, 275. *See also* Strikes;
  Unions
Breckinridge, Sophonisba Preston, 1, 36–37,
  125
Brent, Margaret, 37
Bridge job, 37
Brookwood Labor College, 37, 55
Brown, Charlotte Hawkins, 31
Brown, Olympia, 37–38
Bryn Mawr College, 38, 262
Bryn Mawr Summer School for Women
  Workers, 38, 104, 119, 145, 205, 262,
  290, 302. *See also* Workers' education
Bureau of Vocational Information (BVI), 38,
  274
Burlak, Anna, 59
Burroughs, Nannie Helen, 31
Business and industry, 38–39
Business and Professional Women's Clubs,
  Inc. of the U.S.A. (BPW/USA), 39, 292,
  302

Caldwell, Sarah, 41
California Federal Savings and Loan v. Guerra,
  41
Cambridge School of Architecture and
  Landscape Architecture, 16
Cannery and Agricultural Workers
  Industrial Union, 41
Cary, Mary Ann Shadd. *See* Shadd, Mary
  Ann
Cassatt, Mary, 17
Catalyst, 41
La Causa, 271
Center for Women Policy Studies (CWPS),
  41–42
CETA. *See* Job Training Partnership Act
Chatterton, Ruth, 47
Cheatwood v. South Central Bell Telephone Co.,
  42
Chicago, Judy, 17, 42
Chicago Legal News, 35
Chicago School of Civics and Philanthropy,

36–37

Chicago Training School for Active Workers in the Labor Movement, 46, 55. *See also* Training School for Women Organizers; Workers' education

Chicanas, 7. *See also* Mexican Americans

Child care, 43–45, 242

Children's Bureau, 1, 277, 291

Chinese Americans, 45–46, 216, 282

Chinese Exclusion Act, 45

Chisholm, Shirley Anita St. Hill, 46, 108

Christian Science religion, 77–78

Christman, Elisabeth, 46

Church, Ellen, 94

Cinema, 30, 46–48

Civil Rights, 48–49

Civil Rights Act of 1964, 2, 4, 5, 13, 18, 19, 31, 33, 41, 49–50, 69, 79, 83–84, 94, 96, 101, 105, 106, 138, 181, 186, 194, 203, 205, 212–213, 214, 215, 218, 223, 229, 237, 239, 241, 280, 289

Civil Rights Act of 1991, 50, 240

Civil service. *See* Government workers

Civil War, 23, 29–30, 32, 35, 50–51, 52, 70–71, 107, 191, 278

Civil Works Administration (CWA). *See* New Deal

Clarke, Edith, 51

Class action, 51

Clayton Anti-Trust Act, 51–52

Clearinghouse on Women's Issues, 52

Clergy. *See* Religion

Clerical workers, 52–54

Closed shop, 54. *See also* Unions

Coalition of Labor Union Women, 54, 270

COBRA. *See* Consolidated Omnibus Budget Reconciliation Act of 1986

Coca, Imogene, 58

Cochran, Jacqueline, 55, 209, 296

Cohn, Fannia Mary, 37, 55

Coleman, Bessie, 55

Collar Laundry Union of Troy, New York, 55

Collective bargaining, 55–56

The College, the Market, and the Court, 67

Collins, Jennie, 56

Colonial America, 56–57

Comediennes, 57–58

Coming of Age in Samoa, 166

Commission on the Status of Women. *See* President's Commision on the Status of Women

Committee on Women's Employment and Related Social Issues (WERSI) 58

Communications, 58

Communist Party of the United States of America (CPUSA), 33, 59, 95

Commuter marriages, 59

Comparable worth, 59–60

Compensation, 60

Comprehensive Child Development Act of 1971, 44

Comprehensive Employment and Training Act of 1974 (CETA). *See* Job Training Partnership Act

Computer monitoring. *See* Electronic monitoring

Computer-related health problems. *See* Health hazards; Video display terminals

Conference for Women Artists, 42

Congress of Industrial Organizations (CIO), 11, 26, 54, 60–61, 164, 269. *See also* Unions

Congressional Caucus for Women's Issues (CCWI), 61, 289

Conley, Frances, 3

Consolidated Omnibus Budget Reconciliation Act of 1986, 61, 117

Conspiracy. *See* Criminal conspiracy

Construction workers, 61

Consultants, 62

Consumers' League, 36, 62, 107, 119, 143, 153, 164, 181, 195, 197, 216, 218, 284, 286, 295, 302, 303

Contingent work force, 62

Contract labor, 63

Coolidge, Martha, 48

Cooper Union, 63, 280

Cooperative housekeeping, 63

Cooperative industries, 63–64

Corbally, Kate, 47

Cori, Gerty, 64

Corning Glass Works v. Brennan, 64

Cottage industry. *See* Home work

County of Washington v. Gunther, 64

Coverture, 64

Cowgirls, 65, 193

Crabtree, Lotta, 57

Creative Impulse in Industry, 161

Criminal conspiracy, 65–66

Culture and Commitment: A Study of the Generation Gap, 166

Dall, Caroline Wells Healey, 67

Dancers, 67–68, 74–75, 110, 232, 257

Daughters of St. Crispin, 68, 243

Day care. *See* Child care

Defense Advisory Council on Women in the Services (DACOWITS), 170–172

Deitch, Donna, 48

De la Cruz, Jessie Lopez, 68, 271

DeMille, Agnes, 67
Dentists. *See* Health professionals and paraprofessionals; Taylor, Lucy Beaman Hobbs
Depression. *See* Great Depression
Dewson, Mary Williams, 68–69
The Diary of a Shirtwaist Striker, 159
Dickason, Gladys Marie, 69
Directors. *See* Cinema
Disability insurance. *See* Benefits
Disabled workers. *See* Americans with Disabilities Act of 1990; Networking Project for Disabled Women and Girls; Rehabilitation Act of 1973
Discrimination. *See* Discrimination acts; Americans with Disabilities Act of 1990; Civil Rights Act of 1964; Sex discrimination
Disparate impact, 69
Displaced homemakers, 69–70
Displaced Homemakers Self-Sufficiency Assistance Act of 1990, 70
Displaced workers, 70
Divorce. *See* Displaced homemakers
Dix, Dorothea Lynde, 51, 70–71, 140, 169
Dodge, Grace Hoadley, 244, 265, 294
Dodge, Josephine Jewell, 43
Domestic feminists, 71
Domestic servants, 71–73
Dothard v. Rawlinson, 34, 73
Draper, Ruth, 57
Dreier, Mary, 198
Dress for Success, 73
Dress requirements, 73
Dressler, Marie, 57
Dorr, Rheta, 140
Dual-career couples, 73–74
Dulac, Germaine, 47
Duncan, Isadora, 67, 74–75
Dunham, Katharine, 67
Dunne, Irene, 47
The Duty of American Women to Their Country, 25
Dykes, Eva B., 75

Earhart, Amelia Mary, 77, 209
Eastman, Crystal, 77
Eberle, Mary Abastenia St. Leger, 17
Eddy, Mary Baker, 77–78
Edson, Katherine Philips, 78–79
Education. *See* Academic women; Teachers; Workers' education
Education Amendments Act of 1972, 2, 12, 79, 84–85, 250
EEOC. *See* Equal Employment Opportunity Commission
Eight-hour day, 79
Elder care, 79–80
Electronic monitoring, 80
Elementary Theory of Nuclear Shell Structure, 166
Elizabethton, Tennessee, Strike of 1929, 80, 99
El Paso Laundry Workers' Union (AFL) Strike of 1919, 80
Ellon, Gertrude, 132
Employee Assistance Programs. *See* Benefits
Employment agencies, 81
Employment at will. *See* At-will employment
Employment Retirement Income Security Act (ERISA), 81, 201, 203
Engineers, 81–82
Entertainers. *See* Cinema; Comediennes; Dancers; Musicians; Theater
Entrepreneurs, 82–83
Equal Credit Opportunity Act, 83
Equal Employment Opportunity Act, 49. *See also* Civil Rights Act of 1964; Equal Employment Opportunity Commission
Equal Employment Opportunity Commission (EEOC), 6, 13, 33, 49, 50, 83–84, 112, 218, 268
Equal Pay Act of 1963, 79, 84–85, 233, 237, 289
Equal Rights Amendment, 54, 85, 143, 185, 190, 213, 218, 223, 252, 262, 287, 303
Equity Club, 85
Evans, Elizabeth Gardiner Glendower, 68, 85–86
Executive orders, 86
Executive Orders 11246, 11375, and 12086, 86
Executive women, 132

Factory workers, 87–88
Fair Employment Practices Commissions, 88
Fair Labor Standards Act, 88, 173, 182, 190, 196
Family and Medical Leave Act (FMLA), 79–80, 88–89
Family leave, 89
Family Support Act (FSA), 9
Family wage, 89–90
Farley, Harriet, 90
Farm wives, 90
Farmers, 90–91
Farming out, 91
Federal Council on Negro Affairs, 29
Federal Emergency Relief Administration. (FERA), 187. *See also* New Deal
Federation of Organizations for Professional

Women, 91
Female ghettos. *See* Occupational
  segregation; Velvet ghettos
Female Society of Lynn and Vicinity for the
  Protection and Promotion of Female
  Industry, 91
The Feminine Mystique, 96, 288
Feminist Majority Foundation, 91
Feminization, 91–92
Fern, Fannie, 92
Ferraro, Geraldine, 92, 108
Fertility, 92–93
Fetal protection policies, 93
Filipina Americans, 93
Film. *See* Cinema
Flexible benefits. *See* Benefits
Flexplace. *See* Home workers;
  Telecommuting
Flextime, 93–94
Flight attendants, 94
Flint Auto Workers' Strike, 94–95
Floating population. *See* Transient workers
Flynn, Elizabeth Gurley, 36, 59, 95, 168, 275
Follett, Mary Parker, 95–96
Food service, 96, 115
Force, Juliana Rieser, 17, 96
Frankenthaler, Helen, 17
Franklin v. Gwinett County School District, 96
Fredericks, Pauline, 140
Friedan, Betty, 96–97, 252, 288
Fringe benefits. *See* Benefits
Frontiero v. Richardson, 97

Gastonia, North Carolina, Strike of 1929, 99
Gaynor, Janet, 47
Gender gap, 99–101
Gender-specific occupations. *See*
  Occupational segregation
General Electric v. Gilbert, 101
General Textile Strike of 1934, 101. *See also*
  Strikes
Genetic discrimination, 102
Geyer, Georgie Anne, 140
Gibbs, Katharine, 52, 82, 102
Gibson, Althea, 102
Gilbreth, Lillian Evelyn Moller, 102
Gilder, Jeannette Leonard, 102–103
Gillespie, Mabel Edna, 104
Gilman, Charlotte Anna Perkins Stetson,
  104–105
Gilson, Mary Barnett, 105
Girl Fridays, 105, 160
Given-out work. *See* Piecework
Glass ceiling, 106, 160
Gleason, Kate, 106

Glimpses of Fifty Years, 283
Godey's Lady's Book, 113, 140
Goesaert v. Cleary, 106
Goggin, Catharine, 11
Goldberg, Whoopi, 58
Goldman, Emma, 14, 106–107
Goldmark, Josephine Clara, 107, 161, 177
The Good Neighbor in the Modern City, 228
Government workers, 107–109
Graham, Martha, 67, 110
Great Depression, 31, 54, 69, 110–111, 162,
  181, 187–188, 204, 205, 209, 296
Great Migration, 31, 206. *See also* Black
  Americans
Great Strikes of California, 41. *See also*
  Cannery and Agricultural Workers
  Industrial Union; Strikes
Greeley-Smith, Nixola, 111
Green, Hetty Howland Robinson, 82, 111
Grievances, 112
Griggs v. Duke Power Company, 112
Guerrilla Girls, 18, 112

Hackley, Emma Azalia Smith, 113, 179
Hale, Sarah Josepha Buell, 113, 140
Haley, Margaret Angela, 11, 113–114, 182
Hamilton, Alice, 114, 125, 234
Hamilton, Gordon, 114
Handbook of Labor Literature, 161
Handler, Ruth, 134
Harper, Ida H., 163
*Harriet Hubbard Ayer's Book: A Complete and
  Authentic Treatise on the Laws of Health
  and Beauty*, 19
Harris, Patricia Roberts, 108, 115
Harvey Girls, 115
Hawes, Elizabeth, 115–116
Hayden, Sophia G., 15–16
Hayhurst, Susan, 118
Haywood, "Big Bill," 36
Heads of household, 116
Healey, Dorothy, 59, 116
Health hazards, 116–117
Health insurance, 117
Health professionals and paraprofessionals,
  117–119
Heckerling, Amy, 48
Heilbrun, Carolyn, 2–3
Henrotin, Ellen Martin, 119
Henry, Alice, 119
Hepburn, Katherine, 47
Herford, Beatrice, 58
Herrick, Elinore Morehouse, 119–120
Higgins, Marguerite, 140
Hill, Anita, 50

Hills, Carla Anderson, 120
Hirth, Emma, 38
Hispanic Americans, 120–121, 271
Hishon v. King & Spalding, 18
History of Women's Suffrage, 163
Hobby, Oveta Culp, 121
Home economists, 25, 122, 227
Home workers, 122–123
Homesteaders, 123
Horney, Karen, 123–124
Hosmer, Harriet Goodhue, 124
Hours laws, 217. *See also* Protective legislation
House of Representatives, 46, 92, 223
Househusband, 124
Housekeeping, 124
Huerta, Dolores, 124–125, 271
Hull House, 1, 104, 114, 125, 143, 252
Human resources managers, 125–126, 160
Human Rights Commissions, 126
Hunt, Harriot Kezia, 126
Hutchins, Grace, 59, 126
Hyde, Ida Henrietta, 126–127

Ickes, Anna Wilmarth Thompson, 129
Immigrant women, 129–130
Immigrants' Protective League, 1, 36
Immigration Act of 1965, 45
Indentured servants, 130
Individual Retirement Accounts (IRAs), 130, 203
Industrial Poisons in the United States, 114
Industrial Toxicology, 114
Industrial Workers of the World (IWW), 36, 95, 130–131, 139, 168, 200, 248
Injunctions, 131. *See also* Strikes
Inman, Elizabeth Murray, 131
Institute for Women's Policy Research, 131
Intercollegiate Bureau of Occupations, 131–132
International Alliance (ITA), 132
International Congresses of Working Women. *See* Women's International Labor Conferences
International Ladies' Garment Workers' Union (ILGWU), 11, 21, 22, 35, 37, 55, 60, 132, 161, 172, 177, 205, 233, 258, 269, 272, 283, 293, 303
Inventors, 132, 134
It's Still Spinach, 116
Irwin, Harriet Morrison, 15, 57

Jacobi, Mary Corinna Putnam, 135
James-Rodman, Charmayne, 65
Jane Clubs, 135
Japanese Americans, 7, 135–136
Jarrell, Helen Ira, 136–137

Jeanes teachers, 137
Jemison, Mae Carol, 137
Jewell, Geri, 58
Job sharing, 137–138
Job Training Partnership Act (JTPA), 138
Johnson v. Transportation Agency of Santa Clara, 138
Johnston, Henrietta Deering, 17
Jones, Mary Harris ("Mother"), 36, 123, 138–140, 254
Jordan, Barbara, 140
Journalists, 140–141
A Journey in Brazil, 6
Joyner, Marjorie, 134
Just cause, 141

Kehew, Mary Morton Kimball, 143, 287
Kelley, Florence, 62, 114, 125, 143–144, 161, 253, 277
Kellor, Frances, 144, 229
Kennedy, Kate, 144
Kenney, Mary. *See* O'Sullivan, Mary Kenney
"Keogh" accounts. *See* Individual Retirement Accounts
Kies, Mary, 132
King, Billie-Jean, 144–145
King, Florence, 145, 284
Kingsbury, Susan Myra, 145, 287
Kirkpatrick, Jeanne J., 145
Knight, Margaret, 132
Knights of Labor (KOL), 10, 22, 145–146, 229–230, 243, 246, 252–253. *See also* Unions
Koontz, Elizabeth, 183
Korean Americans, 146
Krasner, Lee, 17
Kreps, Juanita Morris, 146
Kunda v. Muhlenberg College, 2

Labor colleges. *See* Workers' education
Labor force. *See* Work force
Labor legislation, 147
Labor Management Relations Act. *See* Taft-Hartley Act
Labor-Management Reporting and Disclosure Act (Landrum-Griffin Act), 35, 147, 257, 268
Ladies Industry Association, 148
Landrum-Griffin Act. *See* Labor-Management Reporting and Disclosure Act of 1959
Lane, Gertrude Battles, 148
Lanham Act, 43, 148
Lansing, Sherry, 48
Lathrop, Julia, 114, 125
Latina Americans. *See* Hispanic Americans

Lauder, Estée 83
Law enforcement, 148
Lawrence, Massachusetts, Textile Strike. *See* Bread and Roses Strike
League for Equal Opportunity for Women, 149
Lee, Ann, 149
Leisure, 149
Lesbians. *See* Sexual preference
Lewis, Edmonia, 149
Librarians, 149–150
Lin, Maya Ying, 16
Line jobs, 150
Livermore, Mary Ashton Rice, 150–151
Living wage. *See* Family wage
Lockouts, 151
Lockwood, Belva Ann Bennett McNall, 151–152
LoPizzo, Annie, 36
Lothrop, Alice Louise Higgins, 152
Lovejoy, Esther Pohl, 13
Lowell, Josephine Shaw, 152–153, 197, 285
Lowell Female Industrial Reform and Mutual Aid Society. *See* Lowell Girls
Lowell Female Labor Reform Association, 21, 154. *See also* Lowell Girls
Lowell Girls, 87, 90, 153, 254
Lowell Offering, 90, 153
Lozier, Clemence Sophia Harned, 153–155
Ludlow Massacre, 139, 155, 254. *See also* Strikes
Luhring, Marie, 81
Lupino, Ida, 47
Lynn, Massachusetts, Shoe Strike of 1860, 155–156. *See also* Strikes
Lyon, Mary, 1, 156
Lytle, Lutie, 156

Mabley, Jackie ("Moms"), 58
McCarran-Walter Immigration and Nationality Act, 45
McClintock, Barbara, 157
McCormick, Ruth Hanna, 140, 157
McCreery, Maria Maud Leonard, 157–158
McDaniel, Hattie, 47, 57
McDonald, Lois, 249
MacDougall, Alice Foote, 83
McDowell, Anne Elizabeth, 158
McDowell, Mary Eliza, 125, 158
McGee, Anita Newcomb, 158
McLaren, Louise Leonard, 158–159, 249
McPherson, Aimée Semple, 159
Madison, Cleo, 47
Magill, Helen, 159
Mahoney, Mary Eliza, 159
Malkiel, Theresa Serber, 159

Malone, Annie. *See* Turnbo-Malone, Annie Minerva
Management and Technical Assistance 7(J) Program. *See* Small Business Administration
Managers, 160
Manhattan Trade School for Girls, 160
Mann Act, 160
Mansfield, Arabella, 18, 160–161
Manufactory. *See* Factory workers
Marginal workers, 161
Marion, Frances, 48
Marot, Helen, 161, 177
Marriage bars. *See* Married women's employment
Married women's employment, 161–163
Married women's property acts, 64, 163–164
Marshall, Penny, 47
Martin, Anne Henrietta, 164
Martinez, Maria Montoya, 164
Mason, Lucy Randolph, 60, 62, 164
Masters, Sybilla, 164–165
Maternity leave, 165
Mathematics. *See* Science, mathematics, and science-based professions
Matthews, Victoria Earle, 165
May, Elaine, 58
Mayer, Maria Gertrude Goeppert, 165–166
Mead, Margaret, 166–167
Media. *See* Cinema; Comediennes; Communications; Journalists; Theater
Men-only clubs, 167, 228
Mentors, 167
Mercer Girls, 167
Meritor Savings Bank v. Vinson, 49, 167, 239
Mesabi Range Strike, 167–168
Messick, Dale, 17
Mexican Americans, 169, 258, 261. *See also* Hispanic Americans
Meyerowitz, Theresa Bernstein, 17
Midwives, 168–169
Migrant laborers, 169
Military women, 169–172
Miller, Frieda Segekle, 172
Miller, Joyce, 54
Minimum wage, 172–173
Mitchell, Charlene, 59
Mitchell, Joni, 17
Mitchell, Lucy Sprague, 173
Mitchell, Maria, 173–174
Mommy track, 165, 174
Moonlighting, 174–175, 290
Moreno, Luisa, 175
Morgan, Julia, 16, 175
Moskowitz, Belle Lindener Israels, 175–176
Mossell, Sadie Tanner, 176

Mothers' employment, 176
Mothers' pensions, 176–177
Mount Holyoke College, 156
Mourning Dove, 177
Movies. *See* Cinema
Ms. Foundation for Women (MFW), 177
La Mujer Obrera, 177
Muller v. Oregon, 4, 107, 161, 177, 217
Murray, Judith Sargent, 178
Musicians, 178–180

Nashville Gas Co. v. Satty, 181
Nathan, Maud, 181
National Association for the Advancement of
    Colored People (NAACP), 37, 198
National Association for Women in Careers,
    181
National Association of Colored Women, 29
National Association of Commissions for
    Women (NACW), 181
National Association of Women Painters
    and Sculptors, 17
National Association of Working Women,
    181
National Brain Trust on Economic
    Opportunity for Low Income Women,
    42
National Center for Policy Alternatives,
    Women's Economic Justice Center, 181
National Center for Women and Retirement
    Research, 181
National Child Labor Committee, 143, 284
National Commission for Women's
    Equality, 181
National Commission on Working Women,
    189, 282
National Committee for Equal Pay, 182
National Committee on Household
    Employment, 182
National Committee on Pay Equity
    (NCPE), 182
National Congress of Neighborhood
    Women, 182
National Council of Career Women, 182
National Council of Negro Women, 29, 31,
    182
National Council for Research on Women,
    182
National Education Association (NEA), 10,
    11–12, 182–184, 260, 270
National Federation of Business and
    Professional Women's Clubs, Inc. of
    the U.S.A., 39. *See also* Business and
    Professional Women's Clubs, Inc. of
    the U.S.A.
National Federation of Day Nurseries, 43

National Industrial Recovery Act (NIRA),
    88, 110–111, 184, 209, 233
National Labor Relations Act (NLRA),
    55–56, 101, 184
National Labor Relations Board, 119, 147,
    268. *See also* Wagner Act
National Labor Union (NLU), 184
National League for the Protection of
    Colored Women, 144
National League of Women Workers,
    184–185
National Museum of Women in the Arts,
    17–18
National Organization for Women (NOW),
    96, 185, 218, 230, 240
National Task Force on Civil Liberties in
    the Workplace, 10
National Teachers' Association. *See* National
    Education Association
National Workingwomen's League, 155
National Youth Administration (NYA), 29,
    35, 187. *See also* New Deal
Native Americans, 7, 164, 185–186, 257
Navy Nurse Corps. *See* Army Nurse Corps
Nepotism, 186
Nestor, Agnes, 186
Networking, 186–187
Networking Project for Disabled Women
    and Girls, 187
Nevelson, Louise, 17
New Century Guild for Working Women,
    187
New Deal, 88, 110–111, 147, 184, 187–188,
    190, 204, 209, 233, 267, 268, 277, 291
New England Labor Reform League. *See*
    New England Workingmen's
    Association
New England Workingmen's Association,
    188
New York Infirmary for Women and
    Children, 32
New York Working Woman's Protective
    Union. *See* Working Woman's
    Protective Union
New York Working Women's Association.
    See Working Women's Association
Nichols, Minerva Parker, 15
Nine to Five, the National Association of
    Working Women, 54, 188, 270
Ninety-Nines, 77, 188–189
Nontraditional Employment for Women
    (NEW) Act. *See* Job Training
    Partnership Act
Nontraditional occupations, 189–190, 193,
    264
Norris-LaGuardia Act, 190

Norton, Mary Teresa Hopkins, 190
Nurses, 17, 22–23, 29, 191–192, 200, 228, 263, 277
Nutting, Mary Adelaide, 192

Oakley, Annie, 193
Occupational Outlook Handbook, 193
Occupational Safety and Health Act of 1970 (OSHA), 193–194, 281
Occupational segregation, 194–195
Occupational therapy. *See* Health professionals and paraprofessionals; Slagle, Eleanor Clarke
O'Connor, Sandra Day, 18, 108, 195
O'Day, Caroline Love Goodwin, 195–196
O'Keeffe, Georgia, 17
Office of Federal Contract Compliance Programs (OFCCP), 86, 196
Old Age Insurance Program, 196–197, 247
Older women, 197
O'Reilly, Leonora, 197–198, 229
OSHA. *See* Occupational Safety and Health Act of 1970
O'Sullivan, Mary Kenney, 10, 85, 125, 143, 198
Outworkers. *See* Pieceworkers
Overtime, 198

Packard, Sophia B., 199
Palmer, Alice Elvira Freeman, 199–200
Palmer, Sophia French, 200
Parental leave. *See* Family and Medical Leave Act; Family leave; Maternal leave
Parker, Julia Sarsfield O'Connor, 200
Parsons, Lucy Gonzalez, 200
Parton, Sara Payson Willis. *See* Fern, Fannie
Part-time workers, 200–201
Passing, 201–202, 169
Pattern bargaining, 202
Pay equity, 202
Peabody, Elizabeth Palmer, 202
Peale, Anna Claypoole, 202–203
Peale, Margaretta Angelica, 202–203
Peale, Sarah Miriam, 202–203
Peirce, Melusina Fay, 63
Pensions, 203
People v. Charles Schweinler Press, 203
Perkins, Frances, 69, 162, 187, 203–204
Permanent Commissions on the Status of Women, 205
Personnel managers. *See* Human resources managers
Pesotta, Rose, 14, 187, 205
Peterson, Esther, 84
Petition campaigns, 205
Phillips v. Martin Marietta Corporation, 205

Phillis Wheatley Home, 206
Photographers, 24–25, 206
Physicians, 32, 125, 135, 154–155, 206–208
Pickers. *See* Migrant laborers
Pieceworkers, 208–209
Pilots, 55, 77, 209–211
Pin money, 211, 290
Pinckney, Eliza Lucas, 211
Pink-collar workers, 211
Pinkham, Lydia Estes, 82, 211
Plantation system, 212
Police. *See* Government workers; Law enforcement
Politicians. *See* Government workers
Poorhouses, 293–294
Pregnancy, 212
Pregnancy Discrimination Act (PDA) of 1978, 41, 49, 212–213
President's Commission on the Status of Women (PCSW), 213–214
Preston, Ann, 214
Price Waterhouse v. Hopkins, 3, 214
Printers, 214
Privacy rights. *See* Civil rights; Genetic discrimination
Producer cooperatives. *See* Cooperative industries
Producers. *See* Cinema
Productivity, 215
Professional women, 132, 215
Professors. *See* Academic women
Progressive Era, 215–216, 247
Prostitutes, 216
Protective legislation, 201, 217–218
Psychologists and psychiatrists, 218–219
Psychology of Management, 102
Public relations. *See* Communications
Public Relief and Private Charity, 154
Publishers. *See* Writers and publishers
Puerto Rican Americans. *See* Hispanic Americans
Purple Cross Society, 219
Putting-out system. *See* Pieceworkers

Queen bee, 221
Quimby, Harriet, 209, 221
Quintasket, Christine. *See* Mourning Dove

Radcliffe College, 5–6
Radical women, 223
Radice v. New York, 4, 223
Randolph, Virginia E., 137
Rankin, Jeannette Pickering, 108, 223
Ray, Charlotte E., 18
Ray, Dixy Lee, 224
Real estate, 224

Refugee Women in Development, 224
Regan, Agnes Gertrude, 224
Rehabilitation Act of 1973, 224
Reid, Dorothy Davenport, 47
Religion, 77–78, 148, 159, 224–226, 285, 286
Religious Network for Equality for Women, 226
Research science. *See* Science, mathematics, and science-based professions
Restrooms, 42, 226
Retirement Equity Act, 226
Rhoads Dress, 226
Richards, Ellen Henrietta Swallow, 227
Richards, Linda, 227–228
Richmond, Mary Ellen, 228
Ride, Sally, 249
Roberts, Lillian, 228
Roberts v. United States Jaycees, 228
Robins, Margaret Dreier, 14, 125, 198, 228–229, 288
Robinson, Harriet Jane Hanson, 229
Robinson v. Jacksonville Shipyards, Inc. et al., 229
Rodgers, Elizabeth Flynn, 229–230
Roebling, Emily, 230
Roebling, Mary Gindhard, 39
Roosevelt, Anna Eleanor, 14, 29, 164, 230, 233
Rosie the Riveter, 296. *See also* World War II
Ross, Nellie Tayloe, 108
Rostker v. Goldberg, 230
Rubinstein, Helena, 83
Runyon, Brenda Vineyard, 39
Russell, Rosalind, 47
Russell Sage Foundation, 228. *See also* van Kleeck, Mary Abby

Sabin, Florence Rena, 231, 234
Sage, Kay, 17
St. Denis, Ruth, 67, 232–233
Salhany, Lucie, 48
Sanctified Sisters, 285
Sandwich generation, 233
Sanitary Commission, 23, 29, 32, 35, 151
Scab, 233
Schneiderman, Rose, 233, 256, 268
School for Active Workers in the Labor Movement, 233
Schultz v. Wheaton Glass Company, 233–234
Science, mathematics, and science-based professions, 234–235
Scientific management, 235
SCORE. *See* Small Business Administration
Second shift, 235
Seidelman, Susan, 48

Self-employment. *See* Entrepreneurs; Self-Employment Learning Project
Self-Employment Learning Project, 235–236
Sellins, Fannie Mooney, 236
Seneca Falls Convention, 236
Separate spheres, 236
Servants. *See* Domestic servants
Service Corps of Retired Executives (SCORE). *See* Small Business Administration
Service sector, 236–237
Servicewomen. *See* Military women
Seton, Elizabeth Ann Bayley, 237
Settlement houses, 237
Sex, Age and Work, 146
Sex and Temperament, 166
Sex discrimination, 237–239
Sex in the Marketplace: American Women at Work, 146
Sex segregation. *See* Occupational segregation
Sexual harassment, 239–241
Sexual preference, 241
Seymour, Mary Foot, 52, 82, 241
Shadd, Mary Ann, 241
Shakers, 149
Sharecropping. *See* Tenant farmers
Shaw, Anna Howard, 225, 241–242
Sheppard-Towner Act, 242
Sherman Anti-Trust Act. *See* Clayton Act
Shirt Sewers' Cooperative Union, 63, 242
Shirtwaist Makers Strike. *See* Uprising of the 20,000
Shoemakers, 242–243
Shop stewards, 243
Short, Elizabeth, 34
Siebert, Muriel F., 39, 243–244
Simms, Daisy Florence, 244, 303
Simms, Ruth Hanna McCormick. *See* McCormick, Ruth Hanna
Simpson, Georgiana, 244
Sitdown strikes. *See* Strikes
Slagle, Eleanor Clarke, 244
Slavery, 30, 244–245
Slowdown, 245. *See also* Strikes
Small Business Administration (SBA), 245–246
Smith, Charlotte, 246
Smith, Hilda Worthington, 38
Smith, Sophia, 246
Smith, Zilpha Drew, 246
Smith Vocational Education Act, 246
Smith-Hughes Act. *See* Clerical workers; Home economists
Smith-Lever Act. *See* Home economists

Snook, Neta, 77
Social feminists, 247
Social Security Act of 1935, 1, 7, 9, 69,
    196–197, 203, 247
Social Service Review, 1
Social workers, 104, 114, 125, 143, 224,
    247–248
Socialist Party of America, 33, 139, 248, 253
Society of Shoebinders, 248–249
Soldiers' Aid Society, 35
Southern Council on Women and Children
    in Industry, 249
Southern Summer School for Women
    Workers in Industry, 21, 158, 249, 302.
    See also Workers' education
Space, 249–250
Spanish-American War, 23, 158, 191
Speed-up, 250
Spelman College, 199
Sports, 109, 144–145, 250–252
Staff jobs, 252
Stanton, Elizabeth Cady, 22, 163, 295
Starr, Ellen Gates, 125, 252
Steinem, Gloria, 252
Stevens, Alzina Parsons, 125, 252–253
Stewart, Maria W. Miller, 253
Sticky floor, 160, 253
Stockbrokers. *See* Business and industry;
    Kreps, Juanita M.; Siebert, Muriel F.
Stokes, Rose Harriet Pastor, 253
Stoop labor, 253
Stowe, Harriet Beecher, 15, 25, 298
Stretch-out, 253
Strikes, 253–254
Strong, Anna Louise, 254, 256
Successful Women in Business, 12
Suitable occupations, 256
Swartz, Maud O'Farrell, 256, 288
Sweatshops, 256–257

Taft-Hartley Act (Labor-Management
    Relations Act of 1947), 35, 147, 257,
    268
Tallchief, Maria, 257
Tanning, Dorothea, 17
Tarbell, Ida Minerva, 140, 257–258
Taylor, Lucy Beaman Hobbs, 118, 258
Taylor, Rebecca, 258
Taylor, Ruth Carol, 94
Teachers, 258–260, 301
Telecommuting, 260
Telephone Operators' Department of the
    International Brotherhood of Electrical
    Workers (TOD), 53, 200, 260
Television. *See* Comediennes; Journalists
Temporary workers, 260–261

Tenant farmers, 261
Tests, 261
Theater, 261–262
Theory and Practice of Social Casework, 114
Thomas, Clarence, 50
Thomas, Martha Carey, 38, 262–263
Thompson, Dorothy, 263
Thoms, Adah B. Samuels, 263
Thorne, Florence Calvert, 263
Timothy, Elizabeth, 264
Title VII. *See* Civil Rights Act of 1964
Title IX. *See* Education Amendments Act of
    1972
Tomlin, Lily, 58
Trades, 264
*Training for the Professions and the Allied
    Occupations*, 38
Training School for Women Organizers,
    264–265
Training wage, 265
Transformational leadership, 265
Transient workers, 265
Travelers' Aid, 265, 282
Treatise, American Woman's Home, 15, 25
*A Treatise on Domestic Economy for the Use of
    Young Ladies at Home and School*, 25
Triangle Shirtwaist fire, 87, 107, 204,
    265–266, 272
Troup, Augusta Lewis, 266, 295
True Church, 285
Tucker, Sophie, 57
Turnbo-Malone, Annie Minerva, 266
Tuthill, Louisa C., 15
Two-paycheck couples, 266

UAW v. Johnson Controls, 34, 93, 116, 213,
    267
Underemployment, 267
Unemployment, 267
Unemployment Insurance Program,
    267–268
UNESCO. *See* United Nations Educational,
    Scientific and Cultural Organization
Uniform Guidelines on Employee Selection
    Procedures (UGESP), 268
Union for Industrial Progress, 143
Union organizers, 268
Unions, 268–271. *See also* American
    Federation of Labor; Congress of
    Industrial Organizations; Industrial
    Workers of the World; Strikes
United Auto Workers (UAW), 94–95, 271
United Farm Workers (UFW), 124, 271
United Mine Workers, 236
United Nations Educational, Scientific and
    Cultural Organization (UNESCO), 35

United Office and Professional Workers of America (UOPWA), 54, 61, 271
United States Commission on Industrial Relations, 22
United States Employment Service (USES) 81, 271–272
United Tailoresses Society of New York, 272
Unruh Act, 33
Uprising of the 20,000, 159, 272, 290
Urban Institute Program of Policy Research on Women and Families, 272

Valesh, Eva MacDonald, 273
Van Kleeck, Mary Abby, 14, 131, 273
Van Vorst, Bessie, 273
Van Vorst, Marie Louise, 273
Velvet ghettos, 273
Veterans' preference, 273–274
Video display terminals. *See* Health hazards
Vinson v. Meritor Savings Bank. See Meritor Savings Bank v. Vinson
Vocational education, 274
Vocational guidance, 274–275
Vorse, Mary Heaton, 36, 168, 275

Wage discrimination, 277
Wage laws, 218
Wagner Act, 151, 254, 277
Waitresses. *See* Food service; Harvey Girls
Wald, Lillian, 191, 277
Walker, Maggie Lena, 39
Walker, Mary Edward, 169, 277–278
Walker, Sarah Breedlove ("Madame C.J."), 82, 134, 278
Walters, Barbara, 278
Waltham System, 278–279
Walton, Mary, 132
War Brides Act, 45
Ward, Hortense Sparks Malsch, 279
Warren, Mercy Otis, 279
Washerwoman's Strike, 279. *See also* Strikes
Weber, Lois, 47
Welfare secretaries. *See* Human resources managers; Welfare work
Welfare work, 279
Wells-Barnett, Ida Bell, 140, 279–280
West Coast Hotel Co. v. Parrish, 218, 280
Wheeler, Candace Thurber, 280
Wheelock, Lucy, 280
Whistle-blowing, 280–281
White House Conference on Children, 44, 281
White House Conference on the Emergency Needs of Women, 281

White Rose Mission, 165, 206, 281–282
White slavery, 282
White-collar workers, 281
Whitney, Gertrude, 17, 96
Why Is a Dress?, 116
Why Women Cry, 116
Wider Opportunities for Women (WOW), 189, 282
Wildcat strikes. *See* Strikes
Willard, Emma Hart, 282–283
Willard, Frances Elizabeth Caroline, 283
Williams, Kathlyn, 47
Wives, 283–284
Woerishoffer, Emma Carola, 284
Wolfson, Theresa, 284
The Woman Who Toils, 273
Woman's Advocate, 158
Woman's Association of Commerce, 145, 284
Woman's Board of Trade, 284
Woman's Commonwealth, 285
Woman's Medical College of Pennsylvania, 285
Woman's Movement. *See* Women's Movement
Woman's Municipal League, 285
Woman's wage. *See* Women's wage
Women Accepted for Volunteer Emergency Service (WAVES), 170
Women Achieving Greater Economic Status (WAGE$), 285
Women adrift, 285–286
Women and Economics, 105
Women Employed (WE), 286
Women Employed Institute, 286
Women for Racial and Economic Equality (WREE), 286
Women in Community Service (WICS), 286
Women in Crisis (WIC), 286
Women in Industry (Edith Abbott), 1
Women in Industry Service , 14, 273, 286. *See also* Women's Bureau
Women in Transition (WIT), 286
Women Who Work, 126
Women's Airforce Service Pilots (WASPs), 55, 170, 189, 209, 296
Women's Army Auxiliary Corps (WAAC), 121, 170
Women's Bureau, U.S. Department of Labor, 14, 158, 172, 182, 186, 216, 217, 286–287, 290, 302, 303
Women's Business Ownership Act of 1988, 287
Women's Charter, 287

Women's Christian Temperance Union, 211, 283
Women's Computer Literacy Center (WCLU), 287
Women's Educational and Industrial Union (WEIU), 38, 145, 198, 287
Women's Equity Action League (WEAL), 287
Women's Industrial Conference, 288
Women's International Labor Conferences, 256, 275, 288
Women's Legal Defense Fund (WLDF), 288
Women's Movement, 288–289
Women's National Industrial League, 289
Women's National Labor League, 246
Women's Prison Association (WPA), 289
Women's Research and Education Institute, 289
Women's Rights Project. *See* American Civil Liberties Union
Women's Trade Union League (WTUL), 10–11, 14, 22, 38, 46, 80, 85, 104, 119, 126, 143, 158, 161, 172, 186, 196, 197–198, 216, 229, 233, 237, 243, 249, 256, 264, 268, 272, 284, 286, 288, 289–290, 293, 295, 303
Women's Typographical Union, 266
Women's wage, 290–291
Women's World Banking (WWB), 291
Woodbury, Helen Laura Sumner, 291
Woodhull, Victoria C., 108
Woodward Ellen Sullivan, 291–292
Woolman, Mary Raphael Schenck, 160, 292
Work: A Story of Experience, 292
Work Accidents and the Law, 77
Work culture, 292
Work force, 292

Work Incentive Program (WIP), 9, 272, 292
Work Projects Administration (WPA). *See* New Deal
Work Projects Administration Teachers, 11. *See also* New Deal
Work sharing, 292–293
Workers' education, 293
Workfare, 293
Workhouses, 293–294
Working Girls' Clubs, 294
Working mothers. *See* Mothers' employment
Working poor, 294
Working Woman's Protective Union (WWPU), 294–295
Working Women's Association (WWA), 184, 295
Working Women's League, 56, 295
Working Women's Society (WWS), 135, 197, 295
Workmen's Compensation, 295
World War I, 13, 14, 17, 31, 68, 77, 107, 131, 162, 169–171, 183, 191, 207, 223, 234, 295–296
World War II, 13, 14, 16, 17, 31, 43, 53, 55, 93, 94, 110, 136, 148, 162, 170, 183, 186, 191, 207–208, 223, 257, 296–298
Writers and publishers, 298–299

Yalow, Rosalyn S., 301
Yellow-dog contract, 301
Young, Ella Flagg, 183, 301
Young Women's Christian Association (YWCA), 115, 158, 164, 185, 187, 244, 249, 265, 279, 282, 293, 301–303
Younger, Maud, 303

Zakrzewska, Marie Elizabeth, 32, 207–208
Zorach, Marguerite Thompson, 17